BREAK
IT UP

BREAK IT UP

SECESSION, DIVISION, AND THE SECRET HISTORY OF AMERICA'S IMPERFECT UNION

RICHARD KREITNER

LITTLE, BROWN AND COMPANY
New York Boston London

Little, Brown and Company
Hachette Book Group
1290 Avenue of the Americas, New York, NY 10104
littlebrown.com

First Edition August 2020

Little, Brown and Company is a division of Hachette Book Group, Inc. The Little, Brown name and logo are trademarks of Hachette Book Group, Inc.

The publisher is not responsible for websites (or their content) that are not owned by the publisher.

The Hachette Speakers Bureau provides a wide range of authors for speaking events. To find out more, go to hachettespeakersbureau.com or call (866) 376-6591.

ISBN 978-0-316-51060-8
LCCN 2019954347

10 9 8 7 6 5 4 3 2 1

LSC-C

Printed in the United States of America

For Brahna

Contents

Part IV
RETURN OF THE REPRESSED

BREAK IT UP

The Disunited States

Were you looking to be held together by the lawyers?
Or by an agreement on a paper? Or by arms?
—Nay—nor the world, nor any living thing, will so cohere.
—Walt Whitman, *Drum-Taps*, 1865

THE COUNTRY WAS DIVIDED. It had been an explosive election, the culmination of decades of fighting over questions that went to the very heart of the nation's character. The president-elect was at odds with a majority of voters. Citizens had sorted themselves into camps, sects even, swearing the other side's position was unconscionable. Mainstream politicians spoke darkly about a coming conflict, and those on the margins called for revolution. Others wagered the country had seen worse and unity would surely prevail.

The historian Henry Adams called that time "the great secession winter." Republican candidate Abraham Lincoln had won the November 1860 election with less than 40 percent of the popular vote—and without the support of a single slave state. Terrified of the future, alienated from a country they no longer recognized, unwilling to remain loyal to a government that served interests opposed to their own, several Southern states plotted their departure. Fed up with trying to hold together a union that no longer made sense, many Northerners were content to send them on their way.

The onset of war, with the Confederate bombardment of Fort Sumter in Charleston Harbor on April 12, 1861, changed everything. In his memoir *Specimen Days,* Walt Whitman wrote of his joy at the "volcanic upheaval of the nation" that followed. He thought it "the grandest and most encouraging spectacle" in the history of "political progress and democracy."

Before its end, that spectacle brought death to some seven hundred thousand Americans, scores of whom Whitman, as a nurse in army hospitals, comforted in their final hours. But the ever-expansive poet grasped the bigger picture: the rupture revealed the American soul. "It was not for what came to the surface merely," he recalled, "but what it indicated below, which was of eternal importance." Underneath was "a primal hard pan of national Union will." Contrary to prediction, the American people thought their country worth saving after all. The man who had written, back in his blacker-bearded days, that "the United States themselves are essentially the greatest poem" now saw that only after the Union had been sundered did Americans finally realize how much it had meant to them all along. That this disunion could foster a deeper love for the Union was, to Whitman, "the best lesson of the century, or of America, and it is a mighty privilege to have been a part of it."

The 2016 presidential election set off a volcanic upheaval unlike any since the one Whitman welcomed in 1861. The next day, many Americans walked around as if in a daze, their faces the portrait of a divided nation: shock tinged here and there, depending on where one lived, by exaltation or dismay. Across the heartland, Donald Trump's supporters, those he called "the forgotten men and women of this country," swelled with pride and satisfaction, while in New York City, a cold, dreary rain seemed to embody the East Coast's despond. In her concession speech, Hillary Clinton acknowledged that the election revealed a country "more deeply divided than we thought." Classic political understatement, the comment suggested little awareness that downplaying those divisions for years had made them worse. The volcano's sudden eruption was more destructive because so many had convinced themselves it was extinct—it was only dormant.

Meanwhile, something strange seemed to be happening on the other side of the continent. A secessionist group called Yes California rallied on the steps of the state capitol in Sacramento, exchanging American flags for California ones. The leaders of the state legislature released a joint statement saying they had woken up that morning "feeling like strangers in a foreign land." A Silicon Valley investor announced his intention to fund "a legitimate campaign for California to become its own nation"; #Calexit began trending on Twitter.

In the weeks to come, the press covered these separatist stirrings as harmless hiccups. That the same had often been said during Trump's ascent to power—he would never win a single caucus or primary, columnists assured us (and themselves); he certainly wouldn't claim the Republican nomination; he had no chance in the general election—offered little comfort. By Trump's inauguration, pollsters reported that one in three Californians supported seeking independence. Even if that number was inflamed by the heat of a divisive campaign, the election and its chaotic aftermath made it impossible to avoid the conclusion that something was rotten in the United States. At the end of 2016, *Time* magazine named Trump its Person of the Year and gave his title as PRESIDENT OF THE DIVIDED STATES OF AMERICA.

Trump was right when he said, in his first presidential press conference, "I didn't come along and divide this country. This country was seriously divided before I got here." We live in different nations, many said before 2016, and even more have said it since. Now another looming election suggests our nation's descent into perpetual crisis and intractable discord, perhaps even violence, will likely only worsen. For years, mounting evidence has shown that the bonds of our Union are slowly coming undone, from the geographical polarization of the electorate (only 25 out of 435 seats in the House of Representatives were considered up for grabs in 2016) to the percentage of people who say they support their own state's secession (one-quarter, according to a 2014 poll). For much of the country, and certainly for its leading purveyors of establishment opinion, this fact has come· as a shock. It shouldn't have.

Disunion—the possibility that it all might go to pieces—is a hidden thread through our entire history, from the colonial era to the early republic and the Civil War and beyond, through the fabled American Century and up to our own volatile moment. The chronicle of our imperfect union is an epic, untold story of strange origins, accidental creation, and almost two and a half centuries of faltering attempts to hold it together. This book charts for the first time the history of the Union by looking at the ever-present forces that have conspired to divide it. Taking one clear and crucial step outside the confines of how we usually think about our country offers a fuller understanding of both our contentious past and our uncertain future. The Civil War was not an exception to the rest of American history. Diverse, divisible, divided, "these United States," as Whitman and his contemporaries called them, have never really been united. They have always been riven by race and religion, cleaved by class and culture, sundered by section, and fragmented by geography. Our most powerful myth—that the fusion was completed, that the many ever melded into one—is just that: a myth.

Our refusal to recognize this, like patients who insist, against all evidence, that they are not ill, has been a major cause of our political dysfunction and social strife. Secession is the only kind of revolution we Americans have ever known and the only kind we're ever likely to see. The past few years have seen the idea of disunion attain a prominence unseen since the Civil War. With partisan divisions hardening and every branch of government mired in crisis, it's easy to see the appeal. If the massive hodgepodge of a country known as the United States no longer functions as a going concern, maybe it's time to break it up.

While many see secession as a sin peculiar to the South, there are few regions of the country that have not threatened to leave, few groups that have not thought disunion might be a good idea, few eras that have been entirely free from Union-threatening strife. Northerners and Southerners, slaveholders and abolitionists; imperialists and isolationists; nationalists black, white, indigenous, Chicano; Alaskans and Hawaiians, Texans and Californians, Appalachians and Cascadians; spies and secret agents; Mormons and missionaries; hippies, anarchists, feminists, environmentalists, novelists, poets, screenwriters, racists, reverends, soldiers, even presidents—all have questioned the Union's legitimacy, doubted its persistence, plotted its dissolution, or imagined its fall.

Seeing the Union through the eyes of those who seek and have sought to divide it allows us to understand the United States as the tentative proposition it always was and still is, as an experiment that might fail at any time. Paradoxically, disunion has been one of our only truly national ideas. The founding of our country was especially disorderly and vitriolic, even less thought through than the genesis of the similarly beleaguered European Union. The creation of the United States was a means to an end, not an end in itself. There has never been anything inevitable about its survival. Dissension, acrimony, and crisis have been the rule in American politics, consensus and unity the exception, one more often wished for than actually seen. "By an unfortunate necessity which has grown with its growth," Henry Adams wrote in his essay on the secession winter, "the country contained in itself, at its foundation, the seeds of its future troubles."

By tracing the idea of disunion across four centuries, we can perceive the deeper movements of American history. Connecting periods too often treated as distinct and unrelated makes the past less strange, the present less baffling, and the shape of things to come, perhaps, less obscure.

Break It Up is divided into four parts, each of which explores a different era and reflects different ways of thinking about the Union. The battle over the meaning of America has always been a battle of metaphors, and the choice of imagery can be revealing. Part 1, "A Vast, Unwieldy Machine," describes the haphazard process of unification during the colonial and revolutionary periods. The leaders of the American Revolution, many of them dabblers in Enlightenment-era science, thought of their attempt at confederation as an experiment: Could one solution be mixed from disparate elements? Could the "intricate and complicated...Machine of the Confederate Colonies," as John Adams put it, be made to function?

For almost a century and a half, the formation of a union had been not merely unlikely but unthinkable. The first colonial revolution was fought not to create a federation, but to destroy one. After hearing about the overthrow of King James II in 1688, the people of Boston rebelled against the Crown-backed Dominion of New England, a union of several colonies. Bostonians took to the streets to demand a return to local rule. The main obstacle to joining the American provinces together was their reluctance to have anything to do with one another.

Desperate to maintain local autonomy, skittish about their little-known provincial neighbors, colonists resisted all attempts to create a union and finally agreed to join only under duress to avoid an even less appealing consolidation under British imperial rule. Many Americans feared that after seceding from Britain, they would take up muskets and axes against one another. And, in some places, they did.

Only a few years after the first American constitution went into effect, the country nearly collapsed into sectional conflict and populist revolt. An almost certain second revolution was averted at the last moment by the desperate crafting of a new charter that was more protective of the prerogatives of the rich and less responsive to the wealth-spreading inclinations of the aggrieved masses—the "grazing multitude," as George Washington called them. The secret drafting and ratification of this Constitution amid secessionist movements in the West and insurrections in the East was a concerted drive for a "more perfect Union" by the 1 percent of that day, who most perfectly protected themselves and their own interests, including their ownership of slaves. This "peace pact," as David C. Hendrickson calls it, prevented an all-out civil war. But it came at a cost. All these years later, Americans regret the protections afforded slavery by the Constitution, but that remorse comes to us perhaps a little too easily. To honestly reckon with the founding compromises is, necessarily, to question the value the framers put on concord, on the Union, and to wonder if in our own times, blessed as they are, we may be paying more than the enterprise is worth.

When the new government took control, the country was no more united than it had ever been. Even many of the new nation's leaders harbored profound doubts about its prospects. Part 2, "Irreconcilable Differences," traces the thread of disunion through those often skipped-over years between the Revolution and the Civil War. America's rapid expansion in this formative era of the republic created tensions that couldn't be contained by the prevailing constitutional arrangement. Many critics anticipated that the Union would end in divorce. As in many flawed marriages, the only thing keeping Americans together was the fear of coming apart.

The first decades under the new government saw separatist movements arise in every part of the country. Hostile sections and competing parties played a dangerous "game of round-about," Virginia's John Randolph observed, in which those who questioned the Union's worth when they were out of power enforced national unity—with the threat of violence, if necessary—once they retook it.

More than doubling the size of the United States, the Louisiana Purchase made it that much harder to hold the Union together. The stresses of empire would eventually break the country apart. In the short term it proved destabilizing as well. A New England cabal, fearful of losing power in a fast-growing union, conspired to secede and maybe even rejoin Britain. They placed their hopes in Aaron Burr, Jefferson's

frustrated, ambitious vice president, supporting his candidacy for governor of New York on the assumption that he would bring the state into
their "northern confederacy." That prompted Alexander Hamilton to
denounce Burr as a threat to the Union and led to their infamous 1804
duel. Banished from polite society, Burr assembled a posse of ragtag
frontiersmen and schemed to break the West off from the United States
and form an independent empire. On the other side of the Appalachians, Burr found many who—like Jefferson himself—didn't think the
Union's spread across the entire continent was a foregone conclusion.

Burr failed in his breakaway attempt, as did the New Englanders,
whose subsequent threats to secede during the War of 1812 doomed
the Federalist Party to oblivion. But the idea of separation lived on. To
an aged Thomas Jefferson, the clash over slavery's Western spread
sounded like a "fire bell in the night," an early warning of a coming
conflagration. In a test run for secession, South Carolina tried to nullify a federal law within its borders. The God-fearing abolitionist William Lloyd Garrison denounced the Constitution as a pact with the
devil. On the floor of Congress, former president John Quincy Adams
dared to introduce a petition that a brave group of Yankee shoemakers
had drawn up demanding the dissolution of the United States. They
refused to live in a union that protected slavery, and Southerners
refused to live in one that didn't.

The separatist impulse passed from one part of the Union to
another until a critical mass of white Southerners finally took the leap.
Part 3 of this book, "The Earthquake Comes," explores the prolifera-
tion of disunionism in the run-up to the Civil War. Americans on both
sides of the country's starkest sectional and political divide came to
think of the looming collapse of the Union in terms of a ground-
shifting catastrophe that could strike at any time. Though a crack-up
may have been certain, that the South would take the first step was
never assured. The Southern secession movement, in fact, stayed quiet
in the 1850s, as leading slave-state representatives did not puzzle over
how they could leave the Union but how they could expand it, solidify
their control, and ensure it continued to protect their system of racial
oppression and mass bondage. Only when a rising Northern majority
deposed them by electing Lincoln did the slaveholders turn against the
Union and set out to destroy it.

When the Civil War finally began—the "volcanic upheaval" heralded by Whitman—it was because Americans in both the North and the South decided the fundamental differences between them could no longer be ignored. The nominally united country now had a fiercely contested international border running straight across it. One thing was clear: the separation solved nothing. Both the Union and the Confederacy faced the same kinds of internal secessionist movements that had bedeviled the United States since its creation, showing that the fundamental division, the "irrepressible conflict," as New York senator William Seward put it in a notorious 1858 speech, was not just between North and South, freedom and slavery; it reflected something even deeper. The truly "irrepressible" conflict was between union and disunion, those forces bringing Americans together and those tearing them apart.

If the war was an unspeakably messy divorce, the reunion that followed was tepid, unsteady, incomplete. The fourth and final part of this book, "Return of the Repressed," shows how the United States failed to resolve the conflicts that led to and emerged from the breakdown. The pressures of holding together a vast and increasingly varied country required banishing from national consciousness any recognition of competing demands and incompatible interests. In an individual, repression of such conflicts can lead to what Sigmund Freud described as a "civil war" in the patient's mind. After the American Civil War, the conflict was again buried in the nether reaches of the American mind. It's not an uncommon response to trauma for either persons or peoples. But it's also, usually, ineffective. Like anything willfully banished from consciousness, national dissolution seems to be something Americans both desire and fear. When conflicts are silenced rather than addressed, they have a tendency to return.

Reconstruction, the "second founding," ended as the first one had, in a counterrevolution by the rich and powerful, the subjugation of the aspirations of the many to the profit-seeking interests of the few. The fraudulence of the reunion benefited some people (the wealthy and white) at the expense of others (people of color and the poor), and the national prioritization of unity above all else continues to this day. The sanctification of compromise continues to blind us to the costs of union and who has been asked, often at gunpoint, to foot that bill.

After the Civil War, the idea of breaking up the Union never attained the prominence it once had, but it did occasionally reappear in strange, revealing, and often unmanageable ways, as when Mexican revolutionaries tried to take back the Southwest and when black nationalists sought to build a republic on the land their ancestors had been forced to till. The "Civil War of the 1960s," as scholars have called the tumultuous decade, balkanized the country into squabbling subgroups. *E Pluribus Unum,* that once-sacred promise, began to ring hollow, as if the many had never become one—and never would. The end of the Cold War led to infinitely renewable culture wars that powerful economic interests used to drive Americans into the hostile camps we now inhabit.

Over the past twenty years, secessionist movements have cropped up across the country. It is no longer inconceivable that a state might schedule a vote on separation before this decade is out. As the Brexit referendum showed, such plebiscites can have surprising and disruptive results.

Contradictions too long ignored and doubts too long repressed continue to haunt American politics and culture, undermining the legitimacy of our institutions and attracting meddlesome foreign rivals who, as in the early republic, want nothing more than to see the Union break apart. Russia's strategy of sowing discord in American politics has proven a wild success. Yet today's disunion is not a recent development but the return of what for most of our history was the norm: a perpetual war for the soul of America, an ever-present battle over the past and for the future—usually metaphorical but constantly threatening to turn into fact.

Thanks to countless academics, journalists, activists, politicians, and citizens, Americans have in recent years begun having difficult, long-avoided conversations about racism and sexism in this country. This is important and necessary work. But it does not fully address the profundity of our predicament or the depth of our divisions. While pundits and politicians have spent decades bemoaning partisanship and polarization, they seldom pause to consider that today's fractures and fault lines are the result of Americans' refusal to come to terms with lingering doubts about whether the United States should continue to exist— at least in the form we have known. The dewy-eyed version of the country's history—its hallowed revolution against tyranny, its slow but steady march toward democracy, its glorious American Century—fails to explain the moment we find ourselves in today. Despite the bipartisan nostalgia for a golden age of national unity, it never existed. Only after we acknowledge the long history of America's built-in divisions, their causes and consequences, will we be able to plot a path out of the slough in which we find ourselves. Only then will we begin to understand what we can expect in the years to come and what we should do.

For all the gore of the Civil War, Walt Whitman was grateful to have lived to see it. It was a time, he wrote, "when human eyes appear'd at least just as likely to see the last breath of the Union as to see it continue." The same may be true of the eyes reading this book. A reckoning is coming. It will be a grand spectacle to behold, as Whitman put it, "not for what came to the surface merely, but what it indicated below, which was of eternal importance." Beneath the surface of the anxious and agitated American soul, he discovered a deep reservoir of "national Union will." Is that what we will find too? Does living in such an incomprehensibly massive country make each of us more or less significant, our lives more or less meaningful, our rights to life, liberty, and the pursuit of happiness more or less secure?

Far from being unpatriotic, asking this question is a prerequisite for serious discussion about what we Americans want the future to hold for ourselves and this perennially divided union. Americans must choose between joining together to build a truly inclusive, unified country—a multiracial democracy, politically and economically—or going our separate ways. We can't put it off much longer. We must finally finish the work of Reconstruction or give up on the Union entirely.

In 1839, former president John Quincy Adams delivered a speech before the New-York Historical Society to mark the fiftieth anniversary of George Washington's inauguration. At seventy-one, Adams was the last living link to the founding generation. But now he had a sober message for the American people: "If the day should ever come, (may Heaven avert it,) when the affections of the people of these states shall be alienated from each other; when the fraternal spirit shall give away to cold indifference, or collisions of interest shall fester into hatred," Adams said, "...far better will it be for the people of the disunited states, to part in friendship from each other, than to be held together by constraint."

PART I

A VAST, UNWIELDY MACHINE

Tradition holds that the American colonists came together in 1776 to overthrow a detested king and form one nation, indivisible, intended to last for all time. They did nothing of the kind. The Revolution was a civil war, and it created a country perennially prone to a sequel. The fragile Union, a mere means to an end, almost immediately collapsed. This was shocking but not quite surprising. Americans knew that whatever union they, a woefully divided people, managed to form would forever be at risk of breaking down and splitting up. For a century and a half, the colonies had acted as if they were independent nations with little more in common than the wish to remain apart.

CHAPTER 1

Join, or Die

Everybody cries, a Union is absolutely necessary; but when they come to the Manner and Form of the Union, their weak Noddles are presently distracted.

—BENJAMIN FRANKLIN, 1754

WHEN THE *MAYFLOWER* SET SAIL in July 1620, the sixty-five passengers on board called themselves not Pilgrims but Separatists. They wanted to break off from the Church of England and form their own independent congregations. That was illegal, so they left. Their favorite passage in Scripture came from 2 Corinthians 6:17, the verse in which the apostle Paul urges Christians not to mingle with idolaters: "Come out from among them, and be ye separate."

True to their name, the Separatists displayed their fractious tendencies even while their ship crossed the Atlantic. One organizer of the *Mayflower*'s passage described the voyagers as "un-united among ourselves."

From the beginning, would-be Americans were defined by the struggle between union and disunion, the drive to join and the desire to part. Federation offered security from external enemies, easier trade, and a way to manage internal disputes. Separation offered that most enduring of all American longings—freedom from being told what to do.

American communal life from the beginning was marked by fracture and fragmentation. Soon after their boats dropped anchor, the new arrivals began splintering into ever-smaller sects and settlements. Dissidents fell into the habit of leaving existing towns and striking off to start their own. The American colonies were an archipelago of

Benjamin Franklin's 1754 etching failed to convince the colonists to unite. "There would be a lot of dying before there was any joining," one historian quips. (*Library of Congress*)

disjointed settlements connected only by narrow Indian paths and a loose affiliation with the British Empire. Disunion was the natural state of things in America, to be defended and preserved rather than avoided or overcome. After all, it had been the dream of independence, not union, that convinced the early settlers to leave their old world behind for what they desperately tried to convince themselves was a new one.

1. The Serpent in the Garden

The spirit of division was everywhere in colonial America. Far from being tyrannized by the British, the colonists enjoyed a high degree of autonomy. They boasted of their privileges and were "jealous," as they put it, of any new-fangled attempt to govern them by either England or other colonies. Plans devised on both sides of the Atlantic to convince the far-flung, even hostile colonies to work together failed time and again and for many of the reasons the United States would later prove so fragile: regional resentment, ethnic and religious differences, incompatible institutions, and, above all, a widespread suspicion of whose interests a union would serve.

Founded by different groups for different reasons, the colonies nurtured different economies, grew at different rates, and pursued wildly different interests. The provincial governments alone taxed and represented their residents. They proudly held their own separate charters—rudimentary constitutions offering varying degrees of self-government. Each circulated different currency, making travel between them burdensome when the distance didn't make it impossible. In any case, the absence of commercial connections made intercourse unnecessary. Virginia, the profit-seeking project of a private company, became a prosperous tobacco plantation thanks to battalions of servants and slaves. Massachusetts, a few weeks' hard travel up the coast, was founded by Calvinist dissenters desperate to evade their tormentors. Started as an offshoot of Barbados, the Carolinas were rigidly hierarchical, defined by African slavery and aristocratic dominion. Nothing about their origins suggested it would ever make sense to join Georgia, a penal colony; Maryland, a haven for persecuted Catholics; and New York, a bustling commercial port seized from the Dutch. (The vast interior of the continent, populated by untold millions belonging to innumerable Indian tribes, had been penetrated by few European voyagers. That everything from one ocean to the other might someday be one nation crossed the mind of precisely nobody.)

Settlers in the British colonies hailed from all over Europe, a continent not exactly known for fostering peaceful relations among diverse peoples. In America, communication could only be awkward and infrequent between Czech-speaking Moravians and French Huguenots, German-speaking Austrians and Gaelic-lilting Highlanders. And even when all parties spoke English, they had little to talk about if they lived hundreds of miles apart. Hard-drinking Scots-Irish backwoodsmen wanted nothing to do with abstemious Quakers or moralizing Yankees. Rhode Island was founded as a refuge from Massachusetts, so why should the apostates of Providence submit to Boston's rigid theocratic rule? The colonists cherished their self-willed isolation. Yet from the outset, growth and expansion threw them into conflict. New York and New Jersey fought an intermittent boundary war—bullets and all—over where to draw the line between them. Virginians and Pennsylvanians skirmished for control of the region around present-day Pittsburgh.

Colonial divisions endlessly fascinated the era's travelers, at least the few reckless enough to roam the dense woods between distant settlements. Every tour of the colonies became a study in contrasts, conflicts, and contradictions. In 1747, Swedish botanist Peter Kalm, after wandering the continent examining the flora and fauna (especially the species Kalm's mentor, the taxonomist Carl Linnaeus, would soon label *Homo sapiens*), observed that "each English colony in North America is independent of the other." This was especially dangerous during wars with the natives, for it "usually happened that while some provinces have been suffering from their enemies, the neighboring ones have been quiet and inactive, as if it did not in the least concern them." Kalm thought it doubtful they would ever unite.

Things hadn't changed much a decade later when a roving British minister named Andrew Burnaby traveled the length and breadth of the colonies, noting in his diary how vastly different they were, how incompatible their identities and irreconcilable their interests. The history of the colonies was little more than a litany of their disputes over trade, defense, borders. No "voluntary association or coalition" could ever hold it all together, "for fire and water are not more heterogeneous than the different colonies in North America."

Were the colonists ever so brazen as to declare independence, the result, Burnaby predicted, would be "a civil war from one end of the continent to the other." It would take a hundred years, but the prediction would come true.

In 1685, King Charles II decided to unite some of the fractious American colonies under a single government controlled from London. He hoped colonial integration would make the empire run more smoothly and profitably. Ruling the Dominion of New England—which included Massachusetts Bay, Plymouth, Rhode Island, Connecticut, New York, and East and West Jersey—by a royally appointed governor and an advisory council, and without an elected assembly, would make it easier for the Crown to coordinate trade policies, supervise land disputes, and defend against attack, especially from the French and their native allies. Constant squabbling among the colonists was bad for business. Only closer connection to one another and to England could force the colonists into line.

It wasn't the first time a colonial union had been proposed. Fifty years earlier, following the massive Puritan migration of the early

1630s, the fragmenting New Englanders had realized it made little sense to keep splitting into smaller parts. They had spread themselves too thin across the land. William Bradford, the governor of Plymouth Colony, feared the multiplying settlements would "provoke the Lord's displeasure against them." Stretching from the sandy beaches of eastern Long Island to the deep woods of Maine, a territory populated by some twenty-four thousand white inhabitants in 1640, the New England colonies endlessly bickered over issues like immigration, diplomacy, and land. To John Winthrop, Bradford's counterpart in Boston, such "jealousies and differences between us and our friends" could only be the work of "the old serpent"—Satan.

For years, the serpent succeeded in postponing the formation of a confederation. Negotiations dragged on, always faltering over how much power each colony would give up and how disputes between them would be resolved. The separatist impulse proved irresistible.

But when civil war broke out back in England—"a sad *breach* and *disunion*," as one English writer called it—the colonists saw they had nobody to rely on but themselves. Down in New Amsterdam, the Dutch knew all about the tensions among the English colonies and were eager to exploit them. A recent war with the Pequot, a local Indian nation, had ended in colonial victory (and the massacre of hundreds of natives), but it gave the settlers a scare. It was imperative, therefore, that any differences between the colonies be submerged. What doctrine and geography had wrenched apart, only primal, palpable, gut-wrenching fear could bring back together.

In 1643, delegates from the colonies of Massachusetts Bay, Plymouth, Connecticut, and New Haven met in Boston to draw up terms of union. They signed a charter to create "a firme and perpetuall league of friendship and amytie." In the governing council, each province had two votes. A three-fourths majority would be needed to pass any measure.

Despite hopeful beginnings, the United Colonies of New England failed its first major test. In 1652, war broke out between England and the Netherlands. While Massachusetts and Plymouth wanted to keep their distance from European squabbles, Connecticut and New Haven, aggravated by skirmishes with Dutch traders, pushed for war. The confederation council deadlocked. Each colony pursued its own interests. The union collapsed into dissension and disuse.

If a confederation devised by the colonists themselves didn't work, English officials should have seen that one forcibly imposed from abroad would fare no better. Half a century hadn't altered the settlers' ways. To the proud Puritans of Massachusetts Bay, the Dominion of New England, with its taxes on alcohol, prohibitions on town meetings, and onerous regulations, looked like a tyrannical dictatorship. Throughout the region, colonists resisted the unwanted union.

The Crown-appointed governor, a veteran imperial administrator named Edmund Andros, decided to crack down on them. He revoked the colonies' charters, one by one. The semi-independent colonies would be erased, absorbed into the Dominion of New England. The colonists were appalled. According to legend, Connecticut took the lead in resisting the Andros regime. In late 1687, the governor traveled to Hartford to impose order. Meeting with town leaders in a house with low windows open to the warm autumn night, he demanded the colony's charter. Just as the officials laid the document on the table, however, the candles went out. The room went dark. When the candles were relit, the charter was gone. Later it was said that somebody hid it in the hollow of an oak. Andros returned to Boston empty-handed.

Rebellion was brewing—and not only in New England. Back home, Charles II's brother James ascended to the throne. A Catholic convert, James enjoyed little support among the Anglican elite. The birth of a son—a potential Catholic heir—sealed his fate. In 1688, James's Protestant daughter Mary and her husband, William, a Dutch nobleman, invaded England, assumed the throne, and forced James to flee to France.

In England, the Glorious Revolution foreclosed the possibility of a return to Catholicism and cemented the supremacy of Parliament over the Crown. Its effects in the colonies were no less dramatic. Governor Andros tried to suppress the news of James's ouster. Messengers from the home country were arrested for "bringing Traiterous and Treasonable Libels"—fake news. When word leaked out, colonists stormed the cobbled streets of Boston demanding the dissolution of the dominion and the reinstatement of the old charters. Militias began arresting government officials. Andros hid out in a fort in the harbor; he tried to escape—reportedly dressed as a woman—but was caught and sent back to England.

The Dominion of New England was over. Colonial officials, back in charge of their own affairs, debated whether to revive their old confederation. But the colonies were too different, each one too proud of its independence, all too scarred by the trauma of forced union to join together again. It was impossible, Connecticut's leaders finally decided, for the New England colonies to be "accommodated each to other at present." They preferred to remain apart.

That first American revolution was fought not to create a union but to destroy one. The uprising foreshadowed the many times ordinary people would mobilize against distant governments and unaccountable administrators of tossed-together unions that threatened local rule. Though forgotten today, the revolt against the Dominion of New England was a foundational moment of resistance to corruption and despotism, a precedent for later uprisings. Disunion was and would long remain the rule in America. Any attempt to overcome it was seen as an unwelcome aberration.

The rebellious son of a naval officer close to Charles II, William Penn converted as a young man from Anglicanism to Quakerism, a new sect suspicious of established authority. He spent his twenties in and out of prison, charged several times with spreading seditious views and showing contempt for the law. When Admiral Penn died, his subversive son settled a royal debt owed to his father by accepting the title to tens of thousands of square miles in America. The grant turned an eccentric miscreant into the largest private landowner in the world. The day after the king signed over the land, Penn told a friend he was sure God would "bless and make it the seed of a nation."

For his settlement in the woods, Penn drew up a constitution that ensured religious freedom for all. The colony was a "Holy Experiment," a test to determine whether it was possible to create a diverse community free from persecution and strife and dedicated to tolerance, piety, and peace. At Penn's direction, the colony pursued an unusually enlightened policy toward its native neighbors. With a steady inflow of workers and a roaring economy, Pennsylvania boomed.

The experiment's success convinced Penn it might be possible to spread his gospel on a larger scale. In the 1690s, England and France were fighting the first of several world-spanning conflicts, and Penn, who had returned to London, saw the bloodletting as an unfortunate holdover from primitive times.

In 1691, Penn drew up a proposal—the first of its kind—for a European parliament. Diplomacy, rather than war, would patch up international disputes. Meeting every few years, the parliament would adjudicate "all Differences...between one Soveraign and another." By inaugurating a new era of peace, the plan would save "mighty Sums of Money," since towns and whole countries would avoid destruction, and commerce and travel would become easier and more profitable. Anyone with a passport could move freely around this European "Union," as Penn called the federation.

The plan went nowhere; the warring continued. But after writing the essay, Penn realized the New World could benefit from union at least as much as the Old. The fighting between England and France hadn't spared the colonists in America. One winter night a few years earlier, in February 1690, three hundred French soldiers and native warriors had crept on snowshoes to the outskirts of Schenectady, a village of thirty houses set around a square. They found the gate open and tiptoed in. For two hours, moving through a heavy, silent snow, the raiders went from house to house, scalping heads and slitting throats. Then they burned the settlement to the ground. At dawn, residents in nearby Albany were roused from their beds by the screams of survivors who had crawled fifteen miles through the snow.

Like later attacks, the Schenectady massacre helped an otherwise divided people come together—united, for the moment, by fear, shock, and grief. Briefly, the raid scared the colonists out of their separatism. Three months later, delegates from four colonies met in Albany to coordinate a response. They agreed to raise troops for a joint attack on French Canada and sent letters asking the other colonies to contribute.

Yet even this minimal degree of cooperation proved too much to ask of colonial Americans. Most provinces ignored or declined the request. An expedition set out from Albany only to turn back at Lake Champlain, the soldiers ill and outnumbered. The surprising unity that had emerged after the horrifying attack devolved into the usual hostilities and recriminations.

Penn worried that if the bickering colonies failed to resolve their quarrels, America would look a lot like war-torn Europe. Cooperation offered the only alternative to destruction.

Five years after the massacre, Penn was in London testifying before the Board of Trade, a royal commission charged with crafting imperial policy. The bewigged commissioners had grown frustrated by the failure of the colonies to adhere to their agreed-upon military quotas. In a memorandum signed by several of its members (including the philosopher John Locke), the board observed that the colonies were "so crumbled into little Governments and so disunited . . . that they have hitherto afforded but little assistance to each other." The situation was untenable. Though the English colonies in America were wealthier and more populous than the French ones, those advantages were useless "unless they be united."

Penn agreed. Far from helping one another, he told the board, the colonies often went out of their way to do each other harm. Perhaps they should be joined together in a union like the one he had suggested for Europe. Intrigued, the commissioners asked him to draw up a formal proposal.

After a few weeks of work, Penn submitted a "Briefe and Plaine Scheam" for a union of all the English colonies on the Atlantic Seaboard. Delegates, two from each colony—men "well qualified for sence sobriety and substance"—would meet regularly to mediate any disputes and defend against "the publick enemies."

Impressed, the board sent a letter to King William endorsing Penn's plan—in theory. Even the commissioners realized it couldn't work in practice. There would be as many objections as there were colonies. There were no terms on which all would agree.

Penn's scheme for an American congress, like his call for a European parliament, was dead on arrival. But the idea would linger on— for some, an idealistic dream, a plan for perpetual peace; for others, a dangerous threat to their power. To consider themselves a single unit, the colonists would need to set aside their identities as Virginians or New Englanders or even Englishmen and see themselves, above all, as Americans. Given the colonists' manifold differences, that seemed unlikely to happen soon.

*   *   *

Britain, too, began to rethink colonial union. The centralization that once seemed both possible and desirable, an easier way to exert control, had only riled up provincial rebelliousness. Long before the colonists themselves thought of independence, London officials feared that a united America would spin out of the imperial orbit. In the early eighteenth century, they changed tack. Unity had once seemed to serve the Crown's interests; now disunity did. Keeping the colonies separate would ensure their dependence on the mother country. For the next fifty years, Britain tried to prevent the very coordination it had once promoted. It was much easier to rule over divided provinces than united ones, ministers concluded, invoking a strategic principle passed down from the ancients: *divide et impera,* "divide and rule." It was a lesson future foreign rivals would use to their advantage—America's divisions made its inhabitants easier to manipulate.

The colonists had contributed to the new thinking when, rebutting charges that America aimed for independence, they deemed separation impossible because the continent was too divided. In 1721, a New Englander named Jeremiah Dummer wrote that the colonists' numerous differences—"in their Forms of Government, in their religious Rites...and consequently in their Affections"—meant they would never "unite in so dangerous an Enterprize" as independence. It was therefore in Britain's interest "to keep them disunited." A former Pennsylvania governor advised that as long as the colonists remained "seperated by their Independancy," it was "impossible that any dangerous Union can be form'd among them."

At least one official, however, saw things differently. A respected politician and veteran of the Board of Trade, Martin Bladen had long advocated forming an American union. If Britain was to prosper from its colonial possessions, he argued in a 1739 report, the colonies could not remain "divided into so many different Provinces, spread over so immense a Tract of Land...and as devoid of all Care for the Welfare of the whole, as if they were not the Subjects of the same Prince." No wonder the "Independent Common Wealths," as Bladen called the colonies, failed to obey British trade rules and defense quotas. They were, in effect, "Distinct Governments...Absolute within their respective Dominions." From a military perspective, keeping them separate wasn't prudent. With the colonies divided, a foreign power could destroy them, but the same enemy "would not dare to meet them, once United in the Field."

There were other advantages to joining the colonies together. The governor of a colonial union would be the eyes and ears of the king in his American dominions. He could monitor the competence of his servants and the "Dispositions of the People." He would "soon learn to distinguish between the Interest of America, and that of Great Britain," Bladen argued. Evidently, the interests of America and Britain were not the same. The problem was that, before long, the colonists would discover that too.

Bladen's pleas went unheeded. If the push toward union wasn't going to be imported from Britain or home-grown in the colonies, it would have to come from elsewhere in America.

2. Benjamin Franklin and the Iroquois Example

The people were divided and always at war. The habits of good thought—honesty, integrity, forbearance—were everywhere forgotten or ignored. Bitter feuds nobody could remember the origins of had led to endless rounds of violence. Crops failed and families were torn apart as a whole civilization seemed headed for collapse.

Then the Peacemaker came from across the great lake. He told them that if they adopted a "New Mind," their bloody conflicts would end and all could live together under a "Great White Pine" whose branches might someday shade the whole world. In one village, the Peacemaker converted a cannibal to his teachings. Together they set off to convince the warring nations to bury their bloodstained hatchets and form a new alliance. All would live as if in a single dwelling. They would be called Haudenosaunee—"the whole house."

Something happened in the area later known as upstate New York around the middle of the fifteenth century. Cannibalism all but ceased, agriculture advanced by leaps and bounds, and trade in stringed beads—wampum—exploded. The region saw what archaeologists call a "homogenization of material culture" among the Mohawk, Oneida, Onondaga, Seneca, and Cayuga—later known to the English as the Five Nations and to the French as the Iroquois. (A sixth nation, the

Tuscarora, migrated to the area from present-day North Carolina in the early eighteenth century.) Violence among previously hostile tribes disappeared; it was as if they had adopted a new way of thinking, a new mind.

An oral constitution known as the Great Law of Peace united the nations into a confederacy. The fifty-member grand council (convened near present-day Syracuse) adjudicated conflicts. If one nation accused another of wrong, the emissaries pledged to open their eyes, unblock their ears, and clear their throats in order to speak honestly and openly about the injury. When an amendment to the Great Law was proposed, the chiefs debated whether the "new beam" contributed to the strength of the symbolic longhouse. If approved, it was "added to the rafters."

Throughout Iroquois society, the virtues of patience, openness, generosity, and imperturbability were valued in leaders and fostered among the people. The Great Law required chiefs to have skin seven layers deep to prevent them from overreacting to criticism: "Neither anger nor fury shall find lodgment in their minds, and all their actions shall be marked by calm deliberation." Wealth and status were accorded not to those who hoarded riches but to those who gave them away. All decisions were made unanimously. "What kept the universe of political particles generally in orbit around a common nucleus," historian Daniel K. Richter observes, "was a shared belief in the ideal of consensus and in the spiritual power that comes from alliance with others." In Iroquois politics, "the coercive exercise of authority was totally unknown."

The civilization flourished. Its castles (as the fortified towns were called), their entrances adorned with carved wooden heads topped by the scalps of enemies, were more densely populated than any other settlements in eastern North America until the nineteenth century.

Then the floating islands came up from the sea. Contact with Europeans decimated the Iroquois, but unaffiliated tribes fared worse. The Iroquois welcomed the refugees into their league, which any person, regardless of ancestry, could join.

By the end of the seventeenth century, the Iroquois had expanded their domain and emerged as starring actors in the drama of New World diplomacy. Controlling the only level land route between the Hudson River and the Great Lakes—the path the Erie Canal would later follow—the Iroquois sought to hold the balance of power between the contending French and English empires. Iroquois chiefs became master players in a delicate and dangerous game.

So adept was the Iroquois League at statecraft, so tenacious in maintaining its independence, that Europeans began to take note of their sophisticated form of political organization. In 1668, a Jesuit missionary named François Joseph Le Mercier attended a meeting of the grand council. He saw the chieftains calmly submit their complaints and exchange compensatory gifts—"by means of which they maintain a good understanding of one another," Le Mercier explained. He approved of the ritual for it was impossible that during the course of the year "there should not happen some event capable of causing a rupture, and disuniting their minds." The annual meetings of the council served to heal any breach among the nations. "Their policy in this is very wise," he concluded, "since their preservation depends upon their union."

It was just the lesson the colonists needed to learn. A century would pass before they did.

On the morning of July 4, 1744, a tall Onondaga sachem named Canasatego rose to speak in the brick courthouse of Lancaster, a hardscrabble town on Pennsylvania's western frontier. It was the final day of a summit between Iroquois chiefs and officials from Pennsylvania, Virginia, and Maryland. Before everyone headed home, Canasatego had some words of wisdom for his settler friends.

It had been a long two weeks. The meeting had gotten off to a rough start when delegates from Maryland and Virginia began bickering about who would speak first. A Virginia commissioner tried to bribe the Iroquois to side with his colony. The natives were shocked by the breach of custom. There was something wrong—something backward, barbaric even—about a people who publicly quarreled about such petty things. The white men had the most advanced guns, the biggest ships, the finest clothes any Indian had seen, but their ideas about politics seemed shockingly primitive. The Iroquois had overcome their disunity centuries ago. It was time the colonists did the same.

After the initial argument, the conference went more smoothly. The Iroquois sold the colonists another massive parcel of land, which included the Shenandoah Valley, and the colonists presented the chiefs with gifts. But the colonists' unseemly divisions had stuck with the natives. Pacing the courthouse floor, Canasatego used his last speech to implore the newcomers to follow the Iroquois example:

> We have one Thing further to say, and that is, We heartily recommend Union and a good Agreement between you our Brethren. Never disagree, but preserve a Strict Friendship for one another, and thereby you, as well as we, will become the stronger.
>
> Our wise Forefathers established Union and Amity between the Five Nations; this has made us formidable; this has given us great Weight and Authority with our neighbouring Nations.
>
> We are a powerful Confederacy; and by your observing the same Methods our wise Forefathers have taken, you will acquire fresh Strength and Power: therefore whatever befalls you, never fall out with one another.

The colonists ignored him. They were more interested in plying the chiefs with rum than in listening to lectures on political theory. The conference adjourned. The colonial officials returned to Williamsburg, Annapolis, and Philadelphia, the natives to Iroquoia.

We know about Canasatego's advice only because the transcript of the Lancaster meeting fell into Benjamin Franklin's ink-stained hands. In the twenty-one years since he'd fled servitude under his brother in Boston, Franklin had become a wealthy publisher and a civic leader. In his adopted Philadelphia, he was rising in the world, and money was pouring in.

One source of income was a lucrative contract from the Pennsylvania Assembly to print money, laws, and other public papers, including accounts of meetings with the Indians. Information on the natives was hard to come by, and the transcripts made for entertaining reads. Out of his Market Street shop, Franklin sold the pamphlets to colonists curious about their "red brethren."

Franklin left no record of his reaction to Canasatego's speech, but what he did with the Lancaster treaty suggests he was impressed by something it contained: he published far more copies than usual and even sent some to London.

His interest sparked, Franklin began studying up on the Iroquois.

He started with Cadwallader Colden's *History of the Five Indian Nations*, which praised the natives' union. A Scottish-born New Yorker and a trained physician, Colden was interested, like many Enlightenment thinkers, in the origins of human society. To him, the Iroquois offered a glimpse into the deep past. "Here we may with more certainty see the original form of all government, than in the most curious Speculations of the Learned," Colden wrote.

In 1747, Franklin retired from his day job as a printer, and his new-found interest in native affairs turned into a consuming passion. He became involved in Pennsylvania's sensitive Indian diplomacy, and he began arguing for colonial union, just as Canasatego had suggested.

"It would be a very strange Thing," Franklin wrote a friend in 1751, "if Six Nations of ignorant Savages should be capable of forming a Scheme for such an Union, and be able to execute it in such a Manner, as that it has subsisted Ages and appears indissoluble; and yet that a like Union should be impracticable for ten or a Dozen English Colonies, to whom it is more necessary, and must be more advantageous; and who cannot be supposed to want an equal Understanding of their Interests."

If the once-warring Iroquois nations—"ignorant Savages" though they were—could form a lasting confederation, why couldn't the supposedly more civilized colonists? Franklin would soon find out.

In the early 1750s, relations between the colonists and the natives began to fray. Iroquois leaders objected to their treatment by deceitful merchants and the provincial legislatures they controlled. If the Indians broke their long-standing alliance with the British and sided with the French, the balance of power in North America would be upended. In 1753, when a Mohawk chief threatened to burn Albany to the ground, imperial administrators in London realized they faced a problem of urgent geopolitical importance and ordered the colonial governors to solve it.

For the first time, the Board of Trade told all the colonies to sign "one general Treaty" with the Indians rather than each colony negotiating its own separate agreement. After years of intentionally keeping the colonies disunited, British officials now saw that arrangement left too much power in the hands of unreliable provincial legislators, men who had put the entire empire in jeopardy. London still worried about American independence, but colonial cooperation had become necessary.

A few colonial visionaries welcomed the idea. William Shirley, the governor of Massachusetts, hoped "an Union of Councils" to deal solely with Indian affairs might "lay a Foundation for a general one among all his Majesty's Colonies." Half a century after William Penn promoted his ill-fated plan of union, support for an American federation was alive and well. So, too, were the provincial attitudes that had defeated it.

If the Indian threat wasn't enough to inspire joint colonial action, there were other worrisome developments. News soon spread that French soldiers had seized the most strategic location in eastern North America—the Forks of the Ohio River, where the Allegheny and Monongahela Rivers meet and begin a two-thousand-mile journey to the Mississippi and the sea. If the French held that crucial position, they could connect their settlements in Canada with those in Illinois and Louisiana, encircling the seaboard British colonies. Cut off from the interior, the British might have to leave America entirely. Without the profits from colonial trade, Britain wouldn't be able to maintain its powerful navy. France would have control of the high seas, of Europe, and, perhaps, some speculated, of Britain itself. National survival, therefore, depended on the British retaking that backcountry cross-roads, the Forks of the Ohio.

Days after reading reports of the French incursion, Franklin published a now-iconic image, the first American political cartoon. He may not have etched it, but the idea was all his. It was a simple engraving of a snake, broken into sections labeled with the initials of the colonies. Beneath it Franklin added a blunt, boldface message, less inspiring than menacing: "JOIN, or DIE." Union had become a necessity. If affection wasn't enough to hold the colonies together, fear would be the glue.

Franklin's famous image is usually interpreted as anticipating the unity Americans would eventually achieve. But what it really showed was the "disunited State" of the colonies, as Franklin noted in an accompanying editorial. Rather than signaling the beginning of continental solidarity, the image warned that the colonists might prove incapable of even the most basic cooperation necessary for their own survival—not exactly the kind of unifying mythology on which stable nations tend to be built. Nothing could have illustrated Franklin's point better than the colonists' wholesale rejection of his heartfelt plea.

One month later, in June 1754, twenty-five delegates from seven colonies showed up in Albany, New York's sleepy capital, a remote outpost with Dutch architecture and few of the trappings of European civilization. Their main business was to heal the breach with the Iroquois. Only a handful of delegates were authorized even to discuss colonial union; some had been instructed by their assemblies not to. As usual, each colony's elite were reluctant to cede control.

Only the force of Franklin's personality prompted the delegates at the Albany Congress to take up the matter. Ever prepared, he had drawn up a preliminary plan for a federation that looked a lot like the Iroquois one, with a grand council of forty-eight representatives apportioned according to each colony's contribution to the common treasury. But Franklin's plan went further in centralizing power. A governor-general appointed by the king would wield a veto. Taxes on "Superfluities" like tea and strong liquor would fill the union's coffers. The governor and the council would make treaties with the natives, organize land purchases, protect western settlements, and build a navy. The whole plan, once agreed to by the colonies, would go to Parliament for approval.

A robust debate broke out, "almost every Article being contested by one or another," as Franklin reported to Cadwallader Colden. Richard Peters, a fellow Pennsylvanian, suggested the colonies should be made into four separate unions rather than one. Smaller divisions would have more coherence. The delegates rejected the Peters plan, but versions of it would return throughout American history, an appealing option for those who believed a continental union was incompatible with good government.

After approving Franklin's single-union version, the commissioners sent a report to London explaining that the colonies' "Divided Disunited State" made federation necessary, especially as another war with France loomed. For the first time, each colony seemed willing to cede control over its own affairs for the good of the whole.

That, at least, was what the delegates said in Albany. When news of the plan appeared in the press, none could be found to defend it.

This was only prudent, for the union plan was almost universally panned. Maryland's assembly rejected union as "tending to the Destruction of the Rights and Liberties" of the people. Rhode Island instructed its London agent—each colony employed its own—to "be upon his Watch" for any efforts to put the Albany Plan into action. The Pennsylvania Assembly—intentionally—took up the proposal while its author happened to be out of town. The officials dismissed it, Franklin sneered, "without paying any attention to it at all."

Only in Massachusetts, where Governor Shirley supported Franklin's plan, was the idea seriously debated. There, too, however, legislators objected to the "perpetuity of the proposed Union"—they preferred a temporary association to deal only with the immediate emergency. They also criticized "the great sway which the Southern colonies… would have in all the determinations of the Grand Council." Divisions between North and South were already driving Americans apart.

Nearly every Massachusetts representative opposed the plan. Before voting, however, they wanted to hear what their constituents thought. In January 1755, Boston's town meeting debated the proposal. Franklin heard about what happened from a Boston correspondent. Franklin and the Albany commissioners were denounced as "arrant Blockheads," advocates of "a Scheme for destroying the liberties and privileges of every British subject upon the Continent." Bostonians had once overthrown a colonial union, and they weren't about to form a new one. The meeting rejected the Albany Plan, Franklin's friend reported, "by a very great Majority."

Franklin took the defeat stoically, as befitting a scientist faced with the failure of an experiment. But the intensity of colonial opposition had revealed a flaw in his plan. A confederation freely joined could also be freely left, which meant that threats to secede would slowly but surely undermine the union. "As any colony, on the least dissatisfaction, might repeal its own act and thereby withdraw itself from the union," Franklin reflected, "it would not be a stable one, or such as could be depended on." Once one colony left, the others would "one after another, withdraw, till the whole crumbled in its original parts." America would revert to its natural disunity.

The Albany Plan's rejection left only one solution: a push from London to force the colonists to unite. Yet that path, too, proved a dead end. Parliament was no more thrilled about Franklin's plan for an American union than the colonial assemblies had been. The Speaker of the House of Commons warned of the "ill consequence to be apprehended from uniting too closely" the colonies. "An Independency," as he put it, was "to be feared from such an union."

The failure of Franklin's Albany Plan showed how much still divided the colonists, how uninterested they were in anything beyond the hazy, contested boundaries of their own quarrelsome provinces. Told their choice was between two distasteful alternatives—death or union—the colonists still preferred to risk going it alone.

3. Unhappy Divided America

With its seemingly limitless resources, geographical isolation, and explosive population growth, America seemed poised to become richer and more powerful than Britain itself. But to do so, the colonies would first have to come together—and stay together. To a young schoolteacher in Massachusetts, American independence appeared inevitable. Just one obstacle stood in the way: the colonists' refusal to cooperate. "The only way to keep us from setting up for ourselves," John Adams concluded, "is to disunite Us."

Yet, as Adams would learn repeatedly over his long career, Americans didn't need outsiders to disunite them. They were plenty divided on their own.

The world war that began in 1754 saw fighting on five continents and every ocean. Some of the most pivotal battles took place in North America. Yet the same provincial attitudes and local preferences that undermined the Albany Plan kept the colonists from submitting to the top-down coordination needed to win the war. In early 1755, two regiments of Irish troops sailed west under General Edward Braddock, who had been ordered to retake the Forks of the Ohio from the French. Braddock had his work cut out for him. Soon after landing in Virginia, he wrote to London that he found "all want of Union among the Colonies."

That want of union proved one of the main obstacles to victory. After Braddock was killed in battle, French and Indian raids rolled the frontier back to Philadelphia. Spirits plummeted. "The state of these American

Colonies at present looks dark," wrote the president of the college at Princeton, Aaron Burr (whose wife would soon give birth to his better-known namesake). "We are divided in our councils," he wrote.

British generals found it difficult to raise troops among the colonists. In New Hampshire, an ax-wielding mob chased away an army recruiter. Southern colonies wanted their men at home to suppress possible slave insurrections. A Virginia regiment was instructed to fight only those battles necessary to secure the Forks of the Ohio, which the colony claimed as within its domain. The legislature insisted it saw the matter "in a National Light, not as Virginians but as Britons."

The assertion convinced nobody, especially not the leaders of Pennsylvania, who dispatched their own troops to contest Virginia's control. A British commander complained to London about "the Jealousy subsisting betwixt the Virginians and Pensilvanians...as both are aiming at engrossing the commerce and Barter with the Indians, and of settling and appropriating the immense tract of fine country." Those incentives could distort the compass of even the most virtuous colonial gentleman. "Nothing I more sincerely wish than a union to the Colonys in this time of eminent danger," a young militia colonel named George Washington avowed in 1756. But even he and a fellow Virginian were accused by one general of showing greater "attachment to the province they belong to" than to the empire as a whole.

Try as they might, colonial governors couldn't convince their subjects to cooperate. Thomas Pownall of Massachusetts begged soldiers to submit to British commands. "Nothing can hurt and ruin this Country," he insisted, "but a Disunion among the Several Parts of the army." Pownall begged the troops to "most conscientiously maintain a Spirit of union, and Subordination." New York's governor bemoaned "the State of unhappy divided America."

To appalled British officers, the colonists appeared to be some kind of degenerate race, "an Obstinate and Ungovernable People, Utterly Unacquainted with the Nature of Subordination," as one wrote to London. According to James Wolfe, the general later slain outside the walls of Quebec, Americans were "in general the dirtiest, most contemptible cowardly dogs that you can conceive. They fall down dead in their own dirt and desert by battalions, officers and all. Such rascals as those are rather an encumbrance than any real strength to any army."

The colonists seemed to think they were already independent. Most infuriating to one British general was the "Eternal Negotiation" he had to carry on with colonies a thousand miles apart. He could only wonder "what effect it must have in Canada, when they were informed of a disunion" among the colonies. Only after British commanders gave up on the colonists and imported the troops needed to win did its fortunes in the Seven Years' War turn around.

In London, those who saw the officers' dispatches from America blamed the age-old problem of colonial division. Pamphlets poured off the presses with ideas about how to solve it. Malachy Postlethwayt, a merchant and writer on economic themes—his first treatise was a pro-slavery tract bluntly titled *The African Trade, the Great Pillar and Support of the British Plantation Trade in America*—argued for strengthening the empire's control over its American dominions. The colonists' willingness to suffer almost any hardship rather than submit to external rule—to die rather than join—put the whole empire in danger. "Will a wise man stand with his arms folded, when his neighbour's house is on fire?" Postlethwayt asked. "Yet has not this been the conduct of our North-American colonies towards each other?"

He saw only one solution: reviving and extending the Dominion of New England. The defiant provinces had to be "united under a legal, regular and firm establishment" ruled by a "supreme governor." Once they were joined—by force, if necessary—Britain could "unite their military strength...so as to make head against the united military strength of the enemy."

Benjamin Franklin, now living in London as Pennsylvania's agent, soon entered the debate. In 1760, between consorting with the literary elite and founding philanthropic organizations like the Associates for Founding Clerical Libraries and Supporting Negro Schools, Franklin published an essay on colonial affairs. He took aim at the fear among the British that the colonists were aiming for independence—that, freed of the French menace in Canada, they would finally seek it.

Americans were far too divided to pursue such a project, Franklin contended. As architect of the rejected Albany Plan, he knew that they would never voluntarily unite even if it served their own interests. They were essentially different countries with "different forms of government, different laws, different interests, and some of them different religious persuasions and different manners." No enemy had ever been able to unite them. How reasonable was it to think they would ever join forces "against their own Nation...which it is well known they all love much more than they love one another?"

Everything Franklin knew about his countrymen convinced him there was no danger. Americans would never join together to seek independence—"An Union amongst them for such a Purpose is not merely improbable, it is impossible."

And yet there was one exception, Franklin warned, one circumstance in which the colonies might be able to tame all those differences and prejudices and unite in a revolution against the Crown. Only "the most grievous Tyranny and Opposition," he wrote, could lead them into union: "The Waves do not rise but when the Winds blow."

CHAPTER 2

Only United in Name

The States of America cannot be a Nation without War.
—BENJAMIN RUSH, 1776

AMERICANS RELUCTANT TO SACRIFICE THEIR autonomy joined together voluntarily only when they realized they would otherwise be forced to do so against their will and on terms not their own. Partnership offered an alternative to submission. The colonists knew they could never fight the most powerful empire on earth by keeping their efforts separate. To rebel, they had to unite. Compared to imperial consolidation, union was a lesser evil—and even then, only to some. From the start, Americans valued the continental alliance because it served their own and each separate colony's interests. More than a few of its champions would turn against it as soon as they perceived either to be at risk.

Throughout the Revolution, the main obstacle to unity was the widespread belief in its impossibility. The colonists were too different, too divided, to sustain a country of their own. The Union originated as a spontaneous response to emergency; its pretensions to perfection or perpetuity would forever be undermined by the true history of its slapdash formation. Skepticism of the project was voiced from the beginning and could never thereafter be entirely silenced.

Even the most famous work promoting American independence recognized how fragile the experiment really was. In *Common Sense*, his enormously influential pro-independence pamphlet, Thomas Paine noted the provincial attitudes and local differences that had hampered previous efforts to create a union. "The least fracture now," Paine wrote, "will be like a name engraved with the point of a pin on the

The three-dollar Continental bill with its Latin motto, *EXI-TUS IN DUBIO EST* (The outcome is in doubt). (*Museum of the American Revolution*)

tender rind of a young oak; the wound will enlarge with the tree, and posterity read it in full grown characters."

For proponents of American independence, the birth of the Union was, as some parents say of an unexpected pregnancy, a welcome surprise. For opponents, it was a disaster waiting to happen. The United States of America, that ambiguously named creation, was a hypothesis to be tested against its own unfolding history, a proposition its founders hoped would in time become its own proof. In *Names on the Land*, his classic history of American place-names, George R. Stewart observed that the country's awkward appellation revealed its fatal flaw. "The very plurality of States," Stewart wrote, was a "standing suggestion that what had once been united could equally well be taken apart; in the very name, the seeds of nullification and secession lay hidden."

1. Rise of an Unlikely Alliance

After the Seven Years' War, Britain moved to bind the loosely joined colonies closer together. To pay off staggering war debts, Parliament cracked down on smuggling, passed new taxes on sugar and other imports, and required colonists to pay a tax on every piece of paper used for legal purposes; officials would place a stamp on the paper to indicate that the tax had been paid. Given what they knew of American disunity, London ministers expected any opposition to be scattered and weak. The author of the Stamp Act even hoped the measure would divide the colonies and make them more compliant. "All Bonds of Union between them" must be "severed," he wrote.

Instead, the reforms strengthened those bonds more than anything had before. Parliament finally accomplished what no foreign enemy had managed to do. Yet collaboration, after a century and a half of hostility, didn't come easy. It was an arduous and unpleasant task, setting aside differences for the sake of a common cause. As Rhode Island's assembly wrote in a 1764 appeal for colonial solidarity, cooperation was simply "the most probable Method to produce the End aimed at"—the repeal of the unjust taxes. *The most probable method;* not necessarily the most preferred.

Protests broke out up and down the Atlantic Coast as mobs demanded the resignation of officials appointed as stamp-tax collectors, burned them in effigy, ransacked their stately homes. The man Benjamin Franklin handpicked for the job in Pennsylvania wrote to his patron in London that each letter he sent might be his last, for "the Spirit or Flame of Rebellion is got to a high Pitch." The early advocate of American unity was among the first targets of the colonists' wrath; a Philadelphia mob was prevented from tearing down Franklin's house only by armed patrols sent by his allies in the Pennsylvania legislature. Every collector resigned. The law was null and void.

Yet even as the movement spread, the possibility of turning the colonies-wide protests into a more enduring union remained little more than a punch line. "What kind of a dish," one critic asked, could be made by the diverse colonies? "New England will throw in fish and onion; the Middle States flax-seed and flour; Maryland and Virginia will add tobacco; North Carolina, pitch, tar and turpentine; South Carolina, rice and indigo; and Georgia will sprinkle the whole composition with saw dust." It would be an unappetizing stew—not quite the melting pot of later fable. "Such an absurd jumble will you make, if you attempt to form a union among such discordant materials as the thirteen British provinces."

Some tried to formalize the ad hoc colonial cooperation. The Massachusetts assembly suggested that all the colonies meet and craft a

joint petition to Parliament. Though some colonies couldn't participate—
London had instructed the governors to block any "unwarrantable
combination"—nine provinces sent a total of twenty-seven men to New
York's City Hall in October of 1765. All but a few were strangers to one
another. The Stamp Act Congress, like the Albany meeting of 1754, is
often described as a landmark on the road to the Constitution. What it
actually revealed were the conflicts and violence usually associated
with later periods. When Timothy Ruggles of Massachusetts, the wary,
conservative president of the Congress, refused to sign the final product, a Declaration of Rights and Grievances, calling it insubordinate
and possibly treasonous, Thomas McKean of Philadelphia criticized
him harshly. Flustered, Ruggles challenged McKean to a duel. McKean
accepted. They were to meet the next day. Overnight, however, Ruggles
changed his mind and fled home. So ended the Stamp Act Congress,
that "spectacular achievement in unity," as one historian put it.

Still, getting the colonists to cooperate in the past had been impossible, and at least now they were attempting to work together—albeit
reluctantly, having been forced into it by circumstance. Imperial officials dreaded the future. The Massachusetts legislature's outreach to
its neighbors was an attempt to connect "the demagogues of the several Governments in America," Francis Bernard, the colony's panic-
stricken governor, warned officials in London. "A New System of Policy
is now become needful," he wrote. "The Patchwork Government of
America will last no longer."

While they waited for a response to their petition, leading colonists
formed a network known as the Sons of Liberty. Instead of tearing
down houses, they used social ostracism and commercial boycotts to
isolate those who dared to pay the stamp tax. Anyone who did should
be "branded with eternal infamy," one public letter said. "Let him be
alone in the world—let him wish to associate with the wild beasts of
some dark, loathsome cave."

The new sense of solidarity seemed promising, but many doubted
that an alliance forged in such desperate circumstances could last. Two
months after the Stamp Act Congress, one of its breakout stars, an elite
Philadelphia lawyer named John Dickinson, admitted that the colonists
didn't have enough in common to start their own country. Catastrophe
would befall an independent America, Dickinson predicted. The country

would break into a "Multitude of Commonwealths, Crimes, and Calamities, of mutual Jealousies, Hatreds, Wars and Devastations; till at last the exhausted Provinces shall sink into Slavery under the yoke of some fortunate Conqueror. History seems to prove that this must be the deplorable Fate of these Colonies whenever they become independent."

Much to Dickinson's relief, independence wouldn't be necessary— at least not yet. Parliament repealed the Stamp Act in January of 1766, and when the news reached towns in America in May, the streets filled with jubilant inhabitants. Bells rang out; feasts were held in public buildings. Opposition leaders rejoiced not only in their successful fight against an unjust tax but in belonging to an empire responsive to complaints. The Sons of Liberty dissolved. Colonial unity had served its purpose. It was good they had joined together, but even protest leaders hoped they would never need to again.

The Stamp Act's repeal took the momentum out of the resistance. A year later, Parliament passed new duties on paper, glass, paint, and tea. In response, the colonists vowed to boycott British goods. But the movement failed to achieve the unity of the Stamp Act protests. Many New Englanders obeyed the boycott with "religious punctuality," in the words of one observer, but colonists elsewhere seemed to be made of less patriotic stuff. Wealthy merchants scoffed at the idea that "men of liberal Education" should be "dictated to by illiterate Mechanicks." Radicals denounced upper-class holdouts. "When a Country is divided," a newspaper declared, "*Neutrality* is little better than *Treason*."

The movement against the new taxes fizzled out, but it was revived in 1770 after British soldiers panicked and fired on a Boston crowd pestering them with rocks and insults. When the smoke cleared, five people lay dead on the cobblestones. Hoping to douse the flames of discontent, Britain ordered its troops to a harbor fort and rescinded every tax but the one on tea.

It didn't work. Two years later, a crowd in Rhode Island looted and torched a British customs ship. King George III and his ministers responded aggressively, demanding the arrest and prosecution of those responsible. Bostonians formed a "committee of correspondence" to organize the revived resistance movement and coordinate with other provinces.

Many colonists continued to boycott British tea and drank smuggled-in Dutch tea instead. In May 1773, Parliament passed a bill to lower the price of tea and thus undercut smugglers. By purchasing the cheaper tea, Americans would finally concede, implicitly, that Britain had the right to tax them. But the colonists refused to participate. Instead they burned tea in town squares as a sacrifice of "the obnoxious Drug at the Shrine of American Liberty." In Boston, scores of protesters dressed as Mohawk warriors stormed three ships and tossed hundreds of chests into the harbor. The wanton destruction of so much property seemed a point of no return. "The Sublimity of it charms me!" John Adams cheered.

The king retaliated by revoking the Massachusetts charter and closing Boston's port until the city paid for the tea. Assuming "Boston would be left to fall alone," as Samuel Adams wrote, the British government made "no preparation for the effects of an union." But a union was just what the Americans now realized they needed. A Massachusetts paper predicted that Britain's latest attempt at coercion would turn out to be "the very means to perfect that union in America, which it intended to destroy."

Other colonies responded to the crackdown as if they themselves were its targets. The news arrived in Williamsburg like "a shock of Electricity," one paper reported. When Virginia's legislature expressed support for Boston, the royal governor dissolved the assembly. Eighty of its members gathered in a tavern and drew up a declaration: "An attack made on one of our sister colonies…is an attack made on all British America." They called for a continent-wide summit to figure out what to do.

On a September morning in 1774, forty-five men from twelve colonies gathered at the five-floor City Tavern in Philadelphia, "the most genteel one in America," according to Adams. Many had been in town for days; they'd spent most of their time drinking—toasting both to the "Union of the Colonies" and the "Union of Britain and the Colonies, on a Constitutional Foundation"—and reading newspapers aloud. One paper, the *Pennsylvania Journal*, had redesigned its front page to feature a version of Franklin's disjointed snake and the adapted slogan "Unite or Die," still as ominous as ever.

With a cheery hurrah, "the ablest and wealthiest men in America," as one member referred to the group, left the tavern. They walked two blocks west, crossed Dock Creek ("a Receptacle for the Carcasses of dead Dogs," residents complained), went past a putrid tannery, and strode up narrow Whalebone Alley to Carpenters' Hall, an impressive two-story building the city's craftsmen had set up as a meetinghouse and offered as a venue for the Continental Congress.

The delegates were a motley crew. "Here is a Diversity of Religions, Educations, Manners, Interests, Such as it would Seem almost impossible to unite in any one Plan of Conduct," Adams reported to his law partner in Boston. Less a conclave of comrades than a meeting "of Ambassadors from a dozen belligerent Powers of Europe," as Adams wrote, they spent more time talking about what set them apart than what they had in common.

Disunion haunted the Continental Congress like a phantom. The different interests of the colonies led some delegates to call for greater unity and others to insist on preserving each colony's autonomy. "All America is thrown into one mass," a young self-taught lawyer named Patrick Henry exclaimed. "The distinctions between Virginians, Pennsylvanians, New Yorkers and New Englanders are no more! I am not a Virginian, but an American!"

These inspiring words, much quoted ever since, concealed Henry's real intent—to ensure that power in the Continental Congress was distributed unequally among the colonies, with votes accorded to each colony based on its population. His own province, the most populous of all, would then wield the most sway. The distinctions between Virginians and everyone else didn't matter—as long as Virginians had more influence than everyone else. It would be a "great Injustice," Henry declared, "if a little Colony should have the same Weight in the Councils of America as a great one."

The self-serving nature of Henry's speech became clear minutes later when a Virginia ally, Benjamin Harrison (ancestor of two presidents), announced that he and his colony's delegates would leave Philadelphia unless they got their way. So much for all America thrown into one mass.

Smaller colonies objected to Henry's proposal; their only chance for relevance was if each colony had the same amount of votes. Outnumbered, the Virginians conceded, but the underlying issue of how to allocate representation would divide Americans for decades, even centuries, to come.

The weakness of the emerging alliance came into sharper focus when the delegates began to draw up Articles of Association—the terms for a new colonies-wide boycott on trade with Britain. To enforce the ban, local committees would "observe the conduct of all persons" and ensure violators were "universally contemned as the enemies of American liberty." In the coming months, holdouts would be tarred and feathered—tortured—and paraded through the streets. The Continental Association, a "groundbreaking infrastructure of revolution," as historian Holger Hoock writes, was also "an apparatus of oppression." If, as Abraham Lincoln later argued, the articles should be considered the birth certificate of the American union, it was one bound from the beginning by shame, fear, coercion, and conformity.

The seeds of its dissolution, moreover, were present at the creation. New Englanders, facing the brunt of British wrath, wanted the boycott to start immediately, while Virginians, worried about wasting the tobacco they had already planted, demanded a year's postponement. Other delegates wanted to go ahead without Virginia, but Maryland and North Carolina, fearful of being undercut in the market if their neighbor opted out, refused to let that happen. This time, New England had to cave.

Virginia's success showed how much a little brinkmanship could achieve. South Carolina's delegates, every one a wealthy slave owner, took note. That colony's heavy dependence on trade made its leaders suspicious of a self-imposed embargo. Only a small fraction of the North's exports went to Britain, while 65 percent of South Carolina's rice crop and all of its indigo did. "If this association is perfected," John Rutledge of Charleston pointed out, "the northern colonies will suffer very little…while if South Carolina enters into it her chief businesses are ruined." Ruined businesses would mean unfed, inactive, potentially rebellious slaves. To Rutledge, a London-trained lawyer who owned some sixty people, the boycott was "a commercial scheme" cooked up for New England's benefit. It would make his constituents "the dupes of the people of the North"—a humiliation to which they would never submit. At that, Rutledge led his fellow South Carolinians out of Carpenters' Hall.

They, too, found their threats amply rewarded. Samuel Adams negotiated a deal to allow rice exports to continue, although indigo would still be prohibited. The other colonies had no choice but to agree; Georgia—distracted by an Indian war on its frontier—hadn't sent any delegates to Philadelphia, so if South Carolina left, the lower South would have no representation, and the Continental Congress would not be continental at all. South Carolina got its ransom, one patriot later recalled, "only for the sake of preserving the Union of America."

That need, above all, to preserve the fragile Union, even at the cost of its effectiveness, was precisely the problem. In 1861, Lincoln cited the Articles of Association as proof of the Union's perpetuity— evidence, supposedly, that it existed before the states declared independence. Yet whatever rudimentary union the 1774 pact created would forever be weakened by the fact that it could be held hostage by any party willing to break it up—or even threaten to. That lesson would never be forgotten, least of all in South Carolina.

2. The Doomsday Book of America

British redcoats and ragtag colonial militia clashed on a road outside Boston in April of 1775, and three weeks later, seventy-year-old Benjamin Franklin returned to America after a nearly two-decade absence. He marveled at the changes in his native land. No longer did each colony think only of its own interests. The attitudes that defeated his Albany Plan seemed to have slackened. "All parties are now extinguish'd here," Franklin told a London friend. "Britain has found means to unite us."

That hopeful statement, however, was premature. As the Second Continental Congress convened in Pennsylvania's assembly hall in May 1775, John Dickinson cataloged the threats to the colonial cause: "the Danger of Insurrection by Negroes in Southern Colonies—Incursions of Canadians & Indians upon the Northern Colonies—Incidental Proposals to disunite Us—false hopes—selfish designs"—the list went on.

With those obstacles and more ahead of them, Dickinson wanted to try again to reconcile with Britain. "Discord and total Disunion," he believed, would result from a too-hasty rush toward separation. John Adams dismissed the idea of sending another groveling plea to the Crown as ludicrous. But he knew Dickinson and other moderates had to be appeased. Even after fighting broke out, few Americans were ready to embrace independence from the empire they had been raised to revere. The challenge was to keep the bold from leaving the wary behind. "The continent is a vast, unwieldy machine," Adams wrote an ally. "We cannot force events."

Divisions that seemed glaring in Philadelphia were even more so in the crowded Continental army encampment outside Boston. Without milk and vegetables, soldiers suffered from malnutrition and disease. Discipline dissolved. Fights and arguments broke out between troops from different colonies.

For the first time, Americans from distant regions lived in close quarters with one another. They didn't like what they learned. Even George Washington, the Virginian who had been put in command of the New England–dominated army to foster continental unity, called his Yankee troops "an exceeding dirty and nasty people," the privates marked by "an unaccountable kind of stupidity," the officers not much better. Northerners, in turn, looked down on Southerners; one officer complained they were "as Indifferent men as I ever served with… Unwilling for Duty of any kind" and "Exceedingly Vicious."

Come winter, many troops went home. Washington seethed. If nothing was done soon to fix the problem, he wrote to the Continental Congress, "the Army must absolutely break up."

Americans' ties to their own colonies remained stronger than their loyalty to anything larger. Glancing around the assembly hall one day, Adams noted the lingering effects of local attachments on the delegates. It had been easy, back in Boston, to see what made a man tick and why he aligned with one party or another. In Philadelphia, among "a Multitude of Strangers," that was more difficult. The colonies seemed as different from one another "as several distinct nations almost," Adams reflected. If Americans didn't manage their divisions with care and consideration, "they will certainly be fatal."

North and south, east and west, in cities and on the frontier, violent conflicts threatened to tear the fledgling union apart. Local civil wars might have erupted in several places had not the larger war eclipsed them. In the remote uplands east of Lake Champlain, an area claimed by New York but sold off in parcels by an enterprising New Hampshire governor, a group of Connecticut-born frontiersmen headed by a gun-toting farmer named Ethan Allen formed the Green Mountain Boys, a separatist paramilitary organization devoted to overthrowing Albany's rule. In the Wyoming Valley on the upper Susquehanna River, settlers from Pennsylvania and Connecticut fought pitched and bloody battles. Three hundred miles to the southwest, Virginia and Pennsylvania squared off over their long-contested border. In the western Carolinas, irate backwoodsmen rebelled against the seaboard elite whose noisy resistance to the Crown they dismissed as "an artful deception...by the gentlemen of fortune and ambition on the sea coast."

The resolutions of these disputes were postponed by the conflict with Britain, but they would later return to weaken American unity and open the door to foreign meddling.

Loyalists pointed to these mini–civil wars as proof of the colonists' fatal divisions. Could a union of so many different regions, diverse populations, and divergent interests ever last? "O, 'tis a monstrous and unnatural coalition," one critic declaimed. "We should as soon expect to see the greatest contrarieties in Nature to meet in harmony, and the wolf and the lamb to feed together, as Virginians to form a cordial union with the saints of New England."

Patriots, too, worried that American divisions spelled trouble. Look at how the colonists were fighting each other, noted Carter Braxton, a new arrival in the Continental Congress. Observe the "heart burning and jealousy" between provinces. Americans shouldn't break from Britain until they had resolved their own conflicts. If they declared independence now, Braxton warned, "the Continent would be torn in pieces by Intestine Wars and Convulsions."

Yet there wasn't time to worry about disunity. Any delay would only undermine it. "The People are now ahead of you," a friend told John Adams. "The only way to prevent discord and dissension is to strike while the iron is hot."

As for which to do first—declare independence or form a union— Adams thought federation "the most intricate, the most important, the most dangerous, and delicate Business of all." But he had to admit that as long as both got done, "it may not perhaps be of much Importance, which is done first." Decades later, when the Civil War finally came, whether independence or union had come first would seem immensely important, at least as a philosophical matter. But at the time, amid the swirl of events, the question was irrelevant.

In May 1776, cheers erupted in Williamsburg after Virginia's extralegal assembly endorsed independence—the first colony to do so. The British banner came down and a thirteen-striped "Union Flag" went up. Unsure of the new country's name, revelers toasted "the American independent States" and fired off their guns.

One by one, other colonies followed suit. Adams counted the votes: Eight colonies in the South and New England were for independence, but the five middle ones were not. The division could have proven disastrous. Adams later recalled his fear that Pennsylvania and New York, left to themselves, "would have joined the British." Only intimidation by their more radical neighbors forced them into line.

When riders from Williamsburg brought Virginia's resolution to Philadelphia, the Continental Congress appointed three committees: one to draw up a declaration of independence, a second to hammer out terms of union, and a third to draft a model treaty to present to foreign nations. The once unthinkable had become the inevitable. America was setting off on its own. John Adams exulted that even his more conservative rival John Dickinson was "now confessing the falsehood of all his prophecies, and the truth of mine."

But Adams was wrong. Dickinson had one more prophecy to make.

It had been a long, strange revolution for the pale, gaunt lawyer and plantation owner. A leader of the decade-long resistance, Dickinson had won literary celebrity with his 1767 *Letters from a Farmer in Pennsylvania*, which urged Americans to oppose Britain's onerous taxes and commercial regulations. The essays made Dickinson the toast of colonists up and down the seaboard, the namesake for a ship with his narrow visage painted on its hull, and the model for a new sculpture in Patience Wright's famous wax museum. In 1768 Dickinson published a "Song for American Freedom" with lines that echo through the centuries:

> *Then join hand in hand, brave Americans all!*
> *By uniting we stand, by dividing we fall!*

Though we rarely pause to consider its provenance, "United We Stand" has become one of our most popular national mottoes, spanning all identities and ideologies, found on T-shirts and pizza boxes, on bumper stickers adorning pickups and Priuses alike. What's little known, however, is that the man who came up with those words was the only delegate to the Continental Congress who refused to sign the Declaration of Independence and that he did so precisely because he thought Americans weren't united enough to stand together. Actually, he told the Congress, they were divided, and sooner or later their union would fall.

From the moment his fellow delegates began debating independence, Dickinson had been spiked with nervousness, fearful the ship he had helped steer for more than a decade was about to founder on the rocks of irresponsible radicalism and unnecessary haste. He saw how much divided Americans and knew how much more would divide them in the future. He feared America would turn against itself and violently break apart, leaving his own Pennsylvania in the middle of warring Northern and Southern armies. If the delegates voted for independence, Dickinson warned, skeptics like himself "must retire, and possibly their colonies might secede from the Union."

Perhaps to punish Dickinson for his pessimism, his colleagues appointed him chair of the committee tasked with sorting through the colonies' thorny disputes—over Western lands and Atlantic fisheries, slavery and commerce, taxes and representation—and devising a form of government capable of resolving them. Soon after the group began meeting, New Hampshire's delegate reported that drafting a constitution for this government had turned out to be more difficult than expected: "I fear it will take some time before it will be finally settled." He had no idea.

Dickinson saw the committee's struggle as fresh cause for concern. It was, therefore, a tense, haggard man who stood before the Congress on July 1, 1776, holding a barely legible document written in iron-gall ink, full of last-minute insertions and crossed-out scribbles. He had been laboring over his words and hadn't slept much. But he knew what he wanted to say: independence would be a disaster.

The union committee had argued about "almost every Article" in the new constitution. Consensus might prove impossible. "Some of Us totally despair of any reasonable Terms of Confederation," said Dickinson. To leave British protection without a union set up would be to "brave the storm in a skiff made of paper."

The fractures ran too deep; the union would crumble. Before voting to separate, Dickinson wished he could "read a little more in the Doomsday Book of America." He expected it would reveal that the "unwieldy" Union would eventually break in two. "I have a strong Impression on my Mind that this will take Place."

After Dickinson stopped speaking, the delegates sat silent as rain lashed against the windows.

3. The Flaws in the First Constitution

The Declaration of Independence was a divorce notice, drafted and served on behalf of the American people by their lawyers in Congress assembled. As one marriage died, a new one was being born. In his old age, Thomas Jefferson called the Declaration "the fundamental act of union of these states." But the sealing of that union was still years away. Americans seemed reluctant to tie the knot. They had just freed themselves from a relationship that demanded more than they were willing to put in. Unconvinced of their new partners' charms, enjoying their independence, in no position to make financial commitments, they had serious doubts about the viability of a union to which they had consented in the heat of passion, its flaws all too evident in the sober light of morning.

America's first constitution, the Articles of Confederation, was not ratified until after five years of bitter fights, self-serving rationalizations, accusations of infidelity, even blackmail. A decade later, on the verge of a complete breakdown of the marriage, Americans decided to recommit to one another on terms they hoped would make it last. For the sake of harmony, long-simmering doubts had to be silenced, repressed. Little held the Union together but fear of it breaking up.

In addition to announcing America's independence, the Declaration was also a request by separatist rebels for assistance from outside powers, especially France, whose ships, arms, money, and men would prove invaluable. But a tightly integrated monarchy would never deal with thirteen separate squabbling republics. "What contract will a foreign state make with us," one delegate asked, "when we cannot agree among ourselves?" Without union, there would be no alliance; without an alliance, the war would end in defeat; and for the delegates, defeat might mean a firing squad.

The hard work of drafting a constitution had already driven John Dickinson to despair. After abstaining from the final vote on independence, he resigned from the Congress, leaving behind a rough draft of the Articles of Confederation that began: "The Name of this Confederacy shall be 'The United States of America.'" It was Dickinson who, after warning that the new country was anything but united, gave it that clumsy, aspirational name.

Days after declaring independence, the delegates took up the task of forming a confederation. But the work proved no easier then than it had weeks earlier. Time and again, debate broke down on three difficult issues: representation, taxes, and land. Behind all of it lay a single question: Should the Union remain a loose association of sovereign states or become a truly national government? The question divided Americans during the Revolution—and in all the centuries since.

The most heated debate occurred over how to allot votes in Congress. In the First Continental Congress, Patrick Henry had called for a stronger, more solid union in order to give his own colony greater sway. Now, too, soaring rhetoric about unity served the interests of larger states like Pennsylvania and Massachusetts. "We are now One people— a new nation," Benjamin Rush of Philadelphia declared. Deploying a favorite metaphor, John Adams explained that "the confederacy is to make us one individual only. It is to form us, like separate parcels of metal, into one common mass." Anyone who favored a scheme other than population-based representation, Rush insisted, "signs the death warrant of the liberties of America."

The dispute quickly turned ugly. Each side said it would refuse to join a union if the other side won. To small-state delegates, the fate of the Revolution depended on avoiding consolidation into an all-encompassing empire. Eyeing demographic trends, South Carolina's Edward Rutledge (brother of John, who led the 1774 walkout) feared that "destroying all Provincial Distinctions" would guarantee Southern subservience to New England. His state would never unite with the others on such terms.

Because each state had one vote, the smaller ones were again able to protect the status quo. But it was clear the larger states would keep trying to overturn it and give each state congressional votes based on its population. Benjamin Franklin spoke for many opponents of equal state suffrage when he predicted that "a confederation upon such iniquitous principles will never last long."

Nearly as controversial was the matter of taxes. Nobody wanted to give Congress the power to levy taxes on a people who were rebelling to avoid paying them. It was decided that instead, the states would contribute funds to the common treasury. But how much would each state pay? Would their quotas be based on population or property? And in which of those categories were slaves?

The issue opened a breach between North and South—the fault line along which many skeptics of independence expected the Union to someday break. Southerners objected to population-based taxes if those they held in bondage were counted as people. Slaves were property—end of story. If that was even questioned, an angry South Carolinian warned, "there is an End of the Confederation."

The delegates tried to avoid the issue by distributing financial burdens according to each state's land values. But that was only a temporary solution, and it never worked in practice. The thorny questions the debate raised wouldn't go away. "Nothing but present danger will ever make us all agree," a New Jersey delegate wrote home, "and I sometimes even fear that will be insufficient."

Then there was the problem of the Western lands. For years, some of the colonies had verged on open warfare over their competing claims to valuable territory. Virginia's speculators—George Washington among them—claimed that a provision in the colony's 1609 charter gave it almost limitless room to expand from sea to sea. Maryland, New Jersey, Delaware, and other states unblessed by charters with such provisions believed that one reason to form a union was to have it act as steward for the only thing Americans held in common, at least theoretically: the seemingly limitless Western frontier (which they would soon seize from its native inhabitants). Those landless states, as they were known, vowed not to sign a constitution unless it gave the central government ownership of the Western domain.

Because of these issues, the summer of 1776 saw scant progress toward a union. Some began to contemplate a return to the imperial fold. Even the Declaration's author considered independence provisional, a bargaining chip to be used in negotiations with a contrite king. Days after the delegates scrawled their names across the parchment, Jefferson told a friend that Americans might have to reacknowledge "the British tyrant as our king"—although stripped, of course, of the powers he had abused.

So frustrating was the work on the Articles of Confederation that the delegates went days on end without discussing what all of them had recently deemed a matter of the utmost importance. Now it was "of little consequence" whether they formed a Union, Edward Rutledge lamented, "for we have made such a Devil of it already that the Colonies can never agree to it."

At the end of July, the delegates received a much-needed pep talk from Scottish-born Presbyterian minister John Witherspoon. Aaron Burr Sr.'s successor as president of what is today Princeton College, Witherspoon had taught rhetoric, divinity, and moral philosophy to a generation of elite Americans, including members of the Continental Congress. The delegates therefore listened closely, like good students, when Witherspoon spoke on the importance of union.

The moment was ripe for action, but it was fleeting. To further delay cementing the Articles of Confederation might mean postponing a union forever. If the war ended before they were finished, as well it might, Americans would return to their rivalries and hostilities. There could even be a civil war. "The greatest danger We have," Witherspoon warned, "is of Disunion among ourselves."

Even if a confederation was sealed, he acknowledged, "a time must come when it will be dissolved and broken in pieces." All things must pass. Yet the likelihood of the Union's future rupture was hardly a reason not to form one. "Shall we establish nothing good, because we know it cannot be eternal?" Witherspoon asked. The task before the Congress was only to establish a government "upon the best principles and in the wisest manner, that it may last as long as the nature of things will admit."

Not forever— *as long as the nature of things will admit.* From the beginning, a frank acknowledgment of the Union's impermanence was embedded in even the most eloquent argument an American could make on its behalf. Though rhetoricians even abler than Witherspoon would try, the recognition of its essential fragility, lodged deep in the national mind, would never be removed.

In September 1777, with British troops threatening Philadelphia, the delegates fled to Lancaster, Pennsylvania, where they met for a day in the same courthouse that had hosted the Iroquois conference of 1744. Thirty-three eventful years had passed since Canasatego, the Onondaga orator, urged the colonists to unite. Now they had—or were trying to. The next day, looking to put more distance between themselves and the enemy, the delegates moved across the Susquehanna to the rugged village of York. For nine months, that tiny rural outpost, home to just three thousand people, many of whom spoke only German, served as the capital of the United States.

Exiled from the comforts of Philadelphia, the delegates finally found time to finish the Articles of Confederation. The work hadn't gotten easier. "Rely on it," one informed Jefferson, "our Confederacy is not founded on Brotherly Love, and Able Statesmen are Surely wanting here."

By November, the articles were ready to be sent to the states for ratification. Each of the thirteen states had to agree before they went into effect. The delegates attached a letter explaining why this constitution had taken so long to finish and why it should not be rejected even if it was flawed. Americans were a diverse and fractious people. It was difficult to satisfy "the various sentiments and interests of a continent divided into so many sovereign and independent communities." The delegates begged the states to consider the articles, however imperfect, the best possible solution:

> Let them be examined with a liberality becoming brethren and fellow-citizens surrounded by the same imminent dangers, contending for the same illustrious prize, and deeply interested in being forever bound and connected together by ties the most intimate and indissoluble; and, finally, let them be adjusted with the temper and magnanimity of wise and patriotic legislators, who, while they are concerned for the prosperity of their own more immediate circle, are capable of rising superior to local attachments, when they may be incompatible with the safety, happiness, and glory, of the general confederacy.

A perfect union this was not. But the delay had lasted long enough. Congress was broke. The army was on the run. Washington was about to lead thousands of troops and hangers-on—officers, soldiers, spouses, children, nurses, laundresses, and slaves, many of them starving, sick, freezing, clothed in damp rags, and shoeless, their tracks red in the snow—into winter quarters at Valley Forge. Many would never leave. Some of Washington's rivals were scheming to have him fired so they could take command.

"This salutary measure can no longer be deferred," the letter concluded. "It seems essential to our very existence as a free people."

Given that it would take years for the states to ratify the Articles of Confederation and that the final holdout would submit only after being blackmailed by a foreign power, it's clear this union did not seem essential to everyone. To some, it posed almost as great a threat to freedom as the redcoats and their feudal mercenaries. "Only united in name," as one politician said a few years later, Americans remained as divided as ever. And still they had to win the war.

In the fall of 1777, the Americans surprised a British army at Saratoga, New York, and forced its surrender. France, formerly unsure of the rebels' prospects, finally agreed to join the fight.

Almost immediately, this new patron began trying to sway political decisions in its weak client state, dividing the congressmen and the country and opening divisions that would never fully close. Through wartime struggles over how, where, and when to fight and what would follow the return of peace, a pattern of allegiances emerged that would define American politics for decades to come. Two factions became discernible—an English party and a French party. The former dominated the Northern states. Though New Englanders had started the rebellion, they cherished their trade ties to Britain and hoped to renew them after the war. They were suspicious of French intentions and wary lest independence from one power lead to dependence on another. French agents spread rumors that what the New Englanders really wanted was reunion with Britain.

In the South, the French interest prevailed. After Saratoga, the British turned their attention to valuable Southern ports like Savannah and Charleston, where they expected their troops to be joined by thousands of loyalists and fugitive slaves. Southern masters abhorred the British policy of arming slaves in exchange for their freedom. Only France could offer desperately needed protection.

As the war turned south in more ways than one, sectional divisions worsened. The "old prejudices of North against South, and South against North" had again risen to the surface, a Connecticut delegate warned his state's governor. To a New Jersey newspaper, "some malignant disorder" in the body politic seemed likely to cause "a political dissolution." Speaking perhaps too freely with a French diplomat, Samuel Adams confided his belief that the country would split in two.

Late in 1778, the British and their loyalist allies swept into Savannah and marched north toward Charleston. The Continental Congress refused pleas to redirect soldiers from the northern theater. Left to fend for themselves, some Southerners wondered why they had bothered to join the Union if it wasn't going to help them. They could only conclude, as South Carolina's lieutenant governor wrote, that they were being "sacrificed to the resentment of the Enemy"—thrown to the wolves.

The abandonment of Charleston especially saddened Christopher Gadsden, an early resistance leader. His friendships with New Englanders like Samuel Adams had helped build trust and confidence between regions otherwise wary of each other's intentions. Gadsden reminded Adams that, just a few years earlier, South Carolina had rallied to support occupied Boston. "Now the Tables are turn'd, and we in far greater Distress than New England ever was," he noted. "But who feels for us? We seem to be entirely deserted." If his state, facing invasion, didn't receive help from the others, "what advantage have we by the Confederacy?"

Though they couldn't spare troops, Congress didn't ignore the South's appeals. It urged Georgia and South Carolina to enlist their slaves. A few years earlier, when one of John Adams's correspondents had suggested enlisting slaves, Adams had predicted the masters would "run out of their Wits at the least Hint of such a Measure." And so they did. This was a cure worse than the disease. As the British bore down on Charleston, city leaders professed themselves "much disgusted" by the proposal and rejected it "with contemptuous huzzahs." They wished it had never been made.

Months later, when the British demanded Charleston's surrender, officials had to choose whether to surrender or to fight. Alienated by the Congress, they offered to give up if South Carolina could remain neutral in the war. The British refused those terms and made plans to lay siege to the city. Just then, a patriot band showed up and chased the enemy away.

Charleston was saved—for the moment. But that didn't change the fact that South Carolinians, feeling abandoned by the federal government, had been prepared to abandon it in turn. In future fights over slavery, their descendants would come to the same conclusion about how much the Union was worth.

A year later, in May 1780, Charleston fell. It was a devastating loss, the nadir of the war. The Articles of Confederation still hadn't been ratified, and the Union was in dire straits. As so often before, American divisions were hurting the war effort. The French envoy in Philadelphia, Anne-César de La Luzerne, a wily, big-bellied Norman nobleman, liberal in doling out bribes, decided it was time to force the Americans to do what they were evidently unable or unwilling to do themselves—finalize the terms of union.

For three years, Maryland had refused to ratify the Articles of Confederation, objecting to Virginia's insistence on keeping its vast Western domain. Maryland's leaders feared Virginia would grow so wealthy from selling land that it would be able to eliminate all taxes, and since Maryland would have to raise them to pay its share of war expenses, its population would flee. Virginia might swallow its neighbor entirely. The proposed constitution was "contrary to all principles of equity," Maryland's legislature complained. The costs of union outweighed the benefits. Why should small, landless states pay for "subduing and guarantying immense tracts of country" when they weren't going to see a penny from their sale?

Fed up, delegates from Virginia and Connecticut proposed approving the Articles of Confederation even without Maryland signing on. That meant ignoring the provision in the articles that said the constitution—and any subsequent amendments—had to be unanimously approved. Though Maryland's residents would surely "take airs and plague us," one advocate of the idea acknowledged, eventually they would have to buckle. Others suggested forming regional confederations, several instead of one.

Things looked bleak. Vast stretches of the South were in British hands. Congress couldn't afford to print its own journal. The turncoat Benedict Arnold was preparing to lead British forces into Virginia. Frustrated Pennsylvania soldiers mutinied and marched toward Philadelphia, where the frantic congressmen granted the bonuses and discharges they demanded. Then two hundred New Jersey troops revolted. This time, Washington sent a contingent of New Englanders to suppress the uprising. America was "not a nation at war with another nation," a Pennsylvania judge observed, "but a country in a state of civil war."

The Articles had to be ratified; not a moment could be spared. Pressured by Luzerne, Virginia delegates agreed—tentatively—to give up the Western lands, but only on the condition that the prewar claims of private speculators (like Washington) would be secure.

That qualification didn't satisfy Maryland, but with the British army marching through Virginia and Arnold prowling around the Chesapeake, the state had more pressing concerns. Its legislators turned to Luzerne for help. Could France send a few ships to protect Maryland's coast?

Luzerne grabbed the opportunity to use his influence and give France a more stable ally. He couldn't promise anything in the way of aid—although he would see what he could do—but he pointed out to the officials that it might be a good time for Maryland to ratify the Articles of Confederation. It was an offer they couldn't refuse. Reluctantly, state legislators in Annapolis instructed their delegates in Congress to sign the articles. Perhaps it would end Britain's hopes "that the union may be dissolved."

The Articles of Confederation confirmed, the citizens of Philadelphia broke into celebration. Cannons were fired, bells rang out, fireworks lit the sky, the Stars and Stripes flapped in the breeze. What the revelers didn't know was that only brazen meddling by a foreign emissary had pushed the country into union. Americans were content, as posterity has been ever since, to exalt what the *Pennsylvania Gazette* called "a Union, begun by necessity, cemented by oppression and common danger, and now finally consolidated into a perpetual confederacy of these new and rising states: and thus the United States of America... are growing up into consequence among the nations."

Among those other nations, however, even sympathetic observers remained unconvinced that the Union would last. In England, the political writer Josiah Tucker, a critic of the war, argued that Britain should let the colonies go since before long, they would be begging to rejoin the empire. As citizens of an independent nation, "the Americans will have no Center of Union among them, and no Common Interest to pursue," Tucker observed. Geography would do the work of division. Given the mountains and bays and rivers and lakes and ridges dividing the continent—especially "those immense inland Regions, beyond the Back Settlements, which are still unexplored"—it was obvious that "the Americans never can be united into one compact Empire, under any Species of Government whatever. Their Fate seems to be,— A DISUNITED PEOPLE, till the End of Time."

CHAPTER 3

Constitutional Crisis

This country must be united. If persuasion does not unite it, the sword will.

—GOUVERNEUR MORRIS, 1787

FEW WORDS GLADDEN THE AMERICAN heart like the opening of the preamble to the United States Constitution: "We the People of the United States..." The phrase seems to sanctify the charter as the organic emanation of a sovereign citizenry, a timeless testament to indivisibility. But the familiar words did not appear in the first draft of the Constitution. The original formulation was undoubtedly less poetic: "We the People of the States of New Hampshire, Massachusetts, Rhode-Island and Providence Plantations, Connecticut, New-York, New-Jersey, Pennsylvania, Delaware, Maryland, Virginia, North-Carolina, South-Carolina, and Georgia..."

The longer, bulkier formulation was thrown out at the Constitutional Convention in Philadelphia. The new document would go into effect with the approval of only nine states, an egregious violation of the Articles of Confederation—the charter the convention had been called to amend—which required unanimous support for any changes. If any states later refused to ratify the Constitution, it would be awkward for the preamble to list them as authors of a compact they had chosen not to join. "We the People of the United States" eliminated the difficulty. The phrase so often used as shorthand for American unity is actually a vestige of division and disharmony at the moment of the nation's founding.

Ever since thirty-nine men rose from their seats, one state at a time, and scrawled their names on a piece of dried sheepskin, the Constitutional Convention has represented for many Americans a foundational

The Looking Glass for 1787, by Amos Doolittle, shows Federalists and Anti-Federalists arguing. The caption quotes Scripture: "A House divided against its self cannot stand." (*Library of Congress*)

moment of almost miraculous unity. Politicians of both parties invoke the delegates' labors with equal fervor on opposite sides of impassioned arguments, while worldly-wise pundits lament the absence in our time of the framers' spirit. If only Americans today summoned the same scope of vision, the same willingness to compromise, the plea typically goes, the country would be better off.

Shorn of sentiment, the story of the 1787 convention reveals how tenuous the Union was and still is, how odious the compromises required to hold it together were and still are. Repressing the conflicts that beset the fragile Union—over slavery and states' rights, the nature and purpose of government—was the cost of avoiding a civil war. The framers deferred payment on debts they knew were already piling up. But the bill always comes due.

1. Perils of Peace

In the crisis-strewn years after the Revolution, a breakup of the Union often seemed likelier than not. That the country emerged in one piece, if not unscathed, was largely due to the fact that strengthening the federation served the interests of the wealthy.

After a devastating economic downturn, populists in favor of redistributing wealth and abolishing debt came to power in several states. They enacted laws that benefited the poor at the expense of the rich. Taking power from the states became a top priority for elite politicians like George Washington, Alexander Hamilton, and James Madison, who wanted a new constitution that would make it more difficult for economic populists to wield the machinery of government against moneyed men like themselves. It was this small group of affluent statesmen, many of them slave owners, who insisted on keeping the Union together instead of letting it split into three or four smaller confederations that might each be more responsive to popular complaints. They feared a second and more thorough revolution, this one targeting not only political tyranny but also economic inequality. As the historian Carl Becker put it, this revolt would not be over winning home rule but over who would rule at home.

In October 1781, American and French forces managed to trap the British army at Yorktown, Virginia, and force its surrender—a stunning turn of events. The war was effectively over. But there was no time to rejoice. The Union seemed to be on its last legs. The threat of conquest gone, the quarrelsome states reverted to form. Old divisions now returned as threats to a fraying federation torn apart by competing clans: North against South, East against West, debtors against creditors, rich against poor. As European nations circled like buzzards and the states faced their own separatist revolts, the Union's survival after the end of the war that it had been created to help fight seemed anything but a foregone conclusion. James Madison, a new Virginia delegate in Congress, assumed "the present Union will but little survive the present war."

The government was nearly bankrupt, mostly because the states failed to keep up their contributions. Without funds to pay soldiers and suppliers, Congress had begun printing money. But the Continentals, as they were called, quickly depreciated in value and in many places fell out of circulation. People refused to accept the new government's currency, a damning appraisal of how much they believed its word was worth.

Though all knew the Union was in trouble, few Americans had a

plan for fixing it. One who did was a twenty-three-year-old former officer on Washington's staff. Lacking roots in any state, the Caribbean-
born Hamilton thought local ties a distraction. The confederation was
"defective," he wrote while in the army. The little power Congress had
was being ceded to the states. The once-promising confederation
appeared "feeble and preposterous." What America needed, he declared,
was "a solid coercive union."

After Yorktown, Hamilton penned *The Continentalist*, a series of
essays that elaborated on the argument. Congress was weak, ill-equipped
to keep the country together. If things didn't improve, the larger states
might conquer the smaller ones—or else "nourish ideas of separation
and independence," just as the colonies had. Foreign nations were
unwilling to lend Congress money, Hamilton noted, because they
doubted "our continuing united." Unless Americans overcame their
local preferences, "we shall never be a great or a happy people, if we
remain a people at all."

Meanwhile, the victorious Continental army hunkered down in
Newburgh, New York, a convenient base from which to keep an eye on
the British forces in Manhattan. They couldn't disband until diplomats
in Europe finalized a peace treaty. The months ticked by, slowly and
eventlessly, and the troops grew restless. Some threatened to march on
Philadelphia and overthrow Congress unless it fulfilled a wartime
promise of half-pay pensions for officers. Benjamin Lincoln, the confederation's secretary of war, feared the army would be "as difficult to
disband as it has been to raise." Madison expected a "dangerous
eruption."

In late 1782, a committee of officers traveled from Newburgh to
Philadelphia to impress on Congress the extent of the army's disen-
chantment. The pressure was overwhelming. Without the power to tax,
Congress could not raise money to fulfill its promise to the troops.
And some congressmen didn't even want to; they saw military pensions
as a hallmark of the kind of European-style standing army the colonists had rebelled against and feared creating a class of nascent aristocrats in a country that, supposedly, had none.

Robert Morris, the confederation's powerful finance minister and
the richest man in America, worked with Hamilton, now a New York
congressman, and Gouverneur Morris (no relation to Robert) to link

the soldiers' complaints with those of speculators who had loaned the government money during the war. Both groups were willing to hold the country hostage until they were paid what they thought they were owed. The finance crowd wanted to use the officers' implicit threat of violence for its own purposes. Robert Morris seized the moment of the soldiers' intimidating arrival in Philadelphia to present Congress with the grievances of the country's creditors, whom he called a "numerous, meritorious and oppressed body of men." The oppressed speculators of Philadelphia began writing to fellow sufferers in other states, forging a network to push for a stronger central government, one with the power to take money directly from the people—bypassing the states—and to enforce its dictates with the bayonet.

"The army have the sword in their hands," Gouverneur Morris wrote to an ally, John Jay. "You know enough of the history of mankind to know much more than I have said."

The tension in Philadelphia was palpable. Decisions made now, Madison wrote a fellow Virginian, would determine whether the American experiment became a glorious success or an abject failure. Days earlier, during a dispute between New Englanders and Virginians, a Massachusetts delegate had announced that some members were interested in forming separate regional unions if the continental one failed. Madison thought the idea foolish but wondered if it should be considered anyway. "Unless some amicable & adequate arrangements be speedily taken," Madison warned, "a dissolution of the Union will be inevitable."

Tipped off by Hamilton, who tried to enlist the general in the officers' intimidation campaign, Washington masterfully headed off the plot. He agreed with Hamilton about what the country needed but refused to involve the army in politics to achieve it. After summoning his men to a new log building he had built at the Newburgh camp to foster camaraderie among troops from different states, Washington cautioned them not to "open the flood Gates of Civil Discord" and "deluge our rising Empire in Blood." The conspiracy evaporated on the spot. Jefferson later told Washington that he alone prevented the Revolution from ending as so many others had—with the "subversion of that liberty it was intended to establish."

In Philadelphia, news of Washington's triumph helped dispel what one congressman called "the cloud which seemed to have been gathering." Days later, a draft of the peace treaty with Britain arrived. Hamilton sent a letter to Washington congratulating him on winning the war but noting there was still much to be done to keep the country together. "This it is to be lamented will be an arduous work," Hamilton wrote, "for to borrow a figure from mechanics, the centrifugal is much stronger than the centripetal force in these states—the seeds of disunion much more numerous than those of union."

With the arrival of the peace treaty, Washington's army began to fall apart. The Newburgh camp was consumed by riots and mass desertions. Washington hastily sent the men packing with little ceremony and, in lieu of pay, only a few promissory notes, essentially IOUs. Many sold them to pay for the long journey home. One observer summed up the gloomy scene: "The soldiers are loud and insolent, the officers broken, dissatisfied and desponding, the states obdurate and forgetful and Congress weak as water and impotent as old age."

Eager to retire, Washington drew up a farewell letter to the people of the supposedly United States. The country had a bright future ahead. If Americans "should not be completely free and happy, the fault will be entirely their own." The choice was theirs whether to be "respectable and prosperous, or contemptible and miserable, as a Nation."

Washington thought independence would mean little in the absence of some central power. Without it the country would "very rapidly tend to Anarchy and confusion."

Anarchy and confusion came even sooner than the gloomy general anticipated. In June 1783, four hundred Continental soldiers surrounded the Pennsylvania statehouse. As spirits were passed from hand to hand, the troops pointed their muskets at the windows and made it clear they would not leave until Congress paid them. Hamilton and others pleaded with Pennsylvania's governor to send the state militia against the mutineers.

Why the governor refused remains unclear. Perhaps he couldn't be sure the militia wouldn't side with the soldiers. But maybe it was that seven years earlier, he had warned them all it would come to this. "To escape from the protection we have in British rule by declaring independence," John Dickinson had said then, "would be like Destroying a House before We have got another." Now, as Pennsylvania's chief executive, Dickinson may have felt that if the members of Congress needed shelter, it was nobody's fault but their own.

As they were rowed across the Delaware River—New Jersey's government promised to take them in—the delegates must have looked back at the city receding behind them. During the war, they had fled Philadelphia to avoid harm at the hands of enemy troops. Now, with independence secured, they found themselves exiled again, chased away not by British soldiers but by their own army. Every dark prophecy seemed to be coming true. Though the war was over, the Latin phrase stamped on the country's three-dollar Continental bills, now nearly worthless, rang truer than ever: *Exitus in dubio est.* "The outcome is in doubt."

Bitter divisions. Paralyzed government. Separatist movements on the frontier. Tax revolts everywhere. Violent fights over valuable territory. Vast expanses of land, bisected by forbidding mountains, never before ruled by a single government. Enemies circling. The country's apparently irreconcilable divisions made it unlikely Americans could live up to the ambitious—and ambiguous—motto on their new seal: *E Pluribus Unum* ("Out of many, one"). Even true believers like Samuel Osgood, a Massachusetts congressman, found it hard not to be plagued by doubts. "Time will discover whether our Union is natural, or rather whether the Dispositions & Views of the several Parts of the Continent are so similar as that they can & will be happy under the same Form of Government," Osgood wrote. "There is too much Reason to believe they are not."

When the fleeing congressmen regrouped in the second-floor library of the college at Princeton and then, later, in the Maryland statehouse at Annapolis, choosing a new capital was a top priority. The question divided Congress more cleanly along sectional lines than anything had before, as whichever region had the capital would presumably wield outsize influence over confederation affairs. New Englanders favored a site east of the Delaware, while Southerners wanted one closer to home because they feared their interests—slavery, especially—wouldn't be looked after by a government based in the North. With neither side willing to give in, they decided to have two capitals temporarily, one in the North (at Trenton, New Jersey) and one in the South (at Georgetown, Maryland), with meetings of Congress alternating between them. Critics ridiculed the solution. Why not build a whole stage set of a capital city, complete with a statue of Washington on a horse, and move it as needed from place to place? The arrangement satisfied nobody, but since many delegates soon stopped showing up to Congress anyway, it hardly mattered where the nearly defunct body met.

Expecting the Union to falter, foreign nations looked at the young republic as easy prey and seized every opportunity to foment division within it. London ministers hadn't stopped plotting to weaken the confederation and reclaim at least some of the territory they had lost. After the war, British merchants flooded American markets with cheap goods and offered easy credit, an overt attempt to replace political dependence with economic servility. As money flowed out and little came in, much of the Union fell into severe depression. Some proposed a new boycott, but few would make the sacrifice. After years of self-imposed austerity, Americans now had a bottomless "hunger and thirst after cheese and porter," as one Virginian sniffed. Worse, they had grown fond of "trumpery"—trivial, worthless articles of deceptively shiny appearance.

In London, writers and politicians cheered the coming crack-up. Within five years, some wagered, America would be parceled out among the European powers, divided into spheres of influence. Disgruntled Americans would "multiply the examples of independence," one politician predicted; they would secede from the Union as the colonies had from Britain.

Indeed, such examples of independence multiplied fast after the war. Secession was contagious. Discontents across the land saw in the colonists' victory proof that independence was a valid and viable solution to intractable disputes. Usually, the goal was to break off from an existing state, not to start a country of their own. But the result was destabilizing all the same. Just as the arrival of the first separation-minded settlers a century and a half earlier had triggered a wave of fragmentations, so the rebellion of the American colonies led aggrieved communities within the states to ask if they, too, should dissolve political bands and institute governments of their own.

In some places, those bands were already weak or nonexistent. In

1777, the valley dwellers of the Green Mountains had declared Vermont an independent republic. After the war, they sought to join the Union as a state, but Congress refused, deferring to New York's governor at the time, George Clinton, who insisted on calling Ethan Allen and his followers "revolted subjects" of his state—just as the king had labeled the colonists. Scorned, Vermont sought protection from its neighbor to the north. "I shall do everything in my power to render this state a British province," Allen assured the governor-general of Quebec in 1782. A copy of their agreement found its way to Clinton, who published the "traitorous correspondence." Vermont's negotiations with the British ended, but it still remained outside the Union.

Other separatist movements arose in the rich, fertile valleys on the far side of the Appalachians. After the war, thousands of settlers—their wives, children, and slaves in tow—made for the horizon in breathless pursuit of happiness. Within months, remote backwoods clearings with a few rough-hewn log cabins became bustling towns with streets, brick courthouses, taverns, and stores stocked with European finery.

There was a problem, however. Everything but the logs had to be dragged over the mountains from the coast, and everything the region's farmers produced—tobacco, beef, bacon, flour, salt—had to be hauled out the other way, and that was expensive and risky. It made more sense to use the region's abundant rivers—to travel down whatever tributary one had settled along into the Cumberland, the Tennessee, or the Kentucky, then continue on to the Ohio and the mighty Mississippi, drainage ditch of a continent, down to Spanish-held New Orleans, where the lucrative markets of the West Indies were a short sail away. No, the route wasn't easy—there were backwoods bandits, native sharpshooters, and turbulent rapids to contend with, not to mention the most imposing obstacle of all, the brazenly corrupt functionaries of the king of Spain—but at least it went downhill.

That simple fact of geography—which way the rivers ran—had profound implications. If the frontiersmen found it easier to trade through Spanish New Orleans than through Philadelphia or New York, perhaps they would conclude it didn't make sense to remain loyal to the fragile new republic. Disconnected from Eastern markets, the settlers might seek political independence from the states they had already chosen to leave. Nobody better appreciated the dangers of this "separatism of spirit," as the historian Francis S. Philbrick called it, than George Washington, who in 1784, after resigning his command, journeyed to inspect his vast Western landholdings. The trip ended in a protracted legal dispute with headstrong squatters who resented being told by an Eastern interloper, no matter how illustrious, that the land they worked was not their own. If not tied by interest to the coastal states, Washington realized, the Westerners would "become a distinct people from us—have different views—different interests." Instead of bolstering the growing Union, they might ally with a foreign power like Britain or Spain and become "a formidable & dangerous neighbor." The Westerners "stand as it were upon a pivot," Washington warned. "The touch of a feather would turn them any way."

The region he visited—the restive, uncertain border between Virginia and Pennsylvania—had been volatile for more than a decade. In the summer of 1776, inspired by the Philadelphia delegates, residents issued their own declaration of independence. Citing the "vast, extensive, and almost impassible Tract of Mountains" between them and their coastal brethren as proof of a divinely fated separation, they applied for admission to the Union as the state of Westsylvania. Congress refused. For years, infuriated settlers fought off tax collectors and insisted on their right to form a new state. After the war, Pennsylvania declared separatism equal to treason, and the Westsylvania uprising faded. But the tensions in the region survived. Eventually, much of the area would secede from both Virginia and the Confederacy and form the new state of West Virginia. Dreams of independence die hard—or not at all.

For many of the same reasons—distance from the coast, Eastern ignorance of Western concerns—settlers on North Carolina's Appalachian frontier organized a new state and called it Franklin, after the early advocate for the Union they aspired to join. They drew up a constitution making skins, brandy, and tobacco legal tender and banning lawyers from public office. The legislature began meeting, the senate in a humble tavern, the assembly in a log courthouse with the sun shining through the beams.

For years, the Franklin government petitioned Congress for admission, but Southern states, in solidarity with North Carolina and facing their own separatist movements, opposed it. "Our states will crumble to atoms by the spirit of establishing every little canton into a separate state," Jefferson warned. The logic of the Declaration apparently carried only so far. Patrick Henry, Virginia's governor, said Franklin's admission to the Union would "ruin the Western Country." When a new administration in North Carolina sought to assuage Western concerns, some in the breakaway movement renounced statehood. The region fell into chaos as rival militias, courts, and tax assessors harassed the divided residents. After a final battle in which several men died, the Franklin government collapsed. Its territory would eventually be incorporated into the new state of Tennessee.

North of Franklin, arrivals in the Kentucky district of Virginia found themselves in an especially precarious position. Its millions of acres of rolling hillsides and well-watered valleys had been sold to the colonists by the Iroquois in 1768, but the Shawnee and Lenape tribes who actually lived and hunted there did not care for the thousands of interlopers pouring through the mountain passes, and they made their feelings known with gruesome raids on outlying settlements.

Neglected by distant Richmond, Kentucky's residents wanted their own state. As one told Madison, echoing arguments for American independence, it was "better to part in peace than to remain together in a State of Jealousy and Discontent." Following Pennsylvania's example, Virginia declared any push for statehood a capital offense. But the Kentucky movement wasn't going away. Leading residents were already flirting with full-blown secession—leaving not only Virginia, but the United States—when news arrived that pushed them toward active infidelity. Their own government was about to sell them out.

Britain wasn't the only foreign power circling the Union like a vulture around a carcass. Even though it had, with France, aided the patriots' cause, Spain also looked for opportunities to profit from the young country's weakness. As the reigning power in New Orleans, Spain held immense leverage over the Union—it controlled the Mississippi River. At first, Spanish officials let the Western settlers ship their goods downstream. Then, in 1784, they closed the Mississippi to American trade. It was a wily move. Forced to choose between their need to access foreign markets and their allegiance to the United States, the settlers might give up on the fraying confederation. Spain would then have vassals, or at least allies, as far east as the Appalachian foothills, reducing the republic to a coast-bound nonentity and creating a buffer to protect the Spanish empire in the Americas.

In 1785, a Basque arms dealer named Diego María de Gardoqui, Spain's new envoy to the United States, arrived in New York, where Congress had finally found a steady home. His mission: Convince the piddling federation to accept the closure of the Mississippi in exchange for a trade deal that would relieve the Americans of British commercial abuse. Across the negotiating table from Gardoqui was John Jay, secretary of foreign affairs. Like many in the East, Jay knew little of the Western settlements, their surging population and sheer dynamism. He did know, however, that with an army reduced after the war to just a few hundred soldiers, America was in no position to challenge Spain on the Mississippi issue. Congress told the diplomat not to yield Americans' access to the river, but Jay considered that a mere suggestion.

For months, Jay and Gardoqui talked behind closed doors in New York while the country anxiously speculated. Westerners, worried their future would be sacrificed to bail out Eastern merchants, set up committees of correspondence just as their seaboard brethren had a decade earlier. In letters and petitions sent over the mountains, they warned that the crisis could similarly end in secession from a distant, uncaring government. If the Mississippi remained closed, one Kentuckian predicted, Westerners would consider themselves "released from all Federal obligations," free to ally with any nation that offered protection. "This country will in a few years Revolt from the Union, and endeavor to erect an Independent Government," the district's attorney general told Patrick Henry.

Unmoved by Western threats, Jay suggested Congress back off on its demands. Instead of insisting on access to the river or forfeiting the right to it, Americans should agree not to use the right until the Union had grown strong enough to back up its claim with a plausible threat of force. Jay figured that would take at least twenty-five years. As things stood, demanding what they couldn't defend was useless.

Jay's request brought the country's simmering tensions to a boil. "It appears, sir," a French diplomat wrote home, "that the American Confederation has a great tendency toward dissolution."

*   *   *

Every region had its own reasons for embracing partition. Westerners needed access to markets, something the Union couldn't provide. Southerners sided with the West, since any new states carved out of the frontier would likely be extensions of the South. Giving up the Mississippi, even temporarily, would alienate the West from the Union, possibly forever, and benefit the North at the South's expense.

James Monroe, a brooding Virginia congressman of twenty-six, had recently traveled to Kentucky and seen firsthand how disaffected the settlers there had grown. In feverish letters to Madison, Jefferson, and Patrick Henry, Monroe said he suspected that disunion was in fact the secret purpose behind Jay's talks with Gardoqui. Sacrificing the interests of the South and West would break up the Union, freeing the North to go its own way. It was all a conspiracy. He had heard of covert meetings in New York to put the plan into effect, and he had it on good authority that secession was openly discussed in Massachusetts.

If the rumors were true, it wasn't too soon for Virginia to begin preparing for the worst. A former soldier—he had nearly died after taking a bullet to the face at Trenton—Monroe sketched out a military strategy in case of civil war. "If a dismemberment takes place," he told Madison, Pennsylvania "must not be added to the Eastern scale." It had to be kept in the Southern orbit, even if that required a preemptive invasion. If Monroe had gotten his way, the Battle of Gettysburg would have been fought eighty years earlier than it was.

Though paranoid, Monroe wasn't wrong that disunion was seriously being considered in the North too. As the economic depression worsened, merchants demanded retaliation against Britain's unfair trade practices. But any measures taken by the states had little effect, for trade barriers enacted by one state could easily be avoided by sending goods through another. Congress couldn't help, since Southerners thought protecting Northern shippers would raise the cost of selling their crops. New England favored yielding the Mississippi to Spain even if it meant losing the West—or the South. Yankees viewed the Westerners as "little less savage than the Indians." Promoting trans-Atlantic commerce was more important than the hypothetical right to send barrels of tobacco down some distant river none of them had ever seen.

Southerners taunted the New Englanders, saying that "a Separation certainly would not be to their advantage." But some of New England's most prominent citizens begged to differ. Theodore Sedgwick, a lawyer in the Berkshires, called on the Northern and mid-Atlantic states to weigh how much the Union was really worth. Staying attached to the South would "sacrifice everything to a meer chimera"—a once-promising Union that had lost its purpose. The best solution, Sedgwick concluded, was "contracting the limits of the confederacy to such as are natural and reasonable" and within them creating "a real and an efficient government."

In the end, Jay's proposal to temporarily ignore the issue of access to the Mississippi passed Congress on a strictly sectional vote. It had little immediate effect, however, for Jay knew that with the South uniformly opposed, he couldn't get the nine votes he needed to ratify a treaty, and Gardoqui's superiors in Madrid eventually rejected the deal anyway.

Yet the crisis over the Mississippi stripped away what little remained of the veneer of American unity. Dissolution had never seemed more imminent. And dissolution would likely mean civil war.

2. We Are No Longer United States

Late in 1786, armed insurgents in Massachusetts moved to take over courthouses across the state. Fed up with farm foreclosures and stints in debtors' prison, the rebels, many of them veterans of the Revolution wielding the same weapons they had pointed at the British, rose up against a state government ruled by "thieves, knaves, and robbers." The governor tried to call out the militia, but too many of its members had already joined the rebels. Desperate, Boston's rich businessmen put up funds to pay mercenaries. As the hired guns marched west through wintry woods, Daniel Shays, a veteran of Bunker Hill and Saratoga who, like many of his followers, had suffered in the postwar depression, took charge of the insurrection and rode into battle mounted on a white horse.

Sprigs of hemlock in their hats, two thousand rebels marched on the federal arsenal in Springfield, built during the war to store American munitions. If the arsenal fell to them, not only Massachusetts but Congress itself would have to bend to their demands.

Dramatic and well-known, Shays' Rebellion was only the most obvious indication that the country was coming apart. Doubts about the Union were growing in every region. Federal coffers had dried up completely. Unless the states began fulfilling increasingly dire requests by Congress for revenue, one politician wrote, "the federal government must cease and the Union with it." Watching nervously from Mount Vernon, an appalled Washington described the Union as "a perfect nullity" so long as "thirteen sovereign, independent, disunited states" felt free to disobey Congress at will.

Those who wanted to strengthen the confederation believed one reform could turn things around—tariffs. That would help counter Britain's aggressive dumping of cheap goods into American markets and, more important, give Congress a revenue source independent of the capricious states. Instituting such a tax, however, required an amendment to the Articles of Confederation, and an amendment required unanimous approval from all thirteen states.

Twelve signed off on it. One refused. With its bustling port, New York collected its own duties on foreign goods and didn't want to give up those revenues.

Across the Hudson River, New Jersey was appalled by its neighbor's obstinacy. New York's import tax was passed on to consumers in neighboring states who had no vote in the legislature that levied it. New York profited at the expense of states unblessed with deep-water harbors. As relations between the two states deteriorated to the point that some spoke of war, New Jersey's legislature resolved that it wouldn't send any money to Congress until New York approved the tariff amendment—an ultimatum that Congress saw as New Jersey's de facto secession from the Union.

To prevent, if possible, a complete breakdown, Congress sent a delegation to plead with New Jersey to withdraw its incendiary resolution. The commission, led by a South Carolina planter, Charles Pinckney, reminded the New Jersey assemblymen that small states like theirs had the most to fear from disunion. Pinckney had recently introduced a motion in Congress endorsing Virginia's call for an all-states meeting in Annapolis in September to come up with commercial reforms. Instead of abandoning the Union, New Jersey should bring its concerns to Annapolis. The legislators agreed to rescind their provocative announcement, though they still didn't pay Congress what they owed.

The Annapolis meeting proved a bust. A week after its scheduled start, only twelve men from five states had bothered to show up. Suspiciously, the delegates from Massachusetts, New Hampshire, and Rhode Island made it no farther than New York. Some suspected they wanted the conference to fail so New England could secede and form its own confederation. Others thought they hoped its failure would clear the way for a more total overhaul. France's minister to the United States observed that the secret purpose of the Annapolis meeting was "to prepare a question much more important than that of commerce." The economic slump offered "a pretext for introducing innovations" in government that some had wanted all along.

When it became clear the meeting wouldn't have a quorum, Alexander Hamilton read from a wide-ranging report he had already prepared. Nothing less than "an exertion of the united virtue and wisdom of all the members of the Confederacy" could save the Union. He suggested the states send delegates to a more comprehensive convention in Philadelphia the following May "to devise such further provisions as shall appear to them necessary to render the Constitution of the Federal Government adequate to the exigencies of the Union."

The few men who had made it to Annapolis agreed to the Philadelphia idea, even though they had no authority either from their states or from Congress to do so. One delegate privately acknowledged that they had "certainly exceeded" their powers, but they had been justified in doing it in order to prevent foreigners "from Receiving the same impression about the disjointed Counsels of the States as we ourselves felt."

By then, however, it was far too late for that. Nobody knew if the country would survive the eight months until May. A grassroots rebellion was sweeping across the country. There were "contentions and civil discord in almost every state in the union," a Connecticut lawyer observed—the early stirrings of a potential second revolution. In Virginia, protesters burned a courthouse to the ground. New Jersey farmers impaled their governor in effigy. Pennsylvanians set up roadblocks to obstruct foreclosure agents. A mob surrounded the New Hampshire capitol, forcing the governor to call out the militia. When one South Carolina official handed a man a summons to appear in court, the man forced the official to eat it—and gave him a drink to help it go down.

Everywhere, Americans denounced burdensome taxes, outrageous legal fees, and a political system that favored the wealthy. After years of wartime economic stagnation, many had borrowed money and invested it in their homes and businesses, buying plots of land, farm tools, stocks of imported goods. Yet because of the shortage of hard money, few were able to pay off these debts or pay the taxes many states had raised to fulfill their quotas to Congress. Irate citizens demanded immediate tax cuts and debt relief, especially in the form of paper money. Government-printed bills would slowly deteriorate in value, making it easier for the striving many to settle outstanding debts and catch up with the well-off few.

The rich hated paper money. It threw off their balance sheets, cut into their profits. Theodore Sedgwick, the wealthy Massachusetts lawyer who privately favored New England's secession, deemed the calls for paper money an attack on "men of talents and integrity" by "the dregs and the scum of mankind." Within a few months, some of those dregs would break into Sedgwick's Berkshires mansion in search of the family silver.

Despite the opposition, seven states passed laws approving the use of paper money. Nowhere was the issue taken further than in Rhode Island, where a populist coalition swept into power by promising "To Relieve the Distressed." The party acted swiftly to pass paper-currency legislation as well as related measures, including disenfranchisement as punishment for those who refused to accept the new bills. When merchants closed up shop in protest, mobs broke down their doors and took whatever they wanted. Some spoke of putting heads on spikes. Conservatives called for Rhode Island, that "little detestable corner of the Continent," to be ejected from the Union or broken up and "apportioned to the different states."

Next door in Massachusetts, the situation was even more dire. Squeezed between old debts and new taxes, farmers in the western part of the state had complained for years about distant Boston's lack of care for their concerns. Three counties had even sought to secede, possibly to join the republic of Vermont. Now they tried a different method: direct action. When Daniel Shays and his band of rebels approached the Springfield arsenal, wielding swords and muskets, accompanied by fife and drums, they hoped its defenders, fellow veterans, would let them in. Instead, a cannonball landed in their midst.

Four rebels fell in the snow; the rest fled. Pursued through a blizzard by the state's hirelings, the guerrilla army disintegrated. Shays and other rebel leaders fled to Vermont. The insurgency faded.

Even though it failed, Shays' Rebellion horrified American elites. They saw the violence as heralding something "rather worse than anarchy...a pure democracy." Henry Knox, the confederation's secretary of war, tried to explain the rebels' cause to a worried Washington:

> They feel at once their own poverty, compared with the opulent, and their own force, and they are determined to make use of the latter, in order to remedy the former. Their creed is "That the property of the United States has been protected from the confiscations of Britain by the joint exertions of all, and therefore ought to be the common property of all. And he that attempts opposition to this creed is an enemy to equity and justice and ought to be swept from off the face of the earth."

Knox exaggerated the demands of the rebels. They were not protocommunists. But it was true that the short-lived insurgency marked an escalation of class warfare, an alarming radicalization of the Revolution's principles. If something wasn't done soon to prevent the states from succumbing to populist movements, all would be lost.

Holed up at Montpelier, his family's Virginia plantation, James Madison, a short, scholarly thirty-five-year-old bachelor, embarked on a self-designed course of study. What were the historical precedents for combining fractious, jealous, independent states into a tighter, more cohesive whole? And what could those precedents teach Americans? To help him sort through these questions, Madison asked his friend Jefferson, then serving as American minister in Paris, to send him every book he could find related to both ancient and modern confederations, like the Amphictyonic League of Archaic Greece and the United Provinces of the Netherlands. Examining the unions of other times and places might show him how to fix the American one.

As Madison studied these models, working in his second-floor study over the mansion's entrance, he realized the Union was falling victim to the same diseases that had killed others in history. Days before he left for the Philadelphia convention, Madison drew up an essay, "Vices of the Political System of the United States," in which he applied the same coldly appraising eye to the American Union that he had fixed on confederations of the past.

Time was running out. That spring of 1787, proposals to break up the Union appeared in the press for the first time. What only a few frustrated politicos had whispered about a year earlier was now a serious, even commonsense solution to the country's many ills. Bitter years of crisis and contestation had convinced Americans throughout the faltering confederation that its divisions might be ineradicable. Instead of papering them over, maybe it was better to admit that the skeptics had been right, that the Union itself was unsustainable. During the war, a Massachusetts writer observed, Americans had been "bound together by a principle of fear; that principle is gone: we are no longer united states."

The Union had been set up only to secure independence. That end achieved, the coalition was left without a purpose and might as well split apart.

Europe stood ready to pounce if it did. Retaliating for American violations of the peace treaty's requirement that prewar debts to British merchants had to be honored, redcoats continued to occupy forts in the far western reaches of the new republic. It was "difficult to decide," a member of Parliament wryly observed, "whether the United States of America were under one government, whether they consisted of many discordant governments, or whether they were under no government at all." In truth, Americans hadn't yet decided themselves.

In response to the populist turmoil, conservatives all but abandoned their faith in popular government. Noah Webster confessed that while he had once been "as strong a republican as any man in America," he now preferred monarchy, "for I would sooner be subject to the caprice of one man, than to the ignorance and passions of the multitude." Nathaniel Gorham, the impotent president of the obsolete Congress, sent a letter to Prince Henry of Prussia, Frederick the Great's brother, suggesting that if, as seemed likely, the confederation crumbled, Henry should sail across the ocean and become king of the United States. The prince politely declined, observing that Americans had grown too disobedient to be ruled from a throne.

Appalled by the choice between monarchy and disunion—though he considered the latter the "lesser evil"—James Madison tried to figure out how to maintain the foundering federation. The problem, as he saw it, was that the central government was powerless to rescue the country from its economic doldrums. State officials who bent to popular demand for debt relief only made things worse. Unlike those who wanted to return to monarchy, Madison thought the problem wasn't representative government but the size of the territory it governed. Instead of reverting to kingly rule or separating into regional confederations, Madison thought, America should keep the republican form but make it continental.

That, however, meant defying the most influential philosopher of the age: Charles-Louis de Secondat, baron de Montesquieu, whose 1748 treatise *The Spirit of the Laws* was cited by American politicians only slightly less often than the Bible. Montesquieu argued that stable republics could encompass only small territories. Once they grew too big, they succumbed to corruption and decay. "In a large republic, the public good is sacrificed to a thousand considerations," Montesquieu wrote. "In a small one, the public good is better felt, better known, lies nearer to each citizen; abuses are less extensive there and consequently less protected."

Seeing the loose confederation go to pieces around him, Madison decided Montesquieu's ideas were too simplistic. At the state level, majorities easily held sway. If the poor, who formed a majority in all societies, ever organized into a coherent mass, they could seize the government and redistribute property—as they had done in Rhode Island and tried to do in Massachusetts. To a rich person in a time of depression and discontent, to a slave owner amid a rising abolition movement, nothing could have been more unnerving.

In a large republic, Madison realized, the majority's will could more easily be frustrated, for the people would be fragmented across a vast landscape divided by innumerable barriers to coordination. The task of organization would be too daunting. With the right kind of constitution, all those differences of interest, identity, and ideology thought dangerous to the Union could actually secure it against the turmoil that had destroyed past confederations.

To Madison, the purpose of forming a more perfect Union wasn't to unite Americans but to keep them divided, to make the federal government less responsive to popular complaints, to minimize the avenues available for the redress of grievances—especially if those grievances had to do with the woefully unequal distribution of wealth and property, including the kind of property with an inconvenient tendency to run away. In an enlarged republic, Madison wrote, "Society becomes broken into a greater variety of interests, of pursuits, of passions, which check each other, whilst those who may feel a common sentiment have less opportunity of communication and concert." To Madison, that brokenness was a good thing—the less "communication and concert," the better. Fracture would be a feature, not a bug, of the new system he sought to devise. As he put it in *Federalist* 10, written to support ratification of the Constitution:

> Extend the sphere, and you take in a greater variety of parties and interests; you make it less probable that a majority of the whole will have a common motive to invade the rights of other citizens; or if such a common motive exists, it will be more difficult for all who feel it to discover their own strength, and to act in unison with each other.

United by government but disunited by geography, Americans scattered across a massive country would find it difficult to join together. Another Shays' Rebellion would be impossible.

Though he claimed to seek a government "sufficiently neutral between the different interests and factions," Madison was anything but neutral. In *Federalist* 10, he listed the factions that the Constitution would restrain, and they were not slavers, speculators, or self-interested politicians, but workers, debtors, and so-called levelers, popular advocates of greater economic equality: "A rage for paper money, for an abolition of debts, for an equal division of property"—precisely the demands of the Rhode Island populists and Massachusetts rebels—"or for any other improper or wicked project, will be less apt to pervade the whole body of the Union than a particular member of it." Thanks to the Constitution devised by Madison and his Philadelphia coconspirators, those and other such "wicked projects" have been stymied ever since.

3. The Framing of a House Divided

Both an attempt to avoid a crack-up of the Union and a cabal of the rich to protect their own power, property, privilege, and prestige—neither a miracle in Philadelphia nor a solemn conclave of plain, honest men—the Constitutional Convention was a series of intense hostage-takings, high-pressure standoffs with no satisfying resolution in sight. Almost daily throughout the sweltering summer of 1787, one or another of those revered legislators threatened to pull his state out of the talks if he didn't get his way. *Surrender, or we walk* was the constant demand; *Join or die* was the equally hostile response. Day after day, the possibility of dissolution lingered in the hall's stuffy air. If the convention failed, the Union would too.

Most of the delegates regretted the mistakes embedded in the Articles of Confederation. They had been drawn up in the middle of a war when it wasn't possible, or at least not prudent, to air the country's internal divisions. The Union had been a dire response to an immediate need; in a moment of danger, there had been no time to insist on ideals. Perhaps a new constitution, crafted in a time of peace, could correct the mistakes of the old one.

But the Constitution, like the Articles of Confederation, was crafted in the shadow of a violent conflict—this time, a potential civil war. No less than the delegates did in 1776, the men in Philadelphia feared disunion would put American independence in jeopardy. And just as it had then, the need to hold the country together at any cost ultimately won out. Dealing with the Union's divisions had to be postponed again, set aside for a more convenient day, one that would never actually come.

Many delegates felt that the articles had left too much power in the hands of the states, which had failed to protect the rights of property owners like themselves. If anything united the men at the convention, it was a desire to block state-level moves to distribute wealth and power more equally. Early on, speakers expressed a visceral distaste for popular rule, as if that were their only common ground. "Our chief danger arises from the democratic parts of our constitutions," Virginia's Edmund Randolph vowed in his opening-day remarks. Elbridge Gerry of Massachusetts called democracy "the worst of all political evils."

Roger Sherman of Connecticut said ordinary people "should have as little to do as may be about the government." Hamilton, arguing for a return to British-style rule, speculated that European powers hoped for "the preservation of our democratic governments, probably for no other reason, but to keep us weak." James Wilson agreed that the monumental "extent" of the Union might "require the vigour of Monarchy."

This shared antipathy to democracy made it possible for the delegates to coalesce around a handful of crucial reforms, such as banning the states from issuing paper currency and forbidding them to violate the sanctity of private contracts, both of which the elite of the late 1780s deemed necessary to control the populist fervor. But for many delegates, those measures didn't go nearly far enough.

Given the excess of democracy in the states and how incessantly they had bickered since independence, some wanted to abolish them entirely. What were they, really, but the arbitrary creations of irrelevant royal decrees? Others suggested spreading out a map of the Union, erasing the existing state lines, and dividing the whole into thirteen roughly equal parts. While in Philadelphia, Rufus King of Massachusetts received a letter from General Henry Knox. "The vile State governments are sources of pollution, which will contaminate the American name perhaps for ages," Knox wrote. "Smite them, smite them, in the name of God and the people."

For most delegates, however, smiting the states was a nonstarter. The whole point of the Revolution had been to establish the colonies as "free and independent states." Long after Yorktown, Americans still cared more for their own states than the perpetually unstable confederation. If the other delegates even considered abolishing the states, warned South Carolina's Charles Cotesworth Pinckney, they had nothing further to talk about.

But if the states weren't going to be abolished, maybe they could at least be deprived of a veto over national affairs. This applied especially to smaller, troublesome states like Rhode Island, whose populist government refused to send anyone to Philadelphia. Some of the most contentious exchanges of the whole convention regarded an issue that had divided Americans since the early days of the Revolution: how to allocate representation in Congress. Should it be given equally to all the states or proportionally according to each state's population?

Debate over this one subject, Madison wrote to Jefferson, who was still off in distant Paris, produced "more embarrassment and greater alarm...than all the rest put together."

As in the Continental Congress a decade earlier, delegates predictably divided according to which system would benefit their states. Those from the largest states—Virginia, Pennsylvania, Massachusetts—insisted on ending equal state suffrage in Congress. It made no sense for states with tiny populations to obstruct the will of a national majority. "Can we forget for whom we are forming a government?" asked James Wilson of Pennsylvania. "Is it for *men*, or for the imaginary beings called states?" Small states, in turn, vowed never to agree to a system in which their influence would be minimal. Equal representation was inviolable, a delegate from Delaware, the least populous state, insisted. If the convention overturned it, the men from his state would leave.

At that, large-state rivals countered with equally intemperate threats. James Wilson suggested the populous states form "a partial union" among themselves and leave the malcontents out. "Let them unite if they please," retorted New Jersey's William Paterson. His state would "never confederate" if it meant giving up its equal vote in Congress. Paterson said he would "rather submit to a monarch, to a despot, than to such a fate." Stumbling to his feet, Luther Martin, a Maryland lawyer and a notorious, red-faced drunk, declared he "would never confederate if it could not be done on just principles"—his own.

And so the great summit of statesmen, the "assembly of demigods," as Jefferson—thousands of miles away—would later call the convention, devolved into schoolyard temper tantrums and fast-flying taunts. The Union verged on collapse, yet its supposed saviors had come to Philadelphia not "like a band of brothers, belonging to the same family," Elbridge Gerry sighed, but animated by "the spirit of political negotiators," nakedly struggling for power.

For a month the delegates had invoked the airy principles of political theory and referenced the lessons of ancient history. All that was bunk, declared Delaware's Gunning Bedford, conspicuous for his girth even in a room of the affluently plump. Every man looked after only his own interests and those of his state. Pretending to talk philosophy, they were really talking about force. *I do not, gentlemen, trust you,"* Bedford hissed, locking eyes with his opponents. If the Union broke up, Delaware and other small states would "find some foreign ally of more honor and good faith, who will take them by the hand and do them justice."

At this, the delegates sat silent, stunned. The possibility of foreign intervention in Americans' domestic turmoil had been whispered about in private but never threatened out loud.

The next day, a Sunday, George Washington worried that the convention would never meet again. Hamilton, who had impatiently decamped for New York, wrote to his former commander that he was "seriously and deeply distressed" by what he had heard and seen in Philadelphia. He feared the delegates would "let slip the golden opportunity of rescuing the American empire from disunion, anarchy, and misery." Washington concurred with Hamilton's dire predictions and regretted having agreed to attend.

A few weeks earlier, Connecticut's delegates had sketched the outline of a possible deal: equal votes for every state in an upper house of the legislature, population-based representation in a lower house. Amid the free-flowing threats, the proposal was ignored. But the only alternative was ending the convention and going home.

After the delegates returned from a gloomy recess to mark the eleventh anniversary of American independence—some doubted there would be a twelfth—they passed the proposed compromise by a single vote. Splitting the difference, the deal was a major victory for the small-state delegates, who seemed more likely to make good on their threat to leave the convention and abandon the Union than their large-state opponents were, as they had pushed for the Philadelphia meeting in the first place.

The deal that created the different arrangements for the Senate and the House of Representatives reflected no enlightened understanding about how to balance state and national interests, no brilliant theory of divided sovereignty. Rather, it was the only way out of a deadly serious standoff that might have ended the convention, destroyed the Union, and triggered a civil war.

Heralded as the "father of the Constitution," James Madison despised its central compromise. Even if it meant saving the Union, he warned, it would ultimately prove "vain to purchase concord in the convention on terms which would perpetuate discord among their constituents." The price of peace was too high; the Union wasn't worth it. Giving in now would guarantee turmoil in the future when citizens of larger states came to resent a system that accorded them less influence than their small-state neighbors. Instead of capitulating, Madison wanted to call the small states' bluff and dare them to secede. Keeping such an artificial, unworkable system of representation, he said, would "infuse mortality into a constitution which we wished to last forever."

A bastion of aristocratic privilege and an obstacle to popular legislation, the Senate is also a legacy of the Union's origins as more akin to an international assemblage of quarrelsome diplomats than a fully formed nation. It's a living memorial to founding-era disunion. James Wilson predicted that the fatal flaw of equal state suffrage in the Senate would "expand with the expansion, and grow with the growth of the United States." In 1787, the most populous state had thirteen times more people than the least populous had. Today, California has sixty-seven times more people than Wyoming. Because of the Senate filibuster, 11 percent of Americans can veto bills favored by the other 89 percent, and representatives of just 5 percent of the population can block constitutional amendments. No wonder the government is as paralyzed today as it was in the 1780s, when the Articles of Confederation proved incapable of addressing a long list of compounding crises that, but for the Philadelphia conclave, would have destroyed the Union.

As long as the Constitution remains in effect, however, equal state suffrage in the Senate isn't going anywhere. In a last-minute motion by Connecticut's Roger Sherman, it was perpetually protected from amendment unless every state agreed to change it. As an ever-smaller minority of Americans obstruct the will of ever-growing majorities, the effect on the body politic may well be, as Wilson predicted, "disease, convulsions, and finally death itself."

Long before there were states to unite, slavery divided America. In 1759, the British traveler Andrew Burnaby—the one who predicted a "civil war from one end of the continent to the other"—perceived an "imaginary line" separating Pennsylvania and Maryland. It would soon become known as the Mason-Dixon, named for the surveyors who sketched it out. In the North, slavery was horrible but less pervasive and soon to be on the way out; in the South, where people in bondage constituted one-third of the population, slavery infused—and poisoned—every part of politics, society, the economy, life.

Despite the differences between the sections, however, there was initially little tension about the issue. Southerners cared more about maintaining slavery than Northerners did about abolishing it—an imbalance that would hold true, and define American politics, right up to the Civil War. Even after they realized how incompatible human bondage was with their newfound concern for liberty and equality, Northerners willingly suppressed antislavery measures so as not to upset the South—a rare example of comity in an otherwise divided age. In 1777, a bill to abolish slavery in Massachusetts was defeated on the grounds that its passage would, as one legislator put it, have "a Bad Effect on the Union of the Colonies." Early in the Philadelphia convention, the Pennsylvania Abolition Society sent its president, Benjamin Franklin, a petition asking the delegates to ban trade in human chattel. The aged reformer demurred, advising his comrades to let the explosive issue "lie over for the present." Pushing it would have a bad effect on the Union.

Slavery couldn't be avoided, however, bound up as it was with other knots the convention had to untangle, like the already troublesome question of congressional representation. If votes accorded in the lower house were based on population, would slaves be included in the count? The question reopened the old rift between the regions. After a decade of union, the interests of North and South were still, as one Carolinian noted, "as different as the interests of Russia and Turkey," two empires that had warred for centuries. So stark was the divide that some suggested a plural presidency, with one executive to represent each of the sections.

Digging up an old proposal, James Wilson suggested that each enslaved black count only three-fifths as much as a free white. Southerners balked at the fraction, and even threatened to leave the convention if denied full representation for "their blacks." Northerners cocked their own rhetorical pistols in turn. Voters back home wanted to form a union, Rufus King of Massachusetts said, but not so much that they would give the South extra representation for slaves. If the other delegates gave in to the South's threats, King predicted, they would always be able to say, "Do us justice or we will separate."

Tempers flared for days. Gouverneur Morris challenged the delegates to decide whether the conflict between North and South was fictitious or real. "If fictitious, let it be dismissed & let us proceed," Morris said. "If it be real, instead of attempting to blend incompatible things, let us at once take a friendly leave of each other." Slavery threatened to rend the Union in two.

In the end, it was Morris himself who found a way out. He suggested applying the three-fifths ratio not only to representation but also to any direct taxes the government passed. In theory, that would balance the costs and benefits of owning people. If slave owners wanted more sway in the government, they would have to pay. In practice, it had little effect. The federal government didn't pass direct taxes until the Civil War. The compromise did little but allow Northerners to save face while submitting to Southern extortion.

Perhaps for the same reason, the delegates conspicuously left the word *slaves* out of the Constitution. Politicians like Abraham Lincoln would try to argue the omission revealed a hidden pro-freedom bent to the document, but at the time, avoiding the word seemed more damning than putting it in. Luther Martin, who returned home to Maryland and denounced the Constitution, criticized fellow delegates for having "anxiously sought to avoid the admission of expressions which might be odious in the ears of Americans, although they were willing to admit into their system those things which the expressions signified."

Even after the three-fifths clause passed, slavery wasn't done bedeviling the convention or worming its way into the Constitution. Another issue it touched was commerce. The abduction of African people and their sale in America had escalated rapidly since the end of the war with Britain. Disgusted by the practice, some in the North argued for banning outright the importation of human beings. They were joined by representatives of upper South states like Virginia and Maryland, where a glut of supply was driving down prices. They wanted to monopolize the sale of people to the newer, unsettled states of the lower South and the unincorporated West. Foreign competition would sap their profits.

The same economic dynamics made a ban on the foreign slave

trade anathema to the states of the Deep South, which wanted to lower prices on slaves, not raise them. "South Carolina and Georgia cannot do without slaves," Charles Cotesworth Pinckney insisted. Charleston's John Rutledge, who had led the walkout from the Continental Congress thirteen years earlier, warned that his state might bolt once again. "The true question at present is whether the Southern States shall or shall not be parties to the Union," Rutledge insisted.

According to the well-practiced choreography, it now fell to Northern delegates to match the Southerners' threats. Rufus King, regretting his earlier vote for the three-fifths clause, countered that if the South wouldn't approve the Constitution if the slave trade was abolished, "great and equal opposition would be experienced from the other states" if it was preserved. In case of disunion, Northerners said, the South would suffer most, for their discontented slaves would be an irresistible lure to foreign invasion.

Protecting the slave trade was the South's top priority. New England's was to give Congress the power to regulate other aspects of commerce. After all, it had been the confederation's impotence in the face of hostile British trade practices that helped trigger the movement to strengthen the government in the first place. If Congress didn't have the power to regulate trade policy for the whole Union, New England had no desire to stay in it.

The sections' demands suggested the outlines of a new compromise. The Connecticut delegates emerged again as the leading advocates of a deal, even if that meant agreeing to terms overwhelmingly favorable to the South. Slavery helped the whole country, Connecticut's Ellsworth argued. Crops grown on Southern plantations floated to foreign markets on Northern-owned ships. By aligning the economic interests of the states, slavery was itself one of the strongest bonds of Union.

A committee hammered out the final bargain — "a compromise between slavery and capitalism," as the historian Staughton Lynd puts it. That much was clear enough at the time. "Notwithstanding their aversion to slavery," Luther Martin recalled, the Northern delegates were "very willing" to allow the slave trade to continue for twenty years in exchange for enabling Congress to enact new trade restrictions on a simple majority vote — not the two-thirds threshold the South had demanded. Southerners, in turn, were eager to reward the New Englanders for their complicity. Although he had come to Philadelphia with certain "prejudices" about Yankees, South Carolina's Charles Cotesworth Pinckney acknowledged, he found them "as liberal and candid as any men whatever." The essence of that liberality was their willingness to prioritize money over morality, profit over principles—to protect what many delegates, slave owners included, deemed a practice of profound evil that augured catastrophic suffering in the nation's future. The new compromise helped preserve the Union and slavery and sealed the mutual dependence of the two.

Without question, the bargains that produced the three-fifths clause and protection for the slave trade saved the convention—and thus the Union—from failure. Calling for compromise, Connecticut's Oliver Ellsworth observed that if the delegates didn't find a way to overcome their bitter disputes, the states would "fly into a variety of shapes and directions," and the Union would collapse, "probably into several confederations and not without bloodshed."

But the bloodshed, as we know, came anyway and was undoubtedly worse for having been so long postponed. The Constitution that came out of Philadelphia didn't just fail to abolish slavery. It placed insuperable obstacles in the way of any future effort to do so—and it gave slaveholders all the weapons they needed, one of which was a clause, adopted at the end of the convention without debate, requiring states to return fugitive slaves. Only disunion, the catastrophe so narrowly avoided in 1787, would allow the country to repair the most obvious damage done by the framers. Yet almost two and a half centuries later, we still haven't mended the more lasting tears they ripped in the national fabric—nor compensated the workers who wove its threads.

4. The Constitution or Disunion

The day dawned fair in Philadelphia, summer's heat softened by clouds and a cool, steady breeze. Five thousand revelers lined up to march. It was the Fourth of July.

Two weeks earlier, ships had brought news that New Hampshire had ratified the Constitution—the ninth state to do so. Then came word that Virginia, too, had signed on, although its convention ratified it by only a few votes. With the biggest state on board, friends and foes alike began adjusting to the new reality.

To celebrate this timely consummation of American independence, the city where the new Constitution had been drafted decided to put on a lavish parade, a "Grand Federal Procession." Lawyers, merchants, doctors, brewers, blacksmiths, butchers, and other tradesmen and professionals acted out their jobs atop horse-pulled floats, a three-mile-long performance of the work of creating a nation. Shipbuilders hauled a freshly painted vessel named the *Union,* mounted with twenty guns, surrounded by a fake ocean of blue canvas, and crewed by a team of merry boys in sailor costumes calling out commands as they steered through clogged streets. Other floats depicted decisive moments of the Revolution, like the signing of the Declaration of Independence. Singers offered special odes for the occasion. A rabbi locked arms with other clergy—"united in charity and brotherly love," the parade's organizer proclaimed.

For the coup de grâce, a team of white horses pulled a carriage with a monument designed by artist Charles Willson Peale. It featured ten columns for the ten states that had ratified the Constitution, with space for three more. The columns held a dome topped with a statue of Ceres, the Roman goddess of plenty. An inscription at the base read IN UNION THE FABRIC STANDS FIRM.

With its feel-good symbolism and patriotic pomp, Philadelphia's Grand Federal Procession of 1788 has often been depicted as proof of the Constitution's popularity—even, perhaps, of divine favor. "Providence certainly shined on that day," one scholar confidently affirms.

Perhaps. But at the same moment, hundreds of miles away, a very different scene was unfolding. What happened in Albany, New York, on July 4, 1788, says a lot more about the fight over ratifying the Constitution—indeed, about the American political tradition—than does Philadelphia's fabled pageantry, with its stage-managed portrayal of an imaginary consensus.

At nine o'clock that morning, as mirthful Philadelphians lined up for their parade, a group of Albany locals opposed to the Constitution marched from their favorite tavern to the hilltop where the old Dutch fort that had hosted the ill-fated 1754 Albany Congress had once stood.

These Anti-Federalists, as their opponents called them, found little to celebrate in the new Constitution. A tool to make the rich richer, it seemed to revoke rather than reinforce the liberties they had so narrowly won in the Revolution. As the summer sun rose, the rambunctious crowd pinned a copy of the Constitution to a tree. Then they kindled a fire at its base. Flames charred the paper, turned it to ash. Exultant, they raised three cheers, marched back to their tavern, and got roaring drunk.

That afternoon, a pro-Constitution crowd—self-styled Federalists—filed up the same hill carrying a newly cut pine tree; they set it up where their foes had built their bonfire that morning. A man carrying a copy of the Constitution perched at the top of the tree. A few branches below him a bagpiper played, accompanied by drummers on the ground. After singing, firing guns, and burning copies of an Anti-Federalist pamphlet, they pulled the tree back down and marched it through Albany's narrow streets toward the lair of their unsuspecting opponents. "And then," as one report had it, "the action began."

For twenty minutes, the street erupted in a full-on brawl. Stones and bricks went flying and crashing into skulls; clubs, swords, and bayonets drew blood from reddened faces and tensed limbs. The Federalists smashed the windows of the inn and chased their opponents inside. One galloped his horse through the door. An Anti-Federalist leader found hiding under a prostitute's bed was dragged out and thrown in jail, as were several of his allies. When the dust settled, twenty men were injured, some severely.

As inspiring as Philadelphia's procession might have been, observers of the "fracas" in Albany drew a different impression from America's twelfth-birthday celebrations. "Suffer me to remark," one spectator wrote a friend, "that it was the most disagreeable day I ever saw, to behold such a spirit of contestation raised among neighbors, fellow citizens, and near relations." Those who expected that spirit of contestation to vanish under the new government would be sorely disappointed, he concluded, for "'tis probable [it] will not soon subside."

The tumultuous 1780s, a decade scholars have long called the "critical period of American history," a formative time of social turmoil and sectional discord, came to a dramatic climax with the debate over the ratification of the Constitution. The yearlong battle revealed a country starkly divided between proponents of centralized government and those who preferred to keep decision-making at a more local level; between those who thought politics should be the province of the rich and renowned and those who believed it should be open to regular people; between those connected to networks of elite, established opinion and those without access to reliable information.

Celebrated as the most profound debate in American history—"a solemn act of national deliberation and discussion"—the ratification struggle was hardly a fair fight. Throughout the contest, those who favored the Constitution resorted to deceit, censorship, and force. They suppressed critical pamphlets and accelerated votes to keep their predominantly rural opponents from scrutinizing the text. In Massachusetts, historian George Richards Minot wrote that his fellow Federalists faced such headwinds they had "to pack a Convention whose sense would be different from that of the people." As Minot admitted, "Never was there a political system introduced by less worthy means."

Ratification, though it occurred nearly two and a half centuries ago, remains the one time the Constitution was ever put to a vote. Even then, it barely squeaked to passage, and it did so thanks only to a scorched-earth campaign of violence, trickery, and threats. Though even the most skeptical Anti-Federalists would set aside their objections and agree to work within the new system, the ratification struggle left behind submerged resentments, unanswered questions, and poorly patched divisions that haunt the country to this day.

The Federalists' favorite tactic throughout the heated debate was to pose the choice as "the Constitution or disunion," as George Washington put it. There was "no alternative." The country had built-in vulnerabilities, a tendency to break apart. Only a continent-size feat of constitutional engineering would make it hold together. The "Disunited States of America" were like "thirteen distinct, separate, independent, unsupported Columns," one Federalist paper observed. If the overall structure wasn't strengthened soon, it would face "rapid destruction."

The earliest installments of the *Federalist*—pro-Constitution essays authored by Hamilton, Madison, and John Jay (all writing under the pseudonym "Publius")—were aimed squarely at countering disunionists in the Anti-Federalist camp. If the Constitution was not ratified, Hamilton warned, the only recourse would be "splitting ourselves into an infinity of little, jealous, clashing, tumultuous commonwealths, the wretched nurseries of unceasing discord."

In reality, most Anti-Federalists didn't favor disunion or seek chaos. The "hobgoblin" that they did, one essayist sneered, "appears to have sprung from the deranged brain of Publius." Rather, they believed the Constitution's backers were the ones who had ruptured the existing Union by seizing on inevitable setbacks as an excuse to overthrow the government. The Articles of Confederation, which the Philadelphia delegates were supposed to patch up rather than entirely discard, required unanimous approval for any amendment; the Constitution would go into effect with the assent of only nine states. That meant that the old confederation had been dissolved. The Constitution's critics were merely trying to preserve the Union and prevent an illegal attempt by the wealthy and well-heeled to replace it with one more to their liking.

Despite their negative-sounding name, the Anti-Federalists had a positive vision for the Union, one to which later generations of writers, politicians, and activists would return again and again, often unaware of its origins. They believed the Constitution concentrated too much power in the federal government, thus undermining local autonomy and official accountability. "The vast Continent of America," as one Anti-Federalist argued, "cannot be long subjected to a Democracy, if consolidated into one Government—you might as well attempt to rule Hell by Prayer." The states could be either closely united or democratic— not both.

In the North, some Anti-Federalists opposed the Constitution because of the support it gave to slavery, not only in the three-fifths clause and the slave-trade protection but also in the provision requiring the government to suppress insurrections and granting slavers the right to track down their property if it crossed state lines. Any states that agreed to the Constitution, even those that had abolished slavery, would be involved in the unconscionable degradation of humanity. "How does it appear in the sight of heaven," New England theologian Samuel Hopkins asked, "that these states, who have been fighting for liberty and consider themselves as the highest and most noble example of zeal for it, cannot agree in any political constitution, unless it indulge and authorize them to enslave their fellow-men?" Turning a blind eye to evil by signing the Constitution, another critic warned, would make Americans "partakers of each other's sins."

It would be many years before a popular abolitionist movement condemned the proslavery bargains of the Constitution. Even in 1788, though, at least a few Northerners—though not many—favored disunion over compromising on slavery. As one Massachusetts writer noted, "If we cannot connect with the southern states without giving countenance to blood and carnage, and all kinds of fraud and injustice, I say let them go."

However unfair in general, the charge that the leading Anti-Federalists sought to break up the Union may have been true of at least one prominent critic of the new charter. Idolized by modern-day conservatives who fancy themselves acolytes of the true Constitution, Virginia's Patrick Henry actually opposed the Constitution and might even have preferred disunion to ratification. Appalled that during the crisis over Spain's closure of the Mississippi River, New Englanders had been willing to override Southerners on an issue of the utmost urgency, Henry thought that the interests of the people of his state—especially the hill-country farmers he represented—might be more secure outside the Union. Henry declined pleas from George Washington and other fellow Virginians to attend the Philadelphia convention, perhaps because he expected, or even wanted, it and the Union to fail.

A year later, during the ratification debate, rumors spread through Virginia that Henry wanted "to divide the Southern States from the others." The value of Virginia's exports would enable it to form foreign alliances. In a new Southern confederacy, Virginia would be the most prominent state, with Henry, perhaps, at the helm. The famously eloquent lawyer wasn't explicitly calling for "a dismemberment of the Union," a congressman who traveled around Henry's district informed James Madison, but "his Arguments...go directly to that issue. He says that three Confederacies would be practicable and better suited to the good of America than one."

At the pivotal Virginia ratification convention in Richmond, Henry did little to dispel the rumors. "One government cannot reign over so extensive a country as this, without absolute despotism," he warned. "Compared to such a consolidation, small confederacies are little evils." Henry even offered a version of the formulation later made famous by John C. Calhoun. "The first thing I have at heart is American liberty," he declared, "the second thing is American union." If the two came into conflict, he knew which he would choose.

After Virginia's ratification, New York was one of the three holdouts refusing to sign the Constitution. The state was cleanly divided, with Federalists concentrated in the city and its environs and Anti-Federalists dominant upstate. By the early summer of 1788, tensions reached a climax. Even before the July 4 clash in Albany, a newspaper reported "several bloody affrays" throughout New York; in one, a Revolutionary War veteran was killed. When the state convention opened in Poughkeepsie, Anti-Federalists had the edge. Out of sixty-five delegates, forty-five seemed inclined to vote down the Constitution. Now a classic of political theory, the carefully crafted *Federalist* essays, drawn up to push for ratification in New York, hadn't done the trick. As in Massachusetts, Pennsylvania, and elsewhere, Federalists resorted to rough tactics and harsh stratagems to win.

Once the necessary nine states ratified the Constitution, a prominent New York supporter of it, Robert Livingston, said the debate was "reduced to this single point—whether we shall unite with the other states...or separate ourselves entirely from them." New York's failure to ratify, one journal noted, would mean the state's "being repudiated from the grand American confederacy." Even so, Anti-Federalists refused to be intimidated.

The Federalists, however, had a backup plan. Months earlier, John Jay had informed Washington that if the Anti-Federalists successfully blocked ratification, Manhattan, Staten Island, Long Island, and Westchester County would secede from the state, form a new one, and ratify the Constitution on their own—even if it caused a civil war.

The scenario seemed plausible, and the ploy worked. New York's Anti-Federalist holdouts gave in, not because they were convinced by the merits of their opponents' arguments or swayed by the genius of the Constitution but because they were forced to surrender. As one Anti-Federalist put it, such tactics were "the language of tyrants and an insult on the understandings of a free people."

By just three votes, the Poughkeepsie convention ratified the Constitution. But it also adopted a resolution first passed by Virginia's convention a month earlier. The New York version read: "We the Delegates declare and make known that the Powers of Government may be resumed by the People, whensoever it shall be necessary to their happiness." Neither Virginia nor New York would have ratified the Constitution without reserving the right to secede from the Union. Though the Constitution itself was silent on secession, contemporaries clearly believed ratification could be withdrawn the same way it had been tendered: by popularly elected delegates voting at a statewide convention. No state would have joined the Union had its citizens not believed that such a right was necessarily implied.

New York's concession left two states outside the Union. After rejecting the Constitution by an overwhelming margin, North Carolina—dominated by irascible western frontiersmen—would agree to join only in late 1789, after the new government had been up and running for several months.

The paper-money populists in Rhode Island continued to hold out, prompting Providence and Newport to follow the New York model and threaten to secede from the state. The federal government declared it would enforce strict economic sanctions if Rhode Island delayed ratification any longer. Rhode Island's admission to the Union was more like a forceful annexation by a hostile foreign power than a voluntary association. In 1790, after nearly a dozen state conventions—one of which rejected the charter by a margin of ten to one—the Constitution finally passed by only two votes. Like Virginia and New York, Rhode Island claimed the right to leave the Union whenever it chose.

"The American Union Completed," a Boston newspaper triumphantly announced. But there would be little time for celebration. Doubts over the Union had already returned; indeed, they had never gone away. In 1789, just two months after George Washington's inauguration, William Tudor, a Boston lawyer, wrote to John Adams, now vice president, about his fears for the Union. "A Country extensive as the present united States, so differently settled, & so widely dissimilar in Manners & Ideas," Tudor warned, "cannot easily be reduced to a homogenous Body."

In the full-on brawl of the ratification fight, the Federalists carried the vote and the day. But they had vastly underestimated how difficult the task of unification would be. Before long, some of them would give up on it entirely.

PART II

IRRECONCILABLE DIFFERENCES

Americans in the early republic knew how important it was to downplay their tendencies toward disunion if the marriage was to have any chance of success. It was crucial *not* to remember how difficult and divisive the formation of the Union had been. "Now that the tree of liberty has become strong, towering and luxuriant," one orator said, "let us forget the storms that beat upon its youthful branches, and almost shook it from its base." But those storms could not be forgotten. Reminders of all the Constitution had left unresolved were everywhere. During the period now known as the antebellum era, the United States experienced a succession of crises so regular and unbroken as to amount to one fundamental crisis that never went away, and many suspected that war would come. Would the Union survive? Should it? Every attempt to alleviate disaffection in one part of the country riled up the residents of another. Historians have endlessly debated why the Civil War happened when the more apt question is why it didn't happen sooner. The answers are many: fear of the unknown, the profit motive, the mirage of continental conquest, Constitution-worship, the threat of force, sheer dumb luck. Though all helped postpone the breakup of the Union, none could forever hold it off.

CHAPTER 4

Reign of Alarm

I wish to have every American think the union so indissoluble
and integral, that the corn would not grow, nor the pot boil, if it
should be broken.

—FISHER AMES, 1789

THERE WAS NO GOLDEN AGE in America after the ratification
of the Constitution. During the first decade under the new government, the United States split into hostile camps in different parts of
the country, each rooted in a separate reality and nurturing its own set
of facts. Bitter disputes arose over taxation, immigration, inequality,
war and peace, the press, even collusion with foreign powers; all weakened the bonds of union and threatened to rip them apart.

Today's polarization is not a fall from some original ideal. Historian James Roger Sharp notes that Americans in the 1790s "surveyed
the political landscape as if looking through hideously distorting spec-
tacles, seeing grotesque and tormenting shapes and figures that were
products of intense and deeply felt fears." That made it easy to define
one's political opponents as enemies of the country itself.

The Constitution changed the government but without altering the
fundamental nature of American politics. People from different states
and regions remained as hostile toward each other as ever, as divided
by geography as they were by interests, ideas, and identity. By forcing
Americans to settle their differences under a single roof, the new Constitution, meant to stave off dissolution, may actually have made things
worse.

A 1794 engraving shows Washington surrounded by the official seals
of the Union and of the thirteen states, linked together like a chain.
When the first president announced his retirement, a foreign ambassador wrote home: "Disunion will follow." (*Library of Congress*)

1. Washington's Failed Presidency

Threats and predictions of dissolution appeared within weeks of Washington's April 1789 inauguration as the new Congress, still meeting in
New York, took up the difficult work of governing a vast and varied
union. Partisans on all sides came out swinging. It was, fittingly, a
South Carolina slave owner who uttered the first secession threat.
Sooner or later his state would leave the Union, Pierce Butler warned,
"as sure as God was in the firmament."

Watching the dysfunction return, even James Madison had to wonder if saving the Union had been a mistake. Ridiculing self-satisfied

New Englanders in Congress for thinking themselves "the chosen few," Madison imagined that if a prophet had appeared before the Virginia ratifying convention and foretold the rancor that would poison the new Congress, the state would never have joined.

The divisions grew sharpest when talk turned to slavery, still an open wound from the Philadelphia convention, and in early 1790, a group of Quaker activists decided to rub in some salt. Wielding pamphlets and petitions, they waylaid congressmen in the lobby of Federal Hall, on the street, in taverns, at their homes. One petition was signed by the eighty-four-year-old Benjamin Franklin, who, three years earlier, had declined to raise the issue of slavery in Philadelphia. Weeks before his death, Franklin, the godfather of the Union, helped launch the debate that seventy years later would break it up.

As they had when slavery was challenged at the convention, Southern politicians responded furiously to the petitions, denouncing the Quakers and their supposed congressional abettors. Pointing to the activists in the gallery, William Loughton Smith, a South Carolina planter, objected to those "evil spirits hovering over our heads." Ratifying the Constitution had required "compromise on both sides." Smith deadpanned: "The northern states adopted us with our slaves, we adopted them with their Quakers."

Yet Smith was wrong about Northern politicians' complicity with the petitioners; few white Northerners considered the slaves' cause their own. Union, to them, still meant that each state and section retained the right to establish its own laws regulating even as basic a question as whether human beings should be bought and sold like couches or cattle. They would never have joined if it meant putting that arrangement at risk. The Quaker petitions were summarily dismissed. Smith rejoiced at the success of the South's "early and violent opposition." Emancipation, a fellow Carolinian speculated, "would never be submitted to by the southern states without a civil war."

Southerners repelled the challenge to slavery so completely that no similar attempt would be made for nearly fifty years. Still, the episode left some of them in shock. "It was a mortifying thing," Smith wrote a friend, "to see an attempt made to deprive us of our property so soon after we had established a government for the express purpose of protecting it."

All too late, many saw the merit in Patrick Henry's argument that

the Constitution would ensure the "subserviency of Southern to Northern interests." Some turned to a drastic remedy. "To disunite is dreadful to my mind," Virginia's Henry Lee told Madison. "But dreadful as it
is, I consider it a lesser evil than union on the present conditions."

Lee's feeling was widely shared. In his diary of the first federal Congress, Pennsylvania senator William Maclay wrote that many of his colleagues expected "the Union must fall to pieces at the rate we go on.
Indeed, many seem to wish it."

The Constitution had been in effect for one year.

Repeated bouts of near bankruptcy had destroyed the confederation
in the years after the Revolution, as the refractory deadbeat states
refused to fill federal coffers, and Congress went broke. If the Union
was to survive, its chronic money troubles had to be solved.

In January 1790, Alexander Hamilton, Washington's treasury secretary, offered a plan that he thought would put the new government on a
firmer financial footing and finally unite the states. First, the federal
government would assume responsibility for the states' wartime bills; second, a national bank would service those debts and steady the financial
ship; third, a new tax on distilled liquor would raise funds.

Hamilton's alarmed opponents, however, saw the program as
further concentrating wealth and power, just what critics of the
Constitution had warned would happen. Even former Federalist allies
balked. They had wanted to save the Union, not enrich scammers and
speculators. An ardent patriot during the war, Benjamin Rush now
wished his name "blotted out from having contributed a single mite
towards the American revolution." Distressed by the end to which his
own constitutional handiwork was being used—he saw how an
enlarged sphere tended to enlarge certain purses—Madison led the
fight against Hamilton's program in Congress. He and Thomas Jefferson, the secretary of state, began laying the groundwork for an organized opposition. They favored a smaller federal government and a less
centralized union in which most of the power remained with the states.
The country could be united only by affection and common interest,
not force. Though the Jeffersonian faction wouldn't coalesce into a
proper political party for a few years, its members began calling themselves Democratic-Republicans or, more simply, Republicans.

Their ranks included many Anti-Federalists, but the early Republicans didn't repudiate the Constitution. Instead, they argued that Hamilton's programs violated the charter's limits on the powers of the central government. Both parties, Federalist and Republican, agreed to compete within a common constitutional framework rather than in opposition to it—an arrangement that helps explain why America's political culture remains uniquely Constitution-obsessed to this day.

Yet even if all sides accepted the Constitution's legitimacy, Federalists and Republicans strenuously disagreed about what it actually said. Americans of different regions and political predilections agreed to worship the founding charter precisely because they didn't have much else in common. The sanctification of a piece of parchment served as an implicit acknowledgment of the divisions it only barely held in check—a substitute for real unity. As the historian John M. Murrin wrote, "People knew that without the Constitution there would be no America."

As Congress weighed Hamilton's proposals, the question of where to locate the nation's new capital again dominated congressional debate, resurfacing "that odious distinction between Northern & Southern interest," as one congressman put it, that had dominated American politics since independence. Still reeling from the Quaker petitions, Southerners worried that their interests—slavery especially— would be neglected if the government kept its home in the North. They wanted to move the capital to Georgetown, Maryland, on the northern shore of the Potomac. Virginia's Richard Henry Lee, the owner of more than sixty people, insisted that if the Southern states failed to win the capital, they would have to submit to being "slaves in effect, or cut the Gordian knot at once"—that is, separate from the Union.

One day, as Jefferson approached Washington's rented home on Broadway, he saw a dour, disheveled Hamilton nervously pacing outside. He joined him, and the two walked up and down the tree-lined thoroughfare talking about the impasse in Congress. Men from North and South "had got into the most extreme ill humor with one another," Hamilton observed. The Union was breaking apart, and only his plan could save it. If Congress didn't assume the staggering war debts of the New England states, the region might even secede.

Though he objected to Hamilton's program, Jefferson, too, worried the Union was about to break apart. Over dinner at Jefferson's home on Manhattan's Maiden Lane, the famous "room where it happened," Hamilton and Madison, former *Federalist* coauthors, now sworn opponents, came to an agreement: Madison would let the finance measures pass Congress if Hamilton gathered the Northern votes to move the capital, after a decade in Philadelphia, to a new city near Georgetown on the Potomac. This "compromise of 1790" helped avoid national disintegration. Yet Jefferson came to regret agreeing to it, as he said, "merely from a fear of disunion."

In Congress, the debate over the deal featured all the usual threats and histrionics. Richard Henry Lee, thrilled at the selection of the Potomac site, solemnly asked his colleagues to consider "the consequences to be apprehended from disunion," forgetting, apparently, that only a few months earlier, he had suggested the South "cut the Gordian knot" if it didn't get its way.

On the other side, Rufus King, the Massachusetts-born Federalist who moved to New York and won appointment to the Senate after the Philadelphia convention, broke into "lamentations," as diarist William Maclay put it, when it became clear that New York would lose the federal capital: "He sobbed, wiped his eyes, and scolded and railed and accused, first everybody and then nobody, of bargaining, contracting arrangements and engagements that would dissolve the Union."

The country was all but evenly split. Most worrisome, the political alignment reflected geographic divisions—Federalist defenders of Washington's administration were concentrated in the North, and Republican critics were clustered in the South. Jefferson warned the president of the precarious situation. Unless he controlled Hamilton, the country might break up.

In 1792, as his first term neared its end, the sixty-year-old president hoped to make a graceful exit from public life. Nearly two decades of propping up the buckling Union had taken its toll. As he solicited advice from friends and advisers, however, all Washington heard were doubts about whether the country could survive his departure. His resignation "wou'd elate the Enemies of good Government," a Philadelphia friend told him. They "would use it as an argument for dissolving the Union." Though Jefferson and Madison opposed many of the policies of Washington's administration, they too urged him to stay. Only his leadership prevented the ship of state from crashing on the rocks of "violence or secession," Jefferson said. "North and South will hang together, if they have you to hang on."

Reluctantly, Washington agreed not to retire. But he knew changes had to be made. Struck by Jefferson's criticism of how Hamilton was fracturing the country, Washington asked his treasury secretary to answer the charge. Hamilton disavowed responsibility for the divisions and regretted that "party discriminations" had become "so far Geographical as they have been." He confirmed that respectable men in both the North and South spoke openly about the merits of partition. Only "the Efforts of wise men," Hamilton warned, could "prevent a schism."

But even those efforts might not be enough, especially with foreign powers hovering around the margins of the new republic, eager to exploit its divisions.

In the spring of 1787, as James Madison, mulling over the vices of the American political system, sketched out a plan to strengthen the Union, a Kentucky rabble-rouser—also thinking hard about those vices—loaded up a fifty-foot flatboat and launched it down the melt-swelled Ohio River, hoping to break that union up.

For the past year, Virginia's Kentucky district had flirted with seceding from the United States and forming an alliance with Spain, whose control of New Orleans gave it leverage over America's booming Western settlements. Handsome and charismatic but reckless and perennially short of cash, James Wilkinson wasn't satisfied with idle predictions or boastful talk. He had been a general in the Continental army, but his talent for intrigue did not quite equal the eagerness with which he indulged in it, and he was forced out of the service. He decided to head west, and with his wife, a Philadelphia society belle who would later describe frontier life as "torture," Wilkinson moved to Lexington, a small, backwoods settlement, and opened a store.

He had grander ambitions, however, and soon used his boisterous presence and borrowed riches to take charge of the Kentucky separatist movement. Though Spain had closed the river to Americans, Wilkinson convinced locals to trust him with shipments of flour, bacon, butter, and tobacco—goods too costly to haul east over the mountains. He and a twenty-man crew waved farewell to a crowd of well-wishers on the Louisville waterfront, hope-filled settlers "enraptured with his spirit of free enterprise," as one observer put it, "not less than his unbounded patriotism."

Patriotism, that is, to Kentucky, not necessarily to the United States. The people on the docks knew Wilkinson's barge might be blown to smithereens, or at least confiscated, as he approached the first Spanish outpost on the river. If it survived and he somehow managed to cut a deal, they wouldn't ask too many questions.

Through charm and bribery, Wilkinson managed to make it to New Orleans, where he reached an understanding with its shrewd Spanish governor: he would secure Kentucky's secession from the Union in exchange for a handsome pension and a personal monopoly on the Mississippi River trade. The brash adventurer put his quill to a document officially "transferring my allegiance from the United States to his Catholic Majesty." Wilkinson left town as Agent 13 in the service of the Spanish Crown.

He returned to Kentucky a hero. Prices on crops shot up overnight. The profits could be prodigious; the political implications even more so. Just as Wilkinson huddled with the Spanish in New Orleans, the delegates in Philadelphia began hammering out the new Constitution. Thousands of miles apart, the two meetings approached the same problem from opposite directions. As Andro Linklater, Wilkinson's biographer, notes, "One set of negotiations was aimed at partition, the other at union, but each arose from the same divergent tendencies within the United States."

Nothing could be kept secret for long in a world knit together by stagecoach gossip. Eastern statesmen were mortified by rumors of Kentucky's potential secession. "They will either throw themselves on the Spanish government, and become their subjects," one Pennsylvanian feared, "or they will combine, and give themselves possession of that territory and defend themselves in it against the power of the Union." That would mean civil war.

But then, suddenly, the specter of secession dissipated. Support for it waned. Wilkinson's success in unloading goods may have lessened the settlers' frustrations. Now that they had an outlet to the market, their economic desperation abated. The Constitution made a difference too. Anti-Federalists had dominated in Kentucky, yet even the frustrated Wilkinson had to acknowledge, in a coded letter to his Spanish handlers, that while he thought the new government "of doubtful success," it had "inspired the people in general with the loftiest hopes." The mere novelty of the new arrangement convinced the Westerners to give it a try. Several of Wilkinson's coconspirators received appointments as judges or tax collectors, jobs that gave them more money than Spain ever had. By 1790, Wilkinson complained that those "who loudly repudiated all connection with the Union, now remain silent."

Instead of leaving the Union, Kentuckians wanted to join it as a state. But there was a problem. Northerners feared its admission would give the South more votes unless a new Northern state was admitted to balance it out. Hamilton convinced friends in New York to cede the state's claims on Vermont and allow it to enter the Union. Vermonters were mostly content to give up independence, though one representative at the statehood convention warned that the republic's advantages in joining the Union would "by no means be adequate to the sacrifices she must make." Balancing the admission of one state from the North with one from the South set a pattern that would largely hold for decades to come.

Even after Kentucky became a state, however, discontent lingered, because the Mississippi question remained unresolved. Spain still kept the river closed to most American trade. "Patriotism, like every other thing, has its bounds," noted a petition from disgruntled Westerners in 1793. A young country lawyer named Andrew Jackson told a friend the Tennessee territory might have to "seek a protection from some other Source" if Congress didn't look after its interests. Tennessee finally joined the Union in 1796, but Jackson's dabbling with separatism wasn't over.

For both Spain and the United States, the situation seemed untenable. Either the American settlers would attack New Orleans in order to open the river trade, or they would abandon the Union. Both nations had reason to make a deal. In 1795, a new treaty settled border disputes and guaranteed the rights of Americans to trade on the Mississippi.

Yet the threat of frontier separatism wasn't gone. A new Western rebellion compelled the federal government to send an army to enforce national unity. It wouldn't, of course, be the last time.

On a warm summer day in 1794, hundreds of rough-clad frontiersmen, many of them armed, met in a field of sawed-off stumps and fallen trees above a bend in the Monongahela River, south of Pittsburgh.

Covered in buckskins, handkerchiefs tied around their necks, these men from Pennsylvania's four southwestern counties and two neighboring ones in Virginia hoped to transform spontaneous protests against a tax on spirits into a full-blown secessionist movement. Above them, a hand-stitched cloth with six alternating red and white stripes fluttered in the breeze: the flag for a new Western nation.

Hamilton's financial program—especially the tax on whiskey— sparked resistance on the frontier of nearly every state. Malcontents called for revolution. Much of the West suffered from a shortage of hard money, so whiskey was used as currency. A tax on it, as Hamilton knew, would drain the life from the region's agrarian economy. He pushed for it anyway. A show of force in the West, Hamilton told Washington two years before the uprising broke out, would offer an example to the rest of the country: popular resistance to the federal government, though itself founded in rebellion, would be met with deadly force.

The measure provoked an especially ferocious response in western Pennsylvania. Protesters painted their faces black and seized anyone suspected of helping the government collect the tax, including distillers whose only offense was paying it. Roving gangs subjected victims to humiliating ceremonies of degradation and sometimes outright torture. Insurgents patrolled towns and byways talking about guillotines. A gun battle broke out at the elegant hilltop home of the region's tax collector, who, through boarded-up windows, exchanged fire with his neighbors. The insurgents overpowered the defenders and torched every building but the slave quarters.

A full-blown rebellion was brewing in the backcountry. Some spoke of taking the federal garrison at Pittsburgh or posting riflemen at the mountain passes to block an attack from the east. Others looked west and proposed forming a union with their counterparts in other states or even seeking protection from Britain or Spain. Hugh Henry Brackenridge, a local lawyer and novelist who tried to mediate between the rebels and the government, warned Philadelphia officials that unless an army marched west to put down the rebellion, the rebels might march east to seize the capital. "The whole cry was war," Brackenridge later recalled.

Meanwhile, Hamilton, following the plan he had outlined to Washington two years earlier, raised an army and somehow convinced the president to let him—the treasury secretary—lead it. He saw the rebellion as a crisis not to be wasted. "The insurrection will do us a great deal of good," Hamilton wrote, "and add to the solidity of everything in this country."

A month later, thirteen thousand soldiers stormed over the Alleghenies, plundering their way through the countryside. The army cost more than the whiskey tax could ever raise, but the tax had never been the point. "The wrongful Secretary wishes to make us examples," one Westerner observed. Troops arrested more than a hundred and fifty rebels. Some were tied together, kept in dank basements, fed only raw meat, and then marched east in bare feet along icy, muddy roads. When the miserable procession arrived in Philadelphia, Washington stepped out of the executive mansion to watch it pass his door. Satisfaction lit his face. The "father of his country expressed more in his countenance than can be described," one paper reported.

Juries exonerated all but two of the accused, a pair of "simple" farmers who probably had little to do with the insurrection. Washington magnanimously pardoned them. He was grateful the rebellion "happened at the time it did," he wrote, for it gave the government an opportunity to demonstrate its strength. Hamilton, too, saw the new government's first trial as a success. Established in part to suppress popular rebellions like the one led by Daniel Shays in Massachusetts in 1786, by crushing a similar uprising in Pennsylvania, it passed a crucial test.

Fifteen hundred soldiers stayed behind in the rebellious backcountry to extinguish the lingering embers of separatism. Yet the whiskey tax was never enforced, and the spirit of frontier independence endured. To Jefferson, it wasn't the rebellion but Hamilton's policies that were "the instrument of dismembering the Union." The separation of the West from the United States, he wrote, "which perhaps was a distant and problematic event, is now near, and certain, and determined in the mind of every man." The only question was when the breakup would happen, not whether it would.

The quelling of revolt on the frontier did nothing to settle the raging disputes in the seaboard states over whose interests the Union should serve. With polarization on the rise, dissolution seemed ever more likely. In Congress, representatives even began to sound one another out on the merits of divorce. In 1794, Rufus King of New York pulled Virginia's John Taylor into a room off the Senate floor. Taylor had just given a speech denouncing the North. King told him that if the differences between the regions were as stark as Taylor claimed, it was "utterly impossible for the Union to continue." Instead of artificially maintaining the Union, well-meaning leaders should come to an agreement to divide the continent. Everyone knew the country would break up eventually. Why not do it amicably, rather than violently? When Oliver Ellsworth of Connecticut, a fellow Federalist, strolled into the room, King posed the question to him. Ellsworth agreed; separation was the only remedy.

Instead of suspecting a setup (which the encounter probably was), the Virginian took the Northerners at their word. In a memo to his ally Madison, Taylor described his talk with King and Ellsworth in the cloakroom. "The assurances—the manner—the earnestness—and the countenances," he wrote, "all disclosed a most serious intention." Though Taylor had opposed the Constitution, he didn't favor breaking up the country— at least not yet. (Within a few years, he would advocate for Southern secession.) He wondered if the Northerners were colluding with a foreign power. Should New England mend its ties with Britain, Taylor figured, they could together "bring the South to their terms."

Twenty years after independence, fear of Britain remained potent. In 1794, Washington asked John Jay, the veteran diplomat and now chief justice of the Supreme Court, to negotiate a new treaty with Britain. Jay succeeded in winning long-sought trade concessions and a promise from Britain to abandon the forts it still held in the West. But the deal didn't satisfy domestic critics, many of whom thought Jay had failed to sufficiently defend American sovereignty. Kentuckians warned Washington that if he approved the treaty, "western America is gone forever—lost to the Union." In private, the increasingly gloomy president wondered if "a separation of the Union into Northern & Southern" halves was imminent. "We are an unhappy divided People," Vice President John Adams wrote home.

The country was in dire straits. If America wasn't yet experiencing, like France, "the reign of terror," one fellow Virginian wrote to Jefferson, "it is at least the reign of alarm."

Ignoring pleas no less urgent than they were four years earlier, Washington insisted on stepping down at the end of his second term. His presidency had failed by one important measure: the country was even more divided than it had been before he took office. Nobody knew if it could survive without the man admired for his perhaps unique ability to hold it together. Washington alone "saved this nation from...internal dissensions," the Spanish minister Gardoqui, an astute observer of American affairs, wrote to Madrid. "It seems impossible that there could be another man so beloved of all....Disunion will follow."

The president announced his retirement in an address to the American people published in newspapers in the fall of 1796. More than its warning against "entangling alliances"—a phrase Washington did not use (it's from Thomas Jefferson's inaugural speech of 1801)—the Farewell Address focused on the possibility, even the likelihood, that the Union would not last. There would always be bad-faith firebrands seeking to stoke division. Americans should "distrust the patriotism of those who in any quarter may endeavor to weaken its bands." Domestic divisions, the defense-minded general observed, were "the point in your political fortress against which the batteries of internal and external enemies will be most constantly and actively (though often covertly and insidiously) directed." It was only in this context that he warned against "foreign alliances, attachments, and intrigues" that might be used to "stimulate and embitter" already existing enmities.

While insisting that the Union was America's greatest strength, Washington also described it, paradoxically, as the country's weakness— always fragile, a temptation to meddlesome foes.

2. Nullification and the Spirit of '98

Washington's homilies on the importance of national unity were ignored by his successors. Tensions continued to mount as Federalists tested the limits of national power and Republicans tried to figure out how much loyalty was owed by the loyal opposition. Today's supposedly sacred American traditions—the supremacy of the federal government, the constitutional guarantee of free speech, the peaceful transfer of power—were contested at the start; they arose not from fine-tuned philosophical principles but from naked self-interest and the imperatives of partisan conflict.

Both sides saw the election of 1796 as a political Armageddon. The campaign was as vicious as any the country had, or has, seen. Republicans loathed John Adams, believing him an aspiring monarchist, while Federalists called Thomas Jefferson unstable and effeminate, a radical, and a fan of the French Revolution, guillotine and all.

Each predicted there would be a crack-up, and soon, if the other side won. Federalists warned that Jefferson would declare war on Britain and thereby trigger "the fall of the present fabric of government, and a disunion of the states." For Republicans, it was Adams's election that would lead to dissolution, "if not the dreadful alternative of a civil war." A Connecticut essayist observed that the heated campaign revealed differences between North and South so stark that the moment fast approached "WHEN THEY MUST BE DIVIDED." Cowed by Southern blackmail, Northerners had given up too much to ratify the Constitution, the essayist argued; in return they got only "contention, discord, jealousy, and animosity." The Union wasn't working. It was time to break it up.

The election results underscored the sectional nature of the political divide. North of Pennsylvania, Jefferson failed to win a single electoral vote, while Adams took three-fourths of his total from the same region; he won by only three votes. Due to the ill-designed Electoral College, Jefferson, in second place, would become vice president. Some feared he would reject the post, and the country would fall into chaos. When he agreed to serve, the decision raised hopes for some that the Union's political wounds might heal. Others were doubtful. "Fire and frost are not more opposite in their natures than those characters are," one editor observed of Jefferson and Adams.

That was true, too, of the regionally tinged parties they represented. In Philadelphia, the temporary capital, the bitterness lingered long after the campaign ended. "Men who have been intimate all their lives cross the streets to avoid meeting," Jefferson noted, "and turn their heads another way, lest they should be obliged to touch their hat."

A year into the new administration, a diplomatic crisis further unsettled the jittery country. France's revolutionary leaders, angered by the recent thaw in British-American relations, broke off ties with the United States and then demanded bribes from a commission Adams sent to repair them. Faced with the prospect of a new war, Americans split along familiar lines. While the Southern-dominant Republicans, sympathetic to the French Revolution, called for further negotiation, Federalists in the North, especially Hamilton (who, though retired from the cabinet, remained influential), demanded war. Under pressure from hard-liners in his party, Adams called for a military buildup in an address to Congress so strident Jefferson called it "almost insane."

War fever spread through the country as a hastily formed American navy fought skirmishes with France on the high seas. Rumors ran through Philadelphia that Republicans had invited the French to burn the town. "Take care," one Federalist paper cautioned, "or, when your blood runs down the gutters, don't say you were not forewarned of the danger." Adams appeared in full military regalia to accept the allegiance of a belligerent mob. Thousands crowded the streets as fights broke out between rival French- and British-aligned gangs. "The city was so filled with confusion," Jefferson recalled, "that it was dangerous going out." A New Englander told Hamilton that if the choice came to disunion or submission to France, he was "for a Separation."

With the country in an uproar, Federalists moved to crush the opposition. "There will shortly be *national unanimity,*" Hamilton vowed.

In 1798, the Federalist-led Congress passed, and Adams quickly signed, four laws known as the Alien and Sedition Acts. The first three, targeting French and Irish immigrants, a base of Republican support, extended the residency requirement for citizenship and empowered the president to deport foreigners deemed dangerous to public safety as well as those hailing from hostile nations. The bans went unenforced, though some immigrants were seen lining up at the Philadelphia docks having chosen, as a later politician would put it, to self-deport.

A fourth law, the Sedition Act, criminalized "false, scandalous and malicious writing" critical of the president, Congress, or the U.S. government—as vice president, Jefferson, notably, went unprotected. This law *was* enforced. In all, some twenty printers, editors, and politicians would be prosecuted. A Vermont congressman ran for reelection from his jail cell and won.

The laws were immediately controversial. Even Hamilton, looking over a draft of the Sedition Act, warned it might lead to civil war. Republicans, naturally, were appalled by measures more "worthy of the 8th or 9th century," Jefferson wrote, than an age of enlightenment like their own.

As in 1776, the government was undermining the liberties it was supposed to secure. Jefferson drew up a hotly worded resolution and handed it to an ally in the Kentucky legislature. The Union wasn't based on the states' "unlimited submission" to the federal government but on a "compact" drawn up for "special purposes." The states, not Congress or the courts, had the power to determine the constitutionality of federal laws. The Alien and Sedition Acts were therefore void in Kentucky. Though state legislators smoothed the sharpest edges in Jefferson's draft, the gist remained, and the manifesto passed by an overwhelming margin.

In Virginia, Madison followed up with his own ghostwritten resolution. Virginians would consider the "rupture" of the Union "as among the greatest calamities which could befall them," his bill said, "but not the greatest. There is yet one greater, submission to a government of unlimited powers." If the federal government refused to revoke the offending statutes, Republican states would simply ignore them.

This wasn't a fringe theory or a stray remark by some crackpot backbencher. Though they stopped short of calling for disunion, the Kentucky and Virginia Resolutions were stunningly bold in their assertion of a state's right to defy federal law. The authorship of Jefferson and Madison would remain secret for decades, but as the historian Henry Adams—the second president's great-grandson—noted, the Kentucky bills were drafted by the hand that wrote the Declaration of Independence, and the Virginia bills came from the mind that designed much of the Constitution; they are, therefore, as much a part of the American political tradition as those more famous documents. And so, too, are the subversive principles they endorse.

Invocations of "states' rights" have done immeasurable harm throughout American history. Nullification would be most famously taken up by Southern hard-liners defending the ownership of human beings and the system of racial apartheid that replaced it. But worthy and honorable causes have also appealed to the principles of the Kentucky and Virginia Resolutions. Northerners opposed to slavery resisted the Fugitive Slave Act and pronounced the ruling in *Dred Scott* a dead letter. As of this writing, eleven states openly flout the federal prohibition on marijuana sales, while "sanctuary cities" offer residents shelter from harsh immigration laws reminiscent of the Alien Acts. For good and ill, the "Spirit of '98" haunts our politics to this day.

Madison and Jefferson hoped other states would rally to support their resolutions. Instead, the responses ranged from silence to contempt. In

1799, Maryland deemed such arguments "highly *improper*," while Delaware condemned the measures as "a very unjustifiable interference... and of dangerous tendency." To Theodore Sedgwick of Massachusetts, himself a former supporter of New England's secession, the doctrine of nullification stopped "little short of a declaration of war." Henry Lee, a Virginia Federalist who had called disunion a "lesser evil" a few years earlier, now changed his mind. "In point of right, no state can withdraw from the Union," Lee insisted. "In point of policy, no state ought to be permitted to do so." (This was exactly the line Abraham Lincoln would take in fighting the army led by Lee's son.)

The discord grew so fierce that Adams proclaimed a day of fasting so Americans could ask God to save them "from unreasonable discontent, from disunion."

While their countrymen sought divine intervention, Virginians stockpiled arms. The legislature passed measures to strengthen the state militia, increase taxes by 25 percent, purchase weapons from Europe, and build a new armory in Richmond. Southern allies warned Hamilton that Republicans in the Old Dominion were "determined upon the overthrow of the General Government." "Take care of yourself," another advised, for the opposition would stop at "Nothing short of DISUNION, and the heads of JOHN ADAMS and ALEXANDER HAMILTON."

As Hamilton saw it, Republicans were in open rebellion. Discerning "an insidious plan to disunite the people of America, to break down their constitution & expose them to the enterprises of a foreign power," Hamilton thought Virginia needed to be taught the same lesson the whiskey rebels had learned five years earlier. Let the government raise an army, he wrote, "& then let measures be taken to act upon the laws & put Virginia to the Test of resistance."

Hamilton wasn't the only one anticipating a clash. Frustrated by the response to the original resolutions, Jefferson told Madison they should draw up new ones warning that if the laws weren't revoked, Virginians would have no choice but to "sever ourselves from that union we so much value...& in which alone we see liberty, safety & happiness."

These are astonishing words from Jefferson, who, though his stock has fallen in recent years, remains one of the most admired of America's founders: he believed secession was a legitimate response to the abuse of federal power. Madison visited Jefferson and convinced him to drop the idea. The fact that he proposed it, however, reveals a remarkable truth. As his biographer Dumas Malone once observed, Jefferson "no more valued union for its own sake than he did government. He judged it, as he did every other manmade institution, by the ends it served." For the author of the Declaration of Independence, the ends a legitimate government served were life, liberty (at least for whites), and the pursuit of happiness. When the Union threatened to destroy those ends, it was of no value at all.

3. The Civil War Scare of 1801

Few norms in American politics are more cherished than the tradition of the peaceful transition of power. With one obvious exception, each change in presidential administrations has been accomplished in a more or less orderly way and without bloodshed. Even when their successors represent a different party and governing philosophy, outgoing leaders have never tried to hold on to power after losing an election.

But lately, even this supposedly solid-as-bedrock certainty has eroded. It is no longer unthinkable that in the not-so-distant future, it might be tossed aside, and Americans will experience what they have so long prided themselves on avoiding: a hostile takeover, a coup d'état.

Perhaps the mistake was taking the custom for granted. Thomas Jefferson's victory in the 1800 presidential election is often hailed as the first nonviolent handover from one party to another. Yet the real story of that pivotal election shows that the foundations of this long-cherished precedent were never stable. Far from a smooth transfer, the interregnum was the first of several disputed presidential elections. A season now celebrated as America's first peaceful transition looked likelier than not to end in violence. The "Revolution of 1800," as Jefferson proudly called his election, nearly turned into a real one. According to James Roger Sharp, "The country was in as much peril then as in any other era in American history with the single exception of the Civil War."

Republicans and Federalists alike described the contest of 1800, a rematch between Adams and Jefferson, in even more apocalyptic terms than they had used four years earlier—they believed it would determine America's fate for the century to come. Republicans considered it their last chance to save the country from despotism, while Federalists warned that if Jefferson won, "murder, robbery, rape, adultery and incest will all be openly taught and practiced, the air will be rent with the cries of distress, the soil will be soaked with blood, and the nation black with crimes."

Thanks to the three-fifths clause, which gave the South fourteen extra electoral votes, the Republicans notched a decisive win. But the faulty functioning of the Electoral College created a problem even graver than the one that had led to Jefferson serving under his rival. The Constitution didn't provide separate ballots for president and vice president—the man who came in first place took the top job, and whoever came in second took the vice presidency. In 1800, Southerners wary of offending Aaron Burr, a rising young lawyer and the Republicans' preferred pick for the vice presidency, neglected to shave off enough votes to give Jefferson the win. The two Republicans ended up with an equal number of votes.

According to the Constitution, a tie would be broken by the House of Representatives, its members voting not as individuals but as state delegations. With sixteen states now in the Union, nine votes were needed for a majority. As things stood, the Republicans controlled eight delegations, the Federalists six. Two state delegations had an equal number of Republicans and Federalists, so they were deadlocked and couldn't cast a vote for either candidate.

Federalists seized on the tie as a heaven-sent way to overturn the unfavorable results. If they supported Burr for the presidency, he would owe his election to them. Federalists liked that Burr was a New Yorker, not one of those seditionist Virginians, and figured his rumored lack of principles might prove less dangerous than Jefferson's fervent belief in the wrong ones. Both sides began probing Burr's willingness to make a deal. He refused to rule one out. Burr's coy reticence infuriated Republicans and gave Federalists hope.

Nobody knew how or if the crisis could be resolved. "Who is to be president?" asked a fear-struck Virginian. "What is to become of our government?" John Quincy Adams, following events from Berlin, where he served as his father's ambassador, concluded that every outcome pointed to the "dissolution of the Union and a civil war."

Earlier that year, the U.S. government had left Philadelphia and moved a hundred and fifty miles south. After a decade of construction, the new capital city had everything the nation's representatives could want—everything, that is, except a capitol building and a city. Pennsylvania Avenue was less a road than a hastily built causeway stretching a mile and a half through nearly impassable swampland from the shabby executive mansion to the partly finished Senate chamber standing alone on a wind-swept plateau. In this "embryo capital," as a visitor put it, congressmen lived "like bears" in den-like boardinghouses self-segregated by region and party. "By not mixing with men of different or more moderate sentiments," Pennsylvania's Albert Gallatin wrote his wife, "they inflame one another."

The flames weren't only metaphorical. During the transition period, mysterious fires broke out at the War Department and the Treasury. Rumors flew through the makeshift village that Federalists were burning papers that might incriminate them.

The uncertainty of those dark winter months brought up deep-seated fears about the stability of the republic. Would the two parties send armies into the field to fight it out? Some Americans readied for battle. In Philadelphia, a private Republican militia swore to "defend the country against foreign and domestic enemies." A Federalist was overheard suggesting that "every democrat should be put to death in order to secure the government."

A few Federalists hatched a far-fetched scheme: If neither Jefferson nor Burr won a majority of votes by March 4, the date set for the next president's inauguration, the Federalist-dominated Senate would declare the presidency vacant and name an interim executive. Jefferson was appalled. If the Federalists went ahead with that "very dangerous experiment," he warned Adams while the two walked on Pennsylvania Avenue, it would provoke "resistance by force, and incalculable consequences." He asked Adams to denounce the idea.

Adams refused, leaving Jefferson with a grim sense of what lay ahead. "No such usurpation, even for a single day, should be submitted to," he told allies. "If the Union could be broken," Virginia governor James Monroe wrote of the Federalists' plan, "that would do it." A group of Pennsylvania Republicans announced that the day the Senate named a president would be "the first day of revolution and Civil War." A Virginia congressman told a constituent that if Federalists robbed Jefferson of the election, the Old Dominion "would instantly proclaim herself out of the Union." Albert Gallatin, a leading Republican and a relative moderate, suggested that Republican states ignore any actions taken by a pretender in the White House.

Reacting to the rumored Federalist plot, Republicans came up with their own outlandish contingency plans. The semiofficial party newspaper, the *National Gazette*, argued rather creatively that if the House couldn't choose a president, the Constitution would be automatically suspended and the Articles of Confederation reinstated. Jefferson wanted to call a new constitutional convention to settle the matter—a prospect, he noted, that horrified Federalists, "as in the present democratical spirit of America, they fear they should lose some of the[ir] favorite morsels of the constitution."

Two Republican governors quietly began preparing their states for violence. A participant in intra-American squabbling going back to the Stamp Act Congress—during which he nearly fought a duel—Pennsylvania's Thomas McKean later said that in the event of a Senate-backed coup, he would have issued an order for the arrest of every congressman involved in the treasonous scheme. Another proclamation would have instructed all citizens to act as if Jefferson, not the Federalist usurper, was president.

In Virginia, James Monroe sent a secret agent to snoop around the state arsenal under the pretext of protecting it from capture by "a wicked negro or a madman." The spy recruited local militiamen to guard the building against an attempt by the federal government to relocate its contents—thousands of muskets, bayonets, and cartridge boxes, all captured from the British at Yorktown twenty years earlier. Now the munitions might prove useful in case of civil war.

Balloting in the House began on a February afternoon as a blizzard buried the drafty Capitol. Voting continued through the night, once every hour, until eight a.m.—twenty-seven rounds with the same result every time: eight state delegations for Jefferson, six for Burr, two split. The next ten days brought no resolution. "I have not closed my eyes for 36 hours," a Virginian complained.

Relief finally came when Delaware's lone representative, a Federalist named James Bayard, announced that he preferred Jefferson's election to disunion. It helped that, according to Bayard's later claims, Jefferson promised not to purge Federalist officeholders—a vow Burr refused to make. Bayard's fellow Federalists tried to change his mind. "The clamor was prodigious. The reproaches vehement," he told a relative. Die-hard New Englanders "declared they meant to go without a constitution and take the risk of a Civil War."

Yet on the thirty-sixth ballot, enough Federalists left the chamber to give Jefferson the victory, with Burr as his deputy. Still, Jefferson was appalled by the Federalists' "incorrigible" behavior. Their brinkmanship, he felt, amounted to a declaration of partisan war.

Two weeks later, however, Jefferson used his inaugural address to call for a truce, an end to the divisions that had defined the first decade under the Constitution. "We are all Republicans, we are all Federalists," the new president proclaimed, heralding a new era of post-partisanship. It was a stunning about-face, political expediency at its American best: two years after all but endorsing secession, Jefferson preached unity and reconciliation. He even offered protection to those who might adopt the same position he had. "If there be any among us who would wish to dissolve this Union," Jefferson said, "let them stand undisturbed as monuments of the safety with which error of opinion may be tolerated where reason is left free to combat it." Gallant words, although he might not have said them had he known how many such monuments there would be.

Already, some Federalists began to wonder if a union controlled by their enemies could possibly be worth preserving. A few months into Jefferson's administration, William Vans Murray, the ambassador in the Netherlands, wrote to his counterpart in Berlin, John Quincy Adams, and told him, with a touch of paranoia, that he thought Jefferson and the Republicans intended to break the country in two. Adams didn't think that likely to happen. But what if it did? While he cherished the Union, Adams said he was trying to cultivate a habit of "looking coolly" at the possibility of its demise: "If they will break us up—in God's name, let the Union go. I love the Union as I love my wife. But if my wife would ask and insist upon a separation, she should have it, though it broke my heart."

CHAPTER 5

The Lost Cause of the North

Our country is too big for union, too sordid for patriotism, too democratic for liberty.

—FISHER AMES, 1803

WHEN AMERICANS THINK OF SECESSION, we think of the South, the Confederacy, slavery. The idea of breaking up the Union seems so bound up with the slaveholders' drive for independence in the 1860s that earlier attempts to leave have been obscured. Yet the first popular disunion movement in American history developed in the North, not the South. It aimed not to expand and entrench the "peculiar institution," but to counter and contain it, if not quite to destroy it completely.

Once the scope of Jefferson's self-proclaimed revolution became clear, some Federalists began calling for separation from the United States and the establishment of a New England nation. In a development absent from triumphalist versions of our history, political divisions grew so toxic that some of the men who only years earlier had drafted the Constitution came to favor its repeal. Frustrated, out of power, watching the country veer from its rightful path, even once-proud patriots turned into unapologetic disunionists.

American politicians of the time weren't immune from the flip-flopping hypocrisy so pervasive today. In the early republic, each party flirted with secession when its rival was in power and opposed disunion once it took the helm. In the 1790s, Republicans like Jefferson and Madison threatened to abandon the Union rather than submit to the Federalists' autocratic rule. Once they took control, however, Republicans insisted on the sanctity of a Union they had earlier deemed

An 1815 print shows the New England states deliberating whether to leap into the arms of King George III. Timothy Pickering, a Northern separatist, prays he will be made a lord. (*Library of Congress*)

expendable. Now it was the Federalists' turn to weigh the worth of the Union they had formerly championed. Fisher Ames, the New England scribe who said back in 1789 that he hoped to convince Americans their pots wouldn't boil if the Union was dissolved, now questioned if a continental union was even possible. The country was too big for such a union. It would never hold together. Ames didn't think it should.

"What a game of round-about has been played since I was initiated into the mysteries of politics!" exclaimed John Randolph, an acerbic Virginia planter, in 1814. "The question of resistance to any established government is always a question of expediency."

1. The Northern Confederacy

Dawn breaks on a bluff in New Jersey high above the Hudson River. Two men stand ten paces apart, each with a hand on his flintlock. Old friends and political rivals, they're both five feet seven inches tall and nearing fifty years old. One is Aaron Burr, the vice president of the United States, with youthfully dark hair and darker eyes. His adversary is Alexander Hamilton, the former treasury secretary, his sharp features lit up by the rising summer sun.

What happened next has long been the stuff of legend and, more recently, Broadway theater. We think we know what brought them to that fateful precipice on the morning of July 11, 1804. One insulted the other, and the "honor culture" of the time required each to do his duty. Hamilton took a bullet in the stomach, while Burr had to flee; somehow, within three years, he ended up a fugitive on the Western frontier, a traitor to the country he had once aspired to lead.

What's left out of the musical, however, and downplayed in most other accounts is the fact that their deadly feud was rooted not merely in personal animosity but in an explosive debate then roiling the country: whether the United States should remain a single nation or break in two.

That long-standing question had been charged with urgency by Jefferson's purchase of Louisiana from Napoleon in 1803. Three years earlier, the newly crowned emperor had strong-armed Spain into returning to France its former North American territory, ceded after the Seven Years' War. For two decades, Spain, an empire on the decline, had used its control of the Mississippi River to encourage separatist movements in the western reaches of the even weaker American republic. With the return of Louisiana, France could do the same—undoubtedly to greater effect. Napoleon's control of New Orleans and the Mississippi would have "Effects injurious to the Union," an American politician feared. "There is on the globe one single spot, the possessor of which is our natural and habitual enemy," Jefferson observed. "It is New Orleans."

It was imperative, then, to block its occupation by a far more powerful rival. With instructions to buy the city from Napoleon, Jefferson's envoy James Monroe sailed to Paris. Nothing less than "the future destinies of this Republic" depended on his success, the president told him.

When Monroe arrived, Napoleon decided to offload not only New Orleans but the whole of Louisiana, reaching to the Rocky Mountains (wherever those were) in the west. To an adviser's objection that the sale was shortsighted, for someday the United States would be able to dominate any European power, Napoleon had a ready answer: America's ungainly size would lead to its demise. "We may hereafter expect rivalries among the members of the Union," the wily strategist reassured his counselor. "The confederations that are called perpetual last only till one of the contracting parties finds it to its interest to break them."

The new acquisition would be too much for the United States to swallow, Napoleon thought. Expansion, meant to heal divisions, would only make them worse. Decades later, the Civil War, fought over whether slavery would be allowed in the Western territories, proved the emperor right. Eventually, the swollen Union would collapse under the weight of its own contradictions.

Notably, however, Jefferson didn't disagree with his French counterpart about the Union's ability to expand and stay united. A month after the blockbuster deal, Jefferson told an ally that he didn't much care whether the Louisiana Territory remained in the United States or became its own separate nation as long as Americans populated it. "The future inhabitants of the Atlantic and Mississippi States will be our sons," he observed. "God bless them both, and keep them in union, if it be for their good, but separate them, if it be better."

Far from indivisible, the Union remained for Jefferson only a means to certain ends. With all its distant and discordant parts, the country might somehow hold together as one, or it could peacefully break apart, as long as the principles on which it had been founded endured. To him, forming a single sea-to-sea nation wasn't so important.

Ironically, the same opinion was spreading fast among the president's most implacable foes, the Federalists of New England. Agnostic about Louisiana's long-term effects on the Union, Jefferson hoped that acquiring the territory, and thereby freeing the Mississippi Valley from coercion by a foreign power, would end support for secession in the West, at least in the short term. Instead, it brought a new headache: the rise of just such a movement in the East.

If Jefferson had promised to keep Federalists in office—an allegation he denied—he failed to honor the pledge. In fact, he purged the executive branch of his adversaries and then tried to impeach Adams-appointed judges. Seeing through the post-partisan veneer of his inaugural address, Yankee opponents charged Jefferson with pressing a "vindictive attack" on their party and region. The "Virginia lordlings," one Federalist claimed, had "formed a deliberate plan to govern & depress New England."

New Englanders saw the Louisiana Purchase as cause not for celebration but despair. Doubling the size of the Union would dilute their power, especially if the territory was opened to slavery—as, under a

Southern regime, it would be—and if the three-fifths bonus was applied in the new states. "Admit this western world into the Union," New Hampshire senator William Plumer told colleagues, "& you destroy with a single operation the whole weight & importance of the eastern states in the scale of politics."

Northerners, now regretting those Union-saving compromises at the Philadelphia convention, called in vain for repealing the three-fifths clause. In an expanded Union dominated by slave states, why further reward the ownership of human beings? Some even suggested that in buying Louisiana, the old union had been dissolved and a new one formed, leaving out New England. Maybe it was best to separate from the South, one pamphleteer sneered. "Our prospects and politics are as different from theirs as light is from darkness."

It was Timothy Pickering, a former army veteran from Salem, Massachusetts, and a cabinet official under Washington and Adams, who turned the Federalists' despair into a conspiracy. In angst-ridden missives to friends and compatriots, Pickering denounced the purchase as "Mr. Jefferson's plan of destruction" and called for *a new confederacy exempt from the corrupt and corrupting influences and oppression...* of the South." The country, already beginning to fracture, was bound to disintegrate before long. Better to act quickly than wait until it was too late. "The principles of our Revolution point to the remedy,—a separation," Pickering wrote. Invoking the same scriptural passage beloved by his Massachusetts forebears, the independent-minded Pilgrims who had landed on New England's shores nearly two centuries earlier, Pickering wrote, "I am therefore ready to say, 'Come out from among them, and be ye separate.'"

Yet the New Englanders knew their region couldn't defend itself alone. To strengthen the new federation, the British provinces of Quebec and Nova Scotia would be invited to join; Britain might even let them, Pickering thought. The conspirators sought and received encouragement from Anthony Merry, the British ambassador in Washington. Turned off by Jefferson's inattention to diplomatic niceties (the eccentric president wore slippers to their first meeting), Merry despised life in the half-finished capital.

Even foreign support, however, might not be enough to secure independence. To further strengthen the breakaway nation, New York, the second-largest state by population, had to be won over to the conspiracy. With its bustling port and promising land route into the interior, New York would prove indispensable for a Northern nation. Yet the state would join, Pickering saw, only if it was made "the center of the confederacy."

The key to New York's involvement lay in the hands of the vice president. Suspected of having courted the Federalists during the 1800 electoral stalemate, Aaron Burr had been sidelined by Jefferson. He responded by cozying up to the opposition. In early 1802, Burr, still a Republican, stoked gossip in the capital by showing up at a Federalist feast to honor the late George Washington's birthday and offering a toast to "the Union of all honest men!" Many thought the vice president's loyalties might soon be for sale.

Two years later, aware he would be dropped from Jefferson's reelection ticket, Burr decided to run for governor of New York. Once again, the Federalists realized that their plans and Burr's ambitions might align. Over dinner, New England secessionists sounded him out on a bold idea: his election would trigger a declaration of Northern independence, with Burr at the helm of the new country. At first he seemed to approve of the plan. When one plotter, William Plumer, predicted the Union "would soon form two distinct & separate governments," Burr agreed, saying not only that "such an event would take place—but that it was necessary that it should."

Burr's words seemed clear, but Plumer soon realized that Burr hadn't actually committed himself to leading a Northern republic. He refused to say outright that he supported disunion. The Federalists felt uneasy depending on an unreliable ally, but they had no choice. Burr's election, one separatist sighed, was their "only hope" for success.

That the vice president of the United States supported, even tacitly, a plan to divide them was explosive information to possess. The story of what his rival did with that information and what happened next is as often told as it is misunderstood. Alexander Hamilton is worshipped as a martyr for the Union, but his motives were less clear—and, arguably, less commendable—than most people realize.

In early 1804, Pickering and other disunionists were planning to hold a convention for Northern dissidents in Boston that fall. Hamilton agreed to go. He and his fellow Federalists had been removed from power, and his bitterness knew no bounds. Writing to an old friend, Gouverneur Morris, Hamilton called the Constitution a "frail and worthless fabric"—too weak to hold such a fractious people together. He had supported it anyway, only to be repaid with scorn. "Every day proves to me more and more that this American world was not made for me," Hamilton wrote.

His purpose in attending the Boston convention may have been, as his defenders later argued, to discourage his allies from going through with secession. At the time, his Federalist friends were encouraged by the great man's promise to be there.

Hamilton could not abide seeing his longtime nemesis in New York political circles acclaimed as leader in waiting of a new Northern nation. Kept apprised of his Federalist allies' secessionist plans, Hamilton decided to use that knowledge against Burr. At an Albany meeting during which New York's Federalists debated whether to back the renegade Republican for governor, Hamilton denounced his rival's candidacy as a scheme to split the country and raise the shiftless Burr as "chief of the Northern portion."

At a dinner a few days later, Hamilton went even further, and this time, he went too far. In comments later leaked to the press, he called Burr "a dangerous man, and one who ought not to be trusted with the reins of government." Burr was dangerous, of course, precisely because of his rumored complicity with a disunionist plot. But then Hamilton, according to an attendee's leaked letter, offered "a still more despicable opinion" of Burr—a thinly veiled allusion, couched in the parlance of the time, to some kind of sexual deviancy.

The Federalists declined to endorse Burr. He lost the election. Fuming, facing an end to his once-promising career, Burr sent a messenger to Hamilton with press clippings about the Albany dinner, demanding an explanation of the innuendo they contained. Hamilton replied evasively, signaling his willingness to accept a challenge. As their seconds made the arrangements, Burr and Hamilton put their affairs in order.

Given the context of the Northern secession movement and Burr's ambiguous involvement, it's unsurprising that the specter of disunion haunted Hamilton in his final days. After the Civil War, when it was clear such stories would play well, one of Hamilton's sons (only eleven years old when his father died) published a flattering biography of his father filled with unsubstantiated anecdotes he thought important to preserve for posterity. One story told of a dinner Hamilton hosted four days before the tragic duel. After the meal, Hamilton cornered the Connecticut artist John Trumbull, who was headed to Boston, where he would see some of the secessionist leaders. "Tell them from *me*, at *my* request, for God's sake, to cease these conversations and threatenings about a separation of the Union," Hamilton supposedly said. "It must hang together as long as it can be made to."

A similar tale concerned Hamilton's last ride to the Grange, his beloved home in Upper Manhattan, with a fellow lawyer named Samuel Boyd. The pair spoke of recent events, probably Burr's defeat in the election and the New England conspiracy. Suddenly, Hamilton stopped his horse and looked the other man in the eye. "Boyd," he said, clapping a hand on his friend's knee, "to break the Union would break my heart."

It's an attractive line for the historical dramatist—so irresistible, in fact, that Ron Chernow, in his Hamilton biography that inspired the Broadway musical, has the hero utter it several days later while lying prostrate on his deathbed, Burr's bullet lodged near his spine. The error reflects an apparently irresistible need to imagine the dying Hamilton, patriot to the last, using his final breath to grieve not for himself but for his doomed and damaged country.

Such stories, even if true, give us a warped understanding of how Hamilton saw the prospect of national disintegration. The problem for him wasn't that disunion would destroy the country. It was that disunion would prove an inadequate fix to what was wrong with American politics, which was neither partisanship nor slavery nor sectionalism, but democracy. If Madison had been right when he argued, back in 1787, that expanding the sphere of politics by forming a more perfect Union would make it more difficult for the people to organize themselves and push for change, the converse, Hamilton realized, must also be true: dividing the Union would only make the people more powerful in each new part.

The day before Hamilton's friends rowed him across the Hudson River for his "interview" with Burr, he scrawled out a final letter. He addressed it to Theodore Sedgwick, the Massachusetts lawyer and well-connected Federalist who had been one of the first New Englanders to push for separation, back in 1786. "I will here express but one sentiment," Hamilton wrote, "which is, that dismemberment of our Empire will be a clear sacrifice of great positive advantages without any counterbalancing good; administering no relief to our real disease, which is *democracy,* the poison of which by a sub-division will only be more concentrated in each part, and consequently the more virulent."

Secession wouldn't fix anything. It would only make everything the Federalists despised—especially the rising tide of democracy—even worse. These words, some of the last Hamilton ever wrote, are nowhere to be found in the much-loved musical, yet they remain as relevant as anything he ever said. Maybe the revered founder was on to something when he suggested, days before he died, that breaking up the United States would spark a rebirth of American democracy.

Burr's loss and Hamilton's death put New England's secession movement on hold. There would be no Boston convention that fall. That was just as well, since Jefferson already knew about their plans. His postmaster general, a Connecticut Republican named Gideon Granger, snooped through Federalists' mail and kept his boss in the loop about what he found. Though he could have destroyed the opposition by revealing what he knew, Jefferson opted not to disclose the treasonous plot. After Burr's defeat in New York, the threat of Yankee separatism was "gone forever," Jefferson told Granger. "It will be found in this, as in all other similar cases, that crooked schemes will end by overwhelming their authors & coadjutors in disgrace."

That fall, Jefferson romped to reelection, winning even the Federalist stronghold of Massachusetts, while his fellow Republicans expanded their majorities in Congress. Still, Timothy Pickering, chief author of this particular crooked scheme, didn't feel so disgraced as to give up on disunion. He would nurture the embers, keep the flame alive, for even more turbulent years ahead.

He wasn't the only one. On a warm night in July, ten days after he had last crossed the Hudson, the vice president of the United States again left his Manhattan home, climbed into a boat, and was rowed to the New Jersey shore. Opportunity beckoned out west. He would not throw away his shot.

2. The Burr Conspiracy

Burr's enemies had always called him dangerous. Following the 1800 election, one Federalist predicted that Burr's "unbounded ambition, courage, and perseverance might someday prompt him to be a Bonaparte, a King, and an Emperor, or anything else which might place him at the head of the nation." After Hamilton's death, Burr's political career in the United States was over. If he was going to be the head of a nation, he would have to start a new one.

Far from an implausible fantasy doomed to failure, Burr's scheme to break off a massive piece of the United States and form a new Western empire posed a serious threat to American unity. His network of intriguers reached across the country, from New York to New Orleans, South Carolina to Ohio, from the drawing rooms of the national capital to the farthest reaches of the unsettled frontier. An audacious rethinking of the continental map, Burr's plan served as an early warning that the nation's rise to greatness wasn't nearly as inevitable, its destiny not quite as manifest, as its loyal boosters liked to think. That the plot would fail wasn't a foregone conclusion, in part, perhaps, because the president tasked with suppressing it harbored his own doubts about whether the uncharted regions of the recently acquired West should be a single nation or a handful of associated republics.

For an accomplice, Burr had a partner well practiced in deceit. Despite his earlier support for Kentucky's secession and the fact that he was widely suspected to be a Spanish spy, James Wilkinson, like Burr, had done well in the tumultuous politics of the fledgling republic, eventually rising to senior general in charge of the U.S. Army and governor of the immense northern section of the Louisiana Purchase. Still, he was frustrated and restless. In 1803, a French diplomat described Wilkinson as a "rattled-headed fellow, full of odd fantasies… frequently drunk." In boozy, after-dinner talk, General Wilkinson railed against his own government, especially those peace-minded Republicans he called a "set of prating puppies and coxcombs."

Wilkinson knew Burr from their days in the Continental army. They had both served outside the walls of Quebec under Benedict Arnold—perhaps that should have been a clue—and they had stayed in touch over the years, sometimes exchanging letters in code. In spring 1804, the general visited New York and sent Burr a note asking to meet "without observation or intrusion." Secrecy was warranted; Wilkinson brought along hand-drawn maps of the little-known lands between the Louisiana Territory and the Spanish town of Santa Fe, with its clear road into Mexico. With Burr's political talents and Wilkinson's military skills, they could rule a vast empire stretching the breadth of the Mississippi Valley, from the Appalachians to the Rockies, and possibly beyond, all of it funded by cartloads of silver from Mexican mines.

Burr was all ears. The late-night meeting in New York came in the uneasy weeks between his loss in the New York election and the fatal duel, a time when he was carefully considering his options. Hamilton's death made his choice clear. Wanted for murder in New Jersey and for dueling in New York, Burr fled to Washington. He sent a confidant to meet with Anthony Merry, the British minister spurned by Jefferson who had promised support for New England's secession. Burr was eager, Merry explained to his superiors in London, "to effect a Separation of the Western Part of the United States from that which lies between the Atlantick and the Mountains."

Burr's term as vice president was about to expire. He gave a stirring farewell to the Senate, somberly observing that if the Constitution were ever "to perish by the sacrilegious hands of a Demagogue . . . its expiring agonies will be witnessed on this floor." The speech brought business to a halt. An ex-general put his head on a table and wept. "The whole senate was in tears, and so unmanned," one paper noted, "that it was half an hour before they could recover themselves."

Burr's performance was even more impressive given that it was entirely disingenuous. A few days later, he huddled with Merry, the conniving British envoy. For weeks, delegates from New Orleans had been in Washington lobbying for Louisiana's admission to the Union as a state. Denied—American politicians believed the territory was too dominated by foreigners—they left in anger, promising "to seek redress from some other quarter," Merry wrote to London. Burr offered to weaponize their sense of betrayal. The Louisianans were "determined to render themselves independent of the United States," he told Merry. If they could rely on a foreign power for protection, they would set up a separate empire and use the Mississippi as leverage to add the Western part of the United States. Burr proposed himself as "the instrument of effecting such a connection." All he needed was a few ships in the Gulf of Mexico to hold off the American navy.

Impressed by Burr, who seemed to have "all the talents, energy, intrepidity and firmness which are requisite for such an enterprise," Merry urged the British Foreign Office to send help.

That spring of 1805, Burr set out for the West. A fugitive from justice, he meant to "seek another country," he told his son-in-law.

After traveling overland to Pittsburgh, Burr cruised down the Ohio River on a massive, custom-built barge—a two-story "floating house," as he called it, with a dining room, a fireplace, two bedrooms, glass windows, and a walkway along the roof.

Throughout the West, well-placed allies linked Burr into a network of local operators—preachers and politicians, boatbuilders and arms manufacturers. He swept into Kentucky weeks after a promoter showcased a set of wax figures depicting "the LATE UNFORTUNATE DUEL." Now the people of Lexington crowded to see the victor in the flesh. He consulted with the state's leading citizens, including a young lawyer named Henry Clay, soon to be sent to the Senate. Burr's plans were an open secret. After he left, one resident wrote that Burr meant "to separate this western country from the Union." Cincinnati's sheriff expected the Appalachians would shortly become a border.

Despite his later protests to the contrary, Burr's host in Nashville, a thirty-eight-year-old militia officer, must have heard the same rumors. Already known for a violent streak—a year later he would kill a man in a duel and take a bullet to the ribs that would remain there for the rest of his life—Andrew Jackson admired Burr's gumption in killing Hamilton and had appreciated his support for Tennessee's statehood a decade earlier. Burr easily won the grizzled soldier to his side, though he may not have divulged the full extent of his plans.

After leaving Nashville, Burr met with Wilkinson at a frontier fort, then floated down to New Orleans, still dominated by French, Spanish, and Creole elements, where he hoped to shore up support. Assured by Burr that the British would provide cover for a march on Mexico, the city's merchants, who were opposed to the American territorial administration and eager to invade the Spanish lands to their west (Texas) and east (Florida), honored the guest with a banquet. Two weeks later,

Burr traveled north by horseback, stopping again at Jackson's planta-tion and in St. Louis to consult with Wilkinson. Their plan was coming along nicely. The Union would soon "moulder to pieces, die a natural death," Wilkinson later recalled Burr telling him. Westerners were "ready to revolt."

Wilkinson doubted that. He had been trying to get them to revolt for two decades without success. The pair parted on uneasy terms.

Burr returned to Washington. His travels had confirmed that the loosely connected settlers were "so firmly resolved upon separating themselves from their Union," as he told the British minister, that "the revolution there would be accomplished without a drop of blood." Once Ohio, Kentucky, and Tennessee left the Union, New England, too, might strike off on its own. The whole edifice would crumble, Anthony Merry excitedly told his superiors, and "the immense power" of the Union could, "by such a division, be rendered at once informidable."

Yet Burr knew better than to rely solely on Merry's pull in London. (A new U.S.-friendly foreign minister soon ordered the ambassador to return home.) For additional support, he turned, audaciously, to Spain, the country whose territory he planned to invade. He sent a friend, former New Jersey senator Jonathan Dayton, to approach the Spanish ambassador, a vain, redheaded dandy named Carlos Martínez de Yrujo. Instead of conquering Mexico and dividing the Union, as Burr had originally planned, he would launch a revolution in the federal capital. Secret agents would sneak into Washington and arrest Jefferson and the cabinet secretaries—maybe even execute them. If the people sup-ported his coup, Burr would rule. If not, he would sail for New Orleans, declare the independence of a new Western empire, and, taking a page from Spain's own playbook, compel the submission of the trans-Appalachian states.

It was a wild plan. Yrujo, understandably, was skeptical. But he real-ized how much Spain would gain from its success. By triggering the "dismemberment of the colossal power" next door, Burr could save Spain's shrinking American dominion. Yrujo paid Dayton a small tip for the information but held off on committing further until he heard from Madrid.

Impatient, Burr ventured west again in the summer of 1806—not to gather intelligence, but to act. However, the rumors about his motives were finally starting to catch up to him. At a ball thrown in his honor in one Ohio River community, Burr asked a local belle to dance. She refused him, citing a policy not to dance with traitors.

In Kentucky, Burr found the mood had shifted since his last visit. A local newspaper was running exposés of the "Spanish Conspiracy" of the late 1780s, revealing all the officials that had been on the payroll of a foreign power. That conspiracy remained alive, the paper suggested; Burr and Wilkinson were "the two men most to be dreaded in the Union."

Meanwhile, U.S. attorney Joseph Hamilton Daveiss, one of the few Federalists whom Jefferson did not remove from office, visited Louisville, a bastion of separatist support. He found the river town buzzing with activity—boats were being built, heads of cattle purchased, and dozens of young men were signing up for some kind of expedition. "Burr's accomplices," Daveiss reported to James Madison, the secretary of state, were "very busy in disseminating the idea of disunion."

Back in Frankfort, Kentucky's state capital, Daveiss charged Burr with scheming to invade Mexico and separate the Western states from the Union. Burr asked Henry Clay, the best lawyer in town, to defend him in court. Clay compared the trial to the "inquisitions of Europe" and vouched for Burr's honor with his own. The charges were dropped. It helped that the presiding judge was busy defending himself from charges that he had once taken Spanish bribes. If Burr was found guilty of treason, he might be too.

"My present impression is that *all is not right*," the governor of New Orleans wrote to his Mississippi counterpart. Something was afoot. Everyone seemed to know about it but him. The militia refused to muster. Burr's plans formed "almost the sole topic of conversation," another resident reported.

Three hundred miles away, James Wilkinson, camped out with his army, was also growing concerned. The reports of Burr's activities suggested that Wilkinson, too, was party to the scheme. If their project failed, as Wilkinson feared, his decades of secret work for Spain might be revealed, and he would lose everything. Burr's plan depended on the commander of American forces in the West going along with it. That put Wilkinson in a position to make or break the entire scheme.

In early October, a Burr lieutenant scrambled into Wilkinson's tent with a coded letter laying out the progress of their plot. Thousands of men — "a host of choice spirits...a corps of worthies...the best blood of our country" — were being mobilized for the expedition, Burr informed Wilkinson. He was sure they would succeed. "The people of the country to which we are going are prepared to receive us." They would be greeted as liberators.

Protecting himself first, as always, Wilkinson sent a breathless note to Jefferson touting his discovery of a "deep, dark and widespread conspiracy" to dissolve the Union. It involved "young and old, the democrat and the federalist, the native and the foreigner, the patriot of '76 and the exotic of yesterday, the opulent and the needy, the ins and the outs." Then he wrote to the anxious New Orleans governor, warning that Burr's army was headed for the city: "The destruction of the American Union is seriously menaced." Wilkinson would be there soon to defend it. Still, he found time to write a third letter, this one informing his Spanish contacts in Mexico that he had thwarted an invasion and deserved a special reward.

In New Orleans, Wilkinson declared martial law. He arrested a judge, an editor, a former senator, and others whom he was somehow able to identify as Burr associates. He appeared in court in garish military dress — gold buttons, gold stirrups, gold spurs. Wilkinson's five-month reign in the city was "the most compleat scene of confusion and alarm I ever beheld," one observer wrote, a violation of civil liberties unlike any seen in the republic to that time.

What Thomas Jefferson knew of Burr's conspiracy and when he knew it has always been a mystery. He couldn't have missed the banner coverage of his former vice president's Western sojourns. As early as August 1805 — five months after Burr left office — a Philadelphia paper asked, "How long will it be before we shall hear of Col. Burr being at the head of a revolution party on the western waters?" Months later, an anonymous letter informed the president that "Burrs Manouevres," while "ostensibly directed against a foreign power," really aimed at "the distruction of our Government...and the material injury of the atlantic states." Daveiss, the Kentucky attorney, sent the president frantic memos warning that Burr was plotting "a separation of the Union in favor of Spain." He even provided a list of Burr's accomplices. Jefferson, perhaps wary of Daveiss's Federalist ties, ignored the letters and did nothing.

Why, in the face of an organized conspiracy against his government, did Jefferson refuse to take action against it for so long? Was it because Burr's promised invasion of Mexico might prove useful to his own expansionist agenda? Perhaps, rather, Jefferson felt paralyzed by a dilemma of his own creation: How could he prevent the Western people from dissolving the bands that connected them with the East after having once declared inalienable every people's right to do just that? How could he suppress an attempt to divide the continent when he himself remained ambivalent about the need to hold it together?

To Jefferson, the merit of republican government was the willingness of citizens to defend it. The Burr crisis put that faith to the test. For once, the fragile republic passed.

By the fall of 1806, Burr's conspiracy had grown too obvious to ignore. Jefferson no longer doubted that the former vice president aimed at "separating the Western from the Atlantic States, and erecting the former into an independent Confederacy." Even then, however, all he did was send a lone agent to tail Burr around the West. Only weeks later—after receiving Wilkinson's hysterical, self-acquitting letter—did the president issue a proclamation instructing military officers and public officials to do whatever they could to stop Burr.

Westerners proved their loyalty by turning against Burr's traitorous plot. Frail though the Union remained, Jefferson's ascension to the presidency had convinced the region's yeoman farmers that the federal government had their interests at heart. The Louisiana Purchase ensured the Mississippi would never again be closed to their goods. Although the day might come when it made sense to split the country at the Appalachians, it hadn't yet. The mass of frontiersmen that Burr expected to rally to his banners never appeared. Jefferson's agent convinced the Ohio legislature to seize the boats Burr had ordered for the campaign. In Kentucky, those who had been Burr's "warmest advocates," one observer reported, now called him "a rascal, villain, thief and highway robber."

As Jefferson's proclamation was spreading through the Western valleys, Burr was back in Tennessee, again a guest of Andrew Jackson. The alarm went up. Jackson swore he was shocked—*shocked*—to find treason being plotted on his estate. Burr escaped and headed down the Mississippi, intent on meeting Wilkinson. He didn't know Wilkinson had already given him up. Even if there wasn't support in the West for disunion, Burr thought, they could seize New Orleans, take the Mexican mines, and eventually convince the denizens of Kentucky, Tennessee, and Ohio, through bribery and blackmail, to join the new empire.

North of New Orleans, Burr went ashore and read about General Wilkinson's betrayal in a newspaper. He faced a choice. He could allow himself to be captured by Wilkinson's men—already scouring the countryside for the head on which the general had placed a five-thousand-dollar reward—and in all likelihood be executed in New Orleans's public square, or he could submit to Mississippi's territorial governor, who might let him fight the charges in court. Decrying Wilkinson's accusations as the "vile fabrications of a man notoriously the pensioner of a foreign country," Burr surrendered.

In Natchez, the Mississippi capital, Burr went free on bail. The town's high society treated him as a dignitary rather than a traitor. Balls were thrown in his honor. Ever the lothario, he wooed a local widow while awaiting his day in court. Though a grand jury refused to indict him, the judge ordered Burr not to leave town. Nervous that Wilkinson's men were closing in, he fled into the woods, again a fugitive. Two weeks later, though disguised by dirty clothes, a floppy hat, and a short beard, he was spotted in a cabin north of Mobile, given away by his piercing black eyes, which were likened by one early chronicler to "lightning imprisoned and forever playing in a cloud black as death."

Jefferson made sure Burr was tried in the president's own Virginia. Perhaps to redeem himself for his failure to adequately investigate the early reports of Burr's intrigues, Jefferson wanted to see his turncoat ex-lieutenant executed for treason.

Despite the president's efforts, the prosecution's case collapsed. There was no question that a conspiracy existed, but thanks to the Union's massive size and loose federal structure, just which laws had been broken, when, where, how, and by whom proved too difficult for the government to establish. The truth of what Burr really planned may never be known. Yet, as with more recent conspiracies involving foreign agents working with well-placed Americans to foment domestic divisions, it remains hard to explain how there could have been so much smoke without a fire.

After the trial, Burr fled to Europe. He returned to New York in 1812 and lived another twenty-four years, largely in obscurity. James Wilkinson, his actions in New Orleans retroactively approved by Jefferson, retained his command in the U.S. Army for another five years.

Jefferson had no choice but to accept the verdict in Burr's trial as the unsatisfying conclusion to an embarrassing episode. Burr's "enterprise," the president told Congress, was "the most extraordinary since the days of Don Quixote." Yet even he had to admit—in a letter to an aged John Dickinson—that there were "great discontents" in the West. Long after Burr's acquittal, those discontents would remain.

Many Americans hoped the failure of the conspiracy would forever silence the murmurings on both sides of the Atlantic that the Union was about to break apart. Perhaps, as one congressman observed, the "warm, unshaken attachment of the western people" would convince Europeans "of the impossibility of dismembering the Union [and] the futility of tampering with our citizens." That was unlikely, for no sooner had Burr's scheme been stamped out than the specter of New England's secession reappeared, not as the futile project of frustrated men in Washington but as a full-fledged resistance movement with broad popular support.

3. The Civil War of 1812

In June 1807, a British ship fired on an American vessel off the coast of Virginia after its request to search for deserters was denied. The attack finally pushed Aaron Burr's sensational treason trial off the front pages. Jefferson hoped to avoid war at any cost, even if the alternative brought harsh criticism from the opposition and prolonged sacrifice by the government and the people.

At Jefferson's urging, instead of a military response, Congress instituted an embargo on all foreign commerce—sanctions, in effect, against the entire world. To Jefferson, it was the only way to keep the United States out of the latest European war without sacrificing national honor. As long as American vessels sailed the high seas, the British and French would continue to make crushing and incompatible demands on American sovereignty. Keeping the ships in port would avoid such difficulties.

It didn't work out that way. Jefferson overestimated Britain's reliance on American exports. An own-goal of epic proportions, the embargo devastated the domestic economy. With ships stuck in harbors, sailors went without work, merchants without contracts, farmers without buyers of their wheat, flour, fish, pork, and cattle. Not having the advantages of other regions—land in the West, slaves in the South—New England relied on the Atlantic trade. From the beginning, Yankees had called commerce their only motive for federation. Without that, they had none. "The Union is dear," one paper said. "But commerce is still more dear."

New Englanders saw Jefferson's embargo as a drastic escalation of the Southern conspiracy against their region and the commerce it relied on. Barred from power, Federalists had grown more isolated since the collapse of their budding separatist initiative three years earlier. Not only their political influence but their very livelihoods were being taken from them. Economically desperate, geographically isolated, New England was ripe for revolution.

Amid that incendiary situation, Timothy Pickering "hurled a firebrand upon the stage," as fellow Massachusetts senator John Quincy Adams later wrote. In a letter to the state's Republican governor, Pickering described the embargo as the fruit of a secret alliance between Jefferson and Napoleon—a conspiracy to help France at England's (and New England's) expense. Against a president taking orders from the emperor, Pickering called for unflinching, region-wide opposition. "Those States whose farms are on the ocean and whose harvests are gathered in every sea," he wrote, "should immediately and seriously consider how to preserve them."

The governor refused to forward the letter to the state legislature, arguing that it was intended only "to disunite, divide, and dissolve the nation." But Pickering's friends made sure it was widely published. A bestseller, the pamphlet fired up the New England public. "The CONSTITUTION gone!!" one paper declared. The embargo posed "the dreadful, horrible alternative of *Civil War,* or *Slavery,*" unless "New-England

declares firmly... that she will not submit." Seventy towns in Massachusetts petitioned the government to repeal the trade ban. Smugglers
evaded it as they had Britain's restrictions forty years earlier. Armed
crowds helped move goods across the Canadian border and freed ships
taken into custody. Town meetings advocated violating the law and
withholding federal tax revenues.

Yet the president and his fellow Republicans in Congress refused to
buckle. Instead of canceling the embargo, they passed a new act
empowering the administration to use extraordinary means, including
military action, to compel submission. Convinced New England's illicit
trade with Canada "amounted almost to rebellion and treason," Jefferson declared the Lake Champlain region to be in a state of insurrection against the government. He personally oversaw the enforcement
effort down to minute details and even directed troops to enforce the
embargo in recalcitrant states—a remarkable reversal for the supposed champion of limited government and individual rights. "The
United States government," historian Gordon Wood writes, "was virtually at war with its own people."

Jefferson wasn't the only hypocrite. Federalists suddenly found it
convenient to use the states' rights principles put forth by their Republican opponents in the 1790s. They condemned both the "dambargo"
and Jefferson's resort to "Turkish despotism" to enforce it. Juries acquitted anyone charged with violating it. The Massachusetts legislature
condemned the trade ban as "unjust, oppressive and unconstitutional,
and not legally binding on the citizens of this state." Ten years earlier,
when Republicans in Kentucky and Virginia wielded the same doctrine
against a Federalist president from Massachusetts, the legislature had
condemned nullification as near treason. Now the parties' positions
had reversed.

The embargo hurt the United States far worse than it did either
Britain or France. As the economy collapsed, support for secession
began to rise. Boston's leading Federalist newspaper, the *Columbian
Centinel,* maintained that New England had sufficient resources to support independence. The North needed the South less than the other
way around. While disunion was "an evil which can never be sufficiently deprecated by every true patriot," submitting to the embargo
would be worse. Reading the Massachusetts papers, a Republican min-

ister could only conclude that most of the population was "against our own Country [and] in favour of the British." A secret British agent traveling through the United States informed Canadian officials that if war erupted between the empire and the former colonies, Massachusetts would probably leave the Union and ally with its enemy.

"Everyone wishes to preserve the Union if it can be done without ruin," professed Theodore Sedgwick, aging baron of the Berkshires. "But [the] opinion is becoming more and more prevalent, that it will probably become impossible."

Facing such defiance, Republicans had to make an unappetizing choice, as Jefferson later put it, between "repeal or Civil War." They had to either end the unpopular embargo or raise an army from one part of the country to put down a rebellion in the other. The petitions and resolutions passed by Northern protest meetings grew more radical by the day. "I felt the foundations of the government shaken under my feet by the New England townships," Jefferson later recalled. In the 1808 state and congressional elections, Federalists roared back from near irrelevance, an unmistakable sign of public disapproval of the administration's policy.

In March 1809, days before he yielded the presidency to James Madison, his handpicked successor, Jefferson signed a bill repealing the embargo. "We must save the Union," the president concluded, almost ruefully. He preferred to force the "monarchists of the North" to either submit to federal authority or secede from the union. Advised by Madison and others that the Republican Party itself was showing signs of strain, he set aside private doubts for the sake of public duty.

For the first time since the Revolution that Jefferson had helped lead, a mass separatist movement with established leaders and broad support among the population had rocked the political order. The economy, booming before the embargo, would take decades to recover. Yet nothing could cover up the deep divisions it revealed in the foundation of the Union, fractures that became even more hazardous with the onset of another war.

When Jefferson retired, James Madison inherited a divided country and a splintering party. Slight in stature (three inches shorter than Napoleon), the fourth president was often overlooked at gatherings in

the executive mansion—"in danger of being confounded with the ple-
bian crowds," an observer noted, and "pushed and jostled about like a
common citizen."

Madison's lack of charisma left an opening for a rising Republican
faction dubbed the "War Hawks"—young glory-seekers from the South
and West (such as Kentucky's Henry Clay and South Carolina's John C.
Calhoun) who were keen on conquest, eager to flex American muscle.
They convinced Madison that only force would make Britain respect
American rights on the high seas. In June 1812, Congress declared war
by what remains the thinnest margin for such a vote in U.S. history.
Every Federalist voted no.

Intended to shore up national unity, the War of 1812 further
cleaved the country. The first American casualties came neither in
maritime battle nor on the Canadian frontier but in Republican-
dominated Baltimore, where a street mob attacked the office of a Federalist newspaper. Two people died and several were injured. One of
the latter, revolutionary hero Henry Lee, never recovered and succumbed to his wounds six years later. His son Robert grew up without a
father.

The vast majority of New Englanders opposed the war. Caleb
Strong, long-serving Federalist governor of Massachusetts, proclaimed
a day of fasting to lament the hostilities "against the nation from which
we are descended." He and his counterparts in Connecticut and Rhode
Island refused Madison's requests that they lend their state militias for
federal service. A crowd in Plymouth seized its pro-war congressman
and kicked him through the streets.

In New Hampshire, thousands showed up to hear a local lawyer
denounce the war before a countywide convention. The crowd couldn't
fit in the local meetinghouse, so they moved outside into the hot summer air. The speaker had a difficult job; many in the crowd were ready
to give up on the Union entirely. Opposed to secession, he admitted it
might someday be necessary. Disunion would be justified "on some
occasion when one portion of the country undertakes to control, to
regulate, and to sacrifice the interest of another." For many listeners,
that occasion had already arrived. That fall, New Hampshire sent Daniel Webster to Congress.

Support for secession was growing fast. Yankee preachers endorsed revolution from the pulpit. The war was "an outrage against Heaven," one thundered. Anyone who supported it was "a murderer—and no murderer hath eternal life." Another told his flock to "let the southern *Heroes* fight their own battles.... *Forbid this war to proceed in New-England.*" The Union was already dissolved, a Boston rector insisted, adding that "this portion of the *disunited states* should take care of itself."

Poets took up the cause in verse. In 1813, a Massachusetts lyricist recited his latest work to a Federalist crowd:

> *Union we love, and ever would pursue,*
> *Till its great blessings shall escape from view,*
> *Yet, dear as union is, sweet Liberty,*
> *'Tis but a galling chain—unless upheld by thee.*
> *Union is dear: Oh, may we ne'er dissever—*
> *But, if by Union we must bondsmen be,*
> *Let the cords snap*—NEW ENGLAND SHALL BE FREE.

Timothy Pickering thrilled to see the masses finally catching up with him. Historians have depicted Pickering as "the worst-hated man in the nation," but in New England he was popular. Patient for a decade, Pickering decided the region was ready for independence. "I would preserve the Union of the states if possible," he wrote after Congress declared war. "But I would not be deluded by a word. To my ears there is no magic in the sound of union. If the great objects of union are utterly abandoned...let the Union be severed. Such a severance presents no terrors for me."

In November 1812, Madison won a hard-fought bid for reelection, and New England fell deeper into despondency. Many Federalists, believing that the administration did not represent them or their states, gave up on seeking redress within the system. "Instead of wishing to withdraw from the Union, we fear that Government has withdrawn from us," the citizens of one Massachusetts county lamented. Summoning the spirit of the Revolution, a Boston paper concluded, "The determination that was necessary in 1776, is necessary now."

Timothy Pickering, as always, was blunter: "Let the ship run aground."

*　　*　　*

The war was going abysmally. The belief that conquering Canada would be easy—"a mere matter of marching," according to Jefferson—had been quickly revealed as folly.

It didn't help that an entire region of the United States sat out the war and occasionally even obstructed the fight. New Englanders used all the old tricks—smuggling, tax boycotts, anti-recruitment riots. "No sooner is a young man asked to enlist," one congressman observed, "than you see ten or a dozen around him dissuading him from doing so." Britain exempted the region from its naval blockade and coastal sorties. In July 1814, Nantucket's residents agreed to a separate peace with Britain; they wouldn't support the federal government until the end of the war. In Newburyport, Massachusetts, locals raised a flag with five stars and five stripes to represent the five New England states.

For the next half a century, Southerners would use one especially brazen act of anti-war resistance by New Englanders as a political cudgel. On a moonless night in 1813, Stephen Decatur led his squadron out of the harbor of New London, Connecticut, and into Long Island Sound. For six months, the commodore had been trapped by British ships offshore. The people of New London openly traded with the enemy and welcomed its sailors into their homes. They resented Decatur's presence and refused to help him rebuild the town's dilapidated, Revolution-era forts. Worried they might assist a British invasion, Decatur decided to slip out to sea.

As the ships edged toward open water, a sailor noticed blue lights at the mouth of the harbor. Somebody was signaling the ships' movements to the enemy. Decatur turned the fleet around. Twice more that winter he tried to make a break for it; twice more the blue lights appeared. He had no choice but to abandon the ships and travel overland to another part of the coast.

The hot-tempered Decatur, a seasoned duelist, was livid. He tossed off a testy letter to the war secretary that found its way into Republican papers and caused a scandal. A Connecticut congressman condemned "these wicked lights, these torches of treason"—if they existed. He didn't think they did. The lights may have been hung not by American traitors but by British spies. Yet the history of what Alan Taylor has aptly called "the Civil War of 1812" would be written by its Republican victors. "Blue Light Federalists" became a handy epithet for Southerners to argue—correctly—that, despite the sanctimonious prattle of Yankees like Daniel Webster, New Englanders had been the original disunionists.

The Union had always been battered by winds from abroad. The years of Napoleon's reign were especially stormy. But if Napoleon's rise complicated things for the United States, his 1814 abdication threatened to destroy it entirely. Unburdened by other battles, Britain sent new shipments of troops across the Atlantic. They went on the offensive, occupying coastal Maine and torching the federal capital in retaliation for an American raid on Toronto. In burned-out Washington, Madison was distraught. The government was broke, the country divided, the executive mansion smoldering. Three months later, the federal government defaulted on the national debt. Visited by a friend in his rented quarters, the president looked "miserably shattered and woe-be-gone." He was fixated on "the New England sedition." The Union he had helped build seemed now, on his watch, to be falling apart.

As British ships raided areas up and down the coast, the New England sedition entered a more dangerous phase. To pressure the region to capitulate, Britain ended its exemption of New England from the war. That October, Caleb Strong informed the Massachusetts legislature that the Union was on the brink of collapse. The Republican-led Congress would not reimburse the state for defense as long as it refused to place the militia under federal command, which Strong would not do. That left Massachusetts helpless against an enemy it had little reason to fight. Absent divine intervention, Strong declared, Massachusetts could rely only on itself.

At the governor's urging, the legislature called for an emergency New England–wide convention to meet in Hartford, Connecticut, in December, a plan that received broad support. As New Bedford's town meeting solemnly declared, "The time has arrived in which it is incumbent on the people of this state, to prepare themselves for the great duty of protecting, by their own vigor, their unalienable rights."

Whether that meant secession or some remedy just shy of it, New Englanders themselves might not have known. But they were keeping their options open. Connecticut and Rhode Island appointed delegates, and Federalist counties in Vermont and New Hampshire (where Republicans held more sway) did the same. As each state agreed to attend, Federalist newspapers used the same terms they had when the states ratified the Constitution: "SECOND PILLAR *of a New* FEDERAL EDIFICE *Reared*"; "Third Pillar Raised." The crumbling old edifice was being destroyed and a smaller but stronger one erected in its place.

Meanwhile, Governor Strong sent an emissary to see the British governor in Halifax and solicit support for New England's secession. In a memo, Strong's agent said the goal of the upcoming Hartford convention would be to "paralyze the authority of the United States" and force an end to the war. The Canadian official agreed to ask London for advice.

Secession enjoyed support in surprising places. Ever since the Revolution, Gouverneur Morris had been a strong champion of national government, a close ally of Hamilton and Washington. At one point during the Constitutional Convention, Morris had demanded to know whether the differences between North and South were "fictitious or real." A quarter of a century later, he saw they were very real indeed. Over a decade and a half of Republican rule, Morris had watched America turn into something he didn't recognize—an "abused, self-murdered country."

Like most of his business-minded brethren, Morris saw "Mr. Madison's War" as hostile to Northern interests. One of the few delegates in Philadelphia to denounce slavery as immoral, he understood that the extension of the three-fifths bonus to new slaveholding states in the West would destroy the balance of power between the sections. Morris preferred to break up the Union rather than surrender it to the South. "The Union, being the means of freedom, should be prized as such," he wrote in 1813, "but the end should not be sacrificed to the means." He thought Northerners should "examine the Question freely, Whether it be...consistent with the Freedom of the Northern and Eastern States to continue in Union with the Owners of Slaves."

As the war ground on and the government crumbled, Morris struck up a correspondence with Pickering, the preeminent Northern disunionist. "I hear every day professions of attachment to the Union, and declarations as to its importance," he wrote Pickering. "I should be glad to meet with someone who could tell me...to what useful purpose it endures." To Morris, the only question was whether the new border would be drawn at the Delaware, the Susquehanna, or the Potomac.

Later historians—including Morris biographer Theodore Roosevelt—have dismissed the aging statesman's endorsement of disunion as an aberrant, late-career folly. But Morris's secessionism was no less characteristic (or American) than his earlier nationalism had been. In 1814, unlike in 1787, he had the benefit of seeing what the country had become.

And he had much of the Northern public on his side. Never before had secession been so popular. Many in New England—possibly a majority—hoped the Hartford convention would issue a declaration of independence. "The people there are in advance of their leaders," an editor wrote of Massachusetts. Local papers were dominated by disunion talk. One author, using the pseudonym Epaminondas—a Theban general who led his city out of the ancient Greek confederacy—asked the Hartford delegates "not to be entangled by the cobwebs of a compact which has long since ceased to exist." "To the cry of disunion," a Boston paper argued, "the plain answer is, that the States are already separated." The influential *Columbian Centinel* argued that New Englanders were "unquestionably absolved from all obligations to the United States, since the United States have ceased to perform any of its obligations toward them." One reverend warned that half measures wouldn't do. "Union founded upon submission," he noted, "is the Union of slaves."

That fall, Boston trembled—literally. Nobody knew what the future held, but an earthquake seemed to augur nothing good.

In late December 1814, twenty-six men met in the Connecticut capitol building beneath a portrait of George Washington. They saw themselves as continuing what the general had begun, not ending it. Others saw them as traitors. In the square outside, a colonel sent by Madison conspicuously paraded his troops. The president had asked him to keep an eye on things. Leaving nothing to chance, Madison pulled troops off the Canadian border and positioned them near Albany, ready to intervene if New England tried to secede.

He needn't have worried. Leading Federalists, terrified by the swelling support for separation (and reluctant to lose their business connections in other states), stacked the convention with anti-secession moderates. One radical's description of the chief organizer, Boston magnate Harrison Gray Otis—"timid, and frequently wavering, today bold, and tomorrow like a hare trembling at every breeze"—applied to many of the men in Hartford. The convention's president, George Cabot, a white-haired Bostonian who would probably have served as chief executive of a newly created New England nation, told a colleague he was going to Hartford to "prevent you young hot-heads from getting into mischief." John Lowell, a Pickering ally, feared the convention would oppose "any measures which will disturb our sleep."

Like the delegates at the Philadelphia convention, the Hartford delegates swore an oath of secrecy. Little would be revealed of what they said behind closed doors. Yet the official report, written by Otis, suggests a showdown between hard-core disunionists and conservatives seeking delay.

The conservatives won. But as the price for New England's allegiance, the convention demanded a set of constitutional amendments to better balance Northern and Southern interests: repeal of the three-fifths compromise; a two-thirds supermajority requirement for declaring war, blocking trade, or admitting states; a one-term limit for the president; a rule, directed at the Virginia dynasty, that two presidents in a row could not come from the same state; and a prohibition on federal officeholding by any foreign-born citizen (a measure targeted at the treasury secretary at the time, Swiss-born Albert Gallatin).

The delegates knew their amendments would be rejected. In that case, they could take the last fateful step. "Our nation may yet be great, our union durable," the report hinted. "But should this prospect be utterly hopeless, the time will not have been lost which shall have ripened a general sentiment of the necessity of more mighty efforts to rescue from ruin at least some portion of our beloved country."

They agreed to meet in Boston in June 1815 to plan their next move. If the war continued, that would likely mean disunion. Shortly after the Hartford convention adjourned, the British governor in Nova Scotia received an answer from London regarding Massachusetts's request for protection: he should do everything in his power to help New England secede.

*   *   *

The Hartford convention suffered from an epic case of bad timing. A three-man committee, headed by Harrison Gray Otis, set off for Washington to convey the region's demands. From New York to Philadelphia, three black crows seemed to accompany them, marking out the path. Otis worried about the "*ill-omen'd* birds."

He was right to be concerned. The trio rode into Washington just as reports arrived that negotiators in Europe had, weeks earlier, signed a treaty ending the war. It was a stunning development—to some, a miracle, the work of "the Giver of all good things." Only the surprisingly generous peace terms, as one Virginia Federalist observed, saved America from "bankruptcy, disunion, and civil war, combined with foreign invasion; in fine, from national dishonor and ruin." New England's leverage evaporated in a moment. The Hartford convention's urgent appeal for constitutional change seemed irrelevant—even downright traitorous.

A few days later came worse news for the Hartford commissioners. Fresh from a campaign of terror against the Creek on the southern frontier, Andrew Jackson, aided by the timely lifting of a heavy fog, managed to save New Orleans from British attack. Though it happened after the peace treaty had already been signed, Jackson's victory became the crowning American achievement in a war with few of them and started the brash general on his steady rise to the presidency.

It also sent the New England envoys scurrying from the capital. Perusing the list of their proposed amendments, a relieved Madison reportedly laughed out loud. One Republican paper ran a missing-persons notice for the "well looking, responsible men" who had "disappeared suddenly"—an apt epitaph for Federalism itself. Tainted by accusations of disloyalty, the party that had framed and dominated the government dwindled into irrelevance and finally vanished entirely.

That the Union would survive the War of 1812 was far from certain. To the end, it seemed unlikely. That it did was largely coincidence. After the war, a lavish outpouring of patriotic sentiment, as if to bury divisions, showed that the national tradition of repressing conflict was alive and well.

But the underlying issue that divided Americans—more than partisanship, trade, or war—remained. The return of peace brought new waves of settlers lighting out for the territories, for Louisiana and Arkansas, for Indiana and Illinois, for Missouri. Many brought slaves with them. "Old America seems to be breaking up, and moving westward," one emigrant observed—a curious turn of phrase. The reckoning couldn't be postponed forever. Those who went west to avoid it little knew they were helping to bring it on.

CHAPTER 6

This Unholy Union

Disunion startles a man to thought. It takes a lazy abolitionist by
the throat, and thunders in his ear, "*Thou* art the slaveholder!"
—WILLIAM LLOYD GARRISON, 1848

AFTER THE WAR OF 1812, a national identity finally seemed to be
taking shape. Americans were relieved—surprised, perhaps—that the
Union had emerged in one piece, and they agreed to forget divisions
of the past. They set their minds to a future of territorial expansion,
economic growth, and ever-increasing unity.

This was the so-called Era of Good Feelings, an oddly cheery (and
inaccurate) description of a one-party state. With Federalists all but
disqualified from national leadership, the Republicans, held together
by the war, began to split after the return of peace. One issue stood
out: there were those who endorsed federal support for internal
improvements—roads, canals, and bridges, which could move people
and goods more easily across state lines—and those who opposed such
funding as outside the remit of the central government.

John C. Calhoun endorsed improvements. His father, an early settler on South Carolina's Western frontier, had opposed the ratification
of the Constitution as an infringement on state sovereignty. Calhoun
was mentored at Yale by its Federalist president, who defended New
England's right to secede. These influences would later win out. But in
his early career, Calhoun served as a spokesman for union. "Let us...
bind the Republic together," he proclaimed in an 1816 speech. "Let us
conquer space."

Business-minded Americans agreed. They hoped internal improvements would strengthen economic ties even if political ones were weak,

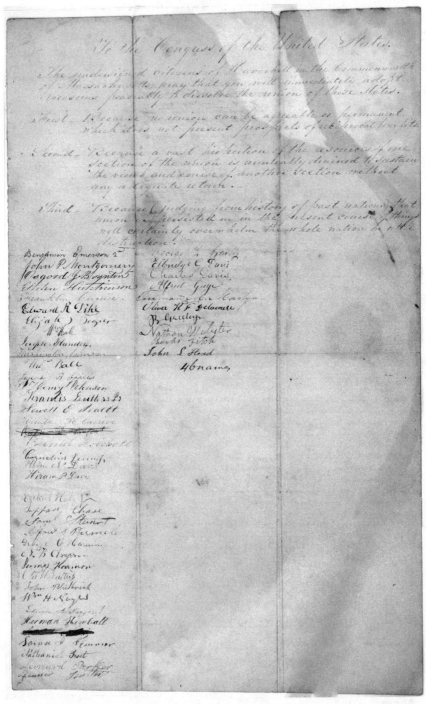

An 1842 petition to dissolve the United States signed by forty-six residents of Haverhill, Massachusetts, an industrial city with business ties to the South. (*Buttonwoods Museum*)

effectively shrinking the country enough to save it from the usual fate of large republics—paralysis, fracture, dissolution. The Union, as Madison's successor, James Monroe, put it, should be "so compacted and bound together that nothing could break it."

To stubborn adherents of the party's original limited-government creed, promises to bind the republic together sounded more like a threat. Federal spending would weaken local rule. Countering Calhoun, a Louisiana politician cautioned against the creation of "one grand, magnificent, consolidated empire." Nathaniel Macon, an old-school states'-rights Republican from North Carolina, said that he didn't "believe in artificial regulations to bind the different sections of the country." His reason? "They must be bound together by love... Good will and a fellow feeling must do it." Weak support for a bridge.

Others worried that a government empowered to build roads and canals was a government empowered to free slaves—an argument Calhoun found so convincing, he soon withdrew his support for the conquest of space.

The debate over internal improvements reveals how disunited the states really were in these supposed halcyon years. The Era of Good Feelings proved a passing illusion, a rush of postwar dopamine. "Sectional harmony was possible," the scholar Paul Finkelman observes, "only as long as no one asked any hard questions about slavery, race, western expansion, or economic development"—that is, about any of the important issues facing the country. The moment one of those forbidden subjects came up, conflict burst through the veneer of harmony that politicians struggled to maintain. The promise of post-partisan politics again collapsed in a crisis that shook the Union to its foundations. Many Americans, in the North and the South, began to regret the compromises of 1787 and concluded that the marriage couldn't be saved.

1. The Missouri Crisis

Nineteenth-century city dwellers dreaded the frantic clang of the municipal bell calling them to bring buckets as volunteers raced their hand-pumped engines toward a fast-spreading blaze. Usually they got there too late. The ringing of the fire bell was no assurance that a building—or a city—would be saved.

When Thomas Jefferson compared the crisis over slavery in Missouri to "a fire bell in the night," he wasn't expressing confidence that the country, having been warned of impending catastrophe, would avoid it. The episode "awakened and filled me with terror," Jefferson wrote. Seventy-six years old, retired at Monticello, he was disturbed by a vision that America itself would burn.

Late one afternoon in February 1819, an obscure freshman congressman rose before the House of Representatives, which was meeting in temporary chambers while the Capitol was rebuilt. James Tallmadge, a tousle-haired lawyer from Poughkeepsie and a devout Christian, was a staunch opponent of slavery. To an otherwise routine bill granting statehood to the Missouri territory, he proposed an amendment banning slavery from the new state.

Southerners saw slavery's exclusion from new states as an existential threat. After Congress banned the foreign slave trade in 1808, it became even more lucrative for older, soil-exhausted states like Virginia to sell laborers to richer lands farther south and out west. Long lines of men, women, and children were chained together and marched barefoot even in winter. Between duels and massacres of Indians, Andrew Jackson led slave coffles down the Natchez Trace. At one point during the Missouri debate, a fifteen-person human train limped past the windows of the House chamber, in full view of the representatives.

Banning bondage in the West would hurt the Southern economy and saddle the older states with a swelling slave population—a recipe for insurrection. Virginians would be "damned up in a land of slaves," one eminent jurist feared. The misspelling, tellingly, was his own.

There were also demographic issues. European immigrants, who didn't care to compete with unpaid labor, had boosted the population of Northern states. Despite the South's extra votes from the three-fifths clause, Northerners dominated the House of Representatives. That made it important for Southerners to retain control in the Senate, where each state wielded equal votes. As long as the pattern held of admitting states in pairs—free Indiana balanced by slave Mississippi, Illinois by Alabama—slavery would be safe. Abandoning it by restricting slavery in Missouri wasn't an option.

By uniting the otherwise divergent interests of the slave states,

James Tallmadge, in a flash, "summoned the South into being," as one historian put it. Before Missouri, even slave owners like Jefferson vaguely imagined a future without slavery. After it, they rarely did. Jefferson wasn't alone in experiencing the controversy as an awakening. Harrison Gray Otis, a Massachusetts veteran of the Hartford convention, wrote that the moment debate began, he saw "terror" in the eyes of his Southern colleagues and knew at once, as if rousing "from a trance," that they would never give up their slaves.

The hall was packed with spectators eager to hear the forbidden issue spoken of, for once, in the open. Southern representatives, noting the presence of slaves in the House galleries, accused Tallmadge of irresponsibly risking servile rebellion. "You conduct us to an awful precipice, and hold us over it," a Mississippi congressman warned. Northerners insisted their Southern colleagues had to make a choice. If Congress missed the opportunity to stop "the growth of a sin which sits heavy on the souls of every one of us," a New Hampshire congressman opined, "let us at least be consistent, and declare that our Constitution was made to impose slavery, and not to establish liberty."

By the second day of deliberations, a run-of-the-mill vote had become "a referendum on the meaning of America," historian Robert Pierce Forbes notes, even "a rhetorical civil war."

It seemed close to sparking a real one. "If you persist, the Union will be dissolved," a slave owner from Georgia threatened Tallmadge. "You have kindled a fire which all the waters of the ocean cannot put out, which seas of blood can only extinguish."

But Tallmadge wouldn't be cowed. Was it possible that a subject essential to America's destiny couldn't be discussed even in the hallowed halls of its legislature? What did that say about the country's stability? "If a dissolution of the Union must take place, let it be so!" he thundered. "If civil war, which gentlemen so much threaten, must come, I can only say, let it come!"

After three weeks of debate, the amendment passed the House with nearly all Northerners in favor and Southerners almost unanimously opposed. But it failed in the Senate, where slavery's bulwark held strong. Congress adjourned for a long recess. The question went out to the country.

*   *   *

Before Tallmadge made his motion, forbidding slavery in new states hadn't excited the Northern public. Even New Englanders opposed to the Louisiana Purchase sought only to keep the three-fifths bonus from applying in future states, not to outlaw slavery entirely. Now restriction became a litmus test of sectional loyalty. Speakers at public meetings urged Northern congressmen to hold firm. Theodore Dwight, a Federalist editor, was so agitated he reached for the upper compartment of his type case: "If…the SIN OF SLAVERY be fastened…upon that boundless region which the United States possesses beyond the Mississippi, THE DEATH-WARRANT OF THE POLITICAL STANDING AND INFLUENCE OF THE FREE STATES WILL IRREVOCABLY BE SEALED."

Nine months later, Congress reconvened in the renovated Capitol, open for the first time since the British attack. In the new House chamber, twenty-six columns of green Potomac marble supported a soaring, windowed dome. Tiered rows of desks in a semicircle faced the Speaker's rostrum, like the seating in an ancient Greek amphitheater. Above the entrance was a sculpture of Clio, the muse of history, standing in a chariot and recording in her ledger the members' words and deeds.

The break hadn't cooled tempers. The incompatibility of Northern and Southern interests was clearer than ever. James Barbour, a Virginia senator, suggested the states meet in convention to sort out the details of going their separate ways. The powerful Speaker of the House, Henry Clay—"the Great Compromiser," "Statesman for the Union," "the Essential American," as biographers have called him—predicted to John Quincy Adams as they walked home one night that within five years, the Union would break apart. Clay accepted the prospect calmly. If civil war erupted, he would return to Kentucky and raise troops for the fight.

The foremost Northern proponent for restricting slavery was Rufus King, New York's long-serving senator and the Federalists' 1816 presidential candidate. During the Constitutional Convention more than thirty years earlier, King had voted for the three-fifths clause but immediately regretted it. Perhaps as penance, he now tried to limit the damage. All laws that upheld slavery, King dramatically insisted, were "absolutely void, because contrary to the law of nature, which is the law of God."

Listening to him, Southerners "gnawed their lips and clenched their fists," John Quincy Adams observed. Remembering the Hartford Convention, the Southerners thought King, having failed to win the presidency, wanted to lead a new Northern nation. King didn't favor separation, but a few Northerners did. "If the alternative be...a dissolution of the Union, or the extension of slavery over this whole Western country," a Pennsylvanian declared, "I, for one, will choose the former."

Even as congressmen traded disunion threats, however, the outlines of a deal emerged. A Massachusetts congressman from the state's Maine district moved to admit that region as a state. Maine residents had been calling for statehood since the Revolution. The movement grew after the War of 1812, when Boston failed to protect the coastline from invasion. In 1819, the state legislature agreed to let Maine go.

Amid the Missouri standoff, the Maine bill handed Southerners leverage. Congress had no more right to ban slavery in Missouri than it had to force it on Maine, they said. Henry Clay, angling to succeed James Monroe in the presidency, hoped to boost his prospects by fashioning a deal. Tying the two statehood bills together—without any rules on slavery in either—would maintain the balance of power in the Senate between free and slave states. To sweeten the deal, Jesse Thomas of nominally free Illinois (the senator owned five "servants") suggested splitting the Louisiana Purchase at the 36°30′ parallel, Missouri's southern border, and banning slavery everywhere north of it except in Missouri itself.

Southerners eagerly supported the deal. They figured slavery was unlikely to spread into the drier, less fertile regions of the upper plains, so the compromise would cost them little. South Carolina's Charles Pinckney, a former delegate to the Constitutional Convention, called the split at the 36°30′ line "a great triumph" for the South.

Northerners had a harder time seeing the bargain's merits. To close the deal, Monroe cajoled and arm-twisted legislators more aggressively than any president had before. He offered wavering congressmen bribes in the form of jobs as tax collectors, postmasters, judges, and land-office clerks. Up for reelection, Monroe promised Southern allies he would fight slavery's restriction in Missouri "even to the hazard of the Union."

The payoffs worked; the compromise passed. Each plank had to be voted on separately, however, since no majority existed for the package as a whole. Without the three-fifths clause, it would have failed. The Union dangled by a thread as thin as air.

Northerners seethed at their turncoat representatives. One was burned in effigy in his hometown. "The Constitution is a creature of compromise," a Connecticut congressman argued in his defense. "It originated in a compromise; and has existed ever since by a perpetual extension and exercise of that principle; and must continue to do so, as long as it lasts."

Yet compromise was losing its constituency. If patched-together agreements only delayed the inevitable, why bother with the pretense? Why not part now rather than wait for a crack-up?

As secretary of state, John Quincy Adams, the only Northerner in Monroe's cabinet, felt he had to back the Missouri deal. In private, however, he had doubts. The Constitution's "bargain between freedom and slavery," especially the three-fifths bonus, was "morally and politically vicious, inconsistent with the principles upon which alone our Revolution can be justified," Adams wrote in his diary. The North never should have agreed to it. Worse, the new compromise only compounded the evil. Maybe it would have been "a wiser as well as a bolder course" for the North to form "a new Union of thirteen or fourteen States unpolluted with slavery." If the Union "must be dissolved," Adams concluded, "slavery is precisely the question upon which it ought to break."

Instead, the inevitable conflict had again been put off for the future. But Missouri was only the beginning, Adams feared, "a mere preamble— a title-page to a great tragic volume." He could already see how it would unfold: A civil war of unimaginable destruction, ending with "the extirpation of slavery from this whole continent." The vision was frightening but also exhilarating. However "calamitous and desolating" such a war would be, Adams wrote, "so glorious would be its final issue, that god shall judge me, I dare not say that it is not to be desired."

Both sides saw that slavery couldn't be discussed without risking an apocalyptic clash. Pledging to defend their property at any cost, Southerners ensured that slavery and the Union would remain inextricably tied; to question one undermined the other.

The strategy convinced Northerners to back off. "The sound of disunion...should never be uttered within these walls," cried Daniel Cook of Illinois. He suggested banning the word *disunion* from being spoken in Congress, as if that would make the specter go away. Nothing could. The Missouri crisis only added kindling to a towering pile just one spark away from all-consuming conflagration.

2. Showdown in South Carolina

For a week in January 1830, a remarkable debate unfolded in the U.S. Senate. Two years earlier, South Carolina had declared its intention to nullify a federal tariff that seemed to violate the interests of the state's powerful slave owners. That crisis was now coming to a head, with Daniel Webster and Robert Hayne representing not only their states—Massachusetts and South Carolina, respectively—but different sections of the Union and their competing visions of its purpose.

The balconies, stairwells, and even the floor of the Senate filled early with onlookers eager for a glimpse of what one called "moral gladiatorship." Webster, a stern-looking forty-eight-year-old with black hair, thick eyebrows, a protuberant forehead, and a voice likened to heavy artillery, was the most famous orator in the country. Elected to the House as a Federalist from New Hampshire, he was now a Republican senator for Massachusetts. Once suspicious of tariffs, Webster now embraced them—and the national strength they were meant to build. The country should be "considered as if there were no State lines," Webster said. There were "no Alleghenies" in his politics.

His opponent, Hayne, a decade younger, short and stocky, was a respected planter and lawyer. Though he was no Webster, he possessed what an admirer called "a seductive eloquence." A strident defender of slavery, Hayne warned that if the federal government ever made an "unhallowed attempt" at emancipation, white Southerners would "consider ourselves as driven from the Union."

Hayne was a true believer, but he served as little more than a ventriloquist's dummy. The puppet master, as everyone knew, was John C. Calhoun, the senator's fellow South Carolinian. As vice president, Calhoun presided over the Senate but wasn't allowed to address the chamber. So instead, throughout the battle with Webster, he silently passed notes to Hayne.

In his opening salvo, Hayne defended South Carolina's right to self-determination. He quoted the Virginia and Kentucky Resolutions, insisting that liberty was superior to union. The Constitution was a mere compact of still-sovereign states. Hayne recalled New England's opposition to federal authority during the embargo crisis and the War of 1812 and even implied that Webster himself had sympathized with the secessionists at the Hartford convention.

Over two days, the New Englander gave a response later heralded as one of the most eloquent addresses ever delivered by an American. (One listener compared Webster's performance to a "Mammoth deliberately treading the cane break.") Contradicting Hayne's insinuations, Webster disavowed any interest in disrupting the settled compromises of the Philadelphia convention, including the three-fifths clause. "I go for the Constitution as it is, and for the Union as it is," he declared. Webster defended "New England men and New England principles" against Hayne's suggestion that they still bore the stain of disunionism. Whatever had transpired in the past, it was now Hayne's own state — and Calhoun's — that claimed the right to defy federal laws. That doctrine, Webster stated, would lead "directly to disunion and civil commotion." The Union was a compact formed not by the states but by the people as a whole. "It is, Sir, the people's Constitution, the people's government, made for the people, made by the people, and answerable to the people," Webster declared — a line that would prove useful to the author of the Gettysburg Address.

Stepping in front of his desk and then pushing it behind him, Webster claimed he wasn't in the habit of looking over "the precipice of disunion, to see whether, with my short sight, I can fathom the depth of the abyss below." But as he stared into the imaginary chasm, he saw "states dissevered, discordant, belligerent, on a land rent with civil feuds, or drenched, it may be, in fraternal blood!" He hoped that in his last moments alive, his eyes would rest on the American flag without a single star removed, "bearing for its motto, no such miserable interrogatory as, *What is all this worth?* Nor those other words of delusion and folly, *Liberty first, and Union afterwards*" — a favorite phrase of Calhoun's — "but every where, spread all over in characters of living light, blazing on all its ample folds, as they float over the sea and over the land, and in every wind under the whole Heavens, that other sentiment, dear to every true American heart—Liberty *and* Union, now and forever, one and inseparable!"

In the battle of oratory, Webster won; one spectator praised his address as sounding like "the steady flow of molten gold." The speech was rushed into print, and as many as a hundred thousand copies of it were circulated. Its most famous passages memorized by generations of schoolchildren, the Webster-Hayne debate made plain there could be no solution to the dispute between North and South short of separation or civil war.

Yet it also bared the hidden fault line beneath the surface-level sectional conflict—the fundamental division wasn't really between slave states and free states but between those Americans who insisted on preserving the Union no matter what and those who dared to ask that "miserable interrogatory... *What is all this worth?*" Webster convinced many Americans, especially in the North, that liberty and the Union were indeed inseparable. But others, in both halves of the divided country, had already begun to see them as intrinsically opposed. The only thing Northern and Southern disunionists disagreed about was whose liberty was worth splitting the country over, the slavers' or the slaves'.

No sooner did the Missouri Compromise ease the strains over slavery's spread than an even more menacing controversy erupted, this time over what Henry Clay called his "American System." A product of the nation-building optimism that followed the War of 1812, the program was meant to stimulate domestic industry and free the country from dependence on foreign trade. It included a new national bank, funding for internal improvements, and high tariffs meant to block cheap European imports. Trade protection found wide support in the Northern and mid-Atlantic states, where manufacturing interests demanded them. Without tariffs, argued Massachusetts congressman Edward Everett, the United States would be "reduced to the condition of dismembered and defenceless provinces."

Southerners, however, blamed the American System for reducing their states to precisely that condition. The South's economy depended on exporting slave-picked cotton to British mills. Trade barriers raised the prices that Southerners had to pay for Northern-made goods.

Southerners denounced the tariffs, noting they benefited the North at the South's expense.

Southerners also worried about the nefarious ends to which the new revenue might someday be used—like federal compensation to masters for slavery's abolition. In 1830, John C. Calhoun told a friend tariffs were only "the occasion, rather than the real cause, of the present unhappy state of things." The real source of Southern discontent, as ever, was the all-consuming anxiety, the constant terror, that slavery would be abolished, and so they fought any threat—present or future, real or imaginary—to the institution. Against the day an emancipation bill came before Congress, the planters needed to set a precedent that a state could defy federal laws.

In South Carolina, where more than half the population was enslaved, the state's low-country planters blamed an economic slump on federal tariffs. By 1827, the line between discontent and disunionism began to blur. Thomas Cooper, an English-born economist and the president of South Carolina College, announced that it was time for the state to "calculate the value of our Union"—to weigh the costs and benefits of staying in the half-century-old federation. "What use to us is this unequal alliance?" Cooper asked. "Is it worth our while to continue this Union of States, where the North demand to be our masters, and we are required to be their tributaries?" If Congress kept instituting higher tariffs on foreign trade, he said, South Carolina should declare independence and make Charleston a duty-free port.

Later that year, a series of provocative essays titled *The Crisis* expanded on Cooper's themes. South Carolina cotton planter Robert J. Turnbull, writing as Brutus, argued that Clay's American System was a hidden assault on slavery and that only secession could protect the state's "domestic institutions." Turnbull fantasized that God might erect a soaring mountain range between the South and North, geological confirmation of their utter incompatibility.

Copies of *The Crisis* flew around the state and rapidly converted Carolinians to the cause. The next year, when Northern manufacturers pushed additional protections through Congress—a measure famously dubbed by Southerners the "Tariff of Abominations"—Calhoun told his son the new taxes would split the country and "make two of one nation."

South Carolina erupted in protest against the new law. Ships in Charleston Harbor flew Union flags at half-mast, while Clay and Webster were burned in effigy. At an anti-tariff dinner, a zealous congressman named George McDuffie, known for his flamboyant rhetorical style, offered a toast to "the stamp act of 1765, and the Tariff of 1828— kindred acts of despotism." The first had sparked a separatist rebellion. The second might too.

Calhoun tried to stay above the fray. He was vice president under John Quincy Adams, but the two had quickly had a falling-out, and he hoped to retain the post under Adams's rival and likely successor, Andrew Jackson, the hero of New Orleans. Calhoun didn't want to jeopardize Jackson's candidacy or his own chances to succeed him in turn by taking too radical a stand.

In private, however, Calhoun seethed. Holed up at Fort Hill, his six-hundred-acre plantation in the western corner of South Carolina (now the grounds of Clemson University), he concluded that Southern interests weren't safe in a union dominated by a growing Northern majority. When the state legislature asked him to write a manifesto justifying the state's opposition to the new tariffs, Calhoun agreed as long as his authorship was kept secret.

Calhoun's *Exposition and Protest,* adopted as an official state paper, picked up where Jefferson and Madison had left off in their 1798 resolutions. It laid out a process to put their principles into practice. If the federal government went beyond its specified limits, each state could declare laws void within its borders. The government would have to back down or seek a constitutional amendment giving itself more power. If the amendment passed, the dissenting state could give up the fight or secede from the Union—though that, Calhoun conceded, would amount to "rebellion."

Secession was a last resort. It was "reformation, not revolution," that South Carolina sought. The *Exposition and Protest* later served as a states' rights road map for Southern secessionists, but at the time, partition was what Calhoun hoped to avoid. Disunion would "falsify all the glorious anticipations of our ancestors, while it would so greatly lessen their high reputation for wisdom," he reflected a few years later. Far from jeopardizing the Union, nullification was the only way to make it last.

*   *   *

Jackson swept into the White House in 1828, and Calhoun stayed on as vice president. South Carolina's nullification threat sat like a loaded gun on the stage of American politics, its hammer cocked, the tension palpable.

On an April night in 1830, two months after the confrontation between Webster and Hayne in the Senate, a lavish dinner was held in a fine Washington hotel to honor the late Thomas Jefferson's birthday. Prior to the dinner, Jackson had perused the list of luminaries slated to offer toasts and realized the event was designed to wrap the new Southern doctrine in Jefferson's good name. He decided to disrupt the festivities with a toast of his own.

After a round of secession-tinged tributes—including one by George McDuffie to "the memory of Patrick Henry: the first American statesman who had the soul to feel, and the courage to declare, in the face of armed tyranny, that there is no treason in resisting oppression"—the floor was opened. Jackson offered a stark salute: "Our Union. *It must be preserved*," he said, glaring at Calhoun, whom he suspected of sympathizing with the nullifiers.

The gauntlet thrown, Calhoun nervously rose, his glass trembling, brown liquid dripping down the side. "The Union—next to our liberty, most dear," he countered. "May we all remember that it can only be preserved by respecting the rights of the States and distributing equally the benefit and the burden of the Union."

The jab was unmistakable. Calhoun's break with Jackson was now public, as were the fundamental questions: Was the Union only, as it had been at the founding, a means to certain ends, such as the preservation of liberty, or had the passage of time made it an end in itself? Were there any conditions that could justify it being dissolved?

The following year, his relationship with the president irreparable— Jackson considered his vice president "one of the most base, hypocritical, and unprincipled villains in the United States"—Calhoun drew up a public letter endorsing nullification. The tariff question had "divided the country into two great geographical divisions, and arrayed them against each other." North and South saw things so differently that "no two distinct nations ever entertained more opposite views." Congressional sessions had devolved into "an annual struggle" among various "sec-

tional and selfish attachments." It was time to call a truce—to suspend
the project of perfecting the Union and return power to the states. Only
by embracing nullification as "the fundamental principle of our system,"
Calhoun claimed, could Americans avoid "a general catastrophe."

By 1832, even Henry Clay realized the tariffs had to be lowered to keep
the country from falling into chaos. The government was close to paying off the national debt, leaving little reason for high taxes. He crafted
a bill to lighten duties on tea, coffee, tropical produce, and other
imports that didn't compete with domestic products. Easing the tariffs
would hopefully appease South Carolina—or, as one supporter put it,
"compromise the different interests, conciliate all parties, and…pre-
serve the Union."

Some parties refused to be conciliated. Northern protectionists
didn't want to lower tariffs at all, while Southern free traders insisted
the cuts didn't go far enough. Both sides summoned the specter of disunion. A meeting in Massachusetts even resolved that secession was
"preferable" to yielding trade protection. South Carolina radical George
McDuffie warned that if the bill passed, "the door of hope will be forever closed upon the South." The slave states would have only one remedy: separation.

Despite the opposition, Clay's measure passed with support from
the middle states and the West. Jackson signed it, hoping to "annihilate the nullifiers" and prove that the disunion fever "only existed in
the distempered brains of disappointed ambitious men."

He assumed that most Southerners, even the citizens of South
Carolina, supported the Union and would back the federal government if it came to a fight. There was some reason for hope. In 1832, an
elderly Continental army veteran, leaning on his crutches, attacked
arch-nullifier Robert Barnwell Rhett for betraying the legacy of the
Revolution. But pro-Union voters were concentrated in the state's
underrepresented up-country, where some threatened to secede from
the state if South Carolina left the Union. Gerrymandering bolstered
the power of the low country's secession-minded planters. State
elections that fall, widely seen as a referendum on nullification, proved
a triumph for the states' rights party, which won control of two-thirds
of the legislature.

Before the rest of the country realized what was happening, delegates at a hastily called South Carolina convention voted in November 1832 to declare the federal tariffs "utterly null and void" as of February 1, 1833. A manifesto announced that Carolinians would no longer be deluded by "that blind and idolatrous devotion which would bow down and worship oppression and tyranny, veiled under a consecrated title." The Union wasn't sacred. Liberty, the statement proclaimed, was "the only idol of our political devotion."

If the federal government tried to enforce the tariffs anyway, the state would secede from the Union. As the convention disbanded to await a response from the federal government, South Carolina's governor called for the formation of an army twelve thousand men strong.

What would Jackson do? A native of the Carolina frontier, the president had spent his first term reining in what he deemed federal overreach. Wielding the veto more than all his predecessors combined, Jackson took a hatchet to Clay's American System—to him, a fancy name for despotism. "For the rights of the state, no one has a higher regard and respect than myself," Jackson assured South Carolina's Robert Hayne. "It is only by maintaining them faithfully that the Union can be preserved." Jackson wasn't for drawing Americans together artificially; he preferred to let them naturally drift apart.

Yet, as he had at the Jefferson Day dinner, Jackson insisted the Union was inviolable. Perhaps compensating for his youthful dabbling with Western separatism, Jackson, as president, had an almost violent reaction to the prospect of dissolution. "There is nothing that I shudder at more than the idea of a separation of the Union," he told one South Carolinian before the 1828 election. "Should such an event ever happen, which I fervently pray to God to avert, from that date, I view our liberty gone."

Like his fellow Southerners, the agrarian-minded president didn't like tariffs, but he thought the 1832 bill fair enough. Now he realized the issue wasn't tariffs at all but setting a precedent for secession. When the South Carolina convention passed its nullification ordinance in early December, Jackson asked one state resident to carry a message back home. "Tell them from me that they can talk and write resolutions and print threats to their heart's content," Jackson said. "But if one drop of blood be shed there in defiance of the laws of the United States, I will hang the first man of them I can get my hands on to the first tree I can find."

Jackson's taste for slaughter was well known, so the scenario seemed more than plausible.

As tensions mounted, the newly reelected president tried to maintain an uneasy balance between his antipathy for the tariff and his inflexible attachment to the Union. In his annual message to Congress in December 1832, Jackson argued that the tax rates should be reduced further or even eliminated lest they encourage "a spirit of discontent and jealousy dangerous to the stability of the Union." He also called for further cuts to government spending. His ousted predecessor, John Quincy Adams, now back in Washington as a congressman, thought Jackson's approach would effectively "dissolve the Union in its original elements"—it would restore the sovereignty of the states. The message represented "a complete surrender to the nullifiers of South Carolina."

Just days later, however, Jackson reversed tack. Addressing the people of South Carolina, the president implored them to abandon the foolish attempt to nullify federal law. Nullification was an "absurdity," a "sophistical construction," a "metaphysical subtlety," meant only, he told South Carolinians, "to prepare you for the period when the mask which concealed the hideous features of DISUNION should be taken off." The Union couldn't be sundered simply on a state's say-so. The federal government was just that—"a *government*, not a league."

Jackson's theory of an unbreakable Union, influenced by Webster, was later adopted by Abraham Lincoln to justify suppressing the Confederate rebellion. It's worth pausing, then, to note how thoroughly that account of American history is contradicted by what we have learned. Jackson's claim that under British rule the colonies "had no separate character" would have surprised those who rejected Franklin's Albany Plan because they wanted to maintain that character. His argument that the adoption of the vague handle "the United Colonies" a year before the Declaration of Independence somehow bound Americans living and unborn in a union unbreachable to the end of time would have alarmed even the most far-seeing patriot. And his observation that from the outbreak of the Revolution to the ratification of the Constitution, Americans never considered themselves "in any other light than as forming one nation" had no basis in fact. On the contrary, the word *nation* was so feared that the framers in Philadelphia ensured it and all its cognates were nowhere in their final product. From John Witherspoon's pep talk to the Continental Congress in 1776 to Washington's Farewell Address twenty years later, the Union's perpetuity was spoken of, even by its warmest partisans, as something to be wished for by all Americans, *not* as an unalterable certainty. Jackson's account was a desperate attempt to cover up the fact that the country remained little more united in his time than it had been in the past.

Friends and foes alike saw the irony of Jackson, self-styled champion of the common man and advocate for small government, issuing "just such a paper as Alexander Hamilton would have written and Thomas Jefferson condemned," one New Yorker observed. The proclamation scrambled alliances, as pro-tariff Northerners for once cheered a president they otherwise deplored. At a "union meeting" in Boston's Faneuil Hall, organized to support Jackson's stand, Daniel Webster called nullification "nothing more nor less than resistance by *force*—it is disunion by force—it is secession by force—it is Civil War!"

The nullifiers, meanwhile, seized on Jackson's edict to position themselves as the true heirs of the Revolution. Some followers, blaming the Proclamation on "the chance ascendancy of this or that counsellor," chose to attribute the aging, inexperienced president's contradictory statements to his tendency to take the advice of the last person who'd spoken to him.

Jackson was unfazed. "I will die for the Union," he told a friend, sounding almost as if he wanted to. Even at sixty-five, Jackson seemed to relish one last chance to lead troops in battle. "South Carolina may raise her ten or twelve thousand men," the president told a visitor, "but Andrew Jackson will raise thirty thousand." He sent reinforcements to Charleston-area forts and ordered his war secretary to be ready to "crush the monster in its cradle."

In January 1833, weeks before nullification went into effect, Jackson asked Congress to grant him extraordinary powers to use armed force to execute federal law. The bill was necessary, he told Congress, to ensure "that the constitution and the laws are supreme and the *Union indissoluble*."

Southerners like Calhoun saw in Jackson's "Force Bill," as they dubbed it, further proof of the despotism that lay behind the tariff all along. Even nullification's opponents didn't think the government had the right to whip a state into line. Wasn't it King George III's decision to do just that that had spurred the colonists to renounce their obligations to the Crown? Washington had allowed Hamilton to run roughshod over the whiskey rebels in western Pennsylvania, but that was a paltry band of lawbreakers, not a people's convention in one of the original states. The issue now wasn't the tariff or even nullification but, in the words of one Southerner, "whether any dotard or miscreant from chance or trickery or popular delusion, may elevate to the presidential chair, may lord over us, and write his vengeance against his opponents in blood."

Jackson's detractors had always called him a barbarous backwoodsman, prone to violence, heedless of law. What further proof was needed than his preparations, as Calhoun said, to "make war on a sovereign state"?

War could have begun at any moment: The federal customs collector in Charleston would ask merchants to pay the tariff. The importers would refuse; their goods would be impounded. The merchants would sue in state court and likely win, but the collector would refuse to obey a state court over federal law. The court would order his arrest. Armed unionists—eight thousand offered to serve—would rally to protect him. The state would fall into chaos as Jackson marched an army toward Charleston to restore order.

If that happened, Carolinians expected the rest of the South would rally to their side. A Southern confederacy would arise. Volunteers from Georgia and Alabama promised their services. If the president ordered a blockade of Charleston Harbor, the city's radical *Mercury* declared, "we will secede—and if he resolves to fight out the right of secession, why on that score he'll find more states in his way than he expected to meet." Even John Marshall, chief justice of the Supreme Court (no nullifier he), realized that "insane as South Carolina unquestionably is," the state wouldn't have "made her declaration of war against the United States had she not counted on uniting the South."

To march on South Carolina, troops would have to cross Virginia.

They would do so only *"over our dead bodies,"* one Virginian warned. "It is on all hands admitted to be the most alarming state of things which has existed since the Revolution," wrote Thomas Ritchie, an influential Richmond editor. He feared events were hurrying to catastrophe and Virginia would have to choose sides.

Across a nervous country, Americans struggled to understand what was likely about to happen. "To think, Louisa," one Carolina woman wrote a friend, "that we should live to see a Civil War!"

"There is one man, and one man only, who can save the Union," Virginia's John Randolph, months from the grave, observed in his last public speech. "That man is Henry Clay."

Seven years earlier, Clay had answered an insult by putting a bullet through Randolph's sleek white coat. With the Union at stake, however, all was forgiven. Though he had lost the 1832 presidential election to Jackson, Clay was the only person in the country able to push a deal through Congress.

Conditions were ripe for a compromise. Under Calhoun's calming influence, South Carolina postponed nullification by a month. Virginia offered to mediate between Charleston and Washington, proof the Palmetto State wasn't as isolated as Jackson had hoped. The Force Bill showed that civil war was a real possibility. Clay hated to see his American System sacrificed to the nullifiers, but he found Jackson's aggression repellent. "We want no sacked cities," he told the Senate, "no desolated fields, no smoking ruins, no streams of American blood shed by American arms!" Only with a new bargain could the country avoid a civil war.

Early in 1833, Clay proposed to lower tariffs slowly, over a decade, to give manufacturers time to adjust. To save face for Jackson, the Force Bill would pass, even if removing the cause of Southern complaints meant there was no rebellion to quell.

At first, the package was unpopular in both sections. Northern protectionists didn't want to condone South Carolina's behavior and thereby confirm—yet again—the efficacy of separatist threats. "The stability of our institutions and the permanency of the Union must some day be tested," one Pennsylvanian argued. "That day may as well be now as tomorrow." Boston's *Courier* wondered how long the country could lurch from crisis to crisis, each more perilous than the last: "Is the Union to be forever a matter of compromise?" John Quincy Adams called Clay's latest bargain "an Act for the protection of John C. Calhoun and his fellow nullifiers"—a pitiful attempt to save the Carolinians from their own recklessness.

Yet the nullifiers rejected Clay's proposal as insufficient and the Force Bill as a nonstarter. They didn't want tariffs lowered gradually, but at once. Further reflection, however, confirmed Adams's conclusion: Clay had offered South Carolina near-total victory. Nullification had worked. The tariffs would be repealed without secession or civil war. Even diehards like George McDuffie voted for the bill. Charleston erupted in celebration. Robert Hayne, now governor, hosted a victory ball. In March 1833, the convention that had adopted the nullification ordinance regrouped to rescind it. Then, for good measure, it nullified the Force Bill too.

The immediate crisis settled, the lesson for South Carolina's leaders was obvious. Their ancestors had first learned it in 1774, when John Rutledge led his delegation out of the Continental Congress: secession threats succeed, resistance is rewarded. The "compromise of 1833" only sowed the seeds for conflicts to come. Indeed, it wasn't a compromise at all, the historian Edward Payson Powell wrote, "but a surrender."

Few Americans thought the demon of disunion had been exorcised for good. James Petigru, a prominent South Carolina unionist, saw only ill omens. "Nullification has done its work," Petigru observed. "It has prepared the minds of men for a separation of the States, and when the question is mooted again it will be distinctly union or disunion." A Jackson supporter in New York agreed that nothing had been resolved. Sure, the country avoided war. "But there is no *peace*," he wrote. "The South will suffer and still rave. And we must go over to the Negro question. That is the rock on which the ship Union will split."

3. The Abolitionist Case for Disunion

One Monday morning in January 1842, a congressman introduced a petition that brought business to a standstill. Signed by forty-six residents of a small New England town, it read: "The undersigned, citizens of Haverhill, in the Commonwealth of Massachusetts, pray that you will immediately adopt measures, peaceably, to dissolve the Union of these States."

The messenger was as shocking as the message. John Quincy Adams had served as ambassador to the Netherlands, Prussia, the United Kingdom, and Russia, senator from Massachusetts, secretary of state, and president. In 1830, two years after he lost to Andrew Jackson, Adams returned to Congress. A short man with a bald dome and silver sideburns, Adams had long believed national divorce preferable to hostile cohabitation. In 1839, the former president had suggested to the New-York Historical Society that it might someday be better for "the people of the disunited states, to part in friendship from each other, than to be held together by constraint."

Adams still didn't think that day had come. Presenting the Haverhill citizens' proposal to dissolve the Union, he said he disagreed with the petition but felt compelled to deliver it.

His colleagues were stunned. One asked permission to burn the petition. For two weeks, Congress debated whether to censure the former president. Some said he should hang.

The rise of the abolitionist movement in the 1830s changed American politics forever. Captivating orators like William Lloyd Garrison and Frederick Douglass railed against "this unholy Union" with slaveholders. They accepted the Southern argument that the Constitution protected slavery, only instead of worshipping the charter, they thought it should be burned. Radical abolitionism heightened the tensions between the North and South. Only in response to its growth did slaveholders begin to think seriously about leaving a union they had created and cherished as long as they remained in control.

Antislavery disunionism has been disparaged by historians and neglected by those seeking inspiration from the past for today's egalitarian causes. Garrison and the Northern disunionists have been belittled as joyless Puritan ideologues little different from Calhoun and the Southern separatists. Similarly, John Quincy Adams has been heralded for fighting the "gag rule" against congressional discussion of slavery, but the essence of Adams's heroism was that he saw, much earlier than most, that the Union might have to be broken if slavery was to end.

While many criticized slavery, only the disunionists spoke with absolute clarity about how deep the rot went. They recognized truths that Americans have only recently begun to grasp—that the Constitution wouldn't have been possible without morally indefensible compromises, that the country was held together by the blood of the enslaved. Nothing short of rupture, they argued, would rouse white Americans from their addiction to the narcotic of compromise.

A shiftless, alcoholic Massachusetts seaman ruined by Jefferson's 1807 trade embargo, Abijah Garrison abandoned his family when his youngest son, William, a good-natured hymn hummer, was only three years old. His mother sent the boy to stay with relatives in various declining port towns north of Boston. At thirteen, Garrison apprenticed with the editor of the *Newburyport Herald,* a conservative paper that had endorsed Northern secession during the War of 1812. While learning the mechanics of newspaper production—tending the kettle of boiling ink, drying the freshly pressed pages—he absorbed the dogmas of the dying Federalist creed. For all his later radicalism, as a young man Garrison identified with "those principles which were promulgated by the Father of his Country."

A few years later, at the mess table in a Boston rooming house, Garrison met a roving Quaker named Benjamin Lundy, publisher of a little-read Baltimore paper called the *Genius of Universal Emancipation.* Lundy was one of the few abolitionists in the country. He suffered occasional beatings for it, but he kept up the crusade, often embarking on long-distance walks to raise awareness for the cause. Hearing Lundy's tales of the agitator's life, Garrison found his purpose. He moved to Baltimore to take over the paper, freeing Lundy for his nomadic proselytizing. The new editor imbued the *Genius* with such fire that local authorities jailed him for libel. Garrison had never been so happy. "Everyone who comes into the world should do something to repair its moral desolation, and to restore its pristine loveliness," he wrote to his former boss in Newburyport. "And he who does not assist, but slumbers away his life in idleness, defeats one great purpose of his creation."

Bailed out by sympathizers, Garrison returned to Boston with some notoriety. The city's Park Street Church asked him to speak on Independence Day 1829 at a meeting to benefit the American Colonization Society. The group was devoted to shipping freed slaves to Africa, a continent few of them had ever seen. The invitation proved a colossal mistake. Garrison seized the occasion to rebuke the ACS. With shocking force, he took aim at the Constitution itself. Thanks to the founding compromises, he said, American life was "rotten to the core." If Northerners "must share in the guilt and danger of destroying the bodies and souls of men, *as the price of our Union*...then the fault is not ours if a separation eventually take place."

Garrison's Park Street address helped initiate a new era of sectional warfare. At the very moment Southerners, angered by the tariff and terrified by the distant possibility of emancipation, began to "calculate the value of the Union," Garrison and other radicalized Northerners started doing the same. Subordinating union to liberty—though they, unlike Calhoun, actually meant liberty for all—the abolitionists precipitated the nation-rending struggle that would only be resolved, and even then not fully, in the crucible of civil war.

On New Year's Day 1831, Garrison launched the *Liberator,* an antislavery weekly. From his small Boston office "within sight of Bunker Hill," Garrison vowed to start a second American Revolution to complete the work of the first. To those who criticized his immoderate language, Garrison replied with thunder:

> I *will* be as harsh as truth, and as uncompromising as justice. On this subject, I do not wish to think, or speak, or write, with moderation...I am in earnest—I will not equivocate—I will not excuse—I will not retreat a single inch—AND I WILL BE HEARD.

Taking advantage of postal rules that allowed editors to send one another free copies of their publications, Garrison scattered issues among opinion-shapers around the country, especially in the South. He was looking for trouble, and trouble he found. Garrison and his acolytes were "doing more to alienate the South from their northern brethren" than the tariff had, a Richmond paper observed. Martha Washington's granddaughter said Garrison deserved the death penalty for making Southerners fear they slept atop "a smothered volcano." Braying for the editor's blood, Virginia's governor warned that the Union was "at an end" if Southerners were "tied up...from doing ourselves justice."

Yet Garrison didn't spend as much time criticizing slavery as he did condemning his fellow Northerners for their complicity with evil, damning the trade-offs Northerners had made at the Philadelphia convention and since. Those supposedly Union-saving deals, Garrison declared, actually sowed the seeds for its destruction.

The nullification crisis of 1832 was a turning point for Garrison. Why should the North cling to the slavery-serving Union when Southerners themselves wanted to break it up? Politicians rhapsodized about the "sacredness" of the Constitution. Far from sacred, that compact served only to protect "a system of the most atrocious villainy ever exhibited on earth." The nullifiers wanted to declare federal laws void? They were too late. The Constitution itself was "null and void from the beginning," for its framers had "no lawful power to bind themselves, or their posterity, for one hour—for one moment—by such an unholy alliance" with slavery.

By selling their consciences to slave owners, Northerners had sent a clear message to their Southern brethren: "Go on—and by this sacred instrument, the Constitution of the United States, *dripping as it is with human blood,* we solemnly pledge to you our lives, our fortunes, and our sacred honor, that we will stand by you to the last." Specifically, the clause in the Constitution requiring the federal government to suppress "domestic insurrections" in the states—including slave rebellions—guaranteed the inherently insecure ownership of human beings. Without that promise, the price of slaves would plummet and the system would collapse.

To Garrison, Northerners who revered the Constitution were guilty of perpetuating slavery. In fact, they were "the main pillars of its support." Only by advocating immediate emancipation could Northern whites redeem the Union and themselves.

"It is said that if you agitate this question, you will divide the Union," Garrison noted. But if that edifice could be propped up only by "treading upon the necks, spilling the blood, and destroying the souls of millions of your race"—to Garrison, there was only one race—"we say it is not worth a price like this." A self-respecting American could take but one position: "Let the pillars thereof fall—let the superstructure crumble into dust—if it must be upheld by robbery and oppression."

*   *   *

By custom, the House of Representatives devoted an hour every second Monday to citizens' petitions. Usually an uneventful affair, the routine turned controversial in the late 1830s when antislavery societies sent wave after wave of petitions with thousands of signatures. Most demanded abolition in the District of Columbia, where the issue was under federal control. The strategy was simple — to use the national legislature as a megaphone.

What followed was the bitterest fighting seen in Congress since the Missouri dispute. A New Yorker recalled that when he first entered the House, he had felt "holy horror" on the few occasions when the prospect of a national divorce was raised. Five years later, disunion threats were "as familiar here as household words."

Annoyed, slave-state congressmen passed a rule requiring any appeal related to slavery to be dismissed without debate. The topic was thus banned from discussion in Congress.

John Quincy Adams fought, often alone, for the repeal of "the gag," as he called the ban. Grim by nature, Adams had grown gloomier as he aged. When he left the White House in 1829, both his parents were dead, and over the next few years he lost one son (to suicide) and then another (to alcohol). With numerous accomplishments behind him, Adams thought it was time "to set my house in order, and to prepare for the churchyard myself."

His neighbors had other ideas. Wishing "to compliment an abused patriot," as one put it, they voted to send the ex-president back to Washington as their congressman. Sixty-four years old, with his wife and children begging him not to go, Adams felt duty-bound to answer the call. He also wanted revenge against the Jackson-led Southern ascendancy that had defeated him. Alarmed by South Carolina's experiment with nullification, Adams saw the nation in peril and hoped to save it — if it could be saved.

He was no abolitionist. The Missouri crisis convinced Adams that ending slavery might even be worth disunion and civil war, but for the sake of his career, he kept the opinion to himself. In 1825, Adams's hope-filled inaugural address had celebrated the "harmony of the nation." He'd known that harmony couldn't last. Still, he strove to uphold the Constitution, flawed as he knew it was.

The nullification crisis convinced Adams to go public with his contempt for slavery and its defenders. Nullification amounted to *"organized civil War,"* he declared on his way out of the White House. Three years later, as storm clouds gathered over Charleston, he warned Henry Clay that the conflict over slavery could be "settled only at the Cannon's Mouth."

As battle lines hardened, Adams became less worried about helping to bring that conflict on. When a vote on renewing the gag rule came to the floor, Adams—"the Madman from Massachusetts," his enemies called him; he was "Old Man Eloquent" to his admirers—refused to reply with an aye or nay. Instead, he denounced the bill as "a direct violation of the Constitution of the United States, the rules of this House, and the rights of my constituents." Southerners howled. But if the "slave-mongers" (as Adams referred to his opponents) thought they could avoid a reckoning over slavery by refusing to talk about it, they were wrong. "Freedom of speech," Adams told them, "is the only safety valve, which under the high pressure of slavery, can preserve your political boiler from a fearful and fatal explosion."

He found ingenious ways to circumvent the ban. Once, he began reading a petition from enslaved people near Fredericksburg, Virginia. "By God, Sir, this is not to be endured any longer!" an Alabama congressman yelled. Others joined in, shouting "Treason! Treason!" and demanding Adams's expulsion from the House. But the petition had a twist—the slaves begged Congress to let them stay enslaved. It was, presumably, a hoax designed by his enemies, but Adams turned the trick against them by using the petition to discuss the forbidden topic.

"Half rabid and half laughing," an observer noted, Adams took a maniacal joy in his bruising exchanges with opponents. Visitors saw the small-statured statesman "growling and sneering...lashing the members into the wildest state of enthusiasm by his indignant and emphatic eloquence." A journalist depicted the crusader at his desk: "Alone, unspoken to, unconsulted, never consulting with others, he sits apart, wrapped in his reveries; and with his finger resting on his nose." The oldest member of the House, Adams was often the first to arrive and the last to leave, and he happily spent the interval eviscerating his enemies for their "never-ending rapacity and persecution."

His performances encouraged new waves of antislavery appeals.

Before long, petitions filled a six-hundred-square-foot room in the Capitol; stacks of papers rose up to its fourteen-foot ceiling. Petitions "flow upon me in torrents," Adams wrote in his diary. Some days he presented five hundred of them to the House. Captivated or enraged by his efforts, Americans around the country sent letters praising or denouncing his work. "You will when least expected, be shot down in the street," one troll informed him, "or your damned guts will be cut out in the dark." Others named the day he would die.

A bustling town of nearly five thousand, Haverhill, Massachusetts, was devoted to tanning leather and manufacturing shoes. Every year, Southern merchants arrived to place their orders. As in the rest of the industrial North, Haverhill relied heavily on Southern markets. "Cotton thread holds the Union together," Ralph Waldo Emerson observed a few years later. In Haverhill's case, it was the soles and laces of shoes.

Yet the town supported a lively abolition society officered by well-off businessmen and lawyers with members from every class and trade. The group met at local churches to hear lectures from Garrison, Douglass, and others. Haverhill native John Greenleaf Whittier, a Quaker poet, contributed antislavery verses and editorials to the town paper. Infuriated by the gag rule adopted by Congress, Haverhill's abolitionists decided to do something about it.

Every Friday afternoon, a group of ten men met in a hat shop on Main Street to talk politics. Lounging by the fire one winter day in early 1842, they decided to send a petition to Congress that, though avoiding the explicit mention of slavery, would be so audacious it couldn't fail to grab attention. They worked on a few drafts, but the one drawn up by "Black Ben" Emerson, so named for his virulent opposition to slavery, stood out for its uncompromising logic and disarming concision. A distant relative of the Concord sage, this Emerson was a shoe manufacturer and church deacon, "a far-sighted, long-headed, strong-minded Baptist," a friend later recalled, "a man of inflexible resolution and absolutely without fear."

Two days later, after Sunday services, Reverend Charles Fitch cleared the Communion table and laid out the petition for his congregants to consider. Thirty-two men lined up to scrawl their names. They were a diverse group: mill owners and blacksmiths, shoemakers and dentists, stable masters and farmers, and the reverend himself. The petition was passed around town, stirring up conversations in shops and homes and on the street. Not everyone approved. Shoe manufacturers, aware the publicity might turn off Southern buyers, pressured employees not to sign or to remove their names if they had. At least one worker, told he'd hang for treason, tracked down the letter and scratched out his name.

To prevent more defections, the paper was returned to the hat shop for safekeeping. Last-minute signers were covertly led late at night through a back door. The next morning, the petition, addressed to the Honorable John Quincy Adams, was handed to a rider bound for Washington.

Adams assumed it was a hoax, most likely the Southerners again trying to make him look bad. Just in case, however, he wrote to a friend who lived in Haverhill. The signers, his friend reported, were "thoroughly in earnest and determined to be heard."

That was good enough for Adams. The intrepid congressman rose from his chair and read the petition. The room was silent. "This," one congressman finally spluttered, "is a petition for the dissolution of the Union."

Indeed it was. The chamber exploded "amid repeated and deafening shouts," according to the official record. Henry Wise, a fiery Virginia populist, called for censuring the Massachusetts congressman. "Fine and imprisonment are infinitely too mild to fit the case," another Virginian observed. "If the ex-president be a traitor, then hanging is the proper punishment for him."

Coolly, Adams said he was surprised to hear condemnation of the petition "from a quarter where there have been so many calculations of the value of the Union."

As the room had fallen into mayhem, the Speaker decided to adjourn before nightfall, on the assumption, as one reporter noted, that "a candle-light sitting would bring in riot, fighting, the use of knives and pistols, and murder." After the gavel fell, congressmen huddled in groups "with knitted brows, compressed lips, and clenched fists," muttering damnations of all " 'agitators' and abolitionists," one of Adams's few allies reported. That night, members from the slave states met to strategize.

Come morning, the House filled with diplomats, journalists, and citizens eagerly anticipating the battle. Henry Clay ventured over from the Senate to watch a spectacle that would "fill every patriot bosom with distress." Thomas Marshall, an ambitious young congressman from Clay's own Kentucky, introduced a resolution to censure the former president. Marshall said he hadn't realized there were "men wild enough, and mad enough, to make a proposition that the Government of the United States should terminate its own existence." Adams was guilty of "high treason." He had offered "the deepest indignity to the House" and an "insult to the people of the United States." He should consider it a mercy he was being censured rather than expelled—or worse.

When he finally could reply, Adams directed his venom at the "slave-ocracy" that tried to silence all criticism. "Up rose that little, feeble, gray tottering old man, his eyes dimmed and his hands trembling," one reporter wrote. He called one opponent a "beef-witted blunderhead" and accused another of being drunk on whiskey and slavery. Slave owners were "befowlers of the nation's sacred freedoms." How dare Marshall accuse him of treason! "It is not for the gentleman from Kentucky, or his puny mind, to define what high treason is," Adams said.

Then he turned to the clerk of the House. "The first paragraph of the Declaration of Independence!" he shouted. Then he called for it again, louder. In a dry monotone, the clerk began reading: " 'When in the course of human events it becomes necessary for one people to dissolve the political bands which have connected them with another' ..." "Proceed, proceed," Adams interjected, "proceed right down to the 'right and duty.' " To an audience of slavers and their sympathizers, the clerk read the embarrassing words that it is the "right and duty" of a people to "alter or abolish" their government if it becomes destructive to life and liberty.

If any principle was sacred, Adams declaimed, it was "the right of the people to alter, to change, to destroy, the Government if it becomes oppressive to them." If the Haverhill petitioners' request to dissolve the Union was treasonous, so was the American Revolution. "I rest that petition," he bellowed, "on the Declaration of Independence!"

It was a masterly performance. His persecutors saw they had made a terrible mistake. Marshall offered to withdraw the censure motion if Adams withdrew the petition. He refused. Two weeks after the clash began—his purpled face dripping with sweat, his weak, wrinkled hands gripping the desk over which, six years later, he would finally slump and die—Adams agreed to yield the floor if the threat of censure was lifted. When it was, he introduced two hundred more petitions.

That summer, the ex-president embarked on a tour of the Northern states that was punctuated by cannon salutes and congratulatory parades. Thomas Marshall's once-promising career never recovered—the debate left him "sprawling in his own compost," Adams sneered. In 1844, the House finally repealed the gag rule. The madman had won.

It's strange the Haverhill petition isn't better known. Here was a group of small-town Americans pleading to destroy their country rather than allow it to continue enslaving their fellow human beings. In a different America, one proud, rather than ashamed, of having fought a war to free people from bondage, it would be on display in some grand building in the capital, a testament to the deeper meanings of patriotism; instead, it is stashed away in the storage room of an obscure local museum, its story seldom told.

Observers at the time believed the episode would never be forgotten. Theodore Weld, an abolitionist who helped Adams prepare his defense, thought it marked "the first victory over the slaveholders... since the foundation of the government." From that moment, Weld predicted, "their downfall takes its date."

A few days later, a traveler arrived in Washington after a depressing tour through Virginia; he'd found its very air laced with "ruin and decay." Everyone was talking about the triumph of the ex-president. Adams was "a lasting honor to the land that gave him birth," Charles Dickens observed. His valiant fight against slavery would be "remembered scores upon scores of years after the worms bred in its corruption are but so many grains of dust."

After Adams's vindication in the House, Northerners began to consider the subversive idea of the Haverhill petition. "People now talk about the value of the Union," Boston lawyer Charles Sumner observed, "and the North has begun to return the taunts of the South." Charles

King, a New York editor (and son of former senator Rufus King), noted that "the horror which used to thrill through all sound hearts at the bare mention of disunion can no longer be expected." Separatist ideas were "floating loosely and largely" in the sea of Northern opinion, finding their way into more and more hearts: "Repulsed at first...it comes again and again...to force an entrance, and at each attempt finds resistance more and more feeble."

In some hearts, there was no resistance at all. William Lloyd Garrison paid close attention to Adams's recent speeches in the House, which, he exulted, had driven "the boastful South almost out of her wits." Studying the congressional debate, Garrison noticed something interesting. Southerners rejected the Haverhill petition, but they confirmed its underlying logic. Once the "bonds of this Union" were broken, Kentucky congressman Joseph Underwood had said, the boundary between free and slave states would become an international border, an irresistible temptation for runaways. Freed from the Constitution's fugitive-slave clause, the Northern republic would welcome the refugees. That, Underwood admitted, would swiftly destroy slavery in Kentucky, Maryland, and Virginia. "The dissolution of the Union," he warned, would mean "the dissolution of slavery."

Reading Underwood's admission, Garrison thought he had found the answer to the riddle of American history. Breaking up the Union could be a practical strategy for ending—instead of merely protesting—the barbaric institution. For the first time, Garrison saw disunion as a political program, not just a moral cry. He flipped Underwood's maxim on its head. "Nothing can prevent the dissolution of the American Union," the editor wrote, "but the abolition of slavery."

Garrison's critics have claimed that he cared more about his own moral purity than alleviating the suffering of the enslaved. Yet disunion was a practical plan for abolition, not an airy idea. The purpose of separation, Garrison said, was "not to leave the slaves to the mercy of their masters: it is to withdraw from those masters all the resources and instrumentalities now furnished to them by the North, without which they are powerless." Deprived of the special guarantees granted slavery in the Constitution, the South would be isolated, weak—"compelled, for self preservation, and from necessity, speedily to liberate all her bondmen."

By convincing the South to emancipate its slaves voluntarily—rather than lose them amid invasion and insurrection—stirring up Northern support for partition might actually prevent it. Facing a choice between slavery and union, the country could avoid the brutality of civil war and the resentment that would linger long after it ended. Following the "overthrow of this blood-stained compact," the states could form a new union "based upon universal freedom, with no root of bitterness to poison our cup." For the first time in history a nation could undergo seismic change not through violence but "the majesty of moral power."

In April 1842, the *Liberator* called for "the REPEAL OF THE UNION between the North and the South." To his father-in-law, a fellow abolitionist, Garrison explained:

> We must dissolve all connexion with those murderers of fathers, and murderers of mothers, and murderers of liberty, and traffickers in human flesh, and blasphemers against the Almighty, at the South. What have we in common with them? What have we gained, what have we not lost, by our alliance with them? Are not their principles, their pursuits, their policies, their interests, their designs, feelings, utterly diverse from ours? Why, then, be subject to their dominion?

The Union was an idol, a golden calf. It is "not of heaven" but rather "founded in unrighteousness, and cemented with blood...It is a horrible mockery of freedom. In all its parts and proportions it is misshapen, incongruous, unnatural."

A daily Bible reader, Garrison urged followers to look at the verses in the book of Isaiah where the prophet denounces an alliance between the kingdom of Judah and some insidious foreign power, probably Egypt. Judah's corrupt rulers think the pact will protect them from calamity: "We have made a covenant with DEATH, and with HELL are we at agreement; when the overflowing scourge shall pass through, it shall not come unto us: for we have made LIES our refuge, and under FALSEHOOD have we hid ourselves." With biting Iron Age sarcasm, Isaiah tells the rulers they will not be safe: "Your covenant with DEATH *shall be annulled,* and your agreement with HELL *shall not stand;* when the overflowing scourge shall pass through, then shall ye be trodden down by it."

Garrison would invoke this passage for twenty years. The Constitution, he said, was a covenant with death, the Union an agreement with hell. In shutting their eyes to reality, Northerners had made lies their refuge. They had agreed to ratify the unholy covenant and to maintain it ever since for the sake of self-protection, out of deference to their Southern allies. Channeling the prophet, Garrison foresaw the coming destruction. He warned Americans that their refusal to root out the evil, to atone for national sins, would be their downfall.

CHAPTER 7

Endangered by Greatness

Ef I'd my way I had ruther,
We should go to work an' part, —
They take one way, we take t'other, —
Guess it wouldn't break my heart.

—JAMES RUSSELL LOWELL, 1846

AS DANGEROUS AS THE NORTH-SOUTH divide had become, other fault lines also threatened the project of perpetual union and ceaseless expansion. Disunion became the cry not only of abolitionists and slaveholders but also of North Woods frontiersmen, persecuted Mormons, border-crossing Texans, and California dreamers, all of whom tried to found nations of their own. The forces fragmenting the Union went beyond slavery and states' rights. Something more fundamental had gone awry—or had never been settled in the first place.

Well into the nineteenth century, the North American map remained up for grabs. Instead of one union from sea to shining sea, the present-day United States might easily have become what a contemporary called "a nest of little republics, spitting and snarling and spattering at each other from morning until night."

Expansionists sought to avoid that outcome. But their aggressive actions didn't silence talk of breakaway movements. Rather, as with the Louisiana Purchase, attempts to preserve unity in the West only exacerbated the breach in the East. The country's expansionist aspirations and internal dissensions presented a paradox: If the government did nothing, the continent would be divided. But if it acted too aggressively, the Union might split. Either way, a fracture was in America's future, a breakup of one kind or another all but inevitable.

The original "Bear Flag" that flew over California for three weeks in 1846, before the United States annexed the breakaway Mexican territory. (*Society of California Pioneers*)

Brought together by common animosity, radicals in the North and South became, oddly enough, ever more united in their calls for divorce. "Disunion must and will come," abolitionist Wendell Phillips predicted. "Calhoun wants it at one end of the Union — Garrison wants it at the other." In an 1850 sermon in Charleston, where war would break out a decade later, the Reverend A. A. Porter urged Americans to acknowledge that there were and always had been "two nations in the womb" of the Union waiting to be born.

1. The Age of Breakaway Republics

On a summer day in 1832, fifty-nine men in homespun wool and moose-hide moccasins filed into a one-room schoolhouse and voted to form their own nation. Their remote region in northern New Hampshire was henceforth "a free, sovereign and independent state," at least until bigwigs in London and Washington figured out "to what government we properly belong," Canada or the United States. They adopted a constitution, levied taxes, established courts and schools. The Republic of Indian Stream was born.

For two years the men acted the part of citizens of a sovereign nation. When pesky officials from either country tried to serve warrants or pursue debtors, the self-styled Streamers invoked their independence as a defense. One man, arrested by New Hampshire authorities for failing to support the mother of his child, argued that U.S. paternity laws didn't apply because conception had occurred within the separate republic. An anxious local sheriff informed state officials that the frontiersmen had even hired "twelve or fourteen Indians...to assist them in case of trouble."

Trouble came in the early spring of 1835, the hills still blanketed with snow, when a shoot-out erupted outside a Canadian magistrate's house where a debtor was being held. New Hampshire's governor readied the state militia to invade the area. Fearing the gallows, the Streamers agreed to annexation by the United States. A few years later, a treaty settled the border dispute in America's favor. The Republic of Indian Stream faded into obscurity.

This border-blurring experiment in self-government is more than a forgotten bit of local lore. The contagion of independence loosed by the American Revolution was still spreading through the landscape. Soon, other breakaway republics emerged, or threatened to, over far vaster stretches of territory, posing more dire threats to the Union's expansion.

As hundreds of thousands ventured into the wilderness, following buffalo trails widened into Indian paths and deepened by wagon wheels, the question arose: Why *would* they want to be governed from thousands of miles away, the same unworkable arrangement the seaboard colonists had fought to overthrow? Inspired by the example of the Revolution, these settlers didn't necessarily feel attached to the Union it had spawned, paralyzed as it was by its own divisions. For many self-exiled Americans, more appealing than annexation to a country "doomed to dissolution," as John C. Calhoun predicted, was seizing the opportunity to start a new one.

Today, few denizens of New Hampshire's North Woods favor reclaiming the sovereignty of their long-lost republic. Yet the same is far from true of other breakaway nations absorbed against the inhabitants' wishes and to the enduring regret of their descendants.

Nowhere was resistance to annexation greater, nowhere has regret been more lasting, than in Texas, the once and possibly future Lone

Star Republic. Generations of American expansionists and adventurers had schemed to pry Texas from Spain by means fair or foul. Aaron Burr saw it as the shimmering Western gem in his new imperial crown. After 1821, when Mexico won independence from Spain, hard-liners in the United States vowed to take the region one way or another.

Demographics accomplished what diplomacy had failed to. Thanks to the efforts of Virginia-born Stephen Austin, who inherited from his father the Mexican government's permission to settle American families in Texas, the nonindigenous population soared from a few thousand to some twenty thousand people by 1830, the majority living along the Gulf Coast. Most had migrated from the United States, especially the South, many with slaves. When the Mexican government passed an emancipation law, the Americans successfully lobbied for Texas to receive a temporary exemption.

Alarmed by the swarm of opportunity-seekers, Mexican officials ordered a total and complete shutdown of Americans entering the country. The border was porous, however, and the migrants continued to come.

Still, Texan independence remained unpopular. Proud of his Mexican citizenship, Austin resisted demands for secession as long as he could. In 1826, when a few American émigrés tried to establish a "Republic of Fredonia" near the town of Nacogdoches, Austin helped put down the rebellion. In 1833 he wrote that "a wise direction of its energies" would make Texas "one of the most efficient, faithful, and devoted States of the Union." He was referring to the Mexican union, not the American one.

Soon, however, the ungainly Mexican federation, even less united than its northern neighbor, began to fracture. A general named Antonio López de Santa Anna dissolved the Mexican congress, overthrew the constitution, and turned the Mexican states into districts subordinate to central rule. Separatists in several outlying regions declared independence. But only one movement would succeed.

On March 2, 1836, from a humble log cabin on the Brazos River, Texan leaders proclaimed the birth of the Lone Star Republic. As in the American colonies sixty years earlier, the rebels believed, according to one newspaper, that Santa Anna meant "to give liberty to our slaves, and to make slaves of ourselves." Inspired by the parallel, thousands of Americans raised funds and arms for Texas. Able-bodied men set out to join the rebel army, eager for the glory their fathers had earned in battle with the British. Without American support, the Texan revolution would have failed, as the American one would have without French assistance.

Six months into the rebellion, a captured Santa Anna saved his own life by signing a treaty recognizing Texan independence. Mexican officials repudiated the surrender, but it was too late.

In New York City, an eighty-year-old lawyer read of the events in Texas with intense interest. A visitor found him clutching the newspaper. "There! You see? I was right!" he shouted. "What was treason in me thirty years ago is patriotism now!" Vindicated, Aaron Burr died a few months later.

Americans dominated Texas, but it was never inevitable that the republic would be absorbed by the United States. Texans wasted no time approving a referendum for annexation, but the federal government did little to encourage them. President Jackson had looked the other way as Americans flocked to support separatists in a country with which their own was at peace. Yet amid a politically sensitive transfer of power to his ally Martin Van Buren, Jackson chose not to act on the Texans' request. Once in office, Van Buren, too, did nothing. As a New Yorker, he knew Northerners opposed the government's upsetting the country's delicate sectional balance by acquiring the vast cotton-growing region. Whigs, as members of the emerging anti-Jackson party were known, warned that adding Texas would bequeath "a deep and lasting curse to the country." Even Van Buren's fellow Democrats, as Jackson followers called themselves, feared broaching the issue.

Jilted by Washington, Texas withdrew its annexation bid and focused instead on building an independent nation. But while the new country was big, some in the Lone Star Republic thought it should be bigger. They proposed annexing the Southern states to Texas rather than the other way around. In 1837, Memucan Hunt Jr., the Texan ambassador in Washington, suggested the arrangement would have "incalculable benefits" for both regions, as the new slaveholders' union, bound "by the strongest ties of a common interest," would be able to "overrun all Mexico" and replace its mixed-race inhabitants with whites. The new South-facing republic might even become "the greatest nation on earth."

Moderates like Austin and Sam Houston, hero of the revolution and the republic's first president, dismissed such "visionary schemes" and preferred to continue seeking annexation. But in 1838, another war hero, Georgia-born poet and lawyer Mirabeau Buonaparte Lamar, was elected to succeed Houston as president. Lamar wanted to keep Texas independent. A free Texas could better protect slavery from the Northern abolitionists. Why should Texas join a nation with many citizens "known to be opposed to her peculiar and essential interests"? As a state, it would be an "unfelt fraction of a giant power." As an independent nation, it could expand to the Pacific.

By 1844, the republic boasted 125,000 residents, one-fifth of them enslaved. Though in debt, it had managed to maintain its independence despite Mexico's attempts to retake it. Sam Houston reclaimed the presidency after Lamar's term expired. Fed up with American inaction, he drafted plans for seizing the unruly Mexican provinces of New Mexico and California. If Washington didn't act soon, Texas would become a transcontinental nation, a rival and a menace to the not-so-United States.

Fifteen hundred miles away, another separatist movement was brewing. California had changed little since the early days of Spanish settlement. Now a peripheral province of independent Mexico, it was largely left alone, deemed too distant for the capital to control. The California of the 1830s was a quiet coastline of abandoned missions, vulnerable forts, and scattered settlements, backed by an all but impassable stretch of mountains. Of the few thousand nonnative settlers, most were *californios*, Mexicans of European descent. Living among them were a few hundred Americans, ocean-borne arrivals, braving it out in a strange land far from home.

After Santa Anna's 1835 coup, California was one of the regions that, like Texas, tried to shake off Mexico's control. American settlers allied with *californios* to expel the governor and declare a "free and sovereign state." Not for the last time, geographical divisions within California impaired its unity and sapped its strength. Residents of southern towns, like sleepy, dusty Los Angeles, who would bear the brunt of a Mexican crackdown were less willing to take risks than northerners. California quickly returned to the Mexican fold.

A few years later, amid a wave of new arrivals, Mexico banned American immigration to California as it had in Texas, aiming to prevent a repeat of the Lone Star revolt. Here, too, the migrants ignored the laws of the country they were entering. Few spoke Spanish. As the foreign-born population rose, locals feared their country was being taken from them, that they were being replaced.

Divided by race, geography, and allegiance, the province verged on civil war. In 1841, a U.S. naval lieutenant named Charles Wilkes warned Washington of the "total absence of all government in California"—an anarchy that might attract foreign rivals. Surrounded by soaring peaks, vast deserts, and the world's largest ocean, California, with its promising harbors and agricultural potential, seemed marked for independence.

That was especially true if it could be combined with the even more anarchic territory to the north. Oregon, a vague handle for the land between California and Russian Alaska, had already drawn interest from a half a dozen countries. In 1818, the United States and Britain agreed to jointly occupy the area. Both could extract resources but neither had sole jurisdiction. The agreement held as long as there weren't enough white people to make it worth going to war over.

In the 1830s, when nine of every ten natives in the area were wiped out by disease, land became available for new settlement. Missionaries led the way, sending back reports depicting Oregon as an Eden-like paradise. Every year, twice as many Americans as the year before loaded up wagons and ventured across the plains. "There is a nation being born in a day," one missionary wrote, "the future eminence and greatness of which needs not a prophet to predict."

The notion of a separate nation on the Pacific Coast was neither new nor controversial. Its earliest champion was the same man who had sent Meriwether Lewis and William Clark into the remote wilderness to see what was there. In 1803, Thomas Jefferson said it didn't matter if the territory just purchased from France someday became a separate republic. That expression of ambivalence wasn't a passing whim. A decade later, after John Jacob Astor established a fur-trading outpost on the Columbia River, Jefferson congratulated the tycoon for planting the seeds of "a great, free, and independent empire on that side of our continent, populated by American settlers, but separated from the United States." In 1825, Missouri's Thomas Hart Benton told the Senate that when the American presence in Oregon grew "strong enough to take care of itself, the new Government should separate from the mother Empire as the child separates from the parent at the age of manhood." That only seemed likelier by the 1840s, when Charles Wilkes, the lieutenant prowling the coast, concluded that the entire region, including California, would eventually form a "powerful maritime nation" that could in time "control the destinies of the Pacific."

Even at the peak of "Oregon Fever," many saw the region's separation as inevitable. The U.S. ambassador to Mexico argued for giving up America's claim to Oregon so it could join with a soon-to-be-independent California. Like their countrymen headed for Texas, takers to the Oregon Trail ventured beyond the United States without any guarantee its borders would be extended to include them. "The bold, restless spirits who have gone to Oregon and California are the very sort of men who are disposed to set up a new government," a St. Louis paper observed. Their willingness to leave the United States, a country that many felt had failed them, was proof enough of their determination. Years later, aging pioneers claimed they had wanted to "save" Oregon for the Union. They said nothing of such intentions at the time. Many spoke instead of independence. They didn't care whether Oregon joined the Union. That uncertainty, as in Texas, would persist long after annexation.

At last, the Prophet had found his followers a home. Over a decade of dislocation, Joseph Smith and his Latter-day Saints trekked from upstate New York to Pennsylvania, Ohio, and then Missouri, where the governor ordered all Mormons "exterminated or driven from the state," and several church leaders escaped death by firing squad only at the last minute. They fled across the Mississippi to Commerce, Illinois, a river town they renamed Nauvoo (from the Hebrew word for "beauty"). From a malarial swamp, they built a teeming, gridded city of ten thousand people, the largest in the state next to Chicago. Voting as a bloc, Mormons held the balance of power between Democrats and Whigs in Illinois politics. In 1840, they convinced state legislators (including a young Abraham Lincoln) to grant Nauvoo an unusually independent city charter. Freed from oversight, the Latter-day Saints built a militia of five thousand men, half the size of the U.S. Army.

But then locals in southern Illinois turned against the Mormons, as locals had elsewhere. After high-profile defections and lurid exposés — such as the rumor that Smith and other church leaders were practicing polygamy (still a closely held Mormon secret) — state officials called for their expulsion. Even a quasi-sovereign city-state wouldn't be enough to protect the Mormons. More drastic measures were needed.

Smith's first idea was to declare his candidacy for president of the United States. He called for abolishing borders by annexing not only Texas and Oregon but all of Mexico and Canada; he also advocated for turning prisons into schools and ending slavery.

His candidacy was a long shot. But the Prophet had a backup plan; he and his followers would leave the United States, a nation "rent from center to circumference, with party strife, political intrigue, and sectional interest," Smith wrote in the official church newspaper in 1842. The only solution was to find a separate realm, far removed from American divisions, where God's true worshippers could build their kingdom.

To help plan the move, Smith formed a top secret committee called the Council of Fifty, the members of which were instructed not to discuss its proceedings even with their wives — any of them — on pain of losing their heads.

When the records of the committee, long protected by the church, were published in 2016, they showed the council resolving, like the seventeenth-century English Separatists, to find refuge from persecution even if it meant setting off for lands unknown. One member, Orson Spencer, argued that "men of congenial religions or other interests, should separate themselves from those of adverse faith & interests and pair off, each to each." For Mormons, as for the Pilgrims, separation was the byword of their politics. Spencer denounced the "promiscuous intermixture of heterogeneous bodies" as a violation of "pure religion & sound philosophy."

The only "government worth asking for," declared Lyman Wight, a close adviser to Joseph Smith (they had stood together before the Missouri firing squad), was one limited to "those whose *interests* are identified with ours." That wasn't the United States, "a damned wrotten thing…full of lice, moth eaten, corrupt, and there is nothing but meanness about it." To build the Kingdom of God, the Saints would have to leave its corruption behind them.

One intriguing possibility arose in early 1844 when Lyman Wight, visiting Wisconsin to oversee lumber production for Nauvoo's ornate temple, wrote to Smith about some local Indians who were planning to move to Texas. Wight thought the Mormons should consider the same. The Saints had closely followed Texan developments, sympathizing with another experiment in independence. Smith liked Wight's idea and sent an emissary to Austin.

Sam Houston was all ears. Warring with Comanches, wary of Mexico's attempts to reclaim its lost province, worried that annexation to the United States would never happen, Houston believed that allowing the Mormons to settle in southern Texas offered advantages for both sides: Texas would have a buffer, defended by the Mormons' impressive militia, between itself and Mexico, while the Saints could finally have a land all their own, far from their American tormentors.

Just as the negotiators got close to a deal, reports arrived in Austin of Joseph Smith's untimely demise. As Nauvoo's mayor, Smith had ordered a marshal to destroy the press of a dissident paper that threatened to divulge the practice of polygamy. That gave local gentiles a pretext to throw Smith and other leading Mormons in jail. The mob got to work; two hundred men, their faces blackened with gunpowder, stormed the building and shot Smith six times.

Soon after, Eliza Snow, one of the Prophet's widows, penned a poem blaming Smith's lynching on the sinful Union:

Once lov'd America! What can atone
For the pure blood of innocence thou'st sown?

A few assailants faced trial for the murder. None were convicted.

After Smith's killing, Brigham Young, one of Smith's disciples, won the succession battle. Practical and business-minded, Young disliked the Texas plan and broke off talks with the Lone Star Republic, whose annexation to the United States now looked likely. Young wanted Mormons to have as little as possible to do with "Satan's Kingdom."

In 1845, Illinois revoked Nauvoo's charter, and Young announced the Saints would set out for the West. Sixteen thousand people walked to temporary camps in Iowa. "We owe the United States nothing," an editorial in Nauvoo's paper said. "We go out by force, as exiles from freedom."

They didn't know their destination. Ideas came from across the country. A letter to Young suggested the Mormons could settle on San Francisco Bay, in northern California, and form a new "United States of the West."

Instead, Young chose the Great Salt Lake, then in a distant corner of Mexican territory, a region attractive for its remoteness. If moving there meant "forsaking the American Republic," as Young put it, so much the better. In a letter to James K. Polk, the Tennessee slaveholder elected to serve the presidential term that Joseph Smith had hoped would be his, Young said the Saints would "rather retreat to the deserts, island or mountain caves than consent to be ruled by governors & judges...who delight in injustice and oppression." That was enough to scare Polk, who wrote worriedly in his diary that the Mormons, once settled out west, would "become hostile to the U.S." and pose an obstacle to expansion.

2. Storm over Texas

The race was on for the far side of the continent. Britain and France, their interest piqued by all the commotion, were already plotting to secure protectorates, convenient Pacific-side perches from which to frustrate America's political and commercial ambitions. The possibility of foreign intervention made it crucial for U.S. expansionists to act quickly lest the moment of uncertainty pass.

The first step—long overdue—was to annex Texas. Meant to strengthen the Union, however, the merger with the Lone Star Republic revealed an unbridgeable divide: Northerners insisted they would leave the Union if the slaveholding republic was annexed, while Southerners threatened to secede if it wasn't. The Texas battle threw the country into a state of crisis and, finally, a fight to the death.

A few far-seeing critics had warned early that that would be its end. While most Americans cheered the Texas Revolution from afar, a lone dissenter raised his voice against it: Benjamin Lundy, the same roving Quaker activist who years earlier had converted William Lloyd Garrison to abolitionism. In the early 1830s, Lundy traveled to Texas to scout land for a colony of former slaves. He spoke with Mexican officials, who supported the plan, and with American transplants, who tried to tar and feather him and then ran him out of town.

When the rebellion broke out, Lundy fumed at the freedom-loving pretensions of the Texans. In a pamphlet, the agitator blasted the depiction of the struggle as "a legitimate contest for the maintenance of the sacred principles of Liberty." It was, in fact, a conspiracy, backed by powerful interests in Washington, *"to wrest the large and valuable territory of Texas from the Mexican Republic, in order to re-establish the* SYSTEM OF SLAVERY; *to open a vast and profitable* SLAVE-MARKET *therein; and, ultimately, to annex it to the United States."*

Lundy sent his observations to John Quincy Adams, then busy fighting the gag rule. As secretary of state and president, Adams had favored acquiring Texas. But now he saw sinister motives at work. Expanding the land devoted to slavery would destroy the balance of power between North and South. Adams condemned the government for supporting the Texans and inviting a clash with Mexico. "You are now rushing into war—into a war of conquest, commenced by aggression on your part, and for the re-establishment of slavery, where it has been abolished," Adams warned Congress. "In that war, the banners of freedom will be the banners of Mexico, and your banners, I blush to speak the word, will be the banners of slavery."

Even the former president, however, could be marginalized as a crank. William Ellery Channing, an establishment-friendly Unitarian theologian in Boston, could not be so readily dismissed. His best-loved sermon, an 1829 discourse titled "The Union" (a response to South Carolina's defiance of the federal government), urged Americans to cherish their federation and avoid a rupture at all costs.

Just a few years later, however, Channing questioned whether the Union was really worth preserving. In an 1837 open letter to Henry Clay, Channing implored the Whig leader to block Texas annexation. A likely war with Mexico would benefit only the South. "Must we of the North buckle on our armor, to fight the battles of slavery?" Channing asked. The United States was already too big—it was "endangered by greatness." Adding Texas would pose "imminent peril to our institutions, union, prosperity, virtue, and peace."

Channing was even open to the case for national divorce. Separating peacefully would "threaten less contention, than a lingering, feverish dissolution of the Union," which would eventually come if such a vast slave territory was added despite Northern objections. Annexing Texas would one day bring "death to our Union."

Inspired by Channing and Adams, Northerners sent Congress hundreds of thousands of petitions opposing annexation. Adams used them to stall a vote, effectively filibustering the bill.

For five years, the issue slumbered. In 1842, John Tyler reawakened it. A rich tobacco planter and slave owner, Tyler was thrust into the presidency when William Henry Harrison, the first Whig elected to the office, died of pneumonia a month into his term. When Tyler, a former Democrat, began vetoing Whig bills, the party abandoned him. Caught without a constituency, the president needed an issue to rally voters. He seized on Texas. Annexation was "neither local nor sectional," Tyler assured Congress, but essential "to the interests of the whole Union."

He was right—as long as the interests of the slave owners were the same as the interests of the Union. To Southerners like Tyler, they were.

Fear of foreign influence played a role in those calculations. In 1833, Great Britain had abolished slavery and began wielding emancipation as a tool of foreign policy. Many Americans feared that the mother country had never stopped trying to halt the United States' expansion, reduce its size, carve it up. The British did little to dispel such concerns. In 1841, an editorial in a London magazine, widely discussed in America, argued that a third war with the United States—sparked by the Oregon dispute—would be "a blessing to mankind," for Britain could divide the Union by sending Jamaican troops to invade the South and ignite a slave rebellion. Two years later, rumor had it that Britain had offered to pressure Mexico to acknowledge Texan independence in exchange for the Lone Star Republic freeing its fifteen thousand slaves. Sam Houston, frustrated by American inaction, was reportedly open to such an overture. Unless Texas was annexed as a slave state, Britain might intercede to ensure it became a free republic.

To Southerners like John C. Calhoun, Tyler's secretary of state, keeping Texas from falling under British influence was of the utmost importance. Failure to act now would hazard "the very existence of the South," Calhoun told an ally. A free republic on the Southern border would become a magnet for fugitives, a staging ground for slave rebellion. Texan independence would turn from a blessing for American slaveholders into an unmitigated curse—just cause for seceding from the Union.

*   *   *

To John Quincy Adams, it was annexing Texas—not letting it go—
that would justify disunion. In 1842, following his victory in the clash
over the Haverhill petition, Adams spent days in government archives
poring over military documents and dusty diplomatic messages, piec-
ing together a secret plot, a decade in the making, to give slavery more
room to expand. Annexing Texas, the aging congressman told his constituents, was part of a larger "slave-breeding conspiracy against the
freedom of the North." America was "no longer a democracy... no longer even a republic—it is a government of 2 or 300,000 holders of
slaves"—roughly 1 percent of the population.

In 1843, Adams and twelve other Whigs published "A Solemn Appeal
to the People of the Free States." The pending merger with Texas would
empower the slave masters "beyond all redemption," the manifesto
declared. To ensure "the continued ascendancy of the Slave Power"—a
new term to describe the slavers' conspiracy to control the government—
Southerners would stop at nothing. They would even sacrifice their own
theories about the limits of federal power. Northerners, however, should
adopt those theories. Any act providing for the acquisition of *"such mis-
begotten and illegitimate progeny"* as Texas would be unconstitutional and
void, the congressmen insisted. Indeed, it "WOULD BE IDENTICAL WITH
DISSOLUTION. It would be a violation of our national compact." The people of the free states "WOULD NOT SUBMIT TO IT."

The Texas issue riled up the North as nothing had since the War of
1812. State after state echoed the nullificationist language recently
heard only from Southerners like Calhoun. In the Massachusetts statehouse, Adams's son Charles Francis argued that merging with another
sovereign nation required a constitutional amendment, if not a new
"Constitution of the United States and Texas."

A few years earlier, Michigan's legislature had resolved that adding
Texas would endanger "this happy Union." Yet as threats to dissolve it
came from every part of the country, the Union looked anything but
happy.

In spring 1844, Calhoun wrapped up negotiations with Texan diplomats and sent the treaty to the Senate for approval. The talks had been
conducted under a cloak of secrecy. The treaty came as "a clap of thun-

der in a clear sky," Missouri's Thomas Hart Benton later recalled. He forgot how stormy the sky had already looked, but still, it was about to get much darker.

Calhoun and Tyler wanted the Senate to consider the treaty in closed session and make it public only after it was ratified. But a rene-gade antislavery Democrat leaked it and related materials to the press. Northerners were outraged by one item in particular, a letter from Cal-houn to the British ambassador in Washington, Richard Pakenham, stating that the purpose of annexing Texas was to protect slavery—an institution Calhoun called "essential to the peace, safety, and prosper-ity of those States of the Union in which it exists."

The Pakenham letter revealed nothing Americans didn't already know, but Calhoun had made the mistake of saying the quiet part loud. Admitting that slavery motivated annexation undermined Tyler's yearslong campaign to convince Northerners it would benefit "the whole Union," not only the South. Now it looked like the Slave Power conspiracy Adams and others had warned about.

Some thought the Pakenham letter no mistake at all but an attempt by Calhoun to sabotage annexation and break up the country. Thomas Hart Benton, a Missouri slave owner who nonetheless had his doubts about the peculiar institution, said the Carolinian's real motive was to give the South an excuse for secession. "Under the pretext of getting Texas into the Union, the scheme is to get the South out of it," the imposing Benton thundered in the Senate. Working with the Texans, Calhoun hoped to create a "separate confederacy stretching from the Atlantic to the Californias."

He wasn't entirely wrong. At least some Southerners sought not to annex Texas but to be annexed by it. Amid the uproar, South Caroli-na's governor, James H. Hammond, told Calhoun that Northern resis-tance to annexation made him wonder if the South should secede. "If the Union is to break there could not be a better pretext," Hammond wrote. "With Texas the slave states would form a territory large enough for a *first rate power* and one that under a free trade system would flour-ish beyond any on the Globe—immediately and forever."

Shortly after the treaty was leaked, the front-runners for the 1844 pres-idential nominations—former president Martin Van Buren, a Democrat, and perennial also-ran Henry Clay, a Whig—issued statements opposing it. Anxious to hold the political center, Clay was content to see Texas remain independent. "We may live as good neighbors, cultivating peace, commerce, and friendship," he wrote. Annexation would "sow the seeds of a dissolution of the Union." Van Buren, a New Yorker, had always known Texas was toxic in the North. Defying Southerners in his party, he hoped to postpone the issue until after the election.

Despite their best efforts, however, neither leader could hold off the storm.

In Texas, news of the treaty's defeat came as a profound disappointment. Sam Houston had thought annexation would finally happen. Earlier maneuvers to secure British-mediated recognition from Mexico had largely been a ruse to stir up jealousy in Washington. But the rejection of the treaty convinced Houston to pursue that option more seriously. Sensing the opening, Britain dropped the antislavery demand and convinced Mexico to recognize Texas if it promised never to join the United States. The Lone Star Republic, once thought temporary, a halfway house between the Mexican and American unions, might be around to stay.

Southerners, too, began working on a backup plan. Forming a union with Texas was even worth destroying the union they already had. In South Carolina, an ominous, familiar call went up in the low country: Disunion now.

Robert Barnwell Rhett answered as if responding to his own name. As a young legislator in the 1820s, Rhett had been inspired by Thomas Cooper's appeals for South Carolina to "calculate the value of the Union." Storming the state with hot-blooded speeches delivered in a rapid, high-pitched voice compared by John Quincy Adams to that of "a howling dog," Rhett emerged as a leading nullifier and unapologetic secessionist. He would rather see America break "into a thousand fragments," he vowed, than live as "a slave—a fearful slave, ruled despotically by those who do not represent me, & whose sectional interests are not mine." (In the minds of white Carolinians, the abolitionists were the masters and they were the slaves.) Unlike Calhoun, Rhett didn't shrink from what that meant. "If to think, to speak, to feel such sentiments as these, constitute me a disunionist and a traitor," he shouted, "then, gentlemen, I am a Disunionist!—I am a Traitor!"

As state attorney general, Rhett reluctantly fell in line with Calhoun on the tariff-lowering compromise of 1833. "If a Confederacy of the Southern States could now be obtained," Rhett asked, "should we not deem it a happy termination — happy beyond expectation — of our long struggle for our rights against oppression?" In the convention that revoked the nullification ordinance, Rhett bellowed: "A people, owning slaves, are mad, or worse than mad, who do not hold their destinies in their own hands."

Rhett entered Congress in 1836, just as antislavery petitions began to flood in. He suggested the state withdraw from Congress or even leave the Union outright "rather than suffer the discussion of the Abolition question in Congress."

For a while, Calhoun kept Rhett in line by lavishing praise on the young firebrand. But Rhett and his clique of radicals schemed to seize power in the state and proclaim a new Southern nation.

By 1844, Rhett thought his moment had come. Two years earlier, the high tariff rates that the 1833 bargain was supposed to phase out had instead been renewed. South Carolinians were outraged. Rhett called abolition and the tariff "two enormous villanies," both caused by "the deep seated and growing animosity of the North to the South." Some accused Rhett of trying to topple Calhoun as the de facto Southern leader, but he was channeling the popular mood. "Nothing alarms and disgusts me so much as the utter prostration of the spirit of the South," veteran nullifier James Hamilton wrote. "We are fit for nothing else but to be overseers of the emancipation of our own slaves whenever our Masters will have decreed it."

On the last day of July 1844, Rhett's followers organized a dinner in his honor in the tidewater town of Bluffton. Under a sprawling oak tree, in a makeshift building put up for the occasion and festooned with palmetto leaves, some five hundred guests listened to speeches and toasts praising their hard-fighting congressman, condemning the "black tariff," invoking the legacy of their revolutionary forefathers, and denouncing those who would betray it.

Rhett took the floor and drew the crowd under his gaze. Forget about half measures, he told them. The only choice was nullification or secession. While for a time it seemed the former had worked, now it was clear that it hadn't. Only secession could safeguard the state's interests.

From Bluffton, the message spread throughout the state. Langdon Cheves, a respected former congressman, published an article endorsing the goal of a Southern confederacy. "Do not deceive yourselves by supposing that the only struggle before you or the greatest is that of the tariff," Cheves wrote. The real issue, "of ten times the importance and danger," was slavery.

By fall, however, the Bluffton movement had collapsed, largely because it failed to overcome Calhoun's opposition. With the 1844 presidential campaign in full swing, the moment wasn't ripe for revolution. Rhett bowed to reality but kept up the fight. In December, during the congressional debate that finally repealed the gag rule, he warned that lifting the ban proved white Southerners had no protection from the federal government. "In the Union or out of the Union," Rhett said of the South, "she can and will be free."

Regardless of Calhoun's motives in publishing the Pakenham letter, it turned support for Texas annexation into a measure of any politician's commitment to slavery. That was a test even Martin Van Buren, long derided as a "Northern man with Southern principles," couldn't pass.

The Democrats scouted for a new nominee and found James K. Polk, a former Speaker of the House and governor of Tennessee. To Southerners, Polk's appeal was obvious. As one Carolinian enthused, "He is a large Slave holder & plants cotton — *free trade* — Texas — States rights *out & out*." (Later, as president, Polk purchased nineteen teenage slaves for his sprawling plantation, separating them from their families.)

To placate Northerners, Polk called for extending American jurisdiction over Oregon as well as Texas. Pairing the two demands again framed Western expansion as a national interest. Texas would be settled by slaveholders, Oregon by free whites — the sectional balance would be maintained.

Polk's Whig opponent, Henry Clay, had opposed annexation when he thought Van Buren would be the Democratic nominee. Facing the pro-Texas Polk, that position cost him in the South. Clay's attempts to appease both sides only confused voters everywhere. In New York and Michigan, enough abolitionists supported a third-party candidate to put Polk over the edge.

All of which left John Tyler, the incumbent, with mixed emotions.

Annexing Texas had been his idea, and he wasn't eager to see Polk take the credit. After the election, Tyler moved quickly to put Texas back on the agenda. Claiming a mandate for the move—dubiously, given that Polk had received a minority of all votes cast—Tyler called on Congress to annex Texas with a simple resolution rather than a treaty. Passage, therefore, would require only a majority in each chamber, not two-thirds support.

Reeling from defeat in the election, congressional Whigs put up a valiant fight. Catastrophe would follow annexation, they warned. An Illinoisan who later died fighting in Mexico said that statehood for Texas would ultimately "shatter this Union to fragments." "As certain as truth and God exist," one New Yorker predicted, "the admission of Texas into this Union will prove, sooner or later, an element of overwhelming ruin to the Republic."

In March 1845, on his way out of the White House, Tyler signed the annexation bill. Mexico's ambassador in Washington denounced the move and left for home. A few days later, after taking the oath of office, Polk sent an army to the disputed borderlands between Texas and Mexico—not to guard against invasion but to find a pretext for war.

Texas had been independent for nearly a decade, and many American-born residents, resenting the country they had left behind, weren't sure they wanted to rejoin it. Mexico's offer of recognition seemed the more attractive option. In late 1844, the Texas presidency passed to Anson Jones, a New England–born doctor who kept five slaves at the presidential plantation. Like many Texans, Jones was ambivalent about annexation, and he received conflicting advice. The republic's diplomat in Europe, influenced by French and British arguments, told Jones that America offered only the "friendship of the lion for the lamb." The Union would swallow Texas whole. A businessman advised Jones to question the value of a merger sealed despite "the Curses of fully one-half of the people of the U.S., who have been deriding us and abusing us for Cutthroats, villains, and bestowing upon us every vile epithet…Just, too, as our Independence was about being acknowledged by Mexico!"

Arguing for annexation were those who saw it as vital for protecting slavery. Memucan Hunt, onetime advocate for preserving independence, reversed his earlier position. In an open letter to the people of

Galveston, a slave-dealing entrepôt, Hunt asked, "Can we close our eyes to the important truth that the Constitution of the American Union is at the moment the strongest bulwark, and almost the only protection against the growing power, the fanaticism, and the reckless violence of Abolitionism?" Abolitionists themselves had been saying so for years.

That argument proved decisive. At noon on February 19, 1846, Jones lowered the Lone Star flag outside Austin's log capitol and raised the Stars and Stripes. "The final act in this great drama is now performed," the president told a hushed crowd. "The Republic of Texas is no more."

3. Gathering of the Forces

Despite its jingoistic associations, the term *manifest destiny* was coined in an anti-war manifesto. In 1845, the pro-expansion *Democratic Review* argued that war against Mexico was unnecessary. The conquest of the continent, including the extirpation of the natives, would proceed more smoothly without it. It was the divine mission of *Americans* to conquer the continent, not necessarily of the United States. California would soon be independent "without agency of our government…in the natural flow of events, the spontaneous working of principles." Eventually, once a railroad connected the Atlantic and Pacific, maybe California would join the Union. But why force it prematurely? Was it really so important for the far West to be governed from the East? Maybe America's real manifest destiny was to break apart, to disunite. The editorial welcomed North America's division into separate nations, at least temporarily, as long as those nations were ruled by English-speaking whites.

To many other expansionists, however, this was the nightmare scenario. Having pledged to serve only a single term, Polk decided he had to act quickly to keep the continent from breaking into smaller republics. Yet the war he launched to ensure continental unity only made the Union's existing divisions worse and led to the very partition he had sought to avoid.

American settlers in California saw the annexation of Texas as a signal to try the same thing. As one new arrival put it, they were eager to "see the repetition of Texas history in this country."

By 1845, California was in upheaval. Early that year, locals again expelled the Mexican governor. European powers took note. Eager to keep California out of American hands, Mexico's president offered to mortgage the province to Britain in exchange for a generous loan. A French diplomat who traveled widely in California reported to Paris that it could be taken by "whatever nation" bothered to send a ship and a few hundred men. Anything seemed possible, and a revolution likely, in a land already independent in all but name.

Yet California remained split between its independence-minded north and the more conservative south. One San Diego businessman, writing to the U.S. consul in Monterey, quoted Scripture to describe the regional divisions: "A house divided against itself cannot stand."

As civil war broke out, American settlers feared they would be blamed for the chaos and ordered to leave. In a divided land falling into disorder, immigrants on the margins of society were willing to do anything to secure a sanctuary. For the outnumbered Americans, armed insurrection, historian Allan Nevins wrote, seemed "their only defense from expulsion, their sole hope for a secure prosperity."

In the spring of 1846, the charismatic explorer John C. Frémont arrived in California at the head of a scientific expedition that, to nervous officials, looked suspiciously like an army. They ordered him to leave. Frémont marched north toward Oregon, then suddenly turned back south. In June, with Frémont's support, twenty-four American settlers seized the Mexican barracks in Sonoma, north of San Francisco, and lowered the national tricolor flag. In its place they raised a white cotton cloth with a single star (inspired by Texas) and a rough-drawn grizzly bear, the words CALIFORNIA REPUBLIC crudely painted below. Then they read a declaration of independence and danced a celebratory fandango.

The "Bear Flag Republic" comprised a single town and boasted the allegiance of very few people. It didn't last long. Three weeks later, a U.S. naval squadron appeared off the coast. The Bear Flag came down. California now belonged to the United States.

Like other once-independent states—Vermont, Texas, Hawaii— California celebrates its brief taste of sovereignty as something of a golden age. Fond memories of the 1846 revolt continue to shape its identity. In 1911, the legislature adopted a version of the Bear Flag as the official state banner, complete with the CALIFORNIA REPUBLIC inscription. For a century, it was a harmless flourish, a historical oddity, but recently the flag has seemed like something more serious—a threat that California, once independent, may soon be so again.

Western separatism was growing outside California as well. In 1845, a federal agent in Oregon reported that settlers, impatient to secure land titles, were embracing independence. A recent outbreak of "disaffection" for the Union might be "but the beginnings" of a broader revolt.

Many Americans continued to think the United States shouldn't even try to assert sovereignty over the isolated region. A New Orleans paper welcomed the declaration of "an empire of Federal Republican States along the Pacific Coast." Whigs who had opposed Texas felt annexing Oregon as well would make the already-bloated Union too big for its own good. Horace Greeley's *New York Tribune* called for America to join Europe in recognizing a "Republic of Oregon and California." The forbidding mountains alone made annexation impractical, Greeley noted; "Cannot a nation sometimes realize that it has territory enough?"

Even Daniel Webster, famed spokesman for an indissoluble Union, admired the "great Pacific Republic" rising on the West Coast. Speaking at a Whig rally in Boston, Webster said it made no sense for Britain and the United States to control a land so distant from both. Far better to establish "a nation where our children may go for a residence, separating themselves from the Government, and forming an integral part of a new government…in the most healthful, fertile, and desirable portion of the globe." Perhaps liberty was not so inseparable from union after all.

In 1846, after much saber-rattling, Polk reached an agreement with Britain to partition the Oregon territory at the forty-ninth parallel. The deal split Polk's party. Oregon had never seemed to offer fertile territory for slavery, so most Southern Democrats didn't care how much of it joined the United States. Northerners, however, felt betrayed by the administration's refusal to follow their rallying cry of "Fifty-four forty or fight"—they wanted a border four hundred miles north. Within months, Northern Democrats' discontent would expose the fragility of a Union that, by agreeing not to criticize slavery, the Northerners had done more than any other group to hold together.

In Oregon, the response was largely positive. "We can look forward now with faith and congratulate one another that we are again citizens of the United States," one paper cheered. But separatism in the Pacific Northwest didn't entirely disappear.

Seizing San Francisco Bay was a top priority of his, Polk told an adviser shortly after taking office in March 1845. The war that erupted a year later on the banks of the Rio Grande had little to do with Texas—Mexico had given up trying to take back its lost territory—and everything to do with Polk's fixation on California and Mexico's refusal to sell it.

In early 1846, Polk ordered General Zachary Taylor to lead his army from the Rio Nueces (which Mexico considered the border) to the Rio Grande (which Texas did), one hundred miles south. Mexican troops ambushed an American detachment, killing eleven soldiers. "Hostilities may now be considered as commenced," Taylor laconically reported to Washington, as if he had already fulfilled his duty by seeing that the war got started. That's what it looked like on the ground. "We have not one particle of right to be here," a young officer wrote in his diary. "It looks as if the government sent a small force on purpose to bring on a war, so as to have a pretext for taking California and as much of this country as it chooses."

Following a rushed, half-hour debate, the time limit strictly enforced by Polk-friendly partisans, Congress resolved that by Mexico's own actions, a state of war existed between the two countries. The formulation meant that an actual declaration of war wouldn't be necessary—a precedent that Whig opponents warned would prove dangerous. Fourteen dissenters voted against the resolution, all of them Whigs, John Quincy Adams among them.

After three decades of relative peace, young glory-seekers, especially from the South and West, rushed to join the fight. States quickly filled their quotas. Early victories fueled calls for the conquest and subsequent absorption into the Union not only of the Texas borderlands and California but of Mexico in its entirety.

In other parts of the country, the war provoked opposition only slightly less virulent than the War of 1812 had. Many Whigs considered the deliberate provocation of Mexico "the great political and moral crime of the period." Polk's willingness to mislead Americans into war was "the grossest act of usurpation and aggression by the President

known to the history of the country." When Polk used a message to
Congress to denounce opponents of the war as providing "aid and
comfort" to the enemy—the same words used to define treason in the
Constitution—Daniel King of Massachusetts shot back, "If an earnest
desire to save my country from ruin and disgrace be treason, then I am
a traitor!"

While conservative Whigs tried to muzzle the critics, others defied
the taboo. One congressman applauded Mexico's "manly resistance" to
the American onslaught, while Joshua Giddings of Ohio, an antislavery
leader, decried the "criminal murder...of an unoffending people."
Abraham Lincoln, a freshman Illinois congressman, introduced his
famous "spot resolutions" demanding the administration cite the exact
location where the first engagement with the enemy occurred, knowing it was on Mexican soil.

Furious that annexing Texas had led, as they had predicted, to a
wasteful proslavery war, some Northerners raised the prospect of
breaking up a Union degraded beyond recognition. The poet James
Russell Lowell based his popular Hosea Biglow character on rustic New
Englanders he met at abolition meetings. The drawling, commonsense
Biglow objected to the war and even endorsed disunion:

> *Man hed oughter put asunder*
> *Them that God hez nowise jined;*
> *And I shouldn't gretly wonder*
> *Ef there's thousan's o' my mind.*

Indeed there were. To the Massachusetts legislature, William Lloyd
Garrison delivered petitions from forty-three towns, listing some 2,834
names, calling for secession from the Union.

On a summer day in Concord, Massachusetts, a local eccentric left
his lakeside cabin for a walk to the cobbler's shop. En route, the con-
stable arrested him for overdue taxes. Henry David Thoreau's mother
and sister subscribed to Garrison's *Liberator;* he was familiar with the
doctrine of disunion. Thoreau took the idea to heart. In his essay about
the night he spent in the Concord jail, Thoreau described civil disobedience as a form of personal secession. "Some are petitioning the State
to dissolve the Union," he observed. "Why do they not dissolve it

themselves—the union between themselves and the State—and refuse to pay their quota into the treasury?"

Like Garrison, Thoreau thought the country could preserve either slavery or the Union, but not both. Indeed, emancipation was necessary even if it meant partition. "This people must cease to hold slaves, and to make war on Mexico," he wrote, "though it cost them their existence as a people."

On a humid night in August 1846, three months into the war, a portly Pennsylvania freshman took to the floor of the House of Representatives. A staunch Democrat, loyal to the Union, David Wilmot was about to become the agent of his party's schism and his country's unraveling.

He and other Northern Democrats felt alienated by the Southern tilt of Polk's administration, which had betrayed them on the Oregon issue, hurt manufacturers by lowering tariffs to appease the Carolinians, and failed to appoint enough supporters of their champion Martin Van Buren to federal office. Their pride in belonging to a unified national party was injured by the realization that it really favored the interests of only one section. "The conviction is forced upon [us]," an Albany Democrat lamented, "that the South is incapable of keeping faith with the North, no matter how sacred the obligation."

The group's demand was simple: no slavery in any new territory acquired after the war. That would mollify the anti-war critics in the free states who worried that conquests of Mexican land would tilt the balance of power further toward the South. It would therefore not only help these endangered Northern Democrats win reelection (by neutralizing Whig criticisms of the war as a proslavery crusade), but also help the country avoid another outbreak of sectional strife.

Instead, Wilmot's proposal immediately divided both Washington politicians and the country. As James Tallmadge's 1819 amendment to the Missouri statehood bill had opened the question of whether slavery would be allowed in states carved from the Louisiana Purchase, Wilmot's bill did the same for lands taken from Mexico. The issue was "fraught with incalculable evil," Polk's vice president wrote. "As if by magic," a Boston paper said, Wilmot "brought to a head the great question which is about to divide the American people." Disunion again seemed more than possible. "I try to avert my eye from such a prospect," a Massachusetts Whig confessed in Congress, "but is it not looming up in the mist—dark and portentous?"

Days later, the House passed the Wilmot Proviso on a strictly sectional vote, winning support from almost every Northern Democrat. Cross-regional party alliances broke down in favor of purely geographical allegiances. The proposal was blocked in the Senate, however, thanks to the two extra votes that annexing Texas had given the South. As Congress adjourned, the issue remained unresolved.

During the recess, every Northern legislature passed resolutions endorsing the proviso. Southerners, by contrast, were appalled. If they couldn't bring slaves to the new lands, it would have been better if the war hadn't been fought at all. Wilmot's proposal, one Virginian observed, showed that abolition was no longer limited to the "insane ravings of associated fanatics" but backed by a majority in Congress. A ban on slavery's westward expansion offered a taste of what was to come—the prohibition of slavery in the South itself. Restricting slavery in the national domain, a North Carolina paper insisted, would "destroy the great principle of equality between the States...and ultimately break up the Confederacy itself." If the Wilmot Proviso became law, the slave states would secede. "Let us be done with compromises," a fired-up Calhoun declared in the Senate. "Let us go back and stand upon the Constitution!"

Perhaps because they shared a proslavery reading of the Constitution, William Lloyd Garrison easily drilled to the core of Calhoun's strategy. "Slave states are to be created indefinitely," he said, summing up the South's latest demand. "On this condition alone is the Union to be maintained. Mark that, ye idolaters of the Union!"

The 1848 Treaty of Guadalupe-Hidalgo ceded what's today California, Nevada, Utah, New Mexico, and Arizona, as well as parts of Colorado and Wyoming, for only fifteen million dollars—a paltry, humiliating price for half of Mexico's territory. Americans tend to forget that a huge part of their domain once belonged to Mexico, but Mexicans have not. Seventy-five years later, revolutionaries in the still-hazy borderlands launched an insurrection to get it back. In the late 1960s, Chicano activists in the Southwest dreamed of independence. Even today, many Mexicans consider the treaty null and void. Xenophobes in the United States, meanwhile, depict northbound migration as a covert scheme aimed at *reconquista,* betraying insecurity about the integrity of a Union bound less by affection than force. After all these years, the artificial border imposed in 1848 remains so unstable it has to be reinforced by a wall.

The land grab immediately heightened the stakes of the sectional dispute. What was to be done with the hundreds of thousands of square miles of mountains, plains, deserts, and coast? Which parts would enter the Union as states, and which would linger in territorial purgatory? Most controversially, where, if anywhere, would slavery be legal? As one Whig observed, "The people of the Union are now involved in a great and overshadowing issue more pregnant for more good or evil in its vast results than any that ever agitated this continent."

Faced with these dilemmas, Congress stalemated. In March 1849, the session ended in loud arguments and drunken fistfights. Buckskin-clad Sam Houston, whittling pine sticks at his desk, declared the spectacle more low-down shameful than anything he had seen on the frontier. "Never in my life have I felt more sorely oppressed with doubt and despondency, or considered the Union more in danger," one Mississippian said.

As Northern legislatures demanded Wilmot's ban on slavery, Southern states vowed resistance to any prohibition. If the proviso went into effect, Virginia's governor warned, "then indeed the day of compromise will have passed, and the dissolution of our great and glorious Union will become necessary and inevitable." His counterpart in South Carolina embarked on a tour of military installations throughout the state as if readying the troops for civil war.

Some Southerners called for a convention of the slave states. As New England had at Hartford in 1814, it was time for the South to issue a joint ultimatum. The idea won support among radicals ready for independence and moderates who hoped the mere threat would intimidate the North. For an aging, ailing Calhoun, a Southern convention would give slave owners one last chance for "saving the Union; or if that should fail, of certainly saving ourselves."

On March 5, 1849, James Polk and Zachary Taylor, the outgoing and incoming presidents, Democrat and Whig, respectively, rode to the latter's inauguration, accompanied by a journalist and the Speaker of the

House. Icy rain lashed the carriage. Someone mentioned the controversy over the Western territories. That night, a still-astonished Polk
recalled in his diary Taylor's opinion that "California and Oregon were
too distant to become members of the Union, that it would be better
for them to be an independent government."

This was horrifying to Polk, for whom bringing California into the
Union had been a priority. Everything had gone to plan. America reached
from sea to sea. The continent was finally, truly united. Now his naive,
unschooled successor—an "illiterate frontier colonel," according to Daniel Webster—shrugged at the prospect of it all slipping away. "These are
alarming opinions to be entertained by the President of the United States,"
Polk reflected. The only possible excuse was that Taylor's words had not
been "well considered." But Taylor wasn't the only one who held those
alarming opinions. They were rapidly taking hold in California itself.

Just over a year had passed since the chance sighting of a few shiny
specks in the Sierra foothills. The place had exploded almost overnight
from scattered, ramshackle settlements into what looked like the beginnings of a mighty, if rambunctious nation. Without a government
under American rule, the new arrivals only heightened the anarchy
and confusion. The U.S. military, nominally in control after the war,
struggled to keep troops from deserting to seek their fortunes; those
who remained alienated the population by failing to impose order. A
local journalist observed in the soldiers "an unparalleled degree of stupidity as to what ought to be done."

Some residents spoke of reestablishing the Bear Flag Republic, or
at least drawing up a constitution; it could lead to statehood or independence, depending on how it was received in Washington. Aware of
the distant rumblings, Polk had begged Californians "to live peaceably
and quietly" until Congress figured out what to do with them.

How long that would take, nobody could say. Tired of waiting, the
Californians set up their own provisional government. At a convention
in Monterey, they drafted a constitution. It prohibited slavery, widely
seen as an unfair advantage in the hills. One of the government's first
acts was to draw up an "Appeal to the American People," asking them
to pressure Congress to grant California statehood. If Congress refused,
the legislators warned, they would send a follow-up message—"a simple request contained in three words: *'Let us alone.'*"

*   *   *

After a grueling trek across the Rockies, Brigham Young and his followers arrived at Salt Lake in the summer of 1847, while war with
Mexico—which still controlled the region—raged. The location was
isolated and inhospitable, perfect for Young's purposes. He wanted the
new Mormon community to be separate, self-sufficient. "The Kingdom
of God," he told the refugees, "cannot rise independent of the gentile
nations, until we produce, manufacture, and make every article of use,
convenience, or necessity among our own people."

Perhaps because the Mormons had finally left the United States,
their relations with the federal government improved. At the outset of
the war with Mexico, Young struck a deal with Polk to raise a battalion
of troops to march into California and reinforce Frémont's men. Publicly, Young supported both the war and the Union.

In private, he and other Mormons said something else. The Wilmot
controversy convinced a Young adviser that "death and dissolution" would
soon come for the United States. After its fall, the Saints would rule; "Gods
will be done, and let him reign whose right it is." Believing the Union
would soon be "broken up and divided into factions," another suggested
the Mormons sign a separate peace with Mexico to secure an outlet on the
Pacific. Still hoping for independence, Young studied maps of the unsettled, war-torn West, measuring the extent of their kingdom to come.

Instead, the treaty with Mexico returned the Saints to the nation
they had tried to escape. To make the best of things, Mormon leaders
drew up a constitution for a vast, semi-autonomous state called Deseret
that took in all of the present-day Southwest, including Los Angeles and
San Diego. An audacious proposal from an unpopular group, the constitution stood little chance of passage in Congress. Yet in staking yet
another claim on the newly acquired territories, the proposal helped
bring about the conflagration that Young and his followers hoped would
end with the Kingdom of God rising to redeem a wicked world.

The Civil War might have begun in Santa Fe in 1850 rather than in
Charleston in 1861. Nowhere did fighting between American citizens
come closer to breaking out than on the frontier between Texas and
New Mexico, inhabited largely by Spanish-speaking villagers and Pueblo
Indians, along with a few English-speaking traders. For years, Texans

had longed to control the trade in one of the oldest European towns on the continent. Deeming the Rio Grande, from source to mouth, the western border of their independent republic, Texans had tried three times to pry Santa Fe from Mexico.

Three times they had failed. New Mexicans had no interest in joining Texas, not least because they didn't want to legalize slavery. After the 1848 treaty put them under American control, Santa Fe's inhabitants called on the United States to protect them from Texas as Mexico had before the war. With federal troops occupying the town, a new invasion by Texas could easily devolve into civil war.

In Texas, the tone quickly turned menacing. Peter Hansborough Bell, an aggressive former Texas Ranger, won the gubernatorial election of 1849 by advocating a fourth march on Santa Fe. Gun-toting residents eagerly offered to join the expedition. Austin's *State Gazette* argued that while Texan patriotism had once meant supporting annexation by the Union, it might soon mean supporting secession. If the federal government blocked Texas from incorporating Santa Fe, the "banner of the Lone Star shall again be unfurled...and those who were foremost to cry aloud for annexation, will be foremost to sever the country from a Union that embraces but to crush and destroy."

Less than five years after Texas had entered the Union, many of the new state's citizens already thought that giving up their independence had been a terrible mistake.

In almost every region, conflicts over slavery and land threatened to plunge the country into chaos. The national Baptist and Methodist Churches split into Northern and Southern associations—a sure sign, to many, of a coming political schism. "No one can say how soon we may be involved in the dangers & calamities of disunion," a Philadelphia diarist wrote in 1849. In Washington, a new session of Congress began. Some members feared, and others hoped, that if they failed to come up with a solution to the impasse, the national legislature would be meeting for the last time.

PART III

THE EARTHQUAKE COMES

Most Americans associate secession solely with the South and the slavery-serving Confederacy. That lets the rest of the country off the hook, as it attributes the impulse to break up a divided, deadlocked Union to a single movement in a single region at a single time, freeing other sections that dabbled with disunionism—New England, the Midwest, the Pacific Coast—of any blame (or depriving them of credit) for bringing on the fatal fracture. The loose-fitting confederation remained, as it had been from the founding, full of contradictions, an ungainly agglomeration of incompatible parts. Behind the oft-told tale of monolithic Northern nationalism and Southern sectionalism is a more complicated reality, a richer tapestry of stories and characters, with messier morals to teach us today.

CHAPTER 8

Wide Awake

If we have suffered our love for the Union to be abused...we have discerned that great error at last.

—WILLIAM SEWARD, 1856

MOST AMERICANS ARE FAMILIAR, or once were, with the land-marks on the road to the Civil War. The Compromise of 1850, Henry Clay's final difference-splitting hurrah, admitted California as a free state, settled the Texas–New Mexico border dispute, passed a stringent fugitive-slave law, and banned the slave trade in the federal capital. The Kansas-Nebraska Act of 1854 repealed the Missouri Compromise by opening the rest of the Louisiana Purchase to slavery if settlers on the ground so chose. A headlong rush into the territories sparked "Bleed-ing Kansas," a vicious proxy war between North and South. Torn over slavery, the Whig Party "died of compromises," leaving an opening for a new Republican Party pledged to ban slavery from all territories. The Supreme Court's 1857 *Dred Scott* decision prohibited such restrictions and barred blacks from American citizenship. John Brown's 1859 raid on the federal arsenal at Harpers Ferry, an attempt to ignite a slave rebellion, failed spectacularly, though his truth went marching on.

These boldface glossary terms offer a convenient way to understand the *how* of the descent into bloody conflict and a basis for still-raging debates about the *why*. Yet most accounts of the 1850s tell only half the story. Knowing how the decade ended—with South Carolina's seces-sion from the Union and the assault on Fort Sumter—historians usu-ally focus on the South's growing self-consciousness, as though it had always been inevitable that if war broke out, the slave states would pull the trigger.

The Tragic Prelude, John Steuart Curry's 1937 mural at the Kansas State Capitol, shows John Brown heralding the approaching conflict. (*Kansas Historical Society*)

Rather than a tale of Southern extremists fed up with federal overreach, the coming of the Civil War can be told as the story of a *Northern* resistance movement, of Northern citizens weighing the meaning of hand-me-down loyalties, questioning whether the Union was still worth preserving at any price the South chose to name. In the free states, a new generation, sensing the future slipping from their grasp, pushed for a thorough overhaul—a political revolution.

This doesn't absolve Southern slave owners of full responsibility for taking the country over the brink and for the catastrophic suffering that followed. But it wasn't the South alone that brought the country to that brink. The slave owners were responding to a more general fragility in the Union, one exposed and exacerbated by Northern radicals. Because the antislavery movement openly rejected the slave owners' stated reason for entering the Union in the first place (to protect their property in the form of men, women, and children), Southerners saw Northerners as the real disunionists. And in a sense, they were right.

After a remarkably brief period of chaotic calculation, white Southerners went from rallying around the flag ("So perish all such enemies of Virginia! All such enemies of the Union!" cried a spectator at John Brown's execution) to deciding they had to rip up the Constitution. The South's secession has been called a "pre-emptive counter-revolution." The real revolution was in the North.

1. The State Rights of the North

Crammed into the 1850 bargain as a sweetener for Southerners, the Fugitive Slave Act was, for slave owners, a win-win. Either it would convince restless slaves there was no freedom to be found stealing away in the night and so end the slow siphoning off of valuable property, or it would provoke popular resistance in the free states that would render the law unenforceable, giving the South an answer to its latest, and last, ultimatum.

Unnecessarily burdensome, gratuitously cruel, the new law seemed designed to fail. With low evidentiary standards, a ban on testimony from alleged runaways, and a prohibition on jury trials, the law offered no protection against cases of mistaken identity or outright fraud. Payment for the federal commissioner appointed to hear each case was twice as high if he returned the accused to slavery—a bribe to hide kidnapping under the cloak of law.

Most galling to Northerners, the law held every American responsible for assisting in the capture of runaways—anyone who refused faced jail time. Ratting out refugees, even hunting them down, became a core responsibility of citizenship, a test of fidelity to the Union and its laws. Residents of the free states could no longer avoid facing up to their complicity.

A massive extension of federal power, the law betrayed the hollowness of Southern talk about states' rights. The federal act preempted Northern states' "personal-liberty laws," which granted accused runaways the right to a jury trial and other legal protections. For slavery's sake, Southerners dropped all pretense of caring about state sovereignty and local control. It was no time for constitutional niceties.

Northerners were equally opportunistic in response. Once enthralled by Daniel Webster's soaring odes to the glorious Union, many now took up the nullification doctrines he had denounced. After the fugitive-slave bill passed Congress, Northern states enacted even stronger personal-liberty laws, directly challenging the new statute. Vermont's legislature extended the right of habeas corpus to accused runaways, essentially voiding the law in the state. Northern juries refused to convict citizens of disobeying the act. While a pro-Southern paper in Washington denounced the North's embrace of "Nullification and

Disunion," New England poet John Greenleaf Whittier proudly called himself a "nullifier."

The epicenter of the revolt, Boston buzzed as it had in the early days of the Revolution. The state's antislavery society, its ranks swelling with converts, demanded the law be "denounced, resisted, disobeyed," and "its enforcement on Massachusetts soil...rendered impossible." Lookouts watched for slave hunters. In 1851, Shadrach Minkins, an escapee waiting tables in a restaurant, was hauled before a federal commissioner, his apron still around his waist. Activists seized the prisoner and shuffled him out of the room. Theodore Parker, an abolitionist, hailed "the most noble deed done in Boston since the destruction of the tea." Eight men stood trial for the raid; none was convicted.

Similar incidents occurred in Philadelphia and Syracuse, Cincinnati and Detroit, Sandusky and Wilkes-Barre. Headlines blared warnings of civil war. Maryland's governor informed Washington that his state "would not remain *one day* in the confederacy" if the government proved unwilling or unable to enforce its own laws.

Designed to destroy the antislavery movement, the Fugitive Slave Act instead breathed new life into it. Northerners resented Southern intimidation and vowed to counter it. "We have had enough of this miserable dictation and menace," announced the *National Era,* an abolitionist paper. "It is the discipline of the plantation, and may do for slaves, but not freemen." Then, speaking for all Northerners, the paper issued the ultimate threat: "A few more measures so atrocious as the Fugitive Slave Bill would turn their love of the Union into hate."

To be sure, most Northerners remained willing to submit to Southern demands. Yet with every passing year, disunionism moved a little closer to the center from the fringe. Ralph Waldo Emerson had long avoided "odious and hurtful" issues and political movements, especially abolition, which he considered the province of the unthinking and unwashed. But the fugitive-slave bill repulsed him. It was hard to imagine, he wrote in his journal, that such a "filthy enactment was made in the nineteenth century, by people who could read and write." He resolved to disobey the law and hoped it would be nullified in the state of Massachusetts. "The Union is at an end as soon as an immoral law is enacted," Emerson proclaimed.

In 1854, a nineteen-year-old Virginia-born runaway named Anthony

Burns was arrested in Boston. Even established politicians and business-men joined the fight to free him. As the wealthy industrialist Amos Law-rence observed, "We went to bed one night old-fashioned, conservative, Compromise Union Whigs and waked up stark mad Abolitionists."

Those who were already stark-mad abolitionists had long been wait-ing for this moment. "Fellow-subjects of Virginia!" Theodore Parker saluted a packed crowd at Faneuil Hall. He called on them to defend "personal liberty and the State Rights of the North." Led by a fiery young preacher from Worcester named Thomas Wentworth Higgin-son, a mob stormed the courthouse where Burns was being held. The attempt to free him failed; a guard died in the melee. Hundreds of federal troops marched Burns to the wharves as fifty thousand grim-faced spectators shouted, "Shame! Shame!"

"The day was brilliant," Parker recalled soon after. "There was not a cloud; all about Boston there was a ring of happy, summer loveliness; the green beauty of June; the grass, the trees, the heaven, the light; and Boston itself was the theatre of incipient civil war!"

In Washington, the mood was dark. Early that year, Stephen Douglas, a pudgy, ambitious Democratic senator from Illinois, had proposed to erase the line laid down thirty years earlier by the Missouri Compromise, the legislation stating that north of 36°30′, there would be no slavery in the former Louisiana Territory, while south of it, there would be. Douglas wanted to create two new territorial governments, Kansas and Nebraska, north of the line. But slavery would not automatically be banned there, as the pact required; in Douglas's bill, "popular sovereignty"—votes by white men on the ground—would determine the issue. Conceivably, slav-ery could spread all the way to the Canadian border.

Douglas hoped his bill would erase the last vestige of disharmony from the maps of the expanding Union. Yet, as with so many efforts to end division, it did exactly the opposite. Repealing the Missouri Com-promise was "a gross violation of a sacred pledge," six antislavery Dem-ocrats from Ohio, New York, and Massachusetts announced in a broadside attack. "The Union was formed to establish justice and secure the blessings of liberty," they observed. "When it fails to accom-plish these ends it will be worthless, and when it becomes worthless it cannot long endure."

Months of agitation followed. Douglas quipped that he could have traveled home to Chicago by the light of his own effigies. Northern conservatives felt especially betrayed. They had assumed, and argued to their constituents, that if the North conceded a little for the sake of unity (by obeying the fugitive-slave law, for instance), the South would return the favor. The Kansas-Nebraska Act revealed that that trust had been woefully misplaced. Drawing support from farmers, laborers, and businessmen in New England and the Midwest, a coalition of alienated Whigs, dejected Democrats, and old-school abolitionists vowed never to allow another slave state into the Union. The faction went by different names, including "the anti-Nebraska interest" and "the Fusion ticket." Soon, members of a few local circles began calling themselves Republicans, an homage to Jefferson's old party. The name caught on, and a new party was born.

Its earliest members weren't crusaders for an indissoluble Union but uncompromising advocates of the rights of the sovereign states. In addition to limiting slavery's expansion, one tenet that united many Republicans was the need to nullify the Fugitive Slave Act. If the slave states wouldn't honor old agreements like the Missouri Compromise, why should the free states honor newer ones? In 1855, William Seward, an antislavery senator from New York and an architect of the Republican coalition, denounced the detestable law for its "invasions of State rights."

After the passage of the Kansas-Nebraska Act, resistance to aiding the return of runaways became more widespread, and Northern politics more extreme. Even in the American heartland, the supposedly solid core of the Union, separatism and states' rights gained support.

Wisconsin took the place of South Carolina as the leading challenger to federal law. In 1854, federal marshals in Racine entered the cabin of a black man named Joshua Glover, busy playing cards with friends. They bludgeoned Glover, put him in chains, and hauled him to Milwaukee to await transport to the South. The next day, a local editor named Sherman Booth, a Connecticut-born, Yale-educated abolitionist, rallied a crowd of five thousand; the mob broke down the jailhouse door and freed Glover. As he made his way through Milwaukee's crowded streets, Glover held up his manacled hands and shouted, "Glory, hallelujah!" (He eventually found refuge in Canada.) Federal officers arrested Booth for aiding Glover's escape, but Wisconsin's high court freed him, deeming the "wicked and cruel" fugitive law a violation of state sovereignty. Booth, whose lawyer boasted that his arguments had been influenced "by the reasoning of Mr. Calhoun," became a hero in the North.

When the federal government appealed to the U.S. Supreme Court, Wisconsin's justices refused to share their records of the case. In 1859, the Supreme Court ruled Booth's arrest lawful, adding that state judges had no power to assess the constitutionality of federal statutes. Carl Schurz, a leader of Wisconsin's community of German émigrés, told a Milwaukee audience that the Constitution was "not worth the paper it is printed on, if the authority to construe it is exclusively and absolutely vested in the central government....People of Wisconsin, we have come to a point where it is loyalty to resist, and treason to submit."

Years later, Schurz, by then a former Union general, left the speech out of his collected works. At the time, however, nullification and states' rights were popular among the Northern public. Horace Greeley's *New York Tribune,* celebrating the North's willingness to take "lessons in Southern jurisprudence," expected a sort of competition to break out among the free states until "all have reached the goal of State independence."

Other states vied with Wisconsin for the title of most defiant. In Ohio, when U.S. marshals arrested abolitionists for subverting the Fugitive Slave Act, the marshals themselves were arrested by state authorities. As in Wisconsin, state and federal courts wrangled over the case. Ohio Republicans called for preserving "the rights of the several States as independent governments." Echoing Calhoun's famous toast a quarter of a century earlier, one Republican said the party's motto should be "Liberty first and Union afterwards." Ohio senator Benjamin Wade argued that "in the last resort" it was up to any state to determine "whether she shall stand on her reserved rights." With Ohio seemingly on the verge of revolution, a warship sailed for Cleveland to intimidate the state into submission.

Even Northerners hostile to abolitionism began to doubt the foundations of the political order. Their desire to divorce the South had nothing to do with ending slavery; they wanted only to block its expansion to the Western territories, a position that was more about political economy and sectional power than moral qualms over forced servitude. In the *New York Tribune,* correspondent James S. Pike wrote that he would rather belong to a "peace-loving, art-developing, labor-honoring, God-fearing confederacy of twenty millions of Freemen, rather than to a filibustering, war-making, conquest-seeking, slavery-extending union of thirty millions, one-sixth of them slaves."

In Portland, Maine, congressman Nathaniel P. Banks, who would soon be elected the first Republican Speaker of the House, told a crowd it might become necessary to "let the Union slide." As with the similar comment from Wisconsin's Carl Schurz, the words later haunted Banks, but they were wildly cheered by his audience and spoke the feelings of his constituents. Benjamin Brown French, a former New Hampshire Democrat and prominent Republican convert, endorsed Banks's sentiment in acerbic lines of verse:

> *"Let it slide" then — this great Union —*
> *Pronounce the compact dead —*
> *With the South no more communion*
> *If slavery still must spread!*
> *There's land, thank God, for Freedom*
> *North of Potomac's tide —*
> *Let the South keep slaves & breed 'em —*
> *But "let the Union slide"*

French, Pike, and others didn't care much about ending bondage. They saw disunion as a chance to get rid of slaves and slave owners alike.

For abolitionists, however, free-state separatism had always been much more — a matter of principle and a practical plan to end slavery everywhere. Now, with Northern discontent rising, William Lloyd Garrison seized the moment to make a forceful statement. On July 4, 1854, six hundred Massachusetts abolitionists gathered in a pond-side grove outside Boston for their annual picnic. An American flag, framed in mournful black, hung upside down over the stage. The attendees were still grieving over the Anthony Burns rendition. Wendell Phillips and Sojourner Truth spoke, then Henry David Thoreau. It was the abolitionists' duty, he said, to "be men first, and Americans only at a late and convenient hour." Garrison then walked onto the stage and placed a stack of papers on a stool beside him. One by one, he lifted them and set them alight — the Fugitive Slave Act, documents from the Burns case. After holding a match to each, he repeated, "And let all the people, say, 'Amen.'" Finally, he picked up a copy of the Constitution. "So perish all compromises with tyranny!" Garrison declared. The paper burst into flames. The crowd roared its approval and broke out in a hymn.

North and South squared off over the West the way European colonial powers would later vie to carve up Africa and Asia. (In neither case, of course, was any regard given to those indigenous nations already occupying the land.) Whether or not slavery spread depended on which section sent more people and guns. Few whites lived in Kansas in early 1854; a year later, there were more than ten thousand. As William Seward told Southerners, "God give the victory to the side which is stronger in numbers as it is in right."

Stronger in numbers and well-organized, free-staters felt confident about their prospects for victory in a fair contest, but Southerners were leaving nothing to chance. Missouri slave owners, anxious to see neighboring Kansas become a slave state, watched nervously as well-organized New Englanders arrived by the hundreds. Kansas was turning into "the unwilling receptacle of the filth, scum, and offscourings of the East," one Missourian wrote. Even as the self-styled "Pro-Slavery Party" in Kansas denounced Northern "Abolitionism and Disunionism," Southern governors warned that the Union would end if Kansas banned slavery.

Only deceit, fraud, and violence could overcome the North's population advantage, so deceit, fraud, and violence became the slave owners' tools. After Missourians swarmed across the border to vote in the first territorial elections, the proslavery legislature expelled the few free-staters who had won seats and outlawed all criticism of slavery. Northerners were appalled. "If Ohio had done to Kentucky, what Missouri has done to Kansas," one minister noted, "the South would have risen as one." The *New York Times* declared the South's crimes in Kansas worse than Britain's abuses eighty years earlier. "If the settlers in Kansas do not resist the enforcement of such laws *to the last extremity*," the paper declared, "they are unworthy of their name and descent."

Sympathizers back east sent rifles in boxes labeled DRY GOODS and BOOKS. "Give us the weapons," a free-state Kansan wrote to his Boston benefactors, "and every man from the North will be a soldier and die in his tracks if necessary...even should it set the Union in a blaze."

Rival governments forced settlers to choose sides. In May 1856, hundreds of armed Missourians marched on the free-staters' provisional capital in the town of Lawrence. They sank a printing press in the Kansas River and destroyed the headquarters of the local abolition society. Over its ruins they raised a crude flag, with *Southern Rights* on one side and *South Carolina* on the other. Only one person died in the so-called Sack of Lawrence, as antislavery publicists called it. Even so, newspapers announced "Civil War in Kansas." In retaliation, a mysterious old man led a handful of free-state followers, including four of his sons, to a cluster of cabins on Pottawatomie Creek, where they hacked to death five proslavery settlers. The attack unleashed rounds of ambushes, robberies, all-out battles, and murder—a proxy war on the plains. Two hundred people lost their lives in the deadliest American-on-American fighting since the Revolution.

Then the violence spread to Congress itself. A day after the Lawrence raid, South Carolina congressman Preston Brooks pummeled Massachusetts senator Charles Sumner with his gold-tipped cane— revenge for a speech Sumner had given in which he not so subtly shamed Southern masters for raping their female slaves. Along with the violence in Kansas, the brutality in Congress heightened the stakes in the sectional struggle.

In Boston, news of the assault on Sumner "produced an excitement in the public mind deeper and more dangerous than I have ever witnessed," one politico observed. "Has it come to this," asked poet and editor William Cullen Bryant, "that we must speak with bated breath in the presence of our Southern masters?" If Northern men weren't safe in Congress, what purpose did the Union serve? "Suppose we raise soldiers in Massachusetts," Ralph Waldo Emerson mused in his journal, "suppose we propose a Northern Union." At one protest meeting, Emerson said he was "glad to see that the terror at disunion and anarchy is disappearing."

Veterans of the disunion movement welcomed the change in public opinion. "Who now needs any more persuasion on the subject?" Garrison asked.

Northern anger over the violence in Kansas and Washington propelled the Republicans into serious contention in the 1856 elections. At its first national convention, in Philadelphia, the party warned that America was "fast falling backwards toward a kingly government—towards an aristocracy founded on slavery such as the world never saw." For a presidential candidate, the Republicans turned to the conqueror of California, John C. Frémont, whose scientific and military exploits out west had earned him national fame. The time had come, as John Greenleaf Whittier put it,

> *When Good and Evil, as for final strife,*
> *Close vast and dim on Armageddon's plain.*

Though Frémont did surprisingly well—winning 33 percent of the popular vote—he lost to James Buchanan, a conventional proslavery Democrat from Pennsylvania. Warning that Frémont's election would rupture the nation, Buchanan framed the election as posing "the grand and appalling issue of Union or Disunion." Privately, however, Buchanan predicted that even if he won, "it might only be the beginning of the end." Neither side seemed willing to back down. The election proved, one observer concluded, that Northerners and Southerners were "countrymen only in name."

2. Clash of Civilizations

Most Republicans had expected to lose the 1856 contest and considered Frémont's impressive showing a "victorious defeat" for the new party. Abolitionists took the defeat harder. They wondered at mainstream Republican opinion-shapers who had argued that liberty itself depended on the Democrats' defeat but then had no plan when Buchanan won. For one Massachusetts minister, that wasn't just hypocritical. Given the millions of lives at stake, it was unconscionable. He thought it was time for a full-on campaign to break up the Union.

A dashing thirty-three-year-old poet, preacher, and calisthenics enthusiast, Thomas Wentworth Higginson would have a long career as a writer and a fighter. During the Civil War, he would serve as colonel of the first regiment of black soldiers to fight in Union blue; he wrote a classic memoir of the experience. Shortly before he went to war, he exchanged letters with an Amherst recluse who had sent him some poems and asked him, "Are you too deeply occupied to say if my Verse is alive?" (After Emily Dickinson's death, in 1886, Higginson edited her work for publication.)

In 1857, Higginson was known as an all-purpose agitator. An advocate for women's suffrage and education, he published statistics on income disparities between the sexes. Condemning "this infernal colorphobia," he led the failed attempt to free Anthony Burns and took a saber blade to the chin. He bore the scar the rest of his life. A self-proclaimed "disunion abolitionist" since the age of twenty-two — timing that coincided with the outbreak of the Mexican-American War — Higginson visited Kansas in fall 1856 to smuggle arms to the beleaguered free-staters. He hoped, as he wrote in his journal, that the clashes there would "result in the disruption of the Union, for I am sure the disease is too deep for cure without amputation."

After Buchanan's election, Higginson decided to organize a convention to promote the idea. Long a rallying cry, disunion couldn't remain an idle dream. It had become, he declared, *"a practical problem which the times are pressing on us."*

An announcement ran in Garrison's *Liberator* the day after Christmas 1856. Buchanan's victory meant "four years more of pro-slavery government, and a rapid increase in the hostility between the two sections of the Union." The fraying federation was "a hopeless attempt to unite under one government two antagonistic systems of society, which diverge more widely with every year." It was "the duty of intelligent and conscientious men...to consider the practicability, probability, and expediency, of a Separation between the Free and Slave States."

On January 15, 1857, the convention opened in Worcester's city hall with the famous Hutchinson Family Singers performing antislavery tunes. The rhetoric was fiery, the demands revolutionary. "It is time, high time, and long has been time," Reverend Samuel May Jr. of Syracuse declared, "when we should cut for ever the bloody bond which unites us to the slaveholders, slave-breeders and slave-traders of this nation." New England should secede, for it had "all the elements of a nation" and could protect its independence "against the world."

Daniel Mann, who had once been ejected from a train after standing up for black passengers, suggested America was "on the eve of a new revolution, which shall repeat the triumphs, but show the mistakes of the old; of a new confederation, which shall not only declare the self-evident truths of humanity, but abide by them and establish them, unterrified by menace, unbribed by flattery, undebased by compromises."

Reflecting on John Quincy Adams's presentation of the Haverhill petition fifteen years earlier, Garrison read the passage in Isaiah that had inspired him to call the Constitution a pact with the devil. The Union was "an insane experiment to reconcile those elements which are eternally hostile." The experiment had failed. "Men of the North!" Garrison exhorted.

> You are constantly assuring the Slave Power that you will yield up every thing to save the Union. You are infatuated! Say to the South that there is a point beyond which she cannot pass, except at the cost of the Union.... Tell her that if she passes beyond that point, she will find no Union existing. Nay, wait for no fresh outrage, but declare the Union to be now at an end!

The convention passed resolutions endorsing dissolution. Whether the crack-up came peacefully or otherwise was a *"secondary consideration."* Even if it meant violence, the Union had to go.

The Hutchinsons sang the hope-filled tune "There's a Good Time Coming," and the convention adjourned.

A fringe gathering, the Worcester convention wasn't popular even in the city where it met. A local paper called the participants a "band of mischievous fanatics, designing demagogues, and weak minded spiritualists"—and suggested South Carolina's separatists should have been invited. "The Lunatics Let Loose," announced a Boston journal. In Faneuil Hall, Caleb Cushing, a South-friendly Massachusetts Democrat, predicted the call for a Northern republic would "kindle the flames of civil and servile war." Leading Republicans repudiated the movement as politically inexpedient, counterproductive. Even Higginson's mother took issue with it in a letter to her son. He replied that he "never was more sure of being right."

Outside New England, disunion continued to gain support. A Michigan group, the Friends of Human Progress, suggested the creation of a "FREE NORTHERN CONFEDERACY, whose atmosphere should never be polluted by the breath of a slaveholder, and whose soil should never shudder under the tread of the Divine image enslaved." In Ohio, disunionists petitioned the legislature to secede. A "national disunion convention," scheduled for Cleveland that fall, was called off only after a financial panic threw the country into depression.

Despite the rhetoric, the purpose of the Worcester meeting hadn't really been to immediately sever ties with the South but to prepare the North to reject another Union-saving compromise when the next crisis came. In that sense, it succeeded. "The vast antagonistic powers are brought into collision," Thomas Wentworth Higginson had declared at the convention. "The earthquake comes—and all we disunionists say is, if it is coming, in God's name, let it come quickly!"

Weeks after the Worcester convention, the Supreme Court handed down its *Dred Scott* opinion: Not only was the plaintiff, an illiterate but spirited man born a slave in Virginia whose master had taken him to free-soil Wisconsin before it became a state, unable to sue for his freedom, since he wasn't an American citizen, but any law banning slavery in a territory was unconstitutional. The once-extreme Southern position was now the law of the land.

Northerners, radical and conservative alike, denounced the opinion and accused the court of judicial activism. "From being expounders, they have become makers of the law," one editor complained. A Wisconsin congressman called the ruling "sheer blasphemy." New York's assembly observed that with its *"inhuman, unchristian, atrocious"* decision, the court had "lost the confidence and respect of the people." An antislavery paper called the ruling "nothing more than the opinion of so many private men," with no force of law. Vermont's legislature called the judges "tyrants."

The case eroded what little remained of Northern trust in the judiciary. But it also definitively gave the lie to the South's prattle about states' rights. "They are now the centralists," noted Connecticut's Gideon Welles. "When their interests and their principles are in conflict, they take care of their interests." Several states passed resolutions recognizing the citizenship of free blacks, nullifying that part of the court's decision. Maine's legislature dismissed the ruling as "not binding, in law or in conscience, upon the government or citizens of the United States." Maine Republicans proclaimed the states "essentially independent sovereignties."

Party leaders like Abraham Lincoln and William Seward stopped short of calling for nullification, but they encouraged the widespread view that *Dred Scott* represented the latest stage in the Slave Power's long-planned coup, a conspiracy to turn the government over to "a pampered and powerful oligarchy of some 350,000 Slaveholders." The plot was "of the most treasonable character," the *New York Post* claimed, involving every branch of government and calling its very legitimacy into question.

Most alarming, the decision threatened to erase the border between North and South. If the Constitution guaranteed slave owners the right to take their "property" into any territory, why didn't that apply to the states as well? Another decision like *Dred Scott*, Lincoln argued, would repeal emancipation in the North and make slavery national. A case moving through New York courts seemed poised to do just that.

That prospect infuriated the Northern public. Frederick Douglass observed that all the measures taken to "diminish the anti-slavery agitation, have only served to increase, intensify, and embolden that agitation." The dynamic was as old as the Union—efforts to enforce unity tended to foster more division. Rather than destroying the Republican Party by declaring its platform unconstitutional, *Dred Scott* highlighted the imperative of the party taking national power, perhaps even stacking the Supreme Court. Only then would the North's political revolution be secure. "Let the next President be Republican," wrote the editors of the *Chicago Tribune*, "and 1860 will mark an era kindred with that of 1776." They little knew how true that would be.

For black Americans, *Dred Scott* wasn't just an outrage—it was a cataclysm. The federal government stopped issuing passports to them, since, according to the court, they were not citizens and never could be. Thousands fled to Canada, joining those who had already crossed to escape fugitive-slave patrols. Voting with their feet, as they couldn't with ballots, they engaged in acts of personal secession from a Union that, as its high court acknowledged, would never truly accept them.

Many more chose to stay and fight. A meeting of free blacks in Philadelphia resolved that "the only duty the colored man owes to a Constitution under which he is declared to be an inferior and degraded being, having no rights which white men are bound to respect, is to denounce and repudiate it, and to...bring it into contempt."

To William Lloyd Garrison and his followers, *Dred Scott* proved the drawbacks of engaging in politics as usual. Taking power through elections wouldn't change the Constitution, the proslavery tendencies of which the justices had accurately interpreted. They weren't surprised to hear the court declare the constitutional order racist to its core. They knew the conspiracy to exclude blacks from citizenship had origins older than the Union. Disavowing sectional compromise would free Northern whites to match their politics with their principles.

Like their white counterparts, black abolitionists were divided over disunion. Once a leading advocate of the doctrine, Frederick Douglass later became its most vociferous critic. The change is often attributed to his break from Garrison, his former mentor. Yet even after 1847, when Douglass moved from Massachusetts to upstate New York and began his own abolitionist paper—a blow to their friendship—he continued to preach disunion. Two years later, he called the Constitution "a most foul and bloody conspiracy against the rights of three millions of enslaved and imbruted men" and called for "this unholy, unrighteous Union" to be dissolved immediately. "Dissolve the Union, and [the slaves] will raise aloft their unfettered arms, and demand freedom," Douglass argued. As for the legality of disunion, Douglass said he shared "the opinion of many, that any State has a right to secede."

Soon after, however, Douglass revised these beliefs. Influenced by Gerrit Smith, a wealthy upstate New York supporter of abolitionism and other reform efforts who believed the Constitution could be used for antislavery purposes, Douglass admitted he had grown "sick and tired of arguing on the slaveholders' side of this question." The framers, he now concluded, had considered slavery "an expiring institution" and sought to make the Constitution "a permanent liberty document."

At an 1851 antislavery meeting in New York, Douglass went public with his change of heart. A startled Garrison, chairing the proceedings, exclaimed that there must be "roguery somewhere"—implying, perhaps, that Douglass had been paid to reverse his position. Douglass never forgave the remark; the two didn't speak for more than twenty years.

In rejecting disunionism, however, Douglass didn't represent all black abolitionists. In fact, he is perhaps better seen as an exception. Long after Douglass moved on, other black leaders continued to call for the North to separate from the South. Perhaps the most prominent was Robert Purvis, a free man born in Charleston, raised in Philadelphia, and educated in Massachusetts. The son of a wealthy English cotton broker and a half-Moroccan, half-Jewish mother, Purvis chose to live as a black man. He married into a family of prominent black activists in Philadelphia, supported the temperance and women's rights movements, and hid runaways in his basement. By his estimate, Purvis helped a fugitive reach freedom every day.

At an 1856 convention, Purvis declared himself a "Disunion Abolitionist." He even applauded the caning of Charles Sumner, calling the deed "timely" and "fitting," for he welcomed "any thing, in God's name, that will tend to establish a backbone for the North, in asserting and maintaining its rights, and without regard to peril or to consequences!" Purvis called *Dred Scott* "in perfect keeping with the treatment of the colored people by the American government from the beginning to this day." It merely recognized the self-evident truth that under the Constitution "the colored people are nothing, and can be nothing but an alien, disenfranchised and degraded class." Purvis endorsed the overthrow of the government, "one of the basest, meanest, most atrocious despotisms that ever saw the face of the sun." In 1860, on the cusp of Lincoln's election, he argued that any self-respecting black American had to look on the Union with *"contempt, loathing,* and *unutterable abhorrence!"*

Charles Lenox Remond, considered by many contemporaries second only to Douglass as a spokesman for black Americans, also endorsed disunion. Born in 1810 in Salem, Massachusetts, a bastion of Federalist separatism at the time, Remond challenged white audiences to recognize that in addition to the black slave of the South there was "a baser slave, the pale face of the North, who patiently submitted to the insults which were heaped upon him by his master, the slaveholder." Why should blacks respect a nation that enslaved them? "Where…is the benefit of this much lauded Union to me?" Remond asked. "Where is the shield of the American Constitution to me? Where is the protection of American law to me? Where is American justice and humanity to me? Nowhere."

Dred Scott sank Remond, like many black activists, into a deep despair. What had the patience of the prim and proper achieved? The Union was an abject failure. It was time to "break into a thousand pieces the American Government." Remond wasn't moved by the argument that disunion might bring violence. "If the result...must be bloodshed, be it so," he told one audience. "I am not only prepared to see it, but I long for the time to come, for I believe it will be a retribution that the American people deserve, and it will be a lesson by which those who come after them will not fail to profit."

On a drizzly night in Rochester a week before the 1858 congressional elections, Republican leader William Seward addressed a packed rally. Jabbing the air with an unlit cigar, Seward observed that the "radically different political systems" of the North and South were approaching a confrontation. An ally in Illinois, Senate candidate Abraham Lincoln, had predicted earlier that summer that the country had to become "*all* one thing or *all* the other"—slavery or freedom would reign, but not both. "A house divided against itself, cannot stand," Lincoln observed, quoting Matthew 12:25. Now Seward switched metaphors, reframing the case. American history could not proceed, the Union could not achieve its full potential, without its fundamental contradiction being resolved. Seward dismissed the idea, popular at the time and since, that the coming conflict was "accidental, unnecessary, the work of interested or fanatical agitators, and therefore ephemeral," and insisted it was fundamental, inevitable—"an irrepressible conflict between opposing and enduring forces."

The irreconcilability of slavery and freedom rendered any bargain fragile and temporary. Either slavery would end and free laborers would pick Southern cotton or slaves would again till the rye and wheat fields of upstate New York—a frightful prospect for the Rochester audience.

"I know, and you know, that a revolution has begun," Seward said in closing. "I know, and all the world knows, that revolutions never go backwards."

Newspapers around the country covered Seward's speech and discussed it beyond Election Day. Southerners read it as a threat of invasion—"the avowal of a distinct design on the part of the Republicans to wage fierce and unrelenting and bloody war upon Slavery wherever it exists." Even in the North, some Republicans condemned Seward for making intemperate, impolitic remarks; he earned a reputation for radicalism that would ultimately cost him the party's 1860 presidential nomination. Others, especially abolitionists, cheered the airing by such a prominent politician of views formerly reserved to the margins of acceptable opinion. Southern radicals, too, agreed that the sectional crisis was no passing disagreement but a fundamental clash of civilizations. Regarding slavery, the secessionist *Charleston Mercury* observed, "The South and the North...are not only two Peoples, but they are rival, hostile Peoples."

Seward's "irrepressible conflict" formulation captured the growing feeling that the fundamental issue could not be forgotten, wished away, postponed, avoided. The conflict had for too long been repressed. Those days were over. The North was awake.

Long before the creation of the world, John Brown believed, his purpose had been determined, every turn of his path through the tangles of earthly existence charted, cleared, and marked. He was born in Connecticut in 1800 to devout Calvinists who taught him to hate slavery. At twelve, living in Ohio, Brown saw a black boy whacked with heavy tools and forced to sleep in the cold. The memory never left him. As an adult he tried some twenty different lines of work—tanning, land dealing, farming, raising sheep, driving cattle. None worked out. Fifty-four years old, Brown followed his sons to territorial Kansas. At a free-state meeting in 1856, Brown declared he would "see this Union dissolved and the country drenched with blood" rather than pay taxes to a proslavery government. A month later, he went to Pottawatomie Creek and drenched the country in blood.

On the run, Brown traveled east to raise money and arms. A mystique-wrapped fighter whose weathered face, a newspaper noted, was "expressive of indomitable will," Brown appealed to Eastern gentlemen who knew little of the Kansas murders and pretended to know even less. "Talk! Talk! Talk!" Brown cried after one abolition meeting. "That will never free the slaves. What is needed is action—action." In Connecticut, he ordered a thousand custom-made pikes (two-sided steel blades attached to six-foot shafts, handy tools for fighters unused to firearms) for newly freed slaves.

Keeping his plans secret, Brown made the rounds of New England abolitionists. Days before the Worcester disunion convention, Thomas

Wentworth Higginson hastened to Boston to meet him. Even if there is no reason to think, as some have claimed, that Brown attended Higginson's separatist conclave, his willingness to kill for the cause strengthened abolitionists' spines. Franklin Sanborn, a Concord schoolmaster who helped raise funds for Brown, praised him to Higginson as "the best Disunion champion you can find."

(What if Brown's raid on Harpers Ferry had succeeded? It's a tantalizing question. One possible answer is offered in *Fire on the Mountain,* a 1988 novel by Terry Bisson. The book imagines an alternate history in which Brown's raid sparked a South-wide slave revolution and the declaration of an independent black republic. In the book, a character in the present comes across an old novel depicting a different scenario: Brown's raid *fails,* the Southern slave owners secede instead, and a bloody civil war ends with the Union intact but the underlying issues of racism and inequality unresolved. Only partially reconstructed, America becomes "a sort of white-supremacist utopia." That bleak reality, Bisson implies, is our own.)

Brown's plan—such as it was—quickly collapsed. Federal troops forced Brown's surrender. Thomas Wentworth Higginson suggested organizing an assault to break him out of jail, but the prisoner refused to cooperate. "The utmost good he could have done by success does not equal the good destined to follow this failure," Higginson assured Brown's wife.

Though Brown failed to achieve the immediate goal of sparking a slave insurrection, he succeeded in his larger purpose of accelerating the conflict between slavery and freedom. A month later, en route to the scaffold, Brown handed his jailer a note: "I John Brown am now quite certain that the crimes of this guilty land: will never be purged away; but with Blood." He rode to the gallows seated on his own coffin, watching the country go by.

Northerners were unsure at first what to make of Brown and his raid, but their opinion underwent a remarkable transformation before his execution. Though they rejected his violent means, many admired his ends. Church bells tolled throughout the day; black drapes adorned public buildings; massive meetings raised funds for his family. "This will be a great day in our history," the poet Henry Wadsworth Longfellow wrote in his diary, "the date of a new Revolution,—quite as much needed as the old one." At a protest in upstate New York, a Republican state legislator inspired by Brown's attack suggested the abolitionists initiate "a free correspondence with the disunionists of the South." One thing alone united them: the belief that it was time to pull the plug and negotiate a separation.

Even in Europe, observers could tell that Brown's hanging marked a fundamental change. "The murder of Brown," Victor Hugo wrote before the execution, "would be an irreparable fault. It would penetrate the Union with a secret fissure, which would, in the end, tear it asunder."

Support for secession ripped through the slave states after Brown's raid, fueled by Northern praise of the martyr and Southern fear of copycat attacks. Formerly fringe voices now earned a respectful hearing. After years of arguing that Congress had no right to pass laws related to slavery anywhere, Southern radicals like Jefferson Davis, a Mississippi senator, demanded federal legislation to guarantee the extension of slavery in the territories, to put into effect *Dred Scott*'s dubious decree.

The question finally broke the beleaguered Democratic Party. In April 1860, when the party convention in Charleston adopted a platform that rejected the South's hard-line proslavery demands, Alabama's delegation marched out, led by arch-secessionist William Lowndes Yancey, who went, one observer noted, "smiling as a bridegroom." They were followed by all the delegates from Florida, Louisiana, Mississippi, Texas, and South Carolina and some from Arkansas and Delaware. "It is right that we should part," a former Mississippi attorney general told his Northern friends. "Go your way, and we will go ours." At separate conventions a month later, the Northern and Southern Democratic factions nominated two different contenders for the presidency (Stephen A. Douglas of Illinois and John C. Breckenridge of Kentucky, respectively).

The Democrats' split boded well for the Republicans. In 1856, Southern secession threats had scared Northerners into choosing Buchanan over Frémont. They would not make that mistake again. Free-state voters were now willing to vote Republican even if it meant risking the country they had been reared to love. The idea, a guiding force from George Washington's time onward, that compromise was always worth seeking no matter the cost had become a bankrupt, widely rejected irrelevancy. Northerners and Southerners alike now

qualified their patriotism with reservations: the Union was worth saving only under certain conditions. The problem was that the do-or-die
demands of each side were utterly incompatible with those of the other.

A new fired-up generation of Northerners refused to pay the price
of peace any longer. Sensing the opening, the Republican Party ran an
even more exuberant campaign than the previous one, only now it
bore an unmistakably militant undertone, as demonstrated by the
explosive rise of the Wide Awakes. The political club for young Lincoln
supporters had chapters around the country, from California to Maine,
and even a few in slave states like Virginia and Missouri. Hundreds of
thousands of farmers, mechanics, stevedores, clerks, students, and
carpenters—many of them first-time voters—turned out for raucous
rallies and parades. Marching in formation, accompanied by brass
bands, the Wide Awakes were easily recognizable in their uniforms of
glazed-cloth caps and capes meant to prevent them from being scalded
by wax dripping from their six-foot torches. In the weeks before Election Day, Wide Awakes staged huge parades through Boston, Cleveland, Chicago, Philadelphia, and New York, where, though it was an
overwhelmingly Democratic city, tens of thousands of men in uniforms
went goose-stepping down Broadway, cheered by spectators from windows and rooftops along the route—"a surging sea of excited humanity," one observer recorded.

The Wide Awakes offered a spectacle unlike anything in American
politics to that point. Their menacing, martial bearing made it easier
for citizens in both sections to imagine their long-standing political
conflict suddenly turning into a military one. The clip-clop of boots on
pavement sounded like "the thunder mutterings of the coming tem-
pest," one fearful Democratic paper observed. Southerners already
wary of Republicans intent on revolution saw the rise of the Wide
Awakes as confirmation of their worst fears. A Texas senator believed
the youth legions meant "to sweep the country...with fire and sword,"
while an Austin newspaper reported that for the first time "the young
and daring element of Abolitionism" had been "enthused with something like a love for military prowess." It was a dangerous development,
all the more objectionable because some Wide Awake clubs allowed
black men to be members. Ohio congressman Owen Lovejoy—a bull-
headed minister whose brother Elijah, an abolitionist printer, had been

killed by a proslavery Illinois crowd in 1837—didn't exactly soothe Southern concerns when he told a rally just before Election Day that instead of torches, the Wide Awakes would soon "shoulder their muskets"—perhaps to invade the South.

Following the advice of his allies, Lincoln stayed stone-silent on every topic throughout the campaign. Others spoke on his behalf. Republican orators gave some fifty thousand speeches. Seward, a former rival for the nomination, eagerly took to the trail, calling Lincoln "a soldier on the side of freedom," a metaphor that only added to the growing expectation of some kind of coming war.

It now seems obvious, even inevitable, that Lincoln had to win the election, given that he faced an opposition split among two Democrats and one so-called Unconditional Unionist (John Bell, a former Whig).

In fact, the outcome was nail-bitingly close. A change of only a few thousand votes in New York could have swung the election. At the last minute, Lincoln's three opponents decided to form a "fusion" ticket to block the Republican in the state. Too little, too late; the ploy failed. Yet given the strong Democratic bent in Manhattan, a more robust effort, begun months earlier, might well have worked. Deprived of New York's electoral votes, Lincoln couldn't have won an outright majority in the Electoral College. The election would have been thrown to the House, as had occurred in 1800 and 1824, each time to destabilizing effect.

As in 1800, Republicans controlled a plurality of state delegations but not a majority, and they had few prospects for making up the difference. The Twelfth Amendment to the Constitution, ratified after that earlier debacle, provided a convoluted way of filling a White House vacancy in case Congress failed to decide. If the House did not choose a president by Inauguration Day, the Senate (dominated by Democrats in 1860) would select a vice president, and that person would then act as president until the House made its choice.

According to the amendment, the Senate could choose from only the top two vote-getters for the vice presidency. In 1860, they were Lincoln's running mate, Hannibal Hamlin of Maine, a swarthy former Democrat smeared by Southerners as part black, and Breckinridge's lieutenant, Joseph Lane of Oregon, a Carolina-born veteran of the

Mexican War and a notorious slavery sympathizer. During the 1860 campaign, Lane pledged to Southerners that if civil war came, he would "fly to your relief from my far-off Pacific home and give all the powers of my arm and my head in your defense, in defense of the rights of the South." Forced to choose, the majority-Democrat Senate likely would have picked Lane.

Seeing the election stolen from them, an already fired-up free-state public would have exploded in anger, perhaps even to the point of violence. Secession and civil war might still have followed the 1860 election, but it would not have been the slave states that appealed to arms. Earlier that year, the influential abolitionist Wendell Phillips told an audience in Brooklyn that if a proslavery Democrat was again elected president, John Brown–style insurrections would break out in the Southern mountains and "every man in the Free States [would] arm himself for a struggle with the Slave Power."

In that event, the origins of the Civil War would be remembered very differently today. Historians would explain its roots in a long history of Northern separatism starting back in colonial days, continuing through the Revolution, the formation of the Constitution, and the early years of the republic, coming to a head with the ill-fated Hartford convention, then returning in the form of abolitionist disunionism and invocations of states' rights in the resistance to the Fugitive Slave Act— all climaxing in a final effort to establish an independent Northern republic free of the old one's original sins. Maybe the South would have resisted the secession of the free states; maybe it would have let them go. Given the North's industrial advantages, it might well have won that hypothetical war to break up the Union just as it did the actual one to preserve it.

It didn't happen that way, of course, partly due to a series of historical accidents, but mostly because a small coterie of secession-minded Southerners conspired to rig the 1860 election so their side would lose, paving the way for the slave states' departure from a Union that had always served their every political desire and economic need. White Southerners turned their nationalism into separatism as soon as they felt their basic interests—preserving mass slavery and racial domination— were in jeopardy. Terrified by the rise of Northern abolitionism, the South responded with a radicalism all its own.

CHAPTER 9

Going, Going, Gone

Whatever happens next, I must say that I rejoice that the old Union is smashed. We never were one people, and never really had a country.

—Nathaniel Hawthorne, 1861

LATE ON A SPRING NIGHT in 1861, Walt Whitman left the opera in Union Square and set off down Broadway toward the ferry that would take him home to Brooklyn. His ears, still ringing with lavish Italian melodies, suddenly picked up a sharp clamor, strange for that hour, echoing through the quiet streets. It grew louder until a clutch of newsboys came tearing up the pavement, their hands gripping late-night extras. Whitman entered a hotel lobby and huddled with strangers below a gas lamp as one read aloud the staggering news: Civil war had begun.

The crowd stood in somber silence, then dispersed into the night.

The days to come found Americans who were still loyal to the United States sifting through confused emotions, disbelief turning to shock and finally a defiant rage. Beneath it all, Whitman noticed, wasn't so much sadness or despair as relief, verging on exhilaration, that war was now inevitable. The South's choice of slavery over union cleared away the messy moral detritus of countless compromises and concessions. Now liberty and union really were on the same side, one and inseparable, as Daniel Webster had prematurely claimed. Not that long ago, they hadn't been so sure. Before Sumter, Henry Adams later recalled, "The Union was a sentiment, but not much more."

As so many had predicted, the Union's foundational frailty, its

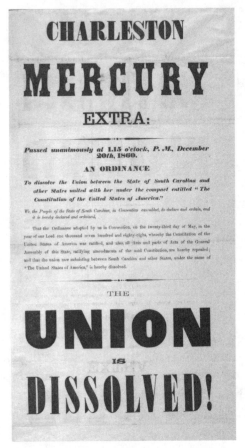

An 1860 handbill announcing South Carolina's secession. (*Library of Congress*)

built-in tendencies to dissolution, resulted in secession and civil war. The bombardment of Fort Sumter was a prism into which all prior American history entered and through which everything since has been refracted.

Little known, however, is that at the time, the South's departure seemed likely to trigger a more general disintegration. New regional confederacies and pint-size republics would spin off in every direction. Powerful figures in states rarely associated with separatism hoped to use the crisis to carve out a division of the continent more logical than the sprawling federation held together by force, fear, and inertia.

1. Birth of a Nation

The 1850s had been good to the South. From the repeal of the Missouri Compromise to the *Dred Scott* decision, national policy consistently favored the wealthy slave owners. "Cotton is king," South Carolina's James Henry Hammond declared in 1858. The South was "satisfied, content, happy, harmonious, and prosperous." After *Dred Scott,* Henry Hilliard of Alabama boasted that "the position of the South in the Confederacy is better than it has been for thirty years."

Three years later, Hilliard swore allegiance to a new confederacy and led troops against the old one. How did this happen? How could Americans who had never imagined rebelling against their own government turn so quickly into its sworn enemies, shooting at the flag they had once claimed to love?

John C. Calhoun had seen it all coming. In 1850, he whispered to a Southern colleague his vision of how the country would divide. "The Union is doomed to dissolution, there is no mistaking the signs," he predicted. Within twelve years, the country would break up. "The mode by which it will be done is not so clear," Calhoun went on. "It may be brought about in a manner that none now foresee. But the probability is it will explode in a Presidential election." Weeks later, after a sip of wine, slavery's greatest champion breathed his last.

Without Calhoun to hold them in line, a new generation of Southerners who had imbibed his ideas were free to follow them to their logical conclusions. "The wild steed of Disunion which he has been training can only be managed by himself," observed the *New York Tribune.* "He is not dead," Calhoun's longtime adversary Thomas Hart Benton said. "There may be no vitality in his body, but there is in his doctrines."

It didn't take long for them to spark back to life. Hard-core Southerners rejected the Compromise of 1850 and sought to build momentum for regional secession. Yet cotton prices were high and the planters were content. At a South-wide convention in Nashville that fall, moderates deemed disunion "a last sad alternative." As long as the North fulfilled its obligations under the Constitution—specifically, to return fugitive slaves—the South would do the same.

In South Carolina, the outburst took longer to quiet down. "May her patriotism be the death of many Yankees!" one toast went. "May she gain her independence, or perish in a blaze of glory!" The next summer, Maryland novelist John P. Kennedy visited the springs resorts in western Virginia and found the place full of Carolinians. "They are generally rabid and intractable seceders—women as well as men," Kennedy wrote his wife. "It is the strangest mania that has ever broke out in this country."

A mania it may have been, but support for secession was no passing fad. "Southern Rights Associations" sprung up in every low-country district. A statewide convention of such groups in Charleston endorsed immediate secession—even if the rest of the South refused to join.

Opponents listed the practical challenges: An army would have to be formed. Taxes would go up. Because slave imports to the United States were illegal, South Carolina could no longer send extra laborers south and west. With a soaring black population, the republic would face the very nightmare it wished to avert—transformation into, as one speaker put it, "a black State."

"I object to the secession movement," a prominent South Carolina judge insisted, "because it is the very thing sought by the Abolitionists. They wish to divide slave-owners from the glorious stars and stripes of '76." Another considered "the Union of these States...the strongest protection that slavery can have." That was as true in 1851 as it had been in 1787. Planters enjoyed "constitutional guarantees for slavery, which we could not have if this Union were dissolved."

Separatists countered that self-interest should give way to loftier ideals. The "overthrow of any government and the establishment of another" was "no holiday affair," one admitted. The public might suffer privations in the short term. But with "a great question of...State existence" at stake, "pecuniary matters ought not to weigh a feather." Even if the other slave states refused to leave the Union, South Carolina could stand on its own. Militarily, the state enjoyed advantages that would enable it to hold off an invading army of one million, one deluded pugilist argued. Whatever the obstacles, the state was "united and prepared for the emergency of disunion."

The conservatives won. Elections of delegates to a secession convention went so badly, its backers called it off. But Southerners who rejected disunion did so only because they continued to believe the

Union the best protection for their ownership of human beings. That judgment made sense as long as the constitutional guarantees they relied on were enforced—meaning as long as Northerners continued to enforce them. When it became clear they would not, proslavery separatism roared back in force.

By the end of the decade, white Southerners felt besieged. The slave states were losing population, wealth, and power. Stagnation formed almost the sole theme of regional literature. "National Decay," a poem by South Carolina's Paul Hamilton Hayne, depicted Southerners as "A People whose true life is in the Past" living in a "desert vast / Of present degradation!"

Though they resented the implied threat in William Seward's "irrepressible conflict" speech, the white South's own spokesmen also described the North and South as akin to clashing civilizations. Slavery was "the single source of all the intestine trouble" in the Union, the *Richmond Enquirer* admitted. America was "divided into two antagonistic sections" with "an intensity of animosity" between them not found "even among separate and distinct nations." The election of 1860 would resolve things one way or the other. Either the "dangerous doctrines of abolitionism" would be defeated or the slave states would "secede at once" and form a separate country.

Even many who rejected disunion believed its time wasn't far away. Georgia's Alfred Iverson pledged in the Senate that the election of an antislavery president would be "cause enough to justify secession." "The electric spark which conveys that intelligence ought to be and will be the silent death-signal of the confederacy," averred a South Carolina congressman. Jefferson Davis, a former secretary of war, declared that if a Republican won the 1860 election, he would personally rip his state's star from the Union flag and place it "on the perilous ridge of battle as a sign round which Mississippi's best and bravest should gather to the harvest-home of death."

Slavers always said they had joined the Union to secure slavery and would leave if it was threatened. Lincoln's election seemed to do just that. The moment had come for them to act, not least to defend themselves against the charge that they had only, once again, been bluffing.

But why secede before Lincoln had taken any action against Southern interests? Democrats still controlled the Senate and the Supreme
Court and could block antislavery legislation. Thanks to the Constitution's guarantees, the peculiar institution could survive a few years of
the government in the hands of its enemies. Why not at least wait until
Lincoln's inauguration and see what he would do?

For secessionists, none of that mattered. Republicans didn't need
legislation to put slavery "in the course of ultimate extinction," as Lincoln had once said—words Southerners never tired of invoking. By
blocking slavery's expansion, the North could confine it to a sliver of
the continent where the soil was already depleted. If antislavery Republicans, or even free blacks, filled the thousands of patronage jobs in
federal forts, post offices, and customhouses, the regime of enforced
silence and censorship that slave masters relied on to keep the abolition menace at bay would be destroyed. Anyone who took such jobs
would risk lynching, yet the governor of Georgia believed plenty of
white non-slaveholders in his state could be "bribed into treachery to
their own section, by the allurements of office." Under a Republican
administration, the radical *Charleston Mercury* pointed out, "the contest
for slavery will no longer be one between the North and the South. It
will be in the South, between the people of the South." Any delay in
leaving the Union would lessen the likelihood of it ever happening.
Only leaving the Union could secure the ends for which the nation had
been established in the first place—namely, preserving slavery. Lincoln's victory, a South Carolina minister declared, was "nothing more
nor less than a proposition to the South to consent to a Government,
fundamentally different on the question of slavery, from that which
our fathers established." He wasn't wrong.

The new Southern nation would be "the real United States," an
Arkansas senator insisted, while the old "rump" Union would be
reduced to "a narrow slip of country...soon to fall to pieces."

In South Carolina, popular fervor swept aside all opposition. Unionists
stood no chance. They were pelted with eggs and turnips, threatened
with worse, and many feared to assemble in public. One complained
that the separatists in their haste were "afraid to trust the second
thought of even their own people." If they waited, the tide would turn.

Privately, secessionists admitted as much: "I do not believe that the common people understand; in fact, I know that they do not understand it...We must make the move and force them to follow."

On December 18, 1860, one hundred and sixty-nine delegates gathered in St. Andrew's Hall on Broad Street in Charleston. All but a handful owned human beings. A steady rain fell as deliberations began. "The Union is being dissolved in tears," a Charleston lady wrote to her daughter. A silk banner stretched over the slave market read "SOUTH CAROLINA — GOING, GOING, GONE!"

Two days later, the delegates voted unanimously to rescind the state's 1788 ratification of the Constitution. "The Union now subsisting between South Carolina and the other states, under the name of the 'United States of America,' is hereby dissolved," the secession ordinance said. Outside the hall, a speaker pronounced South Carolina once again an "Independent Commonwealth." The crowd roared its approval. Agents of the *Charleston Mercury* passed out a broadside with a headline in boldface type: THE UNION IS DISSOLVED. The city lit up with bonfires on every corner as church bells pealed and Roman candles exploded in the air. People massed around Calhoun's grave. "I am somewhat sorry for the old Union," the British consul wrote to London, "although he was a noisy old braggart."

Though nearly every state had at one time or another threatened to leave, up to that point, none had gone through with it. Now South Carolina had. Yet as staggering an event as secession was, little changed immediately. The consequences would take some time to play out. In the Sea Islands off the coast, a planter's wife, getting ready for Christmas, marveled at how life continued as before. "It seems strange we should be, in the midst of a revolution, so quiet, and plentiful," she wrote. "Everything goes on as usual; the planting, the negroes, all just the same, and a great Empire tumbling to pieces around us."

Would there be war? Secessionists dismissed the prospect, skeptical that the North would bother to fight for a union they themselves had recently seemed to turn against. Stereotypes of pacific, profit-minded Northerners convinced Southerners that they would be allowed to leave. "You may slap a Yankee in the face and he'll go off and sue you," one Southerner joked, "but he won't fight." Robert Barnwell Rhett Jr., publisher of the *Mercury,* said it was absurd to think that Northerners, "prone to civil pursuits, should get up and carry out the military enterprise of conquering eight million people." James Chesnut, a South Carolina senator who resigned his seat after Lincoln's election, pledged to drink up any blood that might be spilled. Virginia's Edmund Ruffin, a longtime disunionist, assured Southerners there wasn't "the slightest danger of war from the Northern States," since they couldn't win such a conflict "without the sacrifice of fifty thousand lives...and one hundred million of dollars."

Neither estimate came close to how much it cost in the end. But separatists remained confident. "So far as war is concerned, we have no fear of that in Atlanta," one newspaper insisted. Four years later, the city lay in ruins.

It was vital, above all, to maintain momentum. Howell Cobb, who resigned as federal treasury secretary and returned home to Georgia, acknowledged he was "afraid that the blood of the people will cool down."

Unionists frantically tried to hit the brakes. "It is treason to secede," warned the *Vicksburg Whig.* Secession, a "blind and suicidal course," would not bring peace and plenty but "strife, discord, bloodshed, war, if not anarchy." Alexander Stephens, a former Georgia congressman, argued that "unnecessary changes and revolutions in government" were dangerous. Stephens remembered Lincoln from his single term in Congress and thought him "not a bad man." In Virginia, John Minor Botts predicted the secessionists would earn from posterity the same "scorn and ignominy" as the New England Federalists who had attended the Hartford convention. Elections for state conventions saw unusually low turnouts, suggesting simmering dissent about the path forward.

Yet built-in advantages in state government allowed secessionists to overcome the opposition. Five Southern states—Mississippi, Florida, Alabama, Georgia, Louisiana—quickly followed South Carolina's lead. All made clear, as Mississippi put it, that their position was "thoroughly identified with the institution of slavery."

Except in South Carolina, nowhere was the vote of the state conventions unanimous, and in several states the struggle was fierce. Alabama was typical, sharply divided between plantation-heavy counties and mountainous regions with few slaves. After the state seceded, one up-country delegate declared that his constituents would never agree to leave the Union; he was wrestled to the ground and hauled off to jail. A state senator from north Alabama predicted the region would rebel against the state.

The secession locomotive continued pounding down the tracks. It stopped next in Texas. Sixty-seven-year-old Sam Houston, still hobbling from a Mexican bullet that had been lodged in his ankle since the Texas Revolution, was serving as the state's governor. In the fifteen years since annexation, Houston had resisted proslavery separatism and denounced Southern extremists; he even opposed the Kansas-Nebraska Act, predicting it would divide the country. If a break had to come, however, he preferred to reestablish the Lone Star Republic rather than join a Southern confederacy. Better for Texas to "avoid entangling alliances," he said, "and enter once again upon a national career."

After Lincoln's election, Texan disunionists—those "Demons of anarchy," in Houston's words—demanded that the governor call a secession convention like other Southern states had. When he refused, a rogue justice on the state supreme court did it instead. After irregular elections, the delegates voted to repeal the annexation of 1845. Texas had joined the Union to ensure it remained "a commonwealth holding, maintaining and protecting the institution known as negro slavery—the servitude of the African to the white race," the convention delegates explained. Now the state was leaving for the same reason.

Unlike most other slave states, however, the Texas convention put secession before voters in a snap referendum. Union supporters had little chance. In Waco, a committee warned that every "Lincolnite" who didn't keep quiet would be hanged. Mobs hounded dissidents; some fled the state. Secession easily passed. Texas reclaimed its independence on March 2, 1861, exactly twenty-five years after it first separated from Mexico.

But then the locomotive ground to a halt. In the upper South, ardor for secession had always been cooler. In the seven states that had left the Union, 37 percent of whites owned slaves; in the eight slave states that remained, that figure was only 20 percent. Forty-seven percent of the population of the lower South was enslaved; only 24 percent of the upper South was. Setbacks in Virginia and Kentucky sapped secession's momentum and suggested disunion might not be permanent. Few thought a breakaway nation limited to the Deep South could survive on its own.

In February 1861, representatives of the seceded states traveled to Montgomery, Alabama, to organize a new government. They moved quickly, hoping to present Lincoln with a fait accompli before his inauguration on March 4. Meeting in the state's gleaming capitol, under portraits of Southern heroes like Calhoun, Jackson, Clay, and Washington, thirty-six delegates adopted a constitution modeled closely on the original—though the preamble dispensed with the goal of forming "a more perfect Union" and explicitly proclaimed that each state acted "in its sovereign and independent character."

The delegates had to decide on a name for their country; Appalachia, Alleghenia, Chicora, Atlanta, Panola, Washington, Southland, Secessia, the Allied Republics, and even the League of Nations were all considered. They finally settled on the Confederate States of America, a nod to the looser coalition that had predated the Constitution. Then they adopted a flag (later ditched because of its confusing similarity to the Union banner) and appointed executive officers: Jefferson Davis as president and Alexander Stephens, a skeptic of secession, as vice president.

In astonishingly short order—two months after South Carolina seceded—the Confederacy was up and running. Its prospects seemed bright. If all went well, the South's time in the Union would seem like a brief prelude before it achieved its real destiny. While the delegates met in Montgomery, a young South Carolina schoolteacher named Henry Timrod published a poem later titled "Ethnogenesis," meaning "the birth of a people":

> At last we are
> a nation among nations; and the world
> shall soon behold in many a distant port
> another flag unfurled!

2. Rebellions in the West

There wasn't just one secession crisis but several. The departure of the lower South convinced malcontents elsewhere to wonder if their states and territories should do the same.

Since the early 1840s, settlers on the Pacific Coast had considered separating themselves from the fast-deteriorating situation back east and forming a new country. California newspapers wrote disparagingly about "the other side," referring not to partisan divisions but a physical one—the Continental Divide. After Lincoln's election, the Western separatists saw their chance.

Even after California gained statehood in 1850, pro-independence attitudes didn't disappear; the state's residents felt neglected by Washington, DC. Easterners were profiting from California's gold mines, the U.S. government from duties imposed in its busy ports, but in the distant federal capital, despite lobbying hard for funds and support—post offices, forts, a mint—to serve the soaring population, state representatives found their efforts blocked by Southerners still bitter over the state's ban on slavery. "The fact is, the United States Government has been a tyranny and an oppression to California from the day it was established here," San Francisco's *Alta California* declared. "It has always taxed us without giving the security and benefit we had a right to expect in return."

California wasn't getting much out of its membership in the Union. Maybe it had been a mistake to join. "When the State was admitted to the Union we hailed it with joy," the *Alta* reflected. But that joy had turned to disappointment. Washington's neglect would inevitably "weaken the attachment of our people to the home government," the editors warned, and encourage the growth of separatism. Many residents' attachments to the Union were already weak. Gold-seekers came from Britain, France, Russia, China, South America. "Bred up under different influences, under different governments," the *Alta* noted, they "would require but very little urging to become advocates of a secession movement, aiming eventually to a great western republic."

The West Coast was accessible from the East only by an arduous, weeks-long journey overland or by sea. To separatist-minded Californians, a transcontinental train line was indispensable to ensure the

Pacific Coast's loyalty to the rest of the Union. Deriding the project as a boondoggle, fearing the precedent it might set for government spending, Southerners in Congress blocked federal funding for the railroad. Some Californians advocated the creation of a new "Pacific Party" to promote the interests of the West. "Why do we not, as citizens of the Pacific side, come together and act together for the good of ourselves?" asked the *California Chronicle*. "Why do we embroil ourselves with the controversies and party squabbles of the other side, when in the questions there involved we have no interest?" Others argued the state should secede in order to enact more enlightened policies than were possible in a deadlocked federation. If California "cut loose from Uncle Sam," one writer suggested, it could form a new nation to "carry out the progressive ideas of the age."

In Oregon, some settlers welcomed the resurgence of the Pacific republic idea. Frustrated that their territory hadn't yet been granted statehood, they, too, wanted to secede. The downsides of joining a broken Union seemed to outnumber the advantages. "If nature ever marked out the division of countries, it has done so in North America," the *Portland Standard* argued in 1855. The Rocky Mountains made "an unmistakable boundary…laid down by an overruling providence." East and West were growing more different, not more similar. Easterners were busy "cultivating a spirit of disunion by their altercations." West Coast independence might be "deemed visionary" by the fearful, but so had America's secession from Britain. If the colonists had managed to win independence despite the odds, why couldn't the West?

By 1856, the population of San Francisco, less than one thousand before the gold rush, had hit fifty thousand. That year, a group of roughnecks calling themselves the Vigilance Committee overthrew the corrupt city government, which had failed to control crime. The committee enforced order—if not exactly the law—by hanging a dozen people accused of burglary, arson, and murder. Some members supported seceding from the Union and restoring the Bear Flag Republic or joining a new Western federation.

That summer, thousands of San Franciscans mustered as ad hoc militias; they performed drills with muskets and learned how to fire cannons. Back east, the *New York Herald* urged the federal government to send an army to march on California. By contrast, Horace Greeley's

New York Tribune argued for giving up a distant coast whose protection cost too much money. When a Georgia senator called for letting California "slide" out of the Union, the state's representative retorted that it might do just that.

In San Francisco, defenders of the Vigilance Committee warned that if the federal government sent troops, California would secede. The Union cord had been "very much weakened by the neglect and abuse we have suffered," the *California Chronicle* observed, "and a foray upon us by the United States troops and men-of-war would snap it like a burned tow string." When California legislators began talking about the creation of a university system, a state official suggested it include a military school "following the system of West Point," noting that well-trained officers might be needed to defend a Pacific republic.

Meanwhile, a few hundred miles east, another rebellion brewed. This one would see armies face off in what some historians have called America's first civil war.

In the summer of 1857, Brigham Young gathered thousands of his followers in the mountains outside Salt Lake City to celebrate the tenth anniversary of their arrival in the promised land. Though the proposed state of Deseret, reaching from the Rocky Mountains to the Pacific, had been rejected by Washington, the Utah territory granted in the Compromise of 1850 was a handsome consolation, taking in not only the future state but also today's Nevada and western Colorado. Young was appointed governor as well as commander of the militia. As head of both the church and the territory, he wielded near-absolute power. For the first time, Mormons enjoyed peace and prosperity, and converts flocked in from abroad.

All that ended abruptly, however, when five horsemen galloped into that remote canyon where the Saints were celebrating. A large federal army had been seen crossing Kansas. Young ended the party early and began preparing his people for war.

Relations with the federal government had deteriorated after the church, in 1852, acknowledged the practice of "plural marriage." To other Americans, the Mormons were a fanatical sect, abusers of religious liberty. Attacking them united Southerners and Northerners, Democrats and Republicans. The Republican platform of 1856 condemned slavery and polygamy as "twin relics of barbarism." Stephen Douglas denounced Mormons as "outlaws and alien enemies" and asked Congress to "apply the knife and cut out this loathsome, disgusting ulcer."

For their part, the Mormons chafed under territorial rule. Officials and judges sent from Washington were often incompetent, alcoholic, and hostile to polygamy. "How long, think ye, can such oppression be quietly endured?" asked the official church newspaper. "How long, think ye, will any people submit to the dictates, slanders, corruptions, and abuse of officers whom they have no voice in electing, and whose efforts are constantly put forth to the utmost for the destruction of the people?" After hearing that President Franklin Pierce planned to replace him, Young declared, "I am and will be the governor, and no power can hinder it, until the Lord Almighty says, 'Brigham, you need not be governor any longer.'" Pierce backed down.

Federal appointees fled from Utah and filed reports on what they had seen. The government was "despotic, dangerous and damnable," one wrote; the people obeyed only those laws approved by their church. Young and his functionaries harassed anyone who tried to uphold the Constitution. One account told of a Mormon who had lost faith and tried to leave the church; he and his son were murdered in cold blood. Another said Mormons were allying with neighboring indigenous nations to launch a rebellion against the government or even secede from the United States. (Young had in fact sent emissaries to nearby tribes suggesting they "have either got to help us or the United States will kill us both.") In 1857, a correspondent who visited Utah told James Buchanan's attorney general that Young planned to "erect an immense polygamous Hierarchy in defiance of the United States and entirely independent of its control."

Although most of these reports were exaggerated, they took on a life of their own. Support ran high for subduing the Mormons; some called for the polygamists to be exterminated. Northerners, eyeing a takeover of the federal government in 1860, were eager to set a precedent in case the South tried to secede, while Southerners wanted to divert national attention from conflicts over slavery. One prominent Virginian, Robert Tyler, President John Tyler's son, told his friend Buchanan that only war with the Mormons would distract the "eyes and hearts of the Nation" and make them "forget Kansas!"

Without bothering to confirm the reports, Buchanan replaced Young with a gentile governor and appointed new judges, a territorial secretary, and a marshal. They were accompanied to the territory by twenty-five hundred troops—one-third of the frontier army—and lengthy supply trains in case of protracted hostilities. The president told Congress he meant to overthrow "the despotism of Brigham Young" and suppress the "frenzied fanaticism" of "these deluded people."

News of the army's approach sent Mormons into a panic. "Who would not rather die than bow down to the yoke of the enemy?" one speaker asked. Brigham Young urged Mormons to fight "in the mountains, in the canyons, upon the plains, on the hills, along the mighty streams, and by the rivulets." (Before there was Winston Churchill, there was Brigham Young.) "The time must come when there will be a separation between this kingdom and the kingdoms of this world," Young proclaimed. "Are you prepared to have the thread cut now?" The question was met, an observer recorded, with a "unanimous vote of uplifted hands and a shout of Yea which made the place echo."

Forbidding federal forces to enter the territory, Young declared martial law and ordered a regiment of two thousand men to guard the mountain passes. The church called missionaries from around the world to return home—with weapons. Teams of "Mormon Raiders" went out to destroy federal outposts, burn supply wagons, and seize cattle. Young ordered civilians to evacuate the capital. Thirty thousand refugees headed toward Provo. Soldiers prepared to torch the holy city rather than let it fall. Young once again considered relocating his people outside the United States, perhaps taking them south to Mexico or north to Russian-ruled Alaska.

The mood was ominous; it felt like thunder was about to crack. In southern Utah, a caravan of one hundred and forty emigrants from Arkansas and Missouri, the site of the Saints' worst torments, was traveling west through the territory, bound for California. Nobody would sell them supplies, so some of the travelers resorted to stealing what they needed to survive. In September 1857, a trigger-happy Mormon militia and its native allies ambushed the party in a high mountain meadow, separated the women and children, and executed one hundred and twenty men—possibly the deadliest slaughter of American civilians until the Oklahoma City bombing of 1995.

Outside Utah, the massacre fueled the popular fervor for war. "Virtue, christianity, and decency," a San Francisco newspaper editor cried, "require that the vile brood of incestuous miscreants who have perpetuated this atrocity shall be broken up and dispersed." Buchanan called on Congress to give him more troops to put down the rebellion.

In June 1858, facing certain catastrophe, Young resigned as governor and accepted his replacement, who promised not to infringe on the Mormons' religious practices, including polygamy. Federal troops entered Salt Lake City in a show of strength, then passed through and set up camp on its outskirts. Dozens of Mormons were indicted for treason, then pardoned in exchange for submitting to federal authority. Young and his successors in the church leadership would wield power behind the scenes in Utah for decades to come.

Northerners and Southerners learned different lessons from the Mormon Rebellion. Buchanan's aggressive action satisfied the North that the government would act to put down a Southern rebellion. However, the episode gave slave-state separatists hope that the Mormons, holding the strategic crossroads of the West, were "on the eve of revolution" and would side with the South if a larger war ever came. Young did nothing to disabuse them of that notion.

When the war came, Young saw it as divine retribution for America's sins, especially the murder of Joseph Smith. The conflict signaled the onset of what Mormons called the "winding up scene," the apocalypse that would end with the establishment of God's kingdom on Earth. Although he promised Lincoln that Mormons were "firm for the Constitution," Young told an ally he would welcome a report that Southerners had captured Lincoln and his cabinet. "I will see them in Hell before I will raise an army for them," Young declared. Other than a single mission to help Union soldiers protect the trail to California, Utah sat out the Civil War.

Even after Oregon gained admission to the Union in 1859, West Coast separatism remained strong. States that had recently joined the Union could easily imagine life outside it. In a 1913 memoir, the mining tycoon and former secessionist Asbury Harpending recalled that in 1860 "the ties that bound the Pacific to the Government at Washington were nowhere very strong. The relation meant an enormous loss to California. For all the immense tribute paid, the meager returns consisted of a few public buildings and public works. Besides thousands were tired of being ruled from a distance of thousands of miles."

Though the far-Western states were removed from the crisis in the East, they, too, were sharply divided between Democrats and Republicans. Some in southern California, lamenting the ban on slavery, proposed breaking the state in half. In 1859, the state legislature voted to split off a slave territory that they named Colorado. A referendum in six southern counties returned a clear majority for division. But a distracted Congress failed to act. Tensions ran so high over the issue that a former chief justice of California's supreme court killed a sitting U.S. senator in a duel.

Others wanted to break up not the state but the country itself. A new nation could stretch from the Pacific to the Rocky Mountains, north to Canada and south into Mexico, maybe even west to the Hawaiian archipelago (still an independent kingdom) — all in all, a landmass the size of Europe. California's surviving senator, Milton C. Latham, told colleagues that if the Union divided, as seemed likely, California would join neither North nor South but would form its own nation, one blessed with bountiful resources and an "enterprising and energetic" population. Westerners could then live in peace, free from the turmoil in the war-torn East. "Why should we trust to the management of others," Latham asked, "what we are abundantly able to do ourselves?"

After Lincoln's election, Charles Tyler Botts, the state printer of California and editor of the *Sacramento Standard,* called for a West Coast convention to declare independence. The governor, John B. Weller, even endorsed the idea and called on Californians to side with neither section in the coming contest "but here upon the shores of the Pacific [to] found a mighty republic which may in the end prove the greatest of all."

As the country came apart, the idea gained support from leaders in California and Oregon, including most members of both congressional delegations. Missouri-born J. C. Burch announced in a public letter from gloomy secession-winter Washington that it was time for Californians to "look to our own safety [and] cease our connection with a people bent on self-destruction and political annihilation." Californians should "seek refuge for themselves, from the blighting effects of disunion and civil war, by retiring and establishing a prosperous, happy and successful republic on the Pacific slope." As they had in 1846, Burch said, Californians should "raise aloft the flag of the Bear…and call upon the enlightened nations of the earth to acknowledge our independence."

Because the state's U.S.-born residents hailed from all over the country and retained close ties back home, the state remaining in the Union would inevitably lead to civil war in California itself. If the North tried to conquer the South, Californians would have to pay taxes for the slaughter of fellow citizens—neighbors, parents, siblings, and friends. "I will die before I will ever contribute a dime to prosecute a wicked, unholy, unjust, blackhearted Abolition war upon my Southern brethren," one Democratic assemblyman swore. "If this mighty Government of ours must crumble to pieces and fall, let California look to herself and to her own soil. Let her not remain within these crumbling walls until she, too, is crushed beneath their ruins."

In a rousing speech, one pro-independence politician observed that the ancient liberty-loving spirit of the American people, the spirit of Plymouth and Jamestown, Lexington and Bunker Hill, had crossed the continent with the westering settlers and taken up residence "under the massive arches of the constitutional edifice of a Pacific republic, which will endure, aye, and preserve and shelter it in all coming ages."

In early 1861, the California legislature debated whether or not to stay in the Union. Despite the swelling chorus for separation, a majority remained loyal to the United States. There weren't enough people to guard the state's long coast, an insecurity that would attract European powers still dreaming of colonization. The state's already high taxes would have to be raised to support a military, a diplomatic service, a postal network, and Indian affairs. Secession would destroy all hopes for a transcontinental railroad, a core promise of the Republican platform. The *Alta California*, which had supported secession a decade earlier, now derided the idea as a "burlesque upon disunion." One state legislator dismissed it as a "delusive dream" and called those who favored it traitors.

Separatists had their own calculations. Without trade rules imposed by the United States, independent California could ship gold directly to Europe, and tariffs on imports would supply it with more than

enough revenue. The nation's seemingly unlimited agricultural potential and invaluable mineral deposits, along with easy access to the markets of China, Japan, and the East Indies, would support the "Empire
of California," as one letter-writer put it. If the new nation allied with
the Southern Confederacy, the *Los Angeles Star* argued, "A transcontinental railroad would be built between New Orleans and San Diego in
less than two years."

Bear Flags were seen flying throughout the state—in Stockton and
Sonoma, Los Angeles and San Bernardino. Reports circulated of secret
societies gathering arms and drilling recruits. Squatters were told that
independence would eradicate land titles and open up vast tracts to
free settlement. Before resigning, Buchanan's Virginia-born secretary
of war sent seventy-five thousand muskets to California, possibly to
assist in a coup d'état. In March 1861, a convention in Tucson announced
the secession of Arizona from New Mexico territory and pledged loyalty to the Confederacy. The danger of a similar movement in California became all too clear. Proslavery sympathies were so prevalent in
southern California that partition of the state remained a possibility—
and a Confederate objective—well into the war. "Let it never be forgotten," a San Francisco paper scornfully observed in 1861, "that the
county of Los Angeles, in this day of peril to the Republic, is two to one
for Dixie and Disunion."

In San Francisco, a shadowy cabal of some thirty young men
hatched plans to seize federal military installations scattered around
the bay, including the fort on Alcatraz Island. They raised at least a
million dollars for the operation. To succeed, however, they needed
the blessing of the officer in charge of federal forces in the Pacific,
fifty-eight-year-old Albert Sidney Johnston, a highly regarded veteran
of the Texas Revolution, the Mexican War, and the Mormon Rebellion.
The conspirators visited Johnston at his Presidio headquarters. They
expected wholehearted support for the initiative from Johnston, a Kentuckian by birth and a Texan by choice—"a blond giant of a man with
a mass of yellow hair," as one of the emissaries recalled. Yet Johnston
surprised them by brusquely interrupting the pitch and pledging to
"defend the property of the United States with every resource at my
command, and with the last drop of blood in my body."

In the end, Albert Sidney Johnston gave his blood—and his life—

not to defend the United States but to destroy it. A few weeks after meeting with the separatists, the general learned that his home state of Texas had seceded from the Union. Johnston resigned from the army. Days later, Lincoln, informed that the general had met with California secessionists, relieved him of command. Eluding arrest by Union officers, Johnston made his way to Los Angeles, joined a rebel militia, and crossed into Confederate Arizona. A year later, he took a bullet to the knee at Shiloh and became that battle's highest-ranking fatality on either side. Had events gone somewhat differently—for instance, had Sam Houston not delayed Texas's secession—Johnston might have reigned as dictator of an independent California, allied with the South, financed by piles of Sierra gold. The history of West Coast separatism would be a more familiar story.

3. Let Them Go

Seven states had left the Union, but nothing required the North to fight to keep them in. Ever since the nation's founding, Northerners had resisted federal authority as noisily, assessed the worth of the Union as soberly, doubted its perpetuity as unsentimentally as the Southerners themselves had. Recently, Northern pressmen and politicians—not only radical visionaries but elite opinion-shapers and statesmen—had wondered if the Union had reached the end of its usefulness. During the secession winter, many Northerners otherwise divided among themselves rallied around a policy of peaceful separation. Proslavery Democrats, uncompromising abolitionists, even leading Republicans, including cabinet officials and a future president, argued for allowing the Southerners to leave the Union.

Had they had their way, the Confederacy would have been permitted to stand. The United States as Americans had known it would be destroyed. A Democratic paper in Washington argued that the government had "no power whatsoever to protect itself" if the people "choose to alter, amend, or even annihilate it." That had been the essence of the Declaration of Independence: "If the doctrine was good then, it is good now." A union maintained only by military might wasn't worth keeping. "An attempt to subjugate the seceded States, even if successful, could produce nothing but evil," the *Detroit Free Press* argued. Horace Greeley, an influential Republican, wrote in his *New-York Tribune,* "We hope never to live in a republic whereof one section is pinned to the residue by bayonets." A union shattered by war could never be fully restored.

A rising young Republican lawyer in Cincinnati also favored letting the South go. "The free States alone, if we must go on alone, will make a glorious nation," thirty-eight-year-old Rutherford B. Hayes wrote in his diary after Lincoln's election. Hayes imagined a new union of twenty million people, "full of vigor, industry, inventive genius, educated, and moral; increasing by immigration rapidly, and, above all, free—all free." Maybe it was better for the Union to divide. "Let them go," Hayes wrote of the South. "The experiment of uniting free states and slaveholding states in one nation is, perhaps, a failure."

Inspired by the slaveholders' own arguments against disunion, William Lloyd Garrison had long considered breaking up the country the surest way to abolish slavery. Now the aging agitator was again heartened by the arguments of Southern unionists like the Tennessee politician who predicted "a dissolution of the Union" would prove "the death knell of African slavery." Allowing the South to leave would free Northerners from their constitutional obligations to protect the South from servile insurrections and to return runaways. Before long, the system of bondage would collapse. The sooner the Union split, the sooner slavery would end. "All Union-saving efforts are idiotic," Garrison declared during the secession crisis. "Hail the approaching jubilee, ye millions who are wearing the galling chains of slavery; for, assuredly, the day of your redemption draws nigh, bringing liberty to you, and salvation to the whole land!"

Even Frederick Douglass, Garrison's former acolyte, began to edge back toward the doctrine he had abandoned a decade earlier. He feared Northern whites would again buckle under Southern threats and sign some horrible deal to stave off secession. "If the Union can only be maintained by new concessions to the slaveholders," Douglass argued, "then...let the Union perish." Only after it broke up could it be put back together and finally dedicated to liberty and justice for all.

Nowhere was partition more popular, though in a different way, than in New York, a fiercely Democratic city with business ties to the South, including the illegal slave trade. Every year, dozens of ships left the city for African coasts. The city's *Journal of Commerce* admitted that many "down-town merchants of wealth and respectability are extensively engaged in buying and selling African Negroes." Thanks to well-placed bribes, those caught at sea and hauled into city courts were rarely convicted. Firms sold so many goods—clothing, pianos, tools—to slave plantations that they advertised themselves as devoted "Exclusively to the Southern Trade." Wall Street financiers like the Lehman brothers— German Jews who moved from Montgomery to Manhattan in 1858— grew rich as cotton brokers. "New York belongs almost as much to the South as to the North," the *New York Post* observed.

Though many New Yorkers sympathized with the slave states, Southern secession would have serious repercussions for the city's economy. Deprived of its trade with the slave states, New York would be drained of its wealth and influence. With the South out of the Union, one Democrat predicted during the 1860 campaign, "New York ceases to be the Empire State, this city becomes no more a great national metropolis." Southerners taunted Northern friends with apocalyptic visions of ruination. "What would New York be without slavery?" asked J. D. B. De Bow, a New Orleans editor. "The ships would rot at her docks; grass would grow in Wall Street and Broadway, and the glory of New York, like that of Babylon and Rome, would be numbered with the things of the past."

After Lincoln's election, two thousand frightened businessmen met in the offices of a Carolina-born cotton trader and passed pro-Southern resolutions. "If ever a conflict arises between the races," one attorney declared, "the people of the city of New York will stand by their brethren, the white race."

Despite its proslavery sympathies, however, the city would suffer with the rest of the North if the country broke apart—or went to war. Southerners began boycotting Northern companies. Planters owed millions of dollars to New York firms, debts the speculators feared would be renounced. Within weeks of the election, the city's economy was in free fall. Prices for commodities like wheat and flour plummeted; factories slowed production and laid off workers; money dried up. "The Southern trade is reduced to nothing," the *New York Herald* lamented, "and everything seems to be going to the dogs."

Desperate editors and businessmen began talking up an extraordinary idea—New York City could secede from both the state and the

Union and establish a free and independent city, its ports open to all. A million and a half people wouldn't sit still and starve, the *Journal of Commerce* explained; "they will sooner set up for themselves against the whole world." In December 1860, a New York Democrat named Daniel Sickles took to the floor of Congress to declare that his city would "never consent to remain an appendage and a slave of a Puritan province," a disparaging reference to Republican-majority New England. Better to declare independence than submit to Yankee abolitionists. George B. McClellan, a former railroad president, received a letter suggesting that the city "cut loose from the fanatics of New England & of the North generally, including most of our own State."

The idea caught the attention of Mayor Fernando Wood, a notoriously corrupt proslavery Democrat who had risen from a grocery owner to become a millionaire investor in land, railroads, banks, and insurance companies. Wood loathed the upstate Republicans who controlled Albany. A few years earlier, the state legislature had created a new police force to replace the city's scandal-plagued corps. For months, the two sides battled for control of the city; Wood's men finally surrendered. With Wood as mayor, *Harper's Weekly* commented, New York was "not well-governed nor ill-governed, but simply not governed at all."

Wood knew how valuable Southern trade was to the city economy. The South was its "best customer," he asserted. "The profits, luxuries, the necessities—nay, even the physical existence" of New York "depend upon...continuance of slave labor and prosperity of the slave master!" He openly derided free blacks as inferior and encouraged assaults on abolitionists. Through the *Daily News,* which he purchased and hired his brother to edit, Wood warned that after Lincoln freed the slaves, New Yorkers would "find negroes among us thicker than blackberries swarming everywhere"—unwelcome competition for jobs.

In the first week of 1861, with South Carolina already out of the Union and other states not far behind, the mayor drafted a formal proposal and submitted it to the city council. Secession made as much sense for New York as it did for the slave states. Ruled by upstate Republicans who, sharing the "fanatical spirit" of their New England compatriots, had "wrested control" of the city's almshouses and police, even the new Central Park, the state legislature, Wood argued, had become "the instrument by which we are plundered to enrich their speculators, lobby agents, and Abolition politicians." The city suffered as much from the oppressive state government as the South did from the federal one.

Given that the breakup of the Union had become "inevitable," Wood suggested New York City should seize the opportunity to strike off on its own. "When disunion has become a fixed and certain act," the mayor observed, "why may not New York disrupt the bands which bind her to a venal and corrupt master, to a people and a party that have plundered her revenues, attempted to ruin her commerce, taken away the power of self-government, and destroyed the Confederacy of which she was the proud Empire City?"

By establishing a free city with nominal duties on foreign goods, New York could maintain its ties with the South and become a world-class entrepôt. The city would have so much trade flowing in, it could abolish all internal taxes. The new republic, made up of Manhattan, Staten Island, and Long Island, would be called Tri-Insula—Latin for "three islands."

The city council seemed to like the idea and rushed Wood's message into print. Elsewhere, the plan received scattered support. The mayor's brother at the *Daily News* called it the only alternative to war. If New York stayed in the Union, the paper warned, every white worker should expect to be drafted into the army, forced to "leave his family destitute and unprotected while he goes forth to free the negro." A Democratic paper in Albany opposed the city's secession but favored an "independent existence for our favored state." George Fitzhugh, a Southern polemicist, penned an essay supporting Wood's initiative.

Republicans were horrified that the secession menace had spread to their own city. The port of New York supplied fully two-thirds of federal customs revenues. If the city left the Union, Lincoln would be hard-pressed to find funds to quash the Southern rebellion. The *New York Times* condemned Wood's presentation as "the attempt of a demagogue...to inflame all the passions of the ignorant and needy." The "miserable sophistries and puerilities" of his message were "not really deserving argument." Horace Greeley observed that the mayor "evidently wants to be a traitor."

Well into the spring, however, independence remained popular among businessmen, who didn't want to lose Southern trade, and lower-class laborers, who didn't want to compete for jobs with former slaves. Though Wood had forsworn violence to achieve the city's separation, rumors spread of an association of some five thousand men planning to seize federal warships and storm federal forts along the harbor, even take over the Brooklyn Navy Yard. According to one journal, secret conclaves met regularly at the mayor's residence to plot how to "induce the city to declare its independence of the Hudson River Valley...and the rest of creation."

Even the president-elect of the United States felt the need to address Wood's free-city proposal. "I reckon it will be some time before the front door sets up house-keeping on its own account," Lincoln quipped to a New Yorker visiting him in Springfield. A month later, when Lincoln stopped in New York en route to Washington, the hostility was too palpable to be dismissed with a jest. Wood refused to meet Lincoln at the train station and instead made him call at city hall the next morning. After a private meeting, Lincoln emerged to face a grim, glowering crowd of thirty thousand. He alluded to the independence idea. "There is nothing that can ever bring me to willingly consent to the destruction of this Union, under which not only the commercial city of New York, but the whole country has acquired its greatness," Lincoln said. Walt Whitman, watching from atop a Broadway omnibus, admired the new president's plain-sense talk no less than his gumption in forthrightly facing down the seditious opposition.

Up to the moment that those late-night reports from Charleston roused the city, as Whitman put it, with "a shock electric," making New York an independent city-state remained a real possibility. Even the early rush of war, the onset of what Whitman called the "red business," couldn't end the city's rebelliousness. Two years later, days after the Battle of Gettysburg, civil war broke out in the national metropolis.

Stuck between North and South, the mid-Atlantic states had the most to fear from disunion. A center of manufacturing and agriculture, twin pillars of the national economy, with few radicals of either the Northern or Southern variety, New Jersey, Pennsylvania, Delaware, and Maryland had often acted as a force for national unity. Now they hoped to prevent their farms from becoming blood-soaked battlefields.

Those calculations changed, however, when it became clear that war was imminent. If last-ditch compromise efforts failed, the states stuck in the middle needed a plan. What they came up with, though far-fetched and now little known, was at the time seen as a viable solution: Secede from the Union and establish a "Central Confederacy." Only then could they halt the march to war and broker a peaceful resolution. Caught between the unstoppable force of Northern arms and the immovable object of Southern determination, the area's citizens, even its conservatives, found themselves favoring secession—if only, they hoped, as a temporary measure.

The idea of a Central Confederacy first emerged in Maryland. The state kept nearly ninety thousand people in bondage, but it was as divided as the country. In the South and East, powerful proslavery interests wanted to follow the lower South out of the Union. Before a massed crowd in Baltimore, the lawyer and politician Severn Teackle Wallis condemned any move to coerce the Southern states into remaining. "You cannot shoot and hang men back into union," he thundered. By contrast, Maryland's northern and western counties, closer to Pennsylvania, were filled with antislavery German immigrants. Business interests in Baltimore, tied to the North by rail and river connections, also opposed secession. Complicating matters was the fact that federal troops would have to cross Maryland to reach South Carolina. Residents had to either join the separatists or aid their suppression.

One way to avoid the choice was to secede but not join the Confederacy, to instead create a separate republic as a buffer between the two sides. In December 1860, the novelist John P. Kennedy published a pamphlet, *The Border States,* in which he argued that a mid-Atlantic nation could "serve as a center of reinforcement for the reconstruction of the Union." The region would provide a coolheaded example, and a "beneficent power of gravitation would work with irresistible energy in bringing back the dislocated fragments." Eventually, those fragments could be glued back together.

Maryland's governor, Thomas Hicks, picked up on Kennedy's idea. Though a slaveholder, Hicks opposed disunion. He refused to meet with Confederate commissioners who wanted him to summon a secession convention. He preferred to see what Virginia would do first. But Hicks also valued the state's ties to Pennsylvania, and it pained him to think of choosing between the two. Days after South Carolina's secession, Hicks sent a letter to his Delaware counterpart suggesting that the "honor, safety, and interests" of their states would best be served by forming their own republic. Delaware's governor demurred, thinking small states could prosper only in a large union. One of the state's U.S. senators, however, supported the plan. "Let Delaware preserve her separate and independent position," he said, "until the conservative central states—slaveholding and nonslaveholding, shall unite in a new republic. Whatever may be the fate of the extremes, let the great centre be composed and secure."

Other states responded warmly to Hicks's overtures. John Letcher, Virginia's executive, told his legislature that it was imperative for the middle states to "make their own arrangements to ride out the crisis." Unionists in the mountains of western North Carolina and eastern Tennessee also expressed interest in the proposal. In Pennsylvania, an anti-war meeting called for a state convention to determine "whether Pennsylvania should stand by herself, as a distinct community." George W. Woodward, a Democrat on the state supreme court, not only defended the right of secession but hoped his state would exercise it. "I cannot in justice condemn the South for withdrawing," Woodward said. "I wish Pennsylvania could go with them."

Newspapers throughout the region discussed the Central Confederacy plan, and several supported it. New Jersey, the tip of which reached sixty miles below the Mason-Dixon, had long-standing ties with the South; further, the state had been the scene of numerous battles during the Revolution, and New Jerseyans worried about getting caught in the cross fire again. Joining the Confederacy or forming a new one with Pennsylvania and New York gained support from leading Democrats, including a former governor. The *New Brunswick Times* declared that such a nation "would be formidable in character."

For Central Confederacy proponents, as for Fernando Wood, one motive was fear of falling under New England's sway. Yankee Puritanism and self-righteousness rubbed other Americans the wrong way. With the South out of the Union, the heavily Republican region would have more power than ever. The *New York Herald* called for restoring the Union but "leaving out the New England States." New Englanders were "so fanatical," the paper complained, there could never be "any peace under a Government to which they are parties." Before resigning from the Senate, Louisiana's Judah P. Benjamin mischievously noted that some colleagues "indulged the hope that the Middle States will join the South, and that New England will be left out of the Union to enjoy by herself her fanaticism and the blessings of such freedom as she prefers."

Ironically, leaving out New England might have been fine with some New Englanders. During the secession crisis, Charles Sumner floated the old Federalist dream of the region separating from the South and joining with Canada. The slave states were a moral stain and an economic drain, Sumner thought. Good riddance. Why not annex Canada as "compensation" for the loss of the South and create a new, north-facing union? Kentucky abolitionist Cassius M. Clay suggested Republicans be content, at least for a time, to rule over "a divided empire....Let disunion fever run its course—and let us get Canada."

Others combined the many separatist movements and suggested breaking the Union into four separate nations—an alternative to continental federation that had been proposed as far back as the Albany Congress of 1754 and raised periodically ever since. Now the idea was endorsed by the highest-ranking general in the U.S. Army, Winfield Scott, a soldier since Jefferson's presidency, hero of the Mexican conquest, failed Whig presidential candidate in 1852. Seventy-four years old at the time of Lincoln's election, the Virginia-born Scott disagreed with fellow Southerners that the Republicans posed a dire threat. "I know your little South Carolina," he told a senator's wife. "I lived there once. It is about as big as Long Island, and two-thirds of the population are negroes. Are you mad?"

A week before the 1860 election, Scott sent President Buchanan an unsolicited letter on the "Imminent Danger of a Disruption of the Union." If the nation split, he warned, there could be "no hope of reuniting the fragments except by the laceration and despotism of the sword." Far better to embrace the "smaller evil" of peaceful separation. Surveying the country's "natural boundaries and commercial affinities," Scott sketched rough borders for four new nations: the South, the Northeast, the Midwest, and the Pacific, along with possible locations for their capital cities. He forwarded the memo to friends and to President-elect Lincoln, who replied with a curt, noncommittal note.

When Scott's proposal was leaked to the public, some quibbled with his proposed boundaries, but the notion of splitting the Union into regional confederations gained more support during the secession winter than at any time since the crisis-ridden months of early 1787 before the Constitutional Convention. For some, the general's partition plan offered a last exit from the highway to catastrophe.

A month later, Clement L. Vallandigham, a stridently proslavery Democrat from Dayton, Ohio, introduced a modified version of Scott's proposal in Congress. Though it stopped short of disuniting the country, Vallandigham's version offered a fundamental reordering of the constitutional order. Like many Midwesterners, the handsome forty-two-year-old had close ties to the South, having married into a wealthy slave-owning Maryland family. In the Democrat-dominated southern parts of Ohio, Indiana, and Illinois, farmers and businessmen feared the Confederacy would close the Mississippi River, as Spain had eighty years earlier, leaving them at the mercy of Great Lakes shipping interests and predatory railroad companies backed by Eastern capital. Anxious to avoid war, they found a spokesman in Vallandigham.

In February 1861, as the Montgomery delegates unfurled a new flag, Vallandigham presented a bold plan to avoid permanent division. Two constitutional amendments would create four official regions, roughly those suggested by Winfield Scott. The first measure, focused on the executive branch, aimed to prevent a divisive figure like Lincoln from ascending to high office. A candidate would need support from a majority of electors in all four regions to win the presidency. The term of office would be extended to six years with a ban on reelection unless the incumbent received support from two-thirds of the electors in each section. The second amendment affected Congress. It required support from a majority of senators in each region for the passage of any important piece of legislation. Any region could veto any bill. The goal, as Vallandigham put it, was "to maintain the existing Union...by dividing or arranging the States into sections *within the Union, under the Constitution.*"

Union through division. The congressman's proposal was misreported by the press as a plan to break the country into four nations as

Scott had suggested. Republicans pounced, denouncing Vallandigham as a traitor. The editor of the *Ohio State Journal,* an aspiring poet named William Dean Howells, called the idea "pure and simple treason," while another paper lambasted Vallandigham as "the biggest fool in America."

In fact, as Vallandigham protested, his proposal was meant to *avoid* dissolution, not bring it about. Had it been adopted, the carnage to come might have been averted. In that case, however, slavery might never have been abolished. But at least Vallandigham wanted to deal with America's divisions by forthrightly facing them, even writing them into the Constitution. The idea of devolving power to regional confederations would long outlive the Ohio congressman, who, to stop a war he had sought to avert, soon embraced an even more daring project: Midwestern revolution.

By the time Lincoln took the oath of office, secession seemed regrettable but likely final. The South was never coming back. "I begin to recognize the fact…that treason has triumphed, and that our once glorious and well beloved Union is overthrown," Orville Browning, one of Lincoln's closest Republican allies, wrote. All he could do was to try "slowly, reluctantly, sadly to reconcile myself to it." Maybe the United States should recognize the Confederacy. "It cannot be denied," the *New York Times* observed, "that there is a growing sentiment throughout the North in favor of *letting the Gulf States go.*"

4. Settle It Now

The white South had always insisted that the Union's endurance depended on the systemic violation of its own founding ideals. From the Quaker abolition petitions of 1790 to the slave owners' bombast and bluster over the Compromise of 1850, the country had survived round after round of Southern blackmail only because the South's threats of disunion had bludgeoned the North into silence and submission. Of all the ties that held the Union together, complicity was the strongest bond of all.

During the secession winter, fear of disunion led some in the North to call for yet another South-friendly bargain to head off dissolution. This was the respectable, responsible, conservative opinion. For many other Northerners, however, and certainly for most Republicans, the secession crisis stiffened their spines. It changed the issue from slavery, which divided the free-state public, to the rule of law and democracy, which united it. The Union, whatever its flaws, was too precious to lose over a single election. Compensating, perhaps, for their own rejection of federal authority in fights over the Fugitive Slave Act and *Dred Scott*, Northerners vowed to do whatever was necessary to hold the country together.

For Republicans, that hard-line position was motivated by practical politics (and partisan pique) as much as by pure constitutional principle. Having won the election, they hated to give in. The message sent to the South by a new compromise, one congressman explained, would be unmistakable: "Whenever you are beaten at the ballot-box, you have only to steal the public property and declare war against the Government, and we will make concessions." Every future election would be subject to extortion. The government couldn't last. "Instead of healing the disease," one newspaper warned, "concession will make that disease constitutional, chronic, and fatal."

The loudest calls for war came from Lincoln's own region, the upper Midwest, a bastion of states' rights talk only a few years earlier. With a foreign country again in control of the Mississippi's outlet at New Orleans, farmers feared they would no longer be able to trade on the river. Some Southern-born Midwesterners wanted to join the Confederacy to avoid being severed from the Gulf of Mexico, but many others wanted to force the South back into the Union. In January 1861, when secessionists set up batteries near Vicksburg and briefly closed the river trade, a Cincinnati paper condemned the action as "piracy and murder." Free navigation of the Mississippi was not up for negotiation. "It is *their right*," the *Chicago Tribune* insisted. The conflict had been too long postponed: "Settle it now."

Western Republicans in Congress delivered "flaming tirades against disunion," the *New York Times* reported, and openly threatened war. In a leaked letter, Michigan's senator called for "a little-bloodletting" to show the government meant business. Owen Lovejoy, an outspoken Illinois congressman, warned of a snowball effect if Southern secession was allowed to stand. Pennsylvania would leave the Union in order to demand a higher tariff; New York would secede to secure free trade;

Massachusetts would insist on protection for its fisheries, and Maine on the same for its lumber industry; California would set up a Pacific republic. The Union wouldn't be severed; it would be destroyed. The crisis must be resolved "without compromise, without concession, without conciliation," Lovejoy cried. "It is a crime to make shipwreck of this government."

Though some favored separation or compromise, most Republicans wanted the party to stay true to its promises and principles—refuse to allow slavery in any new states or territories, hold on to federal property in the South, faithfully execute the laws of the land. If that ignited a continent-wide conflagration, so be it. It had been a long time coming. The fault would lie with the separatists rather than the government. "If we must have a civil war," argued Edward Bates, Lincoln's attorney general, "perhaps it is better now than at a future date."

Most figured the war would begin in Washington. John Andrew, the Massachusetts governor, drew up plans for sending troops to protect the capital. Americans should "get accustomed to the smell of gunpowder," he said.

Others suspected it would erupt in Charleston Harbor, where Robert Anderson, a Kentucky-born officer, commanded a few dozen federal troops, their provisions rapidly dwindling, in an unfinished island fortress surrounded by rebel redoubts undergoing round-the-clock reinforcement by battalions of slaves. Some in the North, ready for war, even prayed the Confederates would attack Fort Sumter, though it would mean a massacre. "If Major Anderson and his whole command were murdered in cold blood," Henry Adams wrote, "it would be an excellent thing for the country, much as I should regret it on the part of those individuals."

Waiting out the winter at home in Springfield, the president-elect realized he was about to inherit a fractured country. Lincoln had doubted the South would actually go through with its threats and was as surprised as anyone when it did. Devouring newspapers, interrogating visitors—friends, foes, reporters, supplicants—Lincoln imbibed a steady stream of Northern opinion. He knew that while some Democrats and captains of industry favored another preemptive surrender, most others wanted and expected his administration not to give an inch.

Like many Republicans, Lincoln was willing to make a few concessions for peace. He had always said the free states were responsible for enforcing the Fugitive Slave Act as long as it remained on the books. Now Lincoln endorsed a constitutional amendment to forever guarantee bondage in the Southern states. It would have introduced the word *slavery* into the document for the first time.

The one issue he would not bend on, however, the question on which he described himself as "inflexible," was the expansion of slavery into the territories. To Lincoln, limiting slavery to states where it already existed would herald the dawn of a new era, one that would culminate, he expected, with emancipation measures passed not by Congress—Lincoln acknowledged that was unconstitutional—but by the Southern states themselves. During the secession crisis, as moderate-minded congressmen tried to devise a new compromise, he warned an Illinois ally, Lyman Trumbull, that Republicans shouldn't surrender the main plank of their platform. "Stand firm," he wrote. "The tug has to come, & better now, than any time hereafter."

As for what he *would* do, Lincoln stayed as silent as he had during the campaign. He preferred to speak through political allies and affiliated journals, especially Springfield's *Illinois State Journal.* (Some of its secession-winter editorials may even have been drafted by Lincoln himself.) After South Carolina seceded, the paper adopted a fierce, even bellicose tone. "Disunion by armed force is treason," the *Journal* warned, "and treason must and will be put down at all hazards."

Fighting to preserve the Union, however, meant taking the risk that if the South won, the Union would forever be destroyed. Lincoln has been heralded for his quasi-mystical attachment to the Union, but his choice not to compromise his core principle contained a kernel of the logic that abolitionists like William Lloyd Garrison had been urging for years. The key to Lincoln's genius was precisely that he was *not* willing to do whatever it took to hold the Union together, that he let it break apart—temporarily, he hoped—so that it might be put back together in such a way as to make it, as he had said in an 1854 speech, "forever worthy of the saving."

Even to Lincoln, the Union, that "last best hope of earth," was a means to an end and worth saving only if it continued to serve that end. When the moment of truth came, he rejected the usual response to crisis—patching things over with another problem-postponing compromise—and instead sought to settle the underlying conflict once and for all. That decision was revolutionary. Believing deeply in America's emancipatory mission, he gambled for the highest stakes imaginable. The war to save the Union became a bet that it would, in time, become worthy of having been saved.

Before daylight on April 12, 1861, a ten-inch mortar shell sparked over Charleston Harbor and burst one hundred feet above Fort Sumter—a signal to the batteries ringing the shoreline. Over the next thirty hours, the rebels fired some fifty thousand rounds of artillery at the island garrison. Smoke curled over the fort and wafted toward the city, where residents cheered the action from porches and roofs.

Within Sumter's crumbling walls, soldiers fought with fierce determination fused with a grim bemusement. Three hours into the fighting, one officer went to relieve another and wryly asked what the uproar was about. "There is a trifling difference of opinion between us and our neighbors opposite," the officer replied, "and we are trying to settle it."

CHAPTER 10

The Great Red River

The worst is not only imminent, but already here.
—Walt Whitman, 1861

FOR ALL THE TIMES IT seemed to sputter and stop, the clanging, clattery machine of the federal system had actually broken down only once. "We are now in the midst of what all of us have read of—thought of—and dreamed of before, but never realized," a Georgia woman wrote in her diary. "A revolution."

What was it like to see the country come apart? Churches and businesses saw congregations and supply chains severed. Postal routes were cut off by burned bridges and roadblocks. People on either side of the new border had to enter enemy territory to visit friends and family. The academy at West Point emptied of Southerners. Confederate money had to be thrown into circulation. "War has converted all of the citizens in each of the Confederacies into aliens and enemies," a Nashville paper observed. "It puts an end to intermarriages and traveling into the separate nations. It breaks up all private correspondence and friendship."

Yet the Civil War was not a simple fight between two stable blocs of like-minded states. Though it was the North-South division that finally rent the country, American fractures had never been as clean as a solid South and a unitary North. Southerners were less sure of secession, and the rest of the country less committed to union, than Americans today often suppose. Each side struggled to hold together; each war effort was burdened by the need to suppress internal rebellions and "lesser civil wars." The War Between the States was a war within them as well.

An 1864 map showed "Our Country as Traitors & Tyrants would have it"—"Disunited States" split into four separate nations. Many feared the secession would lead to other fractures. (*Boston Rare Books*)

1. The Union's Disunion

The North's surprising insistence on national unity, based in part on a deep reverence for the founders and faith in the historical destiny of the republic, was also the expression of a bitter hatred for the South that had been building for decades and now burst with the force of a volcanic eruption. Northerners welcomed the schism because on some level, they had wanted it all along. "Civil war is actually upon us," John Sherman, an Ohio senator, wrote to his brother William, "& strange to say it brings a feeling of relief—the suspense is over."

The firing on Sumter produced the unity that had long eluded the North. "The South's attack has made the North a Union," the *New York Times* observed. "One intense aspiring sentiment of patriotism has fused all other passions in its fiery heat." The moment the Stars and Stripes came down from Sumter's flagpole, old divisions seemed to melt away. Democrats and Republicans disagreed about what the flag stood for, but for a moment none of that mattered. Even Lincoln's opponents recalled party founder Andrew Jackson's insistence that the Union had to be preserved. "When the question is whether we shall have a Government or Anarchy," one Democrat said, "I have no hesitancy in declaring my choice."

Few backed the war more enthusiastically than those abolitionists who, months earlier, had called for letting the South go. After Sumter, the crusading abolitionist Wendell Phillips, standing before a display of red, white, and blue bunting, announced that the identity of "abolitionist" was now "merged in citizen, in American." Once the slave owners took aim at the government they had for so long controlled, it finally became possible to be *for* the Union and *against* slavery. Though Lincoln continued to deny any intention to free the slaves, the logic of war, Phillips believed, would make emancipation unavoidable.

William Lloyd Garrison, who had once burned the Constitution, now said that the more the flag was attacked by slave drivers, the lovelier it seemed in his eyes. In 1861, Garrison removed from the *Liberator* his slogan that the Union was a covenant with death. In its place was a verse from Leviticus: "Proclaim Liberty throughout all the land, and to all the inhabitants thereof."

For most Northerners, proclaiming liberty had little to do with the causes or ends of war. "The negro was not the chief thing," Walt Whitman would recall of the days after Sumter. "The chief thing was to stick together."

But sticking together was no easier during the long-drawn-out war than it had been before. The North's newfound unity couldn't survive the pressures of a fight that lasted longer than either side expected. Old divisions returned. Opposition rose as Union armies faced rout after rout, spiking after especially bloody engagements. Peace-minded Democrats joined with outright Confederate sympathizers to criticize and undermine the war. Opponents called them Copperheads for their slithery, snakelike ways.

Copperheads alleged that Lincoln's various efforts to suppress dissent—such as suspending habeas corpus—revealed tyrannical ambitions. In 1862, the Senate expelled Jesse Bright, a long-serving former slave owner from Indiana, after the publication of a letter he had addressed to "His Excellency, Jefferson Davis"—a de facto recognition of Confederate legitimacy. James Bayard, a Delaware senator (his identically named father had cast the decisive vote for Jefferson in the 1801 stalemate), resigned his seat rather than swear an oath of loyalty to the Union. Defending the South's right to secede, Bayard invoked the

philosopher Edmund Burke's words supporting American independence: "Bodies tied together by so unnatural a bond of union as mutual
hatred are only connected to their ruin."

The Emancipation Proclamation worsened wartime partisanship by
changing the nature of the war. Now its purpose was not to save the
Union, Democrats sneered, but to "free the negroes and enslave the
whites." Abolition, they warned, would trigger the mass migration of
freed blacks into Northern cities. To the oft-repeated mantra of those
seeking reconciliation with the South—"The Constitution as it is; the
Union as it was"—some Democrats offered a nasty addition: "the negroes
where they are."

The problem was compounded in the spring of 1863, when the
Union instituted its first-ever draft. All men of military age were eligi-
ble. Yet a draftee could purchase an exemption by paying three hundred dollars (about a year's salary for a laborer) or hiring a substitute
to serve in his place, loopholes that stirred resentment among whites in
working-class districts from Eastern cities to Western coalfields. Democrats denounced the "wicked Abolition crusade" and vowed to "*resist* to
the *death* all attempts to draft any of our citizens into the army."

In a few places, Northern discontent shaded into separatism. In
1862, a Philadelphia businessman named George McHenry published
a fifteen-page pamphlet titled *Why Pennsylvania Should Become One of the
Confederate States*. "The old United States," McHenry declared, "is a
thing of the past." Reunion was impossible. If Pennsylvania was forced
to choose between the new Southern nation or a debt-burdened rump
Union ruled by New England, its commercial rival, the wisest course
was clear— *"secession from Yankeedom."*

A copy of McHenry's essay found its way to Jefferson Davis. A year
later, Robert E. Lee invaded Pennsylvania, expecting Confederate sympathizers to rally to his side. They never appeared.

Days after Gettysburg, an insurrection broke out in Manhattan—
the most violent episode of urban unrest in American history. After
the post-Sumter euphoria wore off, New York reverted to its traditional
role as a stronghold of proslavery feeling and Democratic support. The
day the draft was set to begin, thousands marched through the streets.
They set fire to the draft office, looted hardware stores and a rifle fac-
tory, and burned down the Colored Orphan Asylum off Fifth Avenue,

forcing hundreds of children to flee. The mob swelled and swarmed through the city. Blacks were yanked off streetcars and beaten. Smoke wafted through rubble-strewn streets as gunfire punctuated a chorus of prolonged and tortured screams.

Three days later, after sixty buildings had gone up in flames and well over a hundred people had died—the final toll isn't known—six thousand Union troops arrived fresh from the killing fields at Gettysburg. Building by building, they swept out insurgents and restored order. The draft was reinstated after the city agreed to pay the three-hundred-dollar fee for anyone who didn't want to serve.

New York City hadn't seceded as former mayor (now congressman) Fernando Wood had wanted. But the Draft Riots—what in another part of the world would have been called a pogrom—showed the Civil War as more than a series of set-piece battles between neatly arranged armies. It was also a thoroughgoing breakdown of all kinds of communal bonds. The blood that pooled in Manhattan streets was an omen of the explosive racial and class divisions that imperil the Union to this day and may continue to for ages to come.

Even as he moved troops around the continent like pawns on a chessboard, Lincoln thought the real threat to national unity came not from Confederate armies but from the restive, war-weary populace back home. In January 1863, weeks after issuing the Emancipation Proclamation, Lincoln told Charles Sumner that he feared a "'fire in the rear'"—meaning the Democracy, especially at the Northwest—"more than our military chances."

Strained by war, Lincoln's own region became a hotbed of subversive conspiracies and separatist rebellion. In southern Ohio, Indiana, and Illinois, 40 percent of residents had been born in slave states. Torn between their ancestral and adopted homelands, they tried to avoid the fight. The draft made that impossible. "We stand upon a volcano," wrote an Indiana man, "with a crust so thin that only a spark will explode it."

Wartime tensions between Democrats and Republicans erupted in spasms of violence that looked like miniature versions of the broader carnage. In 1863, an attempt to arrest a deserter in Hoskinsville, Ohio, led to a standoff with hundreds of armed citizens in the snowy woods.

"To think," a local soldier wrote a friend, "that we have sacrificed all, and spent two years hard service on behalf of our glorious Union, to have our own people, yea even our own neighbors, rise up and try to put us down. I tell you I would far rather shoot such a man than the hottest Secesh in the rebel army." A year later, a scuffle between a Union soldier and an anti-war Democrat in a courthouse square in Illinois turned into a bloody melee that left seven soldiers and three civilians dead. A regiment of Indiana troops headed for the front had to be diverted to deal with what seemed like an impending revolt.

Residents of Cairo, Illinois, the state's southernmost city, located at the confluence of the Ohio and the Mississippi, called for the secession of the whole southern half of the state and its absorption by the Confederacy. "There is a wide difference between the wants, the habits, the manner of life, and the modes of thought of the people of North Illinois and those living in South Illinois," proclaimed a local editor. The sentiment pervaded the region. At a meeting at a saloon, men pledged "to use all the means in our power to...attach ourselves to the Southern Confederacy." Illinois's Republican governor sent one thousand troops to quash the movement, but support persisted. An Indiana congressman proposed slicing off the lower parts of Indiana and Illinois and creating a new Confederate state of Jackson.

An idea even more popular than joining the Confederacy was creating a new country—a "Great Brotherhood of the West"—taking in all or part of Ohio, Indiana, Illinois, Michigan, Wisconsin, and Minnesota. In 1862, Thomas Hendricks, a prominent Indiana politician (later Grover Cleveland's vice president), denounced "the capitalists of New England and Pennsylvania" for profiting at Westerners' expense. If the North lost the war and the country divided, "the mighty Northwest must take care of herself and her own interests." Sixteen Democratic county organizations in Indiana backed western secession if, as they thought likely, the Confederacy won.

As war ground on, support for a "Northwestern Confederacy" grew, nurtured in late-night meetings of clandestine societies with "castles" throughout the Midwest: the Knights of the Golden Circle, the Order of American Knights, the Sons of Liberty. Members communicated with secret signs and handshakes, stockpiled arms, drilled at night in forest clearings and quarries, attacked Union draft recruiters, even encouraged enlistment in the Confederate army. One group required members to swear an oath promising to "take up arms in the cause of the oppressed— *in my country first of all*—against any Monarch, Prince, Potentate, Power or Government usurper." When the right moment came, western Copperheads would rise up and proclaim a new Northwestern nation. One member said there were half a million men in his society.

Buoyed by hostility to emancipation, Democrats made gains in the Western states, winning control of the Indiana and Illinois legislatures in 1862 and enough seats in the federal House of Representatives to deprive Republicans of their majority. The new state legislatures called for peace and demanded that Lincoln repeal the "wicked, inhuman and unholy" proclamation. Their Republican governors ignored the Democratic legislatures and essentially ruled as dictators for the duration of the conflict, supported by federal troops stationed in Springfield and Indianapolis. Indiana's chief executive, Oliver P. Morton, a close Lincoln ally with informants in the secret societies, publicly denounced the idea of a Western confederacy as a "wild and wicked dream." The situation was serious, he told Lincoln: "The fate of the Northwest is trembling in the balance."

Confederate agents posted in Canada offered support for the region's would-be rebels. By 1864, the South was running out of options. As Sherman's army marched toward Atlanta and Grant laid siege to Richmond, a new strategy was desperately needed. Revolt in the Union heartland would destroy morale and relieve pressure on the South by forcing the North to redirect troops. Jefferson Davis expected the "separation of the north West from the Eastern States" would lead to civil war within the Union, leaving the Confederacy to enjoy its "peace and prosperity."

Southern politicians wanted to use access to the Mississippi River to pry the Midwestern states away from the Union as Spain had tried to do in the late eighteenth century. In 1863, Mississippi poet Margarita Conedo published an "Appeal to the States of the Northwest," urging the citizens of Ohio, Indiana, and Illinois to free themselves from Yankee domination:

> *South and West are truly brothers, children of a common mother*
> *Why then slaughter one another, at a stranger's dark behest?*

Nobody believed more fervently that South and West were truly brothers than Clement Vallandigham, the charismatic congressman who, during the secession crisis, had proposed writing regional divisions into the
Constitution. The Ohioan emerged as a fiery anti-war leader. Weeks after
the attack on Fort Sumter, he called for Lincoln's impeachment.

Vallandigham doubted the North could conquer the South. He
didn't think it should. A union held together by force was no union at
all. He thought the Western states held the balance of power and could
force an immediate cessation of hostilities. Peace would bring reunion,
Vallandigham insisted, ignoring the fact that peace without Northern
victory would probably mean recognizing Southern independence —
and certainly repealing abolition.

What Vallandigham might really have wanted was to be the founder
of a new nation. "I am not a Northern man, nor yet a Southern man,"
he once declared, "but I am a Western man, by birth, in habit, by education." In 1859, Vallandigham warned Republicans that once the
South left the Union, "the West, the great West, which you now coolly
reckon yours as a province, yours as a fief of your vast empire," might
follow. "Did you ever dream of a Western Confederacy?" He had. Vallandigham said he was a "Western Sectionalist, and so shall continue to
the day of my death."

Despite the Democratic wave of 1862, Vallandigham failed to win
reelection, likely thanks to Republican gerrymandering. He bade farewell to Congress days after the Emancipation Proclamation took effect.
With its adoption, Vallandigham charged, "War for the Union was
abandoned; war for the Negro openly begun." "The people of the West
demand peace, and they begin to more than suspect that New England
is in the way," the Ohioan warned. Pressed too hard, his constituents
might seek an *"eternal divorce between the West and the East."*

That spring, Vallandigham embarked on a tour through the North.
"King Lincoln" was hell-bent on making the country "one of the worst
despotisms on earth," he said, all but begging the military to arrest him
for disloyalty. Union general Ambrose Burnside was happy to oblige. In
the middle of the night, soldiers broke down Vallandigham's door. As
supporters rioted in his hometown of Dayton, the ex-congressman was
tried by a military tribunal and sentenced to prison for the rest of
the war.

Lincoln learned of the arrest from newspapers. Embarrassed by accusations that this amounted to political persecution, he commuted the sentence to exile. Vallandigham was handed over to Confederate troops in Tennessee. From there, he traveled to the Carolina coast and then sailed for Canada, where he set up headquarters in a hotel across the border from Detroit. A hero to Copperheads, Vallandigham was named the Ohio Democrats' nominee for governor. Campaigning from Canada, he received waves of fawning visitors, including Southern agents eager to sponsor Midwestern rebellion.

Vallandigham lost the election, largely because Union victories sapped the peace movement's momentum. But when new setbacks demoralized the Northern public in the spring of 1864, the secret planning for Northwestern Confederacy picked up steam.

Little is known for certain about the particulars — how many agreed to participate, how close they came to putting their plans into effect. After the war, participants weren't exactly eager to save papers that incriminated them in a conspiracy to commit treason.

The broad outline, however, is clear. The Democratic National Convention would be held in Chicago in August 1864. The plan was that, while hundreds of delegates and journalists milled around the city, Southern agents would rally sleeper cells to seize nearby arsenals and liberate the tens of thousands of Confederate prisoners being held in camps on the outskirts of town. The rebel army, swelling to one hundred thousand, would march across the Midwest and overthrow the governments of Illinois, Indiana, and Ohio. A new "empire of northwestern States" would be born.

The uprising ended before it got started. Spies in the secret societies warned Union officers, and when the convention opened, the Copperheads got cold feet. Vallandigham, braving arrest by crossing the border, gave the keynote address at the convention and nominated Lincoln's twice-fired former general George McClellan as the Democrats' presidential candidate. He expected to be arrested, and that would be the pretext for Copperhead insurrection. But the arrest never came. Lincoln decided it would do more harm than good.

Disappointed, the Confederate spies returned to Canada and postponed the Chicago uprising until Election Day, when a simultaneous raid on New York would leave the largest Northern cities in ruins. Before then, however, conspirators in Chicago and Indianapolis were arrested. Authorities found hundreds of loaded revolvers and shotguns, some in boxes labeled "Gospel Tracts." The New York plot failed due to poor execution.

"REBELLION IN THE NORTH!!" one paper blared. The apparent collusion of leading Democrats with Confederates and homegrown traitors became fodder for Republican attacks. Sherman's capture of Atlanta in September 1864, meanwhile, quieted Northern unease. Though Lincoln had considered his defeat in the election "exceedingly likely," support from soldiers furious at the treacherous Democrats gave him the electoral votes of every state still in the Union except Kentucky, Delaware, and New Jersey.

In the end, even those Copperheads who were prepared to obstruct the war effort by discouraging enlistment and subverting the draft balked at the far more difficult and dangerous work of setting up a rival government. "These men were weak amateurs in the rigorous art of conspiracy," one scholar wrote. Yet the periodic outbreaks of violence and discontent in the Midwest required the U.S. government to deploy thousands of troops there that it could have used elsewhere. Confederate officials estimated that their efforts to sow division in the North kept some sixty thousand federal troops off the field of battle.

The South, however, faced even worse home-front problems, including draft resistance and separatism. The Confederacy was even less united than the Union it sought to destroy.

2. Seceding from Secession

A common Southern objection to disunion had always been that disintegration, once set in motion, would never end. In 1798, Thomas Jefferson warned a fellow Virginian that if the Union split at the Potomac, it wouldn't solve the problem of political divisions. "Are we not men still to the south of that," Jefferson asked, "and with all the passions of men?" Secession would splinter any government formed in its name. In a separate Southern nation, Virginia and the Carolinas would have a falling-out, then Virginia itself would break up, and so on.

The antebellum South had never been as cohesive as secessionists wanted it to be. Even after Sumter, white Southerners could only hope their fractures would melt away in the heat of battle. In November 1861, on a day appointed by President Davis for fasting and prayer, a Richmond minister told his parishioners that God had put the divided Southern people "into the furnace of war, that they might be welded into one great, united, and loving people, fused together by common weakness, common suffering, and common triumphs." War would smooth out the South's "diversities"—or those diversities would destroy the Confederacy.

The fusion never happened; the welding was left unfinished. After secession, slaves and pro-Union citizens avoided contributing to the war effort, allied with the United States, and even tried to form free and independent republics. Much of Arkansas and Missouri were consumed by their own mini–civil wars. Lingering loyalty to the Union, particularly in mountainous regions, where there were few slaves and where citizens were resentful of the master class, undermined the Richmond government and contributed to its fall.

To marshal the resources of a divided country, Confederates had to centralize government far beyond what even Republicans had dreamed of (at least before the war). Like a marriage started in adultery, it proved difficult to fight a long, bloody war on a foundation of states' rights. The Confederacy's own founding creed became a luxury it could ill afford.

In April 1862, more than a year before the Union adopted conscription, the Confederate government enacted the first military draft in American history: all able-bodied men had to serve their country, regardless of whether or not they thought it should exist.

Stubborn states' rights devotees condemned the draft as an unprecedented extension of power over the lives and liberties of citizens. The governor of Georgia called it a "dangerous usurpation . . . at war with all the principles for which Georgia entered into the revolution." A popular editor in Raleigh threatened that his state would remain in the Confederacy only "as long as it is to the interest of North Carolina to do so, and no longer."

Defenders of the draft contorted themselves to defend the measure. Jefferson Davis invoked the "necessary and proper" clause that the Confederates had imported into their Constitution from the U.S. charter—the same provision long used by big-government proponents like Alexander Hamilton and Henry Clay to justify innovative uses of federal power. "No man has any individual rights which come into conflict with the welfare of the country," Louis Wigfall of Texas proclaimed in the Confederate senate—the reverse of the South's much-boasted commitment to limited government and states' rights.

However, wary white Southerners didn't resent the Confederacy's ideological hypocrisy so much as the class interests it exposed. An amendment to the draft law exempted any owner of twenty slaves or more. Its logic was simple: Too many absentee masters would weaken the system of racial domination the war was supposed to protect. Without close oversight, even more slaves would flee to Union lines.

But non–slave owners saw the "Twenty-Negro Law" as proof that the conflict was "a rich man's war and a poor man's fight." Up-country farmers, especially in the Appalachians, considered the draft more threatening than Lincoln's armies. Ironically, the secessionists' greatest fear—that the South's non-slaveholding white majority would turn against slavery—was realized only after the war began. Poor whites resented being asked to risk everything in a fight that would gain them nothing. Some even turned the separatists' arguments against them by calling for secession from the Confederacy. In 1863, John A. Campbell, assistant secretary of war, forwarded a disturbing letter to Davis. It read in part: "The condition of things in the mountain districts menaces the existence of the Confederacy as fatally as…the armies of the United States."

Throughout the secession crisis, Virginians west of the Appalachians had warned that the dissolution of the Union would trigger the dissolution of the state. A region too steep for large-scale farming, with far fewer slaves than the tidewater districts, its inhabitants resented slaveholder control over state politics. Western Virginia "suffered more from…her eastern brethren than ever the Cotton States all put together have suffered from the North," a local paper declared.

Closer to Pittsburgh than to Richmond, Virginia's northwestern counties had strong ties to the free states of Pennsylvania and Ohio. They had long dreamed of independence from the coast. In the 1780s, a separatist movement tried to set up a new state called Westsylvania. A decade later, men from western Virginia participated in the separatist Whiskey Rebellion. Now western delegates in Richmond vowed that their constituents would never swear allegiance to the Confederacy. They would secede from the state in order to stay loyal to the Union.

After Sumter, when Lincoln asked the still-loyal states for seventy-five thousand troops to suppress the rebellion, the convention meeting in Richmond voted to take Virginia out of the Union. Most of the dissenters came from western Virginia, which overwhelmingly rejected secession in a subsequent referendum. "We can look to Richmond for taxes and treason, but for little else," a newspaper sneered. At public meetings throughout the mountain counties, residents called for a region-wide convention to consider secession from Virginia.

Standing in their way was the United States Constitution, which prohibits any new state to form within the territory of another without that state's permission. Because Lincoln refused to admit that Virginia had in fact seceded, the clause still applied. With some sly maneuvering, however, a workaround was found: a dissident convention, representing a fraction of Virginians, declared all state offices vacant and claimed itself as the legitimate state government. Despite the "somewhat farcical air" of the proceedings, Lincoln recognized the "Restored Government of Virginia," and Congress welcomed its senators and representatives to Washington. The irregular legislature endorsed the Westerners' bid for statehood, and the ruse was complete.

The position of each side in the broader struggle was thus reversed— Lincoln backed the right of West Virginia to secede, while Southern leaders rejected it. Neither the real Virginia government nor the Confederacy recognized West Virginia. It survived only because tens of thousands of Union troops used long Allegheny ridges to shield it from Confederate attack. After the war, Virginia sued to contest the secession of its western counties, but the Supreme Court denied its claim. Yet even to this day, legal scholars and Confederate apologists continue to debate the legitimacy of West Virginia's existence.

West Virginia's success inspired other anti-Confederate Southerners to try the same thing. East Tennessee, where, as in West Virginia, steep peaks and valleys made slavery impractical, also had a long history of seeking statehood. In the 1780s, the region had collapsed into civil war between North Carolina loyalists and advocates for a new state of Franklin. Congress refused to recognize Franklin, but support for statehood endured even after the admission of Tennessee. In 1842, the state legislature defeated a resolution—sponsored by a young senator named Andrew Johnson—to establish a new state in the mountainous East.

Twenty years later, support for statehood surged as rivals in local politics joined to oppose secession from the Union even if that meant secession from Tennessee. William Brownlow, a shaggy-haired ex-Whig editor and a popular itinerant preacher, had traveled widely through the United States—an experience that gave him, as historian David C. Downing writes, "an almost mystical conviction that the country was all one, that the states were made only by drawing surveyor's lines on a map." No abolitionist—slavery had the blessing of "the Redeemer of the world," Brownlow contended; its critics were "fiery bigots" and "hypocritical freedom-shriekers"—he believed deeply in the perpetuity of the Union. In 1861, Brownlow promised to "fight the Secession leaders till Hell freezes over, and then fight them on the ice."

Brownlow's sworn enemy in Tennessee politics—"an UNMITIGATED LIAR...and a VILLAINOUS COWARD," he called him—was Andrew Johnson, former governor and congressman, proud Jacksonian Democrat, the only U.S. senator who hadn't surrendered his seat when his state seceded. Brownlow had long despised Johnson, but the slaveholders' secession revealed how much they had in common. Both hailed from humble origins and detested the proslavery elite; both had supported East Tennessee's statehood push. Brownlow insisted the poor farmers of the region would "never live in a Southern Confederacy and be made hewers of wood and drawers of water for a set of aristocrats and overbearing tyrants"—the slave masters. Johnson fully agreed.

After Sumter, when Tennessee followed Virginia into the Confederacy, the mountain people hoped their region would be allowed to remain neutral. With its strategic location and valuable resources, however, that soon became impossible. Rising up against the occupying Confederate army, local conspirators burned five railroad bridges to obstruct troop movements. "The whole country is now in a state of rebellion," one officer warned his superiors. Gray-clad troops invaded the region, declared martial law, and used mass imprisonments and executions to command loyalty. Fighting-age men fled for their lives, many of them to Union lines.

But it proved difficult to win hearts and minds in a land one officer deemed a bastion of "unionism and traitorism." The Confederates used the area's forbidding terrain as effectively as the Union did in West Virginia—until 1863, when federal troops finally entered the region, greeted by throngs of cheering residents "almost crazed with joy," as one soldier wrote, some bearing homemade cakes. The region's secession from the state wouldn't be necessary.

Resistance was nearly as strong elsewhere in the southern Appalachians. Some even spoke of linking the rebellious upland counties in several Confederate states and forming a new Union state called Nickajack, after the indigenous name for the area where Tennessee, Georgia, and Alabama met. If created, it would have pointed like a dagger into the heart of the Confederacy.

During the Alabama convention in early 1861, delegates from the state's northern counties had tried to resist the secessionist juggernaut and even spoke of taking their counties out of the state. On July 4, 1861, a meeting at Looney's Tavern in Winston County drew a crowd in the thousands. The attendees declared that the county would remain neutral and asked both armies to leave them "alone, unmolested that we may work out our own political and financial destiny here in these hills and mountains of North Alabama." If a state could secede from the Union, a county could secede from the state.

At that, a Confederate sympathizer in the crowd shouted, "Ho ho! Winston secedes. The Free State of Winston!" The name stuck. Subversion in north Alabama was widespread throughout the war. Hunting for deserters and draft dodgers, officers "burned the woods and sifted the ashes for conscripts," one soldier wrote. Thousands from the region joined a Union cavalry unit and marched with Sherman to the sea.

Perhaps the most famous story of anti-Confederate rebellion unfolded in Mississippi's southeastern Piney Woods region, full of primeval forests and dense, impassable swamps. With few connections to outside markets, farmers eked out a living among the barrens and bogs. Only 12 percent of Jones County's population was enslaved, less than anywhere else in a state where the majority of residents weren't free. Whites in Jones County overwhelmingly opposed secession and were bitterly disappointed when their delegate to the state convention ignored their instructions and voted to leave the Union.

Even so, many Jones County men joined the Confederate army. Among them was a devout Baptist preacher named Newton Knight. Thirty-one years old, Knight was tall, curly-haired, and bearded, with sharp, intense eyes. He attained the rank of sergeant after most of the men in his unit fell ill, but Knight soon grew weary of war, especially after a young nephew was killed. When the Twenty-Negro Law passed, Knight abandoned the army and returned home. To avoid the Confederacy's often vicious draft enforcers, he fled to the lowlands and joined runaway slaves and other outlaws whose backwoods encampment became a fragile sort of fugitives' republic, a swamp society of roughly one hundred outcasts deep in the dimly lit backcountry of the Confederate president's home state. Knight called himself a "Union man." The password to enter the hideaway was "I am of the Red, White, and Blue."

Facing a growing rebellion, Confederate officers sent bloodhounds into the woods to track down Knight and his crew. Fierce, deadly clashes ensued; the insurgents assassinated a Confederate officer and distributed food seized from army wagons to starving local families. Knight and his followers raised the United States flag over a local courthouse and apparently even drew up a declaration of independence. Hoping for Union support, they sent the document to William Tecumseh Sherman, whose Union forces were nearby. Sherman mentioned it in a letter to Henry C. Halleck, general in chief of the Union army. It hasn't survived.

When no help was forthcoming and five regiments of Confederate troops prepared to put down the revolt, the Knight group disbanded. Some escaped to join Sherman. Knight retreated further into the swamps. Shortly before his death in 1922, the former guerrilla leader denied to an interviewer that Jones County had seceded from the Confederacy. He preferred to say it had never left the Union at all.

As much as its industrial weakness and failure to win recognition from European powers—the intervention that had made all the difference for the United States during its own revolution—the South's internal divisions helped bring down the Confederacy. Desertion was endemic. By 1864, half the Confederate army was absent without leave. Half a million Southerners, both white and black, joined the Union army. On the home front, slaves and citizens alike traded with the foe. "We are fighting each other harder than we ever fought the enemy," a Georgia newspaper complained. The rebels had to fight three separate wars: one against the United States, another against poor up-country whites, and a third, perhaps the most decisive of all, against their own freedom-seeking slaves.

Too late, Davis proposed to enlist slaves to fight in exchange for freedom. The last months of the war found white Southerners passionately debating which mattered more, slavery or secession. The jury was still out when Grant cornered Lee at Appomattox and ended the rebellion.

3. The Legality of Secession

The Union's victory didn't resolve the bitterly contested constitutional issue that had precipitated the war in the first place: Had the states, when they entered the Union, reserved the right to secede? The text of the Constitution is silent. The writings of the founders are inconclusive. The question may be unanswerable. Could a continent-wide contest of mass death, strategic maneuvers, and brute force settle a thorny legal and philosophical dispute? It was the "odious nature" of the question, John Quincy Adams once observed, that it could be "settled only at the cannon's mouth."

Legal historian Cynthia Nicoletti has argued that the Civil War can best be understood as a medieval-style "trial by combat," a resort to martial means of conflict resolution when persuasion, politics, and law proved inconclusive. The North won the duel. But that outcome didn't carry the strength of a judicial ruling. For a government ostensibly fighting for the rule of law, mere victory on the battlefield offered a weak foundation on which to rest the legitimacy of national authority. For the sake of appearances, many Republicans wanted to settle the secession question once and for all in an appropriate constitutional forum.

The prosecution of Jefferson Davis offered an opportunity. Captured in Georgia, Davis was imprisoned at Fort Monroe on Virginia's tidewater coast. With much of the North calling for blood, federal attorneys planned to try Davis for treason. But the case never went to trial. Jurors in Richmond, where the trial would be held, might exonerate the former rebel leader. Davis's acquittal would undermine the case for secession's illegality, undermine the result of the war, perhaps even imply that hundreds of thousands had died in vain. Federal prosecutors weren't willing to take the risk. When Andrew Johnson, Lincoln's successor, issued a blanket amnesty for ex-Confederates on Christmas Day 1868, Davis went free. In keeping with the American tradition, the underlying issue remained unresolved.

Four months later, seeing the need for a final statement on secession's constitutionality, the Supreme Court stepped in. The new, pro-Union government of Texas wanted to reclaim U.S. bonds that its Confederate precursor had sold. The case, *Texas v. White*, turned on whether the state had actually seceded or remained in the Union throughout the war. Chief Justice Salmon P. Chase, a founder of the Republican Party and Lincoln's former treasury secretary, seized the opportunity to enshrine in law what the war had seemingly settled in fact.

In a one-paragraph aside, Chase ruled against secession. "The Constitution, in all its provisions," Chase wrote, "looks to an indestructible Union, composed of indestructible states." Texas, therefore, had never left the Union; the sale of bonds by the Confederate-era state government, like all actions of that "unlawful combination of individuals," was null and void.

In lieu of an actual legal argument for the Union's indestructibility, Chase appealed, as Daniel Webster and Andrew Jackson had before him, to a flattened account of American history. The Union was the creation of "common origin, mutual sympathies, kindred principles, similar interests, and geographical relations," Chase pronounced. We have seen otherwise. Americans did not have a common origin; they came from all over Europe and, increasingly, the world. Instead of mutual sympathies, they harbored intense antipathies, from the provincial attitudes of the colonial period to the clashing civilizations of the antebellum era. Their principles, far from kindred, clashed so completely and seemed so incompatible that a devastating war had just been fought over which would rule. Hostile, mutually exclusive interests had led to battles over trade and expansion, race and the role of government, disagreements that survived the Civil War and shaped national politics for another century and more. The country's "geographical relations" were defined by soaring mountain chains, uncharted expanses, and broad rivers that divided Americans more than common possession of an enormous continent united them.

In his dissent, one justice rebuked the majority's willfully warped account of the American past: "This court is bound to know and notice the public history of the nation."

Little discussed at the time, Chase's brief statement against secession remains the only legal confirmation of the military verdict of the Civil War. Far from settling the dispute that led to the cataclysm, *Texas v. White* brushed it aside. "It failed to sort out the weighty legal issues the war left not quite resolved," Nicoletti concludes. The argument for secession was never properly countered through logic or law but suppressed by overwhelming force—a verdict ratified, almost as an afterthought, in a perfunctory judicial diktat. The sense among white Southerners that their consent to be governed by the United States, once withdrawn, was never again solicited or given fueled neo-Confederate nostalgia and the rise of Lost Cause mythology.

In an 1862 essay, "The Contest in America," the English philosopher John Stuart Mill defended the right of secession. But that, he added, did not mean that secession was always right. "Secession may be laudable, and so may any other kind of insurrection, but it may also be an enormous crime," Mill observed. "It is the one or the other, according to the object and the provocation." The consequences of a rebellion were what mattered, and "if there ever was an object which, by its bare announcement, stamped rebels against a particular community as enemies of mankind, it is the one professed by the South." That object was the perpetuation of human bondage.

Seceding for the sake of slavery could only be morally reprehensible and politically illegitimate. Yet the fact that it was the South that finally pulled the plug on the faltering Union has obscured certain distinctions that ought to be kept in mind. Secession may not slumber forever as an arcane legalistic question of merely antiquarian interest. It may prove insufficient in countering Texas or California separatists to dismiss their independence drive with the brusque assertion that the matter was "settled at Appomattox" or in a long-forgotten Supreme Court ruling.

Today, those who defend the right of secession often downplay the evils of slavery and the extent to which the Confederacy was formed to defend it, while those rightly horrified by chattel bondage and clear-eyed about how it caused the Civil War too hastily dismiss one of America's founding principles—the right to alter or abolish a destructive form of government—as irreparably sullied by association with slave-holders. We need not limit our political imaginations to outworn platitudes and simplistic assumptions that have made and would keep us prisoners of an inherited, unalterable past.

PART IV

RETURN OF THE REPRESSED

An old chestnut has it that after the Civil War, the United States turned from a singular noun into a plural one—*they are* became *it is*. Four years of fighting, however destructive, at least united a fractious country. But there is little evidence for this. The change was part of a larger grammatical shift that had nothing to do with the war. America remained divided along sectional, economic, ideological, and, above all, racial lines. The trauma of the war made another attempt at secession by the South nearly unthinkable, but it also revived compromise as the national civic religion. The renewal of the founding bargain—Northern silence for Southern allegiance—lasted well into the twentieth century and underwrote America's rise as a world power. But those lingering divisions couldn't be repressed forever. The effort to ignore them became increasingly difficult, and the possibility of another collapse—a nervous breakdown—more likely. The chased-away specter of dissolution returned time and again in plans and prophecies, fears and fantasies. That is to say, in dreams.

CHAPTER 11

The War Was Fought in Vain

When the armies were disbanded and marched home, there were senses in which the war was not over.

—MURAT HALSTEAD, 1877

THE END OF THE WAR didn't mean the Union was restored. "If an earthquake had cleft this continent in twain, we could not be further separated than we are," William Henry Trescott, a Southern intellectual, noted in 1863. The most important dividing line was not a physical one but that "great, red river of kindred blood, which, swollen by dismal streams from Manassas and Murfreesboro, Antietam and Fredericksburg, now rolls its fearful border between hostile nations."

When the river dried up, it left behind a wrecked and ruined country. It was not only the South that had to be rebuilt—the fractured Union had to be reconstructed from the foundation up. Frederick Douglass called for seizing the moment to create "something incomparably better than the old Union," one more truly perfect, its fusion more complete. There would be no quarter given for sectionalism, no tolerance for supposed states' rights. Wendell Phillips, the former abolitionist, called for "a government so broad, so impartial...that no local prejudice, no local malignity, no local wealth, can hold up its hand against the peaceful exercise of the citizenship under its flag." In his 1871 essay "Democratic Vistas," Walt Whitman announced that "aggregate America" had a cosmic mission to bring forth "a new earth and a new man."

Yet as old divisions reemerged in this aggregate America, conflicts and contradictions were once again stifled, wished away, ignored. The

Cartoonist Thomas Nast ridiculed the Democrats'
post–Civil War slogan "The Union As It Was," as a cover
for white supremacy. (*Library of Congress*)

Union was reconstructed on the same weak foundation it had so
tenuously stood on since the beginning and with the same shoddy
materials. Even the usually ebullient poet was dismayed. American life
had become "canker'd, crude, superstitious, and rotten," Whitman
complained, referring to Gilded Age excess and inequality. Expansion
had done nothing to resolve the nation's flaws and inconsistencies,
Whitman reflected: "In vain have we annex'd Texas, California, Alaska,
and reach north for Canada and south for Cuba." The body had grown
at the expense of the soul. He offered a grim prediction: "The United
States are destined either to surmount the gorgeous history of feudal-
ism or else prove the most tremendous failure of time."

Today, we are still sorting out the conflicts from that era—who
belongs in the Union, who it is for, how much we are willing to give
up to see it preserved. The choice made then—Union without
unity— continues to limit our sense of what's possible. Historians call
Reconstruction "the second founding." Yet just as Americans went to
war over the compromises of the first, today's partisan death match

can be traced to the contradictions the sequel didn't resolve. When our leaders lamely insist—after a divisive election, say, or an act of patriotic gore—that the country needs to come together, unite as one, they are simultaneously reenacting and revealing the limits of the fraudulent reunion that followed but failed to truly end the first American Civil War.

1. A Second Rebellion?

Appomattox had resolved nothing. Fears of treason and visions of subversion haunted the country. Scarred by disunion, Americans dreaded its return. A Union torn apart and only loosely stitched back together might easily be sundered again. Across a country unsettled by war and united by force, the rippling effects of that trauma were—and are—fought over every day.

Anything seemed possible. Politics was as turbulent as before, the restored Union no less fragile. The fundamental tension at the heart of national politics—whether the country would stay together or crack up—remained. The house divided was divided still. Intense partisan battles might bring a second, even bloodier conflict. "The First Southern War may prove not the last," George Templeton Strong, a New York diarist, wrote worriedly in 1866.

Almost immediately, the longed-for peace was shattered by arguments over the same issue that had started the war in the first place: Was it possible for states to leave the Union? Only now it took a new form: Had the Southern states ever really left? Just before his shocking assassination, as the challenges of Reconstruction loomed, Lincoln dismissed the "merely metaphysical question." It wasn't important.

His death left the matter suspended. But it came to dominate postwar politics, prompting whiplash-inducing reversals by almost everyone involved. Republicans who had dismissed secession as impossible now declared that the slave states had committed suicide. By right of conquest, the federal government could demand anything it wanted to before restoring those states to life. Congress could even redraw state lines or redistribute seized lands to former slaves. The task of

Reconstruction, as they saw it, was to rebuild the Union so it could never be broken again.

By contrast, Southerners and their Northern allies, defenders of the right of secession, demanded immediate, unconditional readmission—no punishment for rebels, no help for the four million freedmen. Lincoln's successor, Andrew Johnson of Tennessee, a lifelong Democrat, embraced this position. Though he had supported the Union, Johnson abhorred slaves as much as he resented their masters. Unfree labor victimized poor whites, who couldn't afford to own slaves themselves. After the war, Johnson opposed top-to-bottom political revolution in the South, especially if it empowered blacks. He doled out pardons to any rebel who requested one and allowed Southern states to pass "black codes" that imposed harsh restrictions on the former slaves—a new form of bondage.

The South had lost the war but seemed poised to win the peace. "All is wrong," former Union general Benjamin Butler wrote. "We are losing the just results of this four years struggle."

Bold action was needed to enshrine those just results in the Constitution itself. After the Thirteenth Amendment abolished slavery, Republicans drew up a new amendment guaranteeing the rights and liberties of citizenship to all Americans regardless of race—overturning the *Dred Scott* decision that banned black citizenship. The Fourteenth Amendment would reengineer the structure of the Union, retrofit the ancient, tottering edifice for purposes more inclusive and ennobling than those for which it had originally been built.

The amendment passed Congress and went to the states for ratification. The former rebel states would be readmitted to the Union only after they approved it. Even so, every one of them, except the president's own Tennessee, rejected it out of hand.

Frustrated by Johnson's embrace of the rebels and contempt for former slaves, Republicans in Congress seized control of Reconstruction. Overriding Johnson's vetoes—he issued more than all his predecessors combined—they created five military districts throughout the former Confederacy. Backed by twenty thousand troops, they would overthrow the political structure that had protected slavery and nurtured secession. It was the "most radical hour of American history," one scholar noted. The Union would be remade at the point of a gun.

* * *

Each side accused the other of favoring disunion. Democrats argued that the Republican-led Congress, by excluding Southern members, was an illegitimate, revolutionary body. All its acts—including the Fourteenth Amendment—were void. Johnson called his enemies *"Radical Distructionists"* and "dissolutionists." Keeping the South out of the Union was "secession in another form." "The Black Republicans plunged the country into one civil war," a Democratic editor contended. "Is it unreasonable to suppose that they would not stop at plunging it into another?"

"We are to have another war," wrote William Brownlow, the former East Tennessee separatist and pro-Union preacher who succeeded Johnson as governor. His wartime alliance with Johnson now broken, Brownlow accused the president of treason. Johnson "in the next rebellion will take the place of Jeff Davis," he predicted.

Amid loud, loose talk of a second civil war and coups d'état, any number of Sumter-like showdowns might have sparked another conflagration. Republicans feared Johnson, backed into a corner, would lash out, perhaps even try to seize total power over the divided government. Some Democrats urged him to do so. Every day that Congress met without its duly-elected Southern members was "a triumph of treason," one paper said. The president should summon a volunteer army to invade the Capitol and hang the traitors. When Southerners showed up for the next session, Johnson should have the army escort them to their seats.

The next conflict, if it came, would feature a confusing array of alliances and allegiances. If Johnson used the military to force the South's readmission, one Mississippian assured him, thousands of "trained men, of the late Confederate army...will bear the banner of the Union, to sustain the constitution." A supporter from South Carolina offered Johnson three hundred thousand muskets and men to fire them if it became necessary to "usurp the Government, in order to save the Government." A Confederate veteran promised to take the field on the president's behalf if a new war broke out—but only once his wound from the last one had healed.

As the clashes intensified, Republicans began talking about a tool in the Constitution that had never been applied to the presidency before: impeachment. To them, Johnson's presidency amounted to a vast conspiracy against the Union. He could not be trusted. With large majorities in both houses of Congress, Republicans thought they had the votes to convict.

But what if Johnson refused to yield his office? It wasn't impossible to imagine. As impeachment loomed, Johnson told the cabinet he could never "surrender his office to a usurper, and thus yield the high duty imposed upon him by his oath." During an 1866 cross-country tour, the president, always bombastic and often incoherent and occasionally drunk, remarked, "[I] might have made myself Dictator any day by the aid of the army, if I chose."

If Johnson did try to resist removal, Republicans took heart that Ulysses S. Grant, the top general in the army, would surely refuse any illegal order. Still, Union veterans in Washington began training. Chapters of the Grand Army of the Republic, a new group of war vets, sprouted up across the North, looking to some like a Wide Awake–style army-in-waiting. "The blood and treasure of the country" would rescue Congress from a presidential coup, one Maine resident wrote. A Midwesterner confided to his congressman that he looked forward to slaughtering Democrats "as you would wolves."

Even a sober-minded statesman like William Pitt Fessenden, a respected Maine senator, saw the country tipping toward "another fight… the final one." "I almost fear he contemplates civil war," Senator John Sherman wrote to his brother about Johnson. A Wisconsin representative introduced a bill to distribute the weapons in federal arsenals to Northern governors to keep the president from using them against Congress. Sam Ward, a well-connected lobbyist, thought the country in even "more volcanic danger" than it had been in the secession winter of 1861.

In early 1868, the House finally impeached Johnson—nominally for violating a law barring him from firing cabinet members but really for opposing Reconstruction. The trial in the Senate split the country. Johnson's supporters were breathless in condemning the proceedings. Some wrote to the president offering whatever he needed— *"ballots or bullets"*—to stay in office. "We are in the midst of a revolutionary crisis," warned the *National Intelligencer,* Johnson's unofficial mouthpiece— a "second rebellion."

As the clouds of crisis gathered, a Texas paper got ahead of itself: "WAR! WAR!! WAR!!—THE PRESIDENT IMPEACHED! THE FIRST

GUN FIRED!...GRANT DECLARES HIMSELF DICTATOR!—SECRETARY
SEWARD RESIGNED! GENERAL WAR INEVITABLE!" None of it—except
impeachment—was true. But to Republicans, it was proof of an
unquenched thirst for battle among Southerners unchastened by military defeat. A Massachusetts politician urged Charles Sumner to arrest
the president *before* his conviction in the Senate, even if it triggered
wider violence: "Well, We have been through One War, But rather than
to have treason and traitors triumph, we will fight Again, And Make
Clean Work and Sure, if the Cause demands it."

The president revealed little about his intentions, though he did say
he placed his trust in "the *good sense of the army*" to ensure the Constitution wasn't violated. Disappointing some Democrats, Johnson did
nothing to encourage preparations for battle. Yet it might have been
their fear of violence that convinced enough Republican senators not
to remove him from office (Johnson was acquitted by a single vote). A
fellow Tennessean told the president after the trial that his conviction
"would have resulted either in civil war or despotism, or perhaps both."

Johnson's narrow escape staved off catastrophe. Yet the threat of another
civil war soon loomed amid a hard-fought presidential campaign—the
first since the return of peace. Congress readmitted seven Southern states
that, under military occupation, had ratified the Fourteenth Amendment
and drawn up new constitutions granting black suffrage. That ensured
their loyalty to the Union—and, not incidentally, to the Republican Party.

At their convention in New York, dominated by Confederate luminaries, Democrats adopted a platform condemning military reconstruction
as "unconstitutional, revolutionary, null, and void." For president they
nominated Horatio Seymour, a bland former New York governor and a
Copperhead who in 1863 had called Manhattan's bloodthirsty Draft Riot-
ers his "friends." Francis Blair Jr. of Missouri, an ex-Republican who
switched parties after the war, was his running mate. A former Union
general with a nasty drinking problem, Blair had recently published a letter suggesting the next Democratic administration should use the army
to oust the Republican state governments in the South and restore power
to white people—a move that would have triggered another civil war.

Blair's presence on the ticket enabled Republicans to equate Democratic victory with the resurrection of the Confederacy. "Seymour was

opposed to the late war," they joked, "and Blair is in favor of the next one." Johnson's opponents rallied behind the popular Grant—heralded in the Republican press as "*Union Saving* Grant"—with his upbeat, if ambiguous, slogan: "Let us have peace." Grant swept the election, thanks to the backlash over Blair's remarks and the surge of black votes in the readmitted Southern states.

The next year, Republicans added another amendment to the Constitution expanding suffrage to black men. Reconstruction had reached its peak. Yet the return to normalcy Grant promised was the first sign of faltering Northern will. Republicans believed in Reconstruction, in that "aggregate America" of which Whitman and others continued to dream, but not if it meant another war. For black Americans, however, there would be no peace.

2. The Backward Revolution

One morning in June 1865, after eating breakfast with his grandchildren, Edmund Ruffin of Virginia, a leading secession advocate, ascended to his study, wrapped his mouth around the muzzle of a rifle, and used a forked stick to pull the trigger. His family ran in to find him still upright in his chair, defiant to the last. Ruffin's beloved Confederacy had surrendered two months earlier. On his desk was a diary in which Ruffin had moments earlier declared his "unmitigated hatred to Yankee rule...& to the perfidious, malignant, & vile Yankee race."

Ruffin wasn't the only ex-Confederate who refused to accept the verdict of battle. Thousands of Confederate soldiers and officials fled the country. Some went to Mexico or Brazil, where they established exile communities that still survive. (At annual celebrations, gray-coated boys and bonneted girls quickstep along a dance floor painted with the Stars and Bars.) Others ended up in London, where Louis T. Wigfall, a former general, schemed to start a war between the United States and Britain, thinking that, amid the chaos, a new Southern rebellion would begin.

Even with Jefferson Davis in prison and Robert E. Lee commanding only a small Virginia college, it wasn't inconceivable that the South could rise again. In 1866, as Congress and the president clashed over Reconstruction, a Georgia resident wrote Johnson that his neighbors hoped the partisan bickering would "paralyze the old government and pave the way for the easy achievement of Southern Independence."

For the most part, though, outright secessionism was finally, mercifully, dead. It had brought too much ruin. Ex-Confederates realized they didn't need to secede to get what they wanted. After Appomattox, Southern whites recognized that rejoining the Union was the surest path to getting back their prewar privileges. They rediscovered what generations of their forebears had known: the Union offered the best possible protection for the racist political and economic system they cherished and sought to reestablish in all but name.

Only months after the war, white Southerners were again singing the praises of the Constitution. Blaming Republicans for trying to impose their ideas on the whole country, Southerners tried to reclaim the Union as their own. In July 1867, a former Confederate senator called the Union "the wisest, noblest, and grandest contribution ever made by the human intellect to the science of government."

The South's understanding of the Union, however, was quite different from the "aggregate America" that Whitman and other Northerners longed to forge. Southern whites would remain loyal only if the Union was rededicated to states' rights and white supremacy. After spending time in postwar Georgia in late 1865, Massachusetts lawyer Sidney Andrews denounced the "sham Unionism" of the ex-Confederates. "There may be in it the seed of loyalty," he wrote, "but woe to him who mistakes the germ for the ripened fruit!"

Unrepentant rebels swore to "redeem" the South from federal tyranny and black suffrage. That meant reducing the Reconstruction amendments to "dead letters on the statute-book," in the words of one newspaper, and using vigilante violence to reclaim what they had lost on the battlefield. In Memphis in May 1866, an accidental collision between two carriages led to a three-day bloodbath in which roving gangs led by white police officers rampaged through black neighborhoods, leaving forty-six people dead. Three months later in New Orleans, whites massacred black politicians and activists. According to one Union veteran, the "wholesale slaughter and the little regard paid to human life" were worse than the war. "Does this mean that the rebellion is to begin again?" asked Carl Schurz. Perhaps, rather, it had never ended.

Founded as a social club for Confederate veterans, the Ku Klux Klan marauded through the countryside, assassinating black legislators, shutting down polling stations, terrorizing the black population. Night riders in white cloaks (to make them look like ghosts of Confederate soldiers) targeted blacks who dared to vote, go to school, or start a business—anyone who behaved "like they thought anything of themselves," as one woman said. Blacks were hunted in public and shot in their homes. Thousands were killed, some en masse, others one by one. "Pray tell me," asked a black congressman from South Carolina, "who is the barbarian here?"

White terrorism became so widespread that it amounted to what Ohio's John Sherman called "organized civil war." Some thought it augured a separatist revival. "The idea and the expectation of a Southern Confederacy—of Southern independence of Northern rule—are by no means dead," observed a Tennessee reverend. A New York religious journal, noting the prevalence of former Confederate officers in the Klan, asked "whether rebellion is not resurgent, or at least turning over in its grave and threatening to come forth."

The reign of terror worked to turn the tide of Reconstruction. Rival state governments backed by Union troops and white paramilitary gangs—warlords, essentially—competed for legitimacy, territory, and revenue. By 1876, white Democrats had reclaimed control of nearly every former Confederate state. "It seems that we are drifting back under the leadership of the slaveholders," one black Republican wrote. "Our former masters are fast taking the reins of government." Only another invasion could unseat them. Republicans were divided over whether to counter the violence with force. Many had lost interest in Reconstruction.

There was no mystery in what its end would mean. Vulnerable blacks would be at the mercy of vengeful, embittered whites. As an apprehensive Frederick Douglass later observed, "The law on the side of freedom is of great advantage only where there is power to make that law respected." A fitting epitaph for Reconstruction; it ended not because Southern violence brought it down but because an indifferent North declined to prop it up.

In 1873, a financial panic froze markets and triggered an economic meltdown, ending a decade-long boom and plunging the nation into its longest contraction in history. The depression shattered Americans' faith in progress, exacerbated class divisions, and initiated decades of political gridlock. The following year, Democrats took control of the House of Representatives for the first time since the 1850s. For uneasy Republicans, Reconstruction seemed to be a political vulnerability. Paralyzed by the panic and plagued by scandal, the Grant administration adopted a "let-alone policy" toward the formerly rebellious states. American politics, finally "out of the region of the Civil War," as the *Nation* cheered, would be consumed in the years ahead by new battles and different divisions, fresh opportunities for breakdown and fracture.

The let-alone policy all but undid the surrender at Appomattox. If the Constitution went unenforced in the South, noted one Mississippi Republican, "then the war was fought in vain." In 1875, the South Carolina militia that had fired the first shots at Fort Sumter toured Boston and New York. They found a surprisingly warm reception. Already, the conflicts that had led to war were being repressed, submerged for the sake of unity. Frederick Douglass feared the future. "If war among the whites brought peace and liberty to blacks," he asked, "what will peace among the whites bring?"

Before there could be peace among the whites, however, the country had to face another near eruption of civil war. In 1876, the United States marked its one hundredth birthday. What ought to have been a moment of celebration instead became one of anxious hand-wringing and morose contemplation. Was constitutional breakdown the new normal rather than a regrettable exception? "The chances are by no means inconsiderable," one prominent Democrat mused, "that our form of govt may not survive another 4 of July without serious modification, the results of a perhaps bloody strife."

It all stemmed, as so many American crises had, and would, from a disputed presidential election. The 1876 contest pit Samuel Tilden, New York's Democratic governor and a tremendously wealthy corporate lawyer, against Rutherford B. Hayes, Ohio's governor and a decorated Union general wounded five times in battle but nonetheless a dull, uninspiring figure—a "third-rate non-entity," as Henry Adams wrote. Riding a wave of Americans' discontent with the economy and the Grant administration's shameless corruption, Tilden won the popular vote and, seemingly, the Electoral College. But when Republican officials

in three Southern states—Louisiana, South Carolina, and Florida—
invalidated Democratic votes because of fraud and violent intimidation, Hayes seemed headed for the White House. Democrats vowed not
to let that happen.

"The air is full of coming trouble," one Republican wrote. Some
spoke of a "bloody revolution." Others predicted that "the days of our
republic are numbered." Hard-core Democrats, especially those from
the South, rallied around the ominous slogan "Tilden or War." Rumors
circulated that if Hayes was declared the winner, Tilden would hold a
counter-inauguration in Manhattan, seize the federal treasury building, and fund a shadow government through customs revenues. Democratic state militias would invade Washington and send Hayes back to
Ohio to rule over a Midwestern republic.

Tilden had friends in high places, some of whom seemed willing
and maybe even able to put such a wild plan into effect. George McClellan, the popular Union general and 1864 Democratic candidate,
stumped for Tilden before Election Day and rallied veterans around
the country to support him. Any attempt to prevent Tilden from taking
office would be "revolutionary + must be met by force," McClellan told
his mother. The general's vast network of ex-military admirers encouraged him to take action. One suggested "a little bit of war to inaugu-
rate Mr. Tilden would do us no harm." A Massachusetts ally, referring
to a letter from McClellan detailing certain "potent considerations"
that the general had outlined, wrote, "The few who have seen it open
their eyes wide, and it nerves them on...Any movement to which you
may lend your name...would be the signal for arousing en masse here
all the conservative soldiers and sailors."

Hiding out in his Gramercy Park study, Tilden held himself aloof
from such plans, preferring to labor over a dry legal analysis of the
stalemate and its precedents. He knew, however, as a supporter had
told him, that "well armed men" were ready to march on Washington
and install him in the White House. A single word from Tilden would
plunge the nation "deep in civil war," one journalist wrote. A leading
supporter, financier August Belmont, demanded the candidate show
"radical boldness and recklessness" even if it meant "a revolutionary...
fight." Dutifully, Tilden announced that the inauguration of a "usurper"
as president would justify violent resistance.

Democrats weren't the only ones preparing for war. A Hayes supporter from Texas pledged "hundreds + thousands" of ex-soldiers would
fight for the Republican candidate. Grant, who feared his legacy of ending one civil war would be ruined by his failure to prevent another,
ordered troops to surround the Capitol and re-staffed Washington-area
forts abandoned since Appomattox. William Tecumseh Sherman, Grant's
successor as top general, worried that the military would "be put into a
position to choose between two presidents." Months after marking its centennial, the country was back on the precipice of dissolution.

Pressured by businessmen who disliked the uncertainty, Democrats
and Republicans in Congress agreed to form a fifteen-person commission, composed equally of senators, representatives, and Supreme
Court justices, to sort through the disputed votes. Tilden disparaged
the Democrats' participation as capitulation. "Why surrender now?" he
asked. "Why surrender before the battle, for fear you may have to
surrender after the battle is over?"

In an eight-to-seven party-line vote, the commission gave every
disputed vote to Hayes. Democrats in the House threatened to block certi-
fication of the results in order to force a new election. In a smoke-filled
room at the Wormley Hotel in Washington, party bigwigs agreed to a now-
infamous compromise: Democratic acquiescence to Hayes's inauguration
in exchange for the withdrawal of federal troops from the last Republican
redoubts in the South (Louisiana and South Carolina, where they were
propping up besieged governors). The deal didn't end Reconstruction
overnight, but it ratified what had already begun and brought to a symbolic close the fifteen-year effort to enforce the Constitution in the South.

Wounded by war, devoted to profit rather than principle, grown "tired
of the Negro," as the *New York Herald* put it, Northerners were relieved
to give up on Reconstruction. They would fight to save the Union but
not for the rights of black people. White Southerners would be left to
handle things as they saw fit. Indeed, the new sectional bargain
affirmed the South's contention that union was possible on no other
terms. Georgia's Robert Toombs, a former Confederate general and
cabinet official, said he would "face thirty years of war to get rid of
negro suffrage in the South." No white Northerner would endure the
same to keep it in place. Even former abolitionists sighed and agreed

that the "social, and educational, and moral reconstruction" so desperately needed in the South could "never come from any legislative halls." The essence of the "devil's compromise," as some black Americans called the deal, was a national recommitment to white supremacy, the oldest and strongest union bond of all.

Some had seen the betrayal coming. Years earlier, just after Lincoln issued the Emancipation Proclamation, the former disunion abolitionist Thomas Wentworth Higginson, then commanding the first black Union regiment, worried the country would never fulfill its obligations to former slaves. "Revolutions may go backward," Higginson observed. "The habit of inhumanity" toward blacks was "so deeply impressed upon our people, that it is hard to believe in the possibility of anything better. I dare not yet hope that the promise of the President's proclamation will be kept."

After 1877, the greatest advances for liberty and equality in human history were effectively repealed—except for the abolition of slavery, and even then, the system that replaced it so resembled actual bondage as almost to merit the name. Military withdrawal brought precisely what Frederick Douglass and others had feared: lynchings, voter suppression, segregation. Southern blacks became ensnared in what Eric Foner has called "a seamless web of oppression, whose interwoven economic, political, and social strands all reinforced one another." That web, in a sense, was the Union itself.

In a 1902 memoir, Susie King Taylor, a former slave and Civil War nurse, observed that America remained fatally disunited: "They say, 'One flag, one nation, one country indivisible.' Is this true? Can we say this truthfully, when one race is allowed to burn, hang, and inflict the most horrible torture weekly, monthly, on another? No, we cannot sing 'My country, 'tis of thee, Sweet land of Liberty'! It is hollow mockery."

3. The Great Upheaval

On a glorious spring day in May 1869, two locomotives met at Promontory, Utah, a few miles north of the Great Salt Lake, and forever sealed the permanence of the Union—or so the promoters hoped. The transcontinental railroad had been built in part to keep the Pacific states from spinning out of the American orbit and setting up a separate nation. One of the golden spikes prepared for the ceremony was inscribed by its manufacturer with a fervent prayer: "May God continue the Unity of our Country as this Railroad unites the two great Oceans of the World."

Wood, steel, and steam would help the country heal its wounds. Yet the industrial age they ushered in brought new and dangerous divisions. With the South in ruins, the North emerged as a manufacturing behemoth. But profits accrued to owners rather than workers, widening the divide between haves and have-nots. Within three years of that famous day in Utah, it was revealed that much of the country's political establishment was on the payroll of railroad corporations. Boosterish rhetoric about strengthening the Union had covered for the wealthy and their well-placed cronies to profit at the public's expense. Had hundreds of thousands of Americans died to preserve the blessings of liberty for only an avaricious few?

In the late nineteenth century, a cascade of labor strikes brought new expectations of approaching chaos, even apocalypse. An English visitor observed among the rich "an uneasy feeling that they were living over a mine of social and industrial discontent...and that someday this mine would explode and blow society into the air." Another writer predicted as early as 1871 that the next civil war "would not be sectional and Southern, but internecine and Northern"—a struggle over who would benefit from the consolidation of the Union. "We have not cured the South," the *Nation* informed its Northern readers, "we have ourselves caught the contagion."

The discord subverted Americans' sense of exceptionalism, already tenuous after the Civil War. As the *New York Times* noted, "The days are over in which this country could rejoice in its freedom from the elements of social strife which have long abounded in the old countries."

It wasn't a coincidence that the first major strike took aim at the industry supposedly devoted to uniting the country. In 1877, protests against wage cuts rippled out from the railyards at Martinsburg, West Virginia, spreading to Pittsburgh and then along rail lines throughout the country, reaching as far as Kansas City and San Francisco. "Bread or Blood," the strikers demanded. For two weeks, interstate commerce was effectively shut down as buildings and railcars burned and cities turned into barricaded camps. Enjoying support from locals, the strikes looked like the beginning of an all-out revolution. "Public opinion is almost everywhere in sympathy with the insurrection," the *New York Tribune* reported.

To the elite, this insurrection was no less dangerous than that of 1861. Militia units refused to fire into the crowds; some members joined the picket lines and bunkered in crudely built trenches. In Chicago, businessmen patrolled the streets with loaded rifles. At the request of railroad officials, President Hayes sent three thousand soldiers to suppress the strikes. Troops the government had refused to use to protect blacks in the South were enlisted as unofficial security for private corporations. To businessmen and their handpicked politicians, labor strikes now posed the most severe threat to the Union.

Class conflict replaced sectional division as the likeliest source for a disruption of the constitutional order. Workers and the wealthy were united only in a shared premonition of another collapse. Railroad titan Jay Gould predicted the turmoil was but the beginning of "a great social revolution" that would bring "the destruction of the republican form of government in this country." A pro-labor Pittsburgh paper heralded the onset of "a great civil war…between labor and capital." Before its end, workers would "have our revenge on the men who coined our sweat and muscles into millions for themselves."

In many places, the strikers demonstrated a remarkable cross-racial solidarity; black and white workers marched and fought together. In San Francisco, the story was different. There, down-and-out whites blamed their woes on Chinese immigrants who in the 1850s had begun arriving by the thousands. An 1868 treaty established friendly relations between China and the United States and guaranteed the right of migration. By 1880, Chinese made up one-tenth of California's population and one-fifth of its workforce, most of them men employed in mines and on the railroads.

The backlash against the new arrivals was brutal. In 1871, nineteen Chinese workers were lynched in Los Angeles. After the 1873 financial panic, California's growing labor movement took on a strident anti-immigrant tinge. Strangers from strange lands were being privileged over citizens, demagogues warned—though many of the complainants were themselves of German or Irish descent. Chinese immigrants, encouraged by the money-grubbing railroads, would displace white workers entirely. "Either we must drive out the Chinese slave," the newly formed Workingmen's Party declared, "or we shall soon be slaves our-

selves. There is no other solution of the problem. It is death or victory."
In its first elections, the party won control of the state.

Fears of treachery and subversion, disquieting thoughts about disloyalty and dissolution, continued to shape American life. Unfettered
immigration threatened a new tear in the national fabric, even a fresh
division of the continent. An Oregon senator described the Chinese as
"a distinct and separate nationality"—a threat to American unity.

In 1880, a Californian named Pierton W. Dooner published a novel,
Last Days of the Republic, that was the first of countless "yellow peril" jeremi-
ads to come. Dooner depicted Chinese immigrants as the vanguard for a
takeover of the United States. In the book, the Chinese imperial army over-
throws the Pacific states and then marches east across the continent, revers-
ing manifest destiny. The soldiers occupy Washington and fly the dragon
flag from the dome of the Capitol. The conquest is complete: "The very
name of the United States of America was thus blotted from the record of
nations and peoples." China accomplishes what the Confederacy failed to.

Chinese immigration triggered anxieties about the dissolution of
the Union, but it also awakened California's slumbering separatist
spirit. In 1879, the Sacramento legislature called a state constitutional
convention to enact pro-labor reforms like breaking up monopolies
and raising taxes on the rich. Some wanted to prohibit the Chinese
from testifying in state courts or owning property. Others proposed
banning Chinese immigration entirely, a measure that would have violated the 1868 treaty and resulted in a showdown with Washington.

The more extreme anti-Chinese delegates at the convention
welcomed such a clash. In their opinion, if the United States was to
remain a single nation, it had to be a white Christian nation. Otherwise the country might as well break apart. Only an independent California could control its borders. "If our government don't protect us,
and if our government is to make this State a China Empire," one delegate declared, "I say we have a right to secede." Moderates, alarmed by
secession talk, moved to disavow the state's right to leave the Union.
That motion, initially, was rejected.

The moderates won in the end. The immigration ban didn't make
it into the new constitution, which did, however, prohibit Chinese suffrage and employment on public works projects and instructed the
legislature to do whatever it could to limit the number of new arrivals.

The document also declared that "the State of California is an inseparable part of the American Union." This provision, still in effect,
remains the first obstacle for any movement seeking to realize that
most resilient of California dreams—restoring the Bear Flag Republic.

Yet even if the 1879 California convention stopped short of directly
challenging the federal government, the delegates' secession threats
may not have been inconsequential. Three years later, Congress passed
the Chinese Exclusion Act, the first-ever race-based immigration ban.
To keep the country from rupturing again, any perceived threat to
national unity had to be expunged.

For Gilded Age elites unnerved by European-style class struggle emerging in the United States, the rise of anarchism was an especially disturbing development—the return of disunionism in a new and more
appalling form, one that demanded the dissolution not of a specific
political bond but of all compulsory bonds everywhere.

Indeed, the two ideas—anarchy and disunion—shared a history so
entwined they had often been regarded as synonyms. "Plainly, the central idea of secession is the essence of anarchy," Lincoln had declared
in his first inaugural address. During the Mexican-American War,
Henry David Thoreau had insisted that citizens should "dissolve...the
union between themselves and the State." Ralph Waldo Emerson, after
the caning of Charles Sumner in 1856, said he was "glad to see that the
terror at disunion and anarchy is disappearing." At the Worcester disunion convention, the abolitionist Samuel May Jr. told a story about his
comrade Francis Jackson's response to the question often posed to
secessionists: Where would they draw the border of the new nation? " 'I
would draw it,'" May recalled Jackson saying, " 'directly here'—describing
with his hands a circle round his own person."

The association continued through the Civil War. *True Civilization,* a
manifesto published the same year as the Battle of Gettysburg by an
eccentric Boston-born musician turned inventor named Josiah Warren,
argued for reordering society around radical self-sufficiency. "Individu-
ality, Division, Disconnection, Disunion, is the Principle of Order, Harmony, and Progress," Warren claimed. All individuals were inherently
sovereign; no government could legitimately wield power over them. "A
state or a nation is a multitude of indestructible individualities, and can-

not, by any possibility, be converted into anything else!" Warren declared. He called for "a 'Union' not only on paper, but rooted in the heart."

As for the war, Warren opposed slavery as the most extreme possible violation of individual sovereignty, but he could find no justification for forcing the South back into the Union. As he wrote, "There can be no secession from the freedom to secede!"

Over the next few decades, waves of European immigrants brought similar ideas with them across the Atlantic and applied them to America's political and economic struggles. They sought a wholesale reorganization of society around voluntary and necessarily impermanent associations. A perpetual union, to them, was a contradiction in terms.

Elites feared rising support for anarchism would lead to social violence on an unprecedented scale. While exaggerated, the threat wasn't only in their imaginations. Socialists in St. Louis organized hundreds of Civil War veterans into militia units, and anarchists in Chicago, the epicenter of the new radicalism—some 80 percent of the population was foreign-born—opened a chemistry school to teach "the manufacture and use of explosives."

After an 1886 riot in Chicago's Haymarket Square, during which a bomb killed a police officer and sparked a gun battle, politicians and the press depicted anarchists as akin to the rebels who had fired on Fort Sumter. The *Chicago Tribune* announced that the "soldiers of 1861" were "as ready to fight the Anarchist rebels north of the Ohio as they were secession rebels south of it." The United States was "not big enough," a Washington paper declared, "for men who bring with them from foreign shores the pestilential doctrines of the Commune, and undertake socialistic revolutions in the sign of the red flag." General Nelson Miles, whose military career had begun in the Civil War and would continue through the Spanish-American War, contended that the strikers, like the secessionists, aimed to "blow down the beautiful arch of our sovereignty." A satirist rhymed "Debs" with "Rebs."

Because militia units kept siding with strikers, many states professionalized their armed forces, equipped them with deadlier weaponry, and constructed fortress-style armories in the middle of cities. With thick, castle-like walls, soaring parapets, heavy iron gates, and even backup generators, the urban citadels were equipped to withstand a siege. They had to be "impregnable to mobs," a Boston colonel explained.

The regiments that had once defended the inviolability of the Union in the fields of Maryland and Virginia might have to do so again in the streets of Chicago or New York.

"There's nothing united about these States any more," novelist Owen Wister lamented a few years later, "except Standard Oil and discontent."

In 1868, a newspaper in Virginia cautioned its readers that a new civil war loomed on the horizon. Two sections of the Union, historically hostile, were on the cusp of resorting to arms. "We can discover no extrication from the present national turmoils," the paper warned, "save in a resort to that last agency remaining to distracted nations—a bloody revolution."

Yet this wouldn't be a recurrence of the devastating conflict from which Virginia had barely recovered. Rather, a cleavage between the states on either side of the Mississippi River had become as severe as the divide between North and South before 1861. "There is 'an irrepressible conflict' between the two sections—the bondholder in the East and the taxpayer in the West," the *Petersburg Express* observed. "Blows, given with avaricious hate, must determine, sooner or later, the controversy."

In this new conflict, the issue that divided East and West wasn't slavery but monetary policy. During the Civil War, the federal government had introduced paper bills known as greenbacks to pay for military operations. When the war ended, creditors and financiers pressured the government to retire the bills quickly to prevent inflation from chipping away at their profits. However, many farmers—especially in Western states—called for keeping the greenbacks in circulation, or at least minting silver into coins. Recent discoveries of silver deposits in Nevada and Colorado would loosen the flow of money and spread wealth more evenly.

The "free silver" issue formed the core around which a new political movement coalesced and then swept across the plains and much of the South. Advocates called for nationalizing railroads, regulating banks, creating government-backed farm cooperatives, and enacting a progressive income tax. This "new sectionalism," as some called it, pit the newer states of the West against the richer ones of the East.

In 1891, dissatisfaction with the major parties prompted the insurgents to form their own: the People's Party, also known as the Populist Party. Its platform described "a nation brought to the verge of moral,

political, and material ruin" and called for "permanent and perpetual... union of the labor forces of the United States." The party quickly
became a political force; its candidates for Congress, governorships,
and legislatures were elected throughout the South and West—the
most successful showing by a third party in history. "We as a nation are
dividing ourselves into two classes, the rich and the poor," one supporter observed, "the oppressor and the oppressed."

Opponents equated the insurgents with the Southern rebels of old.
Populism was another "rebellious effort to overthrow constitutional
government," one Union veteran declared.

Sympathizers saw the Gilded Age elite as the true heirs of the slave
masters' revolt. Like the Confederates, corporate bigwigs would see the
streets run with blood to protect their ill-gotten gains. Herbert Newton
Casson, a journalist who favored national ownership of industry, described
inequality as a form of disunion. "The rich, as a class, have seceded from
the great body of citizens, and have formed a dangerous and un-American
aristocracy of ownership," he argued. Socialists, Populists, and other radicals aimed not to divide the country but "to weld the nation into unity
again by repealing the laws that caused it to split asunder."

On both sides of the divide, however, some embraced disunion. In
1894, an influential socialist reported that more than a few of his
acquaintances "bragged that they would delight in shouldering the
musket to bring about a Western secession." Two years later, *Bankers'
Magazine* noted that "the possibility of the formation of a trans-
Mississippi republic has been suggested as not improbable owing to the
lack of homogeneity of Eastern and Western ideas."

The 1896 election marked the peak of the Populist rebellion. At their
national convention in Chicago, Democrats planned to nominate William
Jennings Bryan, a thirty-six-year-old congressman from Nebraska with
free-silver views and a spellbinding voice, for president. Just before Bryan
was scheduled to speak, "Pitchfork Ben" Tillman, a leader of the Southern
Populists, took the stage. An avowed white supremacist, the South Carolina senator had long bragged about his participation in anti-black terrorism in the early 1870s. "How did we recover our liberty?" he once asked,
and candidly answered the question himself: "By fraud and violence."

At the Chicago convention, Tillman declared that the free-silver issue was as much a sectional question as slavery had once been. "I come to you from the South," Tillman said. "From the home of secession." Mayhem broke out in the hall as delegates hissed. Democrats had worked hard to dispel the notion that Populism was a form of sectionalism. Tillman was having none of it. Raising his voice, the disheveled, one-eyed plantation heir said that the last war had been fought for "the emancipation of the black slaves," and he was willing to fight again for "the emancipation of the white slaves."

It was the first time since the Civil War that a politician had threatened secession on a national stage. Party leaders chased Tillman from the podium. In his famous "Cross of Gold" speech that night, Bryan insisted his was "not the platform of section" but of "our common country."

But the damage was done. For the rest of the campaign, Republicans used Tillman's inflammatory words against Bryan and the Democrats. Spooked by Populism, tycoons like John D. Rockefeller and J. P. Morgan raised unheard-of sums for the Republican nominee, former Ohio governor William McKinley. Republicans positioned themselves as the party of sectional reconciliation. "Let us remember now and in all the future that we are Americans," McKinley told a gathering of Confederate veterans during the campaign. The party platform abandoned its customary call for a federal guarantee of black suffrage in the South. The archbishop of St. Paul, Minnesota, published a letter comparing the Democratic platform to "revolution against the United States: it is secession, the secession of 1861." Campaigning for McKinley, New York police commissioner Theodore Roosevelt warned that the Populists were "plotting a social revolution and the subversion of the American Republic." He suggested "taking ten or a dozen of their leaders out, standing them...against a wall and shooting them dead."

The onslaught worked. McKinley won the election, solidifying Republican dominance for another forty years. The Populist movement, divided by Bryan's candidacy and demoralized by defeat, never recovered.

Yet the 1896 campaign had deeper implications for American history. The equating of class politics with Confederate-style disunionism stigmatized any and all bottom-up opposition to entrenched economic power as a threat to national unity. The legacy of the Civil War would be used to marginalize movements committed to defending and expanding the very freedoms the Union had been saved to secure.

CHAPTER 12

Divided We Stand

all right we are two nations

—John Dos Passos, 1936

EVEN AT THE HEIGHT OF the nation's power and prosperity, Americans remained divided. As the centennial of the Civil War approached, in 1961, the contradictions that had caused the conflict were little closer to being resolved. Slavery had been abolished, but it was replaced by a system of court-backed segregation that again rendered African-Americans second-class citizens. Now that system was coming under attack—by a rising civil rights movement about to send Freedom Riders on integrated buses through the South, by a Supreme Court that had ruled against segregation in public facilities, and by a federal government once again willing to deploy military troops to enforce the Constitution at gunpoint. A century after what Walt Whitman had called the "volcanic upheaval" of the secession winter, sulfur was again in the air.

That April, members of the various state Civil War centennial commissions converged on Charleston, South Carolina, to commemorate the one hundredth anniversary of the firing on Fort Sumter. The point was to demonstrate unity, but that plan quickly went off the rails. The local hotel hosting the proceedings refused to serve a group of African-Americans in the New Jersey delegation. Trying to avert a crisis, President John F. Kennedy ordered the National Civil War Centennial Commission to move the festivities to a nearby navy base. As a federal military installation, it was one of the only desegregated venues around.

But the South Carolina commission refused to go along with the

The Republic of New Afrika, a separatist group formed in
1968, demanded an independent black republic in the
South as reparations for slavery. (*Walter P. Reuther Library*)

new plan. Instead, the state decided to secede from the national commemoration, just as it had from the Union a century earlier. At its separate event in the segregated hotel, Strom Thurmond, South Carolina's
proudly segregationist senator, praised the Palmetto State's latest act of
resistance to federal authority. "I am proud of the job that South Carolina is doing," Thurmond said, "and I urge that we continue in this
great tradition no matter how much outside agitation may be brought
to bear on our people and our state." That day, the Confederate battle
flag was raised over the South Carolina capitol building. It would
remain there for more than fifty years.

The fusing of one nation indivisible remained incomplete. Examining how divided the country really was at the peak of its supposed
greatness reveals a hidden history of the American Century. Whether
the Union would hold together no longer plagued national politics.
But that only made the instances when the idea of disunion did crop
up all the more surprising and significant. Whenever divisions became

especially stark, somebody could be counted on to suggest that the United States shouldn't exist at all, at least not in the form Americans had come to take for granted.

1. Trouble on the Border

In the early twentieth century, even as the country occupied itself with fights over monopoly and labor, temperance and suffrage, inequality and foreign affairs, the possibility that the nation might crumble was rarely far from view. On some level, Americans remained aware of the faults and fractures running beneath their ostensibly stable Union. Fears and divisions left over from the previous century—the fear of division, above all—continued to subtly shape national life, how the United States treated its own citizens and related to the rest of the world. Then, too, Americans still had to worry about the paid agents of foreign enemies collaborating with internal discontents to infiltrate the country or even plot to break it up.

In the early 1900s, these fears became focused on the porous Southern border. Three-quarters of a century after the Mexican-American War, the outcome, apparently, was still in doubt—and the borders of the United States still to be determined.

In January 1915, a deputy sheriff in McAllen, Texas, ten miles north of the Rio Grande, arrested a twenty-four-year-old Mexican named Basilio Ramos. The charge wasn't loitering or theft or even murder but conspiracy to levy war against the United States.

Among the suspect's possessions was a strange document, a revolutionary manifesto declaring that one month later, on February 20 at 2:00 a.m., an insurrection would overthrow the U.S. government in those lands of which Mexico had been "robbed in the most perfidious manner by North American imperialism." Hoisting a red flag with a diagonal white fringe and the motto "Equality and Independence," the rebels would declare a new republic. Eventually, it might rejoin Mexico.

According to this "Plan de San Diego," named for the Texas town where the uprising would begin, the "Liberating Army of Races and Peoples" would include not only ethnic Mexicans in Texas and Spanish-speakers on either side of the border but also Southern blacks, who were entitled to a republic of their own, and indigenous nations like the Apache, whose stolen lands would be returned if they joined the rebellion. Perhaps most frightening, it said that all white men older than sixteen would be killed.

The border region was already teeming with plots and intrigues and plagued by political violence. Five years earlier, Mexico had erupted in revolution. Much of the country was reduced to ruins as irregular bands of predatory ruffians vied for control. The unrest sent refugees and fighters into Texas, where ethnic Mexicans, known as Tejanos, and white Anglos lived in tense proximity. Alienated by discrimination, many Tejanos burned with resentment toward the Union that had forcibly absorbed their ancestors. The Plan de San Diego offered, as one plotter said, "a challenge unto death...to the white-faced hogs"—a provocation to the United States.

But Tejanos and Mexicans weren't the only ones looking to weaken the United States and maybe even carve it up. By the time of Ramos's arrest, the Great War had been raging for six months. Both sides—the Central Powers, led by Germany, and the Allied Powers, led by France and Great Britain—scoured the globe for ways to weaken their rivals. The United States was trying to stay out of the fight but sold food and weapons to the Allies.

From the founding of the United States, foreign rivals had tried to exploit its divisions. For imperial Germany, the turmoil in Mexico offered an opportunity. The long, restive southern border was the soft underbelly of the United States. If rebellion broke out in Texas, American arms flowing to Western Europe would have to be redirected there. German diplomats offered guns and money to the shadowy plotters of borderlands revolution.

Officials in Texas didn't know any of this. When February 20, 1915, came and went without incident, they breathed a sigh of relief. Maybe the Plan de San Diego was some horrible hoax. When Ramos went on trial two months later, the judge said that he "ought to be tried for lunacy, not for conspiracy against the United States." Ramos went free and crossed back into Mexico.

But the revolution he had been organizing was far from over. All through the spring of 1915, planning continued. Farmers, butchers, and field hands agreed to join revolutionary cells. A doctor named Jesse Moseley traveled through Texas and Oklahoma trying to recruit fellow African-Americans to support the plan. He met with little success. Moseley was tracked down in a Laredo brothel by a federal investigator and turned over to Texas police. Eleven days later, his body was found in a nearby canyon, the skull caved in.

On July 4—an auspicious date for revolution—forty Mexicans crossed the Rio Grande and killed two white ranchers. Some thirty cross-border attacks followed over the next several months. Raiders robbed stores, burned railroad bridges, cut telegraph wires, shot at soldiers and police officers, and attacked ranchers known for cruelty to Tejano workers. They didn't kill all adult white males, despite what the plan had outlined, but the bandits did occasionally show a propensity for astounding cruelty. A soldier's head was cut off and propped on a pike beside the river. Near Brownsville, brigands derailed a train and went through the cars shooting Anglos. During one attack, armed men asked their captives if any of them were German, and when no one said yes, the men executed them all. Marauding through south Texas, the riders told Tejanos that "this section of the country was taken away from Mexico, and does not really belong to the United States." The bandits moved easily across the dry, broken terrain and vanished as eerily as they had appeared, retreating into Mexico for sanctuary.

For local Anglos, the raids triggered deep-seated fears, not only that their lives might be in jeopardy but that their claim on the land was not as secure as they had thought. After the better part of a century, the annexation of Texas might yet be repealed.

When the U.S. Army proved incapable of defending people and property along the nearly two-thousand-mile border between Texas and Mexico, whites formed vigilante groups known as Law and Order Leagues. With assistance from the Texas Rangers—acting, essentially, as death squads—they attacked ethnic Mexicans, often at random. One rancher called for building "concentration camps along the river" to house suspected insurgents. Others suggested forcing Tejanos across the Rio Grande until the insurrection subsided and shooting all who refused. "The cry was often heard," one local later recalled, "'we have to make this a white man's country!!'"

What followed fit all the criteria of what we now call ethnic cleansing—violence aimed not for vengeance but extermination. A Laredo paper observed that Mexicans in south Texas constituted "a serious surplus population…that needs eliminating." Tejanos were rounded up, taken into the chaparral, and executed. Rows of shot-up skeletons were found in the thick underbrush for decades afterward. Corpses were strung from trees and left for months; others were thrown into the Rio Grande and found floating miles downstream. Amid what some called a "systematic manhunt," untold numbers simply "evaporated," according to one lawyer. Lynchings weren't newsworthy, but a brief lull in them was. The "finding of dead bodies of Mexicans," a San Antonio paper observed, "has reached a point where it creates little or no interest."

The border region all but emptied out as Tejanos fled south and Anglos north. By the time the violence ended, the number of dead ran into the thousands.

In 1916, a new Mexican president agreed to suppress cross-border raiding in exchange for recognition by the U.S. government. But the spasm of racial violence left behind deep hostility among Tejanos and a profound fear among whites that their dominance would always be tenuous, that the land wasn't a permanent part of the Union, that every new swell of Spanish-speaking migrants was an invasion, the first wave of an impending *reconquista*—the retaking by Mexico of its much-missed former lands.

In early 1917, the Associated Press published a secret telegram sent from Berlin to Mexico City. If Mexico declared war on its northern neighbor and joined the German-led alliance, it said, the land it had once ceded to the United States would be returned.

The author of this desperate, foolhardy proposal was Arthur Zimmermann, the German foreign minister. Zimmermann thought the key to German victory was distracting the Americans so they wouldn't intervene in the European war. Fifteen years earlier, as a young diplomat returning to Germany from China, Zimmermann had crossed the United States by train, an experience that gave him special expertise in American affairs—or so he claimed. In cabinet meetings, Zimmermann argued that ethnic and geographical divisions would prevent the United States from coming to Britain's defense. German immigrants in the Midwest would revolt if Congress declared war on their fatherland.

While Zimmermann, who kept a close eye on the turbulence along the Southwestern border, might not have sincerely believed that Mexico could reclaim the land it had lost, he hoped the promise of German support would convince that nation to take the risk. In January 1917, Zimmermann sent the ill-fated note to his Mexican counterpart.

Unfortunately for Zimmermann, the telegram was intercepted by the British government, which was keen to convince the peace-minded president, Woodrow Wilson, to side with the Allies. Plastered across front pages, the "Prussian Invasion Plot" stunned the American public and awakened long-submerged anxieties. The war in Europe, which had seemed remote, now reached deep into the heartland. America had to enter the war to defend not only Western Europe and democracy but the territorial integrity of the Union. One magazine summed up the effect of the telegram in a headline: "How Zimmermann United the United States."

Neutrality became untenable overnight. Former president Theodore Roosevelt declared that if foreign nations plotting to "dismember" the United States wasn't just cause for war, nothing was. The uproar over Zimmermann's note helped turn Wilson's wavering mind toward intervention. Thanks to concerns over its own security, even its geographic cohesion, the United States for the first time entered a European war.

Mexican *reconquista* of the Southwest, through borderland rebellion or geopolitical intrigue, was surely unlikely. But if dismemberment had really been impossible to imagine, neither the Plan de San Diego nor the Zimmermann telegram would have stirred up as much emotion—and violence—as they did. Even today, anxieties that Mexico poses a threat not only to America's stability but also to its unity continue to exert a powerful hold on the American imagination. The man who killed twenty-two people in a Walmart in El Paso, Texas, in August 2019 complained in an online manifesto about the "Hispanic invasion of Texas." His solution: divide the Union into separate regions for each ethnicity and race.

2. Depression and Its Discontents

Manning machine guns and a howitzer, Texas Rangers and Oklahoma National Guardsmen camped out on opposite sides of the Red River, ready for war.

It was the summer of 1931. Construction on a new steel bridge between the two states was nearly complete. A joint project, the free span would compete with a private toll bridge nearby. But before it opened, the toll-bridge owners sued, and a judge in Houston ruled in the company's favor. The governor of Texas, following court orders, barricaded the new bridge.

Across the river, Oklahoma's flamboyant, cigar-chomping governor seethed. "Alfalfa Bill" Murray, a champion of agrarian interests, ordered underlings to destroy the Oklahoma approach to the private bridge and tear down the barricades blocking the public one. Then he declared martial law in a narrow strip along the river. Packing an antique revolver, the governor arrived in what he called the "war zone" to inspect the Oklahoma troops. Cars backed up on both banks as the two sides dug in.

Peace ultimately prevailed. The court lifted its injunction, and the free bridge opened to traffic. The only casualty of the so-called Red River Bridge War was an Oklahoma guardsman who, drunk, tripped and fell on his bayonet.

But that wasn't the last Americans would hear of the episode. A few years later, *Life* magazine reported that Adolf Hitler had learned about the incident and concluded that it proved the United States was about to crack up. Nazi papers published photos of the standoff, evidence that America wasn't strong, like Germany, but "a chaos of little states with different laws." Beneath the nation's surface, a "continuous civil war" was ripping the country apart.

While exaggerated, that wasn't altogether untrue. The stock market crash of 1929 had pulled the rug from under an ebullient nation reveling in a booming economy and its new status as a world power. Darkness and despair spread across the land. Amid diminished hopes and uncertainty about the future, some suggested giving the government emergency powers until the crisis passed. "If this country ever needed a Mussolini," one Republican said, "it needs one now." *Barron's*, the financial weekly, called for "a mild species of dictatorship" to help the country over "the roughest spots in the road ahead."

Like all economic crises, the Depression exacerbated old divisions and dredged up long-submerged grievances. Angered by foreclosures and high taxes, Western farmers saw their position in the nation's economic life slipping away. A few even suggested leaving the Union. "We're going to draw a line at the Mississippi and have our own country west of it," someone shouted at an Iowa foreclosure riot. "Have a capital at Des Moines or somewhere; make our own laws, make our own money!" A Minnesota progressive reported hearing "considerable talk...of secession from the Union by mid-west states if the depression continues." "Unless something is done for the American farmer," an agricultural spokesman told the Senate in early 1933, "we'll have a revolution in the countryside in less than twelve months."

North Dakota emerged as the unlikely epicenter of Depression-era disunionism. The state suffered not only the closure of banks and businesses but also a severe drought and crop-killing grasshoppers that swarmed so thick they blotted out the sun. A few weeks before Franklin Roosevelt's inauguration, William Martin, an eighty-three-year-old state senator, introduced a bill declaring that a "financial oligarchy" based in New England, New York, New Jersey, and Pennsylvania was oppressing the rest of the country. It was time for real Americans "to secede from the above named states, carrying with us the Star Spangled Banner, and leaving them the stripes, which they so richly deserve."

Martin's bill made national news. It was, after all, the first time a state legislature had actually discussed secession since the Civil War. The bill died in committee, but Martin felt satisfied with the results. His threat "woke up those people in the east, and that's more than we've been able to do before," he said. "I guess we scared some of those fellows."

Something was afoot in North Dakota, and the newly elected governor, William "Wild Bill" Langer, an old-school populist, was eager to take advantage of it. Soon after his inauguration, Langer enacted a slate of reforms—deep cuts to state spending, an embargo on wheat exports, a moratorium on farm foreclosures—that earned him popular praise and powerful enemies. In 1934, a jury found Langer guilty of corruption and sentenced him to eighteen months in jail. Langer wanted to appeal, but state law required him to resign immediately. The governor refused to step down. As fans and foes alike took to the streets of Bismarck, the governor barricaded himself in the executive mansion and drew up a "Declaration of Independence for the State of North Dakota." Then he invoked martial law.

Langer didn't issue his declaration. Even for a maverick like the governor, secession seemed a step too far. The next morning, he and his staff left the capitol grounds. North Dakota remained in the Union.

A serious attempt to secede remained all but unthinkable. But the fact that a rabble-rousing demagogue even considered it as a possible solution to a political crisis suggested that beneath the surface of a seemingly solid Union, secession retained its old illicit appeal. The Depression revealed that the country's constitutional order remained more unsettled than prosperity-fueled complacency had led many to suppose.

In the dark months before Roosevelt's inauguration, the country seemed to quiver on the brink of collapse. One in four adults was out of work. Banks were failing. Democracy seemed inadequate to the crisis. Months earlier, tens of thousands of unemployed war veterans had marched to Washington and demanded early payment of promised bonuses. Using tanks, tear gas, and machine guns, General Douglas MacArthur—assisted by Major Dwight Eisenhower—broke up the camp, claiming the veterans had aimed to overthrow the U.S. government.

"For Dictatorship if Necessary," declared a headline in the *New York Herald-Tribune* the day Roosevelt took office. In his inaugural address, Roosevelt threatened to seize "broad executive power" if Congress rejected his program for national recovery. The line received the loudest applause of his speech.

Roosevelt's New Deal was intended to stave off a revolution, unite the country around a common purpose, and serve as the economic equivalent of war. An unprecedented expansion of the federal government, it succeeded in blurring centuries-old geographical divisions. Some New Dealers even wondered if the states themselves were still relevant. In 1935, the *New York Times Magazine* described a radical plan making the rounds on Capitol Hill to abolish the states and replace them with nine regional "departments."

The plan, of course, went nowhere. Yet the new emphasis on national consolidation provoked a backlash from states' rights zealots who believed Roosevelt was altering the terms of the founding compact. One senator denounced the New Deal as a "mutilation of the

Constitution." Others called it a coup d'état. A year into Roosevelt's first term, former Marine general Smedley Butler testified to the Senate that business leaders had tried to involve him in a conspiracy to overthrow the president and establish a dictatorship.

Sectional resentment lay behind much of the opposition. In a 1937 book, *Divided We Stand,* Texas historian Walter Prescott Webb attacked Roosevelt's program as contributing to the massification of American life. Taking aim at everything from Wall Street finance to chain stores and industrial automation, Webb depicted Americans in the heartland as colonial subjects forced to pay tribute to coastal masters.

The sharpest sectional hostility to the New Deal came from the South. Seventy years after Appomattox, white Southerners continued to nurse a grudge, passing resentment from generation to generation like an heirloom. Racial segregation was common throughout the nation, but only in the South was it encoded in law. Virginia had more in common with Louisiana, a thousand miles away, than it did with Pennsylvania. The former Confederacy, journalist W. J. Cash observed, was "another land, sharply differentiated from the rest of the American nation"—if not a separate country, then "the next thing to it."

That lingering sense of Southern distinctiveness grew during the 1930s in reaction to the New Deal's attempt to make the nation more united. New books and periodicals covered every aspect of regional life in the South, while separate professional organizations were created for Southern historians, political scientists, economists, sociologists, and filmmakers. The Confederate battle flag, which had rarely been seen since Appomattox, now appeared on jackets and at football games. A decade later, Southern soldiers brought the Stars and Bars with them to Europe and the Pacific. In 1945, it was the first flag flown over Okinawa after the U.S. victory.

Roosevelt called the South "the Nation's No. 1 economic problem" and sought to solve it. But Southerners resented the description as patronizing, an excuse for outside meddling. Some were even suspicious of the Tennessee Valley Authority, which built massive hydropower and flood-control dams, reforested barren slopes, and brought low-cost electric power to one of the poorest parts of the country. As besuited Ivy Leaguers flocked to these benighted places to bring them up to speed, some had a sense of déjà vu. Donald Davidson, a

Tennessee poet and critic, called the TVA "another Yankee raid into southern territory."

Like the previous one, this new incursion threatened the region's precarious racial order. Nineteenth-century white Southerners like John C. Calhoun had feared that a federal government able to build canals was a government able to free slaves; now their descendants saw the New Deal as the first step toward racial equality. Davidson called for a constitutional convention to give each region the power to tax federal agencies, control its own currency, and "preserve its bi-racial social system"—state-sponsored apartheid. "The recognition of sectional diversity," Davidson argued, echoing Calhoun, "is the true safeguard of national unity." Left to the mercy of "Northeastern imperialism," the South might rise again. He thought historians of the future would someday see the 1930s as the beginning of *"the dismemberment of the United States."*

White Southern racists did more than denounce the New Deal from the outside. They shaped it from within. Bending to Southern pressure, Roosevelt's farm programs benefited landowners rather than tenants, while rural wage earners, mostly black and Hispanic, were excluded from Social Security and collective bargaining. The president refused to use his landslide reelection in 1936 to back an anti-lynching law, the longtime goal of civil rights activists. Despite a surge of killings—in one incident, a man was castrated and forced to eat his own genitals before being dragged from the back of a car—Roosevelt accepted the Southerners' argument that federalizing the issue would infringe on states' rights. Because of the Civil War, Eleanor Roosevelt explained to NAACP head Walter White, a lynching bill signed by a Northerner would "have an antagonistic effect" on the South and therefore the Union. (A century and a half earlier, John Adams had said the same about emancipation in Massachusetts.)

A landmark progressive achievement, the New Deal was also another problem-postponing sectional compromise. The Union continued to exist only on the sufferance of Southern whites. As in the nineteenth century, however, no concession was enough for them. James Byrnes, a South Carolina senator, complained that under Roosevelt, the Democratic Party had been taken over by the "Negroes of the North." The

New Deal offended both whites fearful of its racial implications and a wealthy elite opposed to its progressivism. This alliance between white supremacy and laissez-faire economics formed the core around which modern conservatism would eventually cohere. Racism became a political wedge used to pry millions of Americans, first in the South and then across the country, away from supporting New Deal–style federal action to alleviate inequality. Despite inspirational protest movements and notable legislative victories, the second half of the twentieth century would see the possibility of ever really perfecting the Union recede even further.

3. The Great Exception?

World War II is still fondly remembered as the apogee of American unity. After the United States joined the fight, no troublesome peace movement questioned the government's aims or sided with the enemy. The effort to defeat Nazism and Japanese militarism fused the country as nothing had before.

At least, that's the official story. "World War II unified Americans," journalist John Judis has written. "Business made peace with labor; blacks served alongside whites. And that spirit of national unification lasted for 15 years after the war." The New Deal and World War II laid the foundations for "the great exception," as historian Jefferson Cowie calls the mid-twentieth century, "a rare period of political unity."

But how united was the country? How exceptional could the era have been? Divisions over race, class, region, religion, and sex didn't simply disappear. The superficial unity was undermined by wartime exclusionism, especially the confinement of a hundred and twenty thousand Japanese-Americans—two-thirds of them citizens—in concentration camps. The military did mix Americans of different races and regions. (For the first time, army units weren't organized on the basis of soldiers' home states.) Yet discrimination remained widespread. Except in a few instances, black and white soldiers didn't serve alongside one another. Units were as rigidly segregated as Southern buses. Black and white soldiers often got into brawls or even shootouts. According to historian Gary Gerstle, race tensions in the army "verged on civil war."

Countering the calls for unity, African-American newspapers contrasted the lofty ideals the country was fighting for abroad with realities at home. "Our war is not against Hitler in Europe," the *Pittsburgh Courier* declared, "but against the Hitlers in America." A letter to Roosevelt about military segregation asked, "Is there a democracy for only the white American?" Labor leader A. Philip Randolph threatened to organize a march on Washington to highlight the federal government's hypocrisy. Deadly race riots erupted in cities across the country, especially in New York City's Harlem and in Detroit, where thirty-four people were killed and some six thousand federal soldiers had to be called in to restore order.

The country's contradictions were too obvious to ignore. Enemies took note; Nazi propagandists spread reports of the lynching of a black man in Missouri within forty-eight hours of his death.

Despite these divisions, however, the war did unite the country to some extent. Wartime spending ended the Depression. The economy was roaring. America emerged as an industrial and military juggernaut. A growing rivalry with the Soviet Union gave the country a new sense of national purpose. An increase in military spending, a sharp departure from the usual peacetime drawdown, helped prop up the boom. A vast new state apparatus was devoted to "national security," entrenching as the most secretive, well-funded mission of the government what an earlier age called the preservation of the Union. Historians and literary critics endeavored to prove that the American past was not an endless succession of crises and irresolvable contradictions but instead a shared political "consensus," a nation-defining refusal to be seduced by extremes.

Yet the new outlook betrayed profound insecurity about the durability of national unity. From the earliest days of colonial settlement, fear had often managed to overcome, if temporarily, American divisions—fear of violent incursions by bloodthirsty enemies, of domestic subversives working with foreign powers. After World War II, a Republican senator told President Harry Truman that the government would have to "scare hell out of the American people" to get them to pay the taxes needed to support the higher military spending.

Thus the Red Scare, a society-wide suppression of unpopular views, especially criticisms of racism, capitalism, and militarism. While social strife of all kinds was at an ebb, the lull required rampant violations of civil liberties and bipartisan acquiescence in segregation. The Cold War necessitated a strategic performance of consensus, a national game of make-believe. So the country could present itself as more united than it actually was, the margins of acceptable political discourse had to be strictly policed and national unity enforced. How could Americans demand free elections in Poland, the Soviet foreign minister asked James Byrnes, Truman's secretary of state, when elections were not free in Byrnes's own South Carolina? Cold War competition pressured the United States to bridge its most glaring and enduring divisions.

Running for reelection in 1948, Truman embraced civil rights proposals such as an anti-lynching bill, the abolition of poll taxes, fair employment laws, and desegregation of the armed forces. At the Democratic National Convention, Hubert Humphrey Jr., the youthful mayor of Minneapolis, called on the party to "get out of the shadow of states' rights and walk forthrightly in the bright sunshine of human rights."

As in 1861, the platform split the Democratic Party. "The South we know is being swept to its destruction," warned Mississippi's James Eastland. Southern Democrats, styling themselves the States' Rights Democratic Party (popularly known as the Dixiecrats), nominated South Carolina governor Strom Thurmond for the presidency. The issue wasn't race, Thurmond claimed, but "State Sovereignty." Slave owners had tried the same rhetorical trick a century earlier.

Truman won the election, but Thurmond carried four Southern states, foreshadowing the potential for a fundamental realignment of American politics. As Southerners had predicted in the 1930s, the federal power built up during the New Deal and World War II would indeed be mobilized to force integration. But the attempt would trigger a powerful backlash. The long-suppressed drive toward separatism and disunion was poised for a comeback.

In 1954, the Supreme Court declared racial segregation in public accommodations a violation of the Fourteenth Amendment. Yet *Brown v. Board of Education* addressed more than one divisive issue; it also took on Americans' centuries-old habit, formed in the earliest days of settlement, of using separation as a ready-made solution for stubborn social differences and intractable political quandaries. It called for the country to unify once and for all.

To the white South, *Brown* presented a challenge on the order of Lincoln's election and justified nearly as brazen a defiance of national authority. White-supremacist Citizens' Councils intimidated blacks and pressured officials to ignore court orders or even close public schools rather than integrate them. Now that the Supreme Court had essentially "abolished the Mason Dixon line," a resurgent Ku Klux Klan swore to "establish the Smith and Wesson line."

Virginia senator and power broker Harry Byrd called for "massive resistance" to show that the South would never submit to the Supreme Court's integration rulings. In practice, that meant resurrecting the doctrine of nullification, the idea, first aired in Jefferson and Madison's Kentucky and Virginia Resolutions and later championed by John C. Calhoun, that any state has the right to invalidate federal law. Dormant since the Civil War, the concept was revived by Southerners like James Jackson Kilpatrick, an influential Virginia editor and an ally of Harry Byrd, to fight the long-postponed consolidation of Union victory. Without nullification, Kilpatrick warned, "the States inevitably will be reduced to non-entities." A South Carolina paper suggested nullification could redeem the nation from the evils of an overactive federal government. Its impact would be felt "far beyond...the Mason-Dixon Line. It would help restore the sagging sinews of the Republic itself."

Ten Southern states passed laws that directly contravened *Brown v. Board of Education*. Alabama declared the ruling "null, void, and of no effect" within the state—a direct quote from Jefferson's Kentucky Resolution. Fifty-six percent of Arkansas voters approved a ballot measure to overturn federal laws, a measure its own author later called "damned near a declaration of war against the United States." *U.S. News and World Report* observed that the South was "living through an upheaval, more profound...than the Secession."

In 1956, three Southern senators, including Byrd and former Dixiecrat candidate Strom Thurmond, drew up a "Declaration of Constitutional Principles," also known as the Southern Manifesto—a call for a new counterrevolution. The senators declared federally enforced desegregation an invasion of states' rights and congratulated those states that had moved to block it. The final version carried the signatures of more than four-fifths of Southern representatives in Washington. (Among the holdouts were Lyndon Johnson of Texas and Al Gore Sr. of Tennessee.) "You would think today Calhoun was walking and speaking on the floor of the Senate," scoffed Wayne Morse, an Oregon progressive.

Others saw the shade of another specter: civil war. To William Faulkner, the great man of Southern letters, the crisis revealed how little the country had learned in the past century. "What that war should have done, but failed to do," he wrote in *Life,* "was to prove to the North that the South will go to any length, even that fatal and already doomed one"—secession—"before it will accept alteration of its racial condition by mere force of law or economic threat." It was a staggering suggestion—disunion might again be possible if Northern whites pushed the South too hard on racial integration. A few years later, James D. Martin, one of the first Republicans to run a competitive (but ultimately unsuccessful) campaign in the South, as a Senate candidate in Alabama, suggested "a return to the spirit of '61—1861, when our fathers formed a new nation." Back then, the Party of Lincoln had suppressed that spirit with force. Now, Martin suggested, it should lead the fight.

As in 1833 and 1861, Southerners dared the federal government to use force. The showdown finally came in Little Rock, Arkansas, where Governor Orval Faubus sent the state's National Guard to prevent nine black children from enrolling in the city's Central High School. Dwight D. Eisenhower, the war hero elected president in 1952, didn't want to get involved. Warned by Southern friends that a federal attempt to enforce desegregation would be met with violence, Eisenhower had never endorsed the court's *Brown* decision. After Faubus called up the National Guard to block the children from entering the school, Eisenhower's first instinct was to parrot segregationist talking points. At a press conference, he observed that "you cannot change people's hearts merely by laws." In the clash between white supremacists and civil rights activists, there were good people on both sides.

Yet when a federal court ordered the National Guard to stand down, Eisenhower saw he had no choice but to intervene. Open defiance in a city the size of Little Rock would expose the United States to ridicule abroad. "Our enemies are gloating over this incident," the president groused in a televised address, "and using it everywhere to misrepresent our whole nation." Eisenhower sent the 101st Airborne to escort the nine students into school.

The showdown, historian Taylor Branch observes, was "the most severe test of the Constitution since the Civil War." Segregationists saw it as yet another Northern invasion of Southern soil. For years to come, the slogan "Remember Little Rock" became a fixture of white-supremacist rallies, emblazoned on bumper stickers, stamps, and Citizens' Council literature.

Two weeks after the standoff ended, a tiny light streaked high in the heavens, arcing with remorseless regularity every ninety-six minutes across American skies. For weeks, the fallout from Little Rock shared headlines with the news of Sputnik's launch. Was the United States, paralyzed by its divisions, being left behind in the race for global supremacy? In 1959, the federal government began marking the third week of July as "Captive Nations Week" to honor those countries around the world under the bootheel of Communist tyranny. The coming years, however, would show that the United States had a few captive nations of its own.

4. The Civil War of the 1960s

The idea of carving a separate black republic out of the United States had a long yet little-known history. In the spring of 1861, shortly after the firing on Fort Sumter, Abraham Lincoln received a letter from an Illinois ally. Like many Northerners, Orville Browning encouraged the president to prosecute the war with "utmost vigor." But unlike almost every other Republican at that point, he also urged Lincoln to free the slaves.

That was a radical position so early in the war, but Browning went even further. What was to be done with four million newly freed people? Millions of blacks would never be welcomed in the Northern states; they would compete with whites for jobs. Deportation to Africa— Lincoln's preference—was impractical. "We cannot drive them into the sea," Browning coldly noted. "What are we to do with them?"

He saw only one solution:

Give up the cotton states to them. Let them have the soil upon which they were born.... Let such whites as may remain there at the time get away with all they can carry with them. They cant take away the soil. Give that up to the negroes, and form them into a Republic under the protectorate of this Government.

It was a remarkable suggestion, the establishment of a separate black republic where generations of kidnapped Africans and their descendants had been traded, tortured, murdered. Browning's proposal wasn't wholly humanitarian—his real goal was to keep blacks out of the North. Yet he was sincere. Only black nationhood, Browning believed, would offer justice for the formerly enslaved and lasting security for the Union: "No other course, it seems to me, is open to us. This done our troubles are at an end, and our government planted on the rock of ages."

Lincoln didn't pursue the proposal—Browning seemed "bewildered and dazzled by the excitement of the moment," he told an acquaintance. As an Illinois senator, Browning later turned against Lincoln's emancipation decree. But the idea of black independence would have a long life. From the land worked for centuries by a people ripped from their homelands, their descendants would build a country all their own.

Black separatism returned after World War I when President Wilson proclaimed "self-determination" the right of all peoples. In 1918, the Caribbean-born New York editor Cyril Briggs wrote that black Americans were "a nation within a nation, a nationality oppressed and jimcrowed." Briggs called for establishing an official black enclave in the Pacific Northwest. The following year, race riots in twenty-six American cities convinced thousands to join Briggs's African Blood Brotherhood, a Communist-aligned group devoted to black sovereignty.

A few years later, Harry Haywood, a Nebraska-born war veteran radicalized by the 1919 riots, traveled to the Soviet Union to study how the black freedom struggle in America fit into the worldwide proletarian revolution. Inspired by Vladimir Lenin's description of African-Americans as one of the world's "dependent and underprivileged nations," Haywood concluded that only political autonomy could ensure economic control. At the sixth Comintern Congress, held in Moscow in 1928, Haywood called on the Soviet Union to push for the founding of a black republic in the American South. Stalin endorsed Haywood's proposal. When he returned to the United States, Haywood promoted the idea. "We demand the withdrawal of the armed forces of imperialism from the Black Belt," he wrote.

To be sure, most black leaders hated the idea. The Great Migration, which sent millions of terrorized Southern blacks fleeing to Northern cities, was in full swing. Few wished to return. Community spokesmen wanted to join the American mainstream, not separate from it. The NAACP condemned the call for a black republic as "a plan of plain seg-regation." Though it later counted Langston Hughes, Richard Wright, and Paul Robeson as members, the Communist Party failed to con-vince the masses and eventually withdrew its support for the idea. Out-side the party, Haywood and others continued to promote it.

In the mid-1960s, after years of lying dormant, the idea was revived. Tired of hunger and humiliation, exploitation and neglect, black Americans began venting their pent-up rage. Riots spread from Har-lem to the Watts section of Los Angeles, then around the country. Hundreds died, thousands were wounded, and vast stretches of urban America were left in ruins. "We at home were watching nothing less than the on-the-screen telecast of civil war," screenwriter Budd Schul-berg wrote. In a 1968 book strikingly titled *The Second Civil War*, Garry Wills chronicled how police departments across the country were mak-ing plans to combat guerrilla war. Gathering leftover World War II equipment, from machine guns to gas masks and tanks, the authorities were "arming for Armageddon."

In the "long, hot summer" of 1967, riots erupted in Detroit, New-ark, and over a hundred other cities. President Lyndon Johnson appointed a commission to study "civil disorders." Early the next year, the commission reported that the country was tearing itself apart. "Our nation is moving toward two societies, one black, one white— separate and unequal," the report stated. It outlined programs to alle-viate economic suffering in black ghettos. Martin Luther King called the report a "physician's warning of approaching death, with a prescription for life." A month later, he was assassinated, and riots broke out anew in cities across the country. (White soldiers in Vietnam, meanwhile, raised the Confederate flag after King's death.) The commission's description of a bifurcating nation seemed prophetic.

Black Americans hardly needed a commission to tell them the country was divided. But now some didn't bemoan the fact; they embraced it. They wanted to make it official.

First to demand separation was the Nation of Islam. Territorial sovereignty was (and remains) one of the group's primary demands, as its leader at the time, Elijah Muhammad, spelled out in the manifesto *What the Muslims Want.* Having given whites "400 years of our sweat and blood," black Americans deserved "complete separation in a state or territory of our own." His protégé Malcolm X called for the government to turn over "a few states."

Invoking the Declaration of Independence, the Black Panthers asked for a United Nations–backed plebiscite of all black Americans to decide the question of self-determination. In 1967, the first Black Power Conference, held in Newark, adopted a resolution calling for "a national dialogue on the desirability of partitioning the U.S. into two separate and independent nations," one for blacks and the other for whites. "The Case for Black Separatism," an essay by the economist and anti-war activist Robert S. Browne, criticized those who maintained a sentimental attachment to preserving the Union. Given the apparent permanence of racial oppression, Browne wondered "if there really remains much of a Union to preserve."

On March 31, 1968 — the same day Johnson announced he wouldn't seek reelection — some five hundred activists met in a Detroit church to form a provisional government for a nation to be called the Republic of New Afrika, made up of Louisiana, Mississippi, Alabama, Georgia, and South Carolina. They named various officers, including Betty Shabazz, Malcolm X's widow, as a vice president. A declaration of independence proclaimed its signatories "forever free and independent of the jurisdiction of the United States of America and the obligations which that country's unilateral decision to make our ancestors and ourselves paper-citizens placed on us." An armed wing called the Black Legion would defend against foreign attack. "Consulates" in seven Northern cities encouraged black emigration to the new republic.

Though the goal remained a black Southern nation, the RNA spread the separatist gospel far outside the former Confederacy. During the contentious New York teachers' strike of 1968, RNA activists called for black neighborhoods in Brooklyn to secede from the United States. "If people in Ocean Hill–Brownsville, and anywhere else, really want local control," one member explained, "the only way to achieve it is outside the US federal system."

In 1970, RNA members moved to Mississippi, the state with the largest proportion of black residents, to begin building their nation. They adopted the slogan "Free the Land," and after a black farmer agreed to sell them some property, they hired a contractor to build a school and dining hall. Dozens of activists arrived in a caravan one Sunday, only to find Klansmen and police blocking their way. In a miracle one of the RNA leaders later compared to the parting of the Red Sea, the activists made it through the blockade and christened their capital El Malik—Malcolm X's adopted Muslim name.

The ceremony, however, turned out to be the beginning of the end for New Afrika. Pressured by local whites, the farmer reneged on the land deal. Infiltrated by the FBI's anti-subversive COINTELPRO program, the RNA collapsed. Most of its leaders went into hiding or exile or were sent to prison, often on trumped-up charges. Behind bars, they continued to campaign for black independence as the only compensation for America's founding sin.

African-Americans weren't the only ones reconsidering their place in the Union. Some Mexican-Americans, too, adopted separatism as the cure for societal ills. Inspired by anti-colonial movements around the world and by Black Power at home, young Hispanic activists frustrated by the relative moderation of community leaders like Cesar Chavez and Dolores Huerta began to revive the explosive proposal of the Plan de San Diego of half a century earlier. The Union's sordid history of continental conquest was as bad as slavery, and turning over land to the injured was the only way to heal old wounds.

In March 1969, thousands of young Mexican-Americans gathered in Denver for the first National Chicano Liberation Youth Conference. Amid panel discussions on language and literature and teach-ins on self-defense, delegates drew up a separatist manifesto, *El Plan Espiritual de Aztlán,* named for the mythical Aztec homeland in the American Southwest. "We Declare the Independence of our Mestizo Nation," the plan proclaimed. "We are a Nation, We are a Union of free Pueblos, We are Aztlán. Por La Raza todo, Fuera de la Raza nada." (For my race everything, for outside my race nothing.)

More a symbolic declaration than a literal one, the plan excited the conference-goers and galvanized the left wing of the Chicano movement. A year later, during a fight over a public park in San Diego, activists hoisted a red, white, and green flag to symbolize the reclamation of former Mexican territory. As historian Rodolfo Acuña puts it, many Chicanos "took a hard look at their assigned role in the United States, evaluated it, and then decided that they had had enough, and so they bid good-bye to America."

Puerto Ricans had long dreamed of independence, never having been welcomed into the Union in the first place. Since the island's absorption after the Spanish-American War, there had been periodic bursts of pro-independence feeling. After a 1948 law made it illegal to display the Puerto Rican flag, revolts erupted around the island. Then the violence spread to the mainland. Puerto Rican nationalists tried to kill Harry Truman and opened fire on the floor of the House of Representatives, wounding five congressmen. In 1975, a bomb went off in Fraunces Tavern in Lower Manhattan, the eighteenth-century inn where George Washington had bidden farewell to the officers of the Continental army—another band of colonial irregulars fighting for independence. Four people died. The historical parallel was lost in the smoke. As it had with the Republic of New Afrika, the FBI's COINTEL-PRO decimated the Puerto Rican independence movement.

Separatism was even adopted by some in America's largest group of second-class citizens. A radical fringe of second-wave feminism called on women to free themselves from all connection with men. They wanted to live, as the writer Ariel Levy puts it, in "an alternate, penisless reality." Though one writer published a book in 1972 titled *Lesbian Nation,* the point was not to form a women-only state but to buy land and build up autonomous rural communities far from any trace of the patriarchy. Even male children were barred from some colonies. America was dying of "testosterone poisoning," argued one member of a separatist group who spent years traveling around the country, stopping only to visit communal outposts of "womyn's land." They called themselves the Van Dykes, because they lived in a van.

Turned-on hippies and clued-in radicals also dreamed of leaving behind a war-mad country for a more perfect utopia yet unseen. Radical devolution of power was a primary tenet of the New Left's political philosophy. The anarchist Paul Goodman called "overcentralization… an international disease of modern times." Back-to-the-land communes reflected some people's desire to live not only off the grid but outside the existing constitutional system. In his popular lifestyle guide the *Whole Earth Catalog,* Stewart Brand called for designating official "outlaw areas," places set aside for rogues and renegades to create new forms of society.

In 1966, the *East Village Other,* a trailblazing alt-weekly that once published an ad asking for a pilot to bomb the Pentagon with ten thousand flowers, devised an even more ambitious dream: the Underground States of America, a national home for the "literally thousands of young people…who have, in one form or another, dropped out of the system… and who would benefit once for all by seceding from the Union." With food and shelter provided to all, Allen Katzman, the paper's editor, wrote, citizens of the Underground States would spend their time on creative pursuits like farming, carpentry, painting, and writing. Revenue would be raised by charging squares who wanted to visit the hippie confederacy and absorb its groovy vibes. Such vacations would be like "one great big therapy," Katzman predicted. But there would be rules of decorum: "Any visitor who is not serious about his quest or disturbs the natives, would be asked to leave and his money refunded."

The compromise tradition, America's long refusal to reckon with its contradictions, was again coming apart. The topic of disunion was banished from acceptable discourse, so the impulse was sublimated into all kinds of protest movements, antiestablishment politics, and cultural phenomena. In his multivolume history of "the unmaking of the American consensus," historian Rick Perlstein writes that "year by year, crisis by crisis, America was slowly becoming more divided than it was united." But maybe the mistake was in assuming that it had ever been united, that the consensus had ever been more than a convenient Cold War fiction.

Nothing divided Americans in the 1960s more than the Vietnam War. During a 1967 protest at the Pentagon, Norman Mailer heard a trumpet sound in the distance. It transported him "all the way back through a galaxy of bugles to the cries of the Civil War." Disunion wasn't only in the past. "The ghosts of old battles were wheeling like clouds over Washington," Mailer wrote. The next year, after watching the police assault protesters outside the Democrats' Chicago convention, Mailer wrote that he was pleased to find, "if it came to civil war, there was a side [I] could join."

A wave of bombings and assassinations contributed to the growing sense of breakdown, collapse, and disorder. Terrorist groups like the Weather Underground, the Symbionese Liberation Army, and the FALN, a group of Puerto Rican separatists, were setting off thousands of bombs in banks, colleges, government buildings, airports, and other public places. Violence, the activist H. Rap Brown famously declared, was "as American as cherry pie." Politically motivated shootings, kidnappings, and hijackings became routine. "Oh, another bombing? Who is it this time?' " a New York woman asked a reporter after an attack in 1977. San Francisco, a target of many attacks, became known as "the Belfast of North America." In all, nearly two hundred people were murdered in political violence in the late 1960s and 1970s, and some six hundred were injured.

As the raucous decade came to an end, some Americans believed their divided country couldn't hold together much longer. In 1969, the aged literary critic Lewis Mumford, mourning not only his rudderless country but all the violence modernity had wrought, solemnly wrote a friend, "I think, in view of all that has happened in the last half century, that it is likely the ship will sink."

5. You Are Southerners Too

Remembered largely for its conspicuous displays of political and cultural radicalism, the 1960s also saw—perhaps more important, in the long run—the slow, grinding rise of the New Right. Relegated since the New Deal to the political fringe, conservatism returned to political contention in part by seizing on old sectional attachments and antagonisms. As factories in older, heavily unionized cities closed and

companies opened new operations in less developed Southern and
Western states with looser labor protections, the North and Midwest
lost out. Long before offshoring destroyed American manufacturing,
interstate rivalry hollowed it out in many parts of the country. "The
South is fighting the Civil War all over again in trying to take away our
industry," one New Englander complained.

Meanwhile, the newly prosperous South and West—dubbed the
"Sunbelt" by Republican strategist Kevin Phillips—began to demand
more political power. Echoing New Deal–era critiques, Sunbelt politicians argued that their states suffered a form of colonialism at the
hands of Eastern interests. Decisions made by faceless bureaucrats in
distant boardrooms affected life in small communities. Talented private-
sector workers departed for corporate headquarters in New York, while
their peers in public service swarmed to Washington to staff the new
agencies created by the New Deal and Lyndon Johnson's Great Society.
In culture, too, one section's influence dominated; television projected
the East Coast's vision of America all across the land. In a 1968 essay
about "the new sectionalism," one scholar predicted the country was
about to enter "a rather sensational epoch of ill-will."

That, alas, was an understatement. Southern and Western resentment of Eastern and Northern political and cultural domination crys-
tallized into a strident new conservatism, a combination of free-market
economic orthodoxy, aggressive anti-communism, and unreformed
racism. Holding the motley coalition together was opposition to an
East Coast establishment that supposedly undermined "traditional"
values and surrendered America to its enemies, foreign and domestic—
a gnawing paranoia among blue-collar voters in the heartland that Ivy
League pretenders and parvenus, enamored of Communism and civil
rights, had wormed their way into positions of power in academia, government, and media, eminent perches from which they looked down
on their less sophisticated countrymen.

The idol of the rising conservative movement was Barry Goldwater
of Arizona. A Westerner bidding for Southern support—he refused to
acknowledge *Brown v. Board of Education* as the law of the land—
Goldwater weaponized the growing geographical divide. "Sometimes,
I think this country would be better off if we could just saw off the

eastern seaboard and let it float out to sea," Goldwater told a reporter in 1963.

Yet even conservatism's fiercest advocates knew they could win only by overcoming its Southern origins. When he took office in 1962, Alabama's George Wallace stood on the spot where Jefferson Davis had been inaugurated just over a century earlier and called for "segregation now, segregation tomorrow, segregation forever." But his wasn't a strictly Southern appeal. Wallace wanted all Americans suspicious of federal power to see themselves as heirs to the Confederacy. "You native sons and daughters of old New England's rock-ribbed patriotism, and you sturdy natives of the great Midwest, and you descendants of the far West flaming spirit of pioneer freedom," Wallace sang like a white-supremacist Whitman, "we invite you to come and be with us, for you are of the Southern mind, and the Southern spirit, and the Southern philosophy, you are Southerners too and brothers in our fight."

You are Southerners too. The new conservatism represented the nationalization of traditional white Southernism — its barely disguised racism, its obsession with resistance to the federal government. The Confederate banner began appearing far north of the Mason-Dixon, adopted as "heritage" by those with no familial connection to the antebellum South. (As historian Greg Grandin writes, "The battle flag became the banner not of a specific Lost Cause but of all white supremacy's lost causes.") Wallace's plea for racial solidarity found an enthusiastic response among Northern whites, including members of newly arrived ethnic groups uneasy about their place in the racial hierarchy.

Cementing the emerging realignment depended on conservatives' ability to draw sharp lines of demarcation between worthy and unworthy Americans, patriots and traitors. In 1968, Richard Nixon campaigned for the presidency on behalf of "the forgotten Americans, the non-shouters, the non-demonstrators." Later, he invoked the "silent majority" tired of special assistance for racial minorities and turned off by the counterculture. While Nixon promised in his victory speech to "bring America together," as president he did the opposite.

The clashes of the 1960s gave way to a new era of intensifying political divisions, one in which success required exacerbating the country's divisions, not trying to bridge them. Kevin Phillips, the crafter of Nixon's notorious Southern Strategy, bluntly explained the new thinking: "Who needs Manhattan when we can get the electoral votes of eleven southern states? Put those together with the Farm Belt and the Rocky Mountains, and we don't need the big cities. We don't even want them."

Patrick Buchanan, a Nixon adviser, put the philosophy more succinctly. "If we tear the country in half, we can pick up the bigger half," he told the president. Disunion, in effect, became the modus operandi of the Nixon administration, the reigning ethos of the Republican Party, the defining characteristic of modern American politics.

By the mid-1970s, America's booming postwar economy finally began to stagnate as the country staggered under the weighty burden of Vietnam-fueled inflation. When Arab nations cut off oil exports to the United States (as retribution for its support of Israel in the Yom Kippur War), Americans woke up to how fragile, how unsustainable, their way of life was, how dependent they were on countries over which the United States wielded little control. Ecological disasters showed the cost of unfettered growth, while Watergate tested the limits of American democracy. After Nixon's resignation, the long national nightmare didn't end—it continued unabated. The country seemed to be in free fall.

Given all the division, distemper, and despair, the nation's bicentennial in 1976 brought little to celebrate. "With a choice of red, white and blue decorations," an Ohio paper observed, "the dominant tone seems to be blue." Frank Rizzo, Philadelphia's mayor, braced for an invasion of radicals to America's birthplace and asked for fifteen thousand federal troops to keep the peace. The request was denied, but the invasion never came, and the bicentennial celebration proved a qualified success. Yet the modicum of harmony at picnics and parades was noteworthy mostly for how rare such unity had become. The best President Gerald Ford could say of the bicentennial was that it was wholly atypical: "A spirit of unity and togetherness deep within the American soul sprang to the surface in a way we had almost forgotten." Walt Whitman had noticed something similar at the outset of the Civil War. In neither case would the unity last.

A big, brash birthday party could only patch over national divisions. A fractiousness long suppressed strained to break free. In "The Balkanization of America," a cover story for *Harper's* in 1978, former Nixon strategist Kevin Phillips wrote that "the Union of the United States" was "unraveling." Old wounds reopened in the 1960s had failed to heal. A "crisis of spirit" plagued the United States. The trials of recent years had sent Americans "scrambling after a variety of lesser combinations and self-identifications: ethnicities, regions, selfish economic interests, sects, and neighborhoods." The country was more divided than at any time since the Civil War. If the divisions worsened, Phillips warned, "The heterogeneity of America will become a burden, the constitutional separation of powers crippling, the economy threatened, the cohesion of society further diminished." Ultimately, the balkanization of America would bring on a Rome-like decline. (That his own Southern Strategy had done much to bring that fragmentation about, Phillips did not address.)

By 1979, amid a new gas shortage and polls showing steep declines in trust in government and faith in the future, it was hard not to conclude that the nation was coming apart. Jimmy Carter, a former peanut farmer who had campaigned for the presidency on anti-Washington discontent, met for weeks at Camp David with politicians, experts, and even ordinary citizens to figure out what was ailing the country. America was experiencing "a crisis of confidence," Carter observed in an Oval Office speech. Amassing unheard-of material wealth hadn't compensated for the "loss of a unity of purpose for our nation," a loss that was "threatening to destroy the social and political fabric of America."

Conservatives derided what they called the "malaise" speech—a word Carter had never spoken—but three-quarters of Americans told pollsters they agreed with Carter's diagnosis: the country had lost whatever unity it once had and was hurtling toward ruin.

America's regions had rarely been more opposed; states bickered over energy policy and natural resources, tax incentives and agricultural subsidies, immigration and defense spending. "The attitudes today are the same as those preceding the Civil War," Louisiana's lobbyist in Washington explained. "The North wants everything its own way. This time, it won't get it."

Yet Northerners also felt the Union was giving them a raw deal. "Like blacks, Hispanics, women and homosexuals, Northeasterners are an oppressed minority," one New Yorker said. "We are only beginning to realize how badly the federal government discriminates against us." In a 1981 book, *The Nine Nations of North America,* reporter Joel Garreau surveyed the enduring significance of American regionalism. Garreau argued that the continent's most important geographical divisions cut across national borders and state lines—"those historical accidents and surveyors' mistakes." Political boundaries, he wrote, should be redrawn to accommodate more enduring realities rooted in economy, ecology, and culture.

In a new outburst of Western discontent, the country even experienced an old-school sectional revolt. Adherents of the Sagebrush Rebellion demanded that federally owned lands in the West be turned over to the states or counties to preserve access for grazing and resource extraction. Prodded by angry ranchers, Western officials from senators to county commissioners denounced "federal colonialism." Nevada, Utah, and other states toyed with nullification of federal law. Protesters bulldozed roads into untracked areas to prevent them from receiving wilderness designation. Some advocated violence. A Utah uranium miner named Cal Black, a leader of the movement, threatened to "blow up bridges, ruins and vehicles." Criticizing environmentalists as "selfish" and "radical...dandelion pickers," a "cult of toadstool worshippers," Orrin Hatch, Utah's newly elected senator, heralded the "second American Revolution." "My vision," said Kent Briggs, an assistant to Utah's governor, "is that we might need a new western nation from the Mackenzie River [in Canada] to the Rio Grande." Colorado governor Richard Lamm warned that the Sagebrush Rebellion might lead to civil war.

Just as the Sagebrush Rebellion took off, Ronald Reagan began campaigning for the Republican presidential nomination. "Count me in as a Rebel," he told a roaring crowd in Salt Lake City, identifying himself with the Sagebrush cause. Yet he may have meant it in more ways than one. That same month, following the counsel of his Southern adviser, a Washington lawyer named Paul Manafort, Reagan opened his general-election campaign in Philadelphia, Mississippi, site of the notorious murder of civil rights activists in 1964. "I believe in states' rights," Reagan declared. In the era of Republican dominance that Reagan's presidency inaugurated, "the Confederate theory of the

Constitution," as historian Michael Lind has called it, became the unofficial policy of the United States government.

6. *E Unum Pluribus*

The battles of the 1960s, the "balkanization of America," had divided Americans into camps as distinct, in certain ways, as the North and South in the antebellum period. At the 1992 Republican National Convention, Patrick Buchanan declared that the United States was in the grip of "a cultural war, as critical to the kind of nation we will one day be as was the Cold War itself." It was a war, he said, "for the soul of America."

That war was nothing new. It had been fought since the country's founding. "Consensus" history had covered it up. In this "age of fracture," as historian Daniel Rodgers calls the late twentieth century, the nation returned to old ways. Hoary nostrums of conformity and consensus, used to hide violence, oppression, force, and fraud, came crashing to the ground. What came next, however, wasn't exactly a forthright reckoning with racial inequality and concentrated economic power. The confusing chaos of globalization triggered a return to the safety of the tribe. In part this was a consequence of 1960s-style separatism: if it wasn't possible to form independent nations for each racial group—a future few really wanted—then mainstream politics and society would have to accept a greater multiplicity of voices and perspectives. The surface-level stability of midcentury would have to yield to perennial tension. Conflict would become the norm, not repressed, but valued as more true, fair, and democratic than strictly enforced unity.

On December 25, 1991, the Union of Soviet Socialist Republics abolished its own existence. Member nations had seceded, one after another, until the whole edifice fell apart.

America had schemed for decades to undermine its foe. Yet Western elites were nervous about the crack-up and eager to contain the fallout. Did the collapse of the Soviet Union herald a dangerous period in history, a new world anarchy? Would other governments collapse in turn? "The virus of tribalism risks becoming the AIDS of international politics," the *Economist* tactfully warned.

Yet some in America saw the end of the Cold War as a chance for a fresh start. Perhaps the dissolution of the Soviet Union could serve as a model for its elephantine rival—proof that vast conglomerations of far-flung states could quickly and mostly bloodlessly come undone. (Czechoslovakia's divorce a year later taught a similar lesson, while the ongoing breakup of multiethnic Yugoslavia and its descent into violence offered a disturbing counterpoint.)

The most eloquent skeptic was George Kennan, the U.S. diplomat who had helped start the Cold War with his "Long Telegram" from Moscow half a century earlier in which he advocated a strategy of containment. In a 1993 memoir, Kennan called for the dissolution of the United States—"a monster country" marred by "hubris of inordinate size." The Union had grown too huge for its own interests. "There is a real question as to whether 'bigness' in a body politic is not an evil in itself," Kennan observed. He would divide the country into "a dozen constituent republics." Despite Kennan's reputation, the bipartisan cognoscenti met his proposal with silence.

The end of the Cold War left Americans groping for shared purpose. Suddenly the lid was lifted from the mythical "melting pot" in which diverse ethnic ingredients were supposedly being turned into one tasty mush. What was revealed instead was a boiling, sputtering mess whose varied, clashing ingredients had never quite congealed.

Many pointed out there had never been a truly inclusive America. The compromise tradition—the fetishization of consensus, the national obsession with unity—had always been predicated on violence against marginalized groups, especially people of color. To critics, the "cult of ethnicity" signaled the beginning of "the disuniting of America," as historian Arthur M. Schlesinger Jr. wrote in a 1991 book. Multiculturalism replaced "assimilation by fragmentation, integration by separatism," Schlesinger noted. "It belittles *unum* and glorifies *pluribus*."

For some Americans, race had always been a defining characteristic of the nation. Inspired by black nationalism, militant whites embraced their own form of ethnic separatism: right-wing anarchism in constitutional garb. Deadly showdowns between the FBI and the reactionary fringe—at Ruby Ridge, Montana, in 1992, and in Waco, Texas, a year later—proved that the government had become tyrannical. Cranks and paranoiacs putting their faith in bizarre theories deemed the government illegitimate and massed arms to overthrow it. "Sovereign citizens" forfeited their citizenship and refused to recognize any authority above county sheriff.

The culture wars, however, were about more than race. Republicans used issues like abortion, flag-burning, prayer in public schools, and gay marriage to pry traditional New Deal constituencies from the Democratic Party. Some of the most contentious battles were fought over American history. While liberals called for closer attention to oppression and division, conservatives demanded an uncomplicated, triumphalist story in which America had always been united and right. They hoped cleansing the past of serious disputation and difficulty would keep an already fraying country from falling apart. The anxiety itself betrayed an awareness that the story was a myth.

As the twentieth century ended, America again showed signs of serious strain. The political system fell prey to polarization and gridlock, culminating in a hypocritical, harebrained attempt to remove the president from office. The 2000 election fiasco suggested that the basic functions of democracy had become impossible to perform. The problem wasn't merely partisanship but its increasingly geographic nature. The televised election results showed a sharpening division between Republican states in the South and West and Democratic bastions in the Midwest and on the coasts. Pundits spoke of red states and blue states, after the colors coded on the electoral maps, a handy shorthand for divisions more entrenched with every contest. The Supreme Court's openly partisan intervention to settle the stalemate—it suspended the Florida recount and handed the election to George W. Bush—placed an implicit asterisk beside his name, undermining the legitimacy of his administration and its often controversial acts.

The new president, promising to be a "uniter, not a divider," wasn't unaware of the problem, even if he often exacerbated it. "Sometimes our differences run so deep, it seems we share a continent, but not a country," Bush noted in his inaugural address. In the absence of an enemy, Americans were turning against each other. Was it possible, as Benjamin Rush had suggested in 1776, that the states of America couldn't be a nation without war? The country desperately needed something to unite it.

For a time, the attacks of September 11 seemed to do just that. Since the earliest days of European settlement, deadly attacks by shadowy adversaries had been one of the few things that could bring Americans together—at least for a time. After the towers fell, an otherwise divided people rallied around the suddenly ubiquitous national flag. A tragedy in a city whose supposed arrogance many Americans in the middle of the country had grown to detest prompted an outpouring of cries for unity. "United We Stand, Divided We Fall," John Dickinson's old revolutionary slogan, became the rallying cry of blacks and whites, immigrants and natives, across a shocked and injured land.

The attacks briefly startled the country out of complacency. As citizens wondered why divine favor had been withdrawn, a serious reckoning about America's nature and purpose appeared to be in the offing. Would Americans seize this rare moment of vulnerability to face up to questions long deferred or, by neglecting once again that difficult work, would the United States become, as Walt Whitman feared, "the most tremendous failure of time"?

CHAPTER 13

The Cold Civil War

> The Greeks did not understand each other any longer, though they spoke the same language.
>
> —THUCYDIDES

IN THE FIVE YEARS I spent working on this book, our most intractable conflicts and national contradictions became fodder for the front pages, the nightly news, and the Twittersphere. Disunion, far from a subject of antiquarian interest, became more fraught, more relevant, more *real,* than at any time since the Civil War. I often felt like I was writing a history of hurricanes while a category 5 storm raged all around me.

After the "volcanic upheaval" of 2016, a number of commentators suggested—as so many had before in American history—that instead of letting the country's fabric unravel fitfully and piecemeal, it would be better to come to some kind of formal arrangement to dissolve the Union. The idea had proponents across the spectrum. "Given the divisions among us, deeper and wider than ever, it is an open question as to how, and how long, we will endure as one people," wrote Patrick Buchanan. To anti-war activist David Swanson, "breaking the United States up into a number of pieces" would be "very good for democracy." Social theorist Richard Florida urged liberals to embrace federalism and states' rights. "Let us all have our bubble," Florida pleaded. "Otherwise, we'll continue to see an ongoing, disaggregated civil war." In the *New Republic,* novelist and journalist Kevin Baker published an open letter to Trump voters defending the notion of "Bluexit"—the de facto secession of Democratic states from the Union, at least until

Dueling protests outside a Houston mosque in November 2016 were both organized by Facebook groups secretly set up by Russian operatives. (*Jon Shapley*/Houston Chronicle)

Trump left office. "It's time for blue states and cities to effectively abandon the American national enterprise," Baker wrote, calling for "separation in all but name." By withholding tax payments, the blue states could force voters in the rest of the country to reconsider their principles, priorities, and prejudices.

While a few conservatives cheered Baker's proposal as the belated embrace by progressives of arguments they had been making for decades, most on the left rejected it as vindictive and counterproductive. As the blogger Hamilton Nolan wrote, "The reality is that nobody in America today needs help more than the poor and minority citizens of red states, no matter who they were suckered into voting for."

The abundance of disunion proposals reflected a broader reckoning with the endurance of national divisions. A new term of art soon found its way into political discourse. America had entered a "cold civil war," a clash of competing visions with no room for compromise. It was the job of political leaders to prevent the war from turning hot.

That task, however, became increasingly difficult. In June 2017, a disgruntled Bernie Sanders supporter shot up a congressional baseball practice in Arlington, Virginia, wounding a Republican congressman playing second base. Erick Erickson, an influential conservative, announced that only disunion could prevent political violence from becoming the norm. "If both sides have decided that every hill is a hill to die on and control of Washington means reward for their friends and punishment of their enemies, we need to end Washington," Erickson wrote. "The way to do that is end the union."

Two weeks after the ball-field shooting, I got married. For our honeymoon, my wife and I took a train from New York to Colorado and drove around the Rockies. The trip was supposed to be, among other things, a pleasant diversion from my work on this book and its full-time immersion in disunion, crisis, and civil war.

It worked—until the night before we flew home, when we stayed at a Motel 6 on the outskirts of Denver. Weary from travel, we poured cheap wine into plastic cups and flipped on the television. Having spent two weeks in the mountains, off the internet, away from television, out of reach, we stared in shocked silence as the room filled with horrifying images from Charlottesville, Virginia—neo-Nazis and neo-Confederates marching together, one citizen jabbing another with a flagpole, a car plowing into a crowd. And all of it over a monument to Robert E. Lee. The editor of *American Renaissance,* a white-supremacist magazine, announced his willingness to see the United States break up if it furthered the interests of his people. A century and a half later, the unfinished business of the Civil War looked like it might start a new one.

Watching the coverage, I thought of Charlottesville resident Thomas Jefferson's reaction to the Missouri crisis of 1819–20. With its heated rhetoric and threats of disunion, it sounded to him like a "fire bell in the night," a warning that the country would go up in flames.

A few months earlier, the journalist Thomas E. Ricks had asked a group of national-security experts how likely it was that the United States would experience a civil war in the next ten to fifteen years. Answers ranged from 5 to 95 percent, with an average of around 35 percent. Keith Mines, a veteran diplomat who had seen countries tear themselves apart firsthand, came up with 60 percent. "It is like 1859," Mines observed, "everyone is mad about something and everyone has a gun."

*   *   *

Though networks of communication never reached farther or faster than in the early twenty-first century, they exacerbated the balkanization of American life rather than fostered a deeper integration. As divisions of race, gender, class, education, culture, and geography hardened, possibly to the point of no return, Americans siloed themselves into nonoverlapping realities.

After the September 11 attacks, a fleeting moment of bridge-building and national self-reflection was squandered on another war against an abstract noun—terror. The fact that American leaders' lavish avowals of unity often felt false and forced should have been a sign that the mood wouldn't last. The Bush administration's shredding of constitutional scruples and long-accepted norms in authorizing torture, delegitimizing dissent, and launching an irrelevant and illegal war in Iraq divided and weakened the country, leaving it open to demagogues at home and meddlers abroad.

After Bush's reelection in 2004, frustrated Democrats circulated online maps showing an America crudely divided between a conservative "Jesusland" and a liberal "United States of Canada." Some liberals threatened to leave the country, while others entertained the idea of "Blue State secession." The separatist spirit was strongest in Vermont, where many residents fondly remembered the state's fourteen-year spell of independence in the late eighteenth century. A group called the Second Vermont Republic argued that secession would allow Vermont to recall its National Guard from Iraq and Afghanistan, switch to renewable energy, and tax corporations who wanted access to Vermont's natural resources. A state that, according to one study, received only seventy-five cents in federal spending for every dollar it sent to Washington, secession supporters claimed, could more than hold its own as an independent republic.

Yet 2004 was also the year Barack Obama burst onto the national stage, presenting himself as a latter-day prophet of union. His now-famous speech at the Democratic National Convention resurrected a rhetorical tradition largely dormant since the Civil War. "*E Pluribus Unum:* out of many, one," Obama intoned, rocking from foot to foot, hands slicing through the air. To the "spin masters and negative ad peddlers" plotting to divide and conquer the American people, Obama replied with a riff for the ages:

Well, I say to them tonight, there's not a liberal America and a conservative America; there's the United States of America. There's not a black America and white America and Latino America and Asian America; there's the United States of America. The pundits like to slice-and-dice our country into Red States and Blue States; Red States for Republicans, Blue States for Democrats. But I've got news for them, too. We worship an awesome God in the Blue States, and we don't like federal agents poking around our libraries in the Red States. We coach Little League in the Blue States and, yes, we have some gay friends in the Red States. There are patriots who opposed the war in Iraq and patriots who supported it. We are one people, all of us pledging allegiance to the stars and stripes, all of us defending the United States of America.

Consciously modeling himself after another Illinoisan—launching his presidential campaign in 2007 from the steps of Springfield's Old Capitol, "where Lincoln once called on a divided house to stand together"—Obama invoked the language and symbolism of union. Despite the divisions inflamed by the Bush administration and the sore feelings left over from the culture wars, Obama argued that more united Americans than divided them. "Let us find that common stake we all have in one another," Obama said in one campaign speech, "and let our politics reflect that spirit as well."

Too often reduced to mere post-partisanship or confused with a starry-eyed post-racialism, the proposition was actually quite profound. Amid a collapsing economy, in an overextended empire plagued by violence, inequality, and corruption, rife with bigotry and exhausted by war, could we Americans leave behind partisan grievances and rigid identities—"set aside childish things," as he quoted from Scripture in his inaugural address—and come together to confront the compounding crises facing the country, to continue the work of perfecting the Union, even if the task could never be completed?

No, we couldn't. Somewhere along the line, the dream collapsed. Whether it was on the night of Obama's inauguration, when Republican leaders gathered at a dinner and committed themselves to resisting every initiative of his presidency no matter its merit, or a month later, when CNBC analyst Rick Santelli stood on the floor of the Chicago Mercantile Exchange, spread his arms, yelled "This is America!," and invited "capitalists" to organize a twenty-first-century successor to the Boston Tea Party, it soon became clear that a more perfect Union wasn't in the offing.

During the eight years of Obama's presidency, the Republican opposition perfected their insidious, forty-year-old political strategy of weaponizing American divisions. The party that once led a national crusade to preserve the Union turned into a willing agent of disunion. Its response to Obama's ascension was an experiment in "massive resistance" akin to the Southern revolt against integration in the 1950s. Impugning the legitimacy of a black president, Republicans launched a preemptive counterrevolution less violent and overt, but scarcely less total, than the Confederates had in 1861. Mitch McConnell, the Republican leader in the Senate, vowed that "the single most important thing we want to achieve is for President Obama to be a one-term president." When that failed, he refused to allow the Senate to fulfill its basic constitutional duty of considering the president's nominee to the Supreme Court. "If he was for it, we had to be against it," one Republican senator said.

After Republicans held the federal debt limit hostage in order to make draconian spending cuts to food stamps, children's health insurance, and anti-poverty programs, Standard and Poor's credit agency downgraded the U.S. government's rating for the first time in history. "America's governance and policy making," the agency observed, turned out to be "less stable, less effective, and less predictable than we previously believed."

During Obama's presidency, the division between red-state America and blue-state America collapsed into a more complicated one corresponding roughly to city and country. Yet the other divisions he had dismissed as imaginary or overblown only widened during his eight years in power. Police shootings of unarmed men and women of color revealed that there undeniably was a black America, where residents were condemned to second-class citizenship, and a white America, where even the most desperate and destitute residents could cling to their racial identity as a prized possession. There was an America that prospered after the financial crash and an America that suffered. Losses from the crisis were unevenly distributed, gains from the recovery even more so. In September 2016, a day after reporting new statistics showing significant economic progress, the *New York Times* had to clarify that despite the good news, "large swaths of the country—rural America, industrial centers in the Rust Belt and Appalachia—are lagging behind." In his annual addresses to Congress, Obama described the state of the Union as "strong" (2010), "strong" (2011), "getting stronger" (2012), "stronger" (2013), "strong" (2014), "strong" (2015), and, that's right, "strong" (2016). Unless compelled by tradition or pride of incumbency, few Americans would have said the same thing.

Inflamed by hatred of the president and his policies, some prominent Republican lawmakers echoed John C. Calhoun's arguments that states could nullify federal laws they didn't like. In 2010, the Utah legislature passed a law allowing the state to seize federal land—the same issue behind the Sagebrush Rebellion thirty years earlier. North Dakota declared Obama's Affordable Care Act "null in this state." Governor Sam Brownback signed a law declaring federal regulations "null, void, and unenforceable" with regard to guns manufactured and owned within Kansas. A dozen other states considered similar statutes. In 2013, an Iowa Republican running for the Senate argued that any state with enough "political courage" could nullify federal law. Five years later, Matthew Whitaker became the acting attorney general of the United States.

Other conservative politicians even began talking about secession itself. "We've got a great union. There is absolutely no reason to dissolve it," Texas governor Rick Perry told an interviewer in April 2009. "But if Washington continues to thumb their nose at the American people, you know, who knows what may come out of that?" A Tennessee congressman running for governor said he hoped "the American people will go to the ballot box in 2010 and 2012 so that states are not forced to consider separation from this government." In 2014, the Wisconsin Republican convention considered, before finally rejecting, a resolution defending the state's right to secede. An Oklahoma lawmaker, state senator Joseph Silk, proposed to strip a clause from the state constitution that called Oklahoma "an inseparable part of the Federal Union." While disavowing any immediate need for secession, Silk noted that "30–40 years from now, whenever, you know, my kids are having families, what if the United States comes and turns into a, you know, communist country?"

Within a week of Obama's 2012 reelection, the White House petitions website was flooded with calls for secession from all fifty states. Tyranny was supposedly on the rise, and only another American revolution could save the country from ruin. "We do not want to secede from the Union to destroy the republic, but to restore it," far-right radio host Alex Jones said. Polls showed at least one-quarter of the American electorate supported the idea of their own state peacefully withdrawing from the Union. "The United States hardly seems to be on the verge of fracture," Jim Gaines, a Reuters editor, observed. "But any country where 60 million people declare themselves to be sincerely aggrieved—especially one that is fractious by nature—is a country inviting either the sophistry of a demagogue or a serious movement for reform."

The new secessionism expressed itself not only in the occasional reckless comment by political figures but in real movements with thousands of fired-up followers. Obama-era separatist groups ranged from the polished and earnest to the hateful and violent. The League of the South, an avowedly racist and anti-Semitic group founded in 1994 to reestablish "a free and independent Southern republic," turned rabid during the Obama years. Founder Michael Hill, a former history professor, fantasized about three- to five-man death squads roaming the country and eliminating "political leaders, members of the hostile media, cultural icons, bureaucrats, and other of the managerial elite without whom the engines of tyranny don't run."

Other white nationalists looking to found a whites-only republic eyed, not the former Confederacy, but the inland Pacific Northwest. The survival of whites in a rapidly diversifying America could be secured only by the formation of an "American Redoubt" carved out of Idaho, Wyoming, Montana, and parts of Washington and Oregon— the region of the country with the fewest people of color. Comparing themselves to the seventeenth-century Pilgrims, thousands of hard-core libertarians, conservative Christians, and apocalypse-fearing "preppers" flocked to the area. "Even if God has withdrawn his blessings from our nation as a whole," one declared, "he will continue to provide for and to protect his remnant." The website for a group called the Northwest Front shows a white couple posing on their manicured lawn. From the porch behind them hangs the blue, white, and green flag of the "Northwest American Republic." The site explains: "The sky is the blue, and the land is the green. The white is for the people in between."

The most prominent Obama-era secessionist movement sought to reestablish the Lone Star Republic. Back in 1845, when American imperialists like John Tyler and James Polk pushed for annexation, many Texans hadn't wanted to join the Union. Sixteen years later, they seized on the first opportunity to leave it. After the Civil War, the Supreme Court ruled that the state had never really left—indeed, that no state ever could. But that long-forgotten decision doesn't worry today's Texan secessionists, who have become an unignorable force in the state's politics.

Modern Texas separatism has its roots in the 1990s ferment of right-wing militia movements and anti-government conflicts. In 1997, a West Texas man named Rick McLaren, the self-appointed "ambassador, consul-general and chief foreign legal officer" of a shoestring outfit called the Republic of Texas, engaged in a weeklong armed standoff with local police. The annexation of 1845 was illegal, McLaren and his followers insisted, because it had been effected by a congressional resolution rather than a treaty—the same case Whig opponents had made to try to kill the deal. McLaren kidnapped a couple and was ultimately sentenced to ninety-nine years in prison. Behind bars, McLaren continues to file legal notices on behalf of the "Texian" republic.

A few years later, another, less-trigger-happy faction, the Texas Nationalist Movement, tried to rescue the independence effort from mainstream mockery. The TNM gained supporters after Rick Perry's 2009 comments and continued to grow throughout the Obama years. In 2012, an online petition for Texan independence drew a hundred and twenty-five thousand signatures. Four years later, a committee at the state Republican Party's convention considered adding a call for a secession referendum to its platform. The proposal was rejected, but that the party even considered it showed how far the movement had come. When the United Kingdom voted to leave the European Union in June 2016, many wondered if a similar earthquake could shake up American politics. The TNM's media-savvy leader, Daniel Miller, was prepared for the limelight; #Texit trended on Twitter, along with maps of America without its second-largest state.

In September 2016, a Russian government–funded group called the Anti-Globalization Movement hosted a "Dialogue of Nations," a conference of independence movements from around the world. Among the attendees at Moscow's glitzy Ritz-Carlton, a short distance from the Kremlin, were secessionist groups from Northern Ireland, Catalonia, Azerbaijan, Ukraine, Lebanon, and elsewhere. None came from Russia itself, where advocating for secession is punishable by five years in prison. But there were delegations from several American separatist organizations. Louis Marinelli, president of a group called Yes California, complained that his state had been "conquered and annexed by the American military about 170 years ago," while the self-described "foreign minister" of the Texas Nationalist Movement said he looked forward to the day when the Lone Star Republic and the Russian Federation exchanged ambassadors.

Funded by a charity set up by Russian president Vladimir Putin, the organizers paid the expenses for the American visitors. "The more the West is disunited, the more beneficial it is to Russia," Sergei Markov, an informal adviser to Putin, said at the gathering.

Under Putin's leadership, Russia has openly and actively supported secessionist movements in the United States and elsewhere in the West. RT, the government-backed propaganda channel, gleefully reports on all evidence of a coming American crack-up. Igor Panarin, an influential professor in the training school of Russia's foreign ministry and a close Putin associate, has long predicted the imminent dissolution of the United States and urged the international community to help manage America's decline.

Support from the Russian government brought Texan independence a new level of visibility. During the 2016 campaign, Russian-backed social-media accounts helped spread the message. One group, Heart of Texas, which amassed a quarter of a million followers, was a creation of the St. Petersburg–based Internet Research Agency, the government-backed troll farm later indicted by the U.S. Justice Department for interfering in the election. Before Facebook shut it down, the page spread fake news, conspiracy theories, fabricated quotes, and doctored photographs—one showed Hillary Clinton shaking hands with Osama bin Laden—and made the case, often in conspicuously inept English, for secession: "Texas—homeland of guns, BBQ and ur heart!"

That fall, the Heart of Texas page organized a demonstration outside a mosque in Houston. "Stop Islamization of Texas," it urged followers. Another Facebook group, the United Muslims of America, called on its own members to rally at the same time. On November 5, 2016, three days before the presidential election, the two sides yelled at each other from across police barricades. Some protesters were armed. Only later did it come out that the United Muslims page was also a Russian creation. Neither side's protesters knew they had been sent there at Russia's behest. From thousands of miles away, foreign agents had managed to stoke American divisions and exacerbate racial and religious tensions, nearly to the point of violence. According to a later congressional report, the operation—akin to "arming two sides in a civil war"—cost Russia only about two hundred dollars.

Yet foreign meddling in American politics has been dangerous only when there were homegrown malcontents who welcomed it. According to one poll in the summer of 2016, 26 percent of Texans said they supported independence. But when pollsters asked whether they'd support independence if, as expected, Hillary Clinton won the 2016 election, 40 percent said they would. Sixty-one percent of Trump's supporters in the state said they would support secession if he lost. A retired air force officer named Steve Baysinger, a member of Lieutenant Governor Dan Patrick's advisory board of activists, suggested that America was headed toward an iceberg. "Texas is the only lifeboat left," he said. "If Hillary Clinton is elected, I think that Texas will speed up its move towards independence exponentially."

*   *   *

Even before its stunning result, the 2016 campaign was unlike any in modern American history. Questions about whether the losing side would accept the legitimacy of an unfavorable outcome haunted the nation, as some feared armed hostilities would break out between the two camps—a throwback to the bitter contests, shaded by threats of violence, from the early days of the republic. The governor of Kentucky predicted that, in the event of Clinton's election, his own children's blood might be "needed to redeem something, to reclaim something that we, through our apathy and our indifference, have given away." Trump repeatedly refused to say that he would respect the results if he was not declared the winner. Only "the Second Amendment people," he hinted, would know what to do if he lost.

This openness to violence might have been the irresponsible expression of leaders or it might have filtered up from the grassroots, but the same sentiments were heard from ordinary voters. A week before the election, a Trump supporter in Wisconsin told the *New York Times* that "another Revolutionary War" would erupt if Trump were robbed of his rightful victory. "People are going to march on the capitols," he added. "They're going to do whatever needs to be done to get her out of office, because she does not belong there." After an unusually volatile campaign in which Trump fans physically assaulted protesters with the candidate's openly expressed approval—in Las Vegas, one supporter screamed "light the motherfucker on fire!" as a black demonstrator was dragged away by police—the potential for violence after it ended seemed all too real. "As a Christian, I want reformation," a Trump supporter told the *Times*. "But sometimes reformation comes through bloodshed."

The 2016 election results revealed a country becoming ever more starkly divided, not only between blue and red states—more than half the states voted the same way in every election from 2000 to 2016—but also between blue and red counties, between rural and urban America. When the *New York Times,* days after the election, published maps showing "The Two Americas of 2016"—Trump's map a continental expanse with metropolitan pockmarks, Clinton's a scattered archipelago in a vast, undifferentiated sea—the implication was clear: we don't live in a two-party country but in two one-party countries. Less than 6 percent of congressional seats were considered competitive, while 60 percent of counties nationwide were won by a margin of more than twenty points—a sharp increase from only 38 percent in 1992. Residents of racially diverse, highly educated, and fairly well-off cities in the United States had more in common with their counterparts in other metropolises around the world than with the less sophisticated denizens of more homogeneous, poorer parts of their own country. Americans from different regions and walks of life had lost whatever ability they had once had to understand one another. They lived in different countries.

The movement for Texan independence lost its momentum with Trump's victory. The revolution that had seemed imminent and essential days earlier faded overnight. Support for independence proved an expression more of partisan frustration than of constitutional principle.

The Texas movement's loss, however, was California's gain. It was a fitting reversal, the two most populous states abruptly switching places; the progressives who had defended national authority just weeks earlier now turned against it. As support for Texit, fanned by fake social-media accounts, had soared after the Brexit referendum, Election Night 2016 saw #Calexit go viral, spread by thousands of disappointed Democrats and Russian bots. Perez Hilton, the Hollywood gossip blogger, said he was "100%" for secession, while Shervin Pishevar, an Iranian-born Silicon Valley investor, promised to fund "a legitimate campaign for California to become its own nation." Leaving a Trump-led Union, Pishevar added, is "the most patriotic thing that we can do."

Months earlier, Jerry Brown, the state's long-serving governor, had joked that if Trump won the election, California would build a wall "to defend ourselves from the rest of this country." After Trump's victory, it no longer sounded like a joke. The next day, the leaders of California's state legislature put out a joint statement saying they had woken up "feeling like strangers in a foreign land, because yesterday Americans expressed their views on a pluralistic and democratic society that are clearly inconsistent with the values of the people of California." Zoe Lofgren, a Democratic congresswoman from San Jose, noted that "rational people, not the fringe," were talking about secession. A union that elected Trump might not be worth preserving.

Pishevar later recanted his heat-of-the-moment call for disunion, but Yes California, the separatist group that had attended the Moscow conference of worldwide separatists in September, stood ready to channel the West Coast's rage. "People used to argue with us when we said that America is failing," Marcus Ruiz Evans, a former radio host, told journalists. "With Trump, no one debates that point anymore." Yes California held a rally at the state capitol in Sacramento, accepting unwanted American banners and dispensing Bear Flags in return. They began to gather signatures for an initiative to put the state's independence on the ballot. In December 2016, Louis Marinelli, the group's president, announced the opening of an "Embassy of the Independent Republic of California" in Moscow.

In 2016, California sent $103 billion more in taxes to Washington than it received in federal spending. An independent California would be the fifth-largest economy in the world. Still, naysayers inside and outside California began pointing out the inevitable obstacles. Water rights would have to be negotiated. An arrangement would have to be reached about the future of U.S. military bases. California itself might begin to crack, as it nearly had so often before. The new nation might become a failed state, brought down by staggering debt, teacher shortages, rampant street violence. Some Republicans begged Californians to go through with their threats, noting that its loss would prevent Democrats from ever again being competitive in national politics. Peter Thiel, a libertarian tech investor, welcomed independence since it would "help Mr. Trump's re-election campaign."

Left to itself, the logistical challenges to California's nationhood might doom the project. But there was reason to believe that if the Golden State tried to leave, it wouldn't be alone. The mid-nineteenth-century dream of joining California and Oregon in an independent nation was revived in the wake of Trump's victory. "The election made the Rockies look more like a border than a mountain range," the *Times* commented. Trump's victory, over the objections of voters in Washington, Oregon, and Nevada, as well as California, revived interest in a possible rewriting of the continental map once thought inevitable but long forgotten: the separation of the entire West Coast—including the Canadian provinces of British Columbia and Alberta—and the formation of a progressive republic. With a population of some sixteen million, the region possessed an ecological unity and political distinctiveness that could be encapsulated in a fitting if fantastical name: Cascadia.

After Trump's election, support for Cascadian independence sky-rocketed. In Portland, two activists filed a petition to put an Oregon Secession Act on the statewide ballot. "Oregonian values are no longer the values held by the rest of the United States," one of the organizers told a local paper. Oregon and its like-minded neighbors "could all get together and form a nation that upholds the values that we all share." In an episode of the TV show *Portlandia*, a mayor, played by actor Kyle MacLachlan, called for the city's departure from the Union. It was time to "secede and form our own weird and independent nation," he announced at a city council meeting. The crowd roared its approval as the mayor grabbed a flag and scampered around the room while two hipsters spontaneously started tattooing each other.

Days after announcing the petition drive, however, the activists withdrew it, spooked by how seriously it was being taken by supporters and opponents alike. Apparently, the idea had touched a nerve. Mean-while, conservative residents of the rural, desert-like eastern parts of Oregon and Washington announced that if Cascadia left the Union, they would secede and form their own state of Liberty—a replay of West Virginia's formation a century and a half earlier.

As an organizing principle for the anti-Trump #Resistance, secession proved a nonstarter. Yes California's unsavory Russian connections hindered fundraising and enrollment. In April 2017, the group's president, Louis Marinelli, dropped the referendum campaign and applied for Russian citizenship. Married to a Russian national, he had found in exile "a new happiness, a life without the albatross of frustration and resentment towards one's homeland," he wrote in an e-mail to support-ers. Though others pledged to carry on the movement for California's independence, the momentum, crucial for any revolution, had been lost.

But it had never been likely that a successful Democratic opposition would resort to open rebellion. More likely was a return to states' rights rhetoric typically associated with Republicans. In a 1922 essay, the historian Arthur M. Schlesinger Sr. observed that throughout American history "the group advocating state rights at any period have sought its shelter in much the same spirit that a western pioneer seeks his storm-cellar when a tornado is raging." When Trump took office, Democrats sought shelter in the cellar only recently vacated by their opponents. Blue states began passing laws related to immigration, marijuana, and assisted suicide that directly challenged federal statutes. Progressives had favored an assertive national government under the Obama administration, but with Trump in power, the language of localism thrived on the left.

In California, the state's Democratic attorney general, Xavier Becerra, promised to fight the federal government as Republican attorneys general had sought to stop Obama initiatives on health care, immigration, and environmental protection. By September 2019, the state had sued the Trump administration a record-shattering sixty-two times. California's government even assembled a list of Republican states that public officials were prohibited from using state funds to travel to—punitive sanctions, effectively, for their enactment of discriminatory laws. (Conservatives condemned the practice as a form of "soft secession" that could lead to "a full-blown constitutional crisis, or worse.") Challenged by the Trump administration for refusing to cooperate with federal immigration enforcement, the state invoked the principle of "dual sovereignty," a version of the argument used by nullifiers going back to Calhoun. Perhaps a more apt comparison, however, would be to the Northern states that, in the 1850s, passed laws shielding their citizens from prosecution for failure to comply with the Fugitive Slave Act.

"There is no nullification. There is no secession," Trump's attorney general Jeff Sessions told a gathering of police officers in Sacramento. "Federal law is the supreme law of the land." Liberals in California dismissed the comparison. Jerry Brown mocked the idea of "a fellow coming from Alabama"—a man named for the Confederate president, no less—"talking to us about secession and protecting human and civil rights."

But Sessions had a point. Increasingly, Democrats openly embraced states' rights and federalism. After Trump pulled the United States out of the landmark Paris Agreement to control carbon emissions and combat climate change, California and other Democratic states pledged they would stick to the pact. Within days, Brown flew to Beijing for a high-profile meeting with the Chinese president, Xi Jinping, in a hall that usually played host to leaders of other nations. Brown then traveled around the world to highlight the commitment of America's largest state to fulfill the responsibilities the nation itself had shirked. In 2018, as Brown's time in office neared its end, one magazine profile observed that he was "functioning as the head of something closer to a country than a state."

The twenty-first century has seen an unmistakable resurgence of the idea of leaving or breaking up the United States—a kaleidoscopic array of separatist movements shaped by the conflicts and divisions of the past but manifested in new and potentially destabilizing ways. Earlier periods were defined by the ambitions of one or another region or the separatist impulses of this or that aggrieved minority. The new secessionism has appeared in multiple states at once, each pushing for departure from a Union that no longer functions. If the country as a whole is beyond saving, perhaps one's own state is not. The phenomenon is remarkably bipartisan and transregional. In addition to those in Vermont, Texas, California, and Cascadia, long-simmering separatist movements in Alaska and Hawaii, the last states added to the Union, continue to win adherents to the idea that they never should have joined and that it isn't too late to leave. A reinvigorated movement for indigenous rights has revived the centuries-old idea of uniting long-separate tribes into a federation and reclaiming real sovereignty. Often dismissed as unserious or quixotic, a throwback to the Confederacy, the new secessionism reveals divisions in American life possibly no less intractable than the ones that led to the first Civil War.

Today, there are no simple geographical boundaries separating Americans with different values, incompatible institutions, or opposite political leanings. (As we have seen, the 1860s partition wasn't so simple either.) The complicated nature of the nation's fault lines and fractures renders the likelihood of a conventional civil war, with competing armies facing each other across a field, virtually nonexistent. But that does not make the possibility of a breakdown in order any less disturbing. If the Union again dissolves, it will not be along one clean line but everywhere and all at once.

Trump was right that he didn't divide America, that it was divided long before he arrived. But his presidency certainly made those divisions far worse. The country's built-in impulses toward disunion, so long repressed, were finally released. After 2016, a sharp increase in highly publicized mass murders and outbreaks of political violence — lone-wolf attacks on perceived enemies, organized attempts to foster instability, vigilantes taking the law into their own hands — suggested the trouble lay deeper than Trump. With an average of one mass shooting every day, America has become, by any reasonable measure, a nation at war with itself.

As they had threatened violent revolution if he lost the 2016 election, Trump supporters insisted his removal from office would lead to carnage. "The Christians will finally come out of the shadows," warned televangelist Jim Bakker, who sold buckets of freeze-dried food to those fearful of a coming apocalypse. Steve King, an Iowa GOP congressman with openly white-supremacist views, posted a meme to Facebook bragging that the red states would win the next civil war since conservatives had "8 trillion bullets" while liberals obsessed over bathroom policies. In September 2019, Trump tweeted a quote from evangelical pastor Robert Jeffress warning that the president's removal would "cause a Civil War like fracture in this Nation from which our Country will never heal."

If such a war came, Trump's most loyal followers stood ready to obey his commands. The Oath Keepers, a right-wing militia full of active and former military personnel and police officers, volunteered its services as officially credentialed security guards for Trump rallies. "We ARE on the verge of a HOT civil war," its founder tweeted. A year earlier the group announced its intention to form "a pool of trained, organized volunteers who will be able to serve as the local militia under the command of a patriotic governor loyal to the Constitution, or if called upon by President Trump to serve the nation."

It might be possible to dismiss growing murmurs of a second civil war as exaggerated if the potential dissolution of the Union were not so clearly linked to the broader trend of disintegration roiling politics and economies across the world. Globalization, inequality, and climate change have weakened long-standing borders, revealing how arbitrary and unaccountable massive agglomerations of peoples and geographies have always been. These processes have triggered a nationalist backlash and the erection of new barriers. But walls and travel bans are unlikely to hold back for long the tides of history, the rise and fall of empires, the movement of people, ideas, and goods. A deeper dynamic is at work, one unlikely to be kind to makeshift mash-ups left over from the last millennium, those colossal assemblages known as nation-states. Separatist movements have emerged on every continent and in nearly every country. If America is in any way exceptional in this regard, it might be only for its fragility. Pundits blithely describe fractured countries like Syria and Sudan as struggling to maintain borders set by the arbitrary bureaucratic decrees of former colonial rulers, failing to recognize how well that description applies to the United States itself.

There is no telling what possibilities once deemed unthinkable the future might disclose. According to a 2017 poll, nearly 40 percent of the American electorate believes states have the right to secede at will. A year later, another survey showed that 31 percent of likely voters expected a civil war within the next five years. An academic researcher reported that one-quarter of respondents endorsed breaking the country into ethnically defined subregions. Those who hastily dismiss contemporary proposals for disunion as innocuous thought experiments may be underestimating the potential of these supposedly fringe movements. In a time of profound uncertainty and fragmentation, separatists of all stripes are poised to benefit from the failure of a system so broken, so unmanageable, that progress on issues of the most pressing importance has ground completely to a halt, endangering not just a single sectional or partisan interest but human life as we know it.

Scattered across a vast continent, today's disunionists make up an odd kind of union among themselves. Like the American colonists before the Revolution, what they have in common is the desire to be apart. The idea of breaking up a dysfunctional Union has the potential to appeal to frustrated voters on both the left and the right, a potentially earthshaking combination. The rise of the new secessionists might augur the emergence of a new political coalition—a revived Anti-Federalism—dedicated not to installing one party in office so it can do as much as possible before being replaced by the other but to uprooting the whole system entirely. For a slogan, the movement could do worse than what one citizen wrote in a letter to his local paper during the 2016 campaign: "The United States must die so that America may live."

What Is All This Worth?

Divided we ever have been, and ever must be.

—JOHN ADAMS

FOR NEARLY TWO HUNDRED AND fifty years, we Americans have done whatever we could to avoid deciding once and for all whether we actually want to be one country. Skeptics of the Union have been branded as treasonous malcontents—especially by those who harbor their own doubts. It was the wrong time to talk about it during the Revolution, because there was a war to win. Then the confederation was too fragile to bear such scrutiny. The new Constitution repressed the real causes of nation-rending disputes—slavery, above all. Union-minded propagandists crafted an appealing story about the country's origins in order to argue that an irrevocable federation had been created even before independence. After the Civil War, historians, politicians, and other memory-keepers played down the North's own dalliances with disunionism and dismissed what had once been a national obsession with secession as merely an eccentricity of the antebellum South.

Recovering this long-forgotten history should free us from the shackles of post-Appomattox orthodoxy and complacent, consensus-minded clichés. It should encourage us once again to think of our continent-spanning federation as a means to certain ends—such as those specified in the Declaration of Independence—rather than an end in itself.

Even some of the framers of our Constitution came to feel America had grown "too big for union," as the discouraged New England scribe Fisher Ames put it, and isn't that even more true now, in a country four

times the size with a population sixty times as large? If the radical abolitionists of the 1840s thought the Slave Power held such complete control over the government that no progress toward emancipation could
be made within it, shouldn't we wonder whether we're fast approaching
the day—if it has not already arrived—when the Money Power's control over our politicians has become so deeply entrenched, so ineradicable, that no remedy can be found within the existing political system?
If some of the populists of the 1890s and 1930s considered secession a
possible solution to the unaccountable power of Wall Street, will those
of our day come to that conclusion too?

How long will Americans rightly terrified by the coming climate
chaos work within a system that appears utterly incapable of doing anything to wean our country off a way of life that has rendered human
beings an endangered species? Our government appears to be irrevocably broken, and we are running out of time. "We must, indeed, all
hang together," Benjamin Franklin reportedly warned his fellow delegates in Philadelphia in the summer of 1776, "or most assuredly we
shall all hang separately." It was good advice at the time. But the world
has changed. It's tempting, some days, to take a different view: With
the seas rising much faster than they were in 2008, when Barack
Obama said he hoped posterity would remember his election as the
moment the planet began to heal, we may soon find the only choice is
drowning together or allowing ourselves to part. Should America keep
thwarting international action to address climate change, destroying
the Union rather than preserving it might become, as Lincoln put it,
"the last best hope of earth."

The breakdown in constitutional government is nearly complete. At
the federal level, every branch is mired in a legitimacy crisis from
which the future offers little hope of easy extraction. Whatever happens in the 2020 elections and those to come, Democrats face enormous hurdles to enacting policies that enjoy widespread popular
support—even policies on which the fate of humanity may rely. The
Electoral College favors small, typically conservative states and narrows
the political playing field to a handful of battlegrounds. Partisan gerrymandering, endorsed by an artificially stacked Supreme Court,
means that in some states, Democrats can win nearly half the votes but

fill only a quarter of congressional seats. The Senate remains, as it was in 1789, a bastion of aristocratic privilege and a boon to smaller, typically more conservative states. Thanks to Mitch McConnell's maneuvers to block President Obama from naming judges to federal courts—essentially a coup d'état—Republicans will likely maintain a stranglehold on the judicial system until the middle of this century.

Many Democrats seem to think a coming demographic shift will hand power to them permanently, but there are too many structural obstacles in place that could allow—indeed, that were designed to allow—a small minority of disproportionately wealthy and white people to hold on indefinitely. Consider what has happened in North Carolina and Wisconsin, where the election of Democratic governors in 2016 and 2018, respectively, was swiftly followed by the enactment of laws stripping their offices of power. Will the growing national majority be content to rely on the passing inclinations of a few berobed octogenarians to cement any legislation that does happen to squeak through the stalemated political process? Why should they? Democrats cheered when the Obama administration, stymied by Republicans in Congress, resorted to government by executive fiat, little minding the inconvenient truth that any measure so enacted could be overturned just as easily by a Republican successor—as nearly all of them have been. There's no saying what will happen as the unstoppable force of democratic politics crashes into the immovable object of oligarchic control. Growing talk of abolishing the Electoral College and packing the Supreme Court is only a taste of the norm-smashing to come. Nineteenth-century abolitionists predicted, correctly, that either slavery or the Union might endure, but not both; the same might be said today of the Union and minority rule.

Our political discourse is civil war by other means—we sound as if we do not really want to continue to be members of one country. Well-meaning historians have mined the national past to show that "the soul of America" has triumphed over greater difficulties before and will again. Yet the Union's survival has always been as much a matter of chance and contingency as flag-waving and will. At nearly every step it required morally indefensible compromises that only pushed problems further into the future. There never was any guarantee that the country would survive, and there is none now, no matter how frantically we rap out those mystic chords of memory on keys weakened from overplaying.

The erratic, contingent creation of this country suggests its boundaries are not written in stone. "Everything is negotiable," the current president likes to say. Many things are unimaginable until they become reality.

In the years to come, the idea of pulling the plug on the whole experiment may appeal to some who never imagined themselves as secessionists, especially those who have long defended the exercise of federal power. Progressives may awaken from the century-long dream that a system designed by and for the rich can be wielded for noble ends. Maybe only shrinking the sphere whose extension James Madison defended as necessary for neutralizing movements for "an abolition of debts [and] an equal division of property" can reverse our steady march toward plutocracy. Alexander Hamilton acknowledged as much in 1804, days before his death, when he warned that disunion would make democracy "more concentrated in each part, and consequently the more virulent." Now that so many of us have become devout Hamiltonians, maybe he ought to be taken at his word.

Say we can agree, despite all our differences, that we want to preserve the Union and sort through our whole collection of gripes and grievances within the current system—significant changes in our political and even social behavior will be required. We cannot keep trying to bludgeon one another into submission or indulge fantasies of the sudden evaporation, wholesale extermination, or unconditional surrender of the other side. We will have to find a way out of the morass of nativist exclusivity and racial antagonism—which, of course, is no simple task, thanks to malevolent, moneyed interests using the oldest trick in the book: *divide et impera,* divide and rule. Opportunists preying on divisions have been with us from the beginning. But with not only our country but civilization itself now at stake, we simply can't afford such distractions. It will not be enough to overturn the results of unfavorable elections; we must address the underlying causes of our cleavages. Otherwise, a supposed return to normalcy may prove short-lived. None of this will be easy. We need to re-create our country.

Our shredded national fabric demands attention beyond mere

mending. A new constitutional convention may be necessary to patch the gaping tears revealed in recent years. The House of Representatives, where each legislator represents more than twenty times the number of voters a congressman did in 1790, will have to be radically expanded. Though it's protected from amendment, the Senate, that useless leftover of colonial-era divisions, will somehow have to be abolished or at least see its veto taken away. If not, just as the 1787 compromises over slavery led to the country's first crack-up, those regarding representation may well lead to a second. To avoid that fate, we will have to find a way to truly and thoroughly unite—not *again,* but for the very first time.

"The dogmas of the quiet past are inadequate to the stormy present," Abraham Lincoln told Congress at one of the darkest moments of the Civil War. "The occasion is piled high with difficulty, and we must rise with the occasion. As our case is new, so we must think anew, and act anew. We must disenthrall ourselves, and then we shall save our country."

For Lincoln, that meant finally ending slavery. Today, we must summon the courage to ask that "miserable interrogatory," as Daniel Webster put it: "What is all this worth?" How much does the Union mean to us? What is its purpose, in the twenty-first century and beyond? To ask is not, as Webster thought, to partake of "delusion and folly" but rather the essence of true patriotism, far more respectful of our country's origins in protest, rebellion, and, yes, secession than mindless, mechanical fealty to one nation, indivisible. Neither a nation nor any living thing, Walt Whitman warned in 1865, can be held together by lawyers, or by an agreement on paper, or by arms. Taking the Union for granted, we neglect the work that will be needed not merely to save it, but to do so in such a way as to make and keep it forever worthy of having been saved.

Acknowledgments

I decided to write this book in the spring of 2015, six months after I first began researching the subject for a purpose I did not yet suspect. Warmed by a morning campfire in the Pine Barrens of New Jersey, manically underlining whole pages of Emerson, I halted at these words: *"heed thy private dream."*

Writing this book, I realized, was mine. Yet its fulfillment has not been a private or individual effort. From beginning to end I have been aided by a community of family and friends, colleagues and mentors, without whose unstinting support and invaluable advice I would never have had the courage or the capacity to start, much less to finish it.

That's especially true of my current and former comrades at *The Nation*. Katrina vanden Heuvel took a risk by asking a fresh-faced former intern to help plan the magazine's 150th anniversary issue. For that trust, and for her backing ever since, I remain forever in her debt. Victor Navasky, D. D. Guttenplan, and Scott Sherman have been loyal advisers and steadfast friends. John Palatella assigned me my first serious pieces and improved them, and my approach to writing, immeasurably. He read much of this manuscript and offered characteristically sharp interventions. Lizzy Ratner and Christopher Shay helped me hone themes and arguments that found their way directly and otherwise into these pages. Matthew McKnight, one of the most thoughtful people I know, cheered the project on and read some extremely rough drafts—including a sixty-thousand-word version of the first chapter, bless his heart.

Early conversations with several people, friends and strangers alike, helped confirm that what I had on my hands was indeed a book and that one didn't need a license to write one. William Hogeland, Scott Porch, Mookie Kideckel, Max Fraser, K. Sabeel Rahman, Kirkpatrick Sale, Debbie Engel, Claire Wachtel, Daniel Lo Preto, and Kelly Burdick were generous with their time and sage in their counsel. Without David Waldsteicher's encouragement, I doubt I would have had the confidence to pursue this; he later offered unsurprisingly shrewd and insightful notes on the first four chapters. Eric Foner, Mira Siegelberg, John Pleasants, Rick Carp, and Thomas Richards read sections of the manuscript and offered astute suggestions. David C. Hendrickson welcomed my wife and me to his home in Colorado Springs for a wide-ranging chat—an invigorating and inspiring encounter. Thanks to Thomas Bollier for the author photo.

Without one person in particular, my private dream would have remained just that—a dream. A talented photographer and expert opposite-field hitter, Elias Altman is also a magician, a liaison between parallel dimensions, a deft and diplomatic translator between the languages of art and commerce. His role expanded far beyond literary agent to encompass first-pass editor and round-the-clock confidant; his dedication has been absolute and his guidance indispensable. I don't know how he got so good at what he does so quickly, but it has truly been something to see. Both I and the book have benefited incalculably from his multifaceted labors.

I feel profoundly honored and grateful to have found a home at Little, Brown, the publisher of countless venerable monuments of American historiography cited herein. Reagan Arthur, now at Knopf, supported the book from the first. Vanessa Mobley, a visionary editor, grasped the project immediately and in full. In managing the anxieties and expectations of an ambitious first-time author, she somehow knew, as if mystically, when to intervene and when to let me figure things out for myself. But her greatest service—a reflection of how viscerally she got the idea—was her uncannily casual ability, when I found myself lost in the thickets, to remind me of where it was I had been trying to go. Elizabeth Gassman, Vanessa's assistant, answered with almost unnerving punctuality my innumerable naive questions. Pamela Marshall, production editor, was an effective traffic cop, friendly and forgiving. Deborah P. Jacobs and Tracy Roe gave the book a meticulous copyedit, zeroing in on clunkers that had bothered me for months or even years. My thanks as well to Elizabeth Garriga and Ira Boudah for their painstaking work to promote and market the book in challenging circumstances. That this has found its way into your hands is thanks to them and to my creative and industrious independent publicists, Leah Paulos and Andy Davis.

I researched this book largely in one place and wrote it in another, each ideal for its purpose. Having access to the Frederick Lewis Allen Memorial Room at the New York Public Library, an atmosphere of intense contemplation and commitment to craft, was an unforgettable pleasure. (My apologies for the noisy typing. What can I say? The War of 1812 was exciting.) Thanks to Melanie Locay for her able oversight of the library's research study program. I wrote most of the book in a garden apartment in Sheepshead Bay, Brooklyn, a floor below the residence of my wife's late grandmother, Sara Berkowitz, an author in her own right. I will forever be grateful to my in-laws, Florence Berkowitz and Alan Siegelberg, for making that quiet, peaceful space available to me. Reading the book now, I find it smells like those immaculately dusty rooms, furnished with flotsam I found on the street—including the computer it was typed on.

My loving parents, Robin and Al Kreitner, did everything they could to stoke the manic curiosity and endless love of Americana that led me to pursue this project with single-minded purpose, and their boundless generosity made it possible for me to do so. My sister, Cassie Kreitner; sisters-in-law, Mira Siegelberg and Hannah Siegelberg; and brothers-in-law, Asher Mullokandov, Warren Wertheim, and Michael Bukantz, offered stimulating conversation and unstinting encouragement.

While working on this book, I lost two people very dear to me, both far too soon. It pains me to no end that two of my mother's siblings, Jayne Cohen and Ron Lesonsky, will never read it. I'm proud and delighted, however, that my beloved bubbe, Muriel Lesonsky, will.

I also, in that time, got engaged, married, and became a father twice—the proud charter member of a young and expanding union. The earliest seeds of this book were sown on a long road trip my wife, Brahna, and I took after graduating from college—four months, thirty-three states, twenty thousand miles. We marveled together at the incomprehensible size of the country, its unassimilable multiplicity, at how it often seemed like several countries only pretending to be one. It took some time for those seeds to germinate and grow, but Brahna's thoughts and observations along the way—her accounts of things—served as irreplaceable sources of nutrition. This book is dedicated to her, my navigatrix, in the broadest possible sense: Without her, I know, I would be hopelessly, dopily lost.

I owe something more than gratitude, something unnameable, to my children. Audrey, born during the Civil War (my work on chapter 10, that is), has been a helpful research assistant, a sharp-eyed birding buddy, an endless source of amazement and amusement. Seeing her big, boisterous personality unfurl before my eyes has been the highest privilege of my life. Jeremiah arrived this past spring, radiating pure love and abiding promise in a moment of profound turmoil and pervasive fear. I can't wait to see what you two do in a world that, for all its troubles, remains abundant with beauty and possibility and generosity, yet sorely in need of your intelligence, resilience, wit, compassion, and righteousness. May you each find your own way to heed the call of Jeremiah's namesake: "Set ye up a standard in the land; blow the trumpet among the nations."

Notes

Introduction. *The Disunited States*

"great secession winter": See Henry Adams, *The Great Secession Winter of 1860–61 and Other Essays* (New York: A. S. Barnes, 1963), 1–31.

"volcanic upheaval": Walt Whitman, *Specimen Days and Collect* (Brooklyn, NY: Melville House, 2014), 20.

"the forgotten men and women": Yolanda Arrington, "Donald Trump Claims Victory, Promises to Unite the Nation as President," *Dayton Daily News*, Nov. 9, 2016. https://www.daytondailynews.com/news/national/donald-trump-claims-victory-promises-unite-the-nation-president/AB3hGvs1feVfXIpVx0fKoI/.

"more deeply divided": Colleen McCain Nelson, "Hillary Clinton Concedes: 'This Is Painful, and It Will Be for a Long Time,'" *Wall Street Journal*, Nov. 10, 2016. https://www.wsj.com/articles/hillary-clinton-concedes-this-is-painful-and-it-will-be-for-a-long-time-1478710250.

exchanging American flags: Yes California #Calexit Campaign's Facebook page. Accessed Sept. 10, 2019. https://www.facebook.com/YesCalifornia/posts/join-us-tomorrow-on-the-front-steps-of-the-capitol-in-sacramento-to-hold-one-of-/1819575718326242/.

The leaders of the state legislature: John Myers, "California's Legislative Leaders on Trump's Win: 'We Woke Up Feeling Like Strangers in a Foreign Land,'" *Los Angeles Times*, Nov. 9, 2016.

"a legitimate campaign": Olivia Solon, "Silicon Valley Investors Call for California to Secede from the US After Trump Win," *The Guardian*, Nov. 9, 2016. https://www.theguardian.com/technology/2016/nov/09/trump-win-california-secede-calexit-silicon-valley.

one in three Californians: Alexei Koseff, "'Calexit,' Here We Come? A Third of Californians Back Secession in New Poll," *Sacramento Bee*, Jan. 23, 2017. https://www.sacbee.com/news/politics-government/capitol-alert/article128316519.html.

"I didn't come along and divide": "Full Transcript and Video: Trump News Conference," *New York Times*, Feb. 16, 2017. https://www.nytimes.com/2017/02/16/us/politics/donald-trump-press-conference-transcript.html.

only 25 out of 435 seats: Lee Drutman, "The Divided States of America," *New York Times*, Sept. 22, 2016. https://www.nytimes.com/2016/09/22/opinion/campaign-stops/the-divided-states-of-america.html.

one-quarter, according to a 2014 poll: Jim Gaines, "One in Four Americans Want Their State to Secede from the U.S., But Why?," Reuters, Sept. 19, 2014. http://blogs.reuters.com/jamesrgaines/2014/09/19/one-in-four-americans-want-their-state-to-secede-from-the-u-s-but-why/.

This book charts for the first time: This book pieces together a story strewn across innumerable books and many literatures. A few works have been especially useful. Paul C. Nagel's *One Nation Indivisible: The Union in American Thought, 1776–1861* (1964), organized conceptually rather than chronologically, is a rich resource. Rogan Kersh's *Dreams of a More Perfect Union* (2001) offers a data-oriented analysis of the rhetoric of union up to 1900. William W. Freehling's epic, two-volume *The Road to Disunion* (1990, 2007) and Elizabeth Varon's *Disunion!: The Coming of the American Civil War, 1789–1859* (2008) are landmarks in the field, brisk and invigorating reads, every page bristling with conflict and contestation. Both were indispensable to my research. But the former focuses exclusively on Southern separatism while the latter skips the origins of disunion in colonial and revolutionary America, as well as its afterlife since the 1860s. I aim to chart not only the road to the Civil War, but the road to the road to the Civil War, the road away from it, and, perhaps, the road to the next one.

   Several popular works have been useful as well. *Bye Bye, Miss American Empire: Neighborhood Patriots, Backcountry Rebels, and Their Underdog Crusades to Redraw America's Political Map* (White River Junction, VT: Chelsea Green, 2010), journalist Bill Kauffman's rollicking tour of latter-day secessionist movements, offers a fascinating and highly readable account of the unlikely survival of separatism in the present century. Colin Woodard's *American Nations* (2011) unearths eleven perhaps too cleanly defined mega-regions, with distinct economic interests and cultural mores, whose half-conscious struggles for resources or recognition have served as a hidden force in American political life.

   I have been influenced by "the unionist paradigm," which holds union to have been the central problem—and accomplishment—of the American founding. Its ur-text is David C. Hendrickson's *Peace Pact: The Lost World of the American Founding* (2003), itself inspired by the work of historians like Peter S. Onuf and Jack P. Greene, and somewhat anticipated by the later essays of Frederick Jackson Turner. *Peace Pact* suggests the Constitution is best considered a treaty among quasi-independent nations that prevented them from falling into a ghastly and brutal civil war. I only doubt, given that the war did come, how successful that diplomatic breakthrough really was. For a thorough discussion of the paradigm and its historiographical lineage, see Max M. Edling, "Peace Pact and Nation: An International Interpretation of the Constitution of the United States," *Past & Present* 240, no. 1 (Aug. 2018): 267–303; Alan Gibson, *Interpreting the Founding: Guide to the Enduring Debates Over the Origins and Foundations of the American Republic*, 2nd ed. (Lawrence: University Press of Kansas, 2010), 86–122.

While many see secession: The historian Alexander Johnston observed that in the long sectional struggle from 1789 to 1861, "almost every state in the Union in turn declared its own 'sovereignty,' and denounced as almost treasonable similar declarations in other cases by other states." Yet with few exceptions (i.e., Forrest McDonald, *States' Rights and the Union: Imperium in Imperio, 1776–1876*), that thought has never been fully explored. Johnston is quoted in Arthur M. Schlesinger, "The State Rights Fetish," *New Viewpoints in American History* (New York: Macmillan, 1922), 222.

"By an unfortunate necessity": Adams, *Great Secession Winter*, 29.

"grazing multitude": Joel Achenbach, *The Grand Idea: George Washington's Potomac and the Race to the West* (New York: Simon & Schuster, 2004), 93.

In an individual, repression: Sigmund Freud, *An Outline of Psycho-Analysis*, trans. and ed. James Strachey (New York: W. W. Norton, 1949), 50. For more on Freud's conception of the mind as akin to a society at war with itself, see José Brunner, "On the Political

Rhetoric of Freud's Individual Psychology," *History of Political Thought* 5, no. 2 (summer 1984): 315–32; Mark Edmundson, "Save Sigmund Freud," *New York Times Magazine,* July 13, 1997.

"when human eyes": Whitman, *Specimen Days and Collect,* 24.

"If the day should": John Quincy Adams, *The Jubilee of the Constitution: A Discourse Delivered at the Request of the New York Historical Society* (New York: Samuel Colman, 1839), 69.

Chapter One. *Join, or Die*

"Everybody cries, a Union": Timothy J. Shannon, *Indians and Colonists at the Crossroads of Empire: The Albany Congress of 1754* (Ithaca, NY: Cornell University Press, 2002). I have occasionally altered the punctuation of older quotations—removing a comma, adding a capital letter—without altering the meaning.

"Come out from among them": Nathaniel Philbrick, *Mayflower: A Story of Courage, Community, and War* (New York: Penguin, 2007), 10, 27.

began splintering into ever-smaller sects and settlements: For instance: In 1635, the independent-minded preacher Roger Williams crept out of Massachusetts under cover of a January blizzard. After fourteen weeks' walking through the snow, he found shelter with sympathetic natives and, when the snow melted, founded a new colony at the head of a long, deep bay. Dedicated to religious pluralism and a strict division between church and state, Providence became a haven for rogues and rebels. The same impulse led Anne Hutchinson, the self-styled Boston prophetess, to settle on Aquidneck Island, farther down the same bay, and begin building the town of Portsmouth. Soon a group left Portsmouth to found Newport; another sect started nearby Warwick; and so on. See John M. Barry, *Roger Williams and the Creation of the American Soul: Church, State, and the Birth of Liberty* (New York: Viking, 2012).

The spirit of division: My overview of colonial disunity is indebted to Harry M. Ward, *"Unite or Die": Intercolony Relations 1690–1763* (Port Washington, NY: Kennikat, 1971); D. W. Meinig, *The Shaping of America: A Geographical Perspective on 500 Years of History, Volume 1: Atlantic America, 1492–1800* (New Haven, CT: Yale University Press, 1986); and Colin Woodard, *American Nations: A History of the Eleven Rival Regional Cultures of North America* (New York: Penguin, 2011). For more on local control in the colonial era, see Barbara Clark Smith, *The Freedoms We Lost: Consent and Resistance in Revolutionary America* (New York: New Press, 2010). John M. Murrin, writing about all British colonies in the New World, including the West Indies, described a "broad spectrum of settlements from the Caribbean to New England." Immediate neighbors might share certain characteristics, but the far northern and southern colonies "had almost nothing in common." In the seventeenth century, Murrin concluded, there was "not one, but many Americas, and the passage of time threatened to drive them farther apart, not closer together." John M. Murrin, "A Roof Without Walls: The Dilemma of American National Identity," in *Rethinking America: From Empire to Revolution* (New York: Oxford University Press, 2018), 188.

"each English colony in North America": *Peter Kalm's Travels into North America: The English Version of 1770,* ed. Adolph B. Benson (New York: Dover, 1964), 138.

a roving British minister: Andrew Burnaby, *Travels Through the Middle Settlements in North America in the Years 1759 and 1760, with Observations Upon the State of the Colonies* (London: T. Payne, 1775).

In 1685, King Charles II decided: The best account of the Dominion remains Viola F. Barnes, *The Dominion of New England: A Study in British Colonial Policy* (New York: F. Ungar, 1960). Also see Alan Taylor, *American Colonies: The Settling of North America* (New York: Viking, 2001), 276–78. For the broader imperial background of this little-known revolt, see Owen Stanwood, *The Empire Reformed: English America in the Age of the Glorious Revolution* (Philadelphia: University of Pennsylvania Press, 2011).

"provoke the Lord's displeasure": William Bradford, *Of Plymouth Plantation, 1620–1647,* ed. Samuel Eliot Morison (New York: Alfred A. Knopf, 2002), 254.

"jealousies and differences": *The Journal of John Winthrop, 1630–1649,* eds. Richard S. Dunn, James Savage, and Laetitia Yeandle (Cambridge, MA: Belknap Press of Harvard University Press, 1996), 277.

"a sad *breach* and *disunion*": Isaac Penington Jr., "The Right, Liberty and Safety of the People," in *The Struggle for Sovereignty: Seventeenth-Century Political Tracts,* Vol. 1, ed. Joyce Lee Malcolm (Indianapolis: Liberty Fund, 1999), 466.

A recent war with the Pequot: New Englanders celebrated their victory as proof, one wrote, that "the lord was pleased to smite our Enemies in the hinder Parts, and to give us their Land for an Inheritance." Alfred A. Cave, *The Pequot War* (Amherst: University of Massachusetts Press, 1996), 169.

In 1643, delegates from the colonies: One clause authorized the return of any servant who escaped to a neighboring colony. See Frederick D. Stone, "Plans for the Union of the British Colonies of North America, 1643–1776," *History of the Celebration of the One Hundredth Anniversary of the Promulgation of the Constitution of the United States,* ed. Hampton L. Carson II (Philadelphia, 1889), 439–46; Harry M. Ward, *The United Colonies of New England, 1643–90* (New York: Vantage, 1961).

Connecticut took the lead: Bruce C. Daniels, *New England Nation: The Country the Puritans Built* (New York: Palgrave Macmillan, 2012), 209. Though its veracity is dubious—there are no contemporary records of such an incident, and the story doesn't seem to have taken off until the 1790s—the tale of the Charter Oak remains central to Connecticut lore. When the tree fell in a storm in 1856, Hartford's bells pealed in mourning. Today, a monument stands across the street from the spot it stood on. Its arboreal descendants line the grounds of the state capitol, and an etching of the oak is featured on the back of the Connecticut state quarter. See Dave J. Corrigan, "Exploiting the Legend of the Charter Oak," *Hog River Journal* 6, no. 1 (winter 2007–2008).

"bringing Traiterous and Treasonable Libels": Taylor, *American Colonies,* 280.

"accommodated each to other": Ward, *"Unite or Die,"* 52. In "The Grey Champion," an early short story, Nathaniel Hawthorne describes an incident during the 1689 protests. As Andros and an angry crowd face off in the Boston streets, "the figure of an ancient man," wearing a traditional Puritan cloak and hat, speaking in "accents long disused," appears in the space between them. He forces Andros and his men to retreat, then disappears as mysteriously as he arrived. Who was he? Nobody knows. "His hour is one of darkness, and adversity, and peril," Hawthorne writes. "But should domestic tyranny oppress us, or the invader's step pollute our soil, still may the Gray Champion come, for he is the type of New England's hereditary spirit; and his shadowy march, on the eve of danger, must ever be the pledge, that New England's sons will vindicate their ancestry." Nathaniel Hawthorne, "The Grey Champion," in *Hawthorne's Short Stories,* ed. Newton Arvin (New York: Vintage, 1946), 1–9.

"bless and make it the seed": *William Penn and the Founding of Pennsylvania: A Documentary History,* ed. Jean R. Soderlund (Philadelphia: University of Pennsylvania Press, 1983), 54–55; Andrew R. Murphy, *William Penn: A Life* (New York: Oxford University Press, 2018).

In 1691, Penn drew up a proposal: William Penn, *An Essay Towards the Present and Future Peace of Europe* (Washington, DC: American Peace Society, 1912).

in February 1690: Richard Frothingham, *The Rise of the Republic of the United States* (Boston: Little, Brown, 1873), 88–89; Jonathan Pearson, *A History of the Schenectady Patent* *in the Dutch and English Times* (Albany: J. Munsell's Sons, Printers, 1883), 244–70. Frothingham described the Schenectady raid as "the Fort Sumter of that day." One also thinks of the attacks of September 11, 2001.

Three months later, delegates: Stone, "Plans for the Union," 447; Ward, *"Unite or Die,"* 30, 105–6.

"so crumbled into little Governments": Stone, "Plans for the Union," 449–50; Ward, *"Unite or Die,"* 134.

There would be as many objections: Stone, "Plans for the Union," 451. One supporter of colonial union took issue with Penn's suggestion that the American assembly should always meet in New York. In 1701, an anonymous Virginian suggested in a pamphlet that the American legislature instead rove around the continent, moving from town to town every year. That would help the inhabitants of different regions get to know one another. Soon, "the better sort of People would look upon it as a piece of Gentile Education, to let their Sons go in company of the Deputies of the Province to these Conventions." Through such internships, the people of the colonies would become more closely tied together, willing to cooperate on matters of native affairs, military defense, and more. See "A Virginian's Plan," in Stone, "Plans for the Union," 456–59.

divide et impera: Traditionally attributed to Philip II of Macedon, Alexander the Great's father, the phrase was later associated with the teachings of Machiavelli.

The colonists had contributed: J. M. Bumsted, " 'Things in the Womb of Time': Ideas of American Independence, 1633 to 1763," *William and Mary Quarterly* 31, no. 4 (Oct. 1974): 539–42. To some observers of imperial affairs, it was only natural that a separation with England would eventually occur. "No Creatures suck the Teats of their Dams longer than they can draw Milk from thence, or can provide themselves with better Food," Whig essayists John Trenchard and Thomas Gordon (as Cato) observed in 1722. "Nor will any Country continue their Subjection to another, only because their Great-Grandmothers were acquainted." The Cato essays deeply influenced the American revolutionaries.

At least one official: Jack P. Greene, "Martin Bladen's Blueprint for a Colonial Union," *William and Mary Quarterly* 17, no. 4 (Oct. 1960): 516–30; Ward, *"Unite or Die,"* 10–11.

The people were divided: My account of the Iroquois Confederacy and its relations with European empires is based on William N. Fenton, *The Great Law and the Longhouse: A Political History of the Iroquois Confederacy* (Norman: University of Oklahoma Press, 1998); Francis Jennings, *The Ambiguous Iroquois Empire: The Covenant Chain Confederation of Indian Tribes with English Colonies from Its Beginnings to the Lancaster Treaty of 1744* (Detroit: Wayne State University Press, 1983); Daniel K. Richter, *The Ordeal of the Longhouse: The Peoples of the Iroquois League in the Era of European Colonization* (Chapel Hill: University of North Carolina Press, 1992). An accessible retelling of the Confederacy's founding is Paul A. W. Wallace, *White Roots of Peace: The Iroquois Book of Life* (Santa Fe: Clear Light, 1994). A concise summary of the imperial context is Fred Anderson, *Crucible of War: The Seven Years' War and the Fate of Empire in British North America, 1754–1766* (New York: Vintage, 2001), 11–21. For an interesting legal study of the Great Law, see Donald S. Lutz, "The Iroquois Confederation Constitution: An Analysis," *Publius* 28, no. 2 (spring 1998): 99–127. I should note here: The evidence for an Iroquois influence on Franklin's Albany Plan of Union is largely circumstantial but, to me, compelling. To be clear, that is very different from the claim—as made, for instance, by Donald A. Grinde Jr. and Bruce E. Johansen, in *Exemplar of Liberty: Native America and the Evolution of Democracy* (Los Angeles: American Indian Studies Center, UCLA, 1991)—that in drafting the 1787 Constitution, the founders consciously modeled their new government on the democratic elements they admired in the Iroquois

Confederacy. Though it was endorsed by Congress during the 1987 bicentennial celebrations of the Constitution's drafting, most historians rightly find that claim exaggerated. Indeed, one purpose of the Constitution was to empower the government to
more effectively remove Indians from their ancestral lands, and another was to suppress increasingly democratic tendencies among the settlers themselves. As Timothy
Shannon writes in *Indians and Colonists* (239), the Articles of Confederation and the
Constitution were "decidedly anti-Iroquois in their ramifications." I would argue the
latter at least was also anti-democratic. Yet just because that more ambitious argument about the Constitution has been decisively refuted doesn't mean that the
intriguing evidence of an Iroquois influence on Franklin more than thirty years earlier ought to be ignored. Before 1744, the printer evinced little interest in either colonial union or the structure of the Iroquois Confederation—after, a great deal of
interest in both. Grinde and Johansen overstate the case, but the possibility that the
change can be attributed to Franklin's reading of Canasatego's Lancaster speech cannot be dismissed. For a succinct airing of this sprawling controversy, see "Forum: The
Iroquois Influence Thesis—Con and Pro," *William and Mary Quarterly* 53, no. 3 (July
1996): 587–636.

"homogenization of material culture": Richter, *Ordeal of the Longhouse,* 30–31.

"Neither anger nor fury": The text is in "Great Law of the Iroquois League," *Interpreting a
Continent: Voices from Colonial America,* eds. Kathleen DuVal and John DuVal (Lanham, MD: Rowman & Littlefield, 2009), 87–93.

"What kept the universe": Richter, *Ordeal of the Longhouse,* 45.

the Iroquois welcomed the refugees: Strangers were not only welcome but compelled to
join. The surviving members of many subdued enemy nations were forced to become
Iroquois or face death. This would admittedly seem to mitigate Richter's claim that
coercion in Iroquois life was "totally unknown."

In 1668, a Jesuit missionary: Fenton, *Great Law and the Longhouse,* 251; Richter, *Ordeal of
the Longhouse,* 40.

July 4, 1774: *The Lancaster Treaty of 1744 with Related Documents,* ed. James H. Merrell (Boston: Bedford/St. Martin's, 2008). For background on the Lancaster conference—
and Indian-colonial diplomacy generally—see Merrell's introduction in the above
volume and his *Into the American Woods: Negotiations on the Pennsylvania Frontier* (New
York: W. W. Norton, 1999). Harry M. Ward mentions a telling detail about confer-
ences where several colonies gathered to make deals with the natives: "Indian presents brought by the commissioners were doled out in the name of the crown and all
the colonies so as to avert bad feeling of the Indians towards those colonies which
had not attended or sent gifts." The habit of concealing internal divisions and exag-
gerating national unity would become a staple of American diplomacy. Ward, *"Unite
or Die,"* 133.

the conference went more smoothly: The Lancaster conference has been described as
the beginning of the end of Iroquois power in North America. The ambiguously
worded land sales Canasatego agreed to laid the basis for the coming imperial conflict over the Forks of the Ohio River, and thus the end of the French presence in
Canada and of the Iroquois' ability to play one power off another for their own benefit. In more ways than one, then, the road to the American Revolution passed
through that Pennsylvania frontier town. Anderson, *Crucible of War,* 23.

Benjamin Franklin's ink-stained hands: The best source on Franklin's work printing
Indian treaties for the Pennsylvania government is J. A. Leo Lemay, *The Life of Benja-
min Franklin, Volume 2: Printer and Publisher, 1730–1747* (Philadelphia: University of
Pennsylvania Press, 2006), 394–95.

he published far more copies: James N. Green of the Franklin-founded Library Company of Philadelphia estimates that there were up to 1,500 copies of the Lancaster treaty circulating in England and its colonies, "a really extraordinarily wide distribution for an original American book at that time." See Sandra M. Gustafson, *Eloquence Is Power: Oratory and Performance in Early America* (Chapel Hill: University of North Carolina Press, 2000), 119; Merrell, *Lancaster Treaty*, 5.

Cadwallader Colden's *History of the Five Indian Nations*: Colden lamented how aggressive traders and land-grabbers had taken advantage of the Iroquois and colonial influence corrupted them. "Alas! We have reason to be ashamed that these Infidels, by our Conversation and Neighborhood, have become worse than they were before they knew us," Colden wrote. "Instead of Vertues, we have only taught them Vices, that they were entirely free of before that time. The narrow Views of private interest have occasioned this." Cadwallader Colden, *The History of the Five Indian Nations Depending on the Province of New-York in America* (Ithaca, NY: Cornell University Press, 2016).

"It would be a very strange Thing": "To James Parker, 20 March 1751," *The Papers of Benjamin Franklin, Vol. 4, July 1, 1750, Through June 30, 1753,* ed. Leonard W. Labaree (New Haven, CT: Yale University Press, 1961), 117–21. For Franklin, union meant not only a continental federation but a civic solidarity closer to home. In 1747, French and Dutch privateers began raiding along the Delaware River—stealing clothes and furniture, setting fire to houses, absconding with slaves. Philadelphia seemed to be in jeopardy. But the Quaker-dominated government refused to raise a defensive force. In a pamphlet titled *Plain Truth,* Franklin tried to rally support for forming a militia. "UNION would make us strong and even formidable," he wrote. The enemy privateers never returned, but Franklin had proved his point. Thomas Penn, son of the colony's founder, complained that Franklin had propagated doctrines that were "not fit to be always in the heads of the Wild unthinking Multitude." Franklin was "a dangerous Man," Penn concluded, "and I should be very Glad he inhabited any other Country." See J. A. Leo Lemay, *The Life of Benjamin Franklin, Volume 3: Soldier, Scientist, and Politician, 1748–1757* (Philadelphia: University of Pennsylvania Press, 2009), 49.

A few colonial visionaries: Shirley's support for colonial union was informed by deeply personal frustrations with American division. In 1745, the Massachusetts governor led a successful assault by New England troops on Louisbourg, the imposing French fortress on Cape Breton Island at the mouth of the Gulf of St. Lawrence. It was the most impressive American military accomplishment to that point, and a point of pride in New England for years thereafter. (The seeds of later visions of Canadian conquest were sown early.) Shirley wanted to take the fight to Quebec City, but found himself unable to gather the necessary troops. He blamed the "Disunion of Councils" in the colonies for the failure to follow up. In truth, the British government bore at least as much of the blame. One London minister opposed an American expedition into Canada, fearing "the independence it might create in those provinces, when they shall see within themselves so great an army possessed of so great a country by right of conquest." See Shannon, *Indians and Colonists,* 69–71; Ward, *"Unite or Die,"* 36–37; Carla J. Mulford, *Benjamin Franklin and the Ends of Empire* (New York: Oxford University Press, 2015), 129–30; Lawrence H. Gipson, "Massachusetts Bay and American Colonial Union, 1754," *Proceedings of the American Antiquarian Society* 71, no. 1 (1961): 70.

National survival, therefore, depended: For the next thirty years, as David C. Hendrickson notes, "control of North America was widely seen by European observers as holding the key to the balance of power in Europe." See Hendrickson, "Escaping Insecurity: The American Founding and the Control of Violence," in *Between Sovereignty and*

Anarchy: The Politics of Violence in the American Revolutionary Era, eds. Patrick Griffin, Robert G. Ingram, Peter S. Onuf, and Brian Schoen (Charlottesville: University of Virginia Press, 2015), 216.

Franklin's famous image is usually interpreted: The image was picked up by newspapers up and down the seaboard, tweaked according to the local preferences that made it so urgent in the first place. A newspaper in the Carolinas, resenting the depiction of the southern colonies as the snake's tail, got rid of the animal entirely, rendering the parts as segments of a broken line. Missing from the engraving were Georgia, still largely unsettled, and Delaware, then considered an appendage to Pennsylvania. Timothy J. Shannon calls Franklin's image "a dire warning about disunion....Far from being a confident expression of emerging nationhood, the cartoon had an alarmist tone and predicted the potential extinction of the British colonies." Shannon, *Indians and Colonists,* 85–86.

"a preliminary plan for a federation": L. K. Mathews, "Benjamin Franklin's Plans for a Colonial Union, 1750–1775," *American Political Science Review* 8, no. 3 (Aug. 1914): 398; Shannon, *Indians and Colonists,* 179; Ward, *"Unite or Die,"* 14–15.

"almost every Article being contested": Shannon, *Indians and Colonists,* 175–82. Though Colden, too, wanted to see the colonies follow the Indian example and unite, he doubted the Albany commissioners would be able to sell their plans to the skeptical colonists. "What Authority have they to do this?" Colden, a longtime member of New York's provincial council, wrote Franklin, after perusing a draft of his proposal. "I know of none from either the Council or Assembly of New York." Colden's skepticism of unauthorized colonial action resurfaced a decade later, when, as lieutenant-governor of New York, he opposed the Stamp Act protests. His coach was seized by an irate crowd and thrown on a bonfire in Bowling Green.

Richard Peters...suggested: Franklin countered that those with "selfish views" would be more empowered in regional unions than if they were "swallowed up" in a larger one. Only a single union could vanquish the provincialism that had doomed past efforts to make the colonies cooperate. (Decades later, James Madison would make a similar argument.) Yet Harry M. Ward argues the colonies would have been more willing to accept Peters's proposal for partial unions than Franklin's plan for a general one. Ward, *"Unite or Die,"* 16.

almost universally panned: Shannon, *Indians and Colonists,* 214–20; Robert C. Newbold, *The Albany Congress and Plan of Union of 1754* (New York: Vantage, 1955), 163. Max Savelle explains that Franklin's plan "ran counter to the deepest trend in the thought and practice of the assemblies' struggle, the trend toward complete, particularistic, provincial autonomy for each separate colony, with the greatest possible degree of freedom from interference, either by the mother country, the other colonies, or a combination of them." See David C. Hendrickson, *Peace Pact: The Lost World of the American Founding* (Lawrence: University Press of Kansas, 2003), 331n4.

Only in Massachusetts: Hendrickson, *Peace Pact,* 81–82.

In January 1755, Boston's town meeting: *The Papers of Benjamin Franklin, Vol. 5, July 1, 1753, Through March 31, 1755,* ed. Leonard W. Labaree (New Haven, CT: Yale University Press, 1962), 490–92. The minutes of the Boston meeting are in *A Report of the Record Commissioners of the City of Boston, Containing the Boston Town Records, 1742 to 1757* (Boston: Rockwell & Churchill, 1885), 266.

Franklin took the defeat stoically: *The Writings of Benjamin Franklin, Volume III: 1750–1759,* ed. Albert Henry Smyth (New York: Macmillan, 1907), 203–26.

"ill consequence to be apprehended": Bumsted, " 'Things in the Womb of Time,' " 550–51; Hendrickson, *Peace Pact,* 82. Governor Shirley of Massachusetts, the most prominent advocate, aside from Franklin, of colonial union, tried to assuage London officials wary of American designs on independence. "[I]f it is consider'd, Sir, how different the present Constitutions of their respective Governments are from each other; how much the Interests of some of them clash, and how opposite their Tempers are; such a Coalition among them will seem highly improbable." To some British officials, those colonial differences explained why union could never work. Charles Townshend, a young member of the Board of Trade, said it was "impossible to imagine that so many different representatives of so many different provinces, divided in interest and alienated by jealousy and inveterate prejudice, should ever be able to resolve upon a plan of mutual security and reciprocal expense." If the colonies wouldn't join on their own, Britain shouldn't make them. Ironically, Townshend's own actions as chancellor of the exchequer in the late 1760s would help persuade the colonies to overcome their hostilities and unite. See Theodore Draper, *A Struggle for Power: The American Revolution* (New York: Vintage, 1996), 152; Alison Gilbert Olson, "The British Government and Colonial Union, 1754," *William and Mary Quarterly* 17, no. 1 (Jan. 1960): 22–34.

"The only way to keep us": *The Adams Papers, Papers of John Adams, Vol. 1, September 1755–October 1773,* ed. Robert J. Taylor (Cambridge, MA: Harvard University Press, 1977), 4–7.

"all want of Union": Ward, *"Unite or Die,"* 41.

"The state of these American Colonies": James Parton, *The Life and Times of Aaron Burr* (New York: Mason Brothers, 1861), 43. Burr's wife was then eight months pregnant with a son, the future vice president.

"in a National Light": Ward, *"Unite or Die,"* 250.

"the Jealousy subsisting": Anderson, *Crucible of War,* 284.

"Nothing I more sincerely wish": *The Papers of George Washington,* Colonial Series, Vol. 2, 14 August 1755–15 April 1756, ed. W. W. Abbot (Charlottesville: University Press of Virginia, 1983), 345–47.

"attachment to the province": Anderson, *Crucible of War,* 272.

"Nothing can hurt and ruin": Ward, *"Unite or Die,"* 42–44.

"the State of unhappy divided America": Daniel J. Boorstin, *The Americans: The Colonial Experience* (New York: Random House, 1958), 359.

"To appalled British officers": Ward, *"Unite or Die,"* 45; Anderson, *Crucible of War,* 288.

Most infuriating to one British general: Ward, *"Unite or Die,"* 62; Anderson, *Crucible of War,* 210.

In London, those who saw: Malachy Postlethwayt, *Great Britain's Commercial Interest Explained and Improved* (London: W. Owen, 1759), 471. Samuel Johnson, president of King's College in New York—now Columbia University—offered a similar idea. He proposed to subdue the "disunited state of our Colonies" by installing a "Vice Roi" to rule over the whole continent. Such a ruler would help counter the "republican character" of the provinces, which Johnson thought "pernicious." The only objection he could think of was "the possibility, in the course of time, of an affectation of independency" on the part of the colonists. But that struck Johnson as unlikely. The colonies were "such a distant set of Provinces separate from each other, and dispersed over so large a tract," that so long as "the true loyal principles of Christianity" held sway in America, the colonists would remain docile—"there being the strongest connection between fearing God and honouring the King." See Stone, "Plans for the Union," 482–86.

Franklin published an essay: *The Papers of Benjamin Franklin, Vol. 9, January 1, 1760, Through December 31, 1761,* ed. Leonard W. Labaree (New Haven, CT: Yale University Press, 1966), 47–100. See also Bumsted, " 'Things in the Womb of Time,' " 560.

Chapter Two. *Only United in Name*

"The States of America cannot": Harry M. Ward, *"Going Down Hill": Legacies of the American Revolutionary War* (Bethesda, MD: Academica Press, 2009), 220.

"The very plurality of States": George R. Stewart, *Names on the Land: A Historical Account of Place-Naming in the United States* (San Francisco: Lexicos, 1983), 171.

Given what they knew of American disunity: In 1764, Thomas Pownall, a former governor of Massachusetts, published a landmark work, *The Administration of the Colonies,* a trove of information about how colonial governments worked and why they so often didn't. Pownall was sure the colonies would forever remain "disconnected and independent of each other," unable to mount any significant resistance to British control. In describing the colonies as disconnected and independent, Pownall, who led Massachusetts during the French and Indian War, drew on his close personal acquaintance with "the different manner in which they are settled, the different modes under which they live, the different forms of charters, grants, and frames of government they possess...the rivalship and jealousies which arise from hence, and the impracticability, if not the impossibility, of reconciling and accommodating these incompatible ideas and claims." Jack P. Greene, "A Fortuitous Convergence: Culture, Circumstance, and Contingency in the Emergence of the American Nation," in *Imperatives, Behaviors, and Identities: Essays in Early American Cultural History* (Charlottesville: University Press of Virginia, 1992), 295.

"All Bonds of Union between": Rogan Kersh, *Dreams of a More Perfect Union* (Ithaca, NY: Cornell University Press, 2001), 42. "Nothing is more ironic in the entire span of early American history," John M. Murrin wrote, "than the way in which Britain finally persuaded her North American settlers to embrace a national destiny that virtually none of them desired before the crisis of 1764–1776." See "Roof Without Walls," 192.

"the most probable Method": Draper, *Struggle for Power,* 220.

"the Spirit or Flame of Rebellion is got to a high Pitch": Edmund S. Morgan and Helen M. Morgan, *The Stamp Act Crisis: Prologue to Revolution* (Chapel Hill: University of North Carolina Press, 1995), 258.

"What kind of a dish": Charles A. Beard and Mary R. Beard, *History of the United States* (New York: Macmillan, 1922), 33.

When Timothy Ruggles: David McKean, *Suspected of Independence: The Life of Thomas McKean, America's First Power Broker* (New York: PublicAffairs, 2016), 20. See also Ray Raphael, *The First American Revolution: Before Lexington and Concord* (New York: New Press, 2002), 26.

"spectacular achievement": Morgan and Morgan, *Stamp Act Crisis,* 306. Ruggles later became a loyalist during the Revolution and moved to Canada.

"A New System of Policy": Draper, *Struggle for Power,* 231, 260.

"Let him be alone": Pauline Maier, *From Resistance to Revolution: Colonial Radicals and the Development of American Opposition to Britain, 1765–1776* (New York: W. W. Norton, 1991), 74, 95.

"Multitude of Commonwealths, Crimes": Jack P. Greene, "The Problematic Character of the American Union: The Background of the Articles of Confederation," in *Understanding the American Revolution: Issues and Actors* (Charlottesville: University Press of Virginia, 1995). Dickinson was writing to the former British prime minister, William Pitt, asking him to help secure the Stamp Act's repeal.

"When a Country is divided": John C. Miller, *The Origins of the American Revolution* (Stanford, CA: Stanford University Press, 1943), 298.

"Boston would be left": *The Writings of Samuel Adams, Vol. III: 1773–1777,* ed. Harry Alonzo Cushing (New York: G. P. Putnam's Sons, 1907), 136–39.

"very means to perfect": Richard Frothingham, *The Rise of the Republic of the United States* (Boston: Little, Brown, 1872), 323n2.

"a shock of Electricity": Henry Mayer, *A Son of Thunder: Patrick Henry and the American Republic* (Charlottesville: University Press of Virginia, 1991), 186.

They called for a continent-wide summit: A new congress appealed to moderates who wanted to use the gathering to slow things down. John Dickinson, unnerved by New England's growing radicalism, reminded Boston friends not to get ahead of themselves. "Nothing can possibly throw us into a pernicious confusion but one colony's breaking the line of opposition by advancing too hastily before the rest," he wrote. Thomas Mifflin, a prominent Philadelphia merchant, told Samuel Adams that radical action, such as a new boycott of British trade, would fail to win support from commercial interests. It "may disunite us and ruin the Cause of America," Mifflin warned. See Miller, *Origins of the American Revolution,* 366.

"the ablest and wealthiest": Ibid., 380.

"Ambassadors from a dozen": *The Adams Papers,* Adams Family Correspondence, Vol. 1, December 1761–May 1776, ed. Lyman H. Butterfield (Cambridge, MA: Harvard University Press, 1963), 162–63; John Adams, *Revolutionary Writings, 1755–1775,* ed. Gordon Wood (New York: Library of America, 2011), 323. Connecticut's Silas Deane noted that it was no easy feat "to bring Men From infancy habituated to different modes of Treating Subjects perfectly to harmonize." See *The Declaration of Independence in Historical Context: American State Papers, Petitions, Proclamations, and Letters of the Delegates to the First National Congress,* ed. Barry Alan Shain (New Haven, CT: Yale University Press, 2014), 225–27.

"All America is thrown": David C. Hendrickson offers a corrective to the still-common misconception that Henry was expressing some timeless idea rather than the pressing interests of his own colony at that moment. See Hendrickson, *Peace Pact,* 105. See also Mayer, *Son of Thunder,* 211–13.

"observe the conduct": Ray Raphael and Marie Raphael, *The Spirit of '74: How the American Revolution Began* (New York: New Press, 2015), 144.

"groundbreaking infrastructure": Holger Hoock, *Scars of Independence: America's Violent Birth* (New York: Crown, 2017), 50.

"If this association is perfected": Richard R. Beeman, *Our Lives, Our Fortunes and Our Sacred Honor: The Forging of American Independence, 1774–1776* (New York: Basic Books, 2013), 154–55. The episode is also discussed in John Richard Alden, *The First South* (Baton Rouge: Louisiana State University Press, 1961), 22–24—a useful introduction to sectionalism in the Revolutionary era.

"only for the sake of preserving": William Henry Drayton, *Memoirs of the American Revolution: From Its Commencement to the Year 1776, Vol. I,* ed. John Drayton (Charleston, SC: A. E. Miller, 1821), 168–72. The deal "created an alarming disunion, throughout the whole Colony," South Carolina's Drayton recalled, causing strife between upcountry indigo planters whose interests were sacrificed to aid the more powerful rice-planting coastal elite.

"All parties are now extinguish'd": Robert G. Parkinson, *The Common Cause: Creating Race and Nation in the American Revolution* (Chapel Hill: University of North Carolina Press, 2016), 98. As Franklin knew, all parties were not extinguished. His own son, William, the governor of New Jersey, was an avowed loyalist. "You have now pointed out to you, Gentlemen, two roads," the younger Franklin told his state legislature;

"one evidently leading to Peace, Happiness, and a Restoration of the Public Tranquility—the other inevitably conducting you to Anarchy, Misery, and all the Horrors of a Civil War." The relationship between the father and son never recovered. See Nathaniel Philbrick, *Bunker Hill: A City, A Siege, A Revolution* (New York: Viking, 2013), 172; Daniel Mark Epstein, *The Loyal Son: The War in Ben Franklin's House* (New York: Ballantine, 2017), 200.

"Danger of Insurrection"..."a vast, unwieldy machine": Parkinson, *Common Cause*, 94–97.

"Discord and total Disunion": Hendrickson, *Peace Pact*, 108.

"an exceeding dirty": Merrill Jensen, *The Founding of a Nation: A History of the American Revolution, 1763–1776* (New York: Oxford University Press, 1968), 634. John Adams, who had nominated Washington as commander of the army, recalled that the choice had been "a magnanimous sacrifice of the North to the South; to the base Jealousy, sordid Envy, and ignorant Prejudices of the Southern and Middle States, against New England." Alden, *First South*, 25.

"as Indifferent men as I": Hendrickson, *Peace Pact*, 109. The first Southerners to appear in camp, a regiment of Virginia riflemen, promptly mutinied and tried to liberate a sergeant being punished for "neglect of duty and murmuring." Perhaps out of an affinity for fellow Virginians, Washington let them off with a small fine. The commander was reportedly "chagrined that only one regiment should come from the South, and that set so infamous an example." See *The Papers of George Washington, Revolutionary War Series*, Vol. 1, 16 June 1775–15 September 1775, ed. Philander D. Chase (Charlottesville: University Press of Virginia, 1985), 445–46.

"the Army must absolutely": *The Spirit of 'Seventy-Six: The Story of the American Revolution as Told by Participants,* eds. Henry Steele Commager and Richard B. Morris (Indianapolis: Bobbs-Merrill, 1958), 161–62.

"a Multitude of Strangers": Joanne B. Freeman, *Affairs of Honor: National Politics in the New Republic* (New Haven, CT: Yale University Press, 2001), 20.

"as several distinct nations": Jensen, *Founding of a Nation*, 637.

"an artful deception": Miller, *Origins of the American Revolution*, 479. Patriots throughout the colonies worried about support for the Crown in the western Carolinas. "We have every Thing to fear from the Southward," Washington's aide Joseph Reed informed his boss in early 1776. "A cursed Spirit of Disaffection" ran through the region, which could "prove a most formidable piece of Business, especially when connected with the Hosts of Negroes in the lower Part of the Country." An alliance could emerge among disgruntled frontiersmen and rebellious slaves. Parkinson, *Common Cause*, 205.

"heart burning and jealousy": Trish Loughran, *The Republic in Print: Print Culture in the Age of U.S. Nation Building, 1770–1870* (New York: Columbia University Press, 2007), 69. Daniel Leonard, a loyalist, predicted independent America would be "easy prey, and...parcelled out, Poland like." Robert Beverley, a Virginia planter and a critic of the rebellion, told a friend that America was "an infant Country, unconnected in Interest and naturally disunited by Inclination." He acknowledged there had lately been "a Sort of Union," but it was "only in Appearance." In reality, the bonds were weak. "Ambition, Resentment, and Interest may have united us for a Moment," Beverley wrote. But the pressures of independence would convert those feelings "into Envy, Malevolence, and Faction." Before long there would be "a greater Degree of Opposition" among Americans than between the colonies and Britain, and the Union would fall apart. Hendrickson, *Peace Pact*, 110; Kersh, *Dreams of a More Perfect Union*, 61. I regret not having space to discuss the loyalists' experience of the Revolution as a civil war. See Maya Jasanoff, *Liberty's Exiles: The Loss of America and the Remak-*

ing of the British Empire (London: HarperPress, 2011), 22–53; Hoock, *Scars of Independence.*

"The People are now": Miller, *Origins of the American Revolution,* 485.

"the most intricate": Edmund C. Burnett, *Letters of Members of the Continental Congress,* Vol. I (Washington, DC: Carnegie Institution of Washington, 1921), 446, 471.

cheers erupted in Williamsburg: William Wirt, *Sketches of the Life and Character of Patrick Henry* (Philadelphia: James Webster, 1817), 195.

"would have joined the British": *The Works of John Adams,* Vol. 10, ed. Charles Francis Adams (Boston: Little, Brown, 1856), 63. With tens of thousands of reinforcements expected from Britain at any moment, a fellow Virginian wrote Thomas Jefferson that he was "concerned to find there is danger of disunion at such a crisis, as that only can give Success to our Enemies." *The Papers of Thomas Jefferson, Vol. 1: 1760 to 1776,* ed. Julian P. Boyd (Princeton, NJ: Princeton University Press, 1950), 297.

"now confessing the falsehood": Merrill Jensen, *The Articles of Confederation: An Interpretation of the Social-Constitutional History of the American Revolution, 1774–1781* (Madison: University of Wisconsin Press, 1959), 114.

A leader of the decade-long: Milton Embick Flower, *John Dickinson, Conservative Revolutionary* (Charlottesville: University Press of Virginia, 1983).

"their colonies might secede": *The Life and Letters of Thomas Jefferson: Being His Autobiography and Select Correspondence, from Original Manuscripts* (New York: Edwards, Pratt & Foster, 1858), 13. Jefferson's notes on the debate record only what was said, not who said it. With Dickinson in opposition, initially, were James Wilson, a fellow Pennsylvanian and Dickinson's former law student; Robert Livingston of New York; and Edward Rutledge of South Carolina. Jefferson leaves room for the possibility that any of them could have given the speech. But I think it was likely Dickinson who spoke these words.

"I fear it will take some time": Burnett, *Letters of Members of the Continental Congress,* Vol. 1, 495–96.

"Some of Us totally despair": "John Dickinson's Notes for a Speech in Congress," in *Landmark Debates in Congress: From the Declaration of Independence to the War in Iraq,* ed. Stephen W. Stathis (Washington, DC: CQ Press, 2009), 11–13.

the delegates sat silent: William Hogeland runs through the oddly conflicting descriptions of the weather that day. See *Declaration: The Nine Tumultuous Weeks When America Became Independent, May 1–July 4, 1776* (New York: Simon & Schuster, 2010), 170–71, 240n.

reluctant to tie the knot: As David C. Hendrickson notes, July 4, 1776, should be celebrated "not as their day of betrothal, but as their night of forbidden passion, a glorious consummation to the warm embraces of the previous two years yet an act that fell well short of a regular marriage." So long as they had not yet settled on terms of confederation, the states were "living in sin," as Hendrickson puts it, though "determined to proceed rapidly to the formalization of their vows." Hendrickson, *Peace Pact,* 126.

"What contract will a foreign state": Ibid., 111. As they turned their attention to drawing up articles of confederation, some delegates began studying up on the discarded plans of union from the colonial past. In January 1775, Silas Deane of Connecticut advised Patrick Henry to look up the United Colonies of New England from 1643, by then a dimly remembered curiosity from bygone times. The colonies would have been better off if that early union had survived and expanded to include the other colonies, Deane told Henry. Perhaps it wasn't too late to revive it—or, even better, to create "such an one that…may last forever." Invoking John Dickinson's famous phrase, Deane concluded: "United We stand, divided We fall, is our motto and must be." A few months later, Benjamin Franklin dusted off his old Albany Plan of 1754, refitting its widely panned scheme for "One General Government" into a looser "League of Friendship" under which the colonies would retain as much of their own laws and powers as they saw fit. Even so, the new plan said that if reconciliation with Britain proved impossible, the American union would be "perpetual." A year before independence, that was still more than many were willing to accept. The delegates in Congress tabled Franklin's plan and didn't take up union until the following year. See Jerrilyn Greene Marston, *King and Congress: The Transfer of Political Legitimacy, 1774–1776* (Princeton, NJ: Princeton University Press, 1987), 189; Hendrickson, *Peace Pact,* 119.

he resigned from the Congress: Though he couldn't bring himself to sign the Declaration, Dickinson didn't give up on the American cause. After leaving Congress, he led troops to protect Elizabeth, New Jersey, from the British forces gathering by the tens of thousands off the shores of Staten Island—the largest invasion force the Western Hemisphere had ever seen. Dickinson resigned his commission in the militia in December 1776 and returned to his estate in Delaware. The next year, he freed most of the plantation's three dozen slaves—making him the only prominent patriot to do so during the Revolution.

"The Name of this Confederacy": Dickinson's draft is reprinted in Jensen, *Articles of Confederation,* 254–62. For a brief study of how the name came about, see Edmund C. Burnett, "The Name 'The United States of America,'" *American Historical Review* 31, no. 1 (Oct. 1925): 79–81.

the delegates took up the task: John Adams later wrote that he regretted the "profound Secrecy" with which the Congress went about drafting the Articles. The "whole Record of this momentous Transaction" was almost nonexistent: "No Motions recorded. No Yeas and Nays taken down. No Alterations proposed. No debates preserved. No Names mentioned." All we have are a few notes Thomas Jefferson scrawled out amid the clamor of debate, and letters delegates wrote to friends and family about what went on that first summer in Philadelphia when representatives of the United States sat down to write a constitution. Hendrickson, *Peace Pact,* 127.

"We are now One people"... "signs the death warrant": Ibid., 139, 144.

"destroying all Provincial Distinctions": John Richard Alden, *The South in the Revolution, 1763–1789* (Baton Rouge: Louisiana State University Press, 1957), 216.

"a confederation upon such iniquitous": Edmund S. Morgan, *Benjamin Franklin* (New Haven, CT: Yale University Press, 2002), 239.

"there is an End of": Hendrickson, *Peace Pact,* 139–40. Why, Lynch asked, should slaves be taxed while "Land, Sheep, Cattles, Horses, &c." were not? Benjamin Franklin replied that it was because "Sheep will never make any Insurrections."

"Nothing but present danger": Burnett, *Letters of Members of the Continental Congress,* Vol. II, 32–33.

"the British tyrant": *The Writings of Thomas Jefferson,* Vol. III, ed. Albert Ellery Bergh (Washington, DC: Thomas Jefferson Memorial Foundation, 1907), 276. Jefferson's fellow Virginian, Richard Henry Lee, asked Samuel Adams whether they could ever expect to stop being "teased with the Bugbear Reconciliation, or must we hang for ever on the hagger'd breast of G. Britain?" Miller, *Origins of the American Revolution,* 497.

"we have made such a Devil": Max Savelle, "Nationalism and Other Loyalties in the American Revolution," *American Historical Review* 67, no. 4 (July 1962): 915.

a much-needed pep talk: Hendrickson discusses Witherspoon's speech in *Peace Pact,* 141–43. The text can be found in *Papers of Thomas Jefferson,* Vol. 1, Boyd, 323.

"Rely on it": Hendrickson, *Peace Pact,* 157.

"various sentiments and interests": The letter is in Timothy Pitkin, *A Political and Civil History of the United States of America,* Vol. II (New Haven, CT: Hezekiah Howe and Durrie & Peck, 1828), 17–19.

Congress was broke: The federal coffers were empty because the states refused to make their agreed-upon payments. To remedy the situation, some spoke of empowering Congress to force the states to pay up. It was a South Carolinian, ironically enough, who first proposed this power. In early 1778, the state's chief justice, William Henry Drayton, suggested putting any delinquent state "under the ban of the confederacy, and by the utmost vigor of arms [to] forthwith proceed against such state, until it shall have paid due obedience, upon which the ban shall be taken off and the state shall be restored to the benefits of this confederacy." When latter-day South Carolina secessionists spoke of redeeming the legacy of their forefathers, Drayton was apparently not one they had in mind. See Charles Warren, *The Making of the Constitution* (Boston: Little, Brown, 1937), 8n2.

"Only united in name": *The State Records of North Carolina,* Vol. XVII, ed. Walter Clark (Goldsboro, NC: Nash Brothers, 1899), 172.

Two factions became discernible: Joseph L. Davis, *Sectionalism in American Politics, 1774–1787* (Madison: University of Wisconsin Press, 1977), 17; see also Hendrickson, *Peace Pact,* 177–93.

"the old prejudices of North": Davis, *Sectionalism in American Politics,* 19.

"some malignant disorder": Gordon S. Wood, *The Creation of the American Republic 1776–1787* (Williamsburg, VA: University of North Carolina Press, 1969), 415.

Samuel Adams confided: Savelle, "Nationalism and Other Loyalties," 915.

"sacrificed to the resentment": John Ferling, *Almost a Miracle: The American Victory in the War of Independence* (New York: Oxford University Press, 2007), 386. "I see very plainly," one Marylander observed, "that the Southern States will be obliged to shift for themselves." Virginia's William Lee asked John Adams about a rumor that New Englanders thought it "very immaterial what became of the Southern States"—even if they were reconquered by Britain. Adams tried to reassure Lee that there were no such plans. "A Zeal for the Union of the 13 States," he replied, "is in my opinion one of the first Duties of every American Citizen." Hendrickson, *Peace Pact,* 358n31; Davis, *Sectionalism in American Politics,* 26.

"Now the Tables are turn'd": A known advocate for union, Gadsden was being taunted by neighbors who sneered, *"Did we not tell you so."* Gadsden called himself "an American at large…scorning a Thought in Favor of any one State to the prejudice of the rest." He regretted not all Americans could say the same for themselves. See Hendrickson, *Peace Pact,* 185–86.

"with contemptuous huzzahs": Alden, *First South,* 37–40. South Carolina's Henry Laurens, encouraged by his son John, came up with the slave-soldier idea. He and Richard Henry Lee of Virginia were rare Southern politicians who doubted France's motives. Laurens advised colleagues to avoid dependence "upon a Crafty designing Court, who has never done, & who never will do, any thing for our Interest but what has been or what shall be subservient to their own." Fellow Southerners saw Lee and Laurens as "two Monsters…who pursue points in which the southern states have no interest." Defending himself from the charge that he "favored New England to the injury of Virginia" through his too-close friendships with the Adams cousins, Lee told Patrick Henry: "Our enemies and our friends, too, know that America can only be conquered by disunion….I heartily wish that this greatest of all political evils may not take place before a safe and honorable peace is established." After that, who knew? See Hendrickson, *Peace Pact,* 182–86; Jack Rakove, *Revolutionaries: A New History of the Invention of America* (Boston: Mariner, 2011), 198–241.

officials had to choose: This little-known episode is discussed in James Haw, "A Broken Compact: Insecurity, Union, and the Proposed Surrender of Charleston, 1779," *South Carolina Historical Magazine* 96, no. 1 (Jan. 1995): 30–53.

Anne-César de La Luzerne: See George L. Sioussat and J. Maccubbin, "The Chevalier de la Luzerne and the Ratification of the Articles of Confederation by Maryland, 1780-1781," *Pennsylvania Magazine of History and Biography* 60 (1936): 391–418. "The band of national union, the Confederation, is not yet agreed to by all, nor binding on any," Gouverneur Morris of New York observed. Hendrickson, *Peace Pact,* 152.

"contrary to all principles": Cathy D. Matson and Peter S. Onuf, *A Union of Interests: Political and Economic Thought in Revolutionary America* (Lawrence: University Press of Kansas, 1990), 55.

suggested forming regional confederations: Jensen, *Articles of Confederation,* 196. John Adams opposed the scheme, for the "different divisions of the continent would soon be at War with each other." See *Papers of John Adams, Vol. 10, July 1780–December 1780,* eds. Gregg L. Lint and Richard Alan Ryerson (Cambridge, MA: Harvard University Press, 1996), 359–60.

"not a nation at war": Alan Taylor, *American Revolutions: A Continental History, 1750–1804* (New York: W. W. Norton, 2016), 214.

hopes "that the union may be dissolved": Sioussat and Maccubbin, "Chevalier de la Luzerne," 401. "Luzerne's polite blackmail," as historian Merrill Jensen puts it, paid off. Jensen, *Articles of Confederation,* 236–37.

"a Union, begun by necessity": Savelle, "Nationalism and Other Loyalties," 917.

political writer Josiah Tucker: Loughran, *Republic in Print,* 71.

Chapter Three. *Constitutional Crisis*

"This country must be united": Michael J. Klarman, *The Framers' Coup: The Making of the United States Constitution* (New York: Oxford University Press, 2016), 187–88.

"We the People of the United States...": Kenneth M. Stampp made this point in his classic "The Concept of a Perpetual Union," in *The Imperiled Union: Essays on the Background of the Civil War* (New York: Oxford University Press, 1980), 11.

who would rule at home: For a recent discussion of Becker's framework and its relation to the crisis of the Union, see Max M. Edling, "Peace Pact and Nation: An International Interpretation of the Constitution of the United States," *Past & Present* 240, no. 1 (Aug. 2018): 267–303.

"the present Union will but": Lance Banning, *The Sacred Fire of Liberty: James Madison and the Founding of the Federal Republic* (Ithaca, NY: Cornell University Press, 1995), 23. John M. Murrin: "American national identity was, in short, an unexpected, impromptu, artificial, and therefore extremely fragile creation of the Revolution." Murrin, "Roof Without Walls," 197.

"feeble and preposterous": Davis, *Sectionalism in American Politics,* 31.

"solid coercive union": *The Papers of Alexander Hamilton,* Vol. 2, ed. Harold C. Syrett (New York: Columbia University Press, 1961), 400–418.

"nourish ideas of separation": The "Continentalist" is in *The Works of Alexander Hamilton,* Vol. 1, ed. Henry Cabot Lodge (New York: G. P. Putnam's Sons, 1904), 243–87.

"as difficult to disband": *The Papers of James Madison,* Vol. 5, eds. William T. Hutchinson and William M. E. Rachal (Chicago: University of Chicago Press, 1962), 158–63.

"dangerous eruption": Davis, *Sectionalism in American Politics,* 43. The best book about the tumultuous end to the Revolutionary War is Thomas Fleming, *The Perils of Peace:*

America's Struggle for Survival After Yorktown (New York: Smithsonian, 2007). See also William Hogeland, *Founding Finance: How Debt, Speculation, Foreclosures, Protests, and Crackdowns Made Us a Nation* (Austin: University of Texas Press, 2012). One account of the Newburgh Conspiracy is titled "Fascism—1783." John Corbin, *Two Frontiers of Freedom* (New York: Charles Scribner's Sons, 1940), 50–68.

"numerous, meritorious": Davis, *Sectionalism in American Politics*, 42.

"The army have the sword": Ibid., 45.

"Unless some amicable": *The Papers of James Madison*, Vol. 6, eds. William T. Hutchinson and William M. E. Rachal (Chicago: University of Chicago Press, 1969), 256–58. Madison's first thought was not what a tragedy disunion would be, but what it would hold for his own region: "Will not, in that event, the Southern States…be an easy prey to the Eastern[?]"

"open the flood Gates"…"subversion of that liberty": Richard H. Kohn, *Eagle and Sword: The Federalists and the Creation of the Military Establishment in America, 1783–1802* (New York: Free Press, 1975), 201–7, 220. The officers' demand of lifetime pensions at half-pay was converted to five years at full salary. Though they didn't get everything they had wanted, the conspirators' efforts had gotten them more than they would have had otherwise. There was no coup d'état, but the threat of one worked.

"the cloud which seemed": Davis, *Sectionalism in American Politics*, 47.

"This it is to be lamented": *The Papers of Alexander Hamilton*, Vol. 3, ed. Harold C. Syrett (New York: Columbia University Press, 1962), 304–5.

"The soldiers are loud": James Henry Fowler II, "The Breakdown of Congressional Authority: A Study of the Relations Between the Continental Congress and the States, 1780–1783" (PhD diss., Oklahoma State University, 1977), 261.

"should not be completely free": The full text of Washington's "Circular to the States" appears in John Marshall, *The Life of George Washington*, Vol. II (Philadelphia: Crissy & Markley, 1848), 80–89.

Anarchy and confusion came: See Hogeland, *Founding Finance*, 140.

"Time will discover": Paul C. Nagel, *One Nation Indivisible: The Union in American Thought, 1776–1861* (New York: Oxford University Press, 1964), 26. Charles Thomson, secretary of Congress since 1774, wrote to his wife: "It cannot admit of a doubt that the peace, happiness and prosperity of these new and rising republics depend greatly on a close and intimate Union. And yet the temper, disposition and views of the inhabitants are so discordant, that I have serious apprehensions they will not be long kept together & that the predictions of our enemies will but too soon be verified in the dissolution of our Confederacy." Hendrickson, *Peace Pact*, 203.

choosing a new capital: The best account of sectional politics in this period is Davis, *Sectionalism in American Politics*, 60–69.

After the war, British merchants: Merrill Jensen, *The New Nation: A History of the United States During the Confederation, 1781–1789* (New York: Alfred A. Knopf, 1950), 161–66. The British strategy of fostering American divisions required only taking advantage of already existing fractures. In 1783, a Massachusetts-born spy named Edward Bancroft advised his British superiors that the Union would soon split apart. The only question was whether it would be replaced by thirteen separate states or three confederations. "Having been excited to throw off obedience to the former government," Bancroft observed, "they are but little inclined to submit to any." George Bancroft, *History of the Formation of the Constitution of the United States of America*, Vol. 1 (New York: D. Appleton, 1884), 332.

"hunger and thirst": Bruce A. Ragsdale, *A Planters' Republic: The Search for Economic Independence in Revolutionary Virginia* (Madison, WI: Madison House, 1996), 216.

"multiply the examples": Peter S. Onuf, "Liberty, Development, and Union: Visions of the West in the 1780s," *William and Mary Quarterly* 43, no. 2 (April 1986): 179–213. To Benjamin Franklin, back in London, reports of the Union's death were greatly exaggerated. When a friend in Parliament relayed whispers that "the American States will break to pieces, and then we may still conquer them," Franklin replied that such rumors were "mere London fictions." He was concerned enough, however, to relay the gossip to his Pennsylvania friend Thomas Mifflin, then president of Congress, along with a warning that Americans couldn't be too vigilant in their efforts to preserve the Union. *The Papers of Benjamin Franklin,* Vol. 41, ed. Ellen R. Cohn (New Haven, CT: Yale University Press, 2014), 137–38.

In 1777, the valley dwellers: Edward Countryman, *A People in Revolution: The American Revolution and Political Society in New York, 1760–1790* (Baltimore: Johns Hopkins University Press, 1981), 176. For the Vermont experiment and other 1780s statehood movements, see Peter S. Onuf, *The Origins of the Federal Republic: Jurisdictional Controversies in the United States, 1775–1787* (Philadelphia: University of Pennsylvania Press, 1983).

"I shall do everything": Eliot A. Cohen, *Conquered Into Liberty: Two Centuries of Battles Along the Great Warpath That Made the American Way of War* (New York: Free Press, 2011), 260–63.

"separatism of spirit": Francis S. Philbrick, *The Rise of the West, 1754–1830* (New York: Harper & Row, 1965), 99.

a protracted legal dispute: As it happens, those squatters called themselves "Seceders," after a series of separations from the overly conservative Church of Scotland in the mid-eighteenth century. These backwoods settlers had built houses, cleared fields, set up fences, and tilled the soil. They knew about the general, of course—a nearby town had already been named in his honor—but that didn't mean they recognized this stranger's bizarre claim that he owned the land they had improved. They were a hardy bunch—rough-hewn representatives of the class Washington once dismissed as "the grazing multitude." See Joel Achenbach, *The Grand Idea: George Washington's Potomac and the Race to the West* (New York: Simon & Schuster, 2004).

"become a distinct people": *The Papers of George Washington,* Confederation Series, Vol. 2, ed. W. W. Abbot (Charlottesville: University Press of Virginia, 1992), 86–98. Benjamin Franklin had warned as early as 1755 about the likelihood that those settlers who populated "the great country back of the Appalachian mountains" would become different "from our people, confined to the country between the sea and the mountains." Benjamin E. Park, *American Nationalisms: Imagining Union in the Age of Revolutions, 1783–1833* (New York: Cambridge University Press, 2018), 128–29.

"vast, extensive, and almost impassible": Frederick Jackson Turner, "Western State-Making in the Revolutionary Era," in *The Significance of Sections in American History* (New York: Henry Holt, 1932), 105.

called it Franklin: Kevin T. Barksdale, *The Lost State of Franklin: America's First Secession* (Lexington: University Press of Kentucky, 2010), 83. See also Jason Farr, "A Glorious Failure: The State of Franklin and American Independence," *Tennessee Historical Quarterly* 70, no. 4 (winter 2011): 276–87.

"ruin the Western Country": Turner, "Western State-Making," 126.

"better to part in peace": Lowell H. Harrison, *Kentucky's Road to Statehood* (Lexington: University Press of Kentucky, 1992), 34.

Britain wasn't the only: My account of the Mississippi River controversy relies on Davis, *Sectionalism in American Politics,* 109–26; Jensen, *New Nation;* Hendrickson, *Peace Pact;* and James E. Lewis Jr., *The American Union and the Problem of Neighborhood: The United States and the Collapse of the Spanish Empire, 1783–1829* (Chapel Hill: University of

North Carolina Press, 1998). "It was insanity to suppose that frontiersmen dissatisfied with distant government from New York could imagine themselves happy under
government from Madrid," Francis S. Philbrick has argued. Perhaps, but Westerners
imagined it nonetheless. Far more, however, considered repeating the American
example and declaring independence not to join another country but to form one of
their own. Philbrick, *Rise of the West,* 175.

In 1785, a Basque arms dealer: Davis, *Sectionalism in American Politics,* 121. Gardoqui was
reportedly "very favorably inclined" to offer Spanish protection for the breakaway
state of Franklin, but it dissolved before he could render any assistance. Philbrick,
Rise of the West, 179.

"released from all Federal obligations": Davis, *Sectionalism in American Politics,* 155.

"This country will in a few years": Andro Linklater, *An Artist in Treason: The Extraordinary
Double Life of General James Wilkinson* (New York: Walker, 2009), 79. From Louisville, a
hotbed of western separatism, Thomas Green, a Virginia-born adventurer who had
spent time in a New Orleans jail for claiming the Spanish town of Natchez for Georgia,
penned an open letter to an unnamed eastern friend. "To sell and make us vassals to
the merciless Spaniards is a grievance not to be borne," Green warned. Surrendering
the Mississippi would provoke the West to secede and ally with a foreign nation—
possibly even Britain itself. "When once reunited to them…the province of Canada
and the inhabitants of these waters…will be able to conquer you," Green threatened.
"You are as ignorant of this country as Great Britain was of America." Green's letter is
in *The United States and Spain in 1790,* ed. Worthington Chauncey Ford (Brooklyn, NY:
Historical Printing Club, 1890), 12–14.

Unmoved by western threats: Davis, *Sectionalism in American Politics,* 123.

"It appears, sir": Richard B. Morris, *The Forging of the Union, 1781–1789* (New York:
Harper & Row, 1987), 12.

"James Munroe, a brooding": William Winslow Crosskey and William Jeffrey Jr., *Politics
and the Constitution in the History of the United States, Vol. III: The Political Background of the Federal Convention* (Chicago: University of Chicago Press, 1953), 308–9.
Also see George William Van Cleve, *We Have Not a Government: The Articles of Confederation and the Road to the Constitution* (Chicago: University of Chicago Press, 2017),
175–76.

"If a dismemberment takes place": Hendrickson, *Peace Pact,* 205. Monroe wasn't alone in
seriously considering the merits of disunion. Timothy Bloodworth of North Carolina
reported to his governor on the emergence of "an unhappy division between the
Eastern and Southern delegates" regarding the treaty with Spain. Both sides were
"firm and immovable." "The Confederated compact is no more than a rope of sand,"
Bloodworth wrote, "and if a more efficient Government is not obtained, a dissolution
of the Union must take place." Louis-Guillaume Otto, French minister in the United
States, reported back home that the Mississippi question "may be the germ of a
future separation of the southern states." To be sure, there were Southerners who
supported Jay's request. George Washington, for example, so feared western separatism that he favored closing the Mississippi at least until better trade ties could be
established between the trans-Appalachian territories and the older eastern states—
i.e., through the construction of mountain-defying roads and canals. Van Cleve, *We
Have Not a Government,* 162; Taylor, *American Revolutions,* 351; Klarman, *Framers' Coup,*
64; Philbrick, *Rise of the West,* 174.

any measures taken by the states: Businessmen denounced the "discordant regulations"
in the states. "Each State acts an independent for all its needs and interests," a
French official observed. Davis, *Sectionalism in American Politics,* 99.

Congress couldn't help: With New England's ships blocked from trading with the West Indies, it was easier and cheaper for Southern planters to hire them to ship tobacco, rice, and indigo to Europe. A revival of the fortunes of New England's shipping industry would mean higher prices for Southern planters. New Englanders sought "a most pernicious and destructive Monopoly," which "would be dangerous in the extreme" to the southern States. Matson and Onuf, *Union of Interests,* 84.

"little less savage": Thomas P. Slaughter, *The Whiskey Rebellion: Frontier Epilogue to the American Revolution* (New York: Oxford University Press, 1988), 30.

"a Separation certainly would not": *State Records of North Carolina,* Clark, 174.

Theodore Sedgwick, a lawyer in the Berkshires: Van Cleve, *We Have Not a Government,* 175. Sedgwick's letter appears in "Documents," *American Historical Review* 4, no. 2 (Jan. 1899): 328–30. Benjamin Lincoln, the Confederation's former secretary of war, observed that the interests of the different regions were diametrically opposed—"the necessary consequences of our great extent, of our difference of climate, productions, views, etc." Only by severing the Union could New England's interests be secured. Lincoln wrote to Rufus King, a young Massachusetts congressman, "I do not see how we shall surmount the evils under which we now labor, and prevent our falling into the utmost confusion, disgrace, and ruin, but by a division." King was already thinking along similar lines. In 1785, he wrote to John Adams about the sorry state of American affairs. The thirteen states couldn't agree on anything. But "the eight Eastern states can agree." Why not form a "sub-confederation"—a union-within-the-Union—from Delaware north? To King, it was access to the Mississippi, not the river's closure, that threatened to cleave the West from the Union. If the frontiersmen relied on Spanish ports, "every emigrant to that country from the Atlantic States" would be "forever lost to the Confederacy." King summoned the same bare facts of American geography as proponents of western secession. "Nature has severed the two countries by a vast and extensive chain of mountains," King concluded. "Interest and convenience will keep them separate, and the feeble policy of our disjointed Government will not be able to unite them." See Warren, *Making of the Constitution,* 26; *The Life and Correspondence of Rufus King, Vol. I,* ed. Charles R. King (New York: G. P. Putnam's Sons, 1894), 112–13; "Letters of Rufus King," *Proceedings of the Massachusetts Historical Society* (Oct. 1915–June 1916), 87–89.

armed insurgents in Massachusetts: The best account of the insurrection is Leonard L. Richards, *Shays's Rebellion: The American Revolution's Final Battle* (Philadelphia: University of Pennsylvania Press, 2002). To pay his debts, Shays even had to sell a ceremonial sword given him by the Marquis de Lafayette.

"thieves, knaves, and robbers": Alden T. Vaughan, "The 'Horrid And Unnatural Rebellion' of Daniel Shays," *American Heritage* 17, no. 4 (June 1966).

"federal government must cease": *Collections of the Massachusetts Historical Society, Seventh Series* 4 (1907): 103–5.

"a perfect nullity": *Great Issues in American History: A Documentary Record, Vol. I,* ed. Richard Hofstadter (New York: Vintage, 1958), 82.

Across the Hudson River: My account of this episode is based on Davis, *Sectionalism in American Politics,* 136–37, and David Brian Robertson, *The Constitution and America's Destiny* (Cambridge: Cambridge University Press, 2005), 56–57. As Robertson writes, "To all intents and purposes, New Jersey formally seceded from the congressional requisition system in 1786 and defied the Articles." For an overview of the impost debate, see Jensen, *New Nation.*

"to prepare a question": Klarman, *Framers' Coup,* 109–10n.

"exertion of the united virtue"..."from Receiving the same impression": Ibid., 109.

"contentions and civil discord": Woody Holton, *Unruly Americans and the Origins of the Constitution* (New York: Hill & Wang, 2007), 144–48; Davis, *Sectionalism in American Politics,* 152. See also Terry Bouton, *Taming Democracy: "The People," the Founders, and the Troubled Ending of the American Revolution* (New York: Oxford University Press, 2007).

"men of talents and integrity": Klarman, *Framers' Coup,* 84.

"the little detestable corner": Taylor, *American Revolutions,* 368.

"apportioned to the different states": Warren, *Making of the Constitution,* 133. For more on Rhode Island in the 1780s, see Van Cleve, *We Have Not a Government,* 205–10; Tom Cutterham, "The Republic of Rogue Island," *The Nation,* June 23, 2017, https://www .thenation.com/article/the-republic-of-rogue-island/.

Shays and other rebel leaders fled to Vermont: After reaching Vermont, the rebels sought a meeting with Ethan Allen, who had already denounced the Massachusetts government as "a pack of Damned Rascals" with "no virtue among them." Would he arm them and keep the insurgency going, or even annex western Massachusetts to his independent republic? Allen turned them down. He was hoping to strike a deal normalizing relations with the United States, perhaps even joining the Union, and some members of the republic's legislature feared provoking congressional retribution. Richards, *Shays's Rebellion,* 34, 120.

"rather worse than anarchy": Davis, *Sectionalism in American Politics,* 152.

"They feel at once": Richards, *Shays's Rebellion,* 129–30.

Examining the unions: Madison found no confederation that had ever really worked; most served as cautionary tales. The Amphictyonic League was too weak to prevent war between two members, Athens and Sparta. Shaky, too, was the Achaean Confederacy of the Peloponnese. "Every City was now engaged in a separate interest & no longer acted in concert," Madison wrote of the Achaeans' decline—a judgment he thought also applied to the American Union. Modern confederations were equally unimpressive. Little held together the Helvetic League, a loose alliance of thirteen Swiss cantons. The United Provinces of the Netherlands could collect taxes and conduct diplomacy, but those powers were rarely used. He did like one rule of the Holy Roman Empire, according to which members derelict in their duties could be placed under a "ban" that made "the offenders life & goods…at the Mercy of every one." The example appealed to Madison, who had long thought the Confederation needed the power to use force against uncooperative states. *The Papers of James Madison,* Vol. 9, eds. Robert A. Rutland and William M. E. Rachal (Chicago: University of Chicago Press, 1975), 3–23.

"bound together by a principle": Matson and Onuf, *Union of Interests,* 98. Around the same time, a letter in the Boston-based *Independent Chronicle* said it was time "to form a new and stronger union," composed not of thirteen distant republics, but five "closely confederated" states: Connecticut, Rhode Island, Massachusetts, New Hampshire, and still-independent Vermont. Rather than try to persuade the other states to reform the dysfunctional Confederation, New England should "leave the rest of the continent to pursue their own imbecilic and disjointed plans." The region's members of Congress, that "useless and expensive establishment," should return home to form a "nation of New England." The letter was widely reprinted. Within weeks, a Rhode Islander observed, many in New England had become "warm espousers of separate confederacies." See *The Revolutionary Era: Primary Documents on Events from 1776 to 1800,* ed. Carol Sue Humphrey (Westport, CT: Greenwood, 2003), 113–14; Klarman, *Framers' Coup,* 126–27.

It was "difficult to decide": T. H. Breen, *George Washington's Journey: The President Forges a New Nation* (New York: Simon & Schuster, 2016), 181.

"as strong a republican": Taylor, *American Revolutions,* 372.

Nathaniel Gorham, the impotent president: See Richard Krauel, "Prince Henry of Prussia and the Regency of the United States, 1786," *American Historical Review* 17, no. 1 (Oct. 1911): 44–51.

he considered the latter the "lesser evil": Warren, *Making of the Constitution,* 45.

"In a large republic, the public good": *Montesquieu: The Spirit of the Laws,* eds. Anne M. Cohler, Basia C. Miller, and Harold S. Stone (Cambridge: Cambridge University Press, 2006).

"Society becomes broken": *Papers of James Madison,* Vol. 9, 345–58.

"Extend the sphere"..."A rage for paper money": James Madison, "No. 10: The Same Subject Continued," *The Federalist Papers,* ed. Clinton Rossiter (New York: Signet, 2003), 78. Madison was essentially proposing a return to the divide-and-rule policy pursued by Britain earlier that century. As he explained to Jefferson, "Divide et impera, the reprobated axiom of tyranny, is under certain qualifications, the only policy, by which a republic can be administered on just principles." Woody Holton, "'Divide et Impera': 'Federalist 10' in a Wider Sphere," *William and Mary Quarterly* 62, no. 2 (April 2005): 175–212.

"Our chief danger arises": David Brian Robertson, *The Original Compromise: What the Constitution's Framers Were Really Thinking* (New York: Oxford University Press, 2013), 62.

"worst of all political evils": Taylor, *American Revolutions,* 385.

"should have as little to do": Klarman, *Framers' Coup,* 244.

"preservation of our democratic governments": *Journal and Debates of the Federal Convention, Volume IV,* ed. Jonathan Elliot (Washington, DC, 1830), 115.

"require the vigour of Monarchy": Peter S. Onuf, "Constitutional Politics: States, Sections, and the National Interest," in *Toward a More Perfect Union: Six Essays on the Constitution,* ed. Neil L. York (Albany: SUNY Press, 1988), 41.

"vile State governments": Daniel Lazare, *The Frozen Republic: How the Constitution Paralyzes Democracy* (New York: Harcourt, Brace, 1996), 37.

"more embarrassment": Noah Feldman, *The Three Lives of James Madison: Genius, Partisan, President* (New York: Random House, 2017), 175.

"Can we forget": Klarman, *Framers' Coup,* 184–85.

"Let them unite": Richard Beeman, *Plain, Honest Men: The Making of the American Constitution* (New York: Random House, 2009), 149.

"would never confederate": *Debates Held on the Adoption of the Federal Constitution in the Convention Held at Philadelphia in 1787, Vol. V,* ed. Jonathan Elliot (New York: Burt Franklin, 1888), 267.

"assembly of demigods": Henry Stephens Randall, *The Life of Thomas Jefferson, Vol. I* (New York: Derby & Jackson, 1858), 487.

"like a band of brothers": Beeman, *Plain, Honest Men,* 152.

"I do not, gentlemen, trust you": Klarman, *Framers' Coup,* 193–94; Beeman, *Plain, Honest Men,* 184.

"seriously and deeply distressed": Klarman, *Framers' Coup,* 127.

"vain to purchase concord": Ibid., 198–99.

"infuse mortality into a constitution": *Debates Held on the Adoption,* Elliot, 255, 262, 315, 257.

Today, California has sixty-seven: Daniel Lazare, "Abolish the Senate," *Jacobin,* Dec. 2, 2014. https://www.jacobinmag.com/2014/12/abolish-the-senate.

"a Bad Effect on the Union": Gary B. Nash, *The Unknown American Revolution: The Unruly Birth of Democracy and the Struggle to Create America* (New York: Penguin, 2005), 121.

Free of such obligations, the Republic of Vermont abolished slavery in its 1777 constitution. Pennsylvania did so in 1780, followed by Massachusetts, Connecticut, and
Rhode Island. Even Virginia freed slaves who had served in the militia during the
war, and granted masters the right to liberate their property without permission
from the state. In his 1785 *Notes on the State of Virginia,* Jefferson called slavery "the
most unremitting despotism," degrading to whites and blacks alike. George Washington voiced a vague desire "to see some plan adopted...by which slavery in this
country may be abolished by slow, sure, and imperceptible degrees." Klarman, *Framers' Coup,* 253–57.

"lie over for the present": Beeman, *Plain, Honest Men,* 201.

"as different as...Russia and Turkey": *The Records of the Federal Convention of 1787, Vol. II,*
ed. Max Farrand (New Haven, CT: Yale University Press, 1911), 451.

a plural presidency: Matson and Onuf, *Union of Interests,* 110. "Will not three men so chosen bring with them, into office, a more perfect and extensive knowledge of the real
interests of this great Union?" asked George Mason, Randolph's fellow Virginian, sec-
onding the proposal. Notably, given John C. Calhoun's later advocacy for the same
idea, it fell to a South Carolinian to explain why such a scheme wouldn't work. Pierce
Butler warned that with such an arrangement "there would be a constant struggle for
local advantages." A plural presidency would reflect, not rectify, the Union's stark
divides.

Digging up an old proposal: The ratio had originated in a proposed amendment to the
Articles of Confederation to institute a new population-based system of taxation to
replace the original property-based one that had turned out to be unworkable.
Slaves had "no interest in their labor" and therefore did "as little as possible," James
Madison argued, and therefore should not be taxed as much as free whites — a telling confession. See Klarman, *Framers' Coup,* 269–70, and Beeman, *Plain, Honest Men,*
153–55.

"their blacks": Garry Wills, *"Negro President": Jefferson and the Slave Power* (Boston: Mariner, 2005), 56.

"If fictitious, let it be dismissed": Matson and Onuf, *Union of Interests,* 111. Also Klarman, *Framers' Coup,* 269–71.

The compromise did little: In an important essay, "The Compromise of 1787," Staughton
Lynd suggested that the three-fifths compromise may have been part of a larger
bargain. As the Constitutional Convention met in Philadelphia, the Confederation
Congress in New York was considering the latest version of a Northwest Ordinance to
govern the territory north of the Ohio River. In July 1787, several members of Congress who also served as delegates in the convention traveled back and forth between
the two cities, possibly coordinating the effort to pass the three-fifths clause and the
Ordinance. In the end, Lynd argues, the South voted to support the Ordinance —
even though it outlawed slavery north of the Ohio River — in exchange for Northern
acquiescence to the three-fifths bonus. Both sections were angling for advantage in a
future they assumed would see the sectional divisions of the Confederation era continue unabated. See Lynd, "The Compromise of 1787," in *Class Conflict, Slavery, and
the United States Constitution* (Indianapolis: Bobbs-Merrill, 1967), 185–213.

"anxiously sought to avoid": Klarman, *Framers' Coup,* 265. There was little question at the
time whether the Constitution was for or against slavery. Even where Southern opposition to the charter was rampant, as in Virginia and North Carolina, few Anti-
Federalists criticized the new government as offering insufficient protection for the
ownership of human beings. Slavers were comforted by Charles Cotesworth Pinckney's boast during the ratification debate that, all in all, the Southern delegates in

Philadelphia had "made the best terms for the security of this species of property it was in our power to make." David Waldstreicher makes the important point about the relative absence of proslavery Anti-Federalism—with the exception of Patrick Henry—in *Slavery's Constitution: From Revolution to Ratification* (New York: Hill & Wang, 2009), 114. Pinckney is quoted in Klarman, *Framers' Coup*, 302. For the contrary view—that the Constitution, by not explicitly recognizing the legitimacy of property in slaves, actually undermined the institution—see Sean Wilentz, *No Property in Slaves: Slavery and Antislavery at the Nation's Founding* (Cambridge, MA: Harvard University Press, 2018). Wilentz emphasizes that "the Constitution would tolerate slavery without authorizing it." But slavery wasn't only tolerated: it was rewarded.

"South Carolina and Georgia cannot do": Klarman, *Framers' Coup*, 277–79.

"The true question at present": Charles A. Beard, *An Economic Interpretation of the Constitution of the United States* (New York: Free Press, 1986), 213.

"great and equal opposition": Klarman, *Framers' Coup*, 286.

"a compromise between slavery and capitalism": Staughton Lynd, "On Turner, Beard and Slavery," in *Class Conflict, Slavery, and the United States Constitution*, 136.

"Notwithstanding their aversion": Beeman, *Plain, Honest Men*, 326.

Although he had come to Philadelphia: Klarman, *Framers' Coup*, 290.

The essence of that liberality: Roger Sherman thought "it was better to let the Southern States import slaves than to part with those States." His statue still stands in the rotunda of the United States Capitol as one of two representatives from his state. Ibid., 287.

"fly into a variety of shapes": *Debates Held on the Adoption*, Elliot, 461.

all the weapons they needed: Additionally, the Electoral College appears to have been one of the tools slaveholders built into the Constitution. A popular vote would not give them extra power based on their slaves, while the Electoral College, which gave each state the same number of votes as its senators and representatives combined (including those bonus seats thanks to the three-fifths clause), would.

The day dawned fair in Philadelphia: See Francis Hopkinson, "Account of the Federal Procession in Philadelphia, July 4, 1788," *American Museum* 4, no. 1 (July 1788).

Lawyers, merchants, doctors: According to David Waldstreicher, the tradesmen who participated in federal processions in Philadelphia and elsewhere during the ratification debate deployed elaborate metaphors to relate their work to the task of preserving the Union. Thus the blacksmiths of York, Pennsylvania, proclaimed, "May the Thirteen States be *welded* into the United Empire, by the *hammer* of conciliation, on the *anvil* of peace; and may the man who attempts to *blow the coal* of discord be *burned* by the sparks." Butchers invoked their knowledge of mammalian anatomy: "As the marrow is connected with the bone, or one joint with another, so let us be united, and may no cleaver ever disjoin us." Though their tributes were meant to urge fidelity to the newly strengthened Confederation, their metaphors often revealed how weak it actually remained. As Waldstreicher concludes, "Artisan rhetoric drew attention to the constructed, contingent nature of the new constitutional union." *In the Midst of Perpetual Fetes: The Making of American Nationalism, 1776–1820* (Chapel Hill: University of North Carolina Press, 1997), 105–6.

"Providence certainly shined": John C. Van Horne, "The Federal Procession of 1788: Talk Delivered to the Quarterly Meeting of the Carpenters' Company, July 20, 1987." http://www.carpentershall.org/federal-procession.

a group of Albany locals: *Documentary History of the Ratification of the Constitution, Vol. XXI*, eds. John P. Kaminski, Gaspare J. Saladino, Richard Leffler, and Charles H. Schoenleber (Madison: State Historical Society of Wisconsin, 2005), 1264–75. "For Albany's

Antifederalists and many others," Pauline Maier notes, "burning the Constitution was a perfectly appropriate way to celebrate Independence Day." Maier, *Ratification: The People Debate the Constitution, 1787–1788* (New York: Simon & Schuster, 2010), 374.

"a solemn act": Banning, *Sacred Fire of Liberty*, 1.

"to pack a Convention: Taylor, *American Revolutions*, 390–92.

"the Constitution or disunion": George Bancroft, *History of the Formation of the Constitution of the United States*, Vol. 2 (New York: D. Appleton, 1889), 237.

"Disunited States of America": Peter Onuf, "Anarchy and the Crisis of the Union," in *To Form a More Perfect Union: The Critical Ideas of the Constitution*, eds. Herman Belz, Ronald Hoffman, and Peter J. Albert (Charlottesville: University of Virginia Press, 1992), 284. In November 1787, the *Pennsylvania Journal* observed, "Should the States reject this excellent Constitution, the probability is that an opportunity will never again offer to cancel another in peace—the next will be drawn in blood." Hendrickson, *Peace Pact*, 308n15.

"splitting ourselves": "No. 9: The Union as a Safeguard Against Domestic Faction and Insurrection," in *Federalist Papers*, Rossiter, 68.

most Anti-Federalists didn't favor disunion: As Hendrickson notes, this probably weakened the Anti-Federalists: "The acute vulnerability of their position lay in the fact that they also believed that union was indispensable and that the Articles of Confederation needed correcting." *Peace Pact*, 251.

The "hobgoblin": Maier, *Ratification*, 85.

the ones who had ruptured: At the North Carolina ratification convention, a delegate named William Lenoir warned that just as the original Union had been dissolved by the Constitutional Convention, so in the future "it may be thought proper, by a few designing persons to destroy [the new Union]…in the same manner that the old system is laid aside." Kenneth Stampp observes that by abandoning the unanimous requirement of the Articles, "the Philadelphia Convention made the historical argument for perpetuity invalid, because the Convention and the ratifying states destroyed the existing Union….The result of this dismantling of the 'perpetual' Union created by the Articles of Confederation was a break in historical continuity. The preamble to the Constitution, be it noted, does not propose to make the old Union more perfect but to '*form* a more perfect Union'—that is, to create a new and better one." The framers probably dropped the Articles of Confederation's reference to a "perpetual union" because they realized that their overthrow of the one provided for in that document rendered the repetition of such a claim unwise. Stampp, "Concept of a Perpetual Union," 6–7.

later generations of writers: In a 1983 *Nation* review of Garry Wills's book *Explaining America: The Federalist*, political theorist John H. Schaar wrote: "Some significant part of the American soul has always belonged to the Anti-Federalists. Their disinherited successors have appeared in many forms—the citizens who made the Dorr Rebellion, the Indians who have pleaded for their place and their people, Jane Addams and the Settlement House movement, the Farmers Alliance and the early People's Party, the trade union movement, Dorothy Day and the Catholic Workers, the early Students for a Democratic Society, and Henry Adams, and Mary Parker Follett, and Hawthorne and Faulkner and Edmund Wilson and Jane Jacobs and Kirkpatrick Sale and Wendell Berry—all those who have resisted having their pasts erased and their futures canceled by the waves of forced social change we miscall progress; all those who have cherished the values of conservation, variety and self-government over the values of exploitation, centralism and hierarchy." Schaar, "Anti-Federalists, Arise!," *The Nation*, Jan. 22, 1983, 84–87. See also Herbert J. Storing, *What the Anti-Federalists*

Were For: The Political Thought of the Opponents of the Constitution (Chicago: University of Chicago Press, 1981).

"The vast Continent of America": Jackson Turner Main, *The Anti-Federalists: Critics of the Constitution, 1781–1788* (New York: W. W. Norton, 1961), 129.

"How does it appear": Klarman, *Framers' Coup,* 293.

"partakers of each other's sins": George William Van Cleve, *A Slaveholder's Union: Slavery, Politics, and the Constitution in the Early American Republic* (Chicago: University of Chicago Press, 2010), 176–77. An essay published in western Massachusetts by three delegates to that state's convention, two of them veterans of Shays' Rebellion, declared it "monstrous indeed" to transform a government ostensibly devoted to liberty and equality into "an engine of rapine, robbery, and murder." The essay even took aim at Washington himself, whose name Federalists invoked as if it alone served as a conclusive argument for the Constitution. The hallowed name carried less weight, the writers observed, when the person it belonged to—"at the same time he is brandishing the sword in behalf of freedom for himself—is likewise tyrannizing over two or three hundred miserable Africans, as free born as himself." Klarman, *Framers' Coup,* 300; Waldstreicher, *Slavery's Constitution,* 126–28.

"If we cannot connect": Wilentz, *No Property in Slaves,* 14–15. Rejecting the notion that the North should have chosen disunion, Wilentz uses the same arguments deployed later against abolitionists like William Lloyd Garrison: "Creating a separate northern nation…might have permitted antislavery northerners to verify their righteousness but it would have done nothing to help enslaved southerners, whose fates might well have been all the crueler in a formal, independent slaveholders' republic." This downplays the ample rewards and protections afforded slavery by the Constitution. It is difficult to imagine the fate of enslaved Southerners any crueler in some alternate reality.

"to divide the Southern States"…"his Arguments…go directly": Jon Kukla, *Patrick Henry: Champion of Liberty* (New York: Simon & Schuster, 2017), 313–19.

"One government cannot reign"…"The first thing I have at heart": *The Debates in the Several State Conventions on the Adoption of the Federal Constitution,* Vol. III, ed. Jonathan Elliot (Philadelphia: J. B. Lippincott, 1786), 58, 161.

"several bloody affrays"…"reduced to this single point": Klarman, *Framers' Coup,* 405, 492, 541, 492.

would secede from the state: Ibid., 501; also Main, *Anti-Federalists,* 238–40.

"the language of tyrants": Klarman, *Framers' Coup,* 414n.

We the Delegates declare: David M. Potter, *The Impending Crisis, 1848–1861* (New York: Harper Colophon, 1976), 482n77. Alexander Hamilton was unusual in suggesting that Federalists reject New York's reserved right of secession as equivalent to voting down the Constitution. "My opinion is that a reservation of a right to withdraw…is a *conditional* ratification, that it does not make N. York a member of the New Union," he wrote to Madison. "The Constitution requires an adoption *in toto,* and *for ever.*" Stampp, "Concept of a Perpetual Union," 16.

North Carolina—dominated: See Klarman, *Framers' Coup,* 511–16; Beeman, *Plain, Honest Men,* 403–5.

The paper-money populists…"The American Union Completed": A detailed account of Rhode Island's reluctance to ratify the Constitution is in Klarman, *Framers' Coup,* 516–30.

"A Country extensive": Fergus M. Bordewich, *The First Congress: How James Madison, George Washington, and a Group of Extraordinary Men Invented the Government* (New York: Simon & Schuster, 2016), 4.

Chapter Four. *Reign of Alarm*

"Now that the tree": Park, *American Nationalisms,* 128.

"I wish to have": Nagel, *One Nation Indivisible.*

"surveyed the political landscape": James Roger Sharp, *American Politics in the Early Republic* (New Haven, CT: Yale University Press, 1993), 49, 64. Sharp cites the *Oxford Universal Dictionary on Historical Principles.*

under a single roof: See Murrin, "Roof Without Walls."

***"as sure as God was"...* "It was a mortifying thing":** Bordewich, *First Congress,* 42, 94, 193–207, 213–20, 224. See also Richard S. Newman, "Prelude to the Gag Rule: Southern Reaction to Antislavery Petitions in the First Federal Congress," *Journal of the Early Republic* 16, no. 4 (winter 1996): 571–99.

"subserviency of Southern": Thomas S. Kidd, *Patrick Henry: First Among Patriots* (New York: Basic Books, 224), 2011.

"To disunite is dreadful": Charles Royster, *Light-Horse Harry Lee and the Legacy of the American Revolution* (Baton Rouge: Louisiana State University Press, 1981), 108. Years later, Lee's son Robert, divided between loyalty to his state or his country, also decided that disunion was the lesser evil.

"the Union must fall": Robert G. Parkinson, " 'Manifest Signs of Passion': The First Federal Congress, Antislavery, and Legacies of the Revolutionary War," in *Contesting Slavery: The Politics of Slavery and Freedom in the New American Nation,* eds. John Craig Hammond and Matthew Mason (Charlottesville: University of Virginia Press, 2011), 49.

"blotted out from": Bordewich, *First Congress,* 208.

Madison led the fight: He even reversed his argument for extending the sphere of politics from the state to the Union. In an essay for the *National Gazette* in late 1791, he wrote: "The larger a country, the less easy for its real opinion to be ascertained, and the less difficult to be counterfeited; when ascertained or presumed, the more respectable it is in the eyes of individuals. This is favorable to the authority of government. For the same reason, the more extensive a country, the more insignificant is each individual in his own eyes. This may be unfavorable to liberty." See *The Papers of James Madison,* Vol. 14, eds. Robert A. Rutland and Thomas A. Mason (Charlottesville: University Press of Virginia, 1983), 170.

"People knew that": The 1790s opposition, Murrin noted, elevated the Constitution "into an absolute standard and denounced their opponents for every deviation from its sublime mandates." This superficial consensus "kept the system going and converted its architects into something like popular demigods within a generation." Murrin, "Roof Without Walls," 198–99.

"that odious distinction": Bordewich, *First Congress,* 152.

"slaves in effect": Royster, *Light-Horse Harry Lee,* 108.

One day, as Jefferson... "merely from a fear": "Jefferson's Account of the Bargain on the Assumption and Residence Bills," in *The Papers of Thomas Jefferson, Vol. 17: July 1790 to November 1790,* ed. Julian P. Boyd (Princeton, NJ: Princeton University Press, 1965), 205–8.

"the consequences to be": Jacob E. Cooke, "The Compromise of 1790," in *Establishing the New Regime: The Washington Administration,* ed. Peter S. Onuf (New York: Garland, 1991), 305.

broke into "lamentations": Robert Ernst, *Rufus King: American Federalist* (Chapel Hill: University of North Carolina Press, 1968), 160–61.

The country was all but: Federalists like Hamilton accused their opponents of promoting "National disunion, national insignificance, Public disorder and discredit"; Republicans, in turn, charged Hamilton and his "corrupt squadron" with plotting to subvert the Constitution and set up a monarchy. "The Union: Who Are Its True Friends?" Madison asked in the title of one essay. Not those who accused others of undermining the Union while doing everything in their power to multiply its enemies. Not those who "would force on the people the melancholy duty of choosing between the loss of the Union, and the loss of what the Union was meant to secure." See Brian Steele, *Thomas Jefferson and American Nationhood* (Cambridge: Cambridge University Press, 2012), 210; Nagel, *One Nation Indivisible,* 18; Feldman, *Three Lives of James Madison,* 354–56.

"wou'd elate the Enemies": Beeman, *Plain, Honest Men,* 197.

the rocks of "violence": Noble E. Cunningham Jr., *Jefferson vs. Hamilton: Confrontations That Shaped a Nation* (Boston: Bedford/St. Martin's, 2000), 108.

Hamilton disavowed: Alexander Hamilton, "Objections and Answers Respecting the Administration, August 18, 1792," in *The Political Writings of Alexander Hamilton, Vol. II: 1789–1804,* eds. Carson Holloway and Bradford P. Wilson (Cambridge: Cambridge University Press, 2017), 152.

Kentucky rabble-rouser: The best source is Linklater, *Artist in Treason.* Philbrick, *Rise of the West,* 175–84, downplays Wilkinson's pursuit of Kentucky's secession.

"torture" . . . "One set of negotiations": Linklater, *Artist in Treason,* 74, 79–80, 86, 88.

"They will either throw": Bordewich, *First Congress,* 8. Spain wasn't the only nation trying to pry Kentucky from the Union. In 1787, a suspicious traveler appeared in the Ohio Valley. His job, according to one western official, was "to tamper with the People of Kentuckey and induce them to throw themselves into the Arms of Great Britain" — or, at the very least, to "detach them from the united States." Linklater, *Artist in Treason,* 98.

"of doubtful success" . . . "who loudly repudiated": Linklater, *Artist in Treason,* 100–103.

"by no means be adequate": Samuel B. Hand and H. Nicholas Muller III, "The State of Vermont," in *The Uniting States: The Story of Statehood for the Fifty United States, Vol. III: Oklahoma to Wyoming,* ed. Benjamin F. Shearer (Westport, CT: Greenwood, 2004), 1215.

"Patriotism, like every other": François Furstenburg, "The Significance of the Trans-Appalachian Frontier in Atlantic History, c. 1754–1815," *American Historical Review* 113, no. 3 (June 2008): 666.

"seek a protection": Robert V. Remini, "Andrew Jackson Takes an Oath of Allegiance to Spain," *Tennessee Historical Quarterly* 54, no. 1 (spring 1995): 11.

On a warm summer day: William Hogeland, *The Whiskey Rebellion: George Washington, Alexander Hamilton, and the Frontier Rebels Who Challenged America's Newfound Sovereignty* (New York: Simon & Schuster, 2010), 9, 182–83. Hogeland calls the rebellion "a secessionist insurgency." See also Slaughter, *Whiskey Rebellion,* 1986.

A gun battle: Hogeland, *Whiskey Rebellion,* 144–54; Bouton, *Taming Democracy,* 230–34.

"The whole cry": H. M. Brackenridge, *History of the Western Insurrection in Western Pennsylvania* (Pittsburgh: W. S. Haven, 1859), 162.

"The insurrection will do": Sharp, *American Politics in the Early Republic,* 97.

"The wrongful Secretary": Bouton, *Taming Democracy,* 230.

The "father of his country": Slaughter, *Whiskey Rebellion,* 219.

He was grateful: As Thomas Slaughter notes, the suppression of the insurrection "helped raise the value of Washington's property [in the West] by about 50 percent." Ibid., 224.

"the instrument of dismembering": *The Papers of Thomas Jefferson, Vol. 28, 1794–1796,* ed. John Catanzariti (Princeton, NJ: Princeton University Press, 2000), 228–30. The Whiskey Rebellion wasn't the only threat in the West. Indian nations eyed warily the fast-encroaching settlements. In 1783, thirty-five nations from the Great Lakes and Ohio River regions had met at Sandusky, on Lake Erie, and formed a confederation to resist American expansion. "Congress could not blame them for such a conduct," chiefs told federal agents, "for what had Congress done, but to unite thirteen states as one." Hoping to form an Indian buffer state in what we now call the Midwest, perhaps a step toward dismembering the Union itself, British officials armed the natives. General Anthony Wayne's surprising victory in the Battle of Fallen Timbers in summer 1794, however, sealed the Indians' fate and squelched British plans for reconquest. The natives agreed to move onto reservations or across the Mississippi River. As the historian Alan Taylor writes, "The United States prevailed by shattering the parallel effort by Indians to build their own union." Taylor, *American Revolutions,* 339; see also Taylor, *The Civil War of 1812: American Citizens, British Subjects, Irish Rebels, and Indian Allies* (New York: Alfred A. Knopf, 2010), 54–56.

In 1794, Rufus King: John Taylor of Caroline, *Disunion Sentiment in Congress in 1794,* ed. Gaillard Hunt (Washington, DC: J. H. Lowdermilk, 1905).

"western America is gone": Robert McNutt McElroy, *Kentucky in the Nation's History* (New York: Moffat, Yard, 1909), 193.

"a separation of the Union": Sharp, *American Politics in the Early Republic,* 119.

"We are an unhappy": "Letter from John Adams to Abigail Adams, 26 April 1796," Adams Family Papers: An Electronic Archive, Massachusetts Historical Society. https://www.masshist.org/digitaladams/archive/doc?id=L17960426ja&bc=%2Fdigitaladams%2Farchive%2Fbrowse%2Fletters_JA.php.

"it is at least the reign": *Papers of Thomas Jefferson,* Vol. 28, Catanzariti, 558–59.

"saved this nation from": Gordon S. Wood, *Friends Divided: John Adams and Thomas Jefferson* (New York: Penguin, 2017), 279.

the Farewell Address focused: See John Avlon, *Washington's Farewell: The Founding Father's Warning to Future Generations* (New York: Simon & Schuster, 2017).

"the fall of the present fabric": "Gazette of the United States (Philadelphia), 26 October 1796," in *Revolutionary Era,* Humphrey, 299.

"if not the dreadful"…"Fire and frost": Jeffrey L. Pasley, *The First Presidential Contest: 1796 and the Founding of American Democracy* (Lawrence: University Press of Kansas, 2013), 338, 378–89, 412.

regionally tinged parties: In a letter, Jefferson referred to his party as "the Southern interest." Someone—possibly Jefferson himself—later changed it to "the Republican interest." James Roger Sharp, "Unraveling the Mystery of Jefferson's Letter of April 27, 1795," *Journal of the Early Republic* 6, no. 4 (winter 1986): 411–18.

"Men who have been": Melvin Yazawa, "Dionysian Rhetoric and Apollonian Solutions: The Politics of Union and Disunion in the Age of Federalism," in *Empire and Nation: The American Revolution in the Atlantic World,* eds. Eliga H. Gould and Peter S. Onuf (Baltimore: Johns Hopkins University Press, 2005), 178.

"almost insane": Dumas Malone, *Jefferson and the Ordeal of Liberty* (Boston: Little, Brown, 1962), 370.

"Take care," one Federalist paper cautioned: Sharp, *American Politics in the Early Republic,* 166–67, 175–76.

"There will shortly be": Geoffrey R. Stone, *Perilous Times: Free Speech in Wartime from the Sedition Act of 1798 to the War on Terrorism* (New York: W. W. Norton, 2004), 29n.

the Alien and Sedition Acts: See Terri Diane Halperin, *The Alien and Sedition Acts of 1798: Testing the Constitution* (Baltimore: Johns Hopkins University Press, 2016); James Morton Smith, *Freedom's Fetters: The Alien and Sedition Laws and American Civil Liberties* (Ithaca, NY: Cornell University Press, 1956).

Even Hamilton..."worthy of the 8th or 9th": Sharp, *American Politics,* 177.

Jefferson drew up: William Watkins, *Reclaiming the American Revolution: The Kentucky and Virginia Resolutions and Their Legacy* (New York: Palgrave Macmillan, 2004).

the hand that wrote: Henry Adams, *John Randolph* (New York: Chelsea House, 1983), 34.

the "Spirit of '98" haunts: See *Nullification and Secession in Modern Constitutional Thought,* ed. Sanford Levinson (Lawrence: University Press of Kansas, 2016). Interestingly, Hamilton wrote in the *Federalist* that if the national government became tyrannical it would be possible for the people, "through the medium of their state governments, to take measures for their own defence with all the celerity, regularity and system of independent nations." As Kenneth Stampp notes, Hamilton thus described "both the justification and the method of nullification and secession when they were attempted in later years." Only two years later, however, when Virginia objected to federal assumption of state debts and called the states "guardians... of the rights and interests" of the people, Hamilton denounced "the first symptom of a spirit which must either be killed or kill the constitution of the United States." See Stampp, "Concept of a Perpetual Union," 18, 21.

responses ranged: Sharp, *American Politics,* 200, 209; Frank Maloy Anderson, "Contemporary Opinion of the Virginia and Kentucky Resolutions," *American Historical Review* 5, no. 1 (Oct. 1899): 52; Stampp, "Concept of a Perpetual Union," 23. The most potent rebuke came from Patrick Henry, who had once at least flirted with disunionism. Henry deplored the divisiveness of the 1790s. His health fading, he used his last speech, in early 1799, to denounce the Kentucky and Virginia Resolutions. His voice, at first "slightly cracked and tremulous," by the end "rang clear and melodious," an observer reported. "United we stand, divided we fall," Henry exclaimed. "Let us not split into factions which must destroy that Union upon which our existence hangs." He died two months later.

"from unreasonable discontent": John Adams, "Proclamation: March 6, 1799," in *A Compilation of the Messages and Papers of the Presidents, Vol. I,* ed. James D. Richardson (New York: Bureau of National Literature, 1897), 275.

Virginians stockpiled..."Take care of yourself": Sharp, *American Politics,* 203–8. Though it stopped making weapons in the 1820s, the armory was rebooted in 1861. Built for a civil war that didn't happen, the armory became useful when war finally came.

"an insidious plan": Cunningham, *Jefferson vs. Hamilton,* 119.

"sever ourselves from" ... "no more valued union": Malone, *Jefferson and the Ordeal of Liberty,* 421. Months earlier, before the passage of the Alien and Sedition Acts, Jefferson had rejected secession in a letter to fellow Virginian John Taylor. Four years after rejecting Rufus King's attempt to negotiate a divorce, Taylor now embraced partition. Jefferson disagreed. "It is true that we are completely under the saddle of Massachusetts and Connecticut, and that they ride us very hard," he wrote. But he opposed a division, or, as he put it, a "scission," of the Union. "A little patience," Jefferson assured Taylor, "and we shall see the reign of witches pass over, their spells dissolved, and the people recovering their true sight....Better keep together as we are." It was only after the Kentucky and Virginia Resolutions were rejected by the other states that Jefferson began to consider secession. See *The Papers of Thomas Jefferson, Vol. 30, 1798–1799,* ed. Barbara B. Oberg (Princeton, NJ: Princeton University Press, 2003), 387–90.

"The country was in": Sharp, *American Politics,* 275.

"murder, robbery, rape": Michael A. Bellesiles, " 'The Soil Will Be Soaked With Blood': Taking the Revolution of 1800 Seriously," in *The Revolution of 1800: Democracy, Race,* *and the New Republic,* eds. James J. Horn, Jan Ellen Lewis, and Peter S. Onuf (Charlottesville: University of Virginia Press, 2002), 59.

"Who is to be president?": James E. Lewis Jr., "'What Is to Become of Our Government?':
The Revolutionary Potential of the Revolution of 1800," in *Revolution of 1800,* 13–14.

"dissolution of the Union": Bellesiles, "'Soil Will Be Soaked,'" 66.

"embryo capital": Sharp, *American Politics,* 263.

"like bears": J. D. Dickey, *Empire of Mud: The Secret History of Washington, D.C.* (Guilford,
CT: Lyons, 2014), 14.

"By not mixing": Sharp, *American Politics,* 263.

mysterious fires: Jeffrey L. Pasley, "1800 As a Revolution in Political Culture," in *Revolution of 1800,* 141.

Americans readied…"very dangerous experiment": Sharp, *American Politics,* 250–52,
257; John Ferling, *Adams vs. Jefferson: The Tumultuous Election of 1800* (New York:
Oxford University Press, 2004), 182.

"No such usurpation": Sharp, *American Politics,* 266.

"If the Union could": Lewis, "'What Is to Become,'" 16.

"the first day"…"would instantly proclaim": Bellesiles, "'Soil Will Be Soaked,'" 78, 65.

Albert Gallatin, a leading: Sharp, *American Politics,* 263–65. A Federalist editor in Washington touted Northern military strength. "Are they then ripe for civil war," he taunted
Virginia Republicans, "and ready to imbrue their hands in kindred blood?" Bellesiles,
"'Soil Will Be Soaked,'" 66. Richard Hofstadter overlooked all of this when he wrote of
the 1801 standoff, "Violent resistance was never, at any time, discussed…neither was
disunion." See *The Idea of a Party System: The Rise of Legitimate Opposition in the United
States, 1780–1840* (Berkeley: University of California Press, 1969), 130.

Articles of Confederation reinstated: Nancy Isenberg, *Fallen Founder: The Life of Aaron
Burr* (New York: Penguin, 2007), 214.

"as in the present democratical"…Two Republican governors: Sharp, *American Politics,*
266–71.

"I have not closed": Edward J. Larson, *A Magnificent Catastrophe: The Tumultuous Election of
1800, America's First Presidential Campaign* (New York: Simon & Schuster, 2007), 265.

a vow Burr refused: "The means existed of electing Burr," Bayard wrote, "but they
required his cooperation." Wills, *"Negro President,"* 86.

"The clamor was prodigious": John Sedgwick, *War of Two: Alexander Hamilton, Aaron
Burr, and the Duel That Stunned the Nation* (New York: New American Library, 2015),
304; Sharp, *American Politics,* 271.

Federalists' "incorrigible": James Parton, "The Presidential Election of 1800," *Atlantic
Monthly,* July 1873.

"We are all Republicans": *The Writings of Thomas Jefferson, Vol. VIII,* ed. H. A. Washington
(Cambridge: Cambridge University Press, 2011), 2–3.

"If they will break us up": *Writings of John Quincy Adams,* Vol. II, ed. Worthington C. Ford
(New York: Macmillan, 1913), 525–26.

Chapter Five. *The Lost Cause of the North*

"Our country is too big": Michael G. Kammen, *People of Paradox: An Inquiry Concerning the
Origins of American Civilization* (Ithaca, NY: Cornell University Press, 1990), 74.

"What a game": See *Life of Josiah Quincy of Massachusetts,* ed. Edmund Quincy (Boston:
Fields, Osgood, 1869), 349.

"Effects injurious": James E. Lewis Jr., *The American Union and the Problem of Neighborhood:
The United States and the Collapse of the Spanish Empire, 1783–1829* (Chapel Hill: University of North Carolina Press, 1998), 26.

"There is on the globe": See Jon Kukla, *A Wilderness So Immense: The Louisiana Purchase and the Destiny of America* (New York: Anchor, 2004), 226–31.

"the future destinies"..."We may hereafter": Henry Adams, *History of the United States of America During the Administrations of Thomas Jefferson* (New York: Library of America, 1986), 292, 337.

"The future inhabitants": Robert W. Tucker and David C. Hendrickson, *Empire of Liberty: The Statecraft of Thomas Jefferson* (New York: Oxford University Press, 1992), 160.

"vindictive attack": Kevin M. Gannon, "Escaping 'Mr. Jefferson's Plan of Destruction': New England Federalists and the Idea of a Northern Confederacy, 1803–1804," *Journal of the Early Republic* 21, no. 3 (fall 2001): 429.

"Virginia lordlings": Ibid., 430. A year after his call for an end to partisan division, Jefferson told a friend he intended to "sink federalism into an abyss from which there shall be no resurrection for it." Once-seditionist Virginia was now "a loud declaimer for the Union," Fisher Ames observed; "because she wields it...it is her instrument." Stanley Elkins and Eric McKitrick, *The Age of Federalism: The Early American Republic, 1788–1800* (New York: Oxford University Press, 1993), 754.

"Admit this western world": David C. Hendrickson, *Union, Nation, or Empire: The American Debate Over International Relations, 1789–1941* (Lawrence: University Press of Kansas, 2009), 50.

"Our prospects and politics": Park, *American Nationalisms*, 158.

It was Timothy Pickering: See Gerald H. Clarfield's *Timothy Pickering and the American Republic* (Pittsburgh: University of Pittsburgh Press, 1980); and Wills, *"Negro President."* Pickering had been one of the only officers in the army who, during the 1783 Newburgh Crisis, wanted to press the threat of coup d'état even after Washington asked them to stand down. Later, Pennsylvania's government sent Pickering to bring law and order to the Wyoming Valley, the raucous, war-torn frontier where settlers from Pennsylvania and Connecticut had been engaged in a decade-long bloody battle for supremacy. The Yankees wanted to establish a separate state. Shortly after moving into a fine house in the area, Pickering woke in the middle of the night to find the room he shared with his wife and infant son "filled with men, armed with guns and hatchets, having their faces blacked and handkerchiefs tied round their heads." The masked men tied Pickering's arms and led him north into dense, dark woods. His captors spoke openly in front of Pickering about their expectation of assistance from Connecticut's "great men." But the assistance never arrived. Hunted through the forests by bands of Pennsylvania militia, the abductors finally agreed to let Pickering go. The Connecticut resistance collapsed, and with it the idea of establishing a separate state. See Paul B. Moyer, *Wild Yankees: The Struggle for Independence Along Pennsylvania's Revolutionary Frontier* (Ithaca, NY: Cornell University Press, 2011), 68–75.

"Mr. Jefferson's plan": Gannon, "Escaping 'Mr. Jefferson's Plan,' " 414.

"The principles of our Revolution": *Documents Related to New-England Federalism,* ed. Henry Adams (Boston: Little, Brown, 1877), 338–41, 354–58.

"I am therefore ready": Ibid., 351. Largely, the response was encouraging. No few New Englanders of the sharpest minds and sternest morals thought the Louisiana Purchase justified breaking from the South. To Roger Griswold, a respected Connecticut congressman who shared one of those den-like DC boardinghouses with Pickering and other Federalists, there could be "no safety to the Northern States without a separation from the confederacy." Griswold even crunched the numbers and figured that "a reunion of the Northern States" made economic sense. "Our Constitution is good for nothing," Connecticut's eminent senator, Uriah Tracy, told a friend. Jedidiah Morse, author of a landmark 1794 book on American geography (and the father of telegraph inventor Samuel B. Morse), believed that "a division of the States would become indispensable to the preservation of our dearest interests." Tapping Reeve, a Connecticut law teacher (and Aaron Burr's brother-in-law), noted that many in his state "believe that we must separate, and that this is the most favorable moment." A nephew of Caleb Strong, the powerful Massachusetts governor, reported his uncle "decidedly in favor of forming a new confederated government in New England." Yet not all Northern Federalists supported the scheme. George Cabot, a Massachusetts party leader, told Pickering his plan was foolish. But he objected only to the timing. "The thing proposed is obvious and natural," Cabot said, "but it would now be thought too bold." No doubt its day would come, but that day was not yet. Ibid., 362; Eberhard P. Deutsch, "The Real Origin of the Secession Movement," *American Bar Association Journal* 55 (Dec. 1969): 1136; Gannon, "Escaping 'Mr. Jefferson's Plan,'" 437. See also Charles Raymond Brown, in *The Northern Confederacy: According to the Plans of the "Essex Junto" 1796–1814* (Princeton, NJ: Princeton University Press, 1915), 33. Unlike Brown and Henry Adams, I have chosen not to use the "Essex Junto" label, following David Hackett Fischer's argument that it only existed in the minds of its enemies. But unlike Fischer, I find, with Kevin Gannon, that the New England secession movement was, at least at times, widespread and well-organized. See Fischer, "The Myth of the Essex Junto," *William and Mary Quarterly* 21, no. 2 (1964): 191–235; Kevin M. Gannon, "Calculating the Value of Union: States' Rights, Nullification, and Secession in the North, 1800–1848" (PhD diss., University of South Carolina, 2002).

"center of the confederacy": Wills, *"Negro President,"* 133.

"the Union of all honest men!": Isenberg, *Fallen Founder,* 246.

Over dinner: Gannon, "Escaping 'Mr. Jefferson's Plan,'" 438–39.

their "only hope": *Documents Related to New-England Federalism,* Adams, 355.

"frail and worthless"..."Every day proves": John C. Miller, *Alexander Hamilton and the Growth of the New Nation* (New Brunswick, NJ: Transaction, 2004), 543.

"chief of the Northern": Gannon, "Escaping 'Mr. Jefferson's Plan,'" 440.

"a dangerous man"..."a still more despicable": Ron Chernow, *Alexander Hamilton* (New York: Penguin, 2004), 681; Isenberg, *Fallen Founder,* 257.

"Tell them": John Church Hamilton, *Life of Alexander Hamilton,* Vol. VII (Boston: Houghton, Osgood, 1879), 822–23. Willard Sterne Randall has commented that John Church Hamilton "introduced a plethora of errors into the historical record." See his recent foreword to Allan McLane Hamilton, *The Intimate Life of Alexander Hamilton* (New York: Racehorse, 2016).

"Boyd," he said: This original version of the exchange appeared—before the Civil War—in *Harper's,* vol. 13, no. 76 (Sept. 1856), 569. It is attributed, confusingly, to John A. Hamilton, who did not exist. It should be *James* A. Hamilton, sixteen when his father died, or John C. (for Church) Hamilton, who slightly altered his father's phrasing a decade later in *Life,* 822. In an 1869 memoir, James A. Hamilton, arguing against the apparently persistent rumor that his father sympathized with the 1803–4 secession movement, repeats the "break my heart" quote and cites his brother's biography of their father for "other evidences of his disapproval of dismemberment." He also reprints a letter he wrote to John Quincy Adams in 1829 in which he deemed it a "sacred duty to preserve the memory of my father from all stain." See *Reminiscences of James A. Hamilton* (New York: Charles Scribner, 1869), 111. The best evidence of Hamilton's opposition to the New England secession scheme is Adams's recollection, in that exchange with the younger Hamilton, that Rufus King told him at the time that Hamilton, like King himself, disapproved of the plan. Hamilton supported the

Louisiana Purchase, unlike most Federalists. Still, he felt profoundly alienated from Jefferson's America. See *Documents Related to New-England Federalism,* Adams, 147–48.

while lying prostrate: Chernow, *Alexander Hamilton,* 708. Chernow cites a preface that John Church Hamilton wrote for an edition of *The Federalist* first published in 1868. Yet all the younger Hamilton says there of the quote from his father is that these "were among his latest words." There is no reason to think, as Chernow would have us believe, that Hamilton uttered them on his deathbed, surrounded by friends and family. Indeed, John Church Hamilton's biography of his father explicitly says otherwise.

"I will here express": *The Papers of Alexander Hamilton,* Vol. 26, ed. Harold C. Syrett (New York: Columbia University Press, 1979), 309–11.

"It will be found": Adams, *History of the United States,* 431.

"unbounded ambition": James E. Lewis Jr., *The Burr Conspiracy: Uncovering the Story of an Early American Crisis* (Princeton, NJ: Princeton University Press, 2017), 123.

"rattled-headed fellow"... "without observation": Linklater, *Artist in Treason,* 202–3, 215.

"to effect a Separation"... "The whole senate": Isenberg, *Fallen Founder,* 279–81, 90.

"to seek redress"... "all the talents": Adams, *History of the United States,* 575–76.

"seek another country"... "floating house": David O. Stewart, *American Emperor: Aaron Burr's Challenge to Jefferson's America* (New York: Simon & Schuster, 2011), 91, 97–98.

"the LATE UNFORTUNATE DUEL"... "to separate this western": Lewis, *Burr Conspiracy,* 58–60.

Despite his later protests: Jackson's involvement with Burr has always been debated. "I love my country and my government," Jackson assured Louisiana's governor after the conspiracy collapsed. "I hate the Dons; I would delight to see Mexico reduced; but I will die in the last ditch before I would yield a foot to the Dons, or see the Union disunited!" He may have been protesting too much. "History will never be able to make this episode in Jackson's life satisfactory to honest and loyal citizens," the scholar Edward Payson Powell once sighed. Powell, *Nullification and Secession in the United States: A History of the Six Attempts During the First Century of the Republic* (New York: G. P. Putnam's Sons, 1897), 164.

"moulder to pieces"... "dismemberment of the colossal": Adams, *History of the United States,* 760–66; Stewart, *American Emperor,* 118–20.

She refused him: Norris F. Schneider, *Blennerhassett Island and the Burr Conspiracy* (Columbus: Ohio Historical Society, 1966), 21.

"the two men most"... "Burr's accomplices": Lewis, *Burr Conspiracy,* 72, 76–79.

"inquisitions of Europe": Isenberg, *Fallen Founder,* 310.

"My present impression": Adams, *History of the United States,* 812–17.

"a host of choice spirits"... "the most compleat scene": Lewis, *Burr Conspiracy,* 172–74, 215, 369.

"How long will it": Buckner F. Melton Jr., *Aaron Burr: Conspiracy to Treason* (New York: John Wiley & Sons, 1992), 89.

"Burrs Manouevres": Lewis, *Burr Conspiracy,* 48.

"a separation of the Union": Adams, *History of the United States,* 262, 270.

"separating the Western"... "a rascal, villain": Lewis, *Burr Conspiracy,* 43, 82.

"vile fabrications": Isenberg, *Fallen Founder,* 316.

In Natchez: Ibid., 320–21; Andrew Burstein, *The Passions of Andrew Jackson* (New York: Alfred A. Knopf, 2007), 77; Stewart, *American Emperor,* 195.

"lightning imprisoned": Lewis, *Burr Conspiracy,* 380.

Burr's "enterprise": Walter Flavius McCaleb, *The Aaron Burr Conspiracy: A History Largely from Original and Hitherto Unused Sources* (New York: Dodd, Mead, 1903), 289.

"great discontents": *The Works of Thomas Jefferson,* Vol. 10, ed. Paul Leicester Ford (New York: G. P. Putnam's Sons, 1905), 340.

"warm, unshaken": Lewis, *Burr Conspiracy,* 145.

buyers of their wheat, flour: Alan Taylor, "Dual Nationalisms: Legacies of the War of 1812," in *What We So Proudly Hailed: Essays on the Contemporary Meaning of the War of 1812,* eds. Peter J. Kastor and Pietro S. Nivola (Washington, DC: Brookings Institution, 2012), 74.

"The Union is dear": Gannon, "Calculating," 159.

"hurled a firebrand" . . . "Those States whose farms": Wills, *"Negro President,"* 159, 168.

"to disunite, divide": Clarfield, *Timothy Pickering,* 236.

"The CONSTITUTION gone!!": Richard Buel Jr., *America on the Brink: How the Political Struggle Over the War of 1812 Almost Destroyed the Young Republic* (New York: Palgrave Macmillan, 2005), 74.

Seventy towns in Massachusetts: James M. Banner Jr., *To the Hartford Convention: The Federalists and the Origins of Party Politics in Massachusetts* (New York: Alfred A. Knopf, 1970), 298.

Armed crowds: Gannon, "Calculating," 97.

"amounted almost to rebellion" . . . "The United States government": Gordon S. Wood, *Empire of Liberty: A History of the Early Republic, 1789–1815* (New York: Oxford University Press, 2009), 656.

"dambargo": Gannon, "Calculating," 95.

"Turkish despotism": Clarfield, *Timothy Pickering,* 240.

"unjust, oppressive": Gannon, "Calculating," 104, 120n49.

"an evil which can never be": Buel, *America on the Brink,* 54.

"against our own Country": Wood, *Empire of Liberty,* 655.

A secret British agent: See *Documents Relating to New-England Federalism,* Adams, 118; Henry Adams, "Count Edward de Crillon," *American Historical Review* 1, no. 1 (Oct. 1895): 51–69; Samuel Eliot Morison, "The Henry-Crillon Affair of 1812," *Proceedings of the Massachusetts Historical Society Third Series* 69 (Oct. 1947–May 1950): 207–31. "There is much secret history connected with that individual's mission," John Quincy Adams wrote of the agent, John Henry.

"Everyone wishes": Banner, *To the Hartford Convention,* 304n1.

"repeal or Civil War": Wills, *"Negro President,"* 183.

"I felt the foundations" . . . "We must save the Union": Dumas Malone, *Jefferson the President: Second Term, 1805–1809* (Boston: Little, Brown, 1974), 613, 635.

"monarchists of the North": Sean Wilentz, *The Rise of American Democracy: Jefferson to Lincoln* (New York: W. W. Norton, 2005), 131.

"in danger of being confounded": Wood, *Empire of Liberty,* 662.

cleaved the country: This was Samuel Eliot Morison's judgment during the Vietnam War. See "Our Most Unpopular War," *Proceedings of the Massachusetts Historical Society* 80 (1968): 38–54.

The first American casualties: Donald R. Hickey, "The Darker Side of Democracy: The Baltimore Riots of 1812," *Maryland Historian* 7 (fall 1976): 1–19.

"against the nation": Banner, *To the Hartford Convention,* 307.

A crowd in Plymouth: Henry Adams, *History of the United States of America During the Administrations of James Madison* (New York: Library of America, 1986), 574.

In New Hampshire: Merrill D. Peterson, *The Great Triumvirate: Webster, Clay, and Calhoun* (New York: Oxford University Press, 1987), 36–37; Kenneth E. Shewmaker, "'This Unblessed War,' Daniel Webster's Opposition to the War of 1812," *Historical New Hampshire* 53 (spring/summer 1998). During the War of 1812, when Republicans proposed a military draft, Webster argued that the law would lay the groundwork for "the dissolution of the Government." Gannon, "Calculating," 88, 146.

"an outrage against Heaven": David Osgood, *A Solemn Protest Against the Late Declaration of War* (Exeter, NH: C. Norris, 1812), 9, 11.

"let the southern *Heroes*"..."the *disunited states*": Banner, *To the Hartford Convention*, 307.

"Union we love": Gannon, "Calculating," 163.

"the worst-hated man": David Hackett Fischer, *The Revolution of American Conservatism: The Federalist Party in the Era of Jeffersonian Democracy* (New York: Harper & Row, 1965), 255. As Gannon writes, "Pickering differed from many New England Federalists only in his willingness to bluntly articulate what others might leave unspoken." See Gannon, "Calculating," 186n55.

"I would preserve the Union": *Documents Relating to New-England Federalism*, Adams, 389.

"Instead of wishing"..."The determination": Banner, *To the Hartford Convention*, 313.

"Let the ship run": Gannon, "Calculating," 162. Americans elsewhere thought New England's secession a real possibility. In late 1812, a Virginia lawyer expected the Northeast's secession would "climax a ruinous & disastrous war." Without divine intervention, another Virginian observed, "this union is inevitably dissolved." See Taylor, "Dual Nationalisms," 81.

"a mere matter": Adams, *History of the United States of America*, 528.

"No sooner is": Buel, *America on the Brink*, 195.

Nantucket's residents: Taylor, *Civil War of 1812*, 415.

locals raised a flag: Samuel Eliot Morison, *The Maritime History of Massachusetts, 1783–1860* (Boston: Houghton Mifflin, 1921), 210.

On a moonless night: Robert J. Allison, *Stephen Decatur: American Naval Hero, 1779–1820* (Amherst: University of Massachusetts Press, 2005), 135–36; James H. Ellis, *A Ruinous and Unhappy War: New England and the War of 1812* (New York: Algora, 2009), 154–56.

"these wicked lights": Steven Slosberg, "Site Lines: The Mysterious Blue Lights," *Connecticut Explored* 10, no. 3 (summer 2012).

"miserably shattered": Scott A. Silverstone, *Divided Union: The Politics of War in the Early American Republic* (Ithaca, NY: Cornell University Press, 2004), 105.

"The time has arrived": Banner, *To the Hartford Convention*, 317.

"*SECOND PILLAR of a New*": Gannon, "Calculating," 164.

Meanwhile, Governor Strong: J. S. Martell, "A Side Light on Federalist Strategy During the War of 1812," *American Historical Review* 43, no. 3 (April 1938), 553–66.

"abused, self-murdered country": Buel, *America on the Brink*, 206.

"The Union, being the means": Theodore Roosevelt, *Gouverneur Morris: The Story of His Life and Work* (New York: Charles Scribner's Sons, 1906), 331.

"examine the Question": Samuel Eliot Morison, *The Life and Letters of Harrison Gray Otis, Federalist, 1765–1848*, Vol. II (Boston: Houghton Mifflin, 1913), 84.

"I hear every day": Roosevelt, *Gouverneur Morris*, 331–32.

"The people there": Banner, *To the Hartford Convention*, 346.

"not to be entangled": Samuel Eliot Morison, *Harrison Gray Otis, 1765–1848: The Urbane Federalist* (Boston: Houghton Mifflin, 1969), 366. This volume was an updated and much-altered revision of Otis's *Life and Letters* that Morison—the great-great-grandson of his subject—had first published nearly sixty years earlier, itself based on his Harvard dissertation.

"To the cry of disunion": Brown, *Northern Confederacy*, 109–10.

"unquestionably absolved": Alison L. LaCroix, "A Singular and Awkward War: The Transatlantic Context of the Hartford Convention," *American Nineteenth Century History* 6, no. 1 (March 2005): 19.

"Union founded upon": Nagel, *One Nation Indivisible,* 99.

Boston trembled: Morison, *Harrison Gray Otis,* 363.

In the square outside: Buel, *America on the Brink,* 220–22.

"timid, and frequently wavering": *Documents Relating to New-England Federalism,* Adams, 411.

"prevent you young hot-heads": Banner, *To the Hartford Convention,* 332.

"disturb our sleep": *Documents Relating to New-England Federalism,* Adams, 411.

the convention demanded..."Our nation may yet": *The Proceedings of a Convention... at Hartford, in the State of Connecticut, December 15th, 1814* (Boston: Wells & Lilly, 1815), 4, 20. Gannon notes that the report of the Hartford Convention included language nearly identical to that of Madison's own 1798 Virginia Resolutions, an echo "too close to be coincidental." "Calculating," 173.

***"ill-omen'd birds"...* "the Giver of all good things":** Morison, *Harrison Gray Otis,* 389–90. Straining to exonerate his ancestor of any serious embrace of disunion, Morison argues that "nothing would have happened" even had the war continued—New England would not have seceded. This is doubtful, however, for even Morison admits that the popular mood in New England at the time was not unlike that in the South in 1860. If Madison had resisted signing a peace treaty, he notes, the British would have aided New England in fighting the federal government: "There would have been a civil war." Morison even imagines Andrew Jackson marching north and quashing the rebellion. Had that happened, "Harrison Gray Otis as leader of a lost cause would now have a position in Yankee hagiology similar to that of Jefferson Davis in the South." See 397–99.

"bankruptcy, disunion": Taylor, "Dual Nationalisms," 82.

started the brash general: Thirty years later, on his deathbed, Jackson was reportedly still railing about the "Hartford convention men" and the "blue-light Federalists." Sam W. Haynes, *Unfinished Revolution: The Early American Republic in a British World* (Charlottesville: University of Virginia Press, 2010), 108.

"well looking, responsible": Morison, *Harrison Gray Otis,* 391. Other critics were more severe. "If you attempt to pull down the pillars of the Republic," the Madison-aligned *National Intelligencer* warned, "you shall be crush'd into atoms." Taylor, "Dual Nationalisms," 84.

"Old America seems": Morris Birkbeck, *Notes on a Journey in America: From the Coast of Virginia to the Territory of Illinois* (London: Severn, 1818), 31.

Chapter Six. *This Unholy Union*

"Disunion startles": Ronald Osborn, "William Lloyd Garrison and the United States Constitution: The Political Evolution of an American Radical," *Journal of Law and Religion* 24, no. 1 (2008–2009): 82. See *The Liberator,* Jan. 14, 1848, 3.

John C. Calhoun endorsed: See John Niven, *John C. Calhoun and the Price of Union: A Biography* (Baton Rouge: Louisiana State University Press, 1988); Peterson, *Great Triumvirate.*

"Let us...bind": Calhoun's early nationalism is often overlooked. When they both served in Monroe's cabinet, as secretaries of state and war, respectively, John Quincy Adams observed that Calhoun was freer of "all sectional and factional prejudices...than any statesman of this Union with whom I have ever acted." Robert Pierce Forbes, "The Missouri Controversy and Sectionalism," in *Congress and the Emergence of Sectionalism: From the Missouri Compromise to the Age of Jackson,* eds. Paul Finkelman and Donald R. Kennon (Athens: Ohio University Press, 2008), 78.

"so compacted and bound": Robert Pierce Forbes, *The Missouri Compromise and Its After-math: Slavery and the Meaning of America* (Chapel Hill: University of North Carolina Press, 2007), 18.

"one grand, magnificent": Brian Balogh, *A Government Out of Sight: The Mystery of National Authority in the Nineteenth Century* (New York: Cambridge University Press, 2009), 133.

"believe in artificial": *Register of Debates in Congress...First Session of the Twentieth Congress, Vol. IV* (Washington, DC: Gales & Seaton, 1828), 793.

"Sectional harmony was possible": Paul Finkelman, "Introduction," in *Congress and the Emergence of Sectionalism,* Finkelman and Kennon, 3.

Nineteenth-century city dwellers: Mark Tebeau, *Eating Smoke: Fire in Urban America, 1800–1950* (Baltimore: Johns Hopkins University Press, 2003).

"fire-bell in the night": Daniel Walker Howe, *What Hath God Wrought: The Transformation of America, 1815–1848* (New York: Oxford University Press, 2007), 157.

Long lines of men: Ibid., 129.

a fifteen-person human train: Forbes, *Missouri Compromise,* 44. In older states, changing economics transformed the purpose of owning people from making them work to making them breed. "I consider a woman who brings a child every two years as more profitable than the best man on the farm," Jefferson advised a relative. Ibram X. Kendi, *Stamped from the Beginning: The Definitive History of Racist Ideas in America* (New York: Nation Books, 2016), 136.

"damned up": Howe, *What Hath God Wrought,* 148–49.

"summoned the South": George Dangerfield, *The Era of Good Feelings* (New York: Harcourt, Brace, 1952), 205.

he saw "terror": Forbes, *Missouri Compromise,* 47.

"You conduct us": Elizabeth R. Varon, *Disunion!: The Coming of the American Civil War, 1789–1859* (Chapel Hill: University of North Carolina Press, 2008), 45.

"growth of a sin"..."rhetorical civil war": Forbes, *Missouri Compromise,* 42–44.

"If you persist": William Nester, *The Age of Jackson and the Art of American Power, 1815–1848* (Washington, DC: Potomac, 2013), 73.

"If a dissolution": Howe, *What Hath God Wrought,* 148.

"the SIN OF SLAVERY"...James Barbour: Forbes, *Missouri Compromise,* 51, 94. "You can hardly conceive of the rage & fury which prevail here on this subject," a New Hampshire politician wrote home. "A dissolution of the Union was spoken of as certain, & hardly to be regretted."

Henry Clay: Clay's honorifics are from the subtitles of books by Howard W. Caldwell (1903), Robert V. Remini (1993), and David S. and Jeanne T. Heidler (2010), respectively.

"absolutely void": David Brion Davis, *The Problem of Slavery in the Age of Revolution, 1770–1823* (New York: Oxford University Press, 1999), 332.

"gnawed their lips": Dangerfield, *Era of Good Feelings,* 225. In Charleston, a pamphlet of King's speeches fell into the hands of a formerly enslaved carpenter named Denmark Vesey. At his 1822 trial for leading an attempted slave rebellion, a witness recalled that Vesey had once read a passage to him and called the New York senator "the black man's friend." See Howe, *What Hath God Wrought,* 161.

"If the alternative": Varon, *Disunion!,* 43.

moved to admit that region as a state: See J. Chris Arndt, "The State of Maine," in *Uniting States, Vol. II: Louisiana to Ohio,* Shearer, 517–24.

To sweeten the deal: For more on Thomas, who wanted Illinois to become a slave state, see Matthew W. Hall, *Dividing the Union: Jesse Burgess Thomas and the Making of the Missouri Compromise* (Carbondale: Southern Illinois University Press, 2016), 71–72.

"a great triumph"..."The Constitution is a creature": Forbes, *Missouri Compromise*, 90–93, 97–99.

"bargain between freedom"..."so glorious would be": *John Quincy Adams and the Politics of Slavery: Selections from the Diary*, eds. David Waldstreicher and Matthew Mason (New York: Oxford University Press, 2017), 84–85, 94–95.

"The sound of disunion": *Annals of the Congress of the United States: Sixteenth Congress, First Session* (Washington, DC: Gales & Seaton, 1855), 1105.

"moral gladiatorship": Robert V. Remini, *Daniel Webster: The Man and His Time* (New York: W. W. Norton, 1997), 324.

"considered as if"..."a seductive eloquence": Peterson, *Great Triumvirate*, 157, 174.

"unhallowed attempt": Forbes, *Missouri Compromise*, 206.

New Englander gave: "Speech of Daniel Webster, of Massachusetts, January 26 and 27, 1830," in *The Webster-Hayne Debate on the Nature of the Union: Selected Documents*, ed. Herman Belz (Indianapolis: Liberty Fund, 2000), 81–154.

"Mammoth deliberately": Forbes, *Missouri Compromise*, 239.

author of the Gettysburg Address: Lincoln would call Webster's reply to Hayne "the very best speech that was ever delivered." Howe, *What Hath God Wrought*, 372.

"the steady flow": James Schouler, *History of the United States of America Under the Constitution: Volume III, 1817–1831* (Washington, DC: William H. Morrison, 1885), 487.

hundred thousand copies: Howe, *What Hath God Wrought*, 371.

"reduced to the condition": Peter S. Onuf, "The Political Economy of Sectionalism: Tariff Controversies and Conflicting Conceptions of World Order," in *Congress and the Emergence of Sectionalism*, Finkelman and Kennon, 74.

"the occasion, rather than": Richard Ellis, *The Union at Risk: Jacksonian Democracy, States' Rights and the Nullification Crisis* (New York: Oxford University Press, 1987), 193.

"calculate the value": William W. Freehling, *Prelude to Civil War: The Nullification Controversy in South Carolina, 1816–1836* (New York: Harper & Row, 1965), 128–31. Born in England, Cooper moved to Philadelphia in the 1790s and became active in Republican circles. He was even thrown in prison under the Sedition Act. Jefferson called Cooper "the greatest man in America, in the powers of mind," and tried to hire him for the University of Virginia. Cooper instead moved to Charleston, where he adopted the state's proslavery and free-trade principles. See Dumas Malone, *Jefferson and His Time: The Sage of Monticello* (New York: Little, Brown, 1981), 368.

a series of provocative essays: Robert E. Bonner, *Mastering America: Southern Slaveholders and the Crisis of American Nationhood* (New York: Cambridge University Press, 2009), 54–55.

"make two of one nation": Peterson, *Great Triumvirate*, 154, 161.

"kindred acts of despotism": Haynes, *Unfinished Revolution*, 144.

Holed up at Fort Hill: Niven, *John C. Calhoun*, 158–63.

"reformation, not revolution": Ellis, *Union at Risk*, 53.

"falsify all the glorious anticipations": *John C. Calhoun: Selected Writings and Speeches*, ed. H. Lee Cheek Jr. (Washington, DC: Regnery, 2003), 317–41.

a lavish dinner: Richard R. Sternberg, "The Jefferson Birthday Dinner, 1830," *Journal of Southern History* 4, no. 3 (Aug. 1938): 334–45; Freehling, *Prelude to Civil War*, 192; Peterson, *Great Triumvirate*, 185–86.

"divided the country": *John C. Calhoun*, Cheek, 317–41.

"compromise the different interests"..."only existed": Peterson, *Great Triumvirate*, 200–201, 209; Ellis, *Union at Risk*, 46.

an elderly Continental: Bonner, *Mastering America*, 151.

"utterly null and void": Ellis, *Union at Risk*, 75.

"blind and idolatrous devotion": Powell, *Nullification and Secession*, 306–7.

"For the rights of the state": Ellis, *Union at Risk,* 47. The Carolinians had reason to hope Jackson might endorse nullification. While the tariff dispute led one state to ignore a federal law, another was defying a Supreme Court decision—with Jackson's approval. In 1828, a vein of gold was found in the Cherokee lands of northern Georgia. The state forbade the natives from mining it and sought to remove them. In 1830, Jackson signed a bill providing $68 million—more than the combined price of the Louisiana Purchase and the later annexation of Mexican territory—to purchase land from the so-called Five Civilized Tribes (the Choctaw, Chickasaw, Creek, Seminole, and Cherokee) and pay for their removal to "an ample district west of the Mississippi." Without much trouble, the first three nations were sent away. The Seminoles put up a valiant, decade-long resistance, outrunning the army and its bloodhounds, hiding in the Everglades, fighting a guerrilla war that cost the United States tens of millions of dollars and nearly 1,500 men. But they too—all but a few, at any rate—surrendered. The Cherokee held out longest. With support from top lawyers, including a former attorney general of the United States, the tribe fought Georgia all the way to the Supreme Court, where Chief Justice John Marshall sided with the natives. But Jackson refused to enforce Marshall's decision—and this was what gave the nullifiers hope. Overriding Georgia, the president feared, might provoke a clash between state and federal troops, which, along with the South Carolina situation, could spiral into a region-wide civil war.

One critic accused the president of being "more than half a Nullifier himself," but Jackson didn't see his position in the two cases as contradictory. He feared that recognizing the Cherokee as a separate nation unbound by the laws of Georgia would violate the Constitution's provision that "no new State shall be formed or erected within the Jurisdiction of any other State" without the existing state's permission. The Cherokee threatened to create a nation-within-a-nation, and therefore posed as much of a threat to American unity as nullification. Both threats had to be neutralized. Over several years—removal actually occurred under Jackson's successor, Martin Van Buren—nearly 15,000 Cherokee were sent west. See Howe, *What Hath God Wrought,* 342–57; Peterson, *Great Triumvirate,* 214; Wilentz, *Rise of American Democracy,* 325; Greg Grandin, *The End of the Myth: From the Frontier to the Border Wall in the Mind of America* (New York: Metropolitan, 2019), 62.

"There is nothing": Ellis, *Union at Risk,* 48.

"Tell them from me" … "a *government*": Ibid., 78–84.

Jackson's theory: For more on the dubious history of the Proclamation, see Stampp, "Concept of a Perpetual Union," and Pauline Maier, "The Road Not Taken: Nullification, John C. Calhoun, and the Revolutionary Tradition in South Carolina," *South Carolina Historical Magazine* 82, no. 1 (Jan. 1981): 1–19. Interestingly, the real author was Jackson's secretary of state, Edward Livingston, a former New York City mayor who, thirty years earlier, had moved to Louisiana and became entangled in Burr's Western-empire scheme. Thus two veterans of a disunion conspiracy crafted the most enduring defense of a perpetual Union, one so influential it would be described a half century later by Theodore Roosevelt as "one of the ablest, as well as one of the most important, of all American state papers. It is hard to see how any American can read it now without feeling his veins thrill." Roosevelt, *Thomas Hart Benton: The Story of His Life and Work* (New York: G. P. Putnam's Sons, 1906), 96.

"just such a paper" … "South Carolina may": Ellis, *Union at Risk,* 85–93.

"crush the monster": Nester, *Age of Jackson,* 125.

The bill was necessary: Ellis, *Union at Risk,* 94.

"whether any dotard": Ibid., 96.

"make war on": Peterson, *Great Triumvirate*, 222. A New York paper objected to holding the country together by force: "The Union saved by reasonable concession and a just regard to the RIGHTS OF ALL, will strengthen the fraternal bond....But the Union, saved by the sword, by the butchery of its citizens...will be a mere mockery of the Union." Ellis, *Union at Risk*, 91.

"we will secede"..."It is on all hands": Ibid., 72–73, 79, 91, 98. Just before he died, in 1835, nearly eighty years old, Marshall wrote to his Supreme Court colleague Joseph Story: "I yield slowly and reluctantly to the conviction that our constitution cannot last." Howe, *What Hath God Wrought*, 439.

"To think, Louisa": Park, *American Nationalisms*, 225.

"There is one man"..."We want no sacked": Peterson, *Great Triumvirate*, 217, 230.

"stability of our institutions": Ellis, *Union at Risk*, 99.

"Is the Union to be"...Charleston erupted: Peterson, *Great Triumvirate*, 227–28, 233.

"but a surrender": Powell, *Nullification and Secession*, 276.

"Nullification has done": Wilentz, *Rise of American Democracy*, 387.

"But there is no *peace*": Ellis, *Union at Risk*, 194.

"The undersigned, citizens of Haverhill": A passing reference to the Haverhill Petition is standard in most biographies of John Quincy Adams or accounts of the fight against the gag rule in Congress, but rarely has the episode been explored further. My account is indebted to Kathleen Dacey, "Old Man Eloquent and the Haverhill Petition of 1842," in *Beyond the Battlefield: New England and the Civil War*, ed. Peter Benes (Boston: Dublin Seminar for New England Folklife, 2017). See also William Lee Miller, *Arguing About Slavery: John Quincy Adams and the Great Battle in the United States Congress* (New York: Vintage, 1998), and Joseph Wheelan, *Mr. Adams's Last Crusade: John Quincy Adams's Extraordinary Post-Presidential Life in Congress* (New York: PublicAffairs, 2008). Contrary to Miller, however, the Haverhill petitioners were not Adams's constituents. In 1898, a reporter for the *Boston Globe* visited the town and found ninety-year-old Francis Butters Jr., the sole surviving signer, "deeply engaged in the mysteries of the fascinating game of dominoes." Asked why the petition went to Adams, Butters recalled that he was the only congressman "whom the South could not intimidate." See "To Break Up the Republic," *Boston Daily Globe*, Jan. 9, 1898, 21. The same year the *Globe* article appeared, Haverhill became the first city in America to elect a socialist mayor—a former shoe worker and grocery clerk.

"the people of the disunited states": John Quincy Adams, *The Jubilee of the Constitution: A Discourse Delivered...on Tuesday, the 30th of April, 1839* (New York: Samuel Colman, 1839), 69.

burn the petition: Miller, *Arguing About Slavery*, 431.

A shiftless, alcoholic: The best biography, a model of scholarship and style, is Henry C. Mayer, *All on Fire: William Lloyd Garrison and the Abolition of Slavery* (New York: St. Martin's, 2000).

"those principles which": Osborn, "William Lloyd Garrison," 65. To young Garrison, the name of Timothy Pickering—tribune of New England separatism, and a fellow Newburyport native—was "synonymous with honor, moderation, and intelligence." Gannon, "Calculating," 248.

"Everyone who comes": Mayer, *All on Fire*, 93.

The city's Park Street Church..."must share in the guilt": Osborn, "William Lloyd Garrison," 68–69.

"within sight of Bunker Hill"..."I *will* be as harsh": Mayer, *All on Fire*, 110–13.

"doing more to alienate"..."at an end": Ellis, *Union at Risk*, 191.

"a smothered volcano": Mayer, *All on Fire*, 122–24. Georgetown, in the federal district, banned blacks from taking copies of *The Liberator* at the post office, on punishment of a hefty fine and thirty days in jail, with the risk of being sold into slavery if the fine went unpaid. Georgia offered a five-thousand-dollar reward for Garrison's arrest, a threat that persuaded him to spend some time abroad.

"Go on": Gannon, "Calculating," 253–54.

"holy horror": Varon, *Disunion!*, 122.

"to set my house": Wheelan, *Mr. Adams's Last Crusade*, 53. The presidency proved a disappointment to Adams, but he had met his father's almost abusively high standard for success: "If you do not rise to the head not only of your profession, but of your country, it will be owing to your own *Laziness, Slovenliness, and Obstinacy*," John Adams wrote to his son in 1794, when Washington appointed the twenty-seven-year-old to his first ambassadorship. For their relationship, see Nancy Isenberg and Andrew C. Burstein, *The Problem of Democracy: The Presidents Adams Confront the Cult of Personality* (New York: Penguin, 2019).

"to compliment an abused": Wheelan, *Mr. Adams's Last Crusade*, xiii. See also Samuel Flagg Bemis, *John Quincy Adams and the Union* (New York: Alfred A. Knopf, 1956), 417.

"organized civil War": James E. Lewis Jr., *John Quincy Adams: Policymaker for the Union* (Wilmington, DE: Scholarly Resources, 2001), 124.

"settled only": *The Papers of Henry Clay, Vol. 8: Candidate, Compromiser, Whig*, ed. Robert Seager II (Lexington: University Press of Kentucky, 1984), 397.

"a direct violation"... "Freedom of speech": Wheelan, *Mr. Adams's Last Crusade*, 107, 129. What so angered Adams about the gag rule wasn't so much the evil of slavery itself as the willingness of Southerners to revoke *white* Americans' freedoms in its defense. See *John Quincy Adams and the Politics of Slavery*, Waldstreicher and Mason, 228.

"By God, Sir": Nels Sigurd Jorgenson, "John Quincy Adams and Secession, 1842–1843" (PhD diss., University of Chicago, 1921), 13n3.

"Half rabid"... "You will when": Wheelan, *Mr. Adams's Last Crusade*, 132–37, 157–61.

"Cotton thread holds": Mayer, *All on Fire*, 344.

Haverhill native John Greenleaf Whittier: There is no evidence, as is sometimes suggested, that Whittier wrote the Haverhill petition. He didn't even sign it. According to Kathleen Dacey, he explicitly stated that if asked he would have refused. Dacey, "Old Man Eloquent," 24.

Every Friday afternoon: Ibid., 19–20.

"a far-sighted, long-headed": "To Break Up the Republic," *Boston Daily Globe*, 21.

"a diverse group": Dacey prints the list of signatories in "Old Man Eloquent," 24–26.

"thoroughly in earnest": Ibid., 22.

"This," one congressman: Wheelan, *Mr. Adams's Last Crusade*, 192. The entire exchange is in *The Congressional Globe...Second Session of the Twenty-Seventh Congress, Vol. XI* (1842), 168. See also William W. Freehling, *The Road to Disunion, Vol. I: Secessionists at Bay, 1776–1854* (New York: Oxford University Press, 1990), 350–51.

"a candle-light sitting": Lynn Hudson Parsons, *John Quincy Adams* (Lanham, MD: Rowman & Littlefield, 2001), 249.

"with knitted brows": Miller, *Arguing About Slavery*, 432.

"will fill every patriot": Parsons, *John Quincy Adams*, 249.

"Up rose that little": Dacey, "Old Man Eloquent," 23.

"It is not for"... "befowlers": Wheelan, *Mr. Adams's Last Crusade*, 193.

two hundred more petitions: Miller, *Arguing About Slavery*, 444. Emboldened, Adams spoke more overtly against slavery itself, not only the gag rule. Charged with favoring emancipation even if it meant bloodshed, Adams pled guilty: "I say *now*, let it come....Though it cost the blood of millions of white men, let it come." Wheelan, *Mr. Adams's Last Crusade*, 214–15.

"sprawling in his own": Jorgenson, "John Quincy Adams," 34.

stashed away: I do not take issue with the Buttonwoods Museum's preservation of the petition in storage, where it is least likely to crumble, only to suggest the document deserves greater prominence. When I showed up at the museum one rainy summer morning in 2019, the museum's director, Janice Williams, eagerly pulled out the petition. She also arranged to have it photographed for reproduction in this book and directed me to Kathleen Dacey's article on its origins.

"the first victory" ... "remembered scores": Wheelan, *Mr. Adams's Last Crusade*, 201.

"People now talk": Mayer, *All on Fire*, 315.

"the horror which used" ... "Repulsed": Gannon, "Calculating," 271.

"the boastful South": *Letters of William Lloyd Garrison: No Union with the Slaveholders, 1841–1849*, ed. Walter M. Merrill (Cambridge, MA: Harvard University Press, 1974), 53.

Once the "bonds": W. Caleb McDaniel, "Repealing Unions: American Abolitionists, Irish Repeal, and the Origins of Garrisonian Disunionism," *Journal of the Early Republic* 28, no. 2 (2008): 251. What Garrison probably didn't know was that Underwood, a Whig aligned with Henry Clay, was actually fairly critical of slavery ("a curse of stupendous magnitude"). A supporter of the American Colonization Society, Underwood later freed his own slaves on condition they move to Liberia. See Harold D. Tallant, *Evil Necessity: Slavery and Political Culture in Antebellum Kentucky* (Lexington: University Press of Kentucky, 2003), 39–40.

"Nothing can prevent the dissolution": *William Lloyd Garrison, 1805–1879: The Story of His Life Told by His Children*, Vol. III (Boston: Houghton, Mifflin, 1894), 49.

"not to leave the slaves": Osborn, "William Lloyd Garrison," 81–82.

"the REPEAL OF THE UNION": Gannon, "Calculating," 266. W. Caleb McDaniel, *The Problem of Democracy in the Age of Slavery: Garrisonian Abolitionists and Transatlantic Reform* (Baton Rouge: Louisiana State University Press, 2013), shows how Garrison was inspired by the movement for Irish independence during recent trips to the British Isles.

"We must dissolve" ... "Your covenant": *William Lloyd Garrison, 1805–1879: The Story of His Life Told by His Children*, Vol. III (Boston and New York: Houghton, Mifflin, 1894), 49–53.

Chapter Seven. *Endangered by Greatness*

"Ef I'd my way": James Russell Lowell, *The Biglow Papers* (London: Trubner, 1861).

"a nest of little republics": Thomas W. Richards, "The Texas Moment: Breakaway Republics and Contested Sovereignty in North America, 1836–1846" (diss., Temple University, 2016), 98. Dr. Richards was kind enough not only to share his dissertation with me but to meet to discuss it. His work was indispensable. I am in his debt, and David Waldstreicher's for introducing us. See also Thomas W. Richards, *Breakaway Americas: The Unmanifest Future of the Jacksonian United States* (Baltimore: Johns Hopkins University Press, 2020), which expands on his dissertation.

"Disunion must and will": Mayer, *All on Fire*, 363.

"two nations in the womb": Bonner, *Mastering America*, 144.

"a free, sovereign and independent": Daniel Doan, *Indian Stream Republic: Settling a New England Frontier, 1785–1842* (Lebanon, NH: University Press of New England, 1997), 165. The 1783 peace treaty cited the "northwesternmost head of the Connecticut River" as the border between New England and Quebec. But nobody knew which of three streams was the river's source. By 1830, a three-hundred-square-mile region of lush farmland, named Indian Stream for the middle of the three rivulets, had some four hundred settlers. But because of the vague boundary, their allegiance remained in doubt. See Robert Tsai, *America's Forgotten Constitutions: Defiant Visions of Power and Community* (Cambridge, MA: Harvard University Press, 2014), 18–48; Roger Hamilton Brown, *The Struggle for the Indian Stream Territory* (Cleveland: Western Reserve University Press, 1955).

"twelve or fourteen Indians": Tsai, *America's Forgotten Constitutions,* 39.

faded into obscurity: The Republic is still discernible on the map where Vermont's border with Quebec shoots north at the New Hampshire line. Now called Pittsburg, it's the largest New England town by area.

"doomed to dissolution": Thelma Jennings, *The Nashville Convention: Southern Movement for Unity, 1848–1851* (Memphis: Memphis State University Press, 1980), 7.

"Republic of Fredonia": Andrés Reséndez, *Changing National Identities at the Frontier: Texas and New Mexico, 1800–1850* (Cambridge: Cambridge University Press, 2005), 43–45.

"a wise direction": Stanley Siegel, *A Political History of the Texas Republic, 1836–1845* (Austin: University of Texas Press, 1956), 15.

"to give liberty": Steven Hahn, *A Nation Without Borders: The United States and Its World in an Age of Civil Wars, 1830–1910* (New York: Penguin, 2016), 40.

"There! You see?": James Parton, *The Life and Times of Aaron Burr, Vol. II* (New York: Houghton Mifflin, 1858), 319.

"a deep and lasting curse": John H. Schroeder, "Annexation or Independence: The Texas Issue in American Politics, 1836–1845," *Southwestern Historical Quarterly* 89, no. 2 (Oct. 1985): 142. I have also relied on Joel H. Silbey, *Storm Over Texas: The Annexation Controversy and the Road to Civil War* (New York: Oxford University Press, 2005).

"incalculable benefits"..."visionary schemes": Bonner, *Mastering America,* 26–27.

"known to be opposed": Andrew J. Torget, *Seeds of Empire: Cotton, Slavery, and the Transformation of the Texas Borderlands, 1800–1850* (Chapel Hill: University of North Carolina Press, 2015), 206. In a letter to the citizens of Macon, Georgia, Lamar wrote that slavery could only be preserved by uniting "Texas and the South...two countries drawing their vitality from the same fountain; and therefore involved in a common destiny for good or ill." Changing his metaphor, Lamar compared the neighboring slave-holding regions to "Siamese-twins...bound together by a strong, natural ligament, which if severed, must bring death to both." Bonner, *Mastering America,* 28–30.

Fifteen hundred miles..."There is a nation": Richards, "Texas Moment," 340–49, 361–63, 416–17, 446.

"a great, free, and independent"..."strong enough to take": Daniel Boorstin, *The Americans: The National Experience* (New York: Alfred A. Knopf, 2010), 270; Donald Livingston, "American Republicanism and the Forgotten Question of Size," in ed. Donald Livingston, *Rethinking the American Union for the Twenty-First Century* (Gretna, LA: Pelican, 2013), 139.

"powerful maritime nation": Richards, "Texas Moment," 107, 363, 430, 445, 451.

"exterminated or driven": Bernard DeVoto, *The Year of Decision: 1846* (New York: Truman Talley, 2000), 85.

town they renamed Nauvoo: Howe, *What Hath God Wrought,* 724.

"rent from center to circumference": "The Government of God," *Times and Seasons* 3, no. 18 (July 15, 1842): 856; see also Richards, "Texas Moment," 283–86.

a top secret committee: See Benjamin E. Park, "The Mormon Council of Fifty: What Joseph Smith's Secret Records Reveal," *Religion & Politics,* Sept. 9, 2016. https://religionand politics.org/2016/09/09/the-mormon-council-of-fifty-what-joseph-smiths-secret -records-reveal/. Unfortunately, Dr. Park's *Kingdom of Nauvoo: The Rise and Fall of a Religious Empire on the American Frontier* (New York: W. W. Norton, 2020) appeared too late for me to consult.

One intriguing possibility: See Michael Scott Van Wagenen, *The Texas Republic and the Mormon Kingdom of God* (College Station: Texas A&M University Press, 2002); Richards, "Texas Moment," 292–94.

"Once lov'd America!": Howe, *What Hath God Wrought*, 726.

"Satan's Kingdom": Richards, "Texas Moment," 321–24.

Sixteen thousand people: Daniel Walker Howe has called the Mormon exodus "the best organized large migration in American history." Howe, *What Hath God Wrought*, 727.

"We owe the United States": Craig K. Manscill, "Rumors of Secession in the Utah Territory: 1847–61," in *Civil War Saints*, ed. Kenneth L. Alford (Provo, UT: Deseret, 2012), 84–91.

"United States of the West": Joseph Ellison, "Sentiment in California for a Pacific Republic, 1843–1861" (master's thesis, University of California/Berkeley, 1961), 52.

"forsaking the American Republic": Richards, "Texas Moment," 322.

"rather retreat to the deserts": Manscill, "Rumors of Secession." Before leaving Iowa for the journey over the mountains, Young told his flock—in words William Lloyd Garrison would have approved—that only separation from sin-loving Americans, and the divine retribution they were bound to receive, could secure the future of the children of God: "The whisperings of the Spirit to us have invariably been of the same import, to depart, to go hence, to flee into the mountains, to retire to our strongholds that we may be secure in the visitations of the Judgments that must pass upon this land, that is crimsoned with the blood of Martyrs; and that we may be hid, as it were, in the clefts of the rocks, and in the hollows of the land of the Great Jehovah, while the guilty land of our fathers is purifying by the overwhelming scourge."

"become hostile": Richards, "Texas Moment," 121.

"a legitimate contest": Ibid., 329–32. The title for this section comes from Joel Silbey's indispensable book, *Storm Over Texas*.

"You are now rushing": Wheelan, *Mr. Adams's Last Crusade*, 106.

"Must we of the North" . . . "death to our Union": Gannon, "Calculating," 338–40.

"neither local nor sectional": Silbey, *Storm Over Texas*, 32.

"blessing to mankind": Haynes, *Unfinished Revolution*, 216–17. For more on Britain's role in Texas, see Freehling, *Road to Disunion, Vol. I*, 372–87.

"very existence of the South": Freehling, *Road to Disunion, Vol. I*, 399.

"slave-breeding conspiracy": Schroeder, "Annexation or Independence," 149. Mexican officials, desperate to forestall annexation, seized on Adams's arguments and printed excerpts of his speeches south of the border.

"A Solemn Appeal": Gannon, "Calculating," 345.

"Constitution of the United States and Texas": Mayer, *All on Fire*, 338.

"this happy Union": Gannon, "Calculating," 349–50.

"clap of thunder": Richards, "Texas Moment," 77.

"essential to the peace": Silbey, *Storm Over Texas*, 41.

"Under the pretext": Thomas Hart Benton, *Thirty Years' View, Vol. II* (New York: D. Appleton, 1883), 614. Francis Blair, a Democratic Party founder and former Jackson adviser, begged the ex-president not to endorse annexation. Texas was another scheme by "Calhoun and his old Junto of conspirators . . . to separate the South from the North. They want Texas only as a bone of contention." Calhoun sought a "dissolution of the Union, and a Southern confederacy." Jackson had opposed Calhoun's disunion schemes before. He should again. Jackson didn't take the advice. Silbey, *Storm Over Texas*, 44.

"If the Union is": Chauncey S. Boucher, "The Annexation of Texas and the Bluffton Movement in South Carolina," *Mississippi Valley Historical Review* 6, no. 1 (June 1919), 15.

as if responding to his own name: His name, in fact, was not his name. Along with his brothers, Robert Barnwell Smith adopted the surname of an illustrious colonial-era ancestor. See Eric H. Walther, *The Fire-Eaters* (Baton Rouge: Louisiana State University Press, 1992), 121–27.

"two enormous villanies": Boucher, "Annexation of Texas," 19.

"the deep seated and growing": Varon, *Disunion!*, 171.

"Nothing alarms": Boucher, "Annexation of Texas," 19–20.

Under a sprawling oak tree: The "Secession Oak" still stands in Bluffton. Unmarked by any sign or monument, it towers over a narrow road off a state highway, its gnarled, ivy-clad limbs holding up a broad canopy draped with shaggy moss. See Mike Conklin, "Finding the Tree Where the Confederacy Took Root," *Chicago Tribune*, Dec. 26, 2012.

"Do not deceive": *Letter of the Hon. Langdon Cheves* (Charleston, SC: Walker & Burke, 1844).

"In the Union or out": Varon, *Disunion!*, 173.

"He is a large Slave holder": Howe, *What Hath God Wrought*, 683–84, 702. John Quincy Adams described Polk as "sold body and soul to that grim idol, half albino, half negro, the compound of Democracy and of slavery, which, by the slave-representation in Congress, rules and ruins the Union." Wheelan, *Mr. Adams's Last Crusade*, 210.

put Polk over the edge: In an intriguing essay—written after the divisive 2000 election—Gary Kornblith argues that if Clay had won just a third of the votes in New York that went to the Liberty Party he would have become the next president, Texas would not have been annexed, and the Civil War might never have come. He ignores, however, the rising resistance in South Carolina, silenced only by the hopes Calhoun and others placed in a Polk victory. There is little reason to think a President Clay or his successors could have appeased the hard-core Southerners while keeping the increasingly antislavery North mollified as well. It's possible that in the event of a Clay victory the secession crisis would have come sooner than it did, rather than not at all. See Gary J. Kornblith, "Rethinking the Coming of the Civil War: A Counterfactual Exercise," *Journal of American History* 90, no. 1 (June 2003): 76–105.

"shatter this Union": Gannon, "Calculating," 357–58.

"As certain as truth": Silbey, *Storm Over Texas*, xiii.

"friendship of the lion"..."the Curses of fully": Siegel, *Political History*, 246–54.

"Can we close": Bonner, *Mastering America*, 30.

"The final act": Richard Bruce Winders, *Crisis in the Southwest: The United States, Mexico, and the Struggle Over Texas* (Lanham, MD: SR Books, 2004), 88.

the term *manifest destiny*: "Annexation," *The United States Magazine and Democratic Review*, Vol. XVII (New York: J. L. O'Sullivan & O. C. Gardiner, 1846), 5–10. The editorial may have been written, as long assumed, by the *Review*'s founder and editor, John L. O'Sullivan. But recent scholars suggest the author was Jane McManus Storm Cazneau, a sharp-penned expansionist and—fittingly, given the editorial's argument—ex-mistress of Aaron Burr. See Linda S. Hudson, *Mistress of Manifest Destiny: A Biography of Jane McManus Storm Cazneau, 1807–1878* (Austin: Texas State Historical Association, 2001). The title for this section comes from a collection of Walt Whitman's early journalism, *The Gathering of the Forces*, eds. Cleveland Rodgers and John Black (New York: G. P. Putnam's Sons, 1920).

"see the repetition": Richards, "Texas Moment," 388.

"whatever nation": Howe, *What Hath God Wrought*, 710.

"A house divided": Richards, "Texas Moment," 38–90.

"their only defense": Allan Nevins, *Frémont: Pathmarker of the West* (Lincoln: University of Nebraska Press, 1939), 267–68.

danced a celebratory fandango: Howe, *What Hath God Wrought*, 754–55.

"A recent outbreak"..."Cannot a nation sometimes": Richards, "Texas Moment," 97, 460, 369.

"a nation where our children": *The Writings and Speeches of Daniel Webster, Vol. 13* (Boston: Little, Brown, 1903), 310–24.

The deal split Polk's party: See Howe, *What Hath God Wrought*, 717–20. Southern Democrats wanted to avoid war with Britain over Oregon so they could focus on war with Mexico over California. With that distraction settled, America could "thrash Mexico into decency at our leisure," one paper observed.

"We can look forward": Richards, "Texas Moment," 470.

Seizing San Francisco: Amy S. Greenberg, *A Wicked War: Polk, Clay, Lincoln, and the 1846 U.S. Invasion of Mexico* (New York: Vintage, 2013), 75–76. The adviser was historian George Bancroft, Polk's secretary of the navy.

"Hostilities may now"..."It looks as if": Howe, *What Hath God Wrought*, 732. Polk urged his cabinet to opt for war four hours *before* he received news of the skirmish on the Rio Grande. The real cause was Mexico's rejection of his latest bid to buy California. See Freehling, *Road to Disunion, Vol. I*, 456.

Early victories: Despite battlefield success, the war went on longer than Polk anticipated, mostly because the Mexicans refused to let their government surrender even after crushing defeats. American soldiers responded with massacres, rape, scalping, petty murder. One private told his father that fellow soldiers were "a disgrace to the nation." He saw one shoot a woman washing clothes in a river "merely to test his rifle." US forces indiscriminately bombed the city of Veracruz, hitting a hospital and a post office, killing hundreds of civilians. "My heart bleeds for the inhabitants," Robert E. Lee, a young officer, told his wife; his future adversary, Ulysses S. Grant, would write in his memoirs that he regretted not having had "the moral courage to resign" his service in that "most wicked war." Thousands of soldiers deserted to join the enemy—the most in any American war. Insurgencies broke out in Mexico City, California, and New Mexico. In Taos, rebels carried the American governor's scalp, detached from his arrow-riddled body, through the ancient streets. Allan Nevins, *Ordeal of the Union: Vol. 1, Fruits of Manifest Destiny, 1847–1852* (New York: Charles Scribner's Sons, 1947), 17; Mayer, *All on Fire*, 361.

"great political and moral crime": Silbey, *Storm Over Texas*, 115.

"grossest act": Michael A. Morrison, *Slavery and the American West: The Eclipse of Manifest Destiny and the Coming of the Civil War* (Chapel Hill: University of North Carolina Press, 1997), 71.

"If an earnest desire"..."manly resistance": Howe, *What Hath God Wrought*, 742, 770.

"criminal murder": Mayer, *All on Fire*, 361.

petitions from forty-three towns: Ibid., 360–61. A pacifist, Garrison thought it "a matter of justice to desire the overwhelming defeat of the American troops, and the success of the injured Mexicans."

"Some are petitioning"..."This people must cease": Henry David Thoreau, "Civil Disobedience," in *Walden and Other Writings* (New York: Barnes & Noble, 1993), 283, 286–87. Thoreau's friend and mentor, Ralph Waldo Emerson, expected the war would prove fatal to the republic. "The United States will conquer Mexico," he predicted, "but it will be as the man who swallows the arsenic which brings him down in return. Mexico will poison us." Howe, *What Hath God Wrought*, 821.

On a humid night: Eric Foner, "The Wilmot Proviso Revisited," *Journal of American History* 56, no. 2 (Sept. 1969): 262–79.

"The conviction is forced"..."fraught with incalculable": Silbey, *Storm Over Texas*, 123, 128.

"As if by magic": Robert V. Remini, *At the Edge of the Precipice: Henry Clay and the Compromise That Saved the Union* (New York: Basic Books, 2010), 33. Unlike Tallmadge, who helped abolish slavery in his home state of New York, Wilmot disavowed any "morbid sympathy for the slave." Introducing what he called his "White Man's Proviso," Wilmot claimed to speak only on behalf "of my own race and color." He and other Northerners believed that whites without slaves would never move to a land worked by slaves, because competition with unpaid labor was demeaning. "The question is not whether black men are to be made free," a supporter said, "but whether white men are to remain free." See Freehling, *Road to Disunion, Vol. I,* 458; Nevins, *Ordeal: Vol. 1,* 10; Howe, *What Hath God Wrought,* 768; Morrison, *Slavery and the American West,* 54; Foner, "Wilmot Proviso Revisited," 278.

"I try to avert": Morrison, *Slavery and the American West,* 76.

"insane ravings": Varon, *Disunion!,* 192.

"destroy the great principle": Morrison, *Slavery and the American West,* 78. Tom Corwin of Ohio called it "a sad commentary upon the perfection of human reason" that constitutional principles followed geographical contours. Nevins, *Ordeal: Vol. 1,* 29.

"Let us be done with compromises": Kornblith, "Rethinking the Coming of the Civil War," 104.

"Slave states are": Varon, *Disunion!,* 195; see also Mayer, *All on Fire,* 379–80.

"people of the Union"... "Never in my life": Morrison, *Slavery and the American West,* 86, 103. In 1850, Horace Mann, a Massachusetts congressman, insisted, "Better disunion, better a civil or a servile war—better anything that God in his providence shall send than an extension of the boundaries of slavery." Andrew Delbanco, *The War Before the War: Fugitive Slaves and the Struggle for America's Soul from the Revolution to the Civil War* (New York: Penguin, 2018), 209.

"then indeed the day": Remini, *At the Edge of the Precipice,* 55.

counterpart in South Carolina: Nevins, *Ordeal: Vol. 1,* 248–49.

"saving the Union": Freehling, *Road to Disunion, Vol. I,* 481.

"California and Oregon were too distant": William Henry Ellison, *A Self-Governing Dominion, California, 1849–1860* (Berkeley: University of California Press, 1950), 92; see also John S. D. Eisenhower, *Zachary Taylor* (New York: Times Books, 2008), 95–96.

"illiterate frontier colonel": Nevins, *Ordeal: Vol. 1,* 195. The best even Taylor's admirers could say for his intelligence was that there was "something sublime in his...unaffected child-like simplicity." Taylor had spent his life not in law offices or legislative halls but in the woods, building forts and slaughtering Indians.

"an unparalleled degree": Ellison, "Sentiment in California," 27–31.

"to live peaceably": Morrison, *Slavery and the American West,* 99.

"Appeal to the American People": Ellison, "Sentiment in California," 33. See also Anne Woo-Sam, "The State of California," in *Uniting States, Vol. I: Alabama to Kentucky,* Shearer, 140; Nevins, *Ordeal: Vol. 1,* 22–23.

"The Kingdom of God cannot": Howe, *What Hath God Wrought,* 729.

"Gods will be done": Richards, "Texas Moment," 332. For the Deseret proposal, see 335–39.

The Civil War might have begun: See Nevins, *Ordeal: Vol. 1,* 327; W. C. Binkley, "The Question of Texan Jurisdiction in New Mexico Under the United States, 1848–1850," *Southwestern Historical Quarterly* 24, no. 1 (July 1920): 1–38.

The national Baptist and Methodist: Allen Carden, "Religious Schism as a Prelude to the American Civil War: Methodists, Baptists, and Slavery," *Andrews University Seminary Studies* 24, no. 1 (spring 1986): 1–29; Clarence C. Goen, *Broken Churches, Broken Nation: Denominational Schisms and the Coming of the American Civil War* (Macon, GA: Mercer University Press, 1985).

"No one can say": Holman Hamilton, *Prologue to Conflict: The Crisis and Compromise of 1850* (Lexington: University of Kentucky Press, 1964), 41. Lewis Cass, a Michigan senator, quipped that congressmen spoke as "flippantly of breaking up this Union as we talk about dividing a township." Delbanco, *War Before the War,* 219.

Chapter Eight. *Wide Awake*

"If we have suffered": *The Slaveholding Class Dominant in the Republic: Speech of William H. Seward at Detroit, October 2, 1856* (Washington, DC: Republican Association of Washington, 1857), 13.

"died of compromises": Kenneth M. Stampp, "Lincoln and the Secession Crisis," *Imperiled Union,* 167. The best accounts of the Compromise of 1850 are Hamilton, *Prologue to Conflict;* Fergus M. Bordewich, *America's Great Debate: Henry Clay, Stephen A. Douglas, and the Compromise That Preserved the Union* (New York: Simon & Schuster, 2012); Robert V. Remini, *At the Edge of the Precipice;* Stephen E. Maizlish, *A Strife of Tongues: The Compromise of 1850 and the Ideological Foundations of the American Civil War* (Charlottesville: University of Virginia Press, 2018). See also Delbanco, *War Before the War,* 237–61. "How strong the so-called compromise really was," Delbanco notes, "may be judged by the fact that only four senators voted for all the bills that composed it."

Northern **resistance movement:** LeeAnna Keith, *When It Was Grand: The Radical Republican History of the Civil War* (New York: Hill and Wang, 2020), published as I finished writing this book, offers a useful corrective. "Radicals talked tough—for states' rights, for the local nullification of proslavery federal laws, and in favor of the dissolution of the union," Keith notes on page 4. "They stockpiled armaments, carried weapons on their persons, and used their bodies as weapons. They reveled in war talk, and their militant actions drove the country toward the most destructive war in its history."

"So perish all such": Wilentz, *Rise of American Democracy,* 750.

"pre-emptive counter-revolution": James M. McPherson, *Battle Cry of Freedom: The Civil War Era* (New York: Oxford University Press, 1988), 245.

designed to fail: See Potter, *Impending Crisis,* 131; Paul Finkelman, "The Appeasement of 1850," in *Congress and the Crisis of the 1850s,* ed. Paul Finkelman (Athens: Ohio University Press, 2012), 69. To fugitives and free blacks in the North, the new law presented a dire threat. Fear-stricken, thousands left their settled lives and fled to Canada. Others began arming in self-defense. In Springfield, John Brown formed a black self-defense league and trained its members to shoot slave catchers on sight. A black activist (and Kentucky-born runaway) named Lewis Hayden turned his Boston home, a known refuge for fugitives, into a fortress, and vowed to open fire on any suspicious stranger who approached. Varon, *Disunion!,* 237; Mayer, *All on Fire,* 410.

no time for constitutional niceties: As Henry Adams wrote: "Whenever a question arose of extending or protecting slavery, the slave-holders became friends of centralized power, and used that dangerous weapon with a kind of frenzy. Between the slave power and states' rights there was no necessary connection." Only one prominent Southern politician recognized the inconsistency and opposed the Fugitive Slave Act on the grounds of states' rights: Robert Barnwell Rhett, the South Carolina secessionist. To him, the need for such intrusive legislation to guarantee the performance of a basic constitutional obligation only further proved that the Constitution was "gone, gone forever," and that the Union would "soon come to an end." Adams, *John Randolph,* 273; Matthew Karp, *This Vast Southern Empire: Slaveholders at the Helm of American Foreign Policy* (Cambridge, MA: Harvard University Press, 2016), 5.

Vermont's legislature extended: Horace K. Houston Jr., "Another Nullification Crisis: Vermont's 1850 Habeas Corpus Law," *New England Quarterly* 77, no. 2 (June 2004): 252–72.

"denounced, resisted" ... "the most noble deed": Mayer, *All on Fire,* 406–11. The Minkins episode taught Boston authorities to be hypervigilant when, two months later, a bricklayer from Savannah, Thomas Sims, was snatched up. Taking no chances, officials hired street thugs as extra security and wrapped the building where Sims was being held in chains—a symbol of the bonds holding millions in slavery and the Union together. Watching the elderly chief justice of the state supreme court duck under the chains to enter the building, William Lloyd Garrison called the sight "one of the most disgraceful scenes ever witnessed in this city." Three hundred saber-wielding policemen cleared a path through a swell of angry protesters as the twenty-three year-old Sims, sobbing, was taken aboard a naval warship and back to bondage in Georgia.

"would not remain one day": Hahn, *Nation Without Borders,* 180; Stanley Harrold, *Border War: Fighting Over Slavery Before the Civil War* (Chapel Hill: University of North Carolina Press, 2010), 154.

"We have had enough": Varon, *Disunion!,* 229. "If the Union be in any way dependent on an act so revolting in every regard," Charles Sumner said of the fugitive slave law, "then it ought not to exist." Delbanco, *War Before the War,* 8.

"odious and hurtful": *The Complete Works of Ralph Waldo Emerson, Vol. XI* (Boston: Houghton, Mifflin, 1906), 217.

"filthy enactment was made": *Selections from Ralph Waldo Emerson,* ed. Stephen E. Whicher (Boston: Houghton Mifflin, 1957), 35–55.

"The Union is at an end": *Complete Works of Emerson,* 206. In an 1854 speech denouncing Daniel Webster, who supported the Fugitive Slave Act, as a traitor to New England, Emerson explained the deeper lesson of the senator's betrayal. "No forms, neither constitutions, nor laws, nor covenants, nor churches, nor Bibles, are of any use in themselves," he said. "The Devil nestles comfortably into them all."

"We went to bed": Varon, *Disunion!,* 241. After Burns returned to Virginia, black Bostonians raised money to purchase him. He studied at Oberlin College and moved to Canada to serve as a Baptist minister.

"the State Rights of the North": Adam Freedman, *A Less Perfect Union: The Case for States' Rights* (New York: Broadside, 2015), 79.

"There was not a cloud": Thomas D. Morris, *Free Men All: The Personal Liberty Laws of the North, 1780–1861* (Baltimore: Johns Hopkins University Press, 1974), 166.

Early that year, Stephen Douglas: A canny politician, Douglas knew overturning the Missouri Compromise would be politically dangerous. As he himself noted in 1849, the arrangement had become "canonized in the hearts of the American people as a sacred thing which no ruthless hand would ever be reckless enough to disturb." Five years later, pressured by Southerners, that hand would be his own. Potter, *Impending Crisis,* 156.

"a gross violation": *Great Issues in American History, Vol. 1, 1765–1865: A Documentary Record,* ed. Richard Hofstadter (New York: Vintage, 1958), 354–59.

traveled home to Chicago: Potter, *Impending Crisis,* 165.

one tenet that united many: Not all: Abraham Lincoln believed that the law, though vile, ought to be respected as long as it was on the books. He remained aloof from the party for nearly two years after it was founded. When he finally joined, he didn't give up this position, leaving him somewhat alienated from the party's core membership. Yet this was why he was seen as a moderate choice for the 1860 presidential nomination. Eric Foner, *Free Soil, Free Labor, Free Men: The Ideology of the Republican Party Before the Civil War* (New York: Oxford University Press, 1970), 134.

"invasions of State rights": Varon, *Disunion!*, 263.

In 1854, federal marshals: See Joseph A. Ranney, " 'Suffering the Agonies of Their Righteousness': The Rise and Fall of the States Rights Movement in Wisconsin, 1854–1861," *Wisconsin Magazine of History* 75, no. 2 (winter 1991–1992): 82–116; Morris, *Free Men All*, 173.

"Glory, hallelujah!": Daniel Wait Howe, *Political History of Secession to the Beginning of the American Civil War* (New York: G. P. Putnam's Sons, 1914), 229–30.

"wicked and cruel"... "the reasoning of Mr. Calhoun": Foner, *Free Soil*, 135.

"not worth the paper": Ranney, " 'Suffering the Agonies,' " 104. Schurz wrote in his memoir about the Milwaukee speech: "Here was a striking illustration of the proneness of the human mind to permit itself to be swayed in its logic, its course of reasoning, its philosophical deductions, even in its views of historic events, by moral sentiments, by sympathetic emotions, and by party spirit....All these things co-operated in bringing about a contest in which the Republican party, the natural opponent of the States' rights doctrine...planted itself upon extreme States' rights ground and went to the very verge of actual nullification....It was one of those struggles which, as Mr. Lincoln once said, become so mixed that, in the heat of the wrestle, the combatants worked themselves into one another's coats." *The Reminiscences of Carl Schurz*, Vol. II (London: John Murray, 1909), 113–14.

"lessons in Southern jurisprudence": Forrest McDonald, *States' Rights and the Union: Imperium in Imperio, 1776–1876* (Lawrence: University Press of Kansas, 2000), 174.

"rights of the several States"... "Liberty first and Union afterwards": Foner, *Free Soil*, 136, 140.

"in the last resort": McDonald, *States' Rights and the Union*, 175.

a warship sailed for Cleveland: *History of the Oberlin-Wellington Rescue*, ed. Jacob R. Shepherd (Boston: John P. Jewett, 1859), 111–12.

"peace-loving, art-developing": Robert C. Williams, *Horace Greeley: Champion of American Freedom* (New York: New York University Press, 2006), 215. Many Northerners resented sectional domination far more than they hated actual bondage. Josiah Quincy, a proud New Englander, former mayor of Boston, and ex-president of Harvard, candidly admitted, "My heart has always been much more affected by the slavery to which the Free States have been subjected, than with that of the Negro." Matthew Mason, *Slavery and Politics in the Early American Republic* (Chapel Hill: University of North Carolina Press, 2006), 58.

"let the Union slide": James G. Hollandsworth Jr., *Pretense of Glory: The Life of General Nathaniel P. Banks* (Baton Rouge: Louisiana State University Press, 1998), 25.

" 'Let it slide' then": Joanne B. Freeman, *The Field of Blood: Violence in Congress and the Road to Civil War* (New York: Farrar, Straus & Giroux, 2018), 206–7.

On July 4, 1854, six hundred: Mayer, *All on Fire*, 444–45; Osborn, "William Lloyd Garrison," 83.

"God give the victory": Hahn, *Nation Without Borders*, 167.

"the unwilling receptacle": Potter, *Impending Crisis*, 200.

"Pro-Slavery Party"... "Abolitionism and Disunionism": Hahn, *Nation Without Borders*, 160; Allan Nevins, *Ordeal of the Union: Vol. 2: A House Dividing, 1852–1857* (New York: Charles Scribner's Sons, 1947), 393. See also Morrison, *Slavery and the American West*, 260–65.

"If Ohio had done to Kentucky": Mayer, *All on Fire*, 447.

"If the settlers in Kansas": Morrison, *Slavery and the American West*, 165.

"Give us the weapons": Harrold, *Border War,* 166. While free-state leader Charles Robinson was an abolitionist, most Northerners in Kansas wanted to ban free *and* enslaved
blacks from the territory. "I kem to Kansas to live in a free state," one minister
insisted, "and I don't want niggers a trampin' over my grave." Potter, *Impending Crisis,* 203.

Sack of Lawrence: Mayer, *All on Fire,* 453, 477; Harrold, *Border War,* 169–71.

"produced an excitement": Kenneth M. Stampp, *America in 1857: A Nation on the Brink*
(New York: Oxford University Press, 1992), 11.

"Has it come to this": Mayer, *All on Fire,* 452–53.

"Suppose we raise soldiers": Len Gougeon, *Virtue's Hero: Emerson, Antislavery, and Reform*
(Athens: University of Georgia Press, 2010), 222.

"glad to see that the terror": *Complete Works of Emerson,* 262.

"Who now needs any more": Varon, *Disunion!,* 271.

"When Good and Evil": Wilentz, *Rise of American Democracy,* 700.

"grand and appalling issue": Potter, *Impending Crisis,* 263–64. Southerners were threatening to secede if the Republicans won the 1856 election. A Frémont presidency
"would be the end of the Union, and ought to be," Robert Toombs of Georgia
declared. Preston Brooks, Charles Sumner's assailant, called on Southerners in the
capital to seize "the treasury and archives of the government" if Frémont won. James
Mason called for "immediate, absolute, eternal separation." The *Richmond Examiner*
was "sure as the sun ever shone over her beautiful fields" that Virginia would "treat
the election of an Abolition candidate as a breach of the Treaty of 1789, and a release
of every sovereign State in the South from all part and lot in its stipulations." Henry
Wise of Virginia called on fellow Southern governors to cooperate in case the Republicans won—an outcome he called "an overt act and declaration of war." Wise bolstered the state's militia and prepared to raise tens of thousands of troops. "We will
not remain in confederacy with enemies who endanger our peace and safety by
means the most insidious and dangerous," he declared. The initiative met with little
support. Few Southerners expected Frémont to win, and they didn't want to sully the
Democratic cause by openly preparing for civil war. Though Republican papers dismissed Southerners issuing secession threats as "pretenders simply," Kenneth
Stampp argues that "there is good reason to believe that the states which seceded in
1860–61 would have seceded quite as readily in 1856–57 if Frémont had been
elected." Potter, *Impending Crisis,* 262; Morrison, *Slavery and the American West,* 184;
McDonald, *States' Rights and the Union,* 176; Clement Eaton, "Henry A. Wise and the
Virginia Fire Eaters of 1856," *Mississippi Valley Historical Review* 21, no. 4 (March
1935): 501–9; Stampp, *America in 1857,* 8.

"it might only be the beginning": Morrison, *Slavery and the American West,* 185.

"countrymen only in name": Avery O. Craven, *The Coming of the Civil War* (New York:
Charles Scribner's Sons, 1942), 379.

"victorious defeat": Potter, *Impending Crisis,* 265.

A dashing thirty-three-year-old poet: See Tilden G. Edelstein, *Strange Enthusiasm: A Life
of Thomas Wentworth Higginson* (New Haven, CT: Yale University Press, 1968).

"Are you too deeply": Brenda Wineapple, *White Heat: The Friendship of Emily Dickinson and
Thomas Wentworth Higginson* (New York: Anchor, 2009), 4.

"this infernal colorphobia": Stephen B. Oates, *To Purge This Land with Blood: A Biography
of John Brown* (New York: Harper & Row, 1970), 189–90.

"a practical problem": Edelstein, *Strange Enthusiasm,* 193–94, 203. Higginson joked about
spending the last days of 1856 trimming his Christmas tree while, "in the intervals, I
dissolve the Union & write letters to Kansas."

On January 15, 1857: See *Proceedings of the State Disunion Convention, Held at Worcester, Massachusetts, January 15, 1857* (Boston, 1857).

"band of mischievous fanatics": Edelstein, *Strange Enthusiasm,* 197.

"The Lunatics Let Loose": *Liberator,* Feb. 6, 1857.

"In Faneuil Hall, Caleb Cushing": Gannon, "Calculating," 241.

"never was more sure": Edelstein, *Strange Enthusiasm,* 201.

"FREE NORTHERN CONFEDERACY": Jane H. Pease and William H. Pease, "Confrontation and Abolition in the 1850s," *Journal of American History* 58, issue 4 (March 1972): 935.

"national disunion convention": The Panic of 1857 brought disaster to much of the Union. Banks failed, land values plummeted, farms were foreclosed, ships saw little business except taking disappointed immigrants back to their countries of origin. Angry laborers, demanding public assistance, paraded through the streets of New York in what one observer called "a menacing manner." The U.S. Army called out troops to prevent a crowd from breaking into the Custom House and emptying its vaults. "A nightmare broods over society," a concerned Philadelphian wrote. "God alone foresees the history of the next six months."

Given the turmoil—he attributed the "earthquake shock" to "that Vesuvius of crime, that maelstrom of blood, that pandemonium of oppression, the slave system"— Garrison opted to cancel the Cleveland gathering. There would still be an "informal convention," however, so as not to disappoint the locals who had been looking forward to it. Of course, not all locals were. The *Cleveland Herald* (Oct. 29 and 30, 1857, reprinted in *Anti-Slavery Bugle,* Nov. 14, 1857) dismissed the disunionists as a "small band of dyspeptic men and bilious women....restless, diseased spirits." "What heinous crime has this city committed," the paper asked, "that such a convention of cowardly men, unsexed women, and impudent negroes, should gather within its borders?"

Among those "unsexed women" was Susan B. Anthony, who, having taken a job as New York agent for the American Anti-Slavery Society, toured the state trying to "rouse the sleeping consciousness of the North, by persuading audiences "to feel as if you, yourselves, were the slaves." Anthony admired abolitionists like Garrison and Higginson, and thought "the prophecies of these noble men and women will be read with the same wonder and veneration as those of Isaiah and Jeremiah inspire today."

Another woman at the "Dis. Con." in Cleveland, as Anthony called the lightly attended affair, was veteran activist Abby Kelley. Kelley resented both Garrison's last-minute cancellation of the conference and some positive comments he had recently made about the Republican Party. "Ours is a revolution, not a reform," Kelley insisted. "We contemplate the entire destruction of the present National Government and Union. *We must fire up the opposition,* and create such a spirit of resistance that our opponents will be pushed to extremes. The battle must be fought face to face. This is the work we have to do—this the final issue to which we must come at last. Every year brings us nearer to the impending crisis." See Edelstein, *Strange Enthusiasm,* 200; Stampp, *America in 1857,* 219, 227, 236; McDonald, *States' Rights and the Union,* 181; Wilentz, *Rise of American Democracy,* 720; *The Letters of William Lloyd Garrison: Volume IV: From Disunionism to the Brink of War,* ed. Louis Ruchames (Cambridge, MA: Harvard University Press, 1975), 490; *Liberator,* Nov. 6, 1857; Alma Lutz, *Susan B. Anthony: Rebel, Crusader, Humanitarian* (Boston: Beacon Press, 1959), 56–61; Stanley Harrold, *American Abolitionists* (New York: Routledge, 2001), 87; Mayer, *All on Fire,* 492–93.

"From being expounders"..."nothing more than the opinion": Stampp, *America in 1857,* 104–8.

Vermont's legislature: Allan Nevins, *The Emergence of Lincoln, Vol. I: Douglas, Buchanan, and Party Chaos, 1857–1859* (New York: Charles Scribner's Sons, 1950), 114.

"When their interests": Morrison, *Slavery and the American West,* 192.

"not binding, in law or in conscience" … "essentially independent sovereignties": Eric Foner, *The Fiery Trial: Abraham Lincoln and American Slavery* (New York: W. W. Norton, 2011), 94, 134.

"pampered and powerful oligarchy" … "diminish the anti-slavery agitation": Stampp, *America in 1857,* 106–8.

"Let the next President": Nevins, *Emergence, Vol. 1,* 105.

"the only duty the colored man": Vincent Harding, *There Is a River: The Black Struggle for Freedom in America* (San Diego: Harcourt Brace, 1981), 203. In Chicago, four black men awaiting trial for theft petitioned for release since the Supreme Court had ruled that "they were merely chattels and not persons as alleged in the indictment." Lee-Anna Keith, *When It Was Grand: The Radical Republican History of the Civil War* (Hill & Wang, 2020), 62.

"a blow to their friendship": Mayer, *All on Fire,* 371.

"most foul and bloody conspiracy" … "this unholy, unrighteous Union": *Frederick Douglass: Selected Speeches and Writings,* ed. Philip Foner (Chicago: Chicago Review Press, 1999), 77, 140.

"Dissolve the Union": *The Frederick Douglass Papers: Series One, Vol. II,* ed. John W. Blassingame (New Haven, CT: Yale University Press, 1982), 232.

"sick and tired": David W. Blight, *Frederick Douglass' Civil War: Keeping Faith in Jubilee* (Baton Rouge: Louisiana State University Press, 1989), 31–33. Though Blight covered the strange career of Douglass's disunionism extensively in this first book, his recent biography of Douglass says simply that such "rigid doctrines…no longer sufficed in the political climate of the 1850s." For many others, however, including black abolitionists, they did. Blight, *Frederick Douglass: Prophet of Freedom* (New York: Simon & Schuster, 2018), 214.

"roguery somewhere": Mayer, *All on Fire,* 428–30. Two months later, Douglass folded the *North Star* into Smith's own antislavery paper, thereby doubling its subscription base, and named the new organ *Frederick Douglass' Paper.* Douglass later wrote that if he had stayed in New England he "in all probability [would] have remained firm in my disunion views." Nicholas Bromell, "'A 'Voice from the Enslaved': The Origins of Frederick Douglass's Political Philosophy of Democracy," *American Literary History* 23, issue 4 (2011): 707. Also Benjamin Quarles, "The Breach Between Douglass and Garrison," *Journal of Negro History* 23, no. 2 (April 1938), 144–54.

At an 1856 convention… "contempt, loathing": Margaret Hope Bacon, *But One Race: The Life of Robert Purvis* (Albany: SUNY Press, 2007), 125–26, 136.

"a baser slave": William E. Ward, "Charles Lenox Remond: Black Abolitionist, 1838–1873" (PhD diss., Clark University, 1977), 220–26.

"break into a thousand pieces": *The Black Abolitionist Papers: Volume IV: The United States, 1847–1858,* ed. C. Peter Ripley (Chapel Hill: University of North Carolina Press, 1991), 386.

"If the result…must be bloodshed": Ward, "Charles Lenox Remond," 234. Two other black disunionists are worthy of note. In a tract titled *Disunion Our Wisdom and Our Duty,* Charles E. Hodges, a Baptist preacher in Brooklyn and the son of free black Virginians, argued that destroying the existing Union was a necessary first step toward securing that "more perfect" one promised in the Constitution. Uriah Boston, a Poughkeepsie barber—a "scientific hair cutter," as he had it—advocated snipping off the Southern states like so many dead ends. In 1855, Boston wrote a letter to *Frederick Douglass' Paper* explaining partition's many benefits for free blacks. Douglass blasted Boston's position as "unsafe, unsound, and unwarrantable." But Boston wouldn't back down. In another letter, he argued that after disunion the "disgrace" of supporting slavery "would fall upon the guilty parties only." The North would be freed of the burden of "promoting slave interests." Slavery was "a sick thing, kept alive by its connection with the North," the barber observed. "I say cut it loose and let us see what will come of it." See Charles E. Hodges, *Disunion Our Wisdom and Our Duty*, Anti-Slavery Tracts, No. 11 (New York: American Anti-Slavery Society, 1855); Quincy T. Mills, *Cutting Along the Color Line: Black Barbers and Barber Shops in America* (Philadelphia: University of Pennsylvania Press, 2013), 55; Ripley, *Black Abolitionist Papers*, 304–9.

"radically different political systems": *The Life of William H. Seward, Including His Most Famous Speeches, by a Jeffersonian Republican* (Boston: Thayer & Eldridge, 1860), 129. For useful background, see Bruce Chadwick, *1858: Abraham Lincoln, Jefferson Davis, Robert E. Lee, Ulysses S. Grant and the War They Failed to See* (Naperville, IL: Source-books, 2011), 177–208. The subtitle is unfortunate: Everyone saw some kind of conflict coming.

"avowal of a distinct design": Varon, *Disunion!*, 321.

"The South and the North": John M. Murrin, "War, Revolution, and Nation-Making," in *Rethinking America*, 367–68.

"see this Union dissolved": David S. Reynolds, *John Brown, Abolitionist: The Man Who Killed Slavery, Sparked the Civil War, and Seeded Civil Rights* (New York: Vintage, 2006), 151–52.

"expressive of indomitable will": Stampp, *America in 1857*, 150.

"Talk! Talk! Talk!": McPherson, *Battle Cry of Freedom*, 203.

no reason to think...that Brown attended: In his 1968 biography of Higginson, Tilden G. Edelstein states unequivocally that Brown was "present" at the Worcester meeting, "imbibing the radical spirit of the convention." He cites Oswald Garrison Villard's pioneering *John Brown, 1800–1859: A Biography Fifty Years After* (Boston: Houghton Mifflin, 1910) and James C. Malin's *John Brown and the Legend of Fifty-Six* (Philadelphia: American Philosophical Society, 1942). Neither suggests that Brown attended the convention. Ethan J. Kytle, in his book on the transcendentalists and abolitionism, says that "sitting in the hall that day was John Brown." He cites Edelstein. Given what Edelstein rightly calls the "path which was to wind from Worcester's City Hall to the engine house at Harpers Ferry," the error is understandable—but it does appear to be an error. Edelstein, *Strange Enthusiasm*, 194, 203; Kytle, *Romantic Reformers and the Antislavery Struggle in the Civil War Era* (New York: Cambridge University Press, 2014), 226.

"the best Disunion champion": Reynolds, *John Brown*, 242, 333. This better reflected what Sanborn thought Higginson wanted to hear than Brown's intentions. Though he drew up a "Provisional Constitution" to govern the freedom fighters and emancipated slaves he planned to assemble in the Appalachians after seizing weapons from Harpers Ferry, it wasn't a charter for post-revolutionary Virginia or the declaration of an independent nation. Rather, it was likely a more modest document, meant only to last "for the time being"—until the rest of the country ripped out the cancer at its heart. One article disavowed any attempt to overthrow the federal government or dissolve the Union; the revolution would instead take the form of "Amendment and Repeal."

What if Brown's raid: Terry Bisson, *Fire on the Mountain* (New York: Avon, 1988), 80–81.

"The utmost good": See Kytle, *Romantic Reformers*, 230–35.

"I John Brown am now quite certain": Varon, *Disunion!*, 329.

"This will be a great day": McPherson, *Battle Cry of Freedom*, 209–10.

"a free correspondence": Foner, *Free Soil*, 138.

"The murder of Brown": Reynolds, *John Brown,* 409.

"smiling as a bridegroom": Douglas R. Egerton, *Year of Meteors: Stephen Douglas, Abraham Lincoln, and the Election That Brought On the Civil War* (New York: Bloomsbury, 2010), 76–77. Yancey, a stooping, gray-haired Alabaman, had long pushed for secession, helping to lead a failed campaign for Southern independence after the Compromise of 1850. In 1858, Yancey formed a citizens' advocacy group called the League of United Southerners, with chapters throughout the slave states, as a vehicle to pressure politicians to support radical action in defense of Southern rights. The Montgomery chapter of the group proclaimed that with Seward's Rochester speech the Republican Party had declared "a war of extermination—a war to the knife—upon slavery in the States." The South wouldn't shirk from battle but "embark our fortunes on the open sea of disunion, and trusting to the justness of our cause, leave the issue to Heaven." When a sharply worded private letter by Yancey calling on patriotic politicians to "fire the Southern heart" and "precipitate the Cotton States into a revolution" went public, even sympathetic Democratic politicians had to keep their distance from the League, and the group folded. Yancey concluded that to destroy the Union, he first had to destroy the Democratic Party. Its collapse would let loose "a hungrier swarm of flies." In January 1860, Yancey convinced Alabama's state Democratic convention to threaten to walk out of the coming national convention in Charleston if it didn't adopt a platform that included a call for a federal slave code. When an anti-secession delegate accused Yancey of scheming for disunion, he only smiled. See Walther, *Fire-Eaters,* 253; Egerton, *Year of Meteors,* 9, 54.

"It is right that we should part": Paul Starobin, *Madness Rules the Hour: Charleston, 1860 and the Mania for War* (New York: PublicAffairs, 2017), 56.

an unmistakably militant undertone: See Jon Grinspan, "'Young Men for War': The Wide Awakes and Lincoln's 1860 Presidential Campaign," *Journal of American History* 96, no. 2 (Sept. 2009): 357–78. Walt Whitman may have been alluding to the Wide Awakes in his 1860 poem, "To the States": "With gathering murk—with muttering thunder and lambent shoots, we all duly awake / South, north, east, west, inland and seaboard, we will surely awake."

"the thunder mutterings": Kenneth M. Stampp, *And the War Came: The North and the Secession Crisis, 1860–61* (Chicago: University of Chicago Press, 1950), 6.

"to sweep the country": Egerton, *Year of Meteors,* 183.

"young and daring element"…"shoulder their muskets": Grinspan, "'Young Men for War,'" 370, 375.

"a soldier on the side": Craven, *Coming of the Civil War,* 420.

Deprived of New York's electoral votes: My account of this hypothetical scenario, often discussed during the campaign, is based on Si Sheppard, "'Union for the Sake of the Union': The Selection of Joseph Lane as Acting President of the United States, 1861," *Oregon Historical Quarterly* 115, no. 4 (winter 2014): 502–29.

"fly to your relief": Ibid., 521.

"every man in the Free States": Allan Nevins, *The Emergence of Lincoln, Vol. II: Prologue to Civil War, 1859–1861* (New York: Charles Scribner's Sons, 1950), 115; Wendell Phillips, "THE DISSOLUTION OF THE UNION: A PLEA," *New-York Daily Tribune,* March 21, 1860; "Wendell Philips in Brooklyn," *New-York Times,* March 21, 1860, 8.

Chapter Nine. *Going, Going, Gone*

"Whatever happens next": Susan-Mary Grant, *North Over South: Northern Nationalism and American Identity in the Antebellum Era* (Lawrence: University Press of Kansas, 2000), 157.

Late on a spring night: Whitman, *Specimen Days and Collect,* 19–20.

"The Union was a sentiment": Adam Goodheart, *1861: The Civil War Awakening* (New York: Alfred A. Knopf, 2011), 275.

"Cotton is king": Stampp, *America in 1857,* 230; Wilentz, *Rise of American Democracy,* 724–25.

"the position of the South": Bonner, *Mastering America,* 211.

"The Union is doomed": Bordewich, *America's Great Debate,* 203.

"The wild steed": Nevins, *Ordeal: Vol. 1,* 279.

"He is not dead": Peterson, *Great Triumvirate,* 467–68.

"a last sad alternative": Thelma Jennings, *The Nashville Convention: Southern Movement for Unity, 1848–1851* (Memphis: Memphis State University, 1980), 139.

"May her patriotism be": John Barnwell, *Love of Order: South Carolina's First Secession Crisis* (Chapel Hill: University of North Carolina Press, 1982), 168.

"They are generally rabid": Nevins, *Ordeal: Vol. 1,* 370.

"a black State"... "united and prepared": Barnwell, *Love of Order,* 131, 160–62, 166–67, 189.

"A People whose true life": Bonner, *Mastering America,* 180. Hayne was raised in the home of his uncle, Robert Hayne, the Calhoun ally who had debated Webster in 1830.

"single source of all": Stampp, *America in 1857,* 111–12.

"cause enough to justify": Varon, *Disunion!,* 322.

"The electric spark which conveys"... "on the perilous ridge": Nevins, *Emergence, Vol. I,* 408, 414.

"bribed into treachery": McPherson, *Battle Cry of Freedom,* 242.

"nothing more nor less": *Southern Pamphlets on Secession: November 1860–April 1861,* ed. John L. Wakelyn (Chapel Hill: University of North Carolina Press, 1996), 162. In New Orleans, Rev. Benjamin Morgan Palmer offered a sermon on Thanksgiving Day 1861. "If we cannot save the Union," Palmer said, "we may save the blessings it enshrines. If we cannot preserve the vase, we will preserve the precious liquor it contains." Bonner, *Mastering America,* xiii, 147.

pelted with eggs and turnips: Nevins, *Emergence, Vol. II,* 325.

"afraid to trust the second thought": Starobin, *Madness Rules the Hour,* 164.

"I do not believe that the common": Nevins, *Emergence, Vol. II,* 419.

"GOING, GOING, GONE": Mayer, *All on Fire,* 514.

"dissolved in tears"... "It seems strange we should be": Starobin, *Madness Rules the Hour,* 193, 201, 208. Non-slaveholders were thinly represented at the convention and enslaved people not at all. But that had also been the case when the state ratified the Constitution sixty-plus years earlier.

"You may slap a Yankee": Egerton, *Year of Meteors,* 12.

"the slightest danger of war": Nevins, *Emergence, Vol. II,* 413.

"So far as war is concerned": McPherson, *Battle Cry of Freedom,* 238.

"afraid that the blood of the people": Potter, *Impending Crisis,* 501. To others, there seemed little risk of Southerners' blood cooling, at least in early 1861. Judah P. Benjamin of Louisiana called the South's departure from the Union "a revolution...of the most intense character," which could "no more be checked by human effort...than a prairie fire by a gardener's watering pot." McPherson, *Battle Cry of Freedom,* 237.

"blind and suicidal course": Potter, *Impending Crisis,* 475.

"not a bad man"... "scorn and ignominy": Egerton, *Year of Meteors,* 238, 243.

Elections for state conventions: Potter, *Impending Crisis,* 500.

"thoroughly identified with the institution": Wilentz, *Rise of American Democracy,* 774.

Alabama was typical: Nevins, *Emergence, Vol. II,* 324, 424.

"avoid entangling alliances": Bonner, *Mastering America,* 221; Egerton, *Year of Meteors,* 241–42; Edward R. Maher Jr., "Sam Houston and Secession," *Southwestern Historical*

Quarterly 55, no. 4 (April 1952): 448–58; Howard C. Westwood, "President Lincoln's Overture to Sam Houston," *Southwestern Historical Quarterly* 88, no. 2 (Oct. 1984): 125–44.

"Demons of anarchy": Wilentz, *Rise of American Democracy*, 774; William W. Freehling, *The Road to Disunion, Vol. II: Secessionists Triumphant, 1854–1861* (New York: Oxford University Press, 2007), 449.

In Waco, a committee: Nevins, *Emergence, Vol. II,* 427. Houston refused to swear allegiance to the Confederacy and was stripped of his office. Lincoln offered federal troops to help him restore Texas to the Union, but Houston burned the letter. He didn't want to see his country covered in blood. Born during George Washington's first term, Houston died three weeks after the Battle of Gettysburg.

In the seven states: Egerton, *Year of Meteors*, 243.

Forty-seven percent of the population: McPherson, *Battle Cry of Freedom*, 255; Potter, *Impending Crisis*, 505.

a name for their country: E. Merton Coulter, *The Confederate States of America, 1861–1865* (Baton Rouge: Louisiana State University Press, 1950), 58–59.

"At last we are / a nation": Potter, *Impending Crisis*, 500.

"The fact is, the United States Government": Ellison, "Sentiment in California," 44–46. "The prevalence of disunion sentiments among certain classes of the California pioneers in the years before the war would form an interesting topic for a special research," philosopher and historian Josiah P. Royce wrote in 1891. Ellison took up the challenge in the mid-twentieth century, and young scholars like Thomas Richards and Kevin Waite have addressed it in recent years. But the subject remains understudied. If anything the need for such work has only grown more important with the recent resurgence of California separatism. See Royce, *California: From the Conquest to the Second Vigilance Committee in San Francisco* (Boston: Houghton, Mifflin, 1891), 456.

"When the State was admitted" ... "bred up under different": Ellison, "Sentiment in California," 49.

a transcontinental train line: Joseph Ellison, "Designs for a Pacific Republic, 1843–1862," *Oregon Historical Quarterly* 31, no. 4 (Dec. 1930): 326. The Californians' demand for a railroad convinced Stephen Douglas, an early advocate of how trains could unite the country. But in order for a railroad to be built, the territories lying along the likeliest path of a cross-country route had to be organized. That led him to introduce the Kansas-Nebraska Act of 1854, which reignited the still-simmering sectional debate about slavery in the West.

"Why do we not" ... "cut loose from Uncle Sam": Ellison, "Sentiment in California," 62.

"If nature ever marked out": Ellison, "Designs," 330.

the Vigilance Committee: Ellison, "Sentiment in California," 54–61. See also Dorothy Hull, "The Movement in Oregon for the Establishment of a Pacific Coast Republic," *Quarterly of the Oregon Historical Society* 17, no. 3 (Sept. 1916): 187.

mustered as ad hoc militias ... "following the system of West Point": Ellison, "Sentiment in California," 57–61; Ellison, "Designs," 328–30.

America's first civil war: David L. Bigler and Will Bagley, *The Mormon Rebellion: America's First Civil War, 1857–1858* (Norman: University of Oklahoma Press, 2011).

"outlaws and alien enemies": Stampp, *America in 1857*, 200.

"How long, think ye, can such oppression": Nevins, *Emergence, Vol. 1*, 317–18.

"despotic, dangerous": Manscill, "Rumors of Secession," 84–91.

"erect an immense polygamous" ... "Who would not rather die": Stampp, *America in 1857*, 201–5. One of the federal soldiers who marched west was a German immigrant named

Henry Wilcken. He later deserted to the rebels, converted to Mormonism, and became an assistant to Young's successors as president of the Church. Mitt Romney is his great-great-grandson. Another interesting side note: in 1857, an expedition under Lieutenant Joseph Christmas Ives ascended the Colorado River from the Gulf of California to look for a faster way to get men and arms into Utah. Ives's fifty-foot steamboat crashed on a rock near present-day Las Vegas, so he continued on foot into a rough, uncharted region then known only as "The Great Unknown." Ives and his men thus became the first white men to enter the Grand Canyon. Ives called the region "altogether value-less...intended by nature [to] be forever unvisited and undisturbed." Well, not quite. See William P. MacKinnon, "The Utah War and Its Mountain Meadows Massacre: Lessons Learned, Surprises Encountered," *Review of Books on the Book of Mormon 1989–2011* 20, no. 2 (2008): 244–47; "Explorers," Grand Canyon National Park. https://www.nps .gov/grca/learn/historyculture/explorers.htma.

"in the mountains, in the canyons": Nevins, *Emergence, Vol. I,* 320.

"The time must come": Manscill, "Rumors of Secession."

"unanimous vote of uplifted hands": Bigler and Bagley, *Mormon Rebellion,* 139.

Forbidding federal forces: Stampp, *America in 1857,* 204.

In southern Utah, a caravan: MacKinnon, "Utah War," 240–41.

"Virtue, christianity, and decency": Stampp, *America in 1857,* 207.

"on the eve of revolution": Manscill, "Rumors of Secession"; Nevins, *Emergence, Vol. 1,* 323.

"winding up scene"..."firm for the Constitution": John G. Turner, *Brigham Young: Pioneer Prophet* (Cambridge, MA: Harvard University Press, 2012), 272, 317–18. Young remembered that Lincoln hadn't come to the Mormons' aid when Illinoisans turned against them in the early 1840s.

"ties that bound the Pacific": Asbury Harpending, *The Great Diamond Hoax and Other Stirring Incidents in the Life of Asbury Harpending,* ed. James H. Wilkins (San Francisco: James H. Berry, 1913), 30.

In 1859, the state legislature: Ellison, "Designs," 331.

"enterprising and energetic": Ellison, "Sentiment in California," 69. Also Kevin Waite, "The Slave South in the Far West: California, the Pacific, and Proslavery Visions of Empire" (PhD diss., University of Pennsylvania, 2016), 233. In Oregon, the Republicans' narrow victory in the 1860 election obscured a deep vein of pro-Southern feeling. Senator Joseph Lane, the Southern Democrats' vice-presidential candidate and the state's political boss, so effusively praised the South that some thought Oregon would join their new Confederacy. Meanwhile, Isaac Stevens, governor of Washington territory, hoped joining a separate Pacific republic might offer the fastest way out of territorial purgatory. See Keith A. Murray, "The Movement for Statehood in Washington," *Pacific Northwest Quarterly* 32, no. 4 (Oct. 1941), 36–37.

Charles Tyler Botts..."but here upon the shores": Ellison, "Designs," 332–34. The new Pacific nation would be more united than the old, fractured Union, argued Congressman John Chilton Burch: "The people of California and her neighbors are one in interest and feelings; their pursuits and institutions are not incompatible or inconsistent with each other. We must, then, in order to preserve these elements of harmonious action, unite our fortunes; and, if necessity require it, proclaim for ourselves, and those who come after us, freedom and independence; any other course may plunge us into the same vortex which, I fear will soon swallow up the antagonistic interests on this side of the continent." (He was writing from Washington.) In Sonoma, California, site of the original Bear Flag revolt, the *Democrat* issued a rousing call for a sequel. Why should California involve itself in "the general ruin" of a civil war? "She has all the elements of greatness within her borders," the paper observed. "Situated thousands of miles from the distracted states, she would be an asylum of peace and safety in the eyes of the people of the older states, and thousands would flock to her shores, the effect of which must be to build up on the Pacific a mighty, prosperous and independent nation." "Support for a Pacific republic emanated from a minority of Californians," Kevin Waite writes, "but given the political power of some of its keenest champions, it can hardly be considered a fringe position." Waite, "Slave South in the Far West," 234–35.

Without trade rules: Ellison, "Sentiment in California," 85–86.

"A transcontinental railroad would be built": Waite, "Slave South in the Far West," 235.

Bear Flags were seen: See Ellison, "Sentiment in California," 96; Ellison, "Designs," 341; Waite, "Slave South in the Far West," 233.

"Let it never be forgotten": Waite, "Slave South in the Far West," 252.

In San Francisco, a shadowy cabal: Harpending, *Great Diamond Hoax,* 36–38.

The conspirators visited Johnston: Brian McGinty, "I Will Call a Traitor a Traitor: Albert Sidney Johnston in San Francisco," *Civil War Times Illustrated* (June 1981), 24–31. Before he left San Francisco, Johnston moved Union weapons to Alcatraz for safe-keeping and accelerated construction on area forts.

In the end, Albert Sidney Johnston: See Charles Pierce Roland, *Albert Sidney Johnston, Soldier of Three Republics* (Lexington: University Press of Kentucky, 2001), 246–52.

"no power whatsoever": Jean H. Baker, *Affairs of Party: The Political Culture of Northern Democrats in the Mid-Nineteenth Century* (New York: Fordham University Press, 1998), 329.

"An attempt to subjugate": Thomas J. DiLorenzo, "Yankee Confederates: New England Secession Movements Prior to the War Between the States," in *Secession, State, and Liberty,* ed. David Gordon (New York: Transaction, 1998), 152.

"We hope never to live": Thomas N. Bonner, "Horace Greeley and the Secession Movement, 1860–61," *Mississippi Valley Historical Review* 38, no. 3 (Dec. 1951): 434. David M. Potter has persuasively argued that Greeley did not really support letting the South go, but was playing the role of a parent whose child threatens to run away and who offers to pack their bags and drive them to the bus. He wanted to encourage Northerners not to concede to any compromises that would undermine Lincoln's victory. If rejecting compromise meant a cordial, if regrettable, separation rather than a devastating war, his Republican readers would feel less pressure to bargain away the party's platform. While, in theory, accepting partition, Greeley placed so many qualifications on how a state had to go about secession — the process had to be exceedingly slow, executed with the consent of other parties to the compact, and with support from a clear and overwhelming majority of citizens — that it became clear, in practice, he didn't support it at all. Potter, "Horace Greeley and Peaceable Secession," in *The South and the Sectional Conflict* (Baton Rouge: Louisiana State University Press, 1968), 219–42.

A rising young Republican lawyer in Cincinnati: *Diary and Letters of Rutherford Birchard Hayes, Vol. II: 1861–1865,* ed. Charles Richard Williams (Columbus: Ohio State Archaeological and Historical Society, 1922), 2–4.

the Tennessee politician who predicted: Freehling, *Road to Disunion, Vol. II,* 501. "Freedom & Slavery are incompatible and ought not to exist under the same government," a New Yorker wrote his senator, William Seward. The South should therefore be allowed to leave, while those "who voted for Lincoln and freedom, constitute an independent and free Confederacy by ourselves." Egerton, *Year of Meteors,* 247.

"All Union-saving efforts are idiotic": Mayer, *All on Fire,* 516.

"If the Union can only be maintained": McPherson, *Battle Cry of Freedom*, 251. See also Blight, *Frederick Douglass' Civil War*, 59–79.

Nowhere was partition more popular: See Ron Soodalter, "The Day New York Tried to Secede," *HistoryNet*, Oct. 26, 2011. http://www.historynet.com/the-day-new-york-tried-to-secede.htm. Also Cynthia Nicoletti, "The New York City Secession Movement" (master's thesis, University of Virginia, 2004).

"Exclusively to the Southern Trade": William C. Wright, *The Secession Movement in the Middle Atlantic States* (Rutherford, NJ: Fairleigh Dickinson University Press, 1973), 164. Before the Revolution, New York had more slaves per household than any Southern state. Wilentz, *No Property in Man*, 37.

"New York ceases to be": Stampp, *And the War Came*, 7.

"What would New York be": Edwin G. Burrows and Mike Wallace, *Gotham: A History of New York City to 1898* (New York: Oxford University Press, 1998), 865.

"If ever a conflict arises": Soodalter, "Day New York Tried to Secede."

"The Southern trade is reduced": Chuck Leddy, "New York City's Secession Crisis," *Civil War Times* 45, no. 10 (Jan. 2007): 36.

"they will sooner set up": Wright, *Secession Movement*, 179.

"never consent to remain": Sheppard, "'Union for the Sake of the Union,'" 529.

"cut loose from the fanatics": McPherson, *Battle Cry of Freedom*, 247.

Fernando Wood, a notoriously corrupt: For more on Wood, see Burrows and Wallace, *Gotham*, 831–39. Wood's proposal is in Joseph Warren Keifer, *Slavery and Four Years of War: A Political History of Slavery in the United States, Vol. II* (New York: G. P. Putnam's Sons, 1900), 37. See also Samuel Augustus Pleasants, *Fernando Wood of New York* (New York: Columbia University Press, 1948), 114.

"not well-governed nor ill-governed"..."The profits, luxuries": Soodalter, "Day New York Tried to Secede."

Through the *Daily News*: Burrows and Wallace, *Gotham*, 865.

the new republic...called Tri-Insula: Wright, *Secession Movement*, 177–80. Fitzhugh wrote: "Should New York fail to erect herself into a free port and separate republic; should she remain under the dominion of the corrupt, venal wire-workers of Albany, and of the immoral infidel, agrarian, free-love democracy of western New York; should she put herself under the rule of Puritans, the vilest, most selfish, and unprincipled of the human race; should she join a northern confederacy; should she make New England [and] western New York...her masters; should she make enemies of her Southern friends, and deliver herself up to the tender mercies of her Northern enemies, she will sink to rise no more."

rumors spread of an association: Leddy, "New York City's Secession Crisis," 36; Stampp, *And the War Came*, 235.

"I reckon it will be": Daniel W. Crofts, *A Secession Crisis Enigma: William Henry Hurlbert and "The Diary of a Public Man"* (Baton Rouge: Louisiana State University Press, 2010), 231–32.

"There is nothing that can ever": Leddy, "New York City's Secession Crisis," 36. While in New York, Lincoln met with one hundred pro-compromise businessmen who begged him to give the South whatever it asked for. He refused to be swayed. Privately, Lincoln called bankers and cotton traders *"respectable scoundrels"* who had intentionally provoked the market crunch to spook the Republicans into making concessions. "Let them go to work and repair the mischief of their own making," he told a Connecticut lawyer; "and then perhaps they will be less greedy to do the like again." Nevins, *Emergence, Vol. II*, 336.

"a shock electric"..."red business": Walt Whitman, *Drum-Taps: The Complete 1865 Edition*, ed. Lawrence Kramer (New York: New York Review Books, 2015), 3–5.

a **"Central Confederacy":** This phenomenon remains remarkably little analyzed. See Wright, *Secession Movement*, 21–24; "Efforts Made to Establish a Central Confederacy in 1861," *Southern Historical Society Papers* 28 (1900): 144–48.

"You cannot shoot and hang": Baker, *Affairs of Party*, 328.

In December 1860 . . . "Let Delaware preserve": Wright, *Secession Movement*, 34–35, 47, 88.

"make their own arrangements": Freehling, *Road to Disunion, Vol. II*, 500.

"whether Pennsylvania should stand": Wright, *Secession Movement*, 13–14, 156.

"I cannot in justice condemn": McPherson, *Battle Cry of Freedom*, 685.

New Jersey, the tip: Wright, *Secession Movement*, 105–23. While New Jersey Democrats contemplated joining a new Central Confederacy or even the emerging Southern one, the Republican editor of a newspaper in Toms River, on the Jersey Shore, argued that if proslavery compromise measures passed Congress, the people of Ocean County should meet at the village courthouse and announce their separation from both the state and the Union. "We have all the elements of independence," the editor insisted, rather implausibly. "There is no reason why we should not become a great and a happy people. Let us secede."

"leaving out the New England States" . . . New Englanders were "so fanatical": Sheppard, " 'Union for the Sake of the Union,' " 529.

"indulged the hope that the Middle States": Nevins, *Emergence, Vol. II*, 387.

Why not annex Canada: Robin W. Winks, *The Civil War Years: Canada and the United States* (Montreal: McGill–Queen's University Press, 1998), 27–29.

to rule over "a divided empire": Maury Klein, *Days of Defiance: Sumter, Secession, and the Coming of the Civil War* (New York: Vintage, 1997), 268. Several papers, including the *New York Times*, endorsed buying Canada from Britain. Horace Greeley, Salmon P. Chase (about to become Lincoln's treasury secretary), and John Andrews, governor of Massachusetts, also supported it. In London, the idea won over future prime minister William Gladstone, then chancellor of the exchequer, and the *Economist*, which argued, in classic form, that selling Canada would allow Britain to cut military spending.

"I know your little South Carolina": Elizabeth Brown Pryor, *Six Encounters With Lincoln: A President Confronts Democracy and Its Demons* (New York: Viking, 2017), 22.

A week before the 1860 election: Scott's memo is printed in Edward Davis Townsend, *Anecdotes of the Civil War in the United States* (New York: D. Appleton, 1884), 249–53. See also John S. D. Eisenhower, *Agent of Destiny: The Life and Times of General Winfield Scott* (Norman: University of Oklahoma Press, 1997), 346.

Clement L. Vallandigham . . . Republicans pounced: Frank L. Klement, *The Limits of Dissent: Clement L. Vallandigham and the Civil War* (Lexington: University Press of Kentucky, 1970), 53–56. A New York law professor named William B. Wedgewood proposed breaking the Union into "two, three, or four republics," then calling a convention to reorganize them into a new, looser "Democratic Empire." See Jennifer L. Weber, *Copperheads: The Rise and Fall of Lincoln's Opponents in the North* (New York: Oxford University Press, 2006), 35–36.

"I begin to recognize" . . . "It cannot be denied": Klein, *Days of Defiance*, 305, 340.

"Whenever you are beaten" . . . "Instead of healing": Stampp, *And the War Came*, 144, 152. Carl Schurz, the leader of Wisconsin's German community, surveyed public opinion as he traveled through Pennsylvania, New York, and New England, en route to Lincoln's inauguration. While support for submission was strong among businessmen in large cities, Schurz claimed he couldn't find a single Republican in the countryside who favored yielding to Southern blackmail.

"It is *their right*": McPherson, *Battle Cry of Freedom*, 249; Foner, *Fiery Trial*, 146.

"flaming tirades against disunion": Stampp, *And the War Came*, 69.

Owen Lovejoy, an outspoken: *His Brother's Blood: Speeches and Writings, 1838–1864*, eds. William F. Moore and Jane Ann Moore (Urbana: University of Illinois Press, 2004), 258–60. Two years earlier, Lovejoy had proudly admitted on the House floor that he helped fugitive slaves escape to freedom; he then gave his home address so they would know where to find him. Daniel W. Crofts, *Lincoln and the Politics of Slavery: The Other Thirteenth Amendment and the Struggle to Save the Union* (Chapel Hill: University of North Carolina Press, 2016), 188.

"If we must have a civil war": Egerton, *Year of Meteors*, 293. Northerners were "heartily tired of having this threat stare us in the face evermore," an Indianapolis paper sighed. "If nothing but blood will prevent it, let it flow....We never have been better prepared for such a crisis than now. We most ardently desire that it may come." *Northern Editorials on Secession, Vol. I*, ed. Howard Cecil Perkins (New York: D. Appleton-Century, 1942), 97–98.

"get accustomed to the smell"..."If Major Anderson": Stampp, *And the War Came*, 89, 95. Republicans had every reason to believe their supporters would reject any surrender of the core principle: denying any extension of slavery into the territories. If the party caved, a new antislavery party would likely rise in its place, committed to carrying forward the principles of the one that had betrayed them.

"Stand firm," he wrote: Nevins, *Emergence, Vol. II*, 403. Weeks later, when the tug took the form of Kentucky senator John C. Crittenden's proposal to extend the Missouri Compromise line across the continent—thereby dividing California in two—Lincoln advised friends to oppose the plan. Endorsing Crittenden's idea "would lose us everything we gained in the election," he pointed out, and put the country back "on the high road to a slave empire." Lincoln thought renewing the Missouri Compromise would encourage the South to pursue further imperial conquests below the line, in Central America and the Caribbean. It would prolong the crisis, not end it. Lincoln's letters—along with the disapproval of the Northern public—doomed Crittenden's proposal.

"Disunion by armed force": Ibid., 357. One of his Illinois friends recorded Lincoln's professed belief, during the secession winter, that "far less evil & bloodshed would result from an effort to maintain the Union and the Constitution, than from disruption and the formation of two confederacies." Given the death toll from four years of war, he was surely mistaken. Stampp, *And the War Came*, 189.

"forever worthy of the saving": Abraham Lincoln, *Selected Speeches and Writings* (New York: Vintage, 1992), 99.

"There is a trifling difference": Klein, *Days of Defiance*, 413.

Chapter Ten. *The Great Red River*

"The worst is not only": Whitman, *Specimen Days and Collect*, 23.

"We are now in the midst": *The Secret Eye: The Journal of Ella Gertrude Clanton Thomas, 1848–1889*, ed. Virginia Ingraham Burr (Chapel Hill: University of North Carolina Press, 1990), 185.

"War has converted all": Bonner, *Mastering America*, 215.

"Civil war is actually": Nelson D. Lankford, *Cry Havoc!: The Crooked Road to Civil War, 1861* (New York: Viking, 2007), 232.

"The South's attack has": Baker, *Affairs of Party*, 336.

"When the question is whether": Russell McClintock, *Lincoln and the Decision for War: The Northern Response to Secession* (Chapel Hill: University of North Carolina Press, 2008), 262–65. Dissent hadn't disappeared. It had been driven underground. War had the short-term effect of promoting unity, but it wasn't accomplished without some coercion. In New York, an angry crowd stormed the office of the pro-Southern *Herald*, demanding that it raise the Union flag and change its editorial line. It did both. Another mob tore the Confederate banner from a ship's mast. In Philadelphia, a crowd paraded through the city waving nooses in the air. Goodheart, *1861*, 178; Lankford, *Cry Havoc!*, 179.

the identity of "abolitionist": Foner, *Fiery Trial*, 164.

"Proclaim Liberty throughout": Mayer, *All on Fire*, 518, 525; Stampp, *And the War Came*, 293.

"The negro was not": Goodheart, *1861*, 181.

"His Excellency, Jefferson Davis": Emma Lou Thornbrough, *Indiana in the Civil War Era, 1850–1880, Vol. 3* (Indianapolis: Indiana Historical Society, 2016), 115.

"Bodies tied together": Baker, *Affairs of Party*, 151.

"free the negroes and enslave": McPherson, *Battle Cry of Freedom*, 595.

"the negroes where they are": Hahn, *Nation Without Borders*, 257.

"wicked Abolition crusade": McPherson, *Battle Cry of Freedom*, 609.

In 1862, a Philadelphia businessman: [George McHenry], *Why Pennsylvania Should Become One of the Confederate States of America* (London: J. Wilson, 1862). Secession even reached nearly to the Canadian border. In 1861, residents of Town Line, in Erie County, New York, gathered at the local schoolhouse and voted 85 to 40 to secede from the Union. It has never been clear why they did this. One theory holds that many were recent German immigrants who, having seen war and revolution firsthand (in 1848), didn't want to see it again. At the time, a Buffalo paper called the vote a "very large" joke. The story was largely forgotten until 1946, when a local reporter mischievously noted that the town had never officially rejoined the Union. When some residents refused to withdraw the eighty-five-year-old motion, others appealed to a higher power: Harry Truman. The president played along, and urged the town to revoke the secession ordinance. At a ceremonial gathering in the old schoolhouse (by then a blacksmith shop), it did. Until 2011, Town Line firefighters continued to wear patches on their sleeves showing emblems of the Union and Confederate flags, along with the words "Last of the Rebels." For more on this strange tale, see "WNY Hamlet Seceded from Union During Civil War," News10-WHEC (Aug. 16, 2017), http://www.whec.com/news/western-new-york-union-seceded-civil-war-confederate/4576340/; Daniel Robison, "N.Y. Town Still Uncertain Why It Left The Union," NPR, *All Things Considered*, Oct. 14, 2011. https://www.npr.org/2011/10/14/141362876/n-y-town-still-uncertain-why-it-left-the-union. In 2017, Town Line native Daren Wang published a novel, *The Hidden Light of Northern Fires*, about the incident.

an insurrection broke out in Manhattan: I have relied on John Strausbaugh, *City of Sedition: The History of New York City During the Civil War* (New York: Grand Central, 2016).

"'fire in the rear'"... "We stand upon a volcano": Weber, *Copperheads*, 76, 81–82.

"To think": Gregory Jones, "Violence on the Home Front: Democracy and Disunity in Southeastern Ohio During the American Civil War," in *Lesser Civil Wars: Civilians Defining War and the Memory of War,* ed. Marsha R. Robinson (Newcastle upon Tyne, UK: Cambridge Scholars, 2012), 67.

a courthouse square in Illinois: Stephen E. Towne, *Surveillance and Spies in the Civil War: Exposing Confederate Conspiracies in America's Heartland* (Athens: Ohio University Press, 2015), 166.

Cairo, Illinois: Weber, *Copperheads*, 28; Matthew E. Stanley, *The Loyal West: Civil War and Reunion in Middle America* (Champaign: University of Illinois Press, 2017), 92.

"to use all the means": Ed Gleeson, *Illinois Rebels: A Civil War Unit History of G Company Fifteenth Tennessee Regiment Volunteer Infantry* (Carmel: Guild Press of Indiana, 1996), 5.

new Confederate state of Jackson: Kenneth M. Stampp, *Indiana Politics During the Civil War* (Indianapolis: Indiana Historical Bureau, 1949), 56.

"Great Brotherhood of the West": Stanley, *Loyal West,* 158.

"the capitalists of New England": Stampp, *Indiana Politics,* 166.

Sixteen Democratic county organizations: Stephen Z. Starr, "Was There a Northwestern Conspiracy?," *Filson Club History Quarterly* 38, no. 4 (Oct. 1964): 338.

"take up arms in the cause": David Williams, *A People's History of the Civil War: Struggles for the Meaning of Freedom* (New York: New Press, 2005), 283.

half a million men: Paul D. Escott, *After Secession: Jefferson Davis and the Failure of Confederate Nationalism* (Baton Rouge: Louisiana State University Press, 1978), 198.

"wicked, inhuman and unholy": McPherson, *Battle Cry of Freedom,* 595.

"wild and wicked dream": Stampp, *Indiana Politics,* 136.

"The fate of the Northwest": Towne, *Surveillance and Spies,* 47. A Confederate officer— British-born adventurer George St. Leger Grenfell, who rampaged through Indiana and Ohio on horse-stealing raids—resigned his place in the Southern army and joined the conspiracy to start a western rebellion. "The North Western states are ripe for revolt," Grenfell observed. "We are on the eve of great events."

Jefferson Davis expected: Weber, *Copperheads,* 81. Robert Handy Smith, an Alabama politician, speculated that the Confederacy could eventually expand to incorporate all the "great Northwestern States, watered by the Mississippi." With a little encouragement they might be "drawn by the strong current of that mighty river" into the new Southern nation. Slaveholders could "grasp the power of empire on this continent and announce to a startled North that it has reached its western limit, and must spread, if spread it can, towards the frozen sea." Bonner, *Mastering America,* 230–31.

"South and West are truly brothers": Bonner, *Mastering America,* 236.

"I am not a Northern"..."the West, the great West": Starr, "Was There a Northwestern Conspiracy?," 326–31, 338; Weber, *Copperheads,* 27; Allen C. Guelzo, *Fateful Lightning: A New History of the Civil War and Reconstruction* (New York: Oxford University Press, 2012).

"War for the Union was abandoned": McPherson, *Battle Cry of Freedom,* 592–95; Starr, "Was There a Northwestern Conspiracy?," 328. Any settlement of the nation's difficulties, Vallandigham argued, should "look only to the welfare, peace, and safety of the white race, without reference to the effect that settlement may have on the African"—a position that commanded widespread support throughout the North, especially in the Midwest.

"King Lincoln" was hell-bent: McPherson, *Battle Cry of Freedom,* 592.

conspiracy to commit treason: See Starr, "Was There a Northwestern Conspiracy?," 337–39; Thomas Fleming, "The Northwest Conspiracy," in *What Ifs?: Of American History,* ed. Robert Cowley (New York: G. P. Putnam's Sons, 2003), 103–25; Frank L. Klement, *Dark Lanterns: Secret Political Societies, Conspiracies, and Treason Trials in the Civil War,* 150–217. As James McPherson notes, Klement downplays the western secession conspiracy even as his own research provides much proof that it was real and had allies in high places. McPherson, *Battle Cry of Freedom,* 782.

"empire of northwestern States": Curtis Hugh Morrow, "Politico-Military Secret Societies of the Northwest," *Social Science* 4, no. 4 (Aug.–Oct. 1929): 467.

conspirators in Chicago and Indianapolis: Ibid., 472. In blockbuster trials of the Indianapolis defendants, four of the accused were sentenced to death. After the war, the Supreme Court ruled their military trials unconstitutional because civilian courts in the area were functioning at the time of their arrest. The case, known as *Ex Parte Milligan,* remains one of the most important wartime civil liberties cases in American history.

"REBELLION IN THE NORTH!!": McPherson, *Battle Cry of Freedom*, 782.

"exceedingly likely": Weber, *Copperheads*, 164.

"These men were weak": Starr, "Was There a Northwestern Conspiracy?," 337. The rail-roads that had finally conquered the Appalachians and connected east and west (replacing the traditional Mississippi-centered trading system) meant that many Midwesterners saw their commercial and political interests as bound up with those of the North more than those of the South.

"into the furnace of war": Bonner, *Mastering America*, 246.

"dangerous usurpation"... "No man has any individual rights": McPherson, *Battle Cry of Freedom*, 430–33. Also Emory M. Thomas, *The Confederate Nation, 1861–1865* (New York: Harper Perennial, 1979), 152–55.

"as long as it is to the interest": Escott, *After Secession*, 200.

"a rich man's war": David Williams, *Bitterly Divided: The South's Inner Civil War* (New York: New Press, 2008), 104.

"The condition of things": Eric Foner, "The South's Inner Civil War," *American Heritage* 40, no. 2 (March 1989).

Western Virginia "suffered more": McPherson, *Battle Cry of Freedom*, 298.

"We can look to Richmond": Lankford, *Cry Havoc!*, 223.

claimed itself as the legitimate state government: David C. Downing, *A South Divided: Portraits of Dissent in the Confederacy* (Nashville: Cumberland House, 2007), 65–84. The state was originally to be called Kanawha, after the local river valley where George Washington had had extensive holdings. Many of West Virginia's founders wanted the new state name to have nothing to do with the one they were leaving behind; those who pushed for West Virginia feared nobody would know what Kanawha meant.

legal scholars and Confederate apologists: See Vasan Kesavan and Michael Stokes Paulsen, "Is West Virginia Unconstitutional?," *California Law Review* 90, no. 2 (March 2002): 291–400; David M. Zimring, "'Secession in Favor of the Constitution': How West Virginia Justified Separate Statehood During the Civil War," *West Virginia History* 3, no. 2 (fall 2009): 23–51.

In 1842, the state legislature: See Barksdale, *Lost State of Franklin*, 178.

"an almost mystical conviction": Downing, *South Divided*, 93.

"fight the Secession leaders": McPherson, *Battle Cry of Freedom*, 304.

"an UNMITIGATED LIAR": Downing, *South Divided*, 95.

"never live in a Southern Confederacy": McPherson, *Battle Cry of Freedom*, 304.

"The whole country is now": Noel C. Fisher, *War at Every Door: Partisan Politics and Guerrilla Violence in East Tennessee, 1860–1869* (Chapel Hill: University of North Carolina Press, 1997), 56. One county actually declared its independence from the Confederacy. After a visit in 1861 by Andrew Johnson to Huntsville, Tennessee, the seat of Scott County, the local court voted to secede and establish a free and independent state. The action had little practical effect, and went unrecognized by the Confederacy or the Union, but of the 560 men from Scott County who fought in the Civil War, all but nineteen sided with the Union. Confederate soldiers and bandits targeted the county in revenge attacks. After the war, the episode lived on in local lore. In 1986, in a marketing ploy meant to play up the area's unique history, Scott County's Board of Commissioners finally voted to ceremonially rejoin Tennessee. See Aaron Astor, "The Switzerland of America," *Disunion* (blog), *New York Times*, June 7, 2011. https://opinionator.blogs.nytimes.com/2011/06/07/the-switzerland-of-america/; Blake Fontenay, "The Curious History of the "Free and Independent State of Scott." https://sos.tn.gov/tsla/tri-star-chronicles-scott-county.

"unionism and traitorism": Downing, *South Divided*, 106–7. After Brownlow's newspaper was suppressed, the editor and other rebels fled into the Smoky Mountains and camped in remote mountain coves. He was later arrested and thrown in jail. After appealing directly to Judah P. Benjamin, the Confederate secretary of state whom Brownlow sneeringly referred to in private as "a little Jew, late of New Orleans," he was released and deported across Union lines. Brownlow became a celebrity orator in the North and published a widely read book in which he called disunion a "wasteful disease" that had eaten away at the vitality of the South. When Andrew Johnson became Lincoln's second vice president in early 1865, Brownlow succeeded his former foe as governor of Union-held Tennessee. See E. Merton Coulter, *William G. Brownlow: Fighting Parson of the Southern Highlands* (Knoxville: University of Tennessee Press, 1999).

a new Union state called Nickajack: Clement Eaton, *History of the Southern Confederacy* (New York: Collier, 1961), 26.

On July 4, 1861: Downing, *South Divided*, 120–21; Williams, *Bitterly Divided*, 47–49.

"Ho ho! Winston secedes": Downing, *South Divided*, 121–23. One Winston County farmer wrote to his son about the slaveowners: "All tha want is to git you...to fight for their infurnal negroes and after you do their fightin' you may kiss their hine parts for o tha care." Foner, "South's Inner Civil War."

Perhaps the most famous story: I have relied mostly on Victoria E. Bynum, *The Free State of Jones: Mississippi's Longest Civil War* (Chapel Hill: University of North Carolina Press, 1996). See also Rudy H. Leverett, *Legend of the Free States of Jones* (Jackson: University Press of Mississippi, 1984); Sally Jenkins and John Stauffer, *The State of Jones: The Small Southern County That Seceded from the Confederacy* (New York: Anchor, 2010). Unionism in Mississippi was more widespread than Jones County. In March 1864, a state judge reported to Richmond that the state was "in a most deplorable condition, and is rapidly tending to the most deplorable disgrace. Very many of the middle class, a large number of the more intelligent, and nearly all of the lower class of her people are drifting to the Yankees." Escott, *After Secession*, 207.

a "Union man": Downing, *South Divided*, 131–32.

"We are fighting each other": Williams, *Bitterly Divided*, 164. See also Escott, *After Secession*, 196–225.

Too late, Davis proposed: Thomas, *Confederate Nation*, 290–97. "I do not think I love my country well enough to fight with black soldiers," one North Carolina private confided to his mother. Kevin M. Levin, *Searching for Black Confederates: The Civil War's Most Persistent Myth* (Chapel Hill: University of North Carolina Press, 2019), 63.

"settled only": Stampp, "Concept of a Perpetual Union," 36.

"trial by combat"..."an unlawful combination": Cynthia Nicoletti, *Secession on Trial: The Treason Prosecution of Jefferson Davis* (New York: Cambridge University Press, 2017), 84–120.

In a one-paragraph aside: For the background on *Texas v. White*, see ibid., 313–26.

"This court is bound to know"..."It failed to sort out": Ibid., 318, 322. The author of the dissent, Justice Robert Grier of Pennsylvania, opposed Reconstruction and had voted with the majority in *Dred Scott*.

"Secession may be laudable": John Stuart Mill, "The Contest in America," *Fraser's Magazine for Town and Country* 35, no. 2 (Feb. 1862): 265.

"settled at Appomattox": The legal commentator Eugene Volokh made this point in an astute 2010 blog post. "If in 2065 Alaska, California, Hawaii, or Texas...assert a right to secede," Volokh wrote, "the argument that 'in 1865, the victorious Union government concluded that no state has a right to secede in opposition to the wishes of the

Union, so therefore you lack such a right' will have precisely the weight that the Americans of 2065 will choose to give it—which should be very little." Eugene Volokh, "The Supposed Settling of the Question of 'Secession' at Appomattox," *The Volokh Conspiracy*, Feb. 10, 2010. http://volokh.com/2010/02/10/the-supposed-settling -of-the-question-of-secession-at-appomattox/.

Chapter Eleven. *The War Was Fought in Vain*

nothing to do with the war: Kersh, *Dreams of a More Perfect Union*, 228–29.

"When the armies were disbanded": Gregory P. Downs, "The Mexicanization of American Politics: The United States' Transnational Path from Civil War to Stabilization," *American Historical Review* 117, no. 2 (April 2012), 405.

"great, red river": Bonner, *Mastering America*, 241.

"something incomparably better": Varon, *Disunion!*, 344.

"a government so broad": Kersh, *Dreams of a More Perfect Union*, 212.

"canker'd, crude, superstitious": Walt Whitman, "Democratic Vistas," *Specimen Days and Collect*, 238, 245–46.

A Union torn apart: See Mark Wahlgren Summers, *A Dangerous Stir: Fear, Paranoia, and the Making of Reconstruction* (Chapel Hill: University of North Carolina Press, 2009), and William A. Russ Jr., "Was There Danger of a Second Civil War During Reconstruction?," *Mississippi Valley Historical Review* 25, no. 1 (June 1938).

"The First Southern War": Nicoletti, *Secession on Trial*, 2.

Republicans who had dismissed secession: Thaddeus Stevens of Pennsylvania, a leader of the Radical Republicans, offered to serve as Jefferson Davis's counsel if his case came before a federal court, in order to prove that the states had in fact seceded. Ibid., 9–10.

"All is wrong": Foner, "South's Inner Civil War," 222.

"most radical hour": Rogers Smith quoted in Kersh, *Dreams of a More Perfect Union*, 212.

"*Radical Distructionists*"..."The Black Republicans plunged": Summers, *Dangerous Stir*, 86, 98, 100, 104, 110, 156. To Johnson's closest ally in the Cabinet, naval secretary Gideon Welles, the Republican policy of excluding the Southern states promoted "disunion, dismemberment, alienation, and is extreme partyism rather than patriotism." The very party that had waged war against secession, Welles charged, now wanted to "divide the Union" and plunge the country "into a more wicked rebellion...than that from which we have emerged." With the imposition of military rule in the South, an Ohio editor declared, the old Union was "completely dissolved."

"We are to have another war"..."a triumph of treason": Noel C. Fisher, *War at Every Door: Partisan Politics and Guerrilla Violence in East Tennessee, 1860–1869* (Chapel Hill: University of North Carolina Press, 2001), 112, 169.

"trained men, of the late Confederate army"...A Confederate veteran: Summers, *Dangerous Stir*, 112, 154, 195.

"surrender his office to a usurper": Russ, "Was There Danger," 47.

"might have made myself Dictator"..."more volcanic danger": Summers, *Dangerous Stir*, 108, 113, 116, 142, 211, 213.

the House finally impeached Johnson: Brenda Wineapple, *The Impeachers: The Trial of Andrew Johnson and the Dream of a Just Nation* (New York: Random House, 2019).

"*ballots or bullets*": Russ, "Was There Danger," 41.

"We are in the midst": Summers, *Dangerous Stir*, 176.

"WAR! WAR!! WAR!!"..."Well, We have been through": Russ, "Was There Danger," 53.

"*good sense of the army*"..."would have resulted either": Summers, *Dangerous Stir*, 207, 222.

"Seymour was opposed": Wineapple, *Impeachers*, 405.

"Union Saving Grant": Kersh, *Dreams of a More Perfect Union*, 210.

One morning in June 1865: Walther, *Fire-Eaters*, 228–30.

At annual celebrations: Melia Robinson, "The American Confederacy Is Still Alive in a Small Brazilian City Called Americana," *Business Insider*, June 8, 2015. https://www .businessinsider.com/american-confederacy-is-still-alive-in-brazilian-city -americana-2015-6. See also Gerald Horne, *The Deepest South: The United States, Brazil, and the African Slave Trade* (New York: New York University Press, 2007).

Others ended up in London: Alvy L. King, "Wigfall, Louis Trezevant," Handbook of Texas Online, http://www.tshaonline.org/handbook/online/articles/fwi04.

"paralyze the old government": Russ, "Was There Danger," 39.

"the wisest, noblest, and grandest"...After spending time in postwar Georgia: Kersh, *Dreams of a More Perfect Union*, 204, 220. Gertrude Thomas, the wife of a Georgia planter, wrote in a May 1865 diary entry: "The war is over and again we become a part of the United States—how united will depend alone upon treatment we receive from the hands of the North.... Treated as members of one family—a band of brothers, in time we may have a common interest—but pressed too hard upon, our property taken from us—a desperate people having nothing to lose, the South may again revolt."

"dead letters": Eric Foner, *Reconstruction: America's Unfinished Revolution, 1863–1877* (New York: Harper & Row, 1988), 261–63, 590. Amos T. Akerman, a Southern Republican who served as Grant's attorney general, observed that while the new amendments had made the Union "more national in theory," it was not yet national in fact. "Unless the people become used to the exercise of these powers now, while the national spirit is still warm with the glow of the late war," Akerman argued, "the 'state rights' spirit may grow troublesome again." And so it did. Akerman used the robust powers of the new Department of Justice to prosecute the Klan. He personally led marshals and soldiers into the South Carolina countryside to make hundreds of arrests. Yet his zeal in suppressing white terrorism drew the ire of moderate Republicans and compelled Grant to ask Akerman for his resignation.

the "wholesale slaughter": Russ, "Was There Danger," 39.

"like they thought anything": Summers, *Dangerous Stir*, 251.

"Pray tell me"... "organized civil war": Foner, *Reconstruction*, 443, 454.

"The idea and the expectation"... "whether rebellion is not resurgent": Russ, "Was There Danger," 56–57.

Rival state governments: Downs, "Mexicanization of American Politics," 395.

"It seems that we are drifting": Foner, *Reconstruction*, 444, 454, 458, 524. The most decisive battle in the war of words came over allegations of rampant corruption in black-led Southern governments. An expressly racist propaganda effort painted the reconstructed states as beset by bribery, cronyism, and misgovernment. James S. Pike, the longtime antislavery journalist who, during the Kansas crisis of the 1850s, had filled the pages of the *New York Tribune* with calls for disunion, now argued in a lurid, insinuating book called *The Prostrate State* (1874) that South Carolina was pinned under "a mass of black barbarism...the most ignorant democracy that mankind ever saw." Though Pike's reporting was shoddy and his conclusions exaggerated, the book convinced already-skeptical Northerners that blacks were incapable of self-government and that universal male suffrage had been a mistake—an opinion even Grant embraced, albeit privately, by the end of his second term. (The Fifteenth Amendment, Grant told his cabinet, "had done the Negro no good.") Reports of Southern corruption gave Republicans eager to abandon Reconstruction the cover they needed to begin the gradual process of disengaging the federal presence in the South. See Foner, *Reconstruction*, 525–28; David W. Blight, *Race and Reunion: The Civil War in American Memory* (Cambridge, MA: Harvard University Press, 2001), 138.

In 1873, a financial panic: Foner, *Reconstruction*, 512–13, 525, 537–38, 557–58, 562.

"If war among the whites": Blight, *Frederick Douglass*, 557.

"third-rate non-entity": Foner, *Reconstruction*, 567.

"The air is full of coming trouble": Downs, "Mexicanization of American Politics," 399.

"Tilden or War": Foner, *Reconstruction*, 576.

Rumors circulated that if Hayes…"be put into a position to choose": Downs, "Mexicanization of American Politics," 396–402.

"Why surrender now?": Ibid., 402.

"tired of the Negro": Kevin M. Gannon, "The Civil War as a Settler-Colonial Revolution," *The Age of Revolutions*, Jan. 18, 2016. https://ageofrevolutions.com/2016/01/18/the-civil-war-as-a-settler-colonial-revolution/.

"face thirty years"…"social, and educational": Foner, *Reconstruction*, 556, 590–91.

"devil's compromise": Kersh, *Dreams of a More Perfect Union*, 255.

"Revolutions may go backward": James M. McPherson, *The Struggle for Equality: Abolitionists and the Negro in the Civil War and Reconstruction* (Princeton, NJ: Princeton University Press, 1964), 123.

"a seamless web of oppression": Foner, *Reconstruction*, 598.

"They say, 'One flag, one nation'": Varon, *Disunion!*, 347.

"May God continue the Unity": Simon Winchester, *The Men Who United the States: America's Explorers, Inventors, Eccentrics, and Mavericks, and the Creation of One Nation, Indivisible* (New York: Harper Perennial, 2014), 273.

on the payroll of railroad corporations: In 1862, Republicans passed a bill providing subsidies to private corporations for the construction of a transcontinental route—the price, Californians had always said, for their continued loyalty to the Union. When some in Congress flinched at the cost, its backers said it was necessary to hold the Union together. "What are $75,000,000 or $100,000,000," asked Massachusetts senator Henry Wilson, if the funds were used to "connect the people of the Atlantic and the Pacific? Nothing!" A decade later, it came out that Wilson had benefited handsomely from the largesse of the railroad companies. The intertwined imperatives of perfecting the Union and improving politicians' own wealth—a tradition going back to George Washington and the western lands—was alive and well. See Matthew Josephson, *The Robber Barons: The Great American Capitalists, 1861–1901* (New York: Harcourt, 1962), 78–79.

"an uneasy feeling": Robert M. Fogelson, *America's Armories: Architecture, Society, and Public Order* (Cambridge, MA: Harvard University Press, 1989), 24.

"would not be sectional"…"We have not cured": Downs, "Mexicanization of American Politics," 391, 398.

"The days are over in which": Hahn, *Nation Without Borders*, 416.

"Bread or Blood": Steve Fraser, *The Age of Acquiescence: The Life and Death of American Resistance to Organized Wealth and Power* (New York: Little, Brown, 2015), 109.

"Public opinion is almost everywhere": Foner, *Reconstruction*, 584.

In Chicago, businessmen patrolled: Fraser, *Age of Acquiescence*, 114.

"a great social revolution"…"a great civil war": Fogelson, *America's Armories*, 24–25; Fraser, *Age of Acquiescence*, 115.

By 1880, Chinese made up: Hahn, *Nation Without Borders*, 347.

"Either we must drive out": Edlie L. Wong, *Racial Reconstruction: Black Inclusion, Chinese Exclusion, and the Fictions of Citizenship* (New York: New York University Press, 2015),

124. California didn't ratify the Fourteenth and Fifteenth Amendments until 1959 and 1962, respectively.

"a distinct and separate nationality": Kersh, *Dreams of a More Perfect Union,* 265.

In 1880, a Californian named Pierton W. Dooner: Pierton W. Dooner, *Last Days of the Republic* (San Francisco: Alta California, 1880); see also Wong, *Racial Reconstruction,* 129–37.

"If our government don't protect us": Noel Sargent, "The California Constitutional Convention of 1878–1879," *California Law Review* 6, no. 2 (Jan. 1918): 114–33. Mortified by the renewed talk of California's separation, another delegate expressed astonishment that just a few years after being "put down by force of arms," the doctrine of secession was "still alive, and has its advocates in California and in this Convention."

"'I would draw it'": *Proceedings of the State Disunion Convention,* 16.

an eccentric Boston-born musician: Josiah Warren, *True Civilization An Immediate Necessity and the Last Ground of Hope for Mankind* (Boston: J. Warren, 1863).

"the manufacture and use of explosives"...The United States was "not big enough": Fogelson, *America's Armories,* 22, 27.

the "soldiers of 1861": Patrick J. Kelly, "The Election of 1896 and the Restructuring of Civil War Memory," *Civil War History* 49, no. 3 (Sept. 2003): 271.

"blow down the beautiful arch": Hahn, *Nation Without Borders,* 486.

A satirist rhymed: Heather Cox Richardson, *West from Appomattox: The Reconstruction of America After the Civil War* (New Haven, CT: Yale University Press, 2007), 295.

fortress-style armories: Fogelson, *America's Armories,* 20–21, 47; Fraser, *Age of Acquiescence,* 116.

"There's nothing united about these States": Grandin, *End of the Myth,* 125.

"We can discover no extrication": Russ, "Was There Danger," 57.

This "new sectionalism": Frederick Emory Haynes, "The New Sectionalism," *Quarterly Journal of Economics* 10, no. 3 (April 1896): 269–95.

"a nation brought to the verge": Hahn, *Nation Without Borders,* 437.

"We as a nation are dividing"..."rebellious effort to overthrow": Fogelson, *America's Armories,* 24, 31–32.

"The rich, as a class"..."to weld the nation into unity": Herbert Newton Casson, *The Red Light* (Lynn, MA: Lynn Labor Church Press, 1898), 9, 65. Casson believed the arc of history was bending toward unity, even world government. "The old gray cloud of secession and competition is being everywhere driven back by the blue morning of union and co-operation, and the human race is slowly but irresistibly evolving into a perfect brotherhood," he wrote. Ten years earlier, Edward Bellamy had published *Looking Backward,* a utopian novel imagining how by the year 2000 the United States had managed to overcome its racial, class, and regional divisions and achieve the perfect society. The states had been abolished, Bellamy relates, because "state governments would have interfered with the control and discipline of the industrial army." The Pledge of Allegiance, which introduced the phrase "one nation indivisible," was written in 1892 by Bellamy's cousin, Francis, a socialist. See Freedman, *Less Perfect Union,* 99.

"bragged that they would delight": "After the Election—What?," *Twentieth Century* 13, no. 19 (Nov. 8, 1894): 5–6.

"the possibility of the formation": "Editorial Comment," *Bankers' Magazine* 52, no. 5 (May 1896): 574. The journal's name suggests it wasn't exactly a bastion of Populist sentiment.

"How did we recover our liberty?": See Stephen Kantrowitz, *Ben Tillman and the Reconstruction of White Supremacy* (Chapel Hill: University of North Carolina Press, 2000).

"I come to you from the South": Michael Kazin, *A Godly Hero: The Life of William Jennings Bryan* (New York: Anchor, 2007), 56–57. Tillman lost his left eye to a brain tumor as a teenager. The illness, operation, and recovery kept him out of the Confederate army near the end of the Civil War.

"not the platform of section"... "revolution against the United States": Kelly, "Election of 1896," 255–56, 262–65; Fogelson, *America's Armories,* 27.

"plotting a social revolution": Michael A. Bellesiles, *1877: America's Year of Living Violently* (New York: New Press, 2010), 77.

Chapter Twelve. *Divided We Stand*

John Dos Passos: *The Big Money: Volume Three of the U.S.A. Trilogy* (Boston: Houghton Mifflin Harcourt, 2013), 371.

Civil War centennial commissions: See Justin Worland, "This Is Why South Carolina Raised the Confederate Flag in the First Place," *Time,* June 22, 2015. http://time.com/3930464/south-carolina-confederate-flag-1962/; Maurice Isserman and Michael Kazin, *America Divided: The Civil War of the 1960s* (New York: Oxford University Press, 2000), 1–3; Michael J. Cook, *Troubled Commemoration: The American Civil War Centennial, 1961–1965* (Baton Rouge: Louisiana State University Press, 2007).

"I am proud of the job": Kevin M. Levin, "Will South Carolina Spend Millions on a Fake Flag?," *Daily Beast,* Dec. 25, 2015. https://www.thedailybeast.com/will-south-carolina-spend-millions-on-a-fake-flag.

In January 1915, a deputy sheriff: See James A. Sandos, "The Plan of San Diego: War and Diplomacy on the Texas Border, 1915–1916," *Arizona and the West* 14 (spring 1972); Charles H. Harris III and Louis R. Sadler, "The Plan of San Diego and the Mexican–U.S. War Crisis of 1916: A Reexamination," *Hispanic American Historical Review* 58 (Aug. 1978); Benjamin Heber Johnson, *Revolution in Texas: How a Forgotten Rebellion and Its Bloody Suppression Turned Mexicans into Americans* (New Haven, CT: Yale University Press, 2003); Benjamin Heber Johnson, "Unearthing the Hidden Histories of a Borderlands Rebellion," *Journal of South Texas* 24, no. 1 (spring 2011): 6–21; William Hager, "The Plan of San Diego: Unrest on the Texas Border in 1915," *Arizona and the West* 5, no. 4 (winter 1963): 327–36.

Mexico erupted in revolution: See Hahn, *Nation Without Borders,* 502–6.

"a challenge unto death": Hager, "Plan of San Diego," 331. It's still not clear which faction Ramos and his fellow conspirators were working for, but what is certain was that they wanted to stoke an uprising by ethnic Mexicans in the United States—or the threat of such an uprising—to achieve their own sectarian purposes.

For imperial Germany, the turmoil: Friedrich Katz, *The Secret War in Mexico: Europe, the United States, and the Mexican Revolution* (Chicago: University of Chicago Press, 1981).

A doctor named Jesse Moseley: Sandos, "Plan of San Diego," 10–12; Charles H. Harris III and Louis R. Sadler, *The Plan de San Diego: Tejano Rebellion, Mexican Intrigue* (Lincoln: University of Nebraska Press, 2013), 125.

Some thirty cross-border attacks: Johnson, "Unearthing the Hidden Histories," 9–10.

"this section of the country": Johnson, *Revolution in Texas,* 78.

When the U.S. Army: Harris and Sadler, "The Plan of San Diego," 391.

"The cry was often heard": Hahn, *Nation Without Borders,* 513. Greg Grandin, "The Genocidal Unconscious of American Sports' Naming Practices," *The Nation* (Jan. 4, 2016), https://www.thenation.com/article/the-genocidal-unconscious-of-american-sports-naming-practices/.

"a serious surplus population": Johnson, "Unearthing the Hidden Histories," 6–14.

"evaporated": Johnson, *Revolution in Texas,* 118–19. See also Miriam Elizabeth Villanueva, "Oppression and Violence Along the Border: The Plan of San Diego as Reported in 1915 Newspapers," *Journal of South Texas* 24 (spring 2011): 39.

the German foreign minister..."How Zimmermann United": Barbara Tuchman, *The Zimmermann Telegram* (New York: Ballantine, 1966), 15–16, 59, 64, 163, 200; Katz, *Secret War in Mexico.* The Kaiser's advisers also hoped to sway Japan, then fighting with the Allies, to switch sides. America's rival for supremacy in the Pacific, Japan could use Mexico as a base for an invasion of the United States through the Mississippi Valley, thus splitting the Union in half. The prospect of a Japanese attack, the subject of frenzied speculation for many years, captured the attention of an American culture suffused with terror at Yellow Peril phantoms. Newspapers breathlessly reported that German and Japanese troops were massing in Northern Mexico for an imminent invasion across the border. To a few fearful Americans, the threat to the country's territorial integrity might come from the North as well as the South: former secretary of state Elihu Root called for intervening in the world war to prevent Germany from defeating Britain and invading the United States via Canada.

Neutrality became untenable: See Tuchman, *Zimmermann Telegram,* 175–87. It is not the case, as sometimes suggested, that the Mexican government showed no interest in Zimmermann's proposal. In fact, Venustiano Carranza, then Mexico's president, sent an emissary to meet with the German ambassador. The ambassador, in turn, wired back to Berlin asking whether Germany would provide weapons for the proposed invasion. The Mexicans seemed "not in the least reticent" about the idea, the German diplomat reported. An agent of Mexico's defense ministry toured the American Southwest and told his superiors that "the situation is very favorable to us." Stalling for time, Carranza denied to inquiring American diplomats that his government had received, much less entertained, the German proposal. That was a lie. But with border tensions quieting down, Carranza didn't want to invite further American meddling. More for practical than principled reasons, Mexico rejected Zimmermann's offer and remained neutral for the duration of the war. Tuchman, *Zimmermann Telegram,* 171–73, 200; Katz, *Secret War in Mexico,* 363.

summer of 1931: Jerry B. Lincecum, "The Red River Bridge War," in *Folklore in Motion: Texas Travel Lore,* ed. Kenneth L. Untiedt (Denton: University of North Texas Press, 2007), 25–33; Rusty Williams, *The Red River Bridge War: A Texas–Oklahoma Border Battle* (College Station: Texas A&M University Press, 2016). A similar incident occurred around the same time, when Arizona sent National Guard troops to block California from building a dam on the Colorado River. The fight found its way to the Supreme Court, which sided with Arizona. Construction stopped until Congress passed legislation authorizing the dam's construction. See Scott Harrison, "California Retrospective: How a 1930s Water War Between California and Arizona Delayed Parker Dam," *Los Angeles Times,* Aug. 30, 2015.

"a chaos of little states": Lincecum, "Red River Bridge War," 32.

"If this country ever"..."mild species of dictatorship": Ira Katznelson, *Fear Itself: The New Deal and the Origins of Our Time* (New York: Liveright, 2013), 12.

"We're going to draw a line": Robert Lynn Fuller, *Phantom of Fear: The Banking Crisis of 1933* (Jefferson, NC: McFarland, 2012), 108.

"considerable talk...of secession": "Secession Talk Is Being Heard," *Bismarck Tribune,* Jan. 8, 1934.

"Unless something is done": Michael Golay, *America 1933: The Great Depression, Lorena Hickok, Eleanor Roosevelt, and the Shaping of the New Deal* (New York: Free Press, 2013), 20.

"financial oligarchy": Fuller, *Phantom of Fear*, 108; "Martin Resolution Dies in Committee," *Bismarck Tribune*, Feb. 23, 1933.

William "Wild Bill" Langer: James L. Erwin, *Encyclopedia of American Autonomous and Secessionist Movements* (Westport, CT: Greenwood Press, 2007), 129–31; Jerome D. Tweton, "The Politics of Chaos: North Dakota in the 1930s," *Journal of the West* 41, no. 4 (fall 2002): 30–35. Even after Langer's imprisonment, the prairie renegade's career wasn't over. After successfully appealing the charges, Langer won re-election as governor; North Dakotans sent him to the Senate in 1941. In Washington, senators aware of his rebellious past demanded an investigation into their new colleague's patriotism, or lack thereof. Asked about his secession threats, Langer demurred. An investigating committee concluded that he lacked the necessary "moral fitness to be a senator." But the full Senate agreed to admit him. Langer served in the Senate until his death, in 1959.

In the dark months: See Eric Rauchway, *Winter War: Hoover, Roosevelt, and the First Clash Over the New Deal* (New York: Basic Books, 2018).

"For Dictatorship": Jonathan Alter, *The Defining Moment: FDR's Hundred Days and the Triumph of Hope* (New York: Simon & Schuster, 2007), 4–6. In early 1933, William Randolph Hearst produced a film, *Gabriel Over the White House*, approvingly showing a president dissolving Congress and instituting military rule.

abolish the states: Freedman, *Less Perfect Union*, 128.

"mutilation of the Constitution": Sally Denton, *The Plots Against the President: FDR, a Nation in Crisis, and the Rise of the American Right* (New York: Bloomsbury, 2012), 156.

a former Marine general testified: For more on the "business plot," see Jules Archer, *The Plot to Seize the White House: The Shocking True Story of the Conspiracy to Overthrow FDR* (New York: Simon & Schuster, 2015).

massification of American life: Walter Prescott Webb, *Divided We Stand: The Crisis of a Frontierless Democracy* (Austin, TX: Acorn, 1944). The accusation of unequal treatment also went the other way. New Englanders thought their region bore too heavy a burden supporting "a lot of mendicant States in the West and South," as libertarian writer Albert Jay Nock put it. In a 1934 journal entry, Nock wrote that he had "asked several businessmen what actual good New England is getting out of membership in the Union, and they could not think of any, even though they tried hard. As for myself, I can think of none." Nock, however, was hardly a consistent advocate of Yankee nationalism: the only time he ever voted in a presidential election, he cast a write-in ballot for Jefferson Davis—on the principle, as he put it, that "if we can't have a fine man who amounts to anything, by all means let's have a first-class corpse." Albert Jay Nock, *Journal of Forgotten Days* (Hinsdale, IL: Henry Regnery, 1948), 28; Michael Wreszin, *The Superfluous Anarchist: Albert Jay Nock* (Providence: Brown University Press, 1972), 128.

"another land": Katznelson, *Fear Itself*, 15; Charles W. Pipkin, "The Southern Philosophy of States' Rights: The Old Sectionalism and the New Regionalism," *Southwest Review* 19, no. 2 (Jan. 1934): 176; Morris Berman, *Why America Failed: The Roots of Imperial Decline* (Hoboken, NJ: John Wiley & Sons, 2012), 139.

New books and periodicals: Fletcher M. Green, "Resurgent Southern Sectionalism, 1933–1955," *North Carolina Historical Review* 33, no. 2 (April 1956): 226–28.

the first flag flown over Okinawa: Greg Grandin, "What Was the Confederate Flag Doing in Cuba, Vietnam, and Iraq?," *The Nation,* July 7, 2015. https://www.thenation.com /article/what-was-the-confederate-flag-doing-in-cuba-vietnam-and-iraq/.

"the Nation's No. 1": Katznelson, *Fear Itself*, 170, 253.

"another Yankee raid": Donald Davidson, "Where Regionalism and Sectionalism Meet," *Social Forces* 13, no. 1 (Oct. 1934–May 1935): 26; also Davidson, *The Attack on Levia-*

than: Regionalism and Nationalism in the United States (Chapel Hill: University of North Carolina Press, 1938), 114.

a constitutional convention: Davidson, *Attack on Leviathan,* 109, 128. In the 1950s, Davidson founded Tennessee's version of the White Citizens Councils that fought court-ordered desegregation.

a man was castrated: Katznelson, *Fear Itself,* 167.

"Negroes of the North": Ibid., 177.

"World War II unified Americans": John B. Judis, "The Shutdown Standoff Is One of the Worst Crises in American History," *New Republic,* Oct. 2, 2013. https://newrepublic.com/article/114962/shutdown-standoff-one-worst-crises-american-history.

"the great exception": See Jefferson Cowie, *The Great Exception: The New Deal and the Limits of American Politics* (Princeton, NJ: Princeton University Press, 2016), 7.

especially the confinement: Internment wasn't simply an immediate response to emergency. It was based in long-standing fears of Asian immigrants serving as an advance guard for the kind of mass invasion envisioned in Yellow Peril novels like Pierton Dooner's *Last Days of the Republic.* "It's a question of whether the white man lives on the Pacific Coast or the brown man," said the head of one agricultural organization. Michael J. Klarman, *Unfinished Business: Racial Equality in American History* (New York: Oxford University Press, 2007), 143.

"verged on civil war": Gary Gerstle, *American Crucible: Race and Nation in the Twentieth Century* (Princeton, NJ: Princeton University Press, 2001), 203, 214–16. An internal army memo described black soldiers as "well-meaning but irresponsible children" who "cannot be trusted to tell the truth, to execute complicated orders or to act on their own initiative." Black and white blood donations were kept separate.

"Our war is not against Hitler": Klarman, *Unfinished Business,* 131.

"Is there a democracy": Gerstle, *American Crucible,* 212.

Nazi propagandists: Klarman, *Unfinished Business,* 131.

"scare hell out of": Gore Vidal, "The National Security State," in *United States: Essays, 1952–1992* (New York: Broadway, 1993), 1023. David M. Potter quotes the sociologist Frederick Hertz: "War could be called the greatest instrument of national unification, but for the fact that it also fosters the growth of forces which often imply a new menace to national unity." See Potter, "The Historian's Use of Nationalism and Vice Versa," *American Historical Review* 67, no. 4 (July 1962): 936.

strategic performance: See Klarman, *Unfinished Business,* 133–34. In 1946, Dean Acheson, James Byrnes's understudy and successor at the State Department, warned that the "existence of discrimination against minority groups in this country has an adverse effect on our relations with other countries." Ibram X. Kendi, *Stamped from the Beginning,* 352.

Truman embraced civil rights: Joseph E. Lowndes, *From the New Deal to the New Right: Race and the Southern Origins of Modern Conservatism* (New Haven, CT: Yale University Press, 2008), 27. Though he didn't join the Dixiecrats, a young Senate candidate in Texas named Lyndon Johnson opened his campaign by denouncing Truman's civil-rights proposals as "a farce and a sham—an effort to set up a police state in the guise of liberty." Kendi, *Stamped from the Beginning,* 356.

To the white South: See George Lewis, *Massive Resistance: The White Response to the Civil Rights Movement* (London: Hodder Arnold, 2006); Brent J. Aucoin, "The Southern Manifesto and Southern Opposition to Desegregation," *Arkansas Historical Quarterly* 55, no. 2 (summer 1996).

"abolished the Mason Dixon line": Klarman, *Unfinished Business,* 164.

"the States inevitably will be": Lewis, *Massive Resistance,* 63.

"**far beyond...the Mason-Dixon Line**": Lowndes, *From the New Deal to the New Right*, 41.

"**null, void, and of no effect**": Aucoin, "Southern Manifesto," 183.

"**damned near a declaration**": Rick Perlstein, *Before the Storm: Barry Goldwater and the Unmaking of the American Consensus* (New York: Hill & Wang, 2001), 14.

In 1956, three Southern senators: Lewis, *Massive Resistance*, 65–68.

"**You would think today Calhoun**": Aucoin, "Southern Manifesto," 175.

"**What that war should**": William Faulkner, "Letter to a Northern Editor," *Life*, March 5, 1956.

"**a return to the spirit of '61**": Lowndes, *From the New Deal to the New Right*, 67.

Warned by Southern friends: Lewis, *Massive Resistance*, 86–87.

"**you cannot change people's**": Numan V. Bartley, "Looking Back at Little Rock," *Arkansas Historical Quarterly* 66, no. 2 (summer 2007): 122. Before the Court handed down its decision, Eisenhower told Chief Justice Earl Warren that he sympathized with whites concerned to ensure that "their sweet little girls are not required to sit in school alongside some big black buck." Kendi, *Stamped from the Beginning*, 361.

"**Our enemies are gloating**": Kendi, *Stamped from the Beginning*, 367.

"**most severe test**": Taylor Branch, *Parting the Waters: America in the King Years 1954–63* (New York: Simon & Schuster, 2007), 223.

"**Remember Little Rock**": Lewis, *Massive Resistance*, 88.

"**Captive Nations Week**": Lee Edwards, "Captive Nations Week," *Heritage Foundation*, July 20, 2005. https://www.heritage.org/asia/commentary/captive-nations-week.

The Civil War of the 1960s: I owe the title of this section to the subtitle of the 1999 book *America Divided*, by Maurice Isserman and Michael Kazin.

Abraham Lincoln received a letter: Abraham Lincoln Papers: Series 1. General Correspondence. Orville H. Browning to Abraham Lincoln, April 30, 1861. Retrieved from the Library of Congress, www.loc.gov/item/mal0949600/; see also Goodheart, *1861*, 319.

"**bewildered and dazzled**": David Herbert Donald, *We Are Lincoln Men: Abraham Lincoln and His Friends* (New York: Simon & Schuster, 2007), 113.

"**a nation within a nation**": Susan Campbell, "'Black Bolsheviks' and Recognition of African-America's Right to Self-Determination by the Communist Party USA," *Science & Society* 58, no. 4 (winter 1994–1995): 450.

Harry Haywood, a Nebraska-born: Raymond L. Hall, *Black Separatism in the United States* (Hanover, NH: University Press of New England, 1978), 75–94; Harry Haywood, *Black Bolshevik: Autobiography of an Afro-American Communist* (Chicago: Liberator Press, 1978). Another black separatist movement of the period, the Chicago-based Movement for the Establishment of a 49th State, also fizzled out. George S. Schuyler, "The Separate State Hokum," *Crisis* 42, no. 5 (May 1935).

"**We demand the withdrawal**": Campbell, "'Black Bolsheviks,'" 462.

"**a plan of plain segregation**": Hall, *Black Separatism*, 79. "For most black Americans," sociologist Raymond Hall wrote, "the proposal for a separate nation in America sounded like Jim Crow dressed in clothing made in Moscow." Yet it was because of the Communists' interest in black self-determination in the South that the Party become involved in the key civil-rights fight of the early 1930s—the case of the Scottsboro Boys.

"**We at home were watching**": Garry Wills, *The Second Civil War: Arming for Armageddon* (New York: Signet, 1968), 71.

President Lyndon Johnson appointed: See Stephen M. Gillon, *Separate and Unequal: The Kerner Commission and the Unraveling of American Liberalism* (New York: Basic Books, 2018). Johnson, his political standing eroded by the war in Vietnam, did nothing to push for the Commission's racial-justice recommendations. Instead, he beefed up local police forces for the "war on crime." Kevin M. Kruse and Julian E. Zelizer, *Fault Lines: A History of the United States Since 1974* (New York: W. W. Norton, 2019), 47.

White soldiers in Vietnam: Grandin, *End of the Myth,* 208.

"400 years of our sweat": Elijah Muhammad, *Message to the Blackman in America* (Phoenix: Secretarius MEMPS, 1973), 161–63.

"a few states": Campbell, " 'Black Bolsheviks,' " 450. See also "Message to the Grass Roots," in *Malcolm X Speaks: Selected Speeches and Statements,* ed. George Breitman (New York: Grove, 1965), 3–17.

the Black Panthers asked for: Jennifer B. Smith, *An International History of the Black Panther Party* (New York: Garland, 1999), 68.

"if there really remains": Robert S. Browne, "The Case for Black Separatism," *Ramparts,* Dec. 1967, 46–51. Browne pointed to "the Jewish drama during and following World War II" as proof that "a national homeland is a primordial and urgent need for a people." Browne also adopted the language of union-as-matrimony and disunion-as-divorce that had been used since the founding period: "Divorce is an inherent aspect of the American tradition. It terminates the misery of an enforced but unhappy union, relieves the tension and avoids the risk of more serious consequences. It is increasingly apparent to blacks and whites alike that their national marriage has been a disastrous failure."

the Republic of New Afrika: See Paul Karolczyk, "Subjugated Territory: The New Afrikan Independence Movement and the Space of Black Power" (diss., Louisiana State University, 2014). Florida was excluded because the group deemed it militarily indefensible.

"If people in Ocean Hill–Brownsville": Christian Davenport, *How Social Movements Die: Repression and Demobilization of the Republic of New Africa* (New York: Cambridge University Press, 2015), 199.

In 1970, RNA members moved: Katie Gilbert, "The Socialist Experiment," *Oxford American* 98 (fall 2017). Gilbert's article is a fascinating study not only of the RNA's history but of its legacy. Former RNA founder Chokwe Lumumba was elected mayor of Jackson in 2013. After his sudden death a year later, his son ran for and won the position and continues the push for black self-government, to "Free the Land," though the slogan now refers more to economic than outright political independence.

Some Mexican-Americans: See David M. Reimers, *Unwelcome Strangers: American Identity and the Turn Against Immigration* (New York: Columbia University Press, 1998); Ignacio M. Garcia, *Chicanismo: The Forging of a Militant Ethos Among Mexican Americans* (Tucson: University of Arizona Press, 1997), 93–96; Ernesto B. Vigil, *The Crusade for Justice: Chicano Militancy and the Government's War on Dissent* (Madison: University of Wisconsin Press, 1999), 97–98.

"We Declare the Independence": David A. Sánchez, *From Patmos to the Barrio: Subverting Imperial Myths* (Minneapolis: Fortress, 2008), 101–2.

a fight over a public park: In 2017 and 2018, a series of clashes erupted between Chicanos and a group of right-wing whites called the Bordertown Patriots, who objected to the presence of the Aztlán flag and the absence of the American one. Luis Gomez, "Why San Diego's Chicano Park Is a Battleground in the Trump Era," *San Diego Union Tribune,* Feb. 2, 2018. https://www.sandiegouniontribune.com/opinion/the-conversation/sd-defending-chicano-park-in-the-trump-era-20180202-htmlstory.html.

"took a hard look": Kruse and Zelizer, *Fault Lines,* 53–55.

Puerto Ricans had long dreamed: See Nelson A. Denis, *War Against All Puerto Ricans: Revolution and Terror in America's Colony* (New York: Nation Books, 2016).

"an alternate, penisless reality": Ariel Levy, "Lesbian Nation," *The New Yorker*, March 2, 2009. Feminist separatism also had a long history. In her 1887 story, "A Divided Republic," Lillie Devereux Blake imagined the secession of all women from the United States until men agreed to reform their behavior. The story is reprinted in *Daring to Dream: Utopian Fiction by United States Women Before 1950*, ed. Carol Farley Kessler (Syracuse, NY: Syracuse University Press, 1995), 94–103.

"testosterone poisoning": Levy, "Lesbian Nation." Perhaps the movement wasn't all that peculiar. Author Marilyn Frye noted that while women's separatism was considered strange, even grotesque, male separatism—gentlemen's clubs, sports teams, the military—had become normalized, unworthy of note. Marilyn Frye, "Some Reflections on Separatism and Power," in *The Lesbian and Gay Studies Reader*, eds. Henry Abelove, Michele Aina Barale, and David M. Halperin (New York: Routledge, 1993), 91.

"overcentralization...an international disease": Freedman, *Less Perfect Union*, 166.

the Underground States of America: *The Hippie Papers: Notes from the Underground Press*, ed. Jerry Hopkins (New York: New American Library, 1968), 55–56. The Underground States would be governed by the Ten Commandments, except for those "ridiculous" ones about God. New ones would enshrine such holy maxims as "Thou shall not say anything unless it be beautiful and useful." Sinners would be exiled to the United States: "There they will learn the way of the jungle and the street in its fullest reality and hopefully realize that man cannot exist without love and his fellow human beings." Reformed, they could be welcomed back to the Underground by a majority vote.

"year by year, crisis by crisis": Perlstein, *Before the Storm*, xiii. In 1970, journalist James Reston described the American decade just ended as "the longest and most divisive conflict since the War Between the States." Isserman and Kazin, *America Divided*, 4.

"all the way back"..."if it came to civil war": Isserman and Kazin, *America Divided*, 4, 186.

"as American as cherry pie": Stephan Thernstrom and Abigail Thernstrom, *America in Black and White: One Nation, Indivisible* (New York: Touchstone, 1997), 167.

"Oh, another bombing?"..."Belfast of North America": Brian Burrough, *Days of Rage: America's Radical Underground, the FBI, and the Forgotten Age of Revolutionary Violence* (New York: Penguin, 2016), 5.

nearly two hundred people: Peter Bergen, "The Golden Age of Terrorism," CNN, Aug. 21, 2015. https://www.cnn.com/2015/07/28/opinions/bergen-1970s-terrorism/index.html.

"I think, in view of all": Mumford quoted in Berman, *Why America Failed*, 87.

"The South is fighting": Green, "Resurgent Southern Sectionalism," 234. Also Nicole Mellow, *The State of Disunion: Regional Sources of Modern American Partisanship* (Baltimore: Johns Hopkins University Press, 2008), 38–39.

"a rather sensational epoch": See Daniel J. Elazar, "Megalopolis and the New Sectionalism," *Public Interest* 11 (spring 1968): 67–85.

"Sometimes, I think this country": In the 1964 election, Lyndon Johnson's campaign ran a TV ad showing a piece of wood shaped like the contiguous United States floating in a tub of water. As a saw buzzes south from Ohio to the Gulf Coast, a male voice-over quotes Goldwater and asks, "Can a man who makes statements like this be expected to serve all the people justly and fairly?" As the ad ends, the East Coast splashes into the water and floats offscreen. William L. Benoit, *Seeing Spots: A Functional Analysis of Presidential Television Advertisements, 1952–1996* (Westport, CT: Praeger, 1999), 41.

"You native sons and daughters": Lowndes, *From the New Deal to the New Right*, 82.

"The battle flag became the banner": Grandin, *End of the Myth*, 210.

"the forgotten Americans": Lowndes, *From the New Deal to the New Right*, 113.

"bring America together": Lawrence O'Donnell, *Playing with Fire: The 1968 Election and the Transformation of American Politics* (New York: Penguin, 2017), 407.

"Who needs Manhattan": Mellow, *State of Disunion*, 43.

"If we tear the country": Buchanan quoted in Marshall Berman, "All That Is Solid Melts into Air: Marx, Modernism and Modernization," in *Adventures in Marxism* (New York: Verso, 2002), 92.

"With a choice of red": Rick Perlstein, *The Invisible Bridge: The Fall of Nixon and the Rise of Reagan* (New York: Simon & Schuster, 2015), 711–12.

"A spirit of unity": Daniel T. Rodgers, *Age of Fracture* (Cambridge, MA: Harvard University Press, 2011), 227.

"the Union of the United States": Kevin Phillips, "The Balkanization of America," *Harper's*, May 1978, 37–47.

"a crisis of confidence": Edward Walsh, "Carter Finds 'Crisis of Confidence,'" *Washington Post*, July 16, 1979.

three-quarters of Americans: Kirkpatrick Sale, *Human Scale* (New York: Coward, McCann & Geoghegan, 1980), 420.

"The attitudes today": Phillips, "Balkanization of America," 38.

"Like blacks, Hispanics, women": Kruse and Zelizer, *Fault Lines*, 17.

"those historical accidents": Joel Garreau, *The Nine Nations of North America* (Boston: Houghton Mifflin, 1981), 1.

new outburst of Western discontent: See Richard D. Lamm and Michael McCarthy, *The Angry West: A Vulnerable Land and Its Future* (Boston: Houghton Mifflin, 1982); Jonathan Thompson, "The First Sagebrush Rebellion: What Sparked It and How It Ended," *High Country News*, Jan. 14, 2016; Joseph M. Bauman, "Sagebrush Rebellion: Another View," *Deseret News*, Nov. 7, 1988; Sara Dant, *Losing Eden: An Environmental History of the American West* (Malden, MA: John Wiley & Sons, 2016). Public land had been the subject of disputes between states and the federal government for two centuries. John C. Calhoun had been one of the first to demand transferring public lands back to the states as a way to weaken the federal government and prevent it from selling them to subsidize emancipation.

"blow up bridges, ruins": Raymond Wheeler, "Boom! Boom! Boom!: War on the Colorado Plateau," in *Reopening the Western Frontier*, ed. Ed Marston (Washington, DC: Island Press, 1989), 22.

"radical...dandelion pickers": Dant, *Losing Eden*, 176.

"My vision," said Kent Briggs: Garreau, *Nine Nations of North America*, 11. Even as Canada faced a growing Quebec secession movement, separatism in the western provinces, especially Alberta, was rising as well, fueled by similar issues to those of the Sagebrush Rebellion in the States. Thus Briggs's suggestion of a new nation cutting across old international boundaries might not have been so far-fetched. See *Western Separatism: The Myths, Realities and Dangers*, eds. Larry Pratt and Garth Stevenson (Edmonton, AB: Hurting, 1981). Recently, western Canadian separatism roared back to life after the 2019 federal election.

"Count me in as a Rebel": David F. Salisbury, "Sagebrush Rebels See Open Range in Reagan's Victory," *Christian Science Monitor*, Nov. 18, 1980.

"I believe in states' rights": For the Manafort connection, see Robert P. Jones, "How Trump Remixed the Republican 'Southern Strategy,'" *The Atlantic* (Aug. 14, 2016). https://www.theatlantic.com/politics/archive/2016/08/how-trump-remixed-the-republican-southern-strategy/495719/.

"the Confederate theory": Michael Lind, *Up from Conservatism: Why the Right Is Wrong for America* (New York: Free Press, 1996), 208. In his 1995 dissent in *U.S. Term Limits, Inc. v. Thornton*, Justice Clarence Thomas echoed the theories of John C. Calhoun. The "ultimate source of the Constitution's authority," Thomas wrote, "is the consent of the people of each individual State, not the consent of the undifferentiated people of the Nation as a whole."

"a cultural war, as critical": See Andrew W. Hartman, *A War for the Soul of America: A History of the Culture Wars* (Chicago: University of Chicago Press, 2015).

"The virus of tribalism": Arthur M. Schlesinger Jr., *The Disuniting of America: Reflections on a Multicultural Society* (New York: W. W. Norton, 1998), 14.

The most eloquent skeptic: George F. Kennan, *Around the Cragged Hill: A Personal and Political Philosophy* (New York: W. W. Norton, 1993). Kennan wasn't alone in seeing radical devolution as the only solution to America's problems. Charles Stewart Goodwin, a small-government conservative, wrote several books arguing for a twenty-first -century rebirth of Anti-Federalism. In tracts like *A Resurrection of the Republican Ideal* (1995) and *The Arc of the Pendulum* (1996), Goodwin suggested restructuring the Union into village-size commonwealths with only two or three thousand citizens each.

"assimilation by fragmentation": Schlesinger, *Disuniting of America*, 21. In 1992, when the political scientist Andrew Hacker published *Two Nations: Separate, Hostile, Unequal*, a study of the persistence of racial discrimination, the critic Albert Murray ("How Have We Changed?" *American Heritage* 45, no. 8 [Dec. 1994]) acidly replied, "Two nations? Only two? What about the Asians, Mexicans, Puerto Ricans, Cubans, and other not very white U.S. citizens from Latin America and elsewhere?"

"Sometimes our differences": *My Fellow Citizens: The Inaugural Addresses of the Presidents of the United States, 1789–2009*, eds. Arthur M. Schlesinger Jr. and Fred L. Israel (New York: Facts on File, 2010), 407.

Chapter Thirteen. *The Cold Civil War*

"The Greeks did not understand": In 1860, the jurist Francis Lieber, living in South Carolina, used this quote to describe the acrimony between North and South. According to historian James Ford Rhodes, Lieber quoted the text from memory and muddled the translation. I have given Lieber's version. See Rhodes, "Lecture II," *Lectures on the American Civil War* (New York: Macmillan, 1913), 67.

"Given the divisions": Patrick Buchanan, "Is Secession a Solution to Cultural War?," *RealClearPolitics*, Feb. 24, 2017. https://www.realclearpolitics.com/articles/2017/02/24/is _secession_a_solution_to_cultural_war_133183.html.

"breaking the United States up": Ann Garrison, "Should California Secede? An Interview with David Swanson," *CounterPunch*, Feb. 9, 2017. https://www.counterpunch .org/2017/02/09/should-california-secede-an-interview-with-david-swanson/.

"Let us all have": Daniela Blei, "From California, a Progressive Cry for State's Rights," *New Republic*, Feb. 14, 2017. https://newrepublic.com/article/140606/california -progressive-cry-states-rights.

"It's time for blue states and cities": Kevin Baker, "Bluexit: A Modest Proposal for Separating Blue States From Red," *New Republic*, March 19, 2017. https://newrepublic .com/article/140948/bluexit-blue-states-exit-trump-red-america.

"The reality is that nobody": Hamilton Nolan, "The 'Blue State Secession' Thing Is Not Helping," *Deadspin*, March 17, 2017. https://theconcourse.deadspin.com/the-blue -state-secession-thing-is-not-helping-1793210337.

a "cold civil war": The term was apparently coined in the early 1950s, but was first used in recent years by Angelo M. Codevilla, "The Cold Civil War," *Claremont Review of Books* 17, no. 2 (spring 2017): 24–27. For the history of the term, see Ben Yagoda, "Are We in a 'Cold Civil War'?," *Chronicle of Higher Education*, Oct. 17, 2018. https://www .chronicle.com/blogs/linguafranca/2018/10/07/are-we-in-a-cold-civil-war/.

"If both sides have decided": Erick Erickson, "Let's Consider Secession," *The Resurgent,* June 19, 2017. https://theresurgent.com/2017/06/19/lets-consider-secession/.

Keith Mines, a veteran diplomat: Robin Wright, "Is America Headed for a New Kind of Civil War?," *The New Yorker,* Aug. 14, 2017. https://www.newyorker.com/news/news-desk/is-america-headed-for-a-new-kind-of-civil-war. See also Keith Mines, "Will We Have a Civil War? A SF Officer Turned Diplomat Estimates Chances at 60 Percent," *Foreign Policy,* March 10, 2017. https://foreignpolicy.com/2017/03/10/will-we-have-a-civil-war-a-sf-officer-turned-diplomat-estimates-chances-at-60-percent/.

After Bush's reelection: See Jack Hitt, "Neo-Secessionism," *New York Times,* Dec. 12, 2004. https://www.nytimes.com/2004/12/12/magazine/neosecessionism.html.

"Blue State secession": Kirkpatrick Sale, "Blue State Secession," *The Nation,* Dec. 13, 2004. Before the 2004 Republican National Convention met in Madison Square Garden, journalist Jennifer Senior argued in *New York* magazine for reviving Fernando Wood's idea from 1861: the city—"an island off the coast of the United States"—should secede from a nation with which it had little in common. New York's police department would become the twentieth-largest army in the world, its economy would rank seventeenth, and a city where some 160 languages are spoken on the street "would no longer be identified with a country the rest of the planet hates, fears, and cannot understand." To negotiate an exit deal with the United States, she suggested finding "that special someone, that perfect ambassador who both speaks the red-state language but still unambiguously represents New York." Her half-serious suggestion: bombastic television-tycoon and self-styled deal-maker, Donald J. Trump. See Jennifer Senior, "The Independent Republic of New York," *New York,* July 30, 2004. http://nymag.com/nymetro/news/rnc/9573/.

the Second Vermont Republic: The group included among its ranks, as journalist Christopher Ketcham wrote, "gun nuts and lumberjacks and professors, socialists and libertarians and anarchists, ex-Republicans and ex-Democrats, truck drivers and schoolteachers and waitresses, students and artists and musicians and poets, farmers and hunters and wooly-haired woodsmen." See Christopher Ketcham, "U.S. Out of Vermont!," *American Prospect,* March 19, 2013. https://prospect.org/article/us-out-vermont; and Christopher Ketcham, "The Secessionist Campaign for the Republic of Vermont," *Time,* Jan. 31, 2010. http://content.time.com/time/nation/article/0,8599,1957743,00.html.

His now-famous speech: "The Audacity of Hope," *We Are the Change We Seek: The Speeches of Barack Obama* (New York: Bloomsbury, 2017).

"the single most important thing": Major Garrett, "Top GOP Priority: Make Obama a One-Term President," *National Journal,* Oct. 23, 2010. https://www.nationaljournal.com/member/magazine/top-gop-priority-make-obama-a-one-term-president-20101023.

"If he was for it" . . . "America's governance": Kruse and Zelizer, *Fault Lines,* 298, 313.

"large swaths of the country": Binyamin Appelbaum, Patricia Cohen, and Jack Healy, "A Rebounding Economy Remains Fragile for Many," *New York Times,* Sept. 15, 2016, A1.

"We've got a great union": James C. McKinley Jr., "Texas Governor's Secession Talk Stirs Furor," *New York Times,* April 18, 2009, A15.

"the American people will go": Rachel Rose Hartman, "Congressman Calls for Tennessee Secession," *Yahoo News,* July 26, 2010. https://www.yahoo.com/news/blogs/upshot/congressman-calls-tennessee-secession-185312090.html.

In 2014, the Wisconsin Republican: David Freedlander, "Wisconsin GOP's Secession Panic," *Daily Beast,* May 2, 2014. https://www.thedailybeast.com/wisconsins-gop-secession-panic.

"an inseparable part": Kristen Shanahan, "Lawmaker Says Proposed Bill Would Allow Oklahoma to Secede," KFOR, Jan. 19, 2017. https://kfor.com/2017/01/19/lawmaker

-says-proposed-bill-would-allow-oklahoma-to-secede/. Libertarian spokesman Ron Paul called secession "a deeply American principle." For a country founded in the act of secession, Paul argued, there was "nothing treasonous or unpatriotic about wanting a federal government that is more responsive to the people it represents…. If a people cannot secede from an oppressive government, they cannot truly be considered free." Kevin Cirilli, "Paul: Secession 'Deeply American,'" *Politico*, Nov. 19, 2012. https://www .politico.com/story/2012/11/ron-paul-secession-is-a-deeply-american-principle -084058.

the White House petitions website: Danielle Ryan, "White House Receives Secession Pleas from All 50 States," *Los Angeles Times*, Nov. 14, 2012. https://www.latimes.com /politics/la-xpm-2012-nov-14-la-pn-white-house-secession-50-states-20121114-story .html.

"We do not want to secede": G. Jeffrey MacDonald, "Secession Theology Runs Deep in American Religious, Political History," *Religion News Service*, Nov. 29, 2012. https:// religionnews.com/2012/11/29/secession-theology-runs-deep-in-american-religious -political-history/.

"The United States hardly seems": Gaines, "One in Four Americans."

"free and independent Southern republic": Brett A. Barnett, "League of the South's Internet Rhetoric: Neo-Confederate Community-Building Online," *Journal of Hate Studies* 13 (2015–2016): 156, 161.

three- to five-man: Michael Hill, "A Bazooka in Every Pot," *League of the South* (July 15, 2014). https://leagueofthesouth.com/a-bazooka-in-every-pot/.

"American Redoubt": "The Last Big Frontier," *Economist*, Aug. 14, 2016. https://www .economist.com/united-states/2016/08/04/the-last-big-frontier. In the 1980s, Richard Butler, head of the Aryan Nations, propounded the "Northwest Territorial Imperative," an organized migration to a remote part of the country that whites could officially make their own. The idea was picked up in 2006 by April Gaede, a transplant from California to Kalispell, Montana, who urged white people to "come home." Ryan Lenz, "A Gathering of Eagles: Extremists Look to Montana," *Intelligence Report*, Nov. 15, 2011. https://www.splcenter.org/fighting-hate/intelligence -report/2011/gathering-eagles-extremists-look-montana; Casey Michel, "Want to Meet America's Worst Racists? Come to the Northwest," *Politico Magazine*, July 7, 2015. https://www.politico.com/magazine/story/2015/07/northwest-front-americas -worst-racists-119803.

"Even if God has withdrawn": MacDonald, "Secession Theology Runs Deep."

"The sky is the blue, and the land is the green": See http://northwestfront.org/. The Northwest Front was founded by Harold Covington, author of four self-published novels depicting a coming civil war. The new nation, said Covington, who died in 2018, would be "kind of like the white version of Israel." In 2013 Covington told a reporter that even those who were flocking to the area were doing so for racist reasons even if they didn't say so: "They'll use the right code words, like 'clean air,' 'good schools,' 'friendly neighbors,' 'economic opportunity,' and 'good environment.' What they really mean, of course, is that they're coming to get away from the niggers and the Mexicans and the politically correct crap that's devastated the rest of this country. They're coming to get away from diversity and multiculturalism and live in a predominantly white area. They'll never admit it, but that's why." Matthew Francey, "This Guy Wants to Start His Own Aryan Country," *Vice*, Feb. 12, 2013. https://www.vice.com /en_us/article/4wqe33/this-guy-wants-to-start-his-own-aryan-country.

"ambassador, consul-general": Lily Rothman, "Texas Secession Is Not a New Idea," *Time*, May 13, 2016. http://time.com/4329364/texas-secede-history/.

In 2012, an online petition: Richard Dunham, "White House Nixes Texas Secession Petition," *Houston Chronicle,* Jan. 14, 2013. https://blog.chron.com/txpotomac/2013/01/white-house-nixes-texas-secession-petition/.

Four years later, a committee: David R. Brockman, "Texas GOP Flirts With Secession," *Texas Observer,* May 14, 2016. https://www.texasobserver.org/texas-gop-flirts-with-secession/.

"Dialogue of Nations": Neil MacFarquhar, "Russia, Jailer of Local Separatists, Welcomes Foreign Secessionists," *New York Times,* Sept. 26, 2016, A1; Mansur Mirovalev, "Moscow Welcomes the (Would-Be) Sovereign Nations of California and Texas," *Los Angeles Times,* Sept. 27, 2016. https://www.latimes.com/world/europe/la-fg-russia-separatists-snap-story.html.

Igor Panarin, an influential professor: Andrew Osborn, "As If Things Weren't Bad Enough, Russian Professor Predicts End of U.S.," *Wall Street Journal,* Dec. 29, 2008. https://www.wsj.com/articles/SB123051100709638419.

Russian-backed social-media accounts: Teo Armus, "Texas Secession Was a Key Theme in Russian Disinformation Campaign During 2016 Elections, Report Says," *Texas Tribune,* Dec. 17, 2018. https://www.texastribune.org/2018/12/17/texas-secession-russia-disinformation-2016-social-media-new-knowledge/.

Heart of Texas: Casey Michel, "How the Russians Pretended to Be Texans—and Texans Believed Them," *Washington Post,* Oct. 17, 2017. https://www.washingtonpost.com/?utm_term=.8afe925dc9b4.

organized a demonstration: Claire Allbright, "A Russian Facebook Page Organized a Protest in Texas. A Different Russian Page Launched the Counterprotest," *Texas Tribune,* Nov. 1, 2017. https://www.texastribune.org/2017/11/01/russian-facebook-page-organized-protest-texas-different-russian-page-1/.

"arming two sides": Todd J. Gillman, "Russian Trolls Orchestrated 2016 Clash at Houston Islamic Center, New Senate Intel Report Recalls," *Dallas Morning News,* Oct. 8, 2019.

26 percent of Texans: Russell Berman, "Will Texas Stick Around for a Hillary Clinton Presidency?," *The Atlantic,* Aug. 16, 2016. https://www.theatlantic.com/politics/archive/2016/08/clinton-wins-texas-secedes/496166/.

"Texas is the only lifeboat": Brett Barrouquere, "Texas Secessionists Believe Hillary Clinton Win Speeds 'Texit,'" *Houston Chronicle,* Oct. 31, 2016. https://www.chron.com/news/houston-texas/texas/article/Texas-secessionist-believe-departure-Hillary-10425846.php.

"needed to redeem": David A. Graham, "Matt Bevin's Apocalyptic Warnings of Bloodshed," *The Atlantic,* Sept. 13, 2016. https://www.theatlantic.com/politics/archive/2016/09/matt-bevin-clinton-blood/499754/.

Only "the Second Amendment people": Nick Corasaniti and Maggie Haberman, "Donald Trump Suggests 'Second Amendment People' Could Act Against Hillary Clinton," *New York Times,* Aug. 10, 2016, A1.

"another Revolutionary War": Ashley Parker and Nick Corasaniti, "Some Donald Trump Voters Warn of Revolution If Hillary Clinton Wins," *New York Times,* Oct. 28, 2016, A1.

"light the motherfucker!": Michelle Broder Van Dyke and McKay Coppins, "Trump Supporter Yells 'Light the Motherfucker on Fire' as Protester Is Dragged Away at Rally," *Buzzfeed News,* Dec. 14, 2015. https://www.buzzfeednews.com/article/mbvd/trump-supporter-yells-light-the-motherfucker-on-fire-as-prot. As president, Trump praised a congressman who had body-slammed a reporter as "my kind of guy." In early 2019, he boasted to the website *Breitbart:* "I have the support of the police, the support of the military, the support of the Bikers for Trump—I have the tough people, but they don't play it tough—until they go to a certain point and then it would be very bad, very bad."

"As a Christian": Parker and Corasaniti, "Some Donald Trump Voters."

more than half the states: Sasha Issenberg, "Divided We Stand," *New York,* Nov. 12, 2018.

When the *New York Times:* Tim Wallace, "The Two Americas of 2016," *New York Times,* Nov. 16, 2016. https://www.nytimes.com/interactive/2016/11/16/us/politics/the-two -americas-of-2016.html.

Less than 6 percent: Gregor Aisch, Adam Pearce, and Karen Yourish, "The Divide Between Red and Blue America Grew Even Deeper in 2016," *New York Times,* Nov. 10, 2016. https://www.nytimes.com/interactive/2016/11/10/us/politics/red-blue-divide -grew-stronger-in-2016.html.

"100%" for secession: Ashitha Nagesh, "#Calexit: California Wants to Leave the US After Donald Trump's Election Win," *Metro,* Nov. 9, 2016. https://metro.co.uk/2016/11/09/ calexit-california-want-to-leave-the-us-after-donald-trumps-election-win-6245665/; Solon, "Silicon Valley Investors Call for California to Secede."

"to defend ourselves": Daniel Duane, "I Wish We All Could Be Californian," *New York Times,* Nov. 20, 2016, SR3.

"feeling like strangers": Tim Arango, "In Clash Between California and Trump, It's One America Versus Another," *New York Times,* Jan. 7, 2018, A1.

"rational people, not the fringe": Nikki Schwab, "Desperate Democrats? California Politician Says 'Rational People' Are Talking About States Leaving the Union Because of Trump," *Daily Mail,* Dec. 6, 2016. https://www.dailymail.co.uk/news /article-4007662/Desperate-Democrats-Rational-people-talking-states-leaving -union-Trump.html.

"People used to argue": Matthew Artz, "'Calexit': Just Some Flaky California Dreamin'?," *San Jose Mercury News,* Nov. 26, 2016. https://www.mercurynews.com/2016/11/26 /calexit-just-some-flaky-california-dreamin/.

a rally at the state capitol: Alyssa Pereira, "California Secession Group to Hold Meet-Up at State Capitol," *SFGate,* Nov. 9, 2016. https://www.sfgate.com/news/article/California -secession-group-to-hold-meet-up-at-10594349.php.

"Embassy of the Independent Republic": John Myers, "California Secession Organizers Say They've Opened an Embassy—in Moscow," *Los Angeles Times,* Dec. 20, 2016. https://www.latimes.com/politics/essential/la-pol-ca-essential-politics-updates -calexit-organizers-say-they-ve-opened-1482187671-htmlstory.html.

$103 billion more in taxes: F. H. Buckley, *American Secession: The Looming Threat of a National Breakup* (New York: Encounter Books, 2020), 19.

"help Mr. Trump's re-election": Casey Michel, "Why Russia Loves the Idea of California Seceding," *Politico Magazine,* Jan. 15, 2017. https://www.politico.com/magazine /story/2017/01/why-russia-loves-the-idea-of-california-seceding-214632.

"The election made the Rockies": Thomas Fuller, Jack Healy, and Kirk Johnson, "Amid Tide of Red on Electoral Map, West Coast Stays Defiantly Blue," *New York Times,* Nov. 12, 2016, A1.

"Oregonian values are no longer": Lizzy Acker, "After Donald Trump Victory, Orego-nians Submit Ballot Proposal to Secede from the Union," *Oregonian,* Nov. 10, 2016. https://www.oregonlive.com/politics/2016/11/after_trump_victory_oregonians .html.

conservative residents of the rural: Jim Walz, "Re-consider Western Oregon's Secession from US," *Statesman Journal,* April 18, 2017. https://www.statesmanjournal.com /story/opinion/readers/2017/04/18/re-consider-western-oregons -secession-us/100602252/. In late 2019, Washington state representative Matt Shea, a supporter of the Liberty separatist movement and apparent sympathizer with the Northwest Front, was accused in a legislative report of gathering arms and followers to target minorities and progressives in the event of a second civil war. "He's not about preserving America," the Spokane County sheriff said of Shea and his followers. "They are about starting their own country." As the *New York Times* put it, Shea "laid the groundwork to form an alternative government that would be poised to take over after the expected fall of the United States government." See Mike Baker, "G.O.P. Lawmaker Had Visions of a Christian Alternative Government," *New York Times,* Dec. 24, 2019, 1.

"a new happiness": Katy Murphy, "'Calexit' Campaign Dropped as Leader Bolts for Russia," *San Jose Mercury News,* April 17, 2017. https://www.mercurynews.com/2017/04/17/calexit-leaders-drop-ballot-measure-to-break-from-the-u-s/.

"the group advocating state rights": Schlesinger, "State Rights Fetish," 243.

record-shattering sixty-two times: Hannah Wiley, "Why Humpback Whales and Condors Are at the Center of California's Latest Lawsuit Against Trump," *Sacramento Bee,* Sept. 25, 2019. https://www.sacbee.com/news/politics-government/capitol-alert/article235461192.html.

a form of "soft secession": David French, "California's Soft Secession Accelerates," *National Review,* Jan. 26, 2018. https://www.nationalreview.com/2018/01/california-secession-good-done-soft-correctly/; Jason Willick, "California's Soft Secession," *American Interest,* June 23, 2017. https://www.the-american-interest.com/2017/06/23/californias-soft-secession/.

"There is no nullification": Thomas Fuller and Vivian Yee, "Jeff Sessions Scolds California in Immigration Speech: 'We Have a Problem,'" *New York Times,* March 8, 2018, A22.

Brown flew to Beijing: "It is a little bold to talk about the China–California partnership as though we were a separate nation," Brown said in 2015, "but we are a separate nation." Sammy Roth, "'Nation' of California, China Forge Strong Climate Link," *Desert Sun,* March 5, 2015. https://www.usatoday.com/story/news/2015/03/05/california-climate-china-pollution-jerry-brown/24443923/

"functioning as the head of something": David Siders, "Jerry Brown, President of the Independent Republic of California," *Politico Magazine,* Nov. 11, 2017. https://www.politico.com/magazine/story/2017/11/11/jerry-brown-california-profile-215812.

"The Christians will finally": Josh Delk, "Televangelist Jim Bakker: Christians Will Start a Civil War If Trump Is Impeached," *The Hill,* Aug. 29, 2017. https://thehill.com/blogs/blog-briefing-room/348418-televangelist-jim-bakker-christians-will-start-new-civil-war-if.

"a Civil War like fracture": Donald J. Trump, Twitter post, Sept. 29, 2019, 9:11 p.m., https://twitter.com/realDonaldTrump/status/1178477539653771264.

"We ARE on the verge": Mary B. McCord, "Armed Militias Are Taking Trump's Civil War Tweets Seriously," *Lawfare,* Oct. 2, 2019. https://www.lawfareblog.com/armed-militias-are-taking-trumps-civil-war-tweets-seriously.

According to a 2017 poll: John Zogby, "New Poll on Americans' Support for Secession," *John Zogby Strategies,* Sept. 18, 2017. https://johnzogbystrategies.com/new-poll-on-americans-support-for-secession-webinar-on-tribal-analytics-and-trump-report-card/.

another survey showed that 31 percent: Buckley, *American Secession,* 12.

"The United States must die": Winston McCuen, "Letter: Election Will Break Apart US," *Greenville News,* April 18, 2016. The same writer, I should note, later sent another letter suggesting local schools teach "the virtues of slavery." He had once been fired as a teacher for refusing to remove a Confederate flag from his desk; the League of the South helped raise funds for his legal fight. See Winston McCuen, "Teach Truth

About the Virtues of Slavery," *The State*, Sept. 22, 2017; Allen G. Breed, "Teacher, Wife in Rebel Standoff," Associated Press, April 5, 1999.

Conclusion

"Divided we ever have been": *The Works of John Adams, Vol. X,* ed. Charles Francis Adams (Boston: Little, Brown, 1956), 63.

"We must, indeed, all hang together": D. H. Montgomery, *Benjamin Franklin: His Life* (Boston: Ginn, 1906), 269.

"the last best hope": Abraham Lincoln, *Selected Speeches and Writings,* 364.

boundaries are not written in stone: In a footnote to his important paper, "The Historian's Use of Nationalism and Vice Versa," David M. Potter invokes the work of Czech political scientist Karl W. Deutsch to note the "circularity of the reasoning that Detroit and San Francisco, for instance, are 'united' by lying within a 'common territory,' while Detroit and Toronto are not." Potter, "Historian's Use of Nationalism," 933n7.

"The dogmas of the quiet past": Abraham Lincoln, *Selected Speeches and Writings,* 364.

Index

Note: Italic page numbers refer to illustrations.

About the Author

RICHARD KREITNER is a contributing writer for the *Nation* and the author of *Booked: A Traveler's Guide to Literary Locations Around the World.* His writing on politics, history, and literature has appeared in *Raritan,* the *Baffler, Slate, Salon,* and the *Boston Globe.* Raised in New Jersey and educated at McGill University in Montreal, he currently lives in Brooklyn with his wife and two children.